EDGAR RICE BURROUGHS
The Man Who Created Tarzan

VOLUME 1

EDGAR RICE BURROUGHS

The Man Who Created Tarzan

VOLUME 1

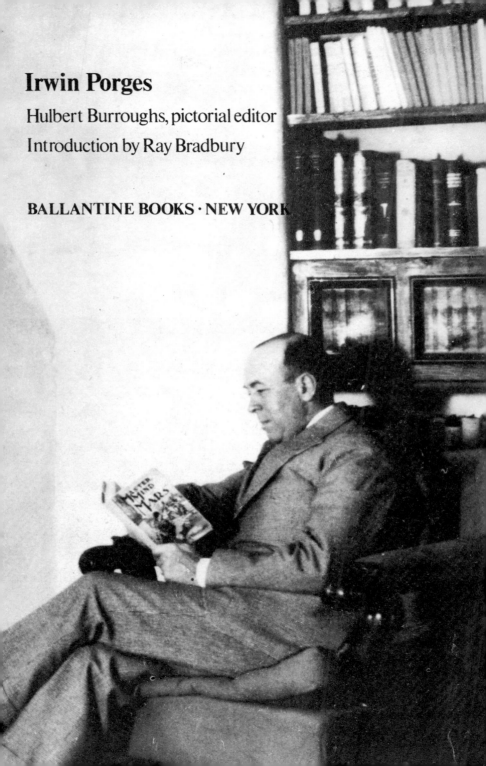

Irwin Porges

Hulbert Burroughs, pictorial editor

Introduction by Ray Bradbury

BALLANTINE BOOKS · NEW YORK

*To my wife Cele,
not only for the years of research, but for
her spirit and enthusiasm that transformed
this formidable task into an adventure.*

Library of Congress Catalog Card Number: 75-15980

ISBN 0-345-25131-8-1000

This edition published by arrangement with
Brigham Young University Press

Manufactured in the United States of America

First Ballantine Books Edition: September 1976

Designed by Gene Siegel

CONTENTS

FOREWORD

The publication of Irwin Porges' biography of Edgar Rice Burroughs is a timely milestone and the ultimate addition to the literature of Burroughsiana. It not only marks the centennial of ERB's birth, but more importantly it is the first and only true and definitive account of the life and work of this remarkably successful author.

Mr. Porges is the first and only researcher who was afforded complete and uncensored access to all of the Burroughs family's personal files as well as those of Edgar Rice Burroughs, Inc. My editorial work on the manuscript involved corrections, addition of interesting material unknown to Porges, and the preparation and production of illustrative matter. No attempt whatever was made to produce a sympathetic book.

Cele Porges, Irwin's talented wife, devoted nearly three years researching the voluminous archives at our company offices and warehouse in Tarzana. The result is a fascinating and well-written story of a man and his career.

Contributing significantly to this volume is the wealth of photographic and illustrative material. Seldom has the subject of a major biography possessed the combined talents of writer, photographer, and artist. Sometime in the 1890s ERB became interested in photography and from then on recorded the people and places in his life. A major portion of the photographs in this book are from his own photo albums and negative files. His pen-and-ink sketches and cartoons are both humorous and documentary. The sheer quantity of good pictorial material available and our realization that only a very limited number could be included because of space limitations presented a rather frustrating challenge. From thousands of photographs and drawings I selected about six hundred for enlargement to 8×10 size. I shall never forget the four days I spent with charming Kerril Sue Rollins, chief project editor of the biography at Brigham Young University Press in Provo, Utah, selecting and placing each picture on the appropriate page of text and the hard and painful decisions we made in reducing the number from 600 to about 270. Had it not been for the firm hand and character of Kerril Sue, the book might well have contained an extra fifty pounds of photos! We swore that some day we would publish an ERB photobiography.

I think my Dad would have been pleased with this book. Irwin Porges has organized and presented a great wealth of material in a way that gives the reader a real insight into ERB the man. I knew him, of course, first as a father. As such he was an extremely loving and kindly man—perhaps overly generous and protective. He set a strong example of love of country, honor, and integrity, as well as loyalty to family and friends. Porges has captured the true essence of ERB with all his strengths and weaknesses. This book will be a prime, standard source for all future Burroughs researchers.

I thank and congratulate Irwin and Cele Porges for their prodigious effort in researching and writing this book. The good people at Brigham Young University Press will always have a special place in my heart. Without the sincere dedication of Gail Bell, Kerril Sue Rollins, Jean Paulson, Mac Magleby, and the other great people of BYU Press, I doubt that this massive volume could have been published.

We are all greatly indebted to Ray Bradbury for his splendid introductory essay. If ERB were alive today, he would be especially pleased for the many times Ray has so generously acknowledged his indebtedness to ERB as the inspiration for his own highly successful writing career. I never cease to wonder at the number and diversity of the minds that have been and are still being influenced by the imagination of Edgar Rice Burroughs. Most important, ERB is gradually receiving the critical acclaim he was denied in his lifetime. No longer is *Tarzan of the Apes* considered mere entertainment—for Tarzan *is* the "Naked Ape," the tribal ancestor of Marshall McLuhan. And ERB's wild imaginings among the stars are no longer beneath the notice of serious men; they have become subjects for scholars and an inspiration to a new generation of writers of imaginative fiction.

Burroughs is remembered as a modest man who never took himself or his work too seriously. His friends recall his ready sense of humor, his great love of the outdoors, and his unbounded pride in his country. One scholar suggests that the very last line of the last Tarzan novel may be taken as ERB's own unintentional valedictory to a very meaningful life: "Thank God for everything."

Hulbert Burroughs
Tarzana, September 1, 1975

PREFACE

THE IDEA OF writing a biography of Edgar Rice Burroughs, which I had only tentatively considered, received a strong stimulus in 1962 as a result of my puzzlement and curiosity.

In my early years I had read the Burroughs stories—a number of the *Tarzan* books and the science-fiction adventures on Mars, Venus, and other worlds. I admired Burroughs for the unlimited bounds of his imagination, for his ingenuity in creating scientific environments for his fantastic civilizations, and for reasons almost impossible to explain that his characters, although unreal and narrowly slanted versions of virtue and vice, somehow lived on vividly and permanently in the reader's mind.

I became convinced that the publicized "ERB," the one known to the readers and the public, was a patchwork of bits and pieces of biography in newspapers and magazines, much of this exaggerated and contradictory. Superficial details—mere lists of data or summary highlights of a person's life—can only produce a superficial man. But an added factor was at work. As a consequence of his wildly imaginative writings and the furor they caused, Burroughs, the individual, was somehow lost—forgotten. *Tarzan of the Apes* alone was potent enough to overwhelm the author. The *author* Burroughs emerged, but not the *man*. Through the years, when he supposedly wrote about himself, he was really supplying the familiar information about his writings or repeating a thin biographical sketch. The *man* Burroughs did not exist—a flesh-and-blood man who had faced conflicts and suffered frustrations and agonies—was unknown.

Why should this have happened? An ironical thought occurred: perhaps there was an assumption that one so strongly identified with worlds of fantasy, a writer who avoided real-life situations, was himself without real-life identification—a disembodied creature. But the puzzling question of why no definitive biography had been written prompted me to get in touch with Edgar Rice Burroughs, Inc., located nearby in the small community that owed its name to ERB—Tarzana, California.

The company is owned and controlled by the author's two sons, Hulbert Burroughs and John Coleman Burroughs. An only daughter, Joan Burroughs Pierce, died in December 1972. My meeting with Hulbert took place in December 1962. The building that housed the Burroughs' offices was unlike anything I had pictured. It was a Spanish-styled bungalow, typical of those popular in Los Angeles from the 1900s on, with one story, walls of yellow-tinged stucco, and a long ivy-festooned veranda across the front. It was the original building, erected by Burroughs in 1927, its exterior unchanged. Set back from busy Ventura Boulevard and secluded behind a weathered redwood fence and huge mulberry trees, the building could easily escape the notice of passers-by who, if they noticed it, might assume it to be a private residence.

Hulbert Burroughs chatted with me, at times seated behind the desk that had belonged to his father, a desk of glowing walnut decorated ornately with Moorish figures—heads of women, rams, circular flowerlike carvings, exotic lamps—and on occasion arising to show me valuable books, illustrations, and Burroughs mementoes. In the adjoining room was a large table, even more elaborate in design than the matching Moorish desk. In facial characteristics Hulbert resembles both his mother and his father; physically, with his broad shoulders, and large hands, he takes after his father. Our discussion was pleasant and the brief tour of the offices highly interesting, but as far as the biography was concerned, I was given no encouragement. Hulbert informed me that he and his brother Jack had plans to write their father's story.

Five years later, the project forgotten, I had turned to other writing when, in October 1967, I received a letter from Robert M. Hodes, the new vice-president and general manager of the Burroughs firm. It contained a proposal that I undertake the biography. After a period of consideration, I agreed to do so. My wife, Cele, an experienced, efficient researcher, began the task of collecting information, much of it contained in documents in the warehouse that adjoined the offices. The warehouse had been built by Burroughs who intended to rent it as a store, but when it remained vacant, he used it at first as a garage. The willing cooperation of the family—Joan, Jack, and Hulbert—was evident from our earliest interviews and tapings. But I had no concept of the complexity of the project I had undertaken.

It was during the early stages of my preparing to write the biography of Edgar Rice Burroughs, and before a single sentence had been composed, that I arrived at a dismaying realization: I had shouldered the task unsuspectingly and with a degree of naivete that already appeared incredible—and would appear increasingly so, I was certain, in the light of developments. For awhile I became convinced that confronting me was a unique situation, unparalleled in the annals of biographies. However, the passage of time (three years of poring through documents on my wife's part, plus the joint searching, sorting, assembling, corresponding, and interviewing by the two of us, and then, of course, the writing and revising) has given me a more temperate and realistic perspective. Undoubtedly my blithe confidence and misapprehension of the difficulties that awaited me have been matched in the experiences of other biographers. But the completion of the biography, accompanied by calm appraisal, has made plain that in one aspect—the huge mass of materials, mainly first sources—the reconstruction of Burroughs' life has posed problems beyond those encountered by the average biographer.

My first view of the warehouse piled to the ceiling with cases of documents and records came as a shock. Before me was a biographer's dream—or nightmare. In the warehouse were seventy-eight large storage file boxes, each the size of a legal file drawer, containing papers that dated to 1911. The labels themselves were an indication of the formidable task that lay ahead: Tarzana Ranch and E.R.B. Personal, 1918-1937, boxes 1-6; Real Estate, 1924-49, boxes 9-12; Motion Pictures, Miscl., and Burroughs-Tarzan Enterprises, Inc., 1918-47, boxes 14-16. Other cases, at random, included Book Publishing—for example, A. C. McClurg & Co., 1914-41—five boxes marked Fans, with letters from every state and from foreign countries; Tarzan Radio Serials, Tarzan Merchandise Franchises, Tarzan Daily Strips, Tarzan Sunday Pages.

Inside some of the sliding file boxes were rows of folders filled with letters, lists, and mimeographed material; many of these had not been examined for years or had not been opened since Burroughs' death in 1950. Valuable original documents had been saved, including correspondence covering Burroughs' first stories —the exchange of letters with Munsey editor Thomas Metcalf concerning "Under the Moons of Mars," *The Outlaw of Torn,* and *Tarzan of the Apes.* Among these was Metcalf's famous eight-word letter: "For the love of Mike! Don't get discouraged!" sent after Burroughs, deeply disappointed and ready to leave the writing field, had remarked, "I can make money easier some other way."

All of these papers would have to be read, and many of them contained material that had to be copied. The amount of general correspondence, letters, and replies by Burroughs was appalling. It had been noted that ERB up to the last years of his life, and except for periods of illness, answered almost everybody who wrote to him. Voluminous is an understated term to describe his letter-writing. With unbelievable patience and care he furnished detailed information to those who sought it, responded to acquaintances, replied to his fans, and even good-humoredly answered cranks who didn't deserve the time and energy he expended. In response to a writer who accused him, because of a scene in one of his stories, of encouraging distressed persons to end their lives, Burroughs wrote, "I thought only of the dramatic value of the situation, and had no intention of glorifying suicide. I feel that very few readers will interpret it as you have. I hope not."

Carbon copies of most of the letters were saved. A survey not only of the warehouse but of other storage rooms and cabinets leads to the indisputable conclusion that Edgar Rice Burroughs was the king of savers. He had inherited a tendency from ancestors who formed a long line of savers of the most meticulous type. The papers in the warehouse were only part of the collection. In other storage places are documents of greater importance to a biographer, those relating personally to Burroughs, revealing his background and illuminating his character and problems, and the family records that in some cases travel back to the ancestral origins in seventeenth-century England.

A favorite means of preservation was the scrapbook. Mary Evaline, Burroughs' mother, kept one, and on the other side Emma Burroughs' parents, the Hulberts, saved several large books of clippings and other references. In addition, Mary Evaline, at her sons' urgings, had written the recollections of her Civil War experiences, and these, together with genealogical information, were printed in a small volume. The family books were augmented by the numerous albums of photos from both the Burroughs family and the Hulberts, photos marked on the backs with vital details.

The custom of keeping records in book form was adopted by Burroughs. His series of desk diaries with brief notations about his stories and comments about daily happenings cover the period of 1921-49. Further records and mementoes are contained in his school scrapbook and other books relating to the past. In the office files are various workbooks in which he methodically

Tarzana storeroom of Edgar Rice Burroughs, Inc., housing files researched by the author, Irwin Porges, and his wife.

prepared story outlines, casts of characters, plot suggestions, definitions for his invented languages, and geographical explanations. His early financial accounts include a precise card index of story sales, dates, and the amounts paid.

But besides all these letters, documents, and records, not to exclude certain personal belongings also saved because, as Burroughs' fame increased, they had a value in themselves, there were of course his writings, both fiction and nonfiction, published and unpublished. A definitive biography is of course written to offer the reader some integration of the man and his works. Awaiting me were some seventy published novels to read—about twenty of these to re-read, since I had read them in my youth—plus many unpublished works. In addition, original manuscripts of published stories, in some cases handwritten, had to be checked for Burroughs' notations and revisions that could be of importance. Applying especially to ERB's writings was a further reading task: his unchanging popularity with science-fiction and Burroughs fan organizations had resulted in the publication of numerous analyses of his works. It was necessary for me to familiarize myself with the ideas expressed in these.

Possibly the most intimate aspects of a man's character emerge through contacts with the people who knew him personally—relatives, friends, business associates. Burroughs throughout his life had a facility for forming friendships, many of these being in the publishing, theatrical, and motion picture fields. Much valuable information has been provided by relatives and friends through correspondence, interviews, and tapings. A list of names is contained under the acknowledgments section.

In summary, I might say that while Burroughs, as with all individuals, revealed himself through his actions, through what he said and what others said about him, as a writer he operated in an additional dimension to expose himself. Even a man who escapes into fantasies of other worlds uncovers himself with every page he creates. Through his writings—and this idea he would have been happy to accept—we obtain a most significant understanding of Edgar Rice Burroughs.

ACKNOWLEDGMENTS

The following people have given me valuable information and assistance in the preparation of this book.

An acknowledgment beyond any words that I could devise must go to my wife Cele for her labors of more than three years among the mounds of paper in the Burroughs storerooms at Tarzana. To the enormous task she brought not only a remarkable ability in research and organization, but also an enthusiasm and a spirit of adventure that swept me through the periods of discouragement. Without her, the biography would have been impossible.

I thank the following members of Edgar Rice Burroughs' family and other relatives: Hulbert Burroughs; John Coleman Burroughs; Joan Burroughs Pierce; James Pierce; Marion Burroughs; Danton Burroughs; Mrs. Carlton D. McKenzie, Harry Burroughs' daughter, for numerous letters and a taped interview; George T. Burroughs, III, for letters and a taped interview; Joyce Burroughs Goetz, George's daughter; Marie Burroughs, Studley Burroughs' widow; June Burroughs, Studley's daughter, for a taped interview; Katherine Burroughs Konkle, Frank Burroughs' daughter, for numerous letters; Dorothy Westendarp Aitchison, niece of Edgar Rice Burroughs, for letters.

I also thank Florence Gilbert, Burroughs' second wife, for a taped interview; Florence's daughter, Caryl Lee (Cindy Cullen), for a taped interview; Lee Chase, Florence's son, for an interview; Ed Gilbert, Florence's brother, for interviews.

I am grateful to the following Burroughs fans who have given me important varied information: Dale R. Broadhurst, for valuable information about Burroughs' Idaho days; Stan Vinson; Vernell Coriell; Henry Hardy Heins; and Sam Moskowitz. I express appreciation to Ray Bradbury for his most appropriate introductory essay.

Mildred Jensen, Burroughs' secretary, has provided interviews and tapings. Ralph Bellamy and Rochelle Hudson have given taped interviews; Sol Lesser, a taped interview; and Hal Thompson, correspondence. General Thomas H. Green, retired, has supplied a letter and a tape; General Kendall Fielder, retired, numerous letters; Phil Bird, an interview; Herbert Weston, Jr., letters; Sterling and Floye Adams, a letter. Mrs. Zeamore Ader has given me information on Burroughs' Chicago background. The Chicago Historical Society, Miss Margaret Scriven, librarian, has provided information on Burroughs' early years in Chicago. The Phillips Academy, Andover, Massachusetts, has also given me valuable information, with special assistance from Charles W. Smith, alumni secretary, and Mrs. Waters Kellogg, associate archivist. I extend my appreciation to all of these people.

Irwin Porges
November 1, 1974

Editor's note: Almost all source material in the book is of a primary nature (i.e., correspondence, poems, drawings, scrapbooks, ERB's *Autobiography,* published novels and stories, and unpublished manuscripts) and is on file at Edgar Rice Burroughs, Inc., at Tarzana, California. Because of this, and because the notes provide thorough information for other sources as well, a separate bibliography has not been included with the back matter. Quoted material has been left in its original form, complete with any misspellings and errors in punctuation and grammar. Only occasionally has a change been made and then only for the sake of clarifying meaning. Burroughs, a prolific writer of notes and letters, often dashed these off in haste, using his own type of shorthand. The term *sic* is used only rarely to call attention to otherwise confusing errors. Titles published in book form appear in italics; titles published in magazines, and also unpublished titles, are placed inside quotation marks. Most of the photographs have been taken by ERB, his son Hulbert, and his daughter Joan.

INTRODUCTION

Tarzan, John Carter, Mr. Burroughs,
and the Long Mad Summer of 1930

In the summer of 1930 if you had got off a train and walked up through the green avenues of Waukegan, Illinois, you might have met a mob of boys and girls running the other way. You might have seen them rushing to drown themselves in the lake or hide themselves in the ravine or pop into theatres to sit out the endless matinees. Anything, anything at all to escape . . .

What?

Myself.

Why were they running away from me? Why was I causing them endless flights, endless hidings-away? Was I, then, that unpopular at the age of ten?

Well, yes, and no.

You see my problem was Edgar Rice Burroughs and Tarzan and John Carter, Warlord of Mars.

Problem, you ask. That doesn't sound like much of a problem.

Oh, but it was. You see, I couldn't stop reading those books. I couldn't stop memorizing them line by line and page by page. Worst of all, when I saw my friends, I couldn't stop my mouth. The words just babbled out. Tarzan this and Jane that, John Carter here and Dejah Thoris there. And when it wasn't those incredible people it was Tanar of Pellucidar or I was making noises like a tyrannosaurus rex and behaving like a Martian thoat, which, everyone knows, has eight legs.

Do you begin to understand why in Waukegan, Illinois, the summer of 1930 was so long, so excruciating, so unbearable for everyone?

Everyone, that is, save me.

My greatest gift has always been falling in love.

My greatest curse, for those with ears, has been the expression of love.

I went to bed quoting Lord Greystoke.

I slept whimpering like Cheetah, growling like Numa, trumpeting like Tantor.

I woke, called for my head, which crawled on spider legs from a pillow nearby, to sit itself back on my neck and name itself *Chessman* of Mars.

At breakfast I climbed trees for my father, stabbed a mad gorilla for my brother, and entertained my mother with pithy sayings right smack-dab out of Jane Porter's mouth.

My father got to work earlier each day.

My mother took aspirin for precipitant migraine.

My brother hit me.

But, ten minutes later I hit the door, the lawn, the street, babbling and yodeling ape cries, ERB in my hand and in my blood.

How came it so?

What was it that Mr. Burroughs did to several dozen million scores of boys all across the world in the last sixty years?

Was he a great thinker?

He would have laughed at that.

Was he a superb stylist?

He would have snorted at that, also.

What if Edgar Rice Burroughs had never been born, and Tarzan with him? Or what if he had simply written Westerns and stayed out of Nairobi and Timbuctoo? How would our world have been affected? Would someone else have become Edgar Rice Burroughs? But Kipling had his chance, and didn't change the world, at least not in the same way.

The Jungle Books are known and read and loved around the world, but they didn't make most boys run amok pull their bones like taffy and grow them to romantic flights and farflung jobs around the world. On occasion, yes, but more often than not, no. Kipling was a better writer than Burroughs, but not a better romantic.

A better writer, too, and also a romantic, was Jules Verne. But he was a Robinson Crusoe humanist/moralist. He celebrated head/hands/heart, the triple H's shaping and changing a world with ideas. All good stuff, all chockful of concepts. Shall we trot about the world in eighty days? We shall. Shall we rocket to the Moon? Indeed. Can we survive on a Mysterious Island, a mob of bright Crusoes? We can. Do we clear the seas of armadas and harvest the deeps with sane/mad Nemo? We do.

It is all adventurous and romantic. But it is not very wild. It is not impulsive.

Burroughs stands above all these by reason of his unreason,

because of his natural impulses, because of the color of the blood running in Tarzan's veins, because of the blood on the teeth of the gorilla, the lion, and the black panther. Because of the sheer romantic impossibility of Burroughs' Mars and its fairytale people with green skins and the absolutely unscientific way John Carter traveled there. Being utterly impossible, he was the perfect fast-moving chum for any ten-year-old boy.

For how can one resist walking out of a summer night to stand in the middle of one's lawn to look up at the red fire of Mars quivering in the sky and whisper: *Take me home.*

A lot of boys, and not a few girls, if they will admit it, have indeed gone "home" because of such nights, such whispers, such promises of far places, such planets, and the creator of the in-habitants of those planets.

In conversations over drinks around our country the past ten years I have been astonished to discover how often a leading biochemist or archaeologist or space technician or astronaut when asked: what happened to you when you were ten years old? replied:

"Tarzan."

"John Carter."

"Mr. Burroughs, of course."

One eminent anthropologist admitted to me, "When I was eleven I read *The Land That Time Forgot.* Bones, I thought. Dry bones. I will go magic me some bones and resurrect a Time. From then on I galloped through life. I became what Mr. Bur-roughs *told* me to become."

So there you have it. Or almost have it, anyway. The explana-tion that we, as intellectuals, dread to think about. But that we, as creatures of blood and instinct and adventure, welcome with a cry. An idea, after all, is no good if it doesn't *move.* Toyn-bee, for goodness sake, teaches us that. The Universe challenges us. We must bleed before the challenge. We must waste ourselves in Time and Space in order to survive, hating the challenge, hating the response, yet in the welter and confusion, somehow loving it all. We are that creature of paradox that would love to sit by the fire and only speak. But the world, other animals more immediately practical than ourselves, and all of outer space says otherwise. We must die in order to live. The settlers did it before us. We will imitate them on the Moon, on Mars, and bury our-selves in graveyards among the stars so that the stars themselves become fecund.

All this Burroughs says most directly, simply, and in terms of animal blood and racial memory every time that Tarzan leaps into a tree or Carter soars through space.

We may know and admire and respect and be moved by Mr. Verne, but he was too polite, wasn't he? You always felt that in the midst of Moon-stalking, his gents might just sit down to tea, or that Nemo, no matter how deep he sank in the Sargasso, still had time for his organ and his Bach. Very nice, very lovely. But the blood does not move so much with this, as does the mind.

In sum, we may have liked Verne and Wells and Kipling, but we loved, we adored, we went quite mad with Mr. Burroughs. We grew up into our intellectuality, of course, but our blood always remembered. Some part of our soul always stayed in the ravine running through the center of Waukegan, Illinois, up in a tree, swinging on a vine, combating shadow-apes.

I still have two letters tucked away in my First Edition *Tarzan of the Apes*. They were written by Mr. Burroughs to me when I was seventeen and still fairly breathless and in fevers over him. I had asked him to come down and speechify the Science Fiction League which met every Thursday night in Clifton's Cafeteria in Los Angeles. It was a great chance for him to meet a lot of mad young people who dearly loved him. Mr. Burroughs, for some strange reason, cared not to join the mob. I wrote again. This time Mr. Burroughs wrote back and assured me that the last thing in the world he would dream of doing was make a public lecture. Thanks a lot but no thanks, he said.

What the hey, I thought, if *he* won't talk about Tarzan, *I will.*

I gabbed and blabbed and gibbered about Tarzan for well over an hour. I had Clifton's Cafeteria emptied in ten minutes, everyone home in twenty, everyone with aspirins for migraine in their mouth five minutes short of an hour.

The summer of 1930 madness had struck again. When I stopped babbling, my arms ached from swinging on all those vines, my head rang from giving all those yells.

I guess that about sums it up.

A number of people changed my life forever in various ways.

Lon Chaney put me up on the side of Notre Dame and swung me from a chandelier over the opera crowd in Paris.

Edgar Allan Poe mortared me into a brick vault with some Amontillado.

Kong chased me up one side and down the other of the Empire State.

But Mr. Burroughs convinced me that I could talk with the animals, even if they didn't answer back, and that late nights when I was asleep my soul slipped from my body, slung itself out the window, and frolicked across town never touching the lawns, always hanging from trees where, even later in those nights, I taught myself alphabets and soon learned French and English and danced with the apes when the moon rose.

But then again, his greatest gift was teaching me to look at Mars and ask to be taken home.

I went home to Mars often when I was eleven and twelve and every year since, and the astronauts with me, as far as the Moon to start, but Mars by the end of the century for sure, Mars by 1999. We have commuted because of Mr. Burroughs. Because of him we have printed the Moon. Because of him and men like him, one day in the next five centuries, we will commute forever, we will go away . . .

And never come back.

And so live forever.

Ray Bradbury
Los Angeles, California
May 8, 1975

CHAPTER 1

PROLOGUE– THE CREATIVE DECISION

On a July day in 1911 Edgar Rice Burroughs sat in a small office at the intersection of Market and Monroe streets in Chicago. He had borrowed desk space from a friend in order to launch his latest enterprise, an agency for the sale of pencil sharpeners. The salesmen who responded to his ads were sent out on a commission basis. "They did not sell any pencil sharpeners," he noted, "but in the leisure moments, while I was waiting for them to come back to tell me that they had not sold any . . ."[1]

What else was there to do? He began to write, the pen seeming oddly small in his heavy fingers. He bore little resemblance to the image of a writer, but there was even less in his appearance to suggest the typical businessman. Since he would seldom draw upon real-life experiences, where would he find the story plots that he needed? His search for excitement, for high adventure in his early years had ended in disappointment. Whatever he found fell far short of his expectations. His youthful spirit of adventure, still unrealized, was temporarily thrust aside. At night, in a happy release from the monotonous daytime routines, it returned to spur his imagination to life. He often lay awake devising fantastic situations and creating his own characters, superhumans who performed incredibly heroic feats in strange worlds and on distant planets.

Now his instincts turned him to the freedom of imagination. His pen swept across the only paper available—orange, blue, and yellow sheets were mixed with white. The blue and yellow ones were old letterheads. He used the backs, shaping words hastily so that they emerged with distinctive flattened or unfinished let-

ERB on the Pacific Coast, 1916.

ters. The *u*'s, *r*'s, *m*'s and *n*'s rose in vague curves above the line, the *i*'s were barely visible, and the crossbars of the *t*'s were dabbed in late beyond the line, out of place, like an afterthought.

Formed in his daydreams and imaginings, the ingredients for many stories—strange encounters, daring rescues, hairbreadth escapes, glorious battles—awaited his summons. As he wrote, the real world of the commonplace became the unreal one; it vanished, and in its place he conjured up a strange fierce civilization set in the midst of a dying planet. The new world closed around him, all sounds of the old were gone, and he was a man lost in a perilous land where science battled against savagery, beauty against ugliness.

The Edgar Rice Burroughs of summer 1911 who entered hesitantly into the field of writing was almost a dual personality. To relatives and close friends he was a delightful man, a humorous practical joker and composer of fairy tales and clever drawings for favorite nieces and nephews. Yet in the business world where he struggled desperately for success he was matter-of-fact, never disclosing the creative imagination of a writer. For example, in a letter discussing his first story he used the stilted jargon of commerce: "It is purely a business proposition with me and I wish to deliver the goods in accordance with your specifications." Though this seems ludicrous, it must be remembered that Burroughs bore not only a suppressed talent but an accumulation of buried hopes, regrets, and frustrations. Approaching thirty-six, he probably viewed his present unhappy circumstances and the past years of random ventures and short-lived occupations with bewilderment and confusion. He had reached a dead end, unable to discover goals or direction.

The reasons for his unplanned, helter-skelter life were unclear to him. All he knew was that he had held on to nothing, that nothing had become permanent. Even the experience he had gained, astonishing in its variety, was of doubtful value. He had floundered about in the business field, vacillating between being an employee and an entrepreneur.

Burroughs lived under the spell of the dominant creed of the times: that success for an individual of the middle-class fringe, especially one without a skill or profession, could be found only in business. A man could begin in a small way with a routine office position, waiting hopefully for promotion, or, if impatient and inclined to gamble, he could invest some tiny capital in business and operate on dreams and a shoestring. There was always the possibility of a get-rich-quick scheme that would work.

Caught in the problems of day-to-day living, Burroughs obtained employment which demanded all his attention and exhausted him; there wasn't time to pause for self-analysis and to identify the creativity that had been struggling for expression since early childhood.

What turned him to writing was not a sudden perception but rather desperation. He wouldn't understand until some time later that a career solely in the business world was not for him. But now, with all the year's efforts adding up to zero, Burroughs was ready to concede that he was a failure. The distinction, subtle but important—the difference between being a failure and being simply a misplaced man—was beyond him. His mind, to elaborate upon the old saw of the pegs, was designed for stretching a round universe of elastic boundaries, for pushing the boundaries out; there was no way he could exist or fit into the universe of square partitions, of offices, of adding machines, sales, profits, and losses.

The turning point came at a time of bitter realization. He had been involved in still another impossible project, hardly knowing why, and with little faith left. Failure was inevitable. "My business venture," he wrote, "went the way of all other enterprises and I was left without money, without a job and with a wife and two babies."[2]

Ironically, with thirty-five years gone and all else tried, he was ready to put his ideas on paper. But strangely, the experiences he had undergone, the colorful characters he had known—soldiers, cowboys, Indians, and miners—these, the stuff of realism and the reminders of an unstable past, he instinctively avoided. These experiences had physically shaped him into what he was—a solid, muscular man, sturdily framed, with broad shoulders and strong arms. His large hands, a family inheritance, with their thick, powerful fingers drew immediate attention. A masseur in a Turkish bath examined Burroughs' hands and remarked, "We get all kinds of people in here, but this is the first time I ever massaged a blacksmith."[3] Athletics, a vigorous outdoor life, cowpunching and horseback riding—at military school he had vaulted easily into the saddle from a standing position—had combined to develop a physique that altered little through the years.

Now, in writing, the strange characters and settings of a favorite fantasy, one to which his mind had often retreated, sprang to life easily with the rapid movement of his pen. Within any man's fantasy there is always a superhero, and of course the role is reserved for him alone. Edgar Rice Burroughs *was* his main character, playing the scene his imagination approved. At the story's opening he, the protagonist, was in a period of enforced return, the wild adventures temporarily over. He was a brooding, suffering man, dragged back without his consent, fated to walk the earth in agony, to tell of events that seemed crowded into the past: "I am a very old man; how old I do not know. Possibly I am a hundred, possibly more; but I cannot tell because I have never been like other men. I remember no childhood . . ."

That was the key, the prayer of all escapists—*not to be like other men.* Burroughs knew little about the techniques of writing but he understood that those who read his story would have their own dreams and fantasies, their own yearnings to get away from painful reality.

As he wrote he compiled a brief glossary of names and of special words used in the story, to him a fascinating task. A man is true master of a civilization when he can dictate its language, concocting such words as *Barsoom*—Mars; *Iss*—River of Death; *Woola*—a Barsoomian calot or dog; *Dejah Thoris*—a Princess of Helium; and *Helium*—the empire of the grandfather of Dejah Thoris.

The list was short, nothing approaching a complete vocabulary, but the words gave a genuine touch to the characters and scenes set on a planet millions of miles distant. The paradox of attempting to weld fantasy with reality and science with the wildest of fiction did not deter him. It was here that Burroughs first demonstrated one of the secrets of his success as a writer—he was able to make the most impossible tale seem as though it were really happening. It had been plausible in his imagination; he was willing to suspend disbelief and he presumed that the reader would respond the same way.

The protagonist, John Carter, was a romantic hero in the most glorious tradition. He was a chivalrous soldier of fortune, an adventurer, a man whose "only means of livelihood" had been fighting. In the foreword, a kind of prologue that is vital to the story, Burroughs describes Carter as:

. . . a splendid specimen of manhood, standing a good two inches over six feet, broad of shoulder and narrow of hip, with the carriage of the trained fighting man. His features were regular and clear cut, his hair black and closely cropped, while his eyes were of a steel gray, reflecting a strong and loyal character, filled with fire and initiative. His manners were perfect, and his courtliness was that of a typical southern gentleman of the highest type.

Burroughs created a character whose background and physical accomplishments were a super version of his own. "His horsemanship, especially after hounds," he wrote, "was a marvel and delight even in that country of magnificent horsemen." Carter had been cautioned about his "wild recklessness," but would respond with a laugh and say "that the tumble that killed him would be from the back of a horse yet unfoaled."

While prospecting in Arizona, Captain Carter strays into the dangerous territory of the Apaches, a situation duplicated by Burroughs in his activities with the Seventh Cavalry. But Arizona was selected as the briefest of settings; once Carter had faced the hostile Indians, all realism was discarded. Mysteriously transported through space, he finds himself among a race of huge green Martians whose young are hatched in glass incubators from eggs two-and-one-half feet in diameter.

It was a beginning, a tentative release of the bonds that had confined Ed's imagination. He wrote freely, all restraints overcome, and by August of 1911 a substantial section of the Mars story was finished. He had worked "very surreptitiously," commenting, "I was very much ashamed of my new vocation and until the story was nearly half completed I told no one about it, and then only my wife. It seemed a foolish thing for a full grown man to be doing—much on a par with dressing myself in a boy scout suit and running away from home to fight Indians."[4] Another, practical circumstance impelled him to secrecy. He still believed his future awaited him in the business world. What would his associates and prospective employers think of a

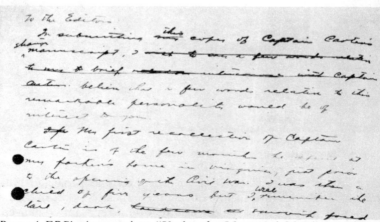

Part of ERB's foreword to "Under the Moons of Mars" in original form; published in book A Princess of Mars, 1917.

STORIES TOLD AND RETOLD

A PRINCESS
OF MARS

Edgar Rice Burroughs

OXFORD UNIVERSITY PRESS

Cover of A Princess of Mars, *Oxford University Press, 1962; book selected for series* Stories Told and Retold.

man who abandoned his sober surroundings and projected himself into unbelievable scenes on another planet? Ed feared that both his reputation and his career would be irreparably damaged.

Moreover, he was a novice to publishing; he knew nothing about magazine editors or the procedures for sending a story to them. When he had written twelve chapters, about 180 pages, he sat back to contemplate his work, convinced he had produced enough to demonstrate that he could write. He was pleased to realize that he still had a great deal of material left. The matter of a title became a problem. Uncertain, he settled for "My First Adventure on Mars," a title both weak and colorless. Shortly afterward he lined it out and inserted "The Green Martians"; this too he found unsatisfactory. He was beginning to appreciate the difficulty that all writers face in selecting titles.

Burroughs considered and in the right corner of the manuscript jotted down "Dejah Thoris Martian Princess," following it with question marks. Beneath the title he wrote an odd nom de plume—*By Normal Bean*. This choice was a measure of his own insecurity and of his modestly humorous appraisal of his writing ability. He wished to stress his ordinariness—that he had a very common head. But his adoption of a pen name was also dictated by his fear of identification with so fantastic a work. The solution was a refuge in anonymity.

Impressed by the popular *All-Story* magazine, he submitted his story to the magazine's editor and offered a brief summary of the plot:

The story is supposedly from the manuscript of a Virginian soldier of fortune who spends ten years on Mars, among the ferocious green men of that planet as well as with the highly developed and scientific race of dominant Martians, who closely resemble the inhabitants of Earth, except as to color. It is a member of this latter race which gives the story its name and at the same time infuses the element of love into the narrative.

Burroughs explained that the manuscript, the first part of *Dejah Thoris, Martian Princess,* totaled about 43,000 words and that he could offer "about two more parts of the same length." He couldn't resist including a personal endorsement that had the tone of a sales-pitch: "The story contains sufficient action, love, mystery and 'horror' to render it entertaining to a large majority of readers."

On August 24, 1911, the answering letter came from the Frank A. Munsey Company in New York, carrying the signature of the managing editor of *All-Story* Magazine, Thomas Newell Metcalf. An analyst par excellence and a man of succinct habits in writing, he mixed the good news with the bad. "There are many things about the story which I like," he said, "but on the other hand, there are points about which I am not so keen. Undoubtedly the story shows a great deal of imagination and ingenuity; but I am unable to judge . . . the total effect, on account of its unfinished condition."

Then he came to grips with the story's weaknesses: it was "too slow in getting under way." Obviously, at least for magazine purposes, he didn't care for the long, wordy foreword that described Captain Carter's background, his return after sixteen years, and his strange death. Metcalf also commented that Burroughs treated "too casually and vaguely Carter's leaving the earth and arriving upon Mars." He complained about the author's "long-windedness" and his tendency to tell many things that were unessential to the story.

Metcalf, with a dry humor, refers to the supposed "taciturnity of the Martians" which Burroughs had emphasized. ". . . yet you have one of the ladies tell a story of a couple of thousand words and often the Tharks talk to a great extent. Somehow, it seems to me you are hardly consistent." The lady was a young green-Martian woman assigned to Carter with combined duties of guide, housekeeper, and tutor. Metcalf, after some hesitation, eliminated the chapter titled "Sola Tells Me Her Story," but Burroughs restored it later in the book form.

Setting a 70,000-word limit, Metcalf went on to end the letter encouragingly: "If it would be possible for you to compress into that length a story as ingenious as is the greater part of what I have read, I should be . . . glad to consider it."

Burroughs was not at all perturbed by the editor's criticisms and suggestions for revision. In his letter of August 26 he displayed an eagerness to rewrite the story. He reverted curiously to the cold, practical philosophy of the businessman in explaining his reasons for writing: "I wrote this story because I needed the money it might bring, and not from motives of sentiment. . . ." (Sentiment was taboo—this from an author who wrote exaggeratedly romantic stories with beautiful heroines and noble, dashing heroes.) His added comment was a giveaway: ". . . although I became very much interested in it while writing." Ashamed to admit any sentiment about the characters who occupied his dreams, he hoped to avoid exposure through this deception and the often-repeated statement, obviously false, that money was his only motive for writing.

When Burroughs showed some confusion about the problem of the garrulous Tharks and the long account given by Sola, Metcalf, struggling to balance a natural asperity against a fear of being overblunt, fell into a style that was amusing in its own longwindedness, ". . . may I say that it will be perfectly easy to correct the inconsistency of which we have talked merely by neglecting to say that the Tharks are a taciturn people? At the same time, I believe that you can eliminate a good deal of their conversation."

In the letter of August 26, Burroughs had also outlined important sections of the last half of the story for Metcalf, including a vague and unsatisfactory ending scene for his hero, John Carter:

. . . later attempts to explore the mysterious Valley Dor at mouth of River Iss. Is caught in mighty air currents above the valley and borne high aloft into cold and darkness. Loses consciousness and awakens in his Arizona cave.

Metcalf, two days later, had his own suggestion for the ending, inquiring, "why would it not be possible to have the Martian city attacked by some kind of a plague, or something of that sort?" The Martian princess would then die, and afterward John Carter would contract the illness and find himself dying; he would awaken in the cave in Arizona.

This suggestion for the last scene proved an inspiration to Burroughs. On September 28 he commented, ". . . worked out the ending along the line you suggested, which is much more satisfactory than that I originally had in mind." But what he had devised far exceeded this modest statement. He had invented an unresolved ending, with the reader (protestingly, as it later developed) clutched and squirming in unbearable suspense. From this first Mars story on, his specialty was to be the unfinished ending and the inescapable sequel.

With the completed revisions the full manuscript was mailed. Perhaps the most thrilling letter of an author's career is the one announcing the first sale. On November 4 Metcalf wrote:

The Martian Princess' story is in perfectly good form now and I should like very much to buy it for publication in The All-Story Magazine. I therefore offer you for all serial rights, $400.00.

His acceptance included a request for permission to change the title and to do some cutting, especially at the beginning. In later years Burroughs commented: "The check was the first big event of my life. No amount of money today could possibly give me the thrill that that first $400 check gave me."

Burroughs' elation was tempered by a businessman's cold

analysis of the payment versus the time consumed. On November 6, he evaluated a future writing profession with considerable skepticism:

This story business is all new to me, but I like the work provided I can make it pay. However, I know that it would not be worth my while to devote all my time to it at this rate, as I started this story in July, which makes the remuneration equivalent to about $100.00 per month.

Metcalf had informed Burroughs that the title would be "In the Moons of Mars," but when the February 1912 *All-Story* appeared with the first installment, the "In" had been changed to "Under." More surprising was the discovery of an alteration in the author's name: it was printed as "Norman" Bean. The assumption was that an enterprising proofreader, dubious that such a name as "Normal" could be correct, had made the change.

Annoyed, Burroughs indicated in his letter of February 2 that as a result of the printer's blunder he was discarding his nom de plume. In sending a new manuscript he commented acidly:

You will also note that I have used my own name as author. I have done this because what little value was attached to my "trade" name was rendered nil by the inspired compositor who misspelled it in the February '11 Story—or was it the artist? ['11 is an obvious error.]

He finished by taking a humorous, more indulgent attitude:

I liked his illustration so well, however, that I easily forgave him; though I cannot forgive the printer who let "animal" get by for "mammal" twice.

The publication of "Under the Moons of Mars" was a beginning. Burroughs, while encouraged, accepted this first sale with caution and would not allow his expectations to soar. A full-fledged writing career was not as yet within his grasp. Nothing had changed, and the necessity to support his family sent him out again on a search for employment. But the most significant thing had been accomplished: he had attained an insight, a vision of his suppressed creativity. A fuller confidence and understanding were not far away. He was on the verge of finding himself.

PART 1
THE
EARLY YEARS

CHAPTER 2

CHILDHOOD AND A FIRST ADVENTURE

Ed Burroughs grew up in a busy environment. The three-story brick house on Chicago's West Side, Washington Boulevard between Lincoln and Robey Streets, solid and substantial, was in itself a symbol of middle-class prosperity. With its many rooms (and the customary basement) the house was well-designed for a large family. Ed, as the youngest child, became a fascinated spectator of the numerous activities of his father and three brothers. He was a sensitive child, observant, and eagerly attentive. An impression of lightness—pale skin and golden-brown hair—conveyed also the image of delicate health that concerned his parents.

Admiring his older brothers, he wished to emulate them, but he was not at all like brothers George, Harry, and Frank. His quick sense of humor was evident in these earliest years, along with his search for creative expression. Curious and imaginative, he liked to shape words and thoughts on paper, turning first, at the age of five, to rhyme:

I'm Dr. Burroaghs come to town,
To see my patint Maria Brown

An account of his education refers jokingly to "an advanced course in a private kindergarten," where the major activity seemed to be "weaving mats from strips of colored paper." [1] But most memorable were the years spent at the old Brown School on the West Side of Chicago, only a few blocks from the Burroughs

---

ERB as a boy of about ten.

Major George Tyler Burroughs, father of ERB, 1861.

home, the same school that George, Harry, and Frank had attended.

Secure within a close-knit circle of family and friends, Ed found this period a happy one. Four blocks to the east was Union Park, a quiet, grassy oasis set in the midst of busy city streets. One of the park's functions was to serve as a grazing area for the neighborhood cows brought there each day by the herdsmen. Major George was among those who kept a cow to supply fresh milk. In their rambles around the neighborhood, Ed and his friends visited the park for another reason: they enjoyed tossing peanuts to Old Bob, the grizzly bear.

The Brown School friends who grew up with Ed were William (Billy) Carpenter Camp; Alson Clark, the painter; Ben Marshall, a successful Chicago architect; and Mancel T. Clark, a wealthy paint manufacturer. Florenz Ziegfeld, the celebrated theatrical producer, was also a pupil at the Brown School. Here, Ed was assigned to what he jokingly listed as his first army experience. Within a list titled My Wonderful Military Career, he

Mr. and Mrs. George Tyler Burroughs and grandson Studley in home at 646 Washington Boulevard, Chicago, 1896.

Mary Evaline Burroughs, ERB's mother.

Alvin Hulbert family home at corner of Robie and Park Avenue, Chicago; the boy in the surrey is Alvin Hulbert, Jr.

noted that he had been "Right Guard, Brown School Cadets," and added in parentheses, "Wooden gun."[2]

Near the Burroughs home on Washington Boulevard resided Alvin Hulbert, his wife Emma Theresa, and their children. For George's four sons the normal neighborly relationships were made more attractive because of the four lively Hulbert sisters—Leila, the oldest, Julia, Jessie, and Emma—who occupied the three-story family residence at 194 Park Avenue. Walking to and from the Brown School, young Ed and Emma often met and formed an early habit of being together.

From the age of six Ed showed an interest and delight in letter writing, enjoying opportunities to correspond with members of his family when they were away from home. On February 19, 1882, his father, while staying in Washington, D. C., received a letter from Ed, written in heavy capitals, reading, "HOW ARE YOU. I MISS YOU VERY MUCH. WE ARE ALL WELL."[3]

In 1885 George Jr. and Henry (Harry) were sent to Yale University by their father, and they enrolled in the Sheffield Scientific School. George, the older of the two, had his education delayed because of illness, and as a result, the brothers entered Yale together.[4] Ed, in this first long separation from his brothers, missed them keenly. He corresponded regularly, eager to hear of

Alvin Hulbert family; seated, left to right: Emma Theresa Hulbert and Alvin Hulbert; standing, left to right: Alvin Hulbert, Jr., Leila, Emma Centennia, Julia, and Jessie.

their activities and to tell about his. These letters reveal much about the beginnings of his creativity, not only in his writing and poetry, but also in his drawings and cartoons, which, often humorous, served as illustrations for his comments, news items, or poems. The letters present an intimate picture of the warm, sympathetic relationships between all of the brothers.

On February 13, 1887, Ed sent his brother George a valentine, and George responded on February 22 to thank him:

". . . it was the only one we received. Did you get many?"

Ed had evidently told of a burglary in the neighborhood, for George wrote:

You must have had quite an exciting time with Dr. Adolphus' burgular. I should think neither the doctor nor Mr. Simington would feel very safe with vacant houses next to them which afford burglars so easy an entrance.

George reveals Ed's interest in reading:

I am glad you are reading "Tales of Ancient Greece" and am not surprised that you enjoy it. I know I did when I read it.

Now if you will take one of our "Barnes General Histories" that I asked Mother to send to us, and read up the history of Greece, which you will find some what closely related to its Mythology, that is the early history, your reading will be more interesting as well as instructive.

39

An 1885 pencil sketch by ERB at age ten.

An 1885 sketch by ERB, at age ten, of an Indian mounted on an elephant.

In continuing, George tells of an incident that might have been serious:

About half the University & half the freshman crew had a nice mud bath down at the boathouse Sat. A platform broke, dropping us about six feet into the slimiest mud I ever saw. I landed square on top of another fellows & so, fortunately, came off somewhat better than I otherwise would, but I was a sight.

George explains about privileges at Yale:

There is still one saloon which we cannot enter and unless our nine, that is the freshman nine defeat the Harvard freshmen in the Spring we are not allowed to sit on the "fence." I think you will find an account of this custom in that book I gave the folks Christmas.

In a joint letter to Harry and George, dated March 27, 1887, Ed, age eleven and one-half, draws a picture, presumably of himself, holding a telephone receiver to his ear while he addresses his brothers. He tells of watching experiments of "crystalizing" under the "microscope" which were "fine." Ed compliments Harry, telling proudly that the man who performed the experiments said that "the fly wing you mounted was mounted as well if not better than any he had. I saw it too." At the close of his letter to Harry he says, "I will be glad when the time comes for you boys to come home."

In the section intended for George, Ed begins:

As I wrote to Harry first I have pretty near emptied my fertile brain but will try to think of some thing more, For instance How are you getting along in your studies? I am getting along first rate backwards. As I lose every letter I get I cant answer them atall. A boy and I have gone into the yeast business x x x x x And broken up. "A Boy" has offered me some pigeons (two) and I expect to get them some time before I die.

At the top of the second page Ed has drawn a picture of the American flag floating from the top of a pole that extends vertically along the left margin of the sheet almost to the bottom. A man in a cowboy suit and hat has climbed more than halfway up the pole. We see that he has dropped his gun and that it is falling through the air. On the ground at the foot of the pole an odd-appearing little animal is waiting. All of this is designed to illustrate the poem which Edgar "made up . . . this morning. . . ."[5]

The lure of cartooning that drove him, even at this early age, to drawing his small illustrations and comical figures in the margins of his letters and poems was also evident in his school textbooks. Within the covers and in the margins of the pages he drew his cartoons; their presence creates the suspicion that his attention could stray from his school work to an activity he found more stimulating.

A more significant part of his creativity was demonstrated in the delight he took in making up stories. Because of his low resistance to colds and infections, he was often confined to bed. At these times he became impatient with the old fables that his mother told him, preferring to create his own imaginative tales and tell them to her.[6]

Ed's poetry writing as an outlet for his imagination was just one part of his youthful development. Major George, always the practical businessman, took the opportunity to provide his son with an experience in the field of commerce. A note dated February 21, 1887, and signed by George Burroughs was evidently used in a business transaction involving Ed. George, using formal terminology, devised a legal form for his twelve-year old son:

On or before March 1st 1888 for value received I promise to pay Edgar R. Burroughs Twenty Seven & 50/100 ($27 50/100) with interest at the rate of six percent per annum.

Whether George purchased something belonging to Ed, or whether he borrowed some of his son's money has not been ascertained. The transaction may have been part of a business game, and not viewed as a real obligation, for George appears to have forgotten about it until years later. But he did discover it and pay it off—with interest. Written across the note is the statement "Paid March 31st 1898 $46.12."

Possibly because of the death of Ed's two infant brothers, his parents became cautious about his health, and when the city was swept by an epidemic of diphtheria, they decided to take him out of the public schools. He was midway through the sixth grade, but his parents, unwilling to take chances, began a search for a private school. The only one available on the West Side was Mrs. K. S. Cooley's School for Girls.

To a twelve-year-old boy the prospect was appalling. Ed reacted to the situation with an attitude of extreme distaste. It was little consolation to him that the parents of a half-dozen of his closest friends were following the Burroughs' example. Billy Camp, Ben Marshall, Mancel Clark, and others were placed in Miss Cooley's school. Ed spent only a brief period there, later commenting, "I know that we all got out of Miss Cooley's Maplehurst School for Girls as quickly as unfeeling parents would permit."

A report card issued by Miss Cooley, dated "April 9th to May 11th 1888," reveals that Ed was a better-than-average student. He received high marks of 98 in geography and 95 in reading. His lowest mark, 80, was in composition.

The Burroughs family had always stressed good health habits and exercise, and this was evidenced in the letters written by brother George while he was at Yale in 1887 and 1888.[7] Concerned about reports of illness, he wrote to his father on December 4, 1887:

I am sorry that Mother & Eddie are not well. I am afraid that neither of them get enough outdoor exercise to keep their systems in order.

Plain food, regular habits, good hours & plenty of exercise keep me in such perfect health that I want to prescribe the same for every one who is not feeling well.

George was both firm and frank in emphasizing his objections to a program of excessive studying at the expense of physical fitness. He clearly had no patience with the student who turned himself into a grind, and in a letter of January 9, 1887, commented:

. . . When I came down here I had hopes that I might distinguish myself in my studies (in some one), but I find that impossible and when I look at those of my classmates who do the best, I feel thankful that I am not like them, for with a few exceptions the "digs" are a poor, sickly looking lot. I hope however that I will know as much as any of them at the end for I will learn from them in recitations & when I get hold of a thing once I remember it. I tell you this for I want you to understand that even if I don't make a mark I am working and not wasting my time.

On April 8, 1888, again from Yale to his father, George, concerned about Eddie's health, wrote:

. . . I am glad Eddie has a bicycle, & hope he will have some inducement to keep him riding it.

I dont think any of us ever realized how much good our bi-cycles did Harry & I how much time we spent on them out of doors when we would otherwise have been in the house.

Frank & Eddie are neither of them as strong & well as they ought to be and I think it is because they do not take exercise enough in the open air. Not that it would do either of them any good to force them to do something distasteful to them. . . .

As Eddie spent more time outdoors, his health improved. Bi-cycle riding became a source of enjoyment, and on Chicago's Warren Avenue, where a first stretch of experimental asphalt pavement had been laid, running west from Ogden Avenue to Western, he rode his bike for many hours.[8]

Although it cannot be documented, it is assumed that during this period the Hulbert and Burroughs families were probably in neighborly association, and Ed found his attachment to Emma growing stronger. A youthful romance was develop-ing, and he soon preferred to devote most of his attentions to her.

Emma's father, Alvin Hulbert, had acquired a position of esteem in Chicago business circles; he was respected as a civic leader, and his reputation in the community was comparable to that held by George Burroughs. Alvin had shown an early in-terest in the hotel business and had worked as a clerk in the old Sherman House in Chicago. He and W. S. Eden later became owners of the Tremont and Great Northern Hotels. Alvin's ven-tures were highly successful, and in October 1871, after the Sher-man House was burned to the ground, he made arrangements

Masthead of cover of Hotel World *magazine, February 10, 1900.*

for the erection of a new hotel with 250 rooms. As its genial landlord, known for his "urbanity and pleasant manners," he received the enthusiastic approval of the hotel guests.[9] He was also associated with the Lindell Hotels in St. Louis.

Alvin's entry into politics in the primary of March 26, 1880, resulted in his defeating his opponent R. P. Williams and being elected Alderman of the Twelfth Ward. He ran on the regular Republican ticket, and in a letter to the *New York Times* (date unknown) protested about the *Times'* error in referring to him as an independent Democrat. He maintained that he had always been a stalwart Republican.[10]

While Emma continued to attend the Brown School, Ed, happy to escape from Miss Cooley's Maplehurst School for Girls, in the fall of 1888 entered the Harvard School on 21st Street and Indiana Avenue. His brother Frank (called Coleman) had been a student at Harvard for a year. Ed remarked, "I was never a student—I just went to school there."[11]

He had vivid recollections of the period:

Benny Marshall, the Chicago architect, was one of my classmates. We used to sneak down to the lake and sit on the breakwater and smoke cubeb cigarettes, thinking that we were regular devils.

While I was attending Harvard School, we lived on the west side on Washington Boulevard, about four blocks west of Union Park; and I often rode my pony to school, keeping it in a livery stable near Twenty-Second Street. It would be difficult to imagine riding a pony from the west side to Twenty-First and Indiana today.[12]

He explained that the West Side was "where everybody made his money in those days and then moved to the South Side to show off." In good weather Ed either drove or rode to school. He remembered other details clearly:

In inclement weather, I took the Madison Street horsecars to Wabash, a cable-car to 18th Street, and another horse-car to school. Sometimes, returning from school, I used to run down Madison Street from State Street to Lincoln Street, a matter of some three miles, to see how many horsecars I could beat in that direction. It tires me all out even to think of it now. I must have been long on energy, if a trifle short on brains.[13]

Of the school staff young Burroughs never forgot Principal John C. Grant, of whom he was "scared to death," and Professor

John J. Schobinger, also listed as principal, who was determined that the students should learn Greek and Latin grammar before turning to a study of English. A *Harvard School* report card, issued on September 7, 1891, covers the period of September 1890 to February 1891, and lists average marks on a scale of 100: Arithmetic, 62; English, 67; Algebra, 79; Latin, 83.

Evidently because of the concentration on Latin, Ed was far stronger in this subject than he was in English.[14] The disparity between the marks on arithmetic and algebra is difficult to explain. In a letter of September 3, 1891, addressed to "Whom this may concern," and signed by both Schobinger and Grant, there is a statement that "he [Ed] leaves the school of his own accord, in good standing." Ed had left the school months earlier, and this certificate of moral character was obviously issued at the request of his father, who needed it for Ed's next school—Phillips Academy. A later combination of report card and character reference, written on the seventh, explains that Ed is "of good moral character and he left our school on account of ill-health." This new version of the reasons for Ed's departure from Harvard may have been demanded by George Burroughs, who was undoubtedly sensitive about his son's weak achievement at the school. Burroughs may have removed his son because of a fear of an epidemic of la grippe which had spread throughout Chicago. Another possibility is that Harvard itself may have been temporarily closed, for a later reference about this school period mentions that ". . . epidemics had closed two schools that I had attended."[15]

That Ed's departure was abrupt is indicated in the exchange of letters (three in all) between Schobinger and Burroughs. On September 7 the Professor wrote:

Your letter being dated Sept 6th and Edgar not having called, I suppose he is gone by this time. I therefore send you the required certificate by mail, as required. . .[16]

At any rate, when Ed left Harvard School in midsemester, some time after February 1891, he must have done so with relief. The typical school studies, the lessons in Greek and Latin, he found dreary tasks. Highly imaginative, he could discover in these subjects nothing to motivate him. But the new plans for the coming months created a feeling of joy and excitement. His destination, for a fifteen-year-old boy, was like something out of his dreams. Awaiting him was the high road to adventure.

Upon their graduation from Yale in 1889, George and Harry returned to Chicago where they went to work in their father's American Battery Company. Harry, at his desk job in an atmosphere filled with battery fumes, quickly developed a cough which worsened as the days went by; his lungs appeared to show the first signs of consumption. The doctor insisted that a change of climate was imperative. Through a friend, Major George arranged at once to purchase land for a cattle ranch in southern Idaho. Lew Sweetser, a Yale classmate, whose father also supplied some of the money, joined in the Burroughs' venture. The vigorous outdoor life of a cowpuncher built up Harry's damaged lungs and restored him to good health.

Located in Cassia County, Idaho, on a section of the extensive ranges owned by "Cattle King" Jim Pierce, the Burroughs-Sweetser spread occupied land along the lower Raft River, in the southeastern part of the state. The ranch was about thirty miles from American Falls, the railway station and shipping point for the cattle. To honor their alma mater the brothers called their ranch the *Bar Y*, and after persuading the federal government to establish a post office near the ranch, paid further tribute to their college by naming the post office *Yale*.

It was to the state of Idaho, newly admitted to the Union on July 3, 1890, that Ed was sent by his father. To a big city boy the sudden removal to a rough, primitive country was a thrilling adventure. From the strict discipline of school and the close supervision of his father he now found himself in the free-and-easy atmosphere of ranch life and under the indulgent care of brothers George and Harry. His friends were rugged and sometimes wild cowboys and miners who because of their vigor and individuality appeared like characters out of a western adventure novel. In contrast, Ed was probably looked upon as a true tenderfoot. His only practical experience, pony riding on city streets, was of only rudimentary value on the *Bar Y* Ranch.

The story of his Idaho cowboy days is colorfully narrated in his *Autobiography:*

I did chores, grubbed sage brush and drove a team of bronchos to a sulky plow. I recall that once, after I unhooked them, they ran away and evidently, not being endowed with any too much intelligence, I hung onto the lines after tripping over a sage brush and was dragged around the country three times on my face. . . .[17]

JONATHAN ABEL, President
HAROLD STURGES, Secretary

GEO. T. BURROUGHS, Vice-Pres't
WILSON AMES, Secretary

AMERICAN BATTERY CO.

MANUFACTURERS OF THE MORRISON

STORAGE BATTERIES

OFFICE, ROOM 709
SECURITY BUILDING, 188 MADISON ST.

TELEPHONE MAIN 3620

Factory, 353 to 361 W. Twentieth St.
TELEPHONE CANAL 170

OVER

.CHICAGO, ILL.

Front of American Battery Company business card.

American Battery Company office, 172-174 South Clinton Street, Chicago, about 1901.

Business card of Sweetser and Burroughs Bar Y Ranch (Y).

He aroused the amazement of the cowboys and won "instant distinction" when he tried to pay for a drink with pennies:

No one in Idaho had ever before seen a penny. Two drinks were "two-bits"; one drink was "two-bits"; a cigar wàs "two-bits"; things were "two-bits," "four-bits," "six-bits." There were no pennies and there was no paper money. Everything was silver or gold; at least I understand there was gold there, though I never saw any of it.

The greenest of ranch hands, young Burroughs began to gain his experience in the most painful ways.[18] His brothers George and Harry were hard put to find some tasks he could do. ". . . as I had proven more or less of a flop as a chore boy," Ed noted, "they appointed me mail carrier." He rode daily to the railroad at American Falls, either on horseback or, if there was freight to bring back, with a team and wagon. When he went on horseback, he made the round trip of sixty miles in one day.

His most exasperating experiences were with horses:

The team that I drove consisted of two outlawed bronchos; one was locoed and the other was too mean to ride. One day the wagon went through a bridge and I had to go about five miles to a ranch house to borrow the necessary tools to get it out. Being a tenderfoot, a horse to me was a horse and not knowing anything about the past lives or reputations of either of the team I naturally climbed aboard the bad one and rode him bareback

ERB at age sixteen in Idaho.

five miles to the ranch. Here I loaded up with shovels, picks and crowbars and climbed back onto the broncho, riding the five miles back to the stalled wagon with assorted hardware bumping him on all his corners, which goes to show that Providence really does look after a certain class of people.

In another incident which demonstrated that naivete and good luck seemed to go together, he was asked to go to the pasture and bring some horses back to the corrals. They belonged to a newly arrived cow outfit. Everybody assumed that Ed would take one of the ranch horses for the trip to the pasture, but instead he chose a strange horse that was standing saddled and bridled. He was unaware of its bad reputation and that it was being ridden by Hi Rice, a famous bronco-buster. Neglecting also to look at the cinch, he climbed hastily aboard and rode away.

As they approached a steep bank of the Raft River, the horse clambered up and the saddle suddenly slipped off over his tail. Ed went head-over-heels, landing on the ground behind the animal. "He should have killed me," Ed said, "but instead he stopped with the cinch around his hind feet and turned an inquiring glance back at me." Later, when he had replaced the saddle, rounded up the horses, and returned to the corrals, a "goggle-eyed group of cowpunchers" was waiting for him, "including a couple of terrified brothers." They all stared as he rode in, "safe and alive, on the worst horse in Cassia County."[19]

These incidents, humorously exaggerated, do not give credit to Ed's knack in handling horses, evident even at this early age. His love of horses and riding—"when I got my leg over a horse I owned the world"—was matched by a sensitive and understanding attitude toward almost all animals.[20]

"At this time," he commented, "I learned . . . to take care of my horses, especially their backs, and I became proud of the fact that I never gave a horse a sore back, nor have I in my life." During a fall roundup he was given two horses with sore backs and both of them were healed while he was riding them.

Ed had noticed one horse, a beautiful black gelding, "fat as butter, with a long mane and a tail that almost dragged the ground." The condition of the tail indicated that the horse hadn't been ridden for some time since it was the custom to thin out the tail hairs so that the tail would not get full of burs and sagebrush.[21] The significance of this and other revealing facts about the horse, Whisky Jack, escaped Ed:

He had killed one man and maimed several others, but he was the only horse that was in good condition and it seemed a shame

*to ride our poor worn out crow baits while he was running in
sleek and glossy idleness.*

Eager to ride Whisky Jack, Ed pleaded with Jim Pierce until
he was given permission. The men had to throw and hogtie the
animal before they could saddle and bridle him. Then they put
a blind on the horse while Ed mounted. When they removed the
blind, Whisky Jack took two jumps, slipped, and fell, with Ed
beneath him.

*He didn't break anything in me, but I certainly hurt. However,
I had to hide it for fear the boss wouldn't let me try it again.
He was surprised when he found that I wanted to; he even grew
enthusiastic. It had now become a sporting proposition with him
and he offered to give me the horse if I could ride him.*

Ed mounted the horse again, doubtful himself that he would
last very long. But Whisky Jack adopted a more tractable attitude: "I stayed on him all that day because I was afraid if I
got off I could never get on again. . . ." He rode the horse as
long as he remained in Idaho, never bridling him but using a
hackamore and a shoelace for a head-stall. Kindness changed
Whisky Jack remarkably; with Ed he was always docile, but he
would still refuse to allow any other man to handle him.

Whisky Jack's reaction was violent, although not unexpected,
the first time Ed used him to carry the mail:

*The Government furnished leather mail bags that went over the
horse's rump behind the saddle and hung down on either side.
They were equipped with metal staples and padlocks that rat-
tled. I had to blindfold Jack to get them on him at all, then I
mounted and jerked off the blind. He took a few steps, felt the
bags against his sides, heard the rattle of the padlocks and started
to leave the country. The road wound through foothills and he
ran for ten miles before he became resigned to the fact that he
couldn't leave the mail bags behind.*

On another occasion Whisky Jack, startled by something, began to buck wildly when Ed mounted him for the return trip
from American Falls to Yale:

*There was a little gulley on the way out of town and some China-
men lived in a dugout there. . . . Whisky Jack elected to buck
up onto the roof of this dugout. That roof must have been constructed of railroad ties. If it had been of any lighter construction,*

we should have gone through. I had a fleeting glimpse of a dozen wild eyed Chinamen scurrying from the interior, and then Jack bucked off down the road relieving me of considerable embarrassment.

Ed recalled those early Idaho days with some nostalgia:

. . . I slept on the floor of a log cabin and in the winter time the snow drifted in under the door. When I got up at four o'clock in the morning to do the chores, I had only two garments to put on, my hat and my boots. The hat went on easy enough, but the boots were always frozen. I wonder why we recall such hardships as among the happiest experiences of our lives.

Cassia County of the 1890s, a section of raw, frontier America, naturally bred rough, violent men. The images of the tough men Ed knew remained vivid in his memory. One, an old man named Blanco, "stammered terribly and cursed like a pirate." Because of his utter fearlessness and uncontrollable temper, nobody dared oppose him in any way. Ed's first experience with him was in a saloon in Albion. Noting the stick pin Ed was wearing, a miniature replica of a cartridge, Blanco walked calmly up to him, removed it from his tie, and stuck it in his own shirt. Ed had heard of Blanco and decided, with discretion, not to offer any protest. "I thought it better to show my deference for age," he said, "and let it go at that."[22]

Texas Pete, a young cowpuncher who arrived at the Burroughs' ranch dead broke, was another one whom Ed remembered. Pete, given a job grubbing sagebrush at seventy-five cents an acre, was charged, according to custom, the usual amount for his board. After working for several weeks, he decided to leave. His earnings were totaled, his board bill deducted, and he was paid the difference. Pete got the full amount—"six-bits"—which Ed then won from him in a crap game.

Ed found Pete to be very likable, "but like most Texans always ready to fight":

I saw him fighting with another puncher one day during a round-up. They went into a clinch on the ground and each one was spurring the other in the back with long roweled Mexican spurs. The foreman used to take their guns away from them in camp; so they had to use spurs.[23]

About Pete, Ed commented, "He had the reputation of being

53

a bad man, but there was nothing bad about him."[24] The events had a tragic outcome. Pete, wanted for some minor law violation, attempted to evade arrest by rowing across the Snake River. He was shot by the sheriff.[25]

Although he was only sixteen, Ed's imagination and powers of observation were stimulated by the colorful characters who surrounded him. Their actions, attitudes, and mannerisms were recorded in his memory. Of the sheriff, Gum Brown, he recalled:

Whenever anyone had to be arrested or a posse was formed, Gum would go around the saloon and point to the cowboys saying, "I deputize yo'; I deputize yo'", and nobody would pay any attention to him. It was a standing joke in Albion.[26]

Other memorable characters were Hank Monk, a cook on the ranch, and Sam Lands, a garrulous cowpuncher who specialized in tall stories. About Monk, Ed remarked, "I could always tell when we were going to have baking powder biscuits: Monk would have flour in his ears and nose. . . . The less one saw of Hank cooking, the better his appetite."[27]

And Lands had an unforgettable story about a bad horse he had ridden:

. . . the horse threw him but his foot caught in the stirrup; and, he said, the horse "drug" him for three days and three nights and that all he had to drink was when he "drug" him through a river, and that all he had to eat was when he "drug" him through a strawberry patch.[28]

To Ed everything that occurred on the ranch was exciting and adventurous. One of his most enjoyable chores was "chasing bulls out of the alfalfa":

There were quite a number of imported Hereford bulls on the range, and there never was a fence built that would hold them. They put their necks under the lower wire and either lifted the post out of the ground or pulled the staples all out. Then we would have maybe three or four of them in our alfalfa. It was my job to take a shotgun loaded with very fine shot, go down on horseback and chase them out. Upon these occasions I played Buffalo Bill, pretending that the bulls were buffalo. I would ride along beside them and pepper them in the seat.[29]

On one occasion Ed had a real scare. The enraged bull

whirled about suddenly to charge him. With the animal very close, Ed fired, hitting him right between the eyes. The bull turned a "complete somersault." Ed rode back to the ranch in a panic, convinced he had killed a three- or four-thousand-dollar bull. Later he was relieved to discover that the animal displayed no symptoms of pain or injury.[30]

Those were the days of bitter rivalry between the cattle and sheep ranches that led to violence and shootings. Unaware at first when the spring roundup began, Ed soon discovered that the man riding with him was a "very likable murderer." As they were resting on a hillside, his friend described how he had killed a man named Paxton and Ed took it in stride:

It was perfectly all right because each of the two men had been hired to kill the other and though Paxton got the drop on him across the dinner table, my friend came out alive and Paxton didn't.[31]

This brief Idaho period in 1891 had given Ed freedom and a touch of the kind of carefree, adventurous life he would seek again. A restlessness and a need to express his masculinity remained with him, governing some of his future actions. But now a summons from his father brought him, regretfully, back to Chicago and a resumption of his education.[32] In contrast to the exciting days he had spent with cowboys and badmen, and the exhilarating physical challenge he had encountered, a program of classroom studies could only appear dull and boring. Major George had already made preparations for Ed's enrollment in school, but he found his son uninterested in a return to books and exams—and even rebellious. The days ahead were to be ones of tension at home, unhappiness for Ed, and disappointment and irritation for his father.

CHAPTER 3

SCHOOLING, REBELLION AND DISCIPLINE

Ed's scrapbook, a bulky collection of papers, cards, and clippings, all reminders of his school days, displays at the beginning a page of the printed entrance examination to Phillips Academy, Andover, Massachusetts, dated September 1891. The page contains problems in mathematics, covering "Algebra to Simple Equations" and "Simple Equations to Quadratics." Written in ink at the bottom is the notation "Passed, Mark 20."

While the Phillips catalog advised that "No age is prescribed for admission," it offered more specific information in its statement that "boys fourteen years of age usually possess sufficient maturity for the responsibilities of school-life here."[1] Ed, just sixteen, and probably overage for a new student, was required to fill out the school's entrance form containing eighteen questions. At the top he listed himself as a candidate for the "Junior Middle E class" (English), adding the projected date of graduation—class of 1894.

He answered the questions in a clear, firm handwriting. Under question six, *Father's business or Profession,* he wrote, "Vice Pres. Anglo American Battery Co." The reason for his own version of the company name is not clear. Under *Father's Titles* he wrote "Major in late war." His mother's birthplace was listed only as "State of Indiana." After *Church Denomination* Ed drew a long line, indicating "none." He of course gave his last school as "Harvard School, Chicago," and the "Chief Instructor" as "Prof. J. J. Schobinger." Other answers revealed that he took room

Tintype photo of four Michigan Military cadets, probably in plebe year; ERB upper left.

and board with Mrs. C. A. Morrill, presumably in Andover, and that his brother Frank Coleman Burroughs had attended the school in 1890 and 1891. To be exact, Frank was in the English Department for two years, 1890-92, as a Junior Middler and Senior Middler.[2]

Phillips Academy, already 113 years old, had first opened for instruction on April 30, 1778. It had been founded by Samuel Phillips, his brother John, and Samuel Phillips, Jr., in that year, although not incorporated until October 4, 1780. As part of the Academy's remarkable history, a most distinguished visitor and speaker, George Washington, on November 5, 1789, addressed the students assembled on the Old Training Field.[3] The fourth principal was John Adams, and during his term the second schoolhouse was burned in 1818, and a new brick Academy was built. This was the "classic hall" described in Oliver Wendell Holmes' centennial poem, "The School-Boy."[4]

The principal at the time of Ed's enrollment was Dr. Cecil F. P. Bancroft, in charge from 1873 until his death in 1901. He is described as "a man of foresight and clear vision, patience and shrewd discrimination."[5] During his administration, attendance increased from 262 to more than 400 pupils. When Ed attended, 1891-92, the exact number was 440, with 184 in the English department and 256 in the Classical department. The pupils came from thirty-eight states and from Hawaii, Japan, Canada, and even Turkey. The tuition for the fall term was $30, winter term, $25, and spring term, $20.

As a Junior Middler in the English department Ed would be required to follow the course of study emphasizing mathematics and the "Natural Sciences, with History, Latin, Modern Languages, and Literature." The catalog states that "The Course of Study is designed to furnish a broad and thorough preparation for the Sheffield Scientific School of Yale University, the Massachusetts Institute of Technology, and other scientific schools and colleges."[6]

All Junior Middle Year students were required to study Latin, but in the Middle Year, French or German was substituted, with Latin becoming elective. The course of study for the Junior Middlers in the Latin department included both Latin (notably Caesar's Gallic Wars) and Greek, plus mathematics and English, in the first term. The second term maintained a Latin sequence with selections from *Ovid* and part of the *Aeneid* of Virgil. Additional Greek, mathematics, and English were required.

The serious scholastic atmosphere of Phillips Academy must have been disconcerting to young Ed Burroughs. But as always he was quick to make friends and was eagerly accepted by the other students. The popularity he quickly achieved with his class-mates may be explained, at least partially, by the colorful anec-dotes he probably told them about his Idaho days. Since for some unexplained reason he arrived with a guitar in his luggage, he was urged to join the Mandolin Club and given a further invitation to the Glee Club.

In regard to the Mandolin Club, he recalled that "I agreed with alacrity, although I cannot conceive that I could have done so without misgivings, inasmuch as I had never played a guitar, am totally devoid of any sense of music and did not know one note from another."[7] He further comments, "They must have been embarrassed when they discovered that I could not play guitar. Anyhow my engagement with the glee club was brief."[8]

While there appeared to be no doubt about his musical limitations, he soon began to express his natural creativity in the familiar directions. Ed turned to the *Mirror,* a publication spon-sored by the Philomathean Society, the literary organization of the school. The *Mirror,* printed once a term, was designed as an out-let for Philomathean members, providing "an opportunity for writing stories, poems and grinds, and for making cuts."[9] Grinds seemed to be quotes by well-known authors, usually witty or humorous, submitted by students who either signed their names or used fictitious names. The grind might apply aptly to the stu-dent himself, in a joking way, or to other students.[10]

Ed submitted material for the *Mirror* of Fall 1891 and Winter 1892. There are no grinds printed with his name beneath, but some may have appeared under a pseudonym, for in the issue of 1891 the editorial review contains an acknowledgment stat-ing, "We are also indebted for grinds and cuts to E. R. Bir-roughs." A number of cuts or cartoons, mainly humorous in nature, are Ed's work (they are initialed E.R.B. in his copy of the 1891 *Mirror*). The first illustration, on the table of contents page, consists of eight human figures spaced about the perimeter of the box that encloses the magazine's contents. These figures perch there or are engaged in various climbing actions. A typical humorous example is a drawing of an odd little machine titled The Mirror Grinding Machine, described beneath as a "Head Reducer." Sketches of a boy are shown, the head at first large and then reduced in size. A caption reads, "Before and After Using."

Another page in the *Mirror* of fall 1891 displays cuts of horses, Ed's favorite subject for drawing. The horses, although small, are skillfully and realistically done.

In the *Mirror* of Winter 1892, the editorial comment refers to a poetry contest and explains, "1st prize for Poem to S. A. Dickerson and in connection with this we are obliged to state that the judges, on account of the lack of competition in poems, deemed it best to award no second prize. . . ." But whether considered worthy of a prize or not, the poem printed in this issue (author unnamed) bears the stamp of Ed's particular humor and style. Titled "Possum et Coona," it stresses a clever distortion of Latin.[11]

The poem tells the story of two boys who go hunting with their dog. When they proudly bring a possum home, displaying him to their parents, comparisons of their glory are made with David, Samson, Caesar, and others. But when they wake in the morning they find that the possum was not really dead, he was playing possum—"the possum est ressurectum." He has fled and they are quite crestfallen. The poem ends: "Pueri think non plus of Caesar, Coad urcum, Shalmeneser;/Take your laurels, cum the honor, Since ista possum is a goner."

The *Mirror* of 1892, in its list of contributors, expresses indebtedness to E. R. Burroughs for cuts only. None of these has been identified. Ed is listed as a member of the Athletic Association and as president of his class. This award of the highest honor by his fellow classmates, presumably stemming from Ed's personal popularity, was also announced on January 20, 1892, in *The Phillipian,* the school newspaper. The brief note contains a misspelling of the new president's name:

Elections. A class meeting of P.S. '94 was held Wednesday noon and the following officers were elected: President, Burrows; vice-president, Clark; secretary and treasurer, Finch.[12]

Commenting on both his selection as class president and the class colors of P.S. '94—pale blue and orange—Ed wrote, "when one considers their choice of a presiding officer the selection of blue seems nothing short of an inspiration, but the fruit should have been lemon."[13]

In the passing days he devoted much of his time to extracurricular activities.[14] A side interest in sports, but neither as a participant nor spectator, is revealed in a letter pasted in his scrapbook. Dated November 23, 1891, the letter, concerned with the placing of a bet, was addressed to him at Andover and came from the office of Stoddard & Kendall in Boston. The firm, according to the items printed on its letterhead, handled a large variety of sports equipment. On the list are fishing tackle, skates, baseball supplies, lawn tennis, and gymnasium goods. The miscellaneous merchandise includes cutlery and hair clippers. The letter to Ed advises:

Dear Sir
I enclose you a check for stake on the Amherst Williams game as it resulted in a tie.
Respty yours
J. L. Crafts[15]

Unfortunately, from the moment of his arrival at Phillips, Ed showed little inclination to concentrate on his studies. His reaction to the formal curriculum at the Academy, with its familiar emphasis upon Latin and Greek, was hardly enthusiastic. He had been equally unimpressed by the same subject requirements at Harvard School.[16] His lack of effort and achievement came to the attention of Principal Bancroft. "Banty," as the students called him, believed that a semester's trial was enough; he reached the limit of his patience. Once the holidays were over, and shortly after school reconvened for the new term on January 15, 1892, Banty made his decision known. George Burroughs received a firm request for the withdrawal of his son. Ed's stay at Phillips terminated as abruptly as it began. It appears that his election as president and his dismissal from the school occurred close enough in date to almost coincide. Obviously, at the class graduation in 1894 President Burroughs would not officiate.[17]

Though his annoyance and disappointment were great, George Burroughs still exhibited unusual control and managed to accept his son's return with an attitude of tolerance and understanding.[18] But he had no intention of abandoning Ed's schooling. Perhaps a more disciplined environment was the answer. Retired Major Burroughs turned to a popular solution, often adopted by parents of problem sons: Ed would be sent to a military school.

The chosen institution was Michigan Military Academy, situated at Orchard Lake, twenty-six miles northwest of Detroit. It had been in existence for fifteen years. Ed later wrote with wry amusement that the academy had a "sub rosa reputation as a polite reform school."[19]

Whether the academy's requirements were really stricter than those of similar schools is doubtful. Certainly, as expected in a military school, the cadets' activities were severely regimented. Emphasis was upon army routine, drilling, and above all discipline and obedience. Physical development was an important goal, and to achieve it the cadets led a hard, rough-and-tumble life.

At the time Ed enrolled, Colonel J. Sumner Rogers was the superintendent and Adelbert Cronkhite, the commandant.[20] Cronkhite's tenure was brief, as was that of Captain Charles King who succeeded him; and in the Michigan Military Academy catalog of 1893 Lieutenant Frederick S. Strong, 4th U.S. Artillery, is listed as commandant. The catalog's register of cadets for 1892-93 displays the name *Edgar Rice Burroughs,* with the course identified as *Sc.* (scientific). Preparatory studies required in the scientific course include English grammar, civil government, arithmetic, and English composition. The curriculum for the first year, divided under first and second terms, contains rhetoric and composition as requirements in both terms. It appears, as far as the catalog is concerned, that the academy did stress the study of grammar and composition.[21]

Among the cadets who entered the academy at the same time as Ed were two who became close and long-lasting friends, Robert D. Lay and Herbert (Bert) T. Weston. Lay's course was listed in the catalog as *Ac.* (academy).[22]

The beginning of Ed's life in a military environment brought no change in his rebellious nature. He was obviously not ready to settle down, and not ready to adapt himself to the academy's strict discipline and regulation. His first semester at the school (second term, 1892) found him in numerous difficulties. A natural nonconformist, he seemed unable to follow school rules or to suppress impulsive actions that usually led him into trouble.

One of Ed's early experiences at the academy during his plebe year had to do with the popular pastime of hazing, carried on by the "old boys" or upper classmen. In Ed's *Autobiography,* where the practice is described as the "refined and unrefined torture of hazing," various details are offered. For what occurred in one particular case, Ed can hardly be blamed. The commandant at the start of the term, Adelbert Cronkhite, who was far from being one of Ed's favorites, appeared to have a pet aversion to plebes:

I think that he looked upon us with absolute contempt and loathing. At noon one day, during the winter, he made a speech in the messhall. It was to the effect that the plebes were too fresh and that it was up to the old boys to put them in their place. This, coming from the high authority of the commandant of cadets, brought immediate effects, one of which was that immediately after the meal the entire plebe class scattered in all directions, taking to the woods, not only figuratively, but literally. Several of us, I recall, just beat it—whither, we did not know.

Michigan Military Academy cavalry platoon; ERB second from left.

"Any place would have been better than the Michigan Military Academy on that bleak Saturday afternoon," Ed remarked. Although he was "as usual" under arrest for "various and diverse infractions of discipline," under these emergency circumstances the arrest became unimportant as did the regulations against going off-limits and, more serious, going off off-limits.

After the panicky escape, Ed and his friends walked twelve miles through the snow to a nearby town. There, although he was wearing rubber boots, he attended a village dance that evening. At a late hour, after the dancing was over, the boys reluctantly decided that they must return to the barracks. This posed a problem:

We also discovered simultaneously that we did not want to walk back and that we had no money. I managed, however, to pawn my watch for three dollars with which we rented a horse and rig, thus coming back to school and sneaking into our quarters while the old boys were asleep.

"I do not recall how much additional punishment I got for this escapade," Ed wrote, "but it could not have meant anything to me as I already was undergoing a life sentence."

Approximately two months after his arrival at the Academy, the Easter vacation began, and all the cadets were excused to return home. From Chicago, where Ed was spending the vacation with his family, his father wrote to Colonel Rogers on March 23, 1892, requesting an extension of Ed's leave. Two days later Rogers replied, ". . . Of course we shall extend cadet Burroughs' permit, as you request, although it is to his disadvantage to be absent from work at this time. School is moving along very pleasantly under our new commandant."[23]

The new commandant, replacing Adelbert Cronkhite, was Captain Charles King, a well-known author of novels centered about army life in the West. Although he remained at the academy for only a brief period, his firm attitude tempered with justice and consideration and his numerous accomplishments created in Ed an intense admiration which was close to worship.

Ed continued to find the discipline and restrictions of a military life impossible to cope with; as described in his *Autobiography,* the penalties seemed endless:

The first year was the hardest. I accumulated so many hours of unwalked punishment that if I had remained there the rest of my life I could never have walked it all, as we had only forty-five minutes a day for recreation, except Saturdays and Sundays and as I recall it we were not compelled to walk punishment on Sunday.

Desperate, and "burdened by a harrowing contemplation of the future," he fled from the academy:

I sneaked out of barracks at dusk and walked four and a half miles to Pontiac. I crept fearfully through the woods, for all the time I heard the cavalry pursuing me, my budding imagination being strong even then.

In Pontiac I hung around the railroad yards waiting for the Chicago train. Every man I saw was a detective searching for me and when the train pulled in and the inspectors passed along it with their flares, I knew they were looking for me, but I hid out between two freight cars until the train started. Those were the good old days before anyone had thought of solid vestibule trains, so I had no difficulty in flipping it and eluding the regiment of detectives that loitered about.[24]

Reaching home on April 15, 1892, Ed told his version of conditions at the academy and the harsh treatment he believed he had suffered. His father, indignant, wrote a letter to Colonel Rogers the same day. But the arrival of a telegram the next day, with its terse, abrupt wording, made Ed's behavior appear serious. The telegram from Commandant Charles King read: "Your son deserted Thursday letter will follow."

That George Burroughs, a retired army major, accustomed to military discipline, should protest about the treatment accorded

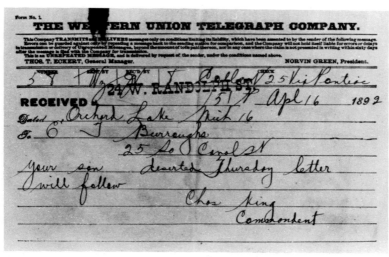

THE WESTERN UNION TELEGRAPH COMPANY.

Form No. 1.

This Company TRANSMITS and DELIVERS messages only on conditions limiting its liability, which have been assented to by the sender of the following message.
Errors can be guarded against only by repeating a message back to the sending station for comparison, and the Company will not hold itself liable for errors or delays in transmission or delivery of Unrepeated Messages, beyond the amount of tolls paid thereon, nor in any case where the claim is not presented in writing within sixty days after the message is filed with the Company for transmission.
This is an UNREPEATED MESSAGE, and is delivered by request of the sender, under the conditions named above.
THOS. T. ECKERT, General Manager.   NORVIN GREEN, President.

RECEIVED   Apl 16   1892

Dated Orchard Lake Mich 16

To E. T. Burroughs
        25 So. Canal St

Your son deserted Thursday letter
will follow

                    Chas King
                        Commandant

"*Your son deserted*" *telegram from General Charles King.*

General Charles King.

Ed indicates that matters can be different when one's own son is involved. Commandant King's reply to Burroughs' letter, written on April 18, in the absence of Superintendent Rogers, revealed also that King, while refusing to budge an inch, was a master of tact and diplomacy:

That you should think, after hearing your son's side of the story, that the commandant is too severe is most natural, and being a father himself, the Commandant has every sympathy with your distress. Now, however, let us look at the soldier side of the question.

He then proceeded to explain in detail the offenses that Ed had committed; George Burroughs must have found the list painfully incredible. "Since his return from vacation, a week or more behind time," King wrote, "Cadet Burroughs has received an extraordinary number of reports for not one of which has he tendered to the authorities the faintest explanation or excuse. They include some of the most serious known to our records both in the Academic and military departments, as you may see from the specimens enclosed herewith."

Of the "specimens" submitted for Burroughs' verification, King commented that the academy had always had a "standard of punishments" for these—the penalties Cadet Burroughs received were nothing new. King offered a mild reproof and reminder to Burroughs:

The severity of which you complain may possibly exist in these long established rules, but as an old soldier yourself, you should understand that the Commandant is simply carrying out the orders in the case, and although he might with propriety say that he feels no obligation to defend his course, on the other hand he prefers to invite the better judgement of a Companion of the Loyal Legion upon the facts in the case.

King remarked with some restraint that "it is to be regretted that Cadet Burroughs for his own sake was not willing to explain." By this time George Burroughs must have realized that his son, to put it euphemistically, had been quite "unwilling" to explain.

Other facts emerged, revealing a debatable question of Ed's supposed "illness":

As to the accusation of harshness in not permitting the young man to remain in bed and have his meals sent to his room, I will say that when one doctor pronounces a Cadet able to be up and about, it is considered ill advised on the part of the Commandant to interpose. In Cadet Burroughs' case, as stated by himself, both *doctors pronounced him able to get up and to go to meals.*

King, continuing to write in his objective third person, stated, "It was the severe Commandant who ventured to oppose his judgement and permit the boy to go to bed again."

As to the confusion arising over Ed's claims that he didn't consider himself "in confinement" even though Professor Loveland had given him the order, following which he had *reported* for confinement, King offered a comment that was a masterpiece of understatement. Ed's explanation "is necessarily looked upon with much surprise, if not with grave doubt as to his sincerity."

King gave further details of Ed's behavior. On the morning of Wednesday, April 13, Ed, while in confinement by orders of Professor Loveland, climbed through the window of the barracks to make his escape. He was accompanied by another cadet "who has since deserted under still more serious accusations." When questioned by the cadet officer, Ed admitted that he was leaving for the depot. Taken before the commandant and "invited to explain his extraordinary breach of orders and discipline," he replied that "he had nothing to say." In the letter King pointed out, "As an old soldier you must know that the Commandant had then no recourse but to administer the punishment required 'by the custom of war' in like cases, as he found it at this Academy."

Ed's attempt to escape, on this morning, had evidently not been very determined. But on the next day, April 14, he made a successful escape and returned to his home in Chicago where, shortly afterward, King's "desertion" telegram was received.

King offered some consoling words to George Burroughs in the letter:

Cadet Burroughs' offenses have been most serious, but not irretrievably so. He has been reckless; not vicious. He has found friends here including the Commandant, who best knew the boy in the Cavalry squad and on drill, and it is not impossible for him to return and wipe out his past.

Ed's father, displaying a most unexpected reaction for a veteran army officer, made demands that King considered unreasonable. They were firmly rejected:

. . . while I am unprepared to say what will be the action of the faculty, this I can say that under no circumstances will your demand that he be given a "clean sheet" and allowed to start in all free again without any punishment whatsoever, be acceded to. If granted to him, it would have to be granted, perhaps, to many another.

King went on to insist firmly that Ed would not be relieved from duty merely because he complained of being sick, but only "when having been examined by the doctor, he is *pronounced* sick." King added to this, with some acidity, that "if cadets were relieved from duty and excused whensoever they complained of feeling ill, at least half the battalion would be off duty every day."

In closing, he referred to George Burroughs' complaint that no boy could undergo the academy discipline without having his spirit crushed. "Permit me to say," King wrote, "that as the result of over thirty years observation of cadets here and elsewhere, I find that more than nine-tenths of the corps take kindly to the discipline and are as spirited and soldierly a lot of young fellows as one could ask to see."

Of the incident and his flight from Michigan Military Academy, Ed noted, "I should have thought that my father would have been about fed up with me by this time." He recalled how he had been received "with open arms and with no reproaches when I was fired from Andover" and added, "but I think that to him, a soldier, this was by far the greater disgrace, yet he put it directly up to me to decide for myself whether I should return or not."[25]

Ed was not long in making a decision. "I think it was the word 'deserted' in the telegram that got me, and the next day I was back at Orchard Lake walking punishment."

By the fall of 1892 Ed had begun to channel some of his excess energies into sports. Football offered the kind of physical challenge that was always important to him; he traveled with the team as they played games away from home.

In a letter of October 19, 1892, in which he explains to his parents, "I owe you all letters I guess so I will write to all of you at once," he discusses the games and school news:

They are not going to send us to Chicago this week, we are going to Pontiac though to march in their procession.

The shin protectors came, and I am much obliged to you

for them. Do not be afraid of my getting hurt in foot-ball. I dont play hard enough, besides its worth while when I can go around to the different towns and play and wear a big M on my sweater and a little MMA on my jacket.

Ed, amused by his parents' concern and their concept of football as a rough and hazardous game, encloses some "illustrations," presumably his typical cartoons, "for the manner in which Foot-Ball is *not* played, though you folks evidently imagined it was." Of the possibility of promotion he notes that "appointments" could be announced within the next two days; "I have been expecting them every day so have not written you hoping to be able to tell you what the fellows whom you know got."

About his own prospects Ed wrote, "I won't get anything, because I haven't been here a year yet." But he added, with some pride, "I am treated by all the fellows that I like and by *all* the fellows who were old-boys last year as if I had been here three or four years. I don't care anyway, so I guess that is the reason."

As a boy away from home for a lengthy period, he was evidently lonely, for he inquired about his brother Harry and Harry's wife Ella (Nellie) Oldham, who had been married less than a year, remarking wistfully that he wished he could see them:

When are some of you coming out? Can't Harry leave his business one Saturday and bring Nell up here: they could leave 8-15 P.M. Friday; spend Sat. here and be back 7 AM Sund. or leave Sat and be back Mon. I will expect Frank most any day.[26]

By the end of the year Ed appeared to be making some adjustments to the academy routine and to be doing better in his studies. His father, continuing an over-solicitous attitude, wrote regularly to Superintendent Rogers about various matters. On December 14, 1892, Rogers reported that "Cadet Burroughs has made excellent progress in his studies during the last three months and is satisfactory in discipline. We hope for still better results after Christmas." Possibly apprehensive, Rogers tempered his praise with a cautionary reminder: "You will aid us materially by him report [sic] promptly January 17th, so that he may have all his lessons on the next day."

Rogers included a laudatory statement about the academy's high reputation and the honor it had recently received:

After fifteen years of earnest effort we feel that we can with becoming modesty claim that we have succeeded in establishing a model school for the complete training of boys. In a list of forty "Leading Secondary Schools in the United States" selected by President Eliot of Harvard University, as President of a special committee of the National Educational Association, this Academy is honored in being one of the number chosen; and the only military school in this important list.

In the letter he also told of plans to increase the academy's attendance during the holiday vacation with a view to creating a battalion of 180 cadets. This battalion would be taken to the World's Fair Columbian Exposition in Chicago in June of the following year. The cadets would camp "in close proximity to if not within, the Exposition Grounds," remaining there for about three weeks. The instructors would accompany the cadets, and the objective was to make a careful and systematic study of the exposition and of exhibits that illustrate and enforce work done at the academy. Rogers explained, "By this plan we are convinced that we shall be able in three weeks to obtain a better knowledge of the people and industries of the World than would probably be acquired in several years' travel."

The change in dates of the Christmas holidays, beginning on December 22 with an extension to January 17, was caused by a decision to omit the Easter vacation. "We think that more satisfactory work can be accomplished by following this plan," Rogers said. The cadets were scheduled to leave about June 10 for the World's Fair, with a possibility that the commencement exercises might be held in Chicago.

On the same date as Rogers' letter, and again on December 16, George Burroughs had written about a problem Ed seemed to be having with his eyes. The exchange of letters appeared to indicate that Ed's father was somewhat annoyed at the fact that Rogers allowed an oculist to treat his son. Burroughs had suggested that Ed be sent to the oculist, and what he had in mind was not clear. Rogers wrote on December 17 with an evidence of impatience:

. . . would say that in accordance with your suggestion in your first dispatch I sent Cadet Burroughs to Detroit to an oculist of high standing to ascertain if his eyes were in a condition to allow him to study. Had no idea that he was to give him any treatment; and thought very likely that he could fit him with a pair of glasses so that he could go on with his work until the vacation began. I do not think that I exceeded my authority in any way.

The nature of the oculist's diagnosis is unknown, but the result was an early vacation dismissal for the patient. Rogers ended his letter with a curt comment, "He returned last night with the report of Dr. Frothingham, and upon his recommendation I have this day sent him home. He will explain the matter fully to you."

Whether Ed had a tendency to exaggerate his illnesses, or even to malinger, is difficult to tell. The record of his early years and the details contained in his brothers' letters from Yale reveal that he had been a delicate child, not as sturdy as his brothers, and more susceptible to common illnesses. That his health had caused both concern and worry to his parents is quite evident.

On January 26, 1893, in a letter to his mother he writes that he has been ill for some time. His complaints about the school are quite bitter; the tone of the entire letter is one of gloom and resentment. However, in this case, there is little doubt that his illness is severe:

Excuse me for not writing sooner but I have been sick and didn't feel very much like writing. I am still in bed. I have had a very sore throat and membraneous formation in my throat, headache, pains all over my body and have been sick to my stomach for the last three days. I am terrible sick at my stomach today but my head and throat are better.

He explained that the doctor had seen him yesterday, and although he had asked them not to send him again, the doctor made a second visit that day. ". . . I guess it was about as well," Edgar wrote, "for if he hadn't called they would have made me get up at noon, as it was he told me to stay in bed and keep quiet." After the vivid description of his illness, he attempts to reassure his parents; "Dont worry as I am not very sick; just thought I would write and let you know that I was still alive," and he adds, "Excuse writing as I am lying down and am rather weak. . . ." His P.S. offers more details and complaints:

To let you see what attention is paid to a fellow on the sick report: There's a jar out in the hall that was brought up yesterday morning and that I have used ever since and thrown up all my meals into it and it has never been emptied; and it never would be if I stayed here ten years with it.

I have lain on this hard bed for so long that my right side is really raw, the bottom of my stomach is raw from having the top sag down and up against it and my throat is raw from the extra work of having each meal go through two ways.

Ed, as with most young people of his age, was not a regular correspondent. He apologizes about his failure to write, and on April 25 offers as an excuse that he had hurt his finger with a sword. He remarks, "I looked over some of my letters the other day and I find that I never acknowledged the letter in which you sent that check I thought I had done so and I am very much ashamed of myself consequently."

He tells of receiving perfume and candy from his mother, adding, "it was fine and went to the right place." The obvious reference is to a girl friend, unidentified, but probably Emma Hulbert.

He inquires, "How is the kid?" a query about his nephew Studley, born only a month before on December 26, 1892, and continues jokingly:

From all of your letters I will expect to find him riding a bicycle and reading Caesar on my return in the summer. Don't rush him too much, he may get brain fever. Just tell him to follow after his uncle:—if he wants to be a blooming idiot.

From his early years, as part of a remarkable sense of humor, Ed exhibited a delight in playing practical jokes. It almost seemed that in devising little schemes at other people's expense he was satisfying some need of his imagination. It was done without malice and no harm was ever intended.[27] But the tendency to lapse into pranks and escapades, to yield to temptations impulsively, was part of his character. He would retain this tendency in lesser degree through his lifetime, and during his school years it would lead him into trouble.

In his letter of April 25, 1893, to his father he reports, with a customary glee, that "Lt. Reeder, who was cadet Capt. and adjutant last year, is going to sleep over in Graves room to-night and Graves, Cox and I were just in there folding up the under sheet in his bed and tying knots in his night shirt. I hope he don't find out who did it."

After telling of this prank he turns to his favorite subject —horses. He had always dreamed of owning one, and now approached the matter obliquely, posing a question to his father with more than a hint of guile:

Would you like to make some money or help me make some? I have an elegant chance to buy Captain, the horse I told you of that I think so much of, for about $150.00 or $125.00—He is a fine Kentucky horse perfectly sound, very showy and well gaited for a saddle horse; he is broken to harness as well; he is a very fine and fast singlefooter; his action is something superb.

There was of course a special reason why the colonel wanted to sell the horse: ". . . he is too fiery and too good a horse for a lot of boys to ride. I am the only cadet that rides him." The story sounds familiar—a scene from Ed's past in Idaho. And one can read between the lines. The fiery and hard-to-handle ones, the outlaws—these were the horses whose beautiful wildness Ed admired, that offered the challenge he couldn't resist. He used a torrent of words to try to persuade his father:

If I had $200 and could buy a horse to keep I would buy him in preference to most any horse I ever rode; in Chicago this year that horse would sell for a good $250.00, I am very sure. If I bought him now for $125.00 or even $150.00 I could have him to ride and get a lot of good out of him until school closes and then or before, ride him down to Detroit and sell him so as to make from $25 to $75.00 off of him anyway.

Carried away by his appeal to his father's practical business instincts, he began to expand the money-making possibilities:

The money I have paid the Col. for cavalry the rest of this term would pay for his board here and I could drop cavalry—for having a horse of my own I would not need to take it as I could do anything I wanted in the way of riding.

"I wish you could see the horse," he said, "I know you would think it a bargain." Another idea occurred: "You might loan me $150.00 for 3 months at 6%." The letter ended on a humorous

A drawing from the Michigan Military Academy Adjutant *depicting an exhibition drill.*

73

note: "Enclosed please find rough sketch of my room mate and myself figuring out the interest on $150.00 for 3 months at 6%."

It appears that Ed's father, powerless to resist his son's blandishments, or to withstand his barrage of dollars and percentages, may have purchased the horse. Ed rode Captain later in exhibitions at the Detroit Riding Club.

As a member of the cavalry troop at Michigan Military Academy Ed had the opportunity to develop a remarkable skill in riding. In recollection, he wrote, "We did a great deal of trick riding in those days—bareback, Cossack, Graeco-Roman and all the rest of it. It was known as 'monkey drill,' and if a man did not lose his nerve and quit, he had to become a good horseman."[28]

News of the astonishing ability of the academy cavalry had reached the ears of the Detroit Riding Club, and a selected group of riders was chosen to appear for an exhibition. A souvenir program of the Columbian Saddle Horse Show describes the events of Tuesday, April 4, through Thursday, April 6, 1893. The Orchard Lake Cadets' exhibition drill, with saddle and full equipment on the first night, was listed as "Event No. 5" on the program. The Drill Master was Hugh Thomason, and of the fourteen cadets in the platoon, Cadet Private E. R. Burroughs is listed as number seven; his friend Robert Lay was number twelve and the color bearer.[29]

On Wednesday April 5 the cadets presented an exhibition drill "with blankets, without equipments." On the final evening, April 6, a newspaper reported the results: "The Orchard Lake cadets took part in a competitive drill, which was an exciting affair. Their vaulting and dismounting and mounting drew applause, and the judges had a hard time picking the winners."[30]

The decision was made: "They finally had T. T. Harker, Ed R. Burroughs and F. R. Graves step out, and after an exhibition by each of them gave the prizes in the order named. . . ."[31] Ed's second prize was a gentleman's riding crop, while his horse, Captain, received a red ribbon. In the newspaper accounts of the exhibition, (April 4-7, 1893) the cadets' riding drew a eulogy:

. . . *These young men ride in the natural and easy position of a cavalry man, and their mounting and dismounting on bareback is wonderful. . . .*

The dashing cavalry from Orchard Lake gave one of the most

attractive exhibits of the evening, commanded by Hugh Thoma-
son, first sergeant troop F, U.S. cavalry. Hard riding and dif-
ficult evolutions, sweep of flashing sabres through the air and a
volley of shots as a wind up, wrought the audience up to a pitch
of applause that was deafening. . . .

The drill wound up in the manner of the wild west show. Draw-
ing their revolvers the cadets dashed madly around the ring, fir-
ing in all directions, and then rallied in the center, after which
they left the ring.

In a news story of April 5, the astonishment of the viewers, and their realization of the differences in style between the sedate, stiff English riders who normally appeared at the horse shows, and the vigorous, natural riding of the cadets is revealed. The writer made it plain that he preferred the American cavalry horsemanship:

These horrid cavalry horses did not have the fashionable
English trot or gallop, nor did the rider sit in the English way,
but they were plain Americans. The cadets ride like the vaqueros
dash through the chapparel, ride like the fleet South American
gauchos, the most skillful and daring riders in the world. But
the cadets are not fashionable riders.

The cadets are what might be called strong riders. Their stir-
rups are long, their seats are firm, they never forsake the motion
of the horse. There is an abandon, a smoothness, a naturalness,
a spirit to their horsemanship, that breathes forth the wild
wind, the long road, the cheerfulness of outdoors. . . .

It is not military horsemanship. It is American horsemanship,
it is Mexican horsemanship, it is South American horsemanship.
It is riding of men who live in the saddle.

A less enthusiastic description of the English rider is added:

The fashionable rider is not part of his horse, he is perched on
his horse; he is bobbing, he is making an art of riding, his
horse is giving an exhibition of what a saddler should be, and
is showing how a rider should retain his seat. . . .

The cadets' type of horsemanship, as reported in a story of April 6, included bareback riding feats that "recalled the exhibitions by Buffalo Bill's cowboys." This riding skill and love of horses developed by Ed in his academy years would always remain with him.

The summer of 1893 saw the start of Ed's lifelong fascination with the automobile when he became involved in the exhibition staged by his father's American Battery Company at the World's Columbian Exposition in Chicago. He was given the enviable assignment of driving an electric automobile around the fairgrounds. George Burroughs had installed the auto at the World's Fair to demonstrate the company's storage batteries. One writer, in calling the vehicle an "electrical horseless carriage," goes on to report that Ed drove "a nineseater horseless surrey about the fairgrounds, starting runaways every hundred feet or so."[32] In another account the writer claims that Ed drove the first automobile in Chicago, and describes how "at night, circling about the Fair grounds, it threw off sparks and flashes of blue flame."[33]

In the passing months Ed became immersed in a variety of school activities. Starting from his plebe year, his interest in football had increased until, after successive semesters, he had made the team. As cadet sergeant major he was evidently responsible for preparing the football lineups. On November 18, 1893, in the game between Michigan Military Academy and Ypsilanti, the lineup lists "Left-H.B.—Burroughs." His friend Bob Lay was scheduled to play fullback, and Bert Weston was right tackle. The name *Ed Burroughs,* together with his rank, is stamped officially at the bottom of the lineup.[34] The score was MMA, 36, Ypsilanti, 22.

The Adjutant, the academy's monthly magazine, reports Ed playing mainly quarterback and on one occasion right end. An article about the games in *The Adjutant* tells of the contest between the school and *Ypsilanti Normal,* with the final score "Academy 24; Normals, 10." Ed is given credit for making one touchdown.[35]

In *The Adjutant,* Senior Number, June 1895, Ed is placed on the Champion Prep School Team of the West, 1894. Statistics show him as "Captain, age 19, weight 169, height 5 feet, 10 ½ in., position Quarter Back." In the December 1895 issue, a listing is again made of a championship team of the year; Ed is shown as "Captain-Quarterback, Height 5-10, Weight 165, Age 20 years, 4 mos."[36]

About his football playing Ed wrote:

I made the football team, which I captained the last two years. We had an unusually good prep school team, cleaning up everything in our class and a number of teams that were out of our class. About the only teams that could beat us were such teams

THIS PASS GOOD ONLY FOR ONE DAILY ADMISSION;
HOLDER WILL OBTAIN PASS CHECK ON LEAVING
THE GROUNDS, TO RETURN.

GOOD FOR
ONE ADMISSION
SEPT. 16, 1893.
No. 28462
NOT GOOD IF DETACHED

ERB passbook to World's Columbian Exposition, Chicago, 1893, where he drove an electric auto powered by batteries.

as Notre Dame and the University of Michigan, and at that we once held to a tie score the University of Michigan team that had held Harvard 4 to 0.[37]

"... In those days," Ed noted, "it was a national football upset of the first magnitude, and our showing against this great Michigan team was equally as remarkable. I know that one of the results was that I was offered flattering inducements to come to Michigan after I graduated from Orchard Lake." Because his brothers George and Harry were graduates of Yale, he had made that college his first choice; as a result, he rejected the Michigan offer.[38]

Michigan Military Academy football team prior to 1895; ERB first on left in front row.

But his interests were not limited to sports. He would always find a fascination in drawing, even if his sketches and humorous figures were done only occasionally in letters or in moments of relaxation.[39] In addition, as at *Phillips Academy,* he could not resist the lure of the school magazine. In *The Adjutant* for October, November, and December 1895, Ed, now a second lieutenant, headed the list of ten editors. It is assumed that he was editor-in-chief or managing editor. *The Adjutant* for January, February, and March of 1896 again displays the name "Lieutenant E. R. Burroughs" above a group of ten other editors. He had returned to the academy after graduation.[40]

The launching of a newspaper, *The Military Mirror,* may have been one of Ed's projects. Volume 1, number 1, is dated January 30, 1894, and on the editorial page the paper is described as "a journal devoted to the Interests of Cadets and ex-Cadets of the Michigan Military Academy." Printed beneath are the names Lt. Burt Barry, Lt. Chas. H. Campbell, Lt. Ed. R. Burroughs, editors. Of interest is the fact that the paper was called *The Mirror,* reminiscent of the Phillips Academy publication to which he had contributed.

By the end of 1893 a continuing improvement in his studies was evident. On December 20 a faculty member, C. Leslie Lewis, wrote a letter of commendation to Ed's father:

ERB in football uniform, Michigan Military Academy, 1895

At the close of the first session of our school year, I take pleasure in speaking of the good record which your son has made here this year.

In spite of the fact that we of the faculty are marking closer than ever before, yet Cadet Burroughs has carried heavy work, and maintained a high standing.

Lewis reported Ed's marks: "Physics 87; French 86; Rhetoric 92; Military Science 90; Junior Rhetoricals 92; giving him an average of 89.4 %. His deportment marks show that he has 16 merits to his credit. We look upon him as one of our best boys."

Ed's marks were in the 60s and 70s at Harvard School, but only three years later show remarkable improvement. He had not, however, become totally angelic. He couldn't resist the temptation to indulge in wild pranks. The wildest of all escapades, one which Ed described amusedly as "the means for breaking the monotony of the long Michigan winters in barracks," was a contrived incident involving Ed and First Lieutenant Charles H. Campbell.[41] "We had quarreled," Ed wrote, "and were not on speaking terms. It occurred to one of us that we might make capital out of our well known dislike for one another. . . ."[42] There is little question about the identity of the "one of us" to whom the idea occurred. On an evening when Ed was officer of the day there was a "prearranged altercation in front of the battalion after it had formed for mess."[43]

The affair, on December 11, 1893, is detailed in Ed's *Autobiography:*

. . . Just before assembly sounded for supper, at a time when the entire corps of cadets was in front of barracks, Campbell made some insulting remark to me and I struck him across the face with my glove, whereupon we immediately mixed, but were presently separated by our friends, one of whom, First Lieutenant Barry, took me into his room until assembly had sounded.

The plan had been for some of the cadets to break up the fight, ". . . but unfortunately for us," Ed wrote, "they were more interested in watching the scrap than in stopping it. Someone finally interfered, much to our relief. . . ."[44]

Later that evening Campbell's second, Captain Risser, delivered the expected challenge:

Sir: For having grossly insulted me in the presence of witnesses and without provocation, I claim it as a right, if you are possessed of any honor, to meet at the earliest possible opportunity and give me the satisfaction my insult demands.
Yours Very Respect.
Charles H. Campbell

In reply, Ed sent his second, Lieutenant Barry, to arrange the details. Someone decided that the weapons should be Springfield rifles at fifty paces. There is some confusion as to who made the choice, but in one account Ed notes, "I . . . being the challenged party, selected the weapons. . . ."[45] They ran into difficulties with Risser, who, Ed observed, was a "solid, substantial sort of chap of a serious turn of mind . . . endowed with a little intelligence, with the result that he positively refused to have anything to do with the matter, and threatened to report the

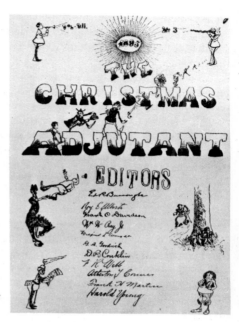

1895 Christmas Adjutant
listing ERB as editor in
chief; pen and ink drawings
were probably ERB's work.

whole thing to the commandant immediately if we did not drop it."[46] Reluctantly, they were forced to let Risser in on the joke; he was then willing to play his part. Captain Buel, selected as referee, was also aware that the whole incident was a hoax.

The duel was to take place at Cass Lake on the ice, about a mile from the academy, at 4:20 Tuesday afternoon. Among the cadets the news of the duel spread rapidly and the entire school was in a fever of excitement. ". . . Why the authorities heard no inkling of it," Ed wrote, "I have never been able to guess, except that the entire corps of cadets was so anxious to see blood shed that none of them wanted to let the powers that be have an opportunity to prevent the meeting."[47]

Wild rumors spread throughout the school. Ed was approached in haste by a friend who informed him that Campbell's group was planning to murder him during the night. The cadet wished to sleep in Ed's room to protect him, and was only dissuaded when Ed explained that he was a light sleeper and would keep a loaded revolver within reach. The "old boys" at the school, determined to keep the entertainment to themselves, had informed the plebes that they were not permitted to watch the event. "But when I approached the field of honor on that bleak Michigan winter morning," Ed wrote, "the bare trees all around the shore of the lake were decorated with plebes who had sneaked off limits ahead of us and gained points of vantage at the ringside."[48]

At 4:00 p.m. Ed had jumped out of the back window of his barracks, and accompanied by his second, started for the "field of honor." Ahead of them, several cadets were carrying the guns. As Ed turned to look at the school, he observed, with satisfaction, that there was a string of cadets "a mile long" following him. The important details of the duel were taken care of: the cartridges were blanks and Ed carried a "bloodied" handkerchief in his blouse.

Shortly afterward some of Campbell's group could be seen hurrying toward the chosen spot. Ed's friends began to shake hands with him and bid him goodbye; overcome at the prospect of his death, several burst into tears. But when the group arrived, headed by Captain Risser, Campbell's second, it was evident that Ed's opponent was not among them. Risser reported that someone had blabbed to the commandant, that Campbell had been placed under arrest and locked up. The commandant, Lieutenant Frederick F. Strong of the 4th Artillery, a West Pointer, sent a very peremptory order to Ed: he was to report to the office immediately. "It was a long, cold walk back to school," Ed wrote. "I would much sooner have faced Campbell with Springfields at twenty paces than to have faced the Commandant, and when I entered his office and saw his face I realized that my judgment was still perfectly good."[49] Ed never forgot Strong's reaction:

. . . He was terrible upset by what had occurred and by the extremely narrow margin by which a bloody tragedy had been averted, for Springfield rifles at fifty paces in the hands of boys who knew how to use them would have meant sudden death for at least one of the principals.

I could see that he was laboring under a great nervous strain and it was with difficulty that he controlled his natural feelings, which I imagine would have prompted him to turn me over his knee and spank me, but as was his custom, he asked me for my story and listened to it, though somewhat impatiently when I told him that the whole thing had been a joke.[50]

Strong asked Ed if discharging Springfield rifles at one another at fifty paces was his idea of a joke. The incident had been so well planned that Ed had difficulty in convincing Strong that it was a hoax. Fortunately, he was able to show Strong the blank cartridges and the white handkerchief stained with red ink. ". . . He was so relieved," Ed wrote, "that we all got off with a simple reprimand and a warning to put a curb in the future on our peculiar senses of humor. But the worst was yet to come. When the cadets learned the truth they wanted to mob us and for a while we were far from being the most popular members of the corps."[51]

On December 15, 1893, soon after the "duel," he wrote a letter to his mother. Both she and his father had evidently written to mention their concern about him and the absence of any news from him. He expressed his regret and said he was in good health, except for "that tired feeling." Then, with pride, he proceeded to give the details of the hoax, telling the story gleefully.

"Campbell, Barry and I started the joke and made all the arrangements before hand, practiced our parts, faked some cartridges etc.," he wrote. Toward the end of the letter he admitted that when the hoax was revealed, "the fellows wanted to kill us both." But he added that "The Lieut. [Commandant Strong] thought it was the best joke he had ever heard of and laughed as much as any one."

At Orchard Lake he had what he described as his "first, last and only stage experience." The cadets formed a company to present a play titled "The End of His Tether." After a school performance the company went on the road during the Easter vacation. The only impression that remained with him, outside of the fact that the play was a "terrible flop," was a most vivid one about the incredible whiskers he wore:

They were a full set fastened to a wire, the ends of which curved over my ears, thus, supposedly, holding the hirsute appendage properly in place, a fact which they accomplished in theory only, since, when I started to speak my lines, my breath blew the whiskers outward until they were suspended at an angle of forty-five degrees and I was talking beneath them.[52]

Of the towns where the cadet actors appeared, Flint, Michigan, was especially memorable. ". . . we played to an audience consisting of the owner of the theater and a couple of members of his family. There was not a paid admission and the only reason the owner was there was because he had to be in order to turn out the lights and lock the doors when we had departed."[53]

When financial matters reached a crisis, the familiar telegram, a duplicate of numerous others sent home by unsuccessful thespians, was dispatched to George Burroughs: "Wire five show busted Hotel Vincent Saginaw."[54]

The year 1894 brought no change in Ed's penchant for ignoring the rules and getting into trouble. An extract of "Special
Order No. 49," issued on April 12, contained serious charges:

*For gross neglect of duty as Officer of the Day on the 11th
Inst. Cadet 2nd Lieut. Burroughs is hereby reduced to the ranks
and confined to "Reduced Limits" until June 10, 1894.*
    By order of Col. Rogers
    R. S. Spilman 2nd Lieut. M.M.A. Adjutant

Ed's father was undoubtedly notified of this; but he received
a further shock when Rogers' letter of April 17 referred to
"Special Orders No. 52." It was Rogers' "unpleasant duty" to
forward an extract of these orders to Burroughs. The Colonel
stated, "Your son has doubtless written you the particulars of his
offense. If not, I will write you fully, explaining to you his
breach of discipline."
    In a reply to Rogers, dated April 20, George Burroughs ex-
hibited mixed emotions of anguish and helplessness. He refers
to the "Special Orders" enclosed in Rogers' letter:

*I need not tell you that its contents brought to me humiliation
and pain. What more can I say? My Son knows what I expect of
him, his sense of duty to his school and his parents should guide
all his actions, and make him obedient to every rule. I do not
know what, if anything, I can do in the premises? If he will
not obey, he must take the consequences, and his parents must
suffer with him.*

But he could not conceal a fear about the extent of his son's
punishment:

*He has not written home about the matter, and I will thank you
to explain fully to me in what his "neglect of duty" consisted,
and also what you mean in "Orders" when you say "Confined
to reduced limits". I hope it does not mean confinement in his
room for such a long time when we are likely to have hot
weather. His offense must have been great, if a reduction to the
ranks would not be regarded sufficient punishment.*

Ed's offense, as described by Rogers on April 23, was almost
beyond the bounds of any that the colonel had ever encountered
at the academy. While on duty as officer-of-the-day, Ed had
"not only permitted but encouraged one of the cadets to assault
one of the cadet officers whom he relieved but a few moments

before for official acts done in the performance of his duty and in accordance with the commands of the Commandant; i.e., he reported this man for smoking."

Rogers stressed that he found it very humiliating to even admit that "such a disgraceful breach of discipline could take place in this Academy." He ended with a softer note, adding that "while it is a severe lesson for your son, I am pleased to say that he seems to consider the punishment merited and is faithfully attending to his duties."

The colonel's belief that Ed, considering himself at fault, had turned contrite, was clearly contradicted in the indignant letter George Burroughs received from his son. On April 20 Ed wrote to explain that he had hesitated to tell his side of the story because he didn't wish to upset them. After reflection he had decided that they would feel much worse if they heard the story from "some other source and without knowing the details."

The account, as Ed gave it, involved one of his friends, Second Lieutenant Ed Rohrbaugh.[55] On April 10 Lieutenant F. B. Ward, officer-of-the-day, was making his customary inspection tour when he saw Rohrbaugh leaning out of a window. "I was also in the room," Ed wrote, "but he says he didn't see me. We had gone in there to call to a cadet in the area." According to Ed, Ward didn't like Rohrbaugh, was quick to assume he was smoking, a violation of rules, and reported him.

The next day, Ed explained, when he was O.D., he saw Rohrbaugh follow Ward up to his room, and, alerted to possible trouble between the two, hurried upstairs after them. It seems plain that Rohrbaugh and Ward were quarreling, and that Rohrbaugh, angry at being reported, made some threats. Ward said he would tell the colonel if "anyone did anything to him." Rohrbaugh then lost his temper and struck Ward in the chest.

Ed, as officer-of-the-day and peacemaker, stepped in to prevent any more blows, and the two men "appeared to cool off." Carrying out his duty, Ed claimed, he reported Rohrbaugh for striking Ward. But unfortunately he couldn't refrain from taking his friend's side and in telling Ward off, including some threats of his own, that Ward "would have to settle with me for some things he had said. . . ." The reference was obviously to some four-letter words which Ed said he couldn't write.

In the meetings with the faculty and administration after the incident, Ed explained to his father that he talked to them "the way I would to you if I were in trouble." He told them not only what he "honestly thought" but also that he despised Ward. "I didn't use any tact," he confessed. "I didn't think I had to, I believed that justice would be given by them, the same way that you would see justice done. It turned out however that I was running down a favorite of the Colonel and Lt. Strong. . . ." Ed said that later Colonel Rogers called him a liar and Rohrbaugh a bully and coward.

In continuing his story, Ed told how all the other cadets gave their support to him. When the order reducing him to the ranks was read in the mess hall, there was a commotion, and "the whole battalion . . . began to hiss and cry 'Lynch him', and 'Kill him,' meaning Ward." Later, when Ward was Officer-of-the-Guard, "the men cut pillows up and threw them at him and spit on him and stepped on him and cryed, 'Drag him out' and 'Lynch him.' It was because the Col. and Comm't liked that . . . man better than they did me that I was reduced."[56] The faculty appeared to be on Ed's side:

Rohrbaugh and I came very nearly being fired, the Col. and Lieut Strong wanted to but most of the younger profs didn't so they compromised. A man said to one of the profs the day I went down that he didn't see why I was reduced and the Prof said: "I'll be darned if I do either."

Ed devoted a section of his letter to urging his parents not to get discouraged, while at the same time making no attempt to conceal his own gloomy attitude:

Please don't feel sorry for me. I have enough sand in me to take my punishment, however unjust without grumbling (too much) but if I could only feel that you and mother hadn't lost confidence in me again on acct of this; it wouldn't be so hard. I have not shown that I felt injured by my reductions. I have done what I thought you would want me to do, braced up and done what I thought would put me on the road to work up all over again. I have been on guard twice and rec'd orderly to the commanding Officer for being the neatest man and having the cleanest gun in the guard.

Toward the end of the letter he found it difficult to control his emotions:

I think I have rec'd no demerits since my reductions, I have studied just as hard if not harder. And I tell you Father its not for myself I am doing it, either, as far as I am concerned I don't give two whoops in hades whether school keeps or not. I am both home-sick and discouraged, because it looks as though a fellow never could get up again, when he had all headquarters to buck against . . .

He signed himself "Your affect. son," using his full name, Ed R. Burroughs, and placing his new, reduced rank beneath in a kind of bitter defiance: "Cadet Private Co. A."[57]

Obviously, his reduction to ranks affected him very deeply; his hurt and resentment were strong because he believed that the punishment was unjustified and that prejudice was involved. Unable to find a release for his anger and frustration, he turned to one of his favorite pastimes—cartooning. On a piece of cardboard he drew a tombstone in a pyramidal shape. In the center he printed his own version of his sentence, giving it the appearance of an epitaph:

April 12, 1894—Cadet 2nd Lieut. Ed. R. Burroughs, Company "A", is hereby reduced to the ranks and confined to reduced limits until the 10th of June 1894, for "Alleged" gross neglect of duty while Officer of the Day. By Col J. S. Rogers and Lt. F. S. Strong without the sanction of the Faculty of M.M.A. . . .

That Ed had sufficient determination to recover from his reduction in rank and start the uphill climb again is demonstrated by the events of the succeeding year. He was advanced to first sergeant, and by his senior year in 1895 was appointed second ranking captain and assigned to the "D" company.[58]

At the academy the fact that he was regularly promoted and given positions of responsibility seemed to indicate he was overly severe in his judgments of Superintendent Rogers and Commandant Smith. His accusations that they were prejudiced against him and in favor of others may have been more emotional than rational. The opinions (and his actions) were part of a period of youthful rebellion. When he examined his academy career in the calmness of retrospect, his estimate was quite different.

In his *Autobiography* he comments:

During my second and third years at Orchard Lake I held various offices, including that of corporal, 1st-sergeant, sergeant-major and 2nd-lieutenant. I was reduced to the ranks a couple of times, for what I do not recall, but realising now what a young ass I must have been it is not so surprising that I was reduced to the ranks as that I was ever reappointed to office again.

ERB on horse "Belle," Michigan Military Academy, April 1895.

From the distance of time he now views the actions of Rogers and others in charge as unbiased:

There was practically no such thing as "pull" at Orchard Lake and little or no favoritism was shown in the appointment of non-commissioned officers and commissioned officers, and as I look back upon it now I cannot understand why it was that I was so often promoted. I was not particularly neat in my personal appearance, except at ceremonies; I was not particularly amenable to discipline, and in the matter of observing regulations I was a rotten soldier, for I broke them all; but I loved everything military. The little United States Infantry Drill Regulations was my bible and I took great pride in the military correctness and precision of my every act and word when on duty.

The lure of military life, the fascination it had for him—these can be understood through a consideration of his age, his nature, and his total personality. He was young and restless, in need of excitement and challenge. But beyond what his age required, he was naturally vigorous and active, bored by too long application to books, in need of a continuous physical outlet. He was fiercely competitive, and in a military life, where in riding and drilling, physical skill was demanded, and promotion depended upon this skill, he found the stimulation that was vital to him.

Strangely, his home environment during that period did not appear to be as important an influence as the factors listed. His father, although an army major, had made no attempt to drive his son toward a military career. His main concern had been to see that Ed received a good education. In his letters Major George Burroughs had been revealed more as an indulgent father rather than as an army disciplinarian. If anything, he appeared to have a mistrust of harsh army regulations and punishments. After all, it was significant that following the Civil War, although an officer, he made no further attempt to find a career for himself in the army, but chose to abandon a military life at the age of thirty-three for a turn at business.

Once promoted to captain, Ed showed a disposition to take quite a different attitude when violations of school rules were committed by the cadets under his command. In an amusing incident, a private was reported by Captain Burroughs for "direct disobedience to orders at supper." The cadet, King Taylor, on March 16, 1895, submitted his own explanation of matters to Commandant Strong:

I would respectfully state that I was laughing when Captain Burroughs told me to wipe it off, and I tried to as quick as I could. But it is not an easy thing to wipe it off when you are laughing hard, and I think I wiped it off so soon after that it would not be called "Dirrect Disobedience to orders" for he didint give me time to wipe it off.

Taylor's protest was sent to Ed with a note attached: "Respectfully referred to Cadet Captain Burroughs for statement of facts in this case." It was signed by the commandant. There is no record of Ed's response.

With his graduation from Michigan Military Academy scheduled for June 1895, Ed realized that plans must be made for his future. The prospect of a military career, especially as a commissioned officer, appealed strongly to him. But the first step to achieve this was a difficult one: somehow he must secure an appointment to the Military Academy at West Point. The support of an influential person, preferably someone in an important government position was needed, and brother George set the political wheels in motion.

George and Harry Burroughs together with their friend Lew Sweetser were still operating as Sweetser & Burroughs, Dealers in Livestock, at their ranch in Yale, Idaho. Their colorful letterhead included an engraving of a steer and a miniature replica of their brand—a large Y with a bar above it. Shipping was still via American Falls. As a respected Idaho businessman, George was able to obtain the help of Congressman Edgar Wilson, a member of the United States House of Representatives. The appointment came through quickly. On May 6, 1895, George sent a telegram to Ed: "You have principal appointment. Prepare for examination on June 13."

George wrote on the same day to give a full explanation:

. . . I enclose letter from Hon. Edgar Wilson to me when you have read same please return. Allow me to extend to you my most sincere congratulations. I consider you very much to be envied and you yourself cannot be any more pleased than I am at the result. Your friends have done all for you now that is in their power to do; your future rests with yourself.

Continuing, George cautioned his younger brother:

I will write you at length in a day or so the steps that have been taken in your behalf and to whom besides yourself you are indebted. Mr. Ramsey, State Auditor, to whom Mr. Wilson refers is a Cassia Co. man and a friend of ours. I feel sure you will pass, Ed, but remember the exam is a rigid one, don't spare yourself in the short time left you to prepare.

George suggested that Ed write a note of appreciation to Congressman Wilson, of whom he noted, "He is a young man and I think a graduate of the University of Mich. If you ever have any opportunity to make his acquaintance do so. I think he has a very bright future before him and he may rise to almost any position."

George's belief was that Wilson would look upon Ed as "a sort of protege," would watch his career with interest, and "will like any man feel gratified if you show that you feel the obligation you are under to him."

Soon after, Ed received the official document from the War Department, dated May 10, 1895. It was addressed to him at what was assumed to be his legal residence, Yale, Cassia County, Idaho, and in an opening notification stated:

You are hereby informed that the President has conditionally selected you for appointment as a Cadet of the United States Military Academy at West Point, New York.

Should you desire the appointment, you will report in person to the Superintendent of the Academy on the 13th day of June, 1895, for examination. . . .[59]

The *Boise Statesman* reported the story at the same time, one of its headlines reading "Edgar R. Burroughs Appointed by Congressman Wilson." The lead paragraph also referred to Albert Brunzell of Reynolds, Owyhee County, who had been named as alternate.

It was interesting to note that Albert Brunzell, the alternate, had been appointed once before, but had failed the examination. The situation was further explained:

Congressman Wilson hopes that one or both of these young men will be successful in the examination so that Idaho may have a creditable representative in the great military school, one who will go through and graduate with honors to himself and to the state.[60]

The statement is puzzling. Whether Wilson was aware of the fact that Ed, born and raised in Illinois, had visited Idaho only briefly, is not clear. But another aspect must be considered. Idaho, a newly-formed frontier state, had only a small number of inhabitants who were born in the state, or who had lived there for any long period. The population consisted mainly of newcomers who had drifted in from other states. Thus a choice of candidates for West Point would be limited.

A further point is that the educational opportunities were limited in this pioneer state. Those hoping for admission to West Point would naturally be forced to choose schools in other states for preparation and training. This would explain the official attitude adopted toward Ed, who, although not in Idaho at the time of his appointment, was noted to be "receiving training and instruction" at Michigan Military Academy.

Unfortunately, as far as candidate Edgar R. Burroughs was concerned, the hopes of Congressman Wilson and the dreams of the state of Idaho were not to be realized. The dismal outcome was reported succinctly in Ed's *Autobiography:* "During the end of my senior year I received an appointment to West Point, where I went for examination with a hundred and eighteen other candidates, only fourteen of whom passed, I being among the one hundred and four." The *Boise Statesman* had mentioned the limited number who had been successful previously: ". . . of 181 examined in March, only 57 passed, while of those examined at New Orleans not one went through successfully." But since on June 13 only fourteen passed, Ed's group made an even poorer achievement than the one that preceded it.

With the news of his failure, both Ed's discouragement and the disappointment at home must have been profound. One can also imagine the humiliation of brother George who had worked so hard to obtain Congressman Wilson's assistance. Ed's father, who had been remarkably tolerant of his son's earlier escapades at the academy, was reaching the limits of his patience. A survey of all the later happenings from 1894 on made it plain that Ed was still not ready to take a serious view of life. He was nearing twenty and groping toward maturity, as yet unsteady and without a goal or objectives.

Nothing awaited; there were no new plans to be formed. He followed the obvious, accepting the only offer: he would return to the academy. On July 4, 1895, Colonel J. Sumner Rogers wrote a letter to "E. P. Burrows," 646 Washington Boulevard, Chicago, explaining:

You will be appointed to the place at the same compensation Spellman [Spilman] & Bisco receive i.e. $35 per month, for the nine school months with room and board. I have not time to write you fully at this time, but I hope that you will take up the work at once with your natural enthusiasm and help us fill every room with desirable cadets—Gentlemen—With kind regards to your father. . . .

Although Ed's behavior had shown improvement in his senior year, it must be admitted that Rogers, like George Burroughs, Sr., displayed great patience and an unusually forgiving nature. Not only did he welcome Ed back, but he was willing to place him in a position of authority. This action proved Rogers to be a man of some discernment. In Ed Burroughs, beyond his erratic and rebellious conduct, were the high spirits, the "natural enthusiasm" Rogers had mentioned, of a young man who took pride in physical achievement, loved military drill and horsemanship, and was willing to work hard at tasks that interested and challenged him.

Ed's position for the fall term of 1895-96 was to be that of assistant commandant, an office which included the duties of cavalry and gatling gun instructor, tactical officer—and professor of geology.

School was out, and the arrival of the summer vacation found Ed at home in Chicago. Too restless to accept the weeks of inactivity, he began a search for employment. His friend and roommate from Orchard Lake, Bob Lay, came forward with an offer. They would both work for the Knickerbocker Ice Company, 134 Van Buren Street, whose owner was Bob's uncle. They were appointed collectors, and Ed's area was in Grand Crossing, a suburb of Chicago.

The job turned out to be anything but mundane. In his *Autobiography,* the experiences he describes most vividly are those involving encounters with unfriendly dogs:

I never was much of a runner, although once I did win a pearl-handled penholder for coming in second in a mile race at Pontiac, after smoking several cigarettes and eating a bag of popcorn, but there was one occasion in Grand Crossing that summer when I broke all existing records for sustained flight without refueling. A dog and I discovered each other simultaneously in a dark hallway upon the third floor of a ramshackle flat building. You know the kind, with the back porches sticking out behind and the stairs zig-zagging from the upper porch to the ground. The dog was young and agile and I only had about fifteen feet start on him, but I beat him down those zig-zag stairs and over the back fence, my banking at the turns being perfect.

On another occasion, in his round of collections, he arrived at a Victorian mansion "set far back from the street in grounds surrounded by a high fence." As he entered he could hear angry barking coming from the stables in the rear of the house. He hesitated, pondering "the advisability of attempting to collect the bill by mail," but he then heard the clank of a chain and felt reassured, believing that the dog was tied up. He walked to the front porch, some distance from the entrance, his fears calmed by the steady clanking of the chain. But as he pressed the doorbell, he became aware of an ominous change in the sound from the rear of the house:

The barking and growling became louder and seemed to be approaching and the clanking of the chain had become a rattle— it was dragging along the ground. I was almost paralyzed, for the dog sounded like a large dog, and when he came careening around the corner of the house I saw that he was a large dog; in fact, he was a Great Dane.[61]

He could think of nothing to do except "gluing" his finger to the bell button as the dog galloped toward him. The memory of what his brother George had once said—that if you stand perfectly still a vicious dog will not bite you—returned to him. "I stood so still," he wrote, "that he must have thought that I was a new statue for the front lawn." The dog sniffed at him for some time and then sprawled at full length across the front of the porch, entirely blocking his escape.

He could hear the continuous ring of the bell and began to fear that there was no one at home:

. . . but presently, to my great relief, a maid opened the door. I told her about the ice bill, but she said that there was no one home to pay it, and then I asked, "Does this dog bite?" To which she replied, "Yes," and slammed the door in my face. Imagine my embarrassment.

Somehow he gathered sufficient courage to step over the dog and start away from the house, managing "to stroll slowly and nonchalantly down to the gate, which was now at least two miles from the front porch." The dog merely stared after him.

His most ludicrous adventure as a bill collector came when he "parked" his horse, tying it to a tree in front of a house. He had several stops to make at homes nearby. He had failed to notice that the horse was stationed near some young trees and also that the horse was hungry. "When I returned," he said, "I found that he had eaten the trees and that an irate householder was waiting for me." The householder happened to be Lieutenant Bondfield of the Chicago Police Department. Bondfield told him off in emphatic language and then sent for one of his sergeants who lived nearby. Ed was placed under arrest. He described what followed:

I was taken to the Police Station and put in a cell in the basement. It was a Saturday afternoon and the Lieutenant evidently planned to keep me there until Monday, for no effort was made to reach either my employers or my father, but I succeeded in making such a damned nuisance of myself that they finally got in touch with the Knickerbocker Ice Company and I was released on bail. Monday, when I appeared in court, my father and the judge discovered that they had won the Civil War together and Lieutenant Bondfield learned that I was going back to Michigan Military Academy as Assistant Commandant, where one of his sons was a cadet, so we all kissed and made up.[62]

When the summer was over, and Ed reported to Orchard Lake for his new position, he could undertake his military tasks with a degree of confidence. But at first consideration his assignment as "Professor of Geology" appeared ludicrous. In his *Autobiography* he describes his return to the academy, the events that followed, and his reactions to the assignment. "The fact that I had never studied geology seemed to make no difference whatever," he commented. "They needed a professor of geology and I was it. . . . The men knew that I knew nothing about geology and naturally they made the most of it, but they did not get away with much because I studied geology harder than they did and always kept about one jump ahead of them."

The commandant was now Captain Fred A. Smith of the regular army. As assistant commandant under him, Ed was responsible for discipline and for detecting any violations of school rules. "Colonel Rogers could scarcely have selected a better man," he noted, "as I had broken every regulation myself while I was a cadet and knew just how it was done."

He would enter the plebes' rooms and go directly to what they presumed was a safe hiding place for their cigarettes or chewing tobacco. They began to view him with awe, not realizing that he had used the same places to hide his own forbidden objects. He describes an inspection of the room of Cadet Martin of Marshalltown, Iowa. Ed went to his desk, pulled out a drawer, and reaching behind it, found a box containing candy:

Now I had not known that there was anything back of that drawer, but Martin was a plebe and the plebes always hid their tobacco, at first at least, in some such obvious hiding place. When I opened the box and found that it was candy I knew that there was something wrong, since candy was not taboo. Therefore I became suspicious and cutting into one of the pieces found that it was chewing tobacco coated with chocolate.

He was well acquainted with all the popular hiding places for the contraband, usually cigarettes or chewing tobacco. The sash weight wells on either side of the windows were often used; at the bottom of the sash was a little panel which could be unscrewed. Other favorite spots were the inside of mattresses or pillows and holes in the floors beneath the rugs. Books were suspect; at times the centers were cut out and the contraband inserted. But the number of hiding places was limited, because the cadets were quartered in small, bare rooms, two to a room. Most of the men learned to carry their tobacco in their socks, "but only when there was little danger of inspection as it was easy to run one's hand down the inside of a man's trouser leg below the knee and feel the package of cigarettes or plug of tobacco beneath."

Ironically, Ed, who had taken delight in breaking many of the rules when he was a cadet, now turned into a strict disciplinarian. Any popularity he may have had began to vanish. In one instance somebody threw electric light bulbs and ink bottles at him when he walked past the barracks at night. Discovering that only one or two men were involved, he gave a stern warning. When it was repeated, he gave the corps an ultimatum: they must produce the guilty man in twenty-four hours. If they didn't, and any more missiles were thrown, the entire corps would be punished. The threat brought no change in the situation:

I did not expect that they would turn in the offender and I should have been ashamed of them if they had, but I thought that at least they would prevent him from throwing any more ink bottles at me. However, the following night I was again attacked whereupon I routed out a bugler, had a long roll sounded and marched the whole corps around the country for about two hours.

This drastic action merely increased his problems. The cadets, exhausted because of a lack of sleep, all failed their recitations the next morning. They blamed Ed, and as a result he was severely criticized by the faculty. A short while later, when he ordered another long roll and a midnight march, he aroused the anger of everybody, and this procedure was strictly forbidden.[63]

The position of assistant commandant with its authority and prestige had at first appeared very enticing to Ed, but as the weeks passed he discovered it had serious disadvantages. Separated from the cadets, viewed by them as a member of the staff, he was now unable to form the friendships that had been so important during his first four years. He realized that he now had a "lonesome job." He lived alone above the quartermaster's office on one side of the quadrangle, while almost all of the other staff and faculty members lived some distance away in cottages. But as far as they were concerned, even if they had lived closer, Ed, at his age, could have little in common with them; what he missed above all was the opportunity to join with the young cadets and be accepted by them.

The weight of his duties as cavalry and gatling gun instructor, tactical officer and professor of geology—plus his responsibilities in supervising the cadets—did not prevent him from being active in sports. On the letterhead of the Michigan Military Academy Athletic Association he is listed as one of the three directors in charge of football. Captain F. A. Smith, the commandant, is the secretary of the organization while Cadet A. T. Conner has replaced Ed as the "Foot-Ball and Base-Ball Captain." But *Lieut. E. R. Burroughs* is now given the title of "Foot-Ball and Baseball Manager."

In these capacities he was given full authority to arrange the game schedules. His contacts with coaches from other schools and universities, evidenced in the original telegrams preserved in his scrapbook, demonstrate that he conducted negotiations and set up times and dates for the games. A telegram from Hyde Park, dated November 13, 1895, is addressed to E. R. Burroughs and reads: "Can Have Them for Morning Game. We Play in Afternoon. Collect 25c. A. A. Stagg."

Another from Notre Dame, Indiana, on November 20, reads: "Will Guarantee $100.00 or One-Half Gate. Reply. (Signed) P. B. McManus."

Other telegrams are indicative of the negotiations. From Faribault, Minnesota, November 19, Newhall writes, "Must stand by my first telegram. This is final." A telegram from Milwaukee, Wisconsin, dated November 19, advised, "Will play if guarantee expenses $90.00 and game is played in afternoon. Answer. Have written." It is signed "Smythe."

He still found time for his duties with the school magazine. The *Adjutants* of November and December 1895 list Lieutenant E. R. Burroughs at the head of ten other editors, and in the issues running from January through March of 1896 his name appears in the same position.

His lonesomeness as assistant commandant was partially alleviated by the friendship of another man who for a few months was given the same title. Emelio Figerallo, Count deGropello, was a captain of cavalry on leave from the Italian army. He and Ed spent time together when they were off duty. To the cadets, Emelio, with his emotional behavior, his typical Italian gestures and expressions, and his blundering attempts at the English language, was a constant source of amusement. It was a period in which Ed, also, had insufficient maturity to understand Emelio. He had noted with some distaste that Emelio's manners at the table were far from what he expected of a European nobleman. But in retrospect, in his *Autobiography,* he describes Emelio with a regret for his old narrowness of vision and with the mature perception of age. Without doubt Emelio was a "great big overgrown boy; a lovable chap who could never understand us or our ways and who, when gauged by the narrow provincialism of a small American private school in those days, could not be understood by us." Emelio, simple and natural, "horrified the members of the faculty by his casual references to natural phenomena, which in those days were not mentioned in the presence of ladies." In summarizing, Ed wrote:

Now, after the passing of years and a broader experience of people, I realize that he was, perhaps, the only human being among us. I know that he had a heart of gold. . . . His family owned a whole town and he had a gorgeous watch that had been presented to him personally by the King of Italy. When he left us he went to South America and I have often wondered what became of him.

By the spring of 1896 Ed's impatience with his confining duties, the routine of school schedules, of supervisory tasks, reached a climax. His restlessness, part of his nature but also of his age, was caused by his urgent need for action and adventure—the challenge of something different. He had spent five years at the academy, was weary of it, and found no interest even in his position of assistant commandant and in chances for future promotions. At twenty Ed was too young and too doubtful about himself to accept permanency or the prospect of being tied down. In contrast to the restrictive atmosphere of a school, he had a dream of a freer, more exciting life. His decision and his departure from the academy came suddenly and, as in the past, impulsively.

PART 2

THE LONG JOURNEY TO ADULTHOOD

CHAPTER 4

THE
SEVENTH CAVALRY
AND BEYOND

Toward the end of 1894, six months before graduation from Michigan Military Academy, Ed had already made his own decision about the future. His studies had improved and he had done better in a variety of subjects, but the army—and especially the cavalry—remained his prime interest. A motivating influence was his love of horses and riding, as well as his love for the outdoors. Added to this was another factor: he had passed four years of military life and had risen in ranks to be a cadet officer. His dream now was to be a commissioned officer in the regular army; and with the experience and training he had acquired at the academy, the appointment might be possible. But if it could not be obtained, he was prepared to serve an apprenticeship as an enlisted man and was planning for the commission that was bound to come.

During the same period Major George Burroughs yielded to pressure from his son and gave him a letter of consent. Required because Ed was underage, the letter of December 1, 1894, gave a complete authorization:

To any Recruiting Officer
  U.S. Army

  This is to certify that the bearer, my son Edgar R. Burroughs who is underage; has the consent of his parents to enlist in the Cavalry Service of the U.S. Army.

                              Very Respectfully
                              Geo. T. Burroughs [1]

Friends and fellow soldiers of ERB, known as "The May-have-seen-better-days Club," Fort Grant, 1896.

As events turned out, the letter was not used. By May of 1895 Ed's plans had changed; awaiting him was the possibility of an appointment to the United States Military Academy. His failure to pass the examination led to his return to Michigan Academy that fall. But with the tediousness of academy duties he once more sought refuge in his dreams of a career in the cavalry.

When Ed had accepted the position of instructor and assistant commandant, Colonel Rogers had assumed he would stay for the school year. Now, sometime in April or the first part of May 1896, he quit his position abruptly. From Orchard Lake he went to the army recruiting station at Detroit. Enlisting was not as simple as he thought. In telling the complete story of his army experience in his *Autobiography,* Ed noted that they wouldn't accept his word that he was twenty-one, adding "which incidentally I was not." He would be twenty-one on September 1. He gave the details:

The fact that I wore good clothes made them suspicious as they had recently had some trouble because of having enlisted a son of Deering, the reaper man, while he was still under age. There was some delay while permission was obtained from my father and then there was a still further delay when I asked to be sent to the worst post in the United States, for they had to get special permission from Washington to send me outside of that department in which Detroit is located.[2]

Ed waited with impatience at the recruiting station, where he recalled having his first experience with wharf rats. "They used to play around at night in the room where we slept and there were some among them that were fully as large as a housecat. We occupied our time throwing shoes at them until we fell asleep."

When permission finally came through from Washington, Ed was assigned to the Seventh Cavalry at Fort Grant, Arizona Territory. He was assured by the recruiting sergeant that it was "absolutely the worst assignment in the United States Army."

In a small brown memorandum book which he had carried with him at Michigan Military Academy, Ed kept a record of his height and weight and jotted down names and addresses. On December 27, 1895, he shows his weight, dressed, as 175 and one-fourth pounds. Some five months later, on May 13, 1896, the date of his enlistment, he notes that his weight stripped is 153 and his height five feet nine inches. Records of ERB's height show some variation. In 1894, as captain of the MMA football team, his height is listed as five feet ten and one-half inches.

Hulbert Burroughs said that his father's height was closer to five feet nine inches. A further entry indicates that his arrival at the Fort was one day early: "Sworn in 9 am. Assigned to Troop B 7th U.S. Cav. May 24th 1896. Arrived Fort Grant May 23rd."[3]

The journey to the fort began with a railroad trip to Wilcox, Arizona. The government paid for coach transportation only, and Ed used his own money to take Pullman accommodations to Kansas City, the first stopover. Viewing the ride as a lark, Ed spent most of his money in Kansas City and as a result was forced to complete the remainder of the long trip in a day coach. He also faced a more urgent problem—what to do about food. "I was very hungry," he said, "so hungry in fact that at one of the stops I swiped the lunch of a Mexican who had gotten off to stretch his legs."

When the train arrived at Wilcox, he discovered he would have to pass the night there; the stage for Fort Grant did not leave until the next morning. His funds were now reduced to a single dollar, and the question was, how to spend it. Although he was "terrible hungry" and "equally sleepy," he settled for a bath, which he wanted most of all. Later, in a hotel, he was allowed to sleep in a sample room used by traveling salesmen. It contained a cot but no lights, and he had barely lain down when he discovered that the cot was swarming with bedbugs. Sleep was impossible, and he dressed, planning to go outside; but as he picked up his suitcase, it burst open, spilling all the contents on the floor. He spent a half hour crawling about on his hands and knees in the dark, searching for his belongings. Then he went out to sit on the edge of the porch for the remainder of the night, his feet dangling into the street.

Fort Grant in 1896 was a dreary collection of dusty barracks and tents set in the midst of parched Arizona country. The bleakness of the natural environment was more than matched by the drudging monotony of the life and work at the fort and the bad relationships between the officers and enlisted men. The duties, a prisonlike form of hard labor, consisted of road work, ditchdigging, and what Ed described as "boulevard building". The commanding officer, enormously fat, and lazy, set an uninspiring example of leadership for the other officers. Ed commented scathingly about the colonel that he "conducted regimental maneuvers from an army ambulance. It required nothing short of a derrick to hoist him onto a horse. He was then and is now my idea of the ultimate zero in cavalry officers."

Similarly lethargic, and reluctant to exert themselves by calling the men out for drill or maneuvers, the officers under the colonel's command were quite willing to accept his philosophy. To the commander, who was known as a "pick-and-shovel man," this philosophy was simple and pragmatic. Ed gave his own version of it: the way to keep soldiers occupied was to have them "building boulevards in Arizona where no one needed a boulevard." Ed further explained that "Fort Grant was superimposed upon a chaos of enormous boulders, some of them as large as a house. . . ." The soldiers' first appalling task was to remove these before the road work began; obviously, as Ed phrased it, the daily labor was "anything but a sinecure."

Ed soon made the acquaintance of two other men from whom he would take orders. About the top sergeant of B Troop, an Irishman named Lynch, Ed wrote, "He would have been nice to me if I had bought beer for him and if I had it to do over again, I would keep him soused indefinitely, for by that route would come favors and promotion." But about the other man, Lieutenant Tompkins, Ed wrote:

Tommy Tompkins was our troop commander. I think he was a first lieutenant then. He had risen from the ranks. Tommy had a set of mustachios that were the pride of the regiment. He could curl the ends back over his ears and the yellow cavalry stripes on his breeches were so wide that little of the blue could be seen. Tommy was a great character and at drill he was a joy. He called us long-eared jackasses and a great many other things, but this is the only one that is printable; yet none of the men ever took offense. There were many other officers in the post who were cordially hated, but Tommy was universally loved.

After being quartered with the rest of the B Troop in Sibley tents, Ed received his initiation in army routine. But it was soon evident that he knew the typical rookie drill by heart; the only new skill to be learned was the use of the saber, and this he mastered quickly. Within a brief period the sergeant was convinced that Ed didn't belong in the beginning dismounted squad, and he was sent to the drill master for instruction in cavalry riding. Ed reported the results with amusement: "I had been in his squad only a few days when he came to Lynch and complained. 'Why in hell did you send me that bird?' he inquired. 'He can ride better than I can.' "[4]

The area surrounding Fort Grant, arid, and baked by the sun to a desertlike dryness, was hardly appealing to a newcomer. Ed was first informed that it hadn't rained for seventeen years; however, soon after his arrival, nature staged a violent reversal of policy. A series of torrential electrical storms began. The drinking water became contaminated and Ed contracted dysentery. Although he resisted for a while, he was finally forced to go to the hospital. The experience was one that remained vivid in his mind, especially as it concerned the hospital steward, a man named Costello, "the one man whom I have ever sworn to kill," and the drunken doctors assigned to the post. Ed described his days in the hospital:

I was so weak that I could scarcely stand and they would not give me anything to eat, which I suppose was the proper treatment; that is they would not give me anything but castor oil, which it seemed to me in my ignorance that I did not need. I was absolutely ravenous for food and one day one of the men on the opposite side of the ward had a crust of toast that he did not want and he told me that I might have it. He was too weak to bring it to me, so I managed somehow to totter over and get it.

Unfortunately, Costello, in hiding, was watching to see if any such attempt would be made, and he appeared in time to take the food away and punish Ed for violating the rules. In a rage, Ed "spent the next few weeks concocting diabolical schemes for killing Costello, after subjecting him to various sorts of torture." He also broadcast the threat that as soon as he was discharged from the hospital and had regained his health, he intended to kill the steward. "I do not know whether he believed it or not," Ed wrote, "but before I was able to carry out my threat he deserted and I have never seen him since."

In later recollections of the incident, Ed could view it with more tolerance: "Time is a mellower; if I should meet him now the chances are that we would have a bottle of home brew together and that I should find him a most delightful fellow."

What Ed termed "the most disagreeable part of his service" centered about his contacts with the doctors. The two medical officers, a major-doctor and a captain-doctor, were a sorry pair:

The principal difference between them being that at times the captain-doctor was not quite so drunk as the major-doctor. However, drunk or sober, their word was law. When they made the rounds of the hospital they referred to us as "this" and "it." To

*them we were less than human beings and if they decided that
one of us was dead, we were dead.*

Costello, the steward, who was given to telling anecdotes
about the hospital and the doctors, relished repeating a story
that fitted his peculiar idea of how to entertain and cure patients:

*A colored trooper was very ill. One of the doctors pronounced
him dead. "Have it taken out," he said to Costello, according
to whom it was their custom to carry the dead from the main
ward and drop them through a trap door into the cellar until the
time for burial arrived. . . . It seems that as they were about to
drop the . . . trooper into the cellar he gained consciousness
and objected, insisting that he was not dead. "The doctor said
you were dead," replied Costello, and pushed him through the
trap door.*

Ed, soon after his arrival at the Fort, was examined by the
major-doctor. To his consternation the doctor recommended an
immediate discharge because of heart disease. Ed hardly knew
what to think. "I did not wish to have heart disease," he commented, "neither did I wish to be discharged from the army."
All he could do was wait to see what procedure would be followed. After awhile, when an order came from Washington
to have him re-examined, the assignment was given to the
captain-doctor. The diagnosis was the same; but Ed believed that
the reason was obvious—the captain didn't dare to differ with his
superior.

After another waiting period a further communication from
Washington ordered Ed to be held for observation. This advice
he evaluated pessimistically, "it evidently being cheaper to bury
me than to pay transportation back to Detroit." Naturally
quite disturbed, he went to the captain-doctor to find out what
his chances were. "He was quite reassuring," Ed wrote. "He told
me that I might live six months, but on the other hand I might
drop dead at any moment."

Ed's recollection of the doctors and their drunkenness led
him to describe an amusing incident:

*The major-doctor had an orderly who had a highly developed
sense of humor. According to military usage, he followed so many
paces behind the major-doctor whenever the latter went abroad.
I have seen them crossing the parade ground with the major-
doctor laying a most erratic course and always, no matter where
or how he staggered, his orderly would stagger similarly the required number of paces to his rear.*

Ed faced the difficulty of adjusting to an existence at the fort where the soldiers' morale and the level of discipline were extremely low. He became convinced that the recruiting sergeant's opinion had been accurate—one could hardly imagine a worse post than Fort Grant.

He was quickly aware of the atmosphere of thinly repressed violence, of enmity between the enlisted men and officers. Ed saw an officer dragged from his mount and beaten up by a soldier; he heard other men in the post canteen who swore that they would kill any officer they found after dark. Few officers walked the grounds at night, and it was seldom that either the officer of the day or the officer of the guard ventured out for evening inspection. The unfortunate situation, Ed believed, was the result of the attitude and behavior of Colonel Sumner, "which was reflected by his subordinates."

Some officers received a measure of respect, and there were others, like Tommy Tompkins, for whom the men showed a comradely affection. As Ed made friends with the men, he realized they were neither incorrigible nor vicious; they had the basic good qualities of good soldiers and would have responded to a fair and reasonable discipline. But their natural response to a callous, repressive treatment could only be one of hostility and hatred.

The fort and its surrounding area teemed with excitement and apprehension. In the wide stretches of Arizona country the actions of the Indians, restless and resentful, could not be predicted. The Apaches had been confined at a nearby post, but everybody expected them to break loose and go on a rampage. A dangerous outlaw, The Apache Kid, was roaming the country side with his band of cutthroats, while there were reports of towns being raided by another bandit called Black Jack. To Ed these depredations became a source of hope rather than fear; he wrote, "We were always expecting boots and saddles and praying for it, for war would have been better than camp life at Fort Grant under Colonel 'Bull' Sumner."

The opportunity came. Ed, having lied himself out of the hospital and still being weak from dysentery, heard that his troop was scheduled to leave on an urgent mission. A man and his daughter had been murdered on the Solomonsville Trail; their wagon had been burned, and the assumption was that the Apache Kid and his band of Indians were the guilty ones. Ed's B Troop, allotted three days rations, was given the task of capturing the Apache Kid. Although in no condition to undertake an active campaign, Ed, by further lying and pleading, managed to rejoin his troop.

The soldiers began a nightmarish journey which took them across the Arizona mountains. Tommy Tompkins was in command, and a young officer acted as a guide to show them a shortcut to Solomonsville. The "shortcut" was revealed as a direct climb across the jagged peaks:

I knew that there was an army wagon with us part of the time, because I remember distinctly assisting it along mountain trails where there was only room for the wheels on one side of the wagon. We would pass ropes from the opposite side over the top of the wagon and the entire troop dismounted and clinging to the mountainside above the wagon would manage to keep the whole business from pitching into the abyss below, while the mules stumbled and slithered along ahead like a bunch of mountain goats.

Ed vaguely recalled that somewhere along the route the wagon was lost. He became a rider weaving blindly in and out of the column, unable to think of anything but his severe abdominal pains. These were aggravated by the fourteen pounds of ammunition and weapons fastened to his waist. As his suffering grew more acute, Ed found it impossible to wait for permission to fall out. He noted that he fell out, "just far enough to clear the horses behind me and then I would tumble off, usually headfirst onto the ground while the troop went on. At first the sergeants used to bawl me out for not getting permission, but after a while they got used to it and paid no attention to me, since I always managed to catch up later."

Their arrival after dark at Solomonsville, a Mormon settlement, launched them on the first of a series of misadventures and blundering escapades. The inhabitants were responsible for the troops being there since they had sent an urgent request for army protection, but their actions in no way resembled those of a welcoming committee. They greeted the exhausted, thirsty soldiers by padlocking the wells, and then proceeded to set their dogs on the men. The enraged B Troopers broke the padlocks and drove the dogs away.

The hunt for the Apache Kid began in the rain. Ed described the soldiers' discomfort:

We each had two blankets that the men, recently from Fort

Sheridan, had nicknamed the Chicago Heralds because they were so thin. One of these blankets we used as a saddle blanket during the day, and the other was in a roll at our cantel, but as it had no protection it was always wet both from rain and horse sweat. At night we laid them on the wet ground with our saddles at one corner and starting at the opposite side we rolled ourselves up in blankets until our heads reached our saddles. This is great for dysentery.

A running guard was kept, and in alphabetical order each enlisted man was required to take one hour of guard duty. The sentry was armed only with a revolver, and because the belt and holster were too heavy and uncomfortable, those on guard followed a custom of jamming the revolver into one of their leggings. The problem was to know when the hour was up and the next man was to be awakened. Fortunately, Ed had brought his watch, the only one in the troop, an open-faced silver watch he had received for a present on his sixteenth birthday. It became indispensable.[5]

The men displayed a naivete about Indians that Ed later viewed as incredible. Two soldiers patrolled the Indian trails all day, exposing themselves easily to attack by the Indians. "It was just as well for us that there were no renegades about," Ed commented, "for these patrols would have been nothing more than animated targets that no self-respecting renegade could have ignored." To him it appeared that the soldiers were being set up as bait; a dead trooper would have proved that there were hostile Indians in the area.

Ed exhibited his own share of blissful ignorance. With a man named Kunze he discovered a hillside cave that was evidently the habitat of a silver-tipped bear. The two men decided to enter the cave and kill the bear, but as Ed noted, "Kunze, having all the brains in the party, remained at the bottom of the hill and held the horses, while I climbed up the steep trail to the cave, armed only with a revolver. A rubber band and a couple of spitwads would have been equally as useful."

Ed was deeply disappointed to find that the bear was not at home. About their actions he wrote in summation, "I mention this incident merely as a suggestion that there must be some power that watches over idiots."

The general ignorance of the men was also revealed in an experience with a gila monster which had been captured and then escaped from its box. The troop, terror-stricken, combed the camp until midnight in a search for the reptile. They believed that its bite meant instantaneous death and that the monster could kill merely by exhaling its venomous breath on any living thing.

Confusion and carelessness were part of normal procedure. Ed, on sentry duty, was given strict orders not to allow anyone to approach the camp, and to follow regulations by challenging twice and then firing. On this dark, rainy night Ed caught the movement of a shadowy figure, apparently dodging from tree to tree. When the figure drew nearer, Ed hurled a challenge, but the man kept moving without any reply. Ed continued to challenge him, and by the time he cried, "Halt or I fire", they were only a few feet apart. In the blackness he couldn't tell whether the man was a soldier or an Indian. He recalled what happened:

I had him covered and my finger was on the trigger of my revolver and then I saw him reach for his hip pocket. That was an occasion where a hunch was worth more than brains for I certainly was warranted in shooting him, and I should have shot him, but I didn't. I waited to see what he was going to pull out of his hip pocket. It was fortunate for one of us that it was a flask instead of a gun. When he asked me to have a drink I recognized his voice and discovered that he was one of our sergeants drunk as a lord.

With their three-days rations gone, the troop was reduced to a diet of potatoes, which they bought in the area, and to a main dish of the only game available—jackrabbits. Ed described the rabbits vividly: "The muscles of those we killed were filled with large white grubworms as big as one's thumb. Sometimes the cook found them and dug them out, though I am under the impression that he missed many." Ravenously hungry, Ed ate the jackrabbit stew.

The men were given an occasional pass to go to the nearby town of Duncan, and Ed got involved in a poker game there, losing all his money to Mexican vaqueros. He conceived the idea of borrowing money from his commanding officer, Tommy Tompkins, hardly dreaming that the attempt would be successful. But Tommy's response raised him forever in Ed's esteem. "He listened to me patiently," said Ed, "told me he only had a dollar and a half and then gave me half of it."

Apparently the hunt for the Apache Kid had long since been forgotten. Since the men never went anywhere and merely lazed around the camp on the Gila River, the possibilities of catching him became quite remote. After a while they were ordered to return to the post. The journey was exhausting and dangerous. A heavy rainstorm turned the arid Arizona flatland into a torrential river; in places it was more than a mile wide, and the soldiers had to march fifty miles out of their way to get around it.

Upon arriving at the post Ed was still weak from his illness and unable to resume his active duties. He refused to go to the hospital, and Tommy Tompkins, again showing an unusual kindness, gave him a special "coffee-cooling" job, an assignment that removed him from drill, guard duty, and boulevard building. But the job was not exactly a sinecure. "I was placed in charge of headquarters stables," Ed noted, "where all I had to do was to take care of fourteen horses. I cleaned them and their stables, hauled manure, hay, and grain, and doctored those that were sick."

For men who led dreary, monotonous lives all year, the Thanksgiving and Christmas holidays were events to look forward to. In these brief periods at least, there was a relaxation of the army discipline; a festive atmosphere prevailed, and the soldiers for a time could escape from the tensions and boredom. Special holiday dinners were prepared, although they could not have been as deluxe as the Thanksgiving dinner displayed on Troop C's menu of November 26, 1896. The menu, found among Ed's souvenirs, included such choice items as Blue Point Oysters, roast venison, and roast pork, probably the result of some soldier's wry sense of humor. The Christmas menu for Troop C listed beef, turkey, and mutton. But about the B Troop and their dinner, Ed noted in disgust:

Our Christmas table groaned beneath a load of bottled beer and I hope to God that for once in his life Lynch got all the beer he wanted. For the rest, B Troop had only an ordinary dinner, but it sloshed in the same beer that one could buy any day at the post canteen.[6]

During this period Ed was part of a trio that organized "The May Have Seen Better Days Club." The men, all from different troops, had one thing in common: they really had seen better days and came from prosperous families. Ed could recall very few names, but wrote:

There was one chap whose father was a wealthy merchant from Boston; another was a Canadian; and the third was a chap by the name of Napier who had been an officer in the English army. We met in my quarters at the headquarters stables once a month, immediately after payday when we were flush. We usually managed to rake up a pretty good feed and plenty of wine, and then through the balance of the month we were broke, for thirteen dollars does not go far, especially when one has a lot of canteen checks to redeem on payday.[7]

By this time it had become apparent to Ed that life as an enlisted man was anything but romantic or adventurous. Still, it wasn't really soldiering that he now viewed with disgust, but the dreary duties of ditchdigging and boulevard building, " 'Bull' Sumner's idea of preparing men to serve their country in time of war." Ed was happiest when he was his own boss at the stables, even though he worked very hard. One of his duties was to haul hay and grain on a two-wheeled army cart pulled by a horse. He would pile the loose hay as high as possible so as to save the work of extra trips, and then climb atop the hay for the return to the stables. His carelessness led to all sorts of mishaps:

Once I slipped off the top bringing most of the load with me, fell astride one of the thills, turned completely over and stood on my head between the horse's hind feet and the cart. Again I had reached my corral and was bouncing down a little incline with the horse at a trot when the top of the load slipped off and took me with it. I bounced off the horse's rump and fell under the wheel, which passed over the small of my back. I thought that I was killed and for several seconds I was afraid to try to move for fear that I should discover definitely that my back was broken.

Although his back was extremely sore for weeks afterward, nothing could have made him disclose his pain to anybody. His fear was that he might lose his "coffee-cooling" job or be sent back to the hospital.

Among Ed's recollections were those of the 24th Infantry, a Negro regiment that was quartered at Fort Grant. He remembers them as "wonderful soldiers and as hard as nails," recalling their belief that "a member of the 24th was a rookie until he was serving his third enlistment." That they were respected by the army is evidenced by the fact that their noncommissioned officers were ranked unusually high, and one of their sergeants had the highest rank in the service.

On several occasions Ed remembered working under a black sergeant in such menial tasks as day labor or cleanup details, and he commented, ". . . without exception they were excellent men who took no advantage of their authority over us and on the whole were better to work under than our own white sergeants."

He made only one friend among the Indian scouts—possibly because he bought whisky for him—a man called Corporal Josh, who may have been a chief at one time. Josh had not surrendered with Geronimo, but had remained a renegade, joining the Apache Kid's band. After a while he decided to give himself up and tried to think of some plan to win favor and forgiveness. There was a reward for the Kid, but Josh didn't dare attempt to bring him in. Ed offered the gruesome details of what followed:

. . . he did the next best thing and killed one of the Kid's relatives, cut off his victim's head, put it in a gunny sack, tied it to the horn of his saddle and rode up from the Sierra Madres in Mexico to Fort Grant, where he dumped the head out on the floor of the headquarters and asked for forgiveness and probably for a reward, so they let him enlist in the Apache scouts and made him a corporal.

Restricted to the monotony of army life, Ed's need for a creative outlet brought him back once more to a field in which he had shown unmistakable talent—that of sketching and water coloring. A keen observer of people and animals, aware always of the unusual and picturesque, he found stimulating subjects for his art in Fort Grant and its environs. He took delight in drawing the soldiers in colorful uniforms, in differing poses, and performing various duties.[8]

Always fascinated by horses, he developed an ability to draw them in precise detail, capturing subtle lines and impressions so that each animal emerged with individuality. No matter what soldier was mounted upon the horse, its beauty and grace were never obscured.

Some of his sketches were highlighted with water colors applied with skill and realism. At the bottom of one page of sketches in various colors he wrote humorously, "Please notice the Impressionist coloring."

Other sketches, typical of his interest, were titled *An Apache Scout, On Herd Guard* (a mounted soldier) and *An Old Soldier.* The Christmas Eve entertainment program provided him with an opportunity to make a group of drawings and cartoons. These included *Wing Dancer,* and one of a soldier carrying a child's hobby horse and toy wagon, with the caption, "How you can tell the 'Married Man'." Ed's sense of humor couldn't be

Sketches ERB made during his service with 7th U.S. Cavalry, Fort Grant, Arizona Territory.

repressed, and one of his cartoons is described as "A Drawing of Sitting Bull presenting Geo. Washington to Victoria of England. The Prince of Wales may be seen in the background." The Prince is shown as a curious but shy child, peering from behind Victoria's skirts.[9]

Ed's disillusionment with the life of an enlisted man at Fort Grant was inevitable. He had arrived on May 23 eager and excited at the prospect of an adventurous career in the cavalry, convinced that this period of training would lead to promotion and the attainment of the commission he had so desired. But two months of drudging labor and monotonous camp life, as well as illness, deflated his romantic ideas and made him realize that a career in the cavalry, especially at Fort Grant, was unthinkable. Whatever were the prospects of advancement, and these appeared remote, Ed couldn't conceive of any circumstances that would persuade him to stay in his present situation.

Toward the end of July 1896 or the first part of August he began writing complaining and even imploring letters to his father. His hopes were centered upon a procedure that had often been followed in cases similar to his: the army permitted a soldier to buy his way out of the service. He discussed this in correspondence with his father and was sustained by a confidence that his father would use money and influence to bring about his discharge. George Burroughs had never wanted Ed to enlist in the army and had undoubtedly yielded against his better judgment. But now, as with his son's impulsive actions and escapades of the past, he would be compelled to come to his rescue.

On August 25 Ed wrote to his father, acknowledging receipt of a letter of August 20, and then went on to reveal his misery and plead for help:

I learned something today which "makes my heart grow sad." A fellow wrote me that he had just heard that some law had been passed lately taking away a soldier's privilege of buying himself out. I don't know whether or not it is so and I can not find out here with-out asking an officer and if Tommy learned that I expected to buy out in the spring he might not like it.

In the event that the rumor was true, and a soldier could not buy his way out, Ed had an alternative suggestion:

I hope it is not true as I was beginning to look forward already to the time when I should be home again. If it is so would you

Sketches ERB made during his service with 7th U.S. Cavalry, Fort Grant, Arizona Territory.

be willing to have me try to borrow the transportation (about $50 including meals) and put in an application for transfer to the 1st Cavalry 2 troops of which are to be stationed at Sheridan (Fort Sheridan, Illinois) if not already there. I should make application for one of those troops. An applicant has to be able to show that he has the cash for transportation.

He also has to have the approval of his troop Commander, Post Commander and Secy of War and the Troop Commander of the troop he is going to has to express his willingness to accept him. I think the only stumbling block would be Col. E. V. Sumner, Post Commander. They say he objects to transfers without good cause.

Ed's youthful bravado and daring that drove him to request the worst assignment in the United States Army had been considerably dissipated by this time. A transfer to Fort Sheridan, near his home in Chicago, was pleasant to contemplate. But he offers to resign himself to his present situation if no change is possible: "If you think best I will make no attempt to transfer. I made my bed and I will lie in it. . . ." He is unable to conceal an acute homesickness:

. . . I think that if I ever get home again that I shall never leave, unless you drive me away and then I will go and sit on the curb stone in front of Rease's house and look at HOME.

I am glad you are to vote for Bryan electors. Hope you are still well at home. Love to all from your affectionate son Ed.

His loneliness may have also provoked wistful thoughts of Emma. From Coldwater, Michigan, where she was spending a vacation, with relatives, she mailed her picture. A notation on the back read, "1896 Sent to E. R. Burroughs—and received on his 21st Birthday at Dunçan Arizona. Camp of the 7th U.S. Cavalry."

As Ed discovered, in matters involving decisions of any type, the army cannot be hurried. By the end of the year he was still waiting. On December 2, 1896, he wrote to Colonel J. Sumner Rogers at the Michigan Military Academy. One can only conjecture as to his reasons. He may have hoped to obtain Rogers' help either in getting a discharge or a transfer to the 1st Cavalry. Possibly, he was contemplating a return to the academy. The letter's main purpose may have been to offer an apology to Rogers. Ed, upon reflection, and with a little more maturity gained through his sequence of shattering experiences, might view his behavior at the academy, and his precipitate departure when the colonel was depending upon him, with guilt and a new understanding of his faults.

Rogers' reply on December 26 showed that the colonel had remarkable powers of patience and forgiveness:

I have read your favor of the 2nd inst with both interest and pleasure. While I still think that you acted imprudently and unkindly to me, I do not permit a single escapade in which your worst qualities were brought into requisition to blind me to the fact that you possess many admirable traits, and your letter still further causes me to forget your mistake.[10]

Ed had evidently stated that he planned to remain in the army, for Rogers referred to this point:

I assure you that I hold no malice against you, and wish you success in your profession of soldier. Your letter confirms my faith in your good heart, which is much to a soldier as well as civilian.

In stressing his friendly feelings, Rogers wrote that Ed would always receive a cordial welcome at the Academy, adding:

It is my desire to remember you just as I remember other ex-cadets who have made a good record at the Academy,— with kindness and sincere good wishes for their prosperity, and I am glad to know that your feelings toward your school are warm and kind.

Concerning the Academy's financial condition, Rogers commented that "Considering the very hard times, we are holding our own in a most encouraging way."

George Burroughs, faced once more with the task of extricating his son from an unpleasant situation, began contacting people of influence. In March 1897 he wrote to a friend, W. D. Preston of the Griffin Wheel Company, requesting him to write to R. A. Alger, secretary of war. Preston, in his letter of March 11, explains the circumstances of Ed's enlistment with his father's consent, and refers to his ambition "to adopt a military profession." Then Preston bases his appeal upon Ed's supposed health problem:

It was his intention, as he is a young man of good ability and education to endeavor to pass the examinations and ultimately to get a commission, but it seems that after he was sent to Arizona he did not pass the proper Medical Inspection and the Medical Inspectors recommended that he be discharged. He has however not been discharged and is still held at Fort Grant.

Ed's main goal, according to Preston, was now unattainable:

This report of the Medical Examiners would undoubtedly prevent his getting a Commission even though he passed the proper examination, and as that was his idea on entering the Service, both he and his parents are now very anxious that he should get a regular discharge, as he has two very fine openings in Commercial lines.[11]

Preston adopted a sentimental tone in mentioning that "His Mother is in poor health and is very much worked up over the matter. . . ." He stated that "from a thorough knowledge of all the circumstances it would appear to me that it would be . . . proper for you to grant the discharge. . . ." George Burroughs' influence with people in high places is revealed in Preston's reference to "Senator Mason of this city," with a comment that the Senator "will undoubtedly present the matter to you in proper form. . . ."

Another of George Burroughs' friends, E. G. Kieth, wrote much along the same lines on March 11 to Secretary Alger, mentioning a "medical examination which was unsatisfactory"; he presented the case from a rather peculiar viewpoint, shifting the blame to Ed's shoulders: ". . . his father is now quite anxious for his discharge, feeling that the young man was inconsiderate in enlisting without a Medical examination."

These intercessions achieved the desired results, and on March 19, 1897, Ed received a telegram from his father which read: "Discharge has been ordered. Will mail draft today."

In his *Autobiography* Ed explains concisely that "owing to the fact that I had twice been recommended for discharge because of heart disease, once by the major-doctor and once by the captain, it seemed wholly unlikely that I should pass a physical examination for a commission, and my father therefore obtained my discharge from the army through Secretary of War Alger."[12]

The discharge, dated March 23, 1897, refers to special orders of March 15 and reports in error that Ed was twenty-one and eight-twelfths years of age at the time of enlistment. He was actually twenty and eight-twelfths years old. His height is listed as five feet eight and one-half inches, his complexion fair with "Brown #3" eyes and dark brown hair, and his occupation as "Student." Tommy Tompkins, his commanding officer, rated his character as "excellent." Information about his military record is contained on the reverse side of the discharge.[13]

His service with the Seventh Cavalry ended, Ed, aware of past failures and disappointments, chose to review his entire sequence of military experiences with a satirical attitude. Beginning with his childhood, he prepared a list of the successive ranks he had held and headed the list "My Wonderful Military Career." On it he listed eleven steps:

1. *Right Guard Brown School Cadets*
   (wooden gun)
2. *High Private Harvard School Cadets (no gun)*
3. *Plebe—Orchard Lake*
4. *Corporal—Orchard Lake*
5. *Sergeant Major—Orchard Lake*
6. *2nd Lieut—Orchard Lake*
7. *Private–Orchard Lake*
8. *1st Sergeant—Orchard Lake*
9. *Captain—Orchard Lake*
10. *2nd Lieut M.M.A. Tactical Officer,*
    Assistant Commandant, Adjutant of the
    Academy—Orchard Lake
11. *Private—7th U.S. Cavalry*

At the bottom he noted, "Between 4 and 5 there should also be a Private and Corporal."

Ed, who had spoken of his homesickness in the letter to his father, may have planned to return to Chicago immediately, but at Fort Grant he learned of his brothers' latest venture in the cattle business and received an invitation from them that was too enticing to turn down. The outfit of Sweetser & Burroughs, while continuing to raise cattle at the Idaho ranch, had discovered that success was becoming more and more elusive. Now, Lew Sweetser had gone to Mexico and purchased an entire brand of cattle, and Harry, at Nogales, Arizona, was awaiting the arrival of the animals. They were to be shipped to Kansas City.

Always eager to be with his brothers, Ed agreed to join Harry at Nogales and help in the loading of the cattle. The experience turned out to be one that he had not anticipated. In his *Autobiography* he gives the details of his second brief period in the cattle business. Accustomed to handling the big Idaho Herefords, Ed was amused by the appearance of the scrubby Mexican animals; they looked "about the size of jackrabbits." He viewed them with contempt, and even went into the loading pens on foot to drive them up the runways to the cars. But he quickly changed his opinion:

They may have been small in stature, but they were large in initiative and they did not wish to go up the runways into the cars. They went part way and then all of a sudden they turned around and came toward me. I was not afraid of them, and on the other hand they appeared to be even less afraid of me. Those in the front rank knocked me down and the others galloped over me, after which I let somebody else load them.

As the train journeyed toward Kansas City, Ed's problems increased. Starting with seven cars of Mexican cattle, he later picked up other cars, including some at La Junta with Texas longhorns. Ed's only helper was an old man whom he described as "a poor consumptive trying to work his way East." The cattle were in poor shape, underfed and underwatered, and at a number of stops they had to drag seven or eight dead animals out of each car. The stops included one at Albuquerque, where, he remembered, he was given a hotel room that apparently belonged to somebody else. ". . . in a drawer were two beautiful six-guns. It was a good thing for the owner that I was honest."[14]

Ed thought he had experienced all possible difficulties, but soon a new one arose. The cattle, weak from starvation, would suddenly fall down. In order to save their lives, somebody would have to crawl into the cars and "tail them up." Since the old man was unable to do it, Ed had no choice but to volunteer for the task. Climbing down through the trap in the roof of each cattle car, he lowered himself among the close-packed, wild Texas steers. He described his task:

After I had got past their horns and down between them it was not so bad for about the worst they could do was step on me. The old fellow helped me at first, but finally he got kicked so badly that I had to do it alone and with the animals swaying and crowding it was a strenuous job to get an animal back on its feet after it had fallen down. Of course it is physically impossible for a man to lift a steer, but if you get hold of the tail and heave up the natural inclination of the beast is to help itself and about all you do is to balance it while it gets its feet under itself, though at that there is considerable heavy lifting.

Ed found that he had to perform this difficult job every time the train stopped; afterward, with the train in motion, his dangerous return route was along the tops of the swaying cars. "As a rule," he wrote, "the wind was blowing so hard across the Kansas prairies that I should have been blown off the top of the train before I reached the caboose, so I used to sit down and cling to a brake handle until the next stop."

With the cattle shipment completed, he was free to return home and to readjust to a family life and activities that must have appeared sedate in comparison to his days in Arizona. In the summer of 1897 he resumed friendships and took part in a varied social life.[15] Separation from Emma Hulbert had, if anything, increased his interest in her. In the small brown memo book that he carried with him at Fort Grant, he had printed the names Jessie D. Hulbert and Emma C. Hulbert, with the address 194 Park Avenue. But there was no question that he now preferred Emma. They dated regularly, went to parties at friends' homes and to the theater. Emma, a year younger than Ed, had been born on January 1, 1876, in Chicago, and her birth year accounted for her unusual middle name of *Centennia* adopted in honor of the 100th anniversary of the Declaration of Independence.

Temporarily, Ed accepted the most readily available occupation—helping his father in the American Battery Company. However, for the first time he considered turning to a creative field for a profession. The lure of drawing and cartooning, especially as a means of using his imagination to present characters in a humorous or satirical way, had always been strong. He had even been intrigued by the possibility of becoming a political cartoonist. Now, with a new surge of interest, he enrolled in classes at the Art Institute on Michigan Boulevard.[16]

Unfortunately, his studies were brief. His lack of perseverance may again be attributed to the personality problems that he still could not conquer. At twenty-two Ed was painfully indecisive, uncertain of goals or directions, and as yet without any understanding of himself or his nature. He was unable to subdue an impatience and a fierce restlessness that drove him into impulsive courses of action. He was motivated by sudden enthusiasms, as in his study of art, but was as quickly discouraged when he perceived that the period of development would be long and difficult. At present only the physical appealed to him: he was still dominated by a desire to obtain a commission and to make the army his career. In the physical and the active lay his confidence

One of ERB's political cartoons.

—in these he had proved himself, but in other areas he felt insecure.

The reasons for his failure to continue his study of art were not only personal. Certainly George Burroughs, impatient with Ed's past mistakes and his tendency to vacillate, could offer little encouragement to his son in this choice of a possible profession. Above all, to George, a hard-headed businessman, the very idea of art as a way of making a living was rejected as unthinkable. Ed's father, while attempting to be tolerant, would view his son's latest project as completely impractical, or as a whim which would soon be forgotten.

In his opinion that Ed would find no serious motivation George Burroughs was correct, for his son was not willing to follow a thorough study of drawing and painting, with exposure to all forms and subjects. According to one report, when Ed was placed in a life class which stressed the ability to understand human anatomy and draw the body realistically, he lost interest at once. Presumably, he made it plain that he cared only to draw horses.[17]

Other influences, powerful in their attraction, were destroying his creative impulse. He wanted to be with his brothers George and Harry, and, as always, he could not resist the lure of the rugged outdoor life of Idaho. But the army still exerted the stronger fascination, and while the 7th Cavalry experience had been an unhappy one, Ed did not believe that this worst post in the army was in any way typical of other units.

On February 22, 1898, Ed wrote to his former commandant from the academy, Captain Fred A. Smith, then stationed at Fort Niobrara, Nebraska, to inquire about enlistment. Smith's reply

One of ERB's political cartoons.

of the twenty-fifth was friendly, but not encouraging about any possibility of enlistment: "I am sorry that I cant hold forth any hope or promise to you just now as I have no place or even expectation at the present writing. . . ."

Ed's plaintive letter to his father at the time he was hoping for an army discharge had contained a promise that if he ever got home again he would never leave unless driven away. But with the passing months he was again confronted with the problem of his future—of choosing some type of career. He could not consider remaining permanently at the American Battery Company; to work there performing routine tasks under the close supervision of his father would hardly be a happy situation. Without any other choice, he decided in April of 1898 to rejoin his brothers at Pocatello, Idaho.

The first stage in the train trip to Pocatello included a stop-over at Denver. Here he ran into an old 7th Cavalry friend, a former member of "The May Have Seen Better Days Club." A celebration seemed in order, and as Ed confessed in his *Autobiography,* the succeeding events became quite hazy. For some reason he and his friend hired a band and paraded along the downtown streets of Denver with the band marching ahead. "This left our exchequer rather depleted, but a kindly disposed gambler came to our rescue the next morning and especially opened his place of business for us at about ten o'clock, so that we could recoup our fallen fortune. But that something must have gone wrong is indicated by a telegram which I find in my scrapbook. It was addressed to my brother, Harry, in Pocatello: 'Lost roll. Wire twenty-five.' "

At Pocatello, where George and Harry greeted him, their

pleasure at his arrival was evident, but it soon became equally clear that they had no permanent employment for him. In fact, the cattle shipping operations had been far from successful, and the brothers were facing financial difficulties. A letter of May 26, 1898, written by Harry from Yale, Idaho, to his father, reveals that he had been unable to make payments on the money that Major George had lent him at an earlier period:

I enclose check for $80 to cover interest on the $1000 note for one year. Had the check made out before I thought of the exchange but will include it in the check I will send for the purchases Mother is making for us. I should have sent this on the 1st when it was due, but did not have the amt. in bank at the time.

After explaining that he would probably go to Denver with the cattle in the following week, Harry wrote, "Ed and I have been driving cattle and will put in the next few days helping Walter and John Sparks gather what we are going to ship. Ed is at the camp up in the hills now, and I start for there tonight."

Even on the small ranch in Idaho, so remote from the center of the nation, Ed had become aware of the turbulent events that were arousing the nation, driving Americans to a fever pitch of patriotism. The sinking of the battleship *Maine* in Havana Harbor on February 15, 1898, had provided a climax to the already tense situation between America and Spain. Congress, in a joint resolution of April 19, authorized President McKinley to use force to drive Spain out of Cuba. Four days later, after being empowered to call on the states for volunteers, McKinley requested 125,000 men.

These stirring actions and the hope that the crisis might create a need for soldiers were a stimulus to Ed's military ambitions. Most exciting to him was the news that Theodore Roosevelt had assembled his Rough Riders to join in the battle. He wrote directly to Roosevelt, volunteering for the Rough Riders; the response was prompt, terse, and disappointing:

First Regt. U.S. Vol. Cavalry
In Camp near
San Antonio, Texas,
May 19th, 1898.

Edgar Rice Burroughs,
Pocatello, Idaho.

Dear sir,

I wish I could take you in, but I am afraid that the chances of our being over-enlisted forbid my bringing a man from such a distance.

> *Yours very truly,*
> *T. Roosevelt*
> *Lt. Col.*

The typed note bore Roosevelt's sprawling signature.

Earlier, in his search for army employment, Ed, on April 26, had sought the help of Colonel Rogers. Rogers' reply of May 3 was cordial: "I know you will be a credit to yourself in such service as you wish to enter. I am just about arranging now to go to Washington and I assure you that I shall gladly say what I can in your behalf. . . ." But a critical report of Ed's attitude toward enlistment contained the accusation that he had refused to join a local group: "A Pocatello barber organized a company of militia that went to the Philippines and served with distinction. But Burroughs was too proud of his military background to go with these raw recruits."[18]

As in the past, Ed's desire to adopt the army as a career was frustrated at every turn. In addition, the employment situation appeared bleak; no openings were available. Adrift without any plans, he was persuaded to launch his first venture as a businessman. Sometime in June 1898, at the urging of his brother Harry, who supplied the money, Ed became the proprietor of a stationery store in Pocatello, Idaho. He bought out the owner, Victor Roeder, a long-time resident of the town. The store, on West Center Street, had a large newsstand and a cigar counter and specialized in the sale of photographic materials and in the development and printing of Kodak pictures.

In his *Autobiography* Burroughs notes that "the girl who attended to that did her work so well that we used to receive films from all over the United States for development and printing." The store, of course, handled books, magazines, and newspapers, and Ed even established a newspaper route. At times, when he couldn't find a carrier, he delivered the papers himself, making his rounds on a black horse he had purchased and named Crow.

He devoted both his imagination and unlimited energies to trying to make the store a success. His printed photo bill an-

Interior of ERB's Pocatello, Idaho, store; dictionary stand in center is still in use in offices of ERB, Inc.

nounces "Finishing for Amateurs a specialty," states that cameras are rented, and refers to "Two Hundred Snap Shot Views of Pocatello and Vicinity from which we print to Order." Beneath the list of charges is a statement, "No deduction can be made for Developing Failures as they require the Same Labor as Successful Exposures."

That Ed was ingenious and enterprising is revealed in the publicity given to the store in the *Pocatello Tribune* (now the *Idaho State Journal*). In the issue of June 25, 1898, a notice under "Local Brevities" announces the change of ownership:

Mr. V. C. Roeder has sold his book and stationery store to Mr. E. R. Burroughs who is now in charge. Mr. Roeder has not yet decided upon what he will do, but if he does not go to war with the volunteer engineers now being recruited by Mr. F. E. J. Mills at Salt Lake, will probably locate somewhere in California. Mr. Roeder's departure from Pocatello is a matter of genuine regret to all. He is one of the old timers of Pocatello and will be missed by everybody. Mr. Roeder's successor, Mr. Burroughs, is a recent arrival in Pocatello, but a young man of fine abilities and we have no doubt "Roeder's", as it has always been known, will continue as popular as ever under his management.[19]

The "Local Brevities" from July through most of October 1898 contained various bits of publicity for the store: "July 2 (?):

128

United States flags from six for five cents to forty cents each; Cuban flags for ten cents at Burroughs, successor to Roeder." The war against Spain and the nationwide sympathy for the oppressed Cubans had made Cuban flags very popular.

July 2: Flags for the Fourth at Burroughs, successor to Roeder.

July 6: E. R. Burroughs, successor to V. C. Roeder, has an assortment of latest vocal and instrumental music.
New novels and magazines every day at Burroughs'. Capt. Chas. King's *latest, "A Wounded Name", just received.*

July 9: Come to Burroughs' and get a photo of your Fourth of July float.
You can get a cigar at Burroughs' that you don't have to go out in the back yard to smoke.[20]

Other publicity notices include offers to deliver any paper or magazine, American or foreign, to the home, and announcements of the Junius Brutus Havana cigars sold at the store. A news story on page one for October 12 and 15 is headed "The Autograph Quilt." It reports that "a feature of the Congregational church Fair will be a new advertising medium—an autograph quilt," and lists "enterprising Pocatello firms who have already secured space. . . ." Among them appears the name E. R. Burroughs.[21]

In spite of the enthusiasm and determination that Ed displayed in launching the business, the stationery store was not destined to be a success. The complete reasons for the failure are difficult to assess. Possibly, his capital was insufficient. A small business, re-established under new ownership, might require time for acceptance and patronage by the community. This would result in a waiting period and a need for a capital reserve. But a personal element was also involved: the new proprietor would have to possess both patience and persistence, plus, of course, a continuing interest in the business. The first two qualities were the ones that Ed had failed to display in the past. After an enthusiastic start he had a habit of losing interest and becoming discouraged. Slowly developing long-range projects that required sustained determination were not for him.

In later years, reminiscing about the store, Ed commented:

I had a book shop in Pocatello, Idaho, when cheap editions cost me fourteen cents and Munsey's Magazine sold for ten cents and cost me nine and weighed over a pound and the postage was a cent a pound and I am still trying to figure where my profits occurred, especially in those recurring periods that it was non-returnable.[22]

Toward the end of 1898 or first part of 1899 the former owner of the stationery store returned and was quite willing to buy the store back. In his *Autobiography* Ed remarked, "My store was not a howling financial success and I certainly was glad when Victor Roeder, the man from whom I purchased it, returned to Pocatello and wanted it back."

To this, he added, "God never intended me for a retail merchant!"

In his unoccupied moments, Ed again turned to creative writing for stimulation. His scrapbook contains newspaper clippings, evidently from the *Pocatello Tribune,* date unknown, of two poems. One, titled "The Black Man's Burden," is a parody of Kipling's famous poem, "The White Man's Burden." While the parody contains no author's name, a brief explanatory note heading the poem supplies reasonable evidence that Ed was the author: "The following clever lines, in imitation of a recent very celebrated poem, are the composition of one of the well-known young men of Pocatello—Ed."

The parody, mocking Kipling's poem, offers a satirical and bitter comment upon the plight of the black man and his mistreatment by the whites. The first line of each stanza, as in Kipling, reads "Take up the white man's burden," but the remaining lines contain a searing description of this "burden" which the Negro has been forced to accept. The poem includes such statements as:

The white man's culture brings you
  The white man's God, and rum.

Take up the white man's burden;
  Take it because you must;
Burden of making money;
  Burden of greed and lust;

Other lines speak of the "poor simple folk" who must "abandon nature's freedom" and then accept the white man's "Liberty" which makes them free only in name, while the white goddess in her heart still "brands" them as slaves.

It is significant that both in tone and content the poem parallels the philosophy so repeatedly expressed by Ed in later years —his bitter indictment of civilization and its destructive, degrading effects upon the simple natives and the animals. (As further supporting evidence of authorship, the very fact that Ed saved these two poems throughout the years must be given some weight.)[23]

Having disposed of the stationery store, Ed, now without any prospect of employment, followed his customary procedure of joining his brothers George and Harry. On Crow, his black horse, he began his journey to the Mule Shoe Ranch on the Snake River, where he planned to help later with the spring roundup.

"There had been a terribly hard winter in Canada and Northern Idaho," he noted in his *Autobiography*, "with the result that timber wolves were driven way down into our back yards, which seemed to be the only places left where they might pick up a bite to eat."

I had never been to the Mule Shoe Ranch before; and the first things that I did was to get myself lost, turning up the Snake after I reached it instead of down.

By the time I was thoroughly convinced that I was going in the wrong direction, night had overtaken me. There was no trail; and so I followed a barbed wire fence, which ran along a side hill. My horse showed signs of unusual nervousness; but he had nothing on me, for I have always been scared of a barbed wire fence and especially so on a trailless side hill after dark.

However, it was not the side hill that seemed to be worrying Crow. It was something above us on the top of the hill, or rather the low ridge below which we were riding. Presently I discovered the cause of his perturbation. A number of animals were paralleling our course along the summit of the ridge. Occasionally I could see them outlined against the sky. I hoped that they were coyotes, but I had never seen so many coyotes together in one pack. I think I counted seven or eight of them. It was about this time that I recalled the fact that the wolves had been driven down by the hard winter. I did not know that they were wolves; I do not know now, but I have never heard of coyotes running in packs or following horsemen; and for the next hour I wished that I were somewhere else, but at that I think I was more afraid of the barbed wire fence than I was of my companions.

I was unarmed, unfamiliar with the country, and it was quite dark; so that it was with a sense of considerable relief that I saw the lights of a ranch house twinkling in the distance; but when I got to the gate and dismounted I found that I had jumped from the frying pan into the fire, for no sooner had I opened the gate than I was set upon by a pack of dogs that seemed much more enthusiastically vicious than whatever had been following me for the past hour.[24]

Once at work on the ranch, Ed demonstrated his love of horses and his ability to handle them. He had a confirmed philosophy about cowboys and their horses which he expounded in his *Autobiography:*

The majority of our cow horses have fool tricks of some nature due exclusively to the fact that they are usually broken by fools. As a horseman, the American cowpuncher is very much overrated. He may be a good rider, but there is lots more to horsemanship than riding.

In civilized countries where they know how to train a horse they have no word analogous to breaking. Their horses are not broken; they are trained. Cow horses were broken, which results in either a disspirited plug or an unruly animal with bad traits.

Ed, as an example, described what had happened to Whisky Jack. The horse had been broken by a Mexican who, according to reports, "beat him over the head and neck with a club until the horse's neck was so swollen that he could not turn his head in any direction and to the day of his death he carried the scars of spur marks almost from his ears to the root of his tail. No wonder that he killed men." Ed maintained that various "tortures" were applied to horses, and that during his years in Idaho "the proper feeding, grooming and care of a horse were practically unknown."

Always indignant about any manifestation of cruelty toward an animal, Ed tells the story in his *Autobiography* of a minister who was his neighbor on the Raft River, and "who had his own ideas about applying the teachings of Christ." The man was especially annoyed because the horse that pulled his buckboard had a tendency to balk. Ed reported the details of what occurred on a day when the minister lost his patience:

Pushing, pulling and beating had accomplished nothing, so he built a fire underneath her. With the stubborn asininity that is one of the symptoms of balkiness, she lay down in the fire, whereupon the sky pilot shoveled coals on top of her.

For the spring roundup the foreman insisted that the men camp near a little mountain stream just below a crossing where the cattle were herded back and forth. As a result, the drinking water turned to "a thick mixture of cow manure and mud." Ed developed a severe case of mountain fever and rode down to the railroad with a temperature in the 100's. ". . . I was, fortunately, out of my head most of the time," he wrote. "How I stuck in the saddle I do not know."

It was during this Idaho period that Ed suffered an odd and distressing experience that he never forgot. As a bystander in a saloon at the time a quarrel erupted, he got in the way of a policeman's billy club. He received a severe blow on the head and wound up in the hospital where stitches were taken in his scalp. Long afterward, he complained of dizziness and reported having strange hallucinations. In later years, responding to a general questionnaire from the Boston Society for Psychic Research, he offered his recollections of the happening and of an unusual incident that followed:

In 1899 I received a heavy blow on the head which, while it opened up the scalp, did not fracture the skull, nor did it render me unconscious, but for six weeks or two months thereafter I was the victim of hallucinations, always after I had retired at night when I would see figures standing beside my bed, usually shrouded. I invariably sat up and reached for them, but my hands went through them. I knew they were hallucinations caused by my injury and did not connect them in any way with the supernatural, in which I do not believe.[25]

Ed then described an occurrence that took place, "for which," he maintained, "I have never been able to find any explanation other than that I was guided by my sub-conscious mind in performing this act."

It was my habit at this time to carry my keys, three or four in number, on a red silk cord about an eighth of an inch in diameter. The ends of the cord were tied in a hard knot and then cut off so closely to the knot that the ends were not visible. I had carried my keys in this way for some time with the result that the silk, which was originally of a very bright color, was much darkened by use, though that portion inside of the knot must have been as fresh and bright as when first tied.

At night I hung my clothes on hooks in a large bathroom which I used for a dressing room. The two doors leading from my bedroom and bath were locked from the inside, yet one morning, when I had occasion to use my keys, I found that one of them had been removed from the cord, though the knot was still tied in precisely the same way that it had been; the ends were not protruding, nor was there any of the clean, bright colored portion visible.

This key could have been removed only by untying the knot and then re-tying it precisely as it had been, which would have been practically impossible for anyone to accomplish without evidence of the knot having been tampered with being apparent.[26]

Ed added a theory he had developed as a result of this odd incident: "While the above appears to have not much bearing upon the subject of your investigation, it has suggested to me, when considered in the light of the fact that it is the only occurrence of its kind in a lifetime of over fifty years, that much other, perhaps all, so-called supernatural phenomena are the result of injured or diseased brains. Prior to my injury I had no hallucinations; subsequent to my recovery I have had none."[27] Being a creator of fantasies of other worlds filled with unrealistic incidents that might be considered wilder than any hallucinations was one thing. But as a man of science in a real world, he firmly rejected the improbable or unprovable.

Before the spring roundup was over, Ed, again in his desperate search for employment, continued his efforts to obtain a commission in the army. He had heard the news that on March 3, 1899, the War Department obtained official authorization to organize a volunteer army of 25,000. On March 25, he wrote to the War Department to inquire. But the reply that he received four days later offered nothing definite. The acting secretary of war, after acknowledging Ed's application for a commission, wrote, "As it has been decided not to organize at this time the 25,000 volunteers, authorized by the act of March 3, 1899, your letter has been placed on file for consideration should the future turn of events make this possible."

Also on March 25, Ed took the opportunity to seek the help of Congressman Edgar Wilson of Idaho who had sponsored his appointment to West Point. Wilson responded, ". . . I am advised that Idaho has received her full quota of appointments in the Army, so there would not be an opportunity for you to secure a place. However, if you could bring to bear any influence from Michigan, or the east anywhere, I would be glad to second the application and give the best endorsement possible." Wilson further suggested that Ed write to friends in Chicago and Michigan who might have influence with the secretary of war.

July of 1899 found Ed in New York. Whether he was there because of some business transactions in connection with the

American Battery Company, or whether he was in search of employment or trying to contact someone who might help him get a commission is impossible to ascertain. A letter of July 16 was sent to Colonel Rogers, and Rogers' reply of the twenty-second is addressed to Ed at "No. II East 17th Street" in New York. Rogers, writing from the Pay Department of the Army in Washington, where he had evidently been assigned because of the Spanish-American War, refers to not having a vacation "since entering the service" and states that "the work has been very arduous during the war." About to take a short leave, he anticipates "a good rest at Orchard Lake."

Rogers indicates that he would be quite willing to help Ed, but points out that "an army officer's influence amounts to little where Senators and Congressmen, and in fact, Cabinet Officers, are so numerous." He urges Ed to get one of these to intercede for him if he wishes to get a commission in the regular service. "I am sure your father could get some influential politician in Chicago to look after your case," Rogers writes.

But all of Ed's attempts to get a commission were in vain.[28] Resigned to the inevitable, he returned to Chicago to accept a job again in his father's American Battery Company. In his *Autobiography* he comments, "I started at the bench and learned the business from the ground up." Some time afterward he became the treasurer of the company.[29]

An 1899 item, possibly of minor import, could, however, lead to some interesting speculations. The item, a book preserved throughout the years in Burroughs' personal library, is *Descent of Man,* by Charles Darwin (2nd Edition, Century Series, American Publishers Corporation, N.Y., 1874). On the flyleaf appears a notation "E. R. Burroughs Jan '99," and beneath it a pencil drawing by Ed of a large monkey or ape in a typical position, somewhat crouching, knuckles resting on the ground. On the right of the drawing he had written "Grandpa." Young Ed, only 23, and given to mischievous pranks, was poking fun at Abner Tyler Burroughs, his grandfather. The drawing and his early exposure to Darwin's theories can naturally raise questions about *when* the Tarzan-of-the-apes idea was born. Was there a mere glimmering, an intriguing notion of an ape-man at this time, and did the idea lie dormant for many years until some creative necessity summoned it?

CHAPTER 5

MARRIAGE, WANDERINGS AND REALITY

Through the years, Ed's unchanging devotion to Emma had proved to be an element of constancy in his erratic life. It was not surprising, therefore, that their attachment to each other should reach its natural romantic peak. Since Ed had presumably given up his wandering ways and was ready to settle down to the sober role of a businessman, marriage was obviously on the horizon. He had shown some adjustment to his position in the American Battery Company and to the social activities of his circle of friends.[1]

From the earliest days when they both attended the Brown School, he had considered Emma to be his girl. According to one account, "When Ed was fourteen . . . he began proposing to a little girl named Emma Hulbert. . . . For ten years 'Ed' Burroughs haunted her, when he wasn't out West, or in the army, or at school, and for ten years he kept proposing and she continued to say 'no.' "[2]

The growing-up period for Emma, the youngest of four sisters, was one of calm and security. Alvin Hulbert, her father, highly successful in his hotel enterprises, had ample income to provide not only the material comforts for his family, but to afford some of the luxuries typical of wealthy families. These even included a trip to Europe for his daughter Leila. An unidentified clipping reports the event: "Miss Leila Hulbert, eldest daughter of Mr. Alvin Hulbert, of the Tremont and Great Northern Hotels, left on Tuesday via the Michigan Central Railway for New York, where she will spend a few days prior to sailing on Saturday for a three months' tour of Europe."

Emma Hulbert prior to her marriage to ERB in 1900.

Emma spent her early years in the normal patterns of schooling, home duties, and social affairs, but displayed a special interest in music, taking private voice lessons. Her formal education ended with her graduation from the Brown School in 1892; however, she continued her work in music. The family suffered a serious tragedy and an interruption of all activities with the death of the only son, Alvin, Jr., at the age of fourteen.[3]

The Hulberts, as with both sides of the Burroughs family, could establish a British ancestry. The family line, traced by Emma Theresa (Mrs. Alvin) Hulbert, went back to as early as 1413 when a certain John Drake married Christiana Billett. Thomas Drake, born in Colyton, Devon County, England, about 1635, then carried the Drake lineage to America in 1653-54.[4] Distinguished members of the Drake family fought in the Continental Army at Lexington and at Bunker Hill. Emma Theresa Drake and her husband Alvin were both born in Rochester, New York, she on July 24, 1850, and he on January 29, 1829. With their marriage on October 12, 1868, the two lines, Hulbert and Drake, were joined. On the birth certificate of their daughter, Emma Centennia, the twenty-two year difference stands out: Alvin was forty-six at the time, Emma Theresa, twenty-four.[5]

Although their daughter Emma had grown quite serious about Ed, the Hulberts could hardly view him with any enthusiasm as a prospective son-in-law. In fact, his visits to the Hulbert home provoked vigorous opposition. Ed could recall the circumstances at a later period:

. . . *as you probably know, parental interference often results in defeating its own purpose. Mrs. Hulbert forbade me the house before Emma and I were married. Perhaps, had she adopted an opposite policy and insisted on my coming to dinner every day, Emma would have gotten so fed up on seeing me around that she would have dropped something in my coffee some evening. . . .*[6]

The Hulberts, leading stable, sedate lives, with the emphasis upon regularity in one's tasks, whether at home or in the business world, had observed Ed's past antics with disapproval. A young man who appeared unable to settle down, unable to choose some type of career or occupation, was not one they could consider suitable for their daughter. But the lovers' determination made it plain that resistance was futile. Alvin and Emma Theresa Hulbert had to capitulate, and on Wednesday, January 31, 1900, Ed and Emma were married in Chicago.[7]

That made three brothers who were married in the same

Emma and ERB about 1900.

month and year. George T. Burroughs, Jr., and Edna McCoy of Bellvue, Idaho, were married in Minidoka, Idaho, on January 10; and Frank (Coleman) married Grace Stuart Moss on January 24 in Chicago. Harry had wed Ella Frances Oldham in 1891. Soon after the wedding of Ed and Emma the Hulbert family experienced another tragedy. On February 4, 1900, Alvin Hulbert, Sr., died at the age of 71.

Working at his father's battery company and starting married life with Emma seemed to pose no problems for Ed at first. In his *Autobiography* he wrote, "When I was married I was getting fifteen dollars a week and immediately thereafter received a raise to twenty. Owing to the fact that we could eat as often as we pleased at Mrs. Burroughs' mother's home or at my mother's, we got along very nicely."

During the years 1901-2 Ed made a serious attempt to adjust to his work and to assume the responsibilities of a married man. He and Emma, as with all newlyweds, were experiencing the ordinary problems of running a household. Ed's salary of twenty dollars was barely sufficient to meet daily expenses, and little was left to pay for extras. He had taken out an insurance policy with the New York Life Insurance Company, but in October 1902 was forced to borrow on the policy in order to meet his premium.[8] In the same year he was ill for some time with typhoid fever.[9]

By 1903 he was finding the situation at the American Battery Company increasingly difficult. Working under the supervision of his father, as in the past, created tension and conflict. Also, Ed could generate little interest in the business. His impatience was sharpened with envy at the thought that his brothers were in Idaho, living the kind of active, unrestricted life that had always appealed to him.

George and Harry, discouraged after years of struggle and small profit, had given up their cattle ranch. They conceived of a new enterprise, one that offered rich opportunities. From their Bar Y Ranch property, as it bordered on the Snake River, the brothers and their partner Lewis Sweetser had observed the many itinerant miners who traveled along the river banks panning for gold. To the three Yale engineers, graduates of the Sheffield Scientific School, this method appeared slow and antiquated. They discussed the possibility of removing the gold by suction with a large dredge. As a result, in about 1897, the Yale Dredging Company was formed, and soon after, a dredge was constructed. At a later period, at the end of 1898 or the first part of 1899, the partners had another inspiration: in order to be close to their operations, and to have a mobile home that could accompany the dredge to new sites, they began to build a houseboat. They and their families had been living in Pocatello. The Yale Dredging Company was now expanded to the Sweetser-Burroughs Mining Company, which at first listed only three officers: George T. Burroughs, Jr., as president and treasurer; Walter S. Sparks, vice-president; and Lewis H. Sweetser, secretary. Sweetser, the brothers' close friend and Yale classmate, had been with them since graduation. The company's location was at Minidoka, Idaho. Frank and Harry Burroughs had joined in the project, and later, Harry assumed the position of treasurer.

The houseboat, christened El Nido (the nest), was an example of remarkable planning and construction. Providing accommodations for all the members of the company and their families, it contained eighteen rooms and included a spacious living room thirty feet long and fifteen feet wide. The double-decked houseboat, with dimensions of sixty by thirty feet, had porches six feet wide, railings on the upper porches, and two twelve-foot planks to allow for walking along the sides.

On the houseboat were George and Edna Burroughs; Harry Burroughs and his wife Nellie and their children Studley and

Evelyn; Walter and Frieda Sparks; Lewis Sweetser, then un-married; and of course Frank Burroughs who had arrived alone, but had returned to Chicago to marry his fiancée, Grace Moss. In February 1900, after their honeymoon, the couple came back to live on the houseboat.

The dredge, a platformlike contrivance with a towering fun-nel, contained a suction hose to draw up the gravel, sand, and gold. At the front of the dredge were tables covered with burlap; as the sand washed over the tables, the gold particles were left behind, caught in the burlap. The houseboat and dredge, natu-rally, were inseparable. The dredge worked up- or down-stream, floating through whatever open channels it could find, leaving large mounds of gravel and sand in its wake. Each move required a new campsite; the dredge had to work within reason-able distance of some level shoreland where the houseboat, a tug, and some barges could be tied up.

The various tasks were apportioned, and Frank (Coleman) and Grace were given the job of traveling along the shore to find suitable campsites. George, whose specialty was organiza-tion and planning, took charge of the daily work schedules. The dredge ran on three eight-hour shifts, 6 a.m. to 2 p.m., 2 p.m. to 10 p.m., and 10 p.m. to 6 a.m., and since the men were dependent upon rowboat transportation up and back, George made certain that the changing shifts were ready on time. The company employed a crew of four to six men who were assigned living quarters on a smaller houseboat.[10]

Ella Oldham Burroughs and ERB's brother Henry Studley Burroughs in 1891 shortly after their marriage.

El Nido *(the nest), houseboat built by partners in gold-dredging adventure.*

Sweetser-Burroughs tug, Snake River, Idaho.

142

Sweetser-Burroughs Mining Company dredge, Snake River.

While the operation of the dredge was generally smooth and uneventful, there was at least one occasion when an emergency arose. The main danger area, always to be watched, was in the dredge's caulking; if this were washed away, the dredge could quickly sink to the bottom. In her recollections of these gold-mining days, Grace Moss Burroughs tells of a frightening occurrence:

A signal had been set up so that in case of an emergency the men on the dredge could blow a whistle. Early one morning, shortly after midnight, this terrifying whistle resounded as though from a cannon, routing all of us from our beds. . . . The men

*all made for the rowboats which were fastened to the houseboat
at all times, and made for the dredge some several hundred feet
away. The wives waited tensely for some sound which would
indicate the nature of the problem and what was being done
about it. Soon we realized that the caulking must have loosened,
permitting the dredge to take in water; for, almost immediately,
the pumps began to operate. After hours of strenuous labor, the
caulking was replaced and the dredge floated again. But it had
been a tense ordeal. We wives sent coffee in relays all night long,
for the men could not leave their posts and risk the terrible loss
which loomed as a very real and disastrous possibility.*[11]

The wives, Edna, Nell, Freda, and Grace shared the housekeeping chores among them.[12] The only two children, Studley
and Mary Evelyn, about eight and five years old at the time,
were delighted with the adventurous outdoor living and never
forgot their experiences.

Although during this period Ed's lifelong creative com-
pulsion became more and more manifest, it would be another ten
years before he would finally discover the talent that had been
struggling beneath the surface for so many years. In 1900-
1901 his interest in poetry, drawing, and cartooning took a more
concrete form. About this time he composed his first complete,
unified works. Dedicated to his niece Evelyn, with some poems
written for her, the three booklets contained original verses and
accompanying cartoons.

The booklet that appears to represent his earliest work is of a
family nature, featuring humorous references to Ed's brothers,
offering advice to little Evelyn on future marriage choices, and
commenting about the family ancestral line. Idaho gold-dredging
activities are also mentioned. The first page with its poem about
the distinguished genealogy of Evelyn's (Marie's) family indicates clearly that the original emphasis upon ancestry resulted
from Ella Oldham Burroughs' interest and research into this
subject. The page contains a large drawing of George Washington holding a baby on his knee, and the poem follows:

You're descended from the Burghs *of
    Normandy
From the Naegles and the Burkes
And in your veins there lurks
The blue blood of the Washingtons, Marie
You never can complain*

144

Of Your Old ancestors fame
For your Great Grandmother sat on George's
  Knee.[13]

Ed is not hesitant about ridiculing himself and in one poem mentions his drawing ability and concludes that it is best demonstrated when he hastens to draw his pay. A cartoon portrays him running frantically to do so. In the same family booklet he has devised a page of "Uncle Ed's Finger Plays" for his niece Evelyn. Drawings of the fingers and hands show how to create impressions of certain objects, animals, and places that are listed in the poem. These include a well, a corral, a long-horned steer, a bucking bronco, a milking stool, and a mule.[14]

A second booklet of poems, handwritten, artistically lettered and dated 1900, is titled "Snake River Cottontail Tales." The booklet, marked "Author's Autographed Edition E. R. Burroughs Limited To One Copy of Which This is No. 1," contains children's poems with watercolor drawings, all composed expressly for Evelyn Burroughs. In its twelve pages with alternating poems and cartoons, the booklet features rabbits as the main characters and observers of animal antics; at times a baby rabbit is being informed about events by its mother. In these creations Ed also reveals that he is a keen and careful observer of nature. He shows his proclivity for puns and double puns. One cartoon depicts a bull fiercely rushing toward a man who is leaping headlong over the fence to escape the animal. A rabbit onlooker comments:

"A Bull Rush in the meadow,
As the Blue-Jay on the wing,
Informs me," said the rabbit,
"That we'll see an early spring."

In the play on words the "bullrush" is also a plant, the cattail, and of course the "early spring" is matched by the man's "spring" over the fence.

Another cartoon shows a cow sliding down a steep incline on its rump, while two rabbits watch through a fence. A poem describes the action:

"When I see the little cow-slip,"
Said the Rabbit to his chum,
"I can read the story plainly
That another Fall has come."

Ed cannot resist the puns on "cow-slip" and the animal's "fall."

A baby rabbit, peering in confusion at a hen, remarks to its mother:

"That great big ugly egg-plant, ma,
Just bit me on the leg."
"That is a hen you foolish child."
"Well I saw her lay an egg."[15]

The third booklet of fourteen pages, displaying alternate recipes and cartoons, is titled *Grandma Burroughs' Cook Book,* and the dedication reads, "For Miftrefs Evelyn Christmas 1901." The recipes, real ones, are deliberately prepared in small quantities for a child's use—gills, drops, and pinches. They include ingredients and instructions for the making of cookies, fried chicken and gravy, angel's food cake, three kinds of candy and ice cream, and sponge cake.

Ed again reveals himself as a close observer, even in the kitchen. The meticulous nature of the recipes is demonstrated by the one for strawberry ice cream; after the details are presented, an admonition follows: "mixing the sugar with the berries prevents cream from curdling." Instructions for the preparation of other dishes are offered with equal care and accuracy.[16]

Ed, convinced that he could not remain with the American Battery Company, waited for some encouragement from his brothers to rejoin them in Idaho. The invitation finally came, and in the spring of 1903 he and Emma said goodbye to Chicago and started their journey west. It appears that the trip may have been financed through a loan from his brother Coleman through a series of notes totaling $300.[17]

Since they planned to establish a permanent home in Idaho, Ed and Emma brought all of their possessions, their furniture, and even their collie dog, Rajah. They soon discovered that transporting Rajah posed problems. Whether a dog was allowed on the train at all depended upon the consent of the express messenger in whose car the passengers rode. ". . . as there were seven divisions on the Union Pacific between Chicago and Pocatello," Ed noted in his *Autobiography,* "it was necessary to beseech the aid of seven express messengers en route."

Because he had fortunately brought with him "the ingredients for numerous cocktails," he was able to smooth the way and eliminate any difficulties: "We spent practically all of our time in the express cars, going back to our Pullman only at night,

Cover (upper left), autograph page (upper right), and first two pages (bottom) of ERB's Snake River Cotton-Tail Tales.

Emma Burroughs on stage coach at watering stop for horses between Challis and Robinson's Bar, Stanley Basin country, Idaho, May 1903.

Emma Burroughs in baggage car between Blackfoot and Mackay, Idaho, May 1903.

ERB on train platform en route to Stanley Basin, Idaho, on Union Pacific, 1903.

and we were usually surrounded by the entire train crew with the exception of the engineer and fireman."

From Pocatello, Ed and Emma proceeded to Mackay and then on from there to the Stanley Basin, where the Burroughs brothers' dredge was located. Riding on what Ed described as "an old-time Concord stage coach drawn by four horses," they perched on top during the day and slept inside at night. Ed remembered the vivid beauty of the wild country:

Stanley Basin is in the heart of the Sawtooth Mountains, the most beautiful spot in the United States. There granite peaks rise far above the timber line and the summits of the higher mountains are covered with perpetual snow, while nestled in the valleys is a series of beautiful lakes and numerous mountain streams.

The country itself he recalled was "almost untouched even as late as 1903 and abounded in game of many varieties, including deer, mountain sheep and grizzly bear." Ed and Emma set up housekeeping in a tent at first and then began planning a more permanent home. Lumber was no problem; they selected a site, and with the aid of the men who worked at the mine, felled some of the adjacent trees. Ed gave details of the building of the cabin: "My plan was to set posts in the ground to the height of the eaves, nail slabs on the inside and outside and fill the interstices with dirt. It was an excellent idea or would have been if the dirt had not leaked out through the sides between the slabs."

While working on the new house, Ed employed an Italian to construct a "one-holer" for him, he disclosed in his *Autobiography*. The results were not at all what he had anticipated:

The Italian could not understand English and I could not understand Italian, so I marked out a rectangle on the ground and handed him a long handled shovel, then I went away and left him. I think I must have forgotten him until late in the afternoon for when I got back he had dug himself out of sight and I found him at the bottom of a deep shaft from which I had to drag him into the light of day at the end of his shovel. Nothing short of a parachute could have imparted a feeling of safety in the subsequent use of this famous one holer, which was, to be technically accurate, of the Kansas single rail type.

The Sweetser-Burroughs Mining Company was doing very well. A newspaper story describes the placer mining in the vicinity of Minidoka and notes that "The owners do not make boasts of what they are doing, but their success is attested by the fact that they have kept the plant in operation night and day all this season."[18] The company was also reported as having moved the machinery that year, drifting downstream during the winter and starting dredging in a new place in the summer.

In this hectic period with the dredge working around the clock and the company employing four to six additional men, the feverish activities seemed to duplicate those of the Gold Rush of '49. For the three brothers and their wives and the two children, Studley and Mary Evelyn, life on the houseboat was a far cry from the quiet days in Chicago. About the only possible resemblance was that the brothers, as in Chicago, kept a cow to provide milk for the children.[19]

When the gold production in the Minidoka area began to dwindle, the company sought richer fields. Ed recalled the various enterprises, noting that his brothers had operated gold dredges on the Snake River in Idaho "over a stretch of about sixty miles, until they had worked out the gravel in this district." Following this, George moved a dredge up to Stanley Creek in the Sawtooth Mountains of Idaho, while Harry took over the management of a dredge on the Snake River in Oregon near Parma, Idaho.[20]

His employment at the Stanley Basin evidently had little appeal for Ed. After a short stay he and Emma decided to join Harry at Parma. The move may have been made as a result of some differences with George or even an outright quarrel. One account indicates that Ed showed little inclination to do his share of mining and preferred to spend his time in romantic walks with Emma along the river bank. George, annoyed, is supposed to have told him to stop the walks and get down to work. Ed's departure soon followed.[21]

Traveling usually created hazards and temptations for Ed; the short trip to Parma was no exception. He described the journey in his *Autobiography:*

We loaded our belongings onto a freight wagon and started for Hadley, where we arrived in due time with a collie dog and forty dollars. Forty dollars did not seem much to get anywhere with, so I decided to enter a stud game at a local saloon and run my capital up to several hundred dollars during the night.

One member of the poker game whom he never forgot was a "one-eyed tinhorn, who would put the side of his head with the good eye flat on the table, raise the corner of his hole card and while he was pretending to look at it endeavor to see mine if I raised it off the table." Based upon Ed's previous gambling

ERB and Emma waiting for train in Parma, Idaho, 1904.

Main Street of Parma, Idaho, 1904.

escapades, the outcome of this one was easily anticipated. He noted the aftermath briefly: "When I returned to the room that we had rented we still had a collie dog; otherwise we were flat broke."

As usual, brother Harry came to the rescue, providing him with funds to reach Parma. There Ed showed some temporary adjustment to his gold-mining chores. But in his spare time he turned again to creative expression. He still maintained an interest in his drawing and water coloring. A letter of October 9, 1903, to his father reveals that Ed was taking correspondence lessons in drawing. His main purpose in writing was to send a birthday greeting: on October 13 his father would be seventy. The letter contains one of Ed's typical illustrations at the top, that of a man bent to drink from an outdoor pump, a cowboy hat held in his hand. After writing, "Here's wishing you many happy returns of the day," he continues with, "Have completed three of my drawing lessons. Two have returned and the criticisms are very favorable."

He refers to a previous letter from his father: "Am glad you are going to close Saturday afternoon. Am also very glad to hear of your good sales for this year. Am always interested in hearing about the business. . . ."

From at least one source there is evidence that Ed had not relinquished his dream of being a cartoonist. In a biography sent to Charles Lederer of the Chicago Press Club, he remarks, "It was while I was at Parma, Idaho, that you had hopes of making a cartoonist of me. . . ."[22] But more important evidence reveals that during this period or shortly thereafter he made his first creative venture into the field of fiction, improvising a delightfully fanciful story titled "Minidoka 937th Earl of One Mile Series M. An Historical Fairy Tale."[23] The recent discovery of this unnoticed manuscript clearly established that it antedates the story assumed to be Burroughs' first—"Under the Moons of Mars."

Handwritten on odd sheets of paper including the backs of letterheads of the Yale Dredging Company, Minidoka, Idaho, photo bills from the stationery store at Pocatello, and letterheads of the American Genealogical Society, 1102 Woman's Temple, Chicago, the story is composed of eighty-two pages. The Burroughs handwriting, unmistakable, sweeps across the pages in a hasty scrawl, as though his pen were dashing to keep pace with the ideas that tumbled forth. Yet, despite the apparent haste, there are not many corrections. The first part of the story is somewhat scratchy, with lined-out phrases and with sentences and words inserted or changed; but the author's imagination soon breaks free, and the incidents, as improbable as any ever created, soon flow along with only brief and minor corrections.

"Minidoka" is a captivating, highly imaginative fairy story that presages the Edgar Rice Burroughs talent that was to flower ten years later. Idaho was naturally the setting for the fairy tale, and Ed created two imaginary kingdoms separated by the Raft River and "forever at war." The tone of the writing is of course humorous and satirical, and in the opening Ed pokes fun at the Irish.

The year 1903 passed with Ed aiding his brother Harry in the gold dredging on the Snake River in Oregon near Parma, Idaho. In the spring of 1904 Ed conceived of a new idea—he would enter politics and run for the office of town trustee. Competition in Parma was between the incumbent Citizens' Ticket and an opposing group seeking office. In the election of April 5, 1904, 104 of the 108 registered voters cast their ballots. The *Parma Herald* of April 9 broadcast the result, the headline reading "Old Board of Trustees Re-Elected With One Exception. Large Vote Cast." The lead paragraph reported, "Parma's first election since becoming a municipality passed off in a very dignified manner."

The "one exception" was E. R. Burroughs; and his winning

margin, in defeating Pat Hanratty, was *one vote,* 49 to 48. Ed had run as an independent, not being selected for either ticket, but had still managed to secure enough votes to edge his way in. In his *Autobiography* Ed humorously disclosed the secret of his success:

. . . There was to be an aldermanic election. I do not know how I came to be nominated unless I nominated myself. I was running against a popular party named Hanratty, who was already an alderman. My campaigning methods were simple. I button-holed every voter that I met, told him that I was running for office and that I did not want to be embarrassed by not getting a single vote and asking him as a personal favor to cast his vote for me, with the result that enough of them tried to save me from embarrassment to cause my election.

Ed's Certificate of Election reads:

Know all men by these presents:
This is to certify that E. R. Burroughs was duly elected as a Trustee of the Village of Parma, Canyon County Idaho, at the General Election held within said Village on the 5th day of April 1904, for the term of one year, or until his successor is duly elected, appointed and qualified.

Attest.
R. K. (?) Sammons
Clerk of the Village
Parma, Canyon County, Idaho, April 11th 1904[24]

But fate, appearing to have other plans for Ed, yanked him abruptly from his first and only political office. The gold-dredging enterprise, which had first operated profitably, ran into disaster. According to one story, an eastern syndicate persuaded the brothers to take over property on the Salmon River and dredge there. The gold deposits were ample, and success seemed assured, but because the period allowed for the payment of their various obligations was impossibly short, they were unable to meet their creditors' demands and went bankrupt.[25] Another account stresses that the brothers' troubles began when they bought a new claim on the Snake River. After taking their dredge apart, they faced the difficult and dangerous feat of hauling the heavy equipment over the rapids—accomplished by their throwing lines across. The move took weeks. And when the exhausted men arrived, they found they had been swindled. The claim was salted.[26]

154

ERB hanging out laundry, probably in Salt Lake City.

Ed in his *Autobiography* records briefly, "The company for which my brother was working failed and Mrs. Burroughs and I found ourselves again in possession of nothing but a collie dog." Again through the efforts of his brother Harry he was to find a new type of employment. The sight of the luxurious private cars reserved for railroad executives (especially presidents and vice-presidents) caused Ed to drift temporarily into a world of illusion. "I decided to devote my life and talents to railroading," he wrote in his *Autobiography,* recalling his willingness to start at the bottom and "work up to a private car." He added, "As a matter of fact the only interest that I had in railroading, I think, was the ultimate private car. . . ."

To oblige his friend Harry Burroughs, Howard V. Platt, a division superintendent of the Oregon Short Line Railroad Company at Salt Lake City, offered Ed a job. Ed had been willing to start in as a fireman, but there were no vacancies. He was persuaded to accept the only opening available—that of railroad policeman. When notified that Ed was broke, the accommodating Platt even sent passes for the trip from Parma to Salt Lake.

In April of 1904 Ed and Emma said their farewells to Idaho, the adventurous days of a near-frontier life forever behind them, and departed for Salt Lake City. Upon arrival they took rooms at 111 North First West.[27] The procedure for appointment as a special railroad policeman included the approval of the chief of

Emma in rooms at 111 North Fifth West Street, Salt Lake City, Utah, 1904.

police and Salt Lake City Council. A letter of May 12 from the recorder's office to Ed contains the official statement: "At a meeting of the City Council held May 9th, 1904, your appointment by the Chief of Police as special policeman to serve without pay from the City, was presented and the appointment confirmed on unanimous roll call vote." He would of course be paid by the Oregon Railroad Company. His classification was "depot policeman," and he was outfitted with a blue uniform with gleaming brass buttons and carried a club.[28]

For Bob Davis's column in the *New York Sun,* July 20, 1940, Ed recalls the days:

. . . now an experienced man, I married, settled down in Salt Lake City with a job on the police force as a special officer. My beat was in the railroad yards where after nightfall I rambled and fanned bums off the freight cars and the blind baggage of the Butte Express. Kept good hours and always came home with fifty pounds of highgrade ice, which I swiped while the watchman slept. I was always a good provider.

In his *Autobiography* Ed provides details of his and Emma's experiences in Salt Lake City, noting that he was kept busy "rushing bums out of the railroad yards and off the passenger trains." He adds, "It was not very exciting for the bums and yeggs were seldom as hard boiled as they are painted and only upon one or two occasions did I even have to flash my gun."[29] He considered drunks to be the worst. "If you have never tried to eject a drunk from a day coach," he wrote, "you have no idea how many arms and legs a man can have."

Notified that a murderer was hiding in the railroad yard, and "being more conscientious than intelligent," he hunted through numerous dark coaches and box cars without finding the man.

On their own for the first time, without any help from their families or from Ed's brothers, the young couple struggled to solve their household problems. Because his small salary was barely sufficient to meet necessary expenses, Ed had to perform all sorts of unaccustomed tasks:

Neither one of us knew much about anything that was practical, but we had to do everything for ourselves including the family wash. Not wishing to see Mrs. Burroughs do work of this sort I volunteered to do it myself. I took all of our soiled clothes and put them in the bath tub, turned the water on them and let them soak over night. I did not know until next morning that I

*should have separated the white clothes from the colored ones
and thereafter it would have made no difference since they were
all colored. I got along fairly well, however, until I came to iron
the sheets. I tried to iron them flat on a little ironing board without folding them. The sheets were so large that they trailed on
the floor and got tangled up in my feet. They had not been
very clean—the sheets I mean—when I got through washing
them. When I got through ironing them no one could have recognized them as sheets.*[30]

During those months in Salt Lake City Ed half-soled his own
shoes—and even bottled his own beer. Meanwhile, he could
hardly feel any enthusiasm about his duties as a railroad policeman, and the prospect of a fireman's job seemed too remote to
contemplate. In a letter home, undated, he wrote:

*. . . Made an arrest last night and after waiting half an hour for
the wagon turned the man loose. I can imagine the Chicago pa-
trol taking a half hour to answer a call.
The fellow was drunk, dressed up and disorderly, refused to
leave the yd. and resisted me.
Can't say I am stuck on the job of policeman. . . .*

Once again his illusions had vanished, and with them went his
vision of the glamorous private car, dissipated by the cold light
of reality. Seeing no future in railroading, on October 14, 1904,
Ed resigned. An official acceptance letter from the Oregon
Short Line Railroad Company, dated October 17, states, "Conduct, services and capabilities satisfactory."

On October 16 he wrote home, addressing his letter to "Dear
Little Mother," explaining that the exact time of departure for
Chicago was uncertain, but that he and Emma would, upon arrival, go directly to the Hulberts' home on 194 Park Avenue,
and not to the Burroughs' place at 493 Jackson Boulevard until
a later evening. "I quit work yesterday," he wrote, "as they had
my successor down here from Ogden." He speaks of his cold
being so bad that he "welcomed the opportunity of staying in-
doors nights," and explains that "Emma also has a bad cold
and as we have no heating stove we are longing for Tuesday to
come so that we can go somewhere and get warm."

Ed illustrates his letter with a small cartoon in a lower corner; the caption beneath it reads, "The Passing of the Cook and
the Cop" and he symbolizes his and Emma's duties in Salt Lake
by outlining the dotted forms of a policeman and cook, and then
drawing Emma and himself in heavy lines as they emerge in

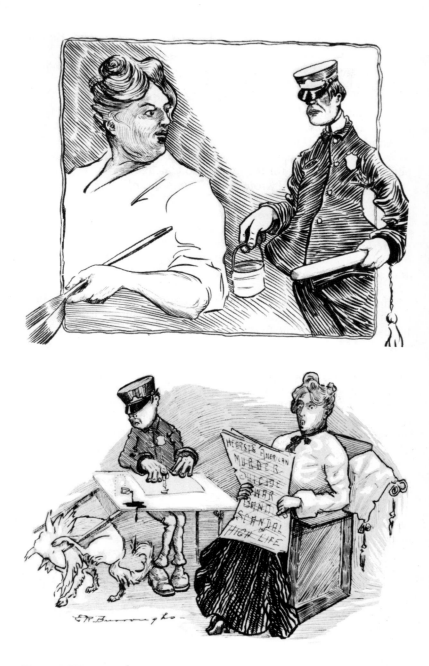

Two of ERB's sketches of the "cop" and the "cook," made during his
employment as a policeman in Salt Lake City.

their new forms—Ed jaunty, with derby and cane, and Emma all dressed up and wearing a flowered hat. Clearly, Ed had little regret at the passing of their Salt Lake period. But, his policeman's job had lasted only five months.

In their plans to return home, the couple encountered their most serious obstacle: they had no money for the railroad fare. At this time they conceived a brilliant idea. All they possessed of value was the household furniture, dragged with them "all over Idaho and Utah." This they would auction off, hoping to obtain enough money for the journey to Chicago.

About the results Ed wrote in his *Autobiography:*

That auction was a howling success. I never imagined people would buy such utterly useless things and pay real money for them. The only decent things that we had brought little or nothing, but the junk brought about ten times what it was worth, and so we got home again, traveling first class.

The pattern was depressingly repetitive—he was again unemployed. When his search for a job proved futile, he appealed to his close friend and former Michigan Military Academy classmate, Bob Lay. The only opening Bob could find was that of a timekeeper at a site where a seventeen story brick and concrete warehouse was being constructed. Ed was willing to take anything, and although he had no experience in this field and was made dizzy by heights, he soon found himself crawling about on narrow steel girders high in the air. One day he saw a workman tumble from the heights, pulling a wheelbarrow of concrete after him. Ed was shaken by this and grew even more apprehensive, but he forced himself to walk across the girders. He described the closest he came to catastrophe:

Once I was tight-roping across a steel girder on the ninth or tenth story with nothing on either side of me. About twelve feet ahead of me planks were laid across two other girders, making an oasis in the desert of mid-air. Somehow I lost my balance after I started across that girder. At an angle of about forty-five degrees I ran a few steps and jumped for the oasis. That I am here today is sufficient evidence that I hit it, but thereafter I swallowed my pride, straddled the girders and hitched myself across.[31]

The job, obviously, was one that Ed could not endure, and the hunt continued. Work that promised interest and stimulation, a position with permanency and a future, seemed nonexistent.

Ed grabbed at the only work available; he became a door-to-door book salesman, peddling Stoddard's collected lectures. As part of his training he memorized a sales talk he was prepared to deliver at the moment a housewife opened the door. In a letter of February 12, 1921, to Herbert Hungerford, editor of the *American News Trade Journal,* Ed supplied the details:

. . . I was equipped with a long thing that telescoped like an accordion and Mrs. Burroughs made me a little black bag with a shoulder strap, that I put on over my vest. I carried the thing in the little black bag hidden under my coat tails. It might have looked as though I was ashamed of it; but I was not supposed to be and I was. And I wandered around a large city shoving my foot inside front doors before weary house-wives could slam the doors in my face and if I succeeded in getting in and planting myself on their best plush furniture I commenced to recite, parrot-like, a long and hideous lie, interspersed occasionally with facts. The initial and most colossal falsehood of that shameful aggregation still haunts my memories. It was: "Mr. Stoddard has asked me to call on you, Mrs. Brown." Even now I blush as I type it.

The "thing" must have been a folding series of book covers and illustrations, in facsimile, which Ed displayed to the house-wives. He recalled that he had actually sold several sets of Stoddard's Lectures, but commented, "I think my victims were moved more by compassion for me than for any desire for the lectures."[32] During these months he also tried selling electric light bulbs to janitors and candy to drugstores. Unsuccessful in this, he found an advertisement in the *Chicago Tribune* for an "expert accountant." Without having the faintest idea of the duties of an accountant, he applied for the job at E. S. Winslow Company and was accepted.

In his *Autobiography* Ed notes that the breaks or luck are as important as one's ability and explains that "my employer knew even less about the duties of an expert accountant than I did." Winslow was so impressed by Ed's procedures in opening an entire new set of books that he gave him a permanent job as his office manager. "I was with him for a couple of years," Ed wrote, "and I think that in all that time he never really found me out, for when I left him it was of my own accord."

Ed's jobs and business ventures cannot always be identified. For example, a postcard saved in Emma's album is dated January 18, 1906, and addressed to Ed at Room 409, Western Union Building, Jackson and La Salle Streets, Chicago. Whether this was his office or his place of employment has not been determined. But his search for success through a bewildering variety of occupations brought him into two strange mysterious enterprises. He had saved the stationery of what appeared to be defunct businesses. One yellow letterhead reads American Genealogical Society with the address beneath as 1102 Woman's Temple, Chicago, and to the left the phone number, Main 949. A blue letterhead reads "Moss & Burroughs, Forwarding Agents," with the same address and phone number. On this stationery, in addition, appear two printed names: E. R. Burroughs at top right and Earl C. Moss at top left.[33]

The precarious living, the changes from job to job, and the inability to find a type of employment that could challenge him and sustain his permanent interest, brought him back once more to an ambition that had never died. His hope of obtaining some kind of military position, either as an instructor or as a commissioned officer, where his skill in horsemanship could be utilized, became dominant again. In March 1906 he wrote a series of letters to acquaintances to inquire about possible openings for instructor in horsemanship and cavalry tactics or to request letters of recommendation for such a position. The first person he wrote to, naturally, was the man whom he still idolized in his memory—Charles King, Brigadier General U.S.A. (West Point, 1866). King was then superintendent of St. John's Military Academy in Delafield, Wisconsin.

On March 3 King replied to a letter from Ed that had evidently contained a request for his advice. A logical assumption is that Ed was uncertain that he still possessed the skill and knowledge needed to qualify as a cavalry instructor in a military academy. King, in his response, offered Ed reassurance:

You rode well in 1892 and with all your later experience ought now to be an expert teacher of the soldier school of horsemanship—which is far more exacting than the Park or English system. For civil life, however, one needs to be at home in the latter, as I dare say you have discovered and have made it, too, a study.

Ed wrote again, hard on the heels of his first letter, but whether he hinted about the possibility of a position at St. John's Academy is difficult to tell. King, three days later, does not refer to any request, but states, "Your letter went right to my heart. Twelve of the boys wrote me in '98 asking for staff positions but I had none to give. Every now and then I meet some of the old battalion and it does me good." King enclosed some photos of himself.

Although King had been commandant at Michigan Military Academy for only a short period, and his dealings with Ed had been brief, his forthrightness, attitude of simple humanity, and emphasis upon principle and justice had left an indelible impression in Ed's mind. In recollections of the academy, Ed wrote glowingly of King:

. . . The Commandant was Capt. Charles King, author of the best army stories that ever were written; a man who has been an inspiration to me all my life because of his outstanding qualities as a soldier, a cavalryman and a friend. But the inspiration he gave me had nothing to do with writing. He made me want to be a good soldier.[34]

King, whose blunt telegram of April 16, 1892, to Ed's father read, "Your son deserted yesterday," a telegram that Ed preserved and reread in the passing years, was the same man who became a well-known author of novels about army life in the West. Ed communicated with him periodically and sought his advice about writing and publishing.[35]

That Ed, a boy of sixteen separated from his home and family, lonesome, and possibly seeking a father figure in the stern but kindly King, may have created an unreal image of the general, in certain aspects is entirely possible. The picture of King may have been exaggerated or romanticized, especially because of his soldierly qualities and colorful horsemanship. An exchange of letters with a former Orchard Lake classmate offers some evidence in this direction. C. C. Matteson, who had read a biography of Ed in the *Los Angeles Times,* wrote to him about King, commenting, "Why stress the short term as commandant of Captain King, as I remember it he was there for only three months, during which time he was mostly drunk. . . ."

Ed replied on November 6, 1929:

. . . The article in the Times *was a condensation of an autobiography that my publishers hounded out of me. They picked the parts that they thought would prove interesting. In the original you may be sure that I did not neglect General Strong, for whom I had and still have the highest admiration. I gave Adelbert Cronkhite hell and possibly it was just as well that they left that out.*

As for General King—I conceived a boyish enthusiasm for him because he was a strict disciplinarian and at the same time just, and because he stood so high in the estimation of the regular army as a tactician. I fully understood his weakness—a weakness for which he paid very dearly and which he regretted more than any man, but it did not lessen my admiration for him. He is a fine character and very much loved by everyone with whom I have come in contact who has known him at all well. . . .

Another former commandant of Michigan Military Academy to whom Ed wrote in 1906 was Frederick F. Strong, a major in the artillery corps, stationed in Washington. Ed requested a letter of reference and Strong was happy to oblige, commenting on March 5, "Of course I must rely upon my knowledge of you some years ago, but am confident you have not changed very much." In his reference, headed "To Whom it May Concern," Strong described Ed as "one of the best horsemen ever at the academy and a good soldier in all respects," adding that "unless he has greatly changed I am glad to recommend him for the position of Cavalry Instructor and Tactical Officer."

Ed, motivated by the hope of finding a position of interest that would provide a degree of security, turned March into a month of busy correspondence. He received letters of recommendation from various friends and business acquaintances: one on March 12 from George C. Ball of the firm of T. A. McIntyre and Company, stockbrokers, and separate letters on March 14 from the partners in a Chicago insurance company, C. E. Rollins, Jr., and Arch O. Burdick.[36] An old friend, Lew Sweetser, wrote from Yale, Idaho, on March 15 to contribute his recommendation.

The two letters Ed also wrote in March addressed to Fred A. Smith, another former commandant from the academy, were sent to Governor's Island and, since Smith had been assigned elsewhere, did not reach him until mid-July. Smith, now a colonel in the 8th United States Infantry, responded from the headquarters at Camp Jassman, Guimaras, Philippine Islands, on July 17, 1906. His letter of reference described Ed as "energetic and fully qualified to instruct in all the branches, Infantry, Cavalry or Artillery but particularly excellent in Cavalry." His accompanying note read:

I would not have you think for a moment that I did not esteem your friendship and often think of the pleasant hours we spent together in the Commandant's office. I take pleasure in forwarding with this a letter such as I think you desire but for God's sake if you have a good position do not forfeit it for the military business.

The scare in China seems to have blown over but I was reading today that the Chinese are employing Japanese Officers as Instructors and why not you.

Smith explained that he was in charge of operations in the island of Samar, where his task would be "to subjugate the 'Pulajanes' a disaffected crowd who rob their friends and foes." Smith's suggestion about seeking a position with the Chinese Army had already been anticipated by Ed. On March 12 he wrote to Major George W. Gibbs, addressing him "% Chinese Imperial Reform Assn.," at 345 South Clark Street in Chicago. Ed stated, "Am seeking a commission in the Chinese Army and beg to ask if you can give me information relative to the proper parties to whom I should go."

Gibbs's lengthy hand-written reply of March 19 was on the letterhead of the 1st Battalion, 2nd Regiment Infantry, 1st Brigade Imperial Army and was sent to Ed at 194 Park Place. Gibbs supplied a detailed explanation of the circumstances:

. . . I have no information that the Chinese Gov't is looking for military men for their army. From items published in the press, it would appear that they were seeking such men, but from the best authority of the Chinese themselves they tell me it is false. From the numerous letters I have on file I believe I could furnish several hundred such parties if they were needed. I presume these letters were sent me because I am mentioned as an instructor at the American Chinese Empire Reform Academy, an institution incorporated under the State Laws of Ill.

He described the academy as a school "maintained by the Chinese Empire Reform Ass'n, another incorporated organization, for the purpose of instructing the Chinese in the English Language, Western Civilization, International Law and Military Science and Tactics." He then wrote with some fervor about China's new role among the nations of the world:

China has no idea of attacking any other nation, but she is going to create an army on modern ideas, for the purpose of defending herself, for example she don't propose to have any more outside countries use the chinese territory for a place to settle disputes of war to the distress and loss of her own people. She is also going to demand the respect of other countries in the treatment of Chinese subjects that they may receive at least the treatment and courtesy that other nations receive.

Major Gibbs (a "late 1st Lieutenant, Utah Artillery, U.S. Volunteers") promised that if military men "with first class records" were needed in the future he would notify Ed. He commented that "the newspapers seem to be writing up a lot of fairy stories in an endeavor to get next to the inside." But he did reveal that a commission for the Chinese Army had "a specification for a contract for 1 million rifles and 3 thousand guns for light artillery." Gibbs invited Ed to visit the drill hall and school at 345 South Clark Street, third floor, and closed with the statement, "I write you at length for the trouble you took to reach me."

On March 17, two days before receiving Gibbs's reply, Ed wrote to the Imperial Chinese Legation in Washington. Their response of the 20th was blunt: ". , . there are no openings in the Chinese army for American officers or those of any other nationality, so far as this Legation is informed. The report that the Chinese Government is engaging such officers has no foundation whatever."

Thus, from the Spanish-American War period of 1898 through March of 1906 all of Ed's efforts to return to military life either as a soldier, officer, or instructor had proved fruitless. His attempts to find a permanent career in the army or at a military academy were at an end. But his interest in military life and his intense patriotism would drive him to seek other associations with the army in the future. It is significant to note that in all of Burroughs' attempts to obtain a commission in the army or as an instructor at an academy, he relied on letters of recommendation. Invariably he sought the help of someone who might have influence with the authorities in obtaining for him officer's rank. Except for the relatively brief stint with the 7th Cavalry, Burroughs made no attempt to enlist in the Army with the idea of working his way up the ladder for a commission. He wanted to start as an officer.

For Ed and Emma the early period of their marriage, the years of struggle and discouragement, were also the years of constant moving, often from one shabby flat to another. When their marriage was launched in 1900 they took a room in the large, three-story Hulbert home at 194 Park Avenue. The collection of photos in the old family album, with precise notations on their backs, chronicles the frequent changes of address. They are shown at 88 Park Avenue in 1901; 35 South Robey Street from April 1902 to May 1903; and upon their return from Idaho and Salt Lake City in 1904, they stayed with

ERB's drawing of Sears, Roebuck stenographic department.

ERB's drawing of activity in stenographic department at Sears, 1907.

Emma's family again at 194 Park Avenue. By 1908 they had moved across the street, taking a flat at 197 Park Avenue in a building owned by the Hulberts. The addresses of cards sent through the mail indicate that in July 1909 they still lived at 197 Park Avenue, but by October had moved to 2008 Park Avenue. 1910 found them at 821 South Scoville Avenue in Oak Park, a suburb of Chicago.[37]

The search for employment continued. Impressed by the reports of unusual opportunities in the mail order business, Ed, in 1907, applied for a job at Sears, Roebuck and Company. He was given a position in the correspondence department. His promotion came quickly; an interoffice bulletin, addressed to managers and assistant managers, dated April 17 and issued by L. E. Asher, reads, "Mr. E. R. Burroughs has been appointed Manager of the Stenographic Department (159)." Ed, in describing the Sears, Roebuck period in his *Autobiography*, said, "After a few months, I was made manager of a clerical department, in which all the correspondence was handled and typed."

That Ed's efficient methods and business ingenuity focused attention upon him is illustrated in a letter of November 30, 1907, sent by R. C. Blanchard to the general office manager, P. V. Bunn. It opens with enthusiastic praise:

I found the Stenographic Department to be in very satisfactory condition. The department is well managed by Mr. Burroughs, who is handling the department in a business like and rather professional manner. He seems to be conversant with every detail of the department; knows all that goes on, and is in every respect all that could be expected of a Manager.

After further complimentary remarks, Blanchard says, "In all the department shows a remarkable improvement over its condition a year ago, and I think that Mr. Burroughs and his division heads should be given due credit for what they have done."

Ed, the man who "knows all that goes on," was quick to demonstrate that even the most minor of inefficiencies and unwarranted expenditures could not escape his scrutiny. A discovery of his, which Mr. Blanchard considered of great value, was that from January of that year the graphophone and shorthand letters had gradually increased in length from about twelve lines to an average of sixteen lines per letter. As a result of Ed's perception, Blanchard analyzed the letters and reported that in some cases "eight or ten lines could be cut out of a letter and it would be equally if not more forcible." At the rate of 4,000 letters a day, and a cost of thirty cents per hundred lines, if four lines were removed, the savings would be $48 per day, $288 a week, or $14,976 a year.[38]

About the situation Ed wrote, "It was a large department in which we turned out a tremendous volume of business and as I was able to cut costs materially, I was acclaimed as a howling success. I had my problems there, including the young lady who couldn't do as much work in the winter time as she could in the summer time because the days were shorter."

On December 7, 1907, Ed issued a comparison report of the four weeks ended November 23 against the corresponding four weeks of 1906 to explain how he had cut costs. L. E. Asher described the results as "indeed very satisfactory," forwarded the paper to Mr. Bunn who in turn sent the report to Julius Rosenwald, the head of Sears, Roebuck, with the comment "interesting and gratifying." He wrote across the paper, "Very Fine. J.R." The figures were impressive: Ed had turned out 36 percent more lines while reducing the payroll 21 percent. His cost per 100 lines was 35.2 cents as compared with the 1906 cost of 61.5 cents, an improvement of 42.7 percent.

Ed's recollections of Mr. Rosenwald were pleasant. He noted in a letter of March 3, 1937, to M. R. Werner of New York that "my contacts with Mr. Rosenwald were not of any great importance, either to Sears, Roebuck & Co. or to the world at large, but they did give me a slight insight into Mr. Rosenwald's character." As manager of a stenographic department which employed approximately 150 stenographers and typists, all of whom worked in one room, Ed could expect regular visits and inspections by company executives, who often brought business acquaintances and friends. The department was a kind of showroom. Ed remembered that although he was "a very minor cog in the machinery of the mail-order business," Mr. Rosenwald was always very careful to ask his permission courteously before bringing anyone to his department and never forgot to thank Ed when he left the room.

In a letter of September 13, 1926, to John M. Stahl of Sears, Roebuck radio station WLS in Chicago, while noting that he still kept up an acquaintance with O. C. Doering, a general superintendent for Sears, Roebuck,[39] Ed recalled Julius Rosenwald's visits again and remarked, "Only a thorough gentleman would remember always to accord an inferior such a courtesy."

Even the cold efficiency of the mail order business could not stifle Ed's creative impulses. He was happy to find an opportunity to write some of his humorous verse. On January 16, 1908, a letter sent to Rosenwald encloses a copy of a screed "which has been going around through the country press, entitled 'Ninety and Nine,' and which has just appeared in the Emporia Kansas Gazette." The letter refers to "Mr. Burroughs of 159" who has added a verse of his own "from the Seroco standpoint" (Seroco was a brand of Sears pants). The author of the letter, an unidentified company official, explains that the plan is to get both verses started around among the country papers. A memo to Ed at the bottom of the typed note reads: "I took a few liberties with your verses but not many."

The original screed poked fun at Sears, Roebuck and the type of customers who dealt with them:

There were ninety and nine who blew their wads, in Emporia stores each day, when they purchased their clocks or their lightning rods, their soap or their bales of hay; but one would send to the roebuck sears and he was the object of gibes and jeers. . . .

It pictured the ninety and nine as "rich and fat" and living on "oysters and pumpkin pie"; but the one "who bought of roebuck sears, had never the price of a pair of beers." While the ninety and nine at death could look forward to a ride in "the smoothest hearse in town," the sorry creature "who deals with the roebuck sears, will be hauled away by a pair of steers."

Ed responded with his own screed, composed in the same verse form, and offered a defense of Sears, Roebuck by explaining what would happen in the hereafter. The ninety and nine found quite a different situation when they approached the "golden gates" where St. Peter commented that "oysters and pie weren't served in Heaven with beer." He identified the one "intelligent ghost, with elegant coat and vest" and recognized the Seroco pants of Sears. The others are sent to a place "where fires are furnished free," because they "hadn't the brains to know Sears, Roebuck quali-tee."[40]

In December 1907, Ed addressed letters to a book dealer and to public libraries in Chicago requesting information about certain types of publications. Attempts to explain the reasons for these inquiries have led to a number of speculations. A response from A. C. McClurg & Company, 215 South Wabash Avenue, dated December 12, was sent to Ed at 194 Park

Avenue. After referring to his letter "of recent date," it listed books and prices:

Holt. Care and Feeding of Children	net 75 cts.
Finger Prints, Classification and uses, by Henry.	net 80 cts.
Finger Print Directories by Galton.	net $2.00
Decipherment of Blurred Fingerprints.	net 1.00

McClurg's noted that the "first mentioned title" was in stock, but that the others "would have to be imported from England, which would require at least two months time."

A logical explanation for Ed's interest in books on the raising of children may be found in his anticipation of the birth of his first child, only a month away. But his unusual inquiry about books on fingerprints, plus two additional requests for information sent out at the same time, does not yield so easily to explanation. On December 10 he wrote to both the John Crerar Library in Chicago and the Chicago Public Library, and in response these libraries offered lists of books on the same subject, including those by Francis Galton and E. R. Henry, and others by Roscher and Windt, German language publications. These replies from McClurg's and the libraries have been preserved in one of Ed's notebooks along with an article "The Telltale Fingers" by Harry H. Seckler (source unknown) that describes the fingerprint system of identification used by departments of the federal government. It presents case histories and stresses the superiority of this system to the Bertillion method.

As indicated, there have been various conjectures as to what lay behind Ed's curious interest in fingerprints during this 1907 period. The explanations either deal separately with his inquiries for children's books and fingerprinting books, or attempt, ingeniously, to unite the two. The reasoning and evidence will be familiar to readers of Tarzan of the Apes.[41]

By 1908, Ed's record at Sears, Roebuck and his business efficiency and imagination had marked him in the eyes of the company executives as a man to be watched. A successful, stable career with steady advancement awaited him. Then, in a typically impulsive gesture, he abandoned his prospects and his future at Sears, Roebuck.

The previous failures to find anything permanent had left him undaunted. He decided to go into business for himself.

He left Sears, Roebuck during August of 1908, and on August 14 received a letter of commendation from P. V. Bunn, the general office manager. Bunn, who was away on a vacation and had missed saying goodbye to Ed, wrote to him at 197 Park Avenue:

Your record with the house has been a fine one, and the work you have done in straightening out the Stenographic Department and bringing it down to a proper level as to cost output has been much appreciated, and if ever at any time you wish to return to us, I am sure the House will be glad to give your request for reinstatement its best consideration.

Contrary to his own statements in various brief autobiographical articles that he failed in every job he attempted, Ed did not fail at Sears. He obviously performed well there and had excellent chances for a successful future.

Ed's action appears even more bewildering in view of the anticipated event that occurred early that year: on January 12, 1908, at the Park Avenue Hospital, Emma had given birth to a daughter. The arrival of Joan Burroughs meant, of course, a new responsibility for Ed to shoulder. It seemed hardly a time to throw over security and an established future.

At a later period, in his *Autobiography,* Ed could joke about the birth of Joan: ". . . the collie dog, that had shared our vicissitudes with us for so many years, was compelled to take a back seat along with me. . . ." The arrival of a daughter was also the occasion for some humorous writing, in this case an article that joked about the care of babies, the selection of a nurse and doctor, and the duties of the mother, father, and grandmother. In the 1908 article, titled "What Every Young Couple Should Know," Ed, evidently enjoying himself, went on at length creating some 3,000 words of comical exaggeration about a home with a baby. This tone is set at once in the opening.[42]

Although Burroughs made no attempt to submit "What Every Young Couple Should Know" to any publication at that time, the article had a later revival, far in the future. On May 5, 1937, in a letter to Gertrude Lane, Editor of *Woman's Home Companion,* he wrote:

I am sending you, herewith, copy of a manuscript that I wrote about twenty-nine years ago, shortly after the birth of my first child. This was before I started writing and was merely for the

amusement of my family and friends. I recently found it among
some old papers; and as it seems to be quite as up-to-date today
as it was twenty-nine years ago, I thought it might have some
interest for your readers. . . .

The manuscript referred to was undoubtedly "What Every Young Couple Should Know"; there is no record of acceptance by any magazine.

In 1908, while capable of joking about the advent of a daughter, Ed must have faced reality, understanding that as a married man with a child it was time to view his obligations more seriously. But what he did not understand was the uncontrollable part of his nature—the part that would not allow him to settle for a routine life, the part that drove him on blindly in a quest, undefinable, for something different, something that matched his imagination.

THE ALL-STORY

VOL. XXII   FEBRUARY, 1912.   No. 2

Under the Moons of Mars

by Norman Bean

RELATIVE to Captain Carter's strange story a few words, concerning this remarkable personality, are not out of place.

At the time of his demise, John Carter was a man of uncertain age and vast experience, honorable and abounding with true fellowship. He stood a good two inches over six feet, was broad of shoulder and narrow of hip, with the carriage of the trained fighting man. His features were regular and clear-cut, his eyes steel gray, reflecting a strong and loyal character. He was a Southerner of the highest type. He had enlisted at the outbreak of the War, fought through the four years and had been honorably discharged. Then for more than a decade he was gone from the sight of his fellows. When he returned he had changed, there was a kind of wistful longing and hopeless misery in his eyes, and he would sit for hours at night, staring up into the starlit heavens.

His death occurred upon a winter's night. He was discovered by the watchman of his little place on the Hudson, full length in the snow, his arms outstretched above his head toward the edge of the bluff. Death had come to him upon the spot where curious villagers had so often, on other nights, seen him standing rigid—his arms raised in supplication to the skies.

—*Editor's Note.*

CHAPTER I.

IN THE MOUNTAINS.

I AM a very old man; how old, I do not know. Possibly I am a hundred, possibly more; but I cannot tell, because I have never aged as other men, nor do I remember any childhood. So far as I can recollect, I have always been a man, a man of about thirty. I appear to-day as I did forty years and more ago, and yet I feel that I cannot go on living forever; that some day I shall die the real death from which there is no return.

I do not know why I should fear death, I who have died twice and am still alive; yet I have the same horror of it as you who have never died, and it is because of this terror of death, I believe, that I am so convinced of my mortality.

FRANTIC YEARS
AND A
TASTE OF SUCCESS

In preparing to write his *Autobiography,* Ed made a rough outline, jotting down in words or phrases the events still sharp in
his memory. Whatever a man recalls from the past—and especially from a past of fifty years crowded with experiences—
must be of importance to him. In the eight pages that he headed
"Thoughts on Auto Biog," the section relating to the seven or
eight years that followed his return from Salt Lake City is quite
detailed. "The next few months encompassed a series of horrible
jobs," Burroughs wrote. The list of positions or projects abandoned, the impression of deep discouragement, are reminders
of the years when Ed's fortunes deteriorated steadily to their
lowest point:

I get a job as Time Keeper on a construction job
  dizzy heights
I sell Stoddards lectures
  candy
  lt bulbs
  I am a Flop
Get job as expert accountant
make good
Office Manager for E. S. Winslow
Go to Sears
Joan born
Go into business with Dentzer
Fail

*First page of ERB's first story, "Under the Moons of Mars," as
published in February 1912 issue of* All-Story *magazine.*

Get job with Stace
Hulbert born about this time
Stace-Burroughs Co
Flop
Head aches for years—no vacation—lunches
Sell pencil sharpeners
Am just about ready to give up
Start writing A Princess of Mars
in corset jobbers office at Market & Monroe
Champlain Yardley Co
½ story accepted
My first check
Write Outlaw of Torn   rejected
Great poverty
pawning watch
Get job with System
E. W. Shaw
Jack born
Give up my job & decide to depend solely on writing
Everyone thinks I am crazy including myself

Impatient with any moderate and gradual climb up the ladder of success, Ed preferred to exchange a career at Sears, Roebuck for a more stimulating scheme with get-rich-quick possibilities. The enterprise, a partnership, was started with a man named Dentzer. A small brown business card, saved in one of Ed's scrapbooks, reads, "Burroughs & Dentzer, Advertising Contractors/610—134 E. Van Buren Street, Chicago."

One writer has described the business as an advertising agency based upon a correspondence course in salesmanship that prepared the students for active selling.[1] Ed, not at all deterred by his meager knowledge of salesmanship, had supposedly written the course. The situation and its outcome are vividly pictured in a magazine article:

Burroughs and his partner thought there were millions in it. They regarded themselves as aluminum kings about to corner the pot-and-pan trade with the help of peddlers who would pay tuition fees for the privilege of peddling. But the students all quit when they got to the field-work stage. Some failed to send back either the money or the pots and pans.[2]

This type of project, involving a few weeks of study by correspondence followed by door-to-door selling of pots and pans,

176

appears to duplicate, in many respects, an enterprise that occurred at a later period during Ed's partnership with Dr. Stace.

Ed left Sears, Roebuck in August 1908, and the card he sent to Emma from South Bend, Indiana, shortly afterward indicates that he was preparing for some new enterprise or engaged in making contacts or purchases for his partnership with Dentzer. Dated September 15, 1908, the card was addressed to Emma at 197 Park Avenue. It reads: "This isn't a half bad little town. Haven't accomplished much yet. Not even my lunch—12:15 p.m." On the same date he sent little Joan a card containing one word: "Google."

Whatever the business was, Ed, in his *Autobiography,* could summarize its collapse with wry amusement: "Having a good job and every prospect for advancement I decided to go into business for myself, with harrowing results. I had no capital when I started and less when I got through."

The circumstances were familiar; the struggle continued. From the run-down flat at 197 Park Avenue where he, Emma and baby Joan lived, Ed resumed the quest for employment. Meanwhile, the fortunes of Ed's own family had undergone some change. With the failure of their gold dredging projects in Idaho, brothers George, Harry, and Coleman returned to Chicago. Major George Tyler Burroughs, at an advanced age, still headed his company, but the income had declined steadily. During this difficult period his deep love for Ed and the unfailing kindness of his nature were demonstrated in the letter he sent to his son on December 25, 1908. Written on the letterhead of the American Battery Company at 172 South Clinton Street, it is addressed to "My Dear Son Edgar" and contains a most unusual Christmas present:

Kindly accept from me the within paid notes. I have had them for quite a long time, and I think it only right, at this time to give them to you, that your mind may be relieved of just this burden. They would never have troubled you, had I retained them, it is just as well for you to have them. Coleman has been paid in full. It is better for you not to mention this transaction to either Geo. or Coleman as the latter did not wish to let me have them and only did so after repeated importunities. He did not wish to hurt your feelings. There is no reason why they should be. Coleman could not afford to carry these notes and you could not take them up at that time, therefore I did the only proper thing, I think. I took them myself. I hope you will soon be in shape to pay any other indebtedness you have, and now wishing you & Emma a Merry Christmas & a happy New Year.

Thus, Major George, without saying anything, had paid off the notes for the $300 Ed had borrowed from Coleman in May 1903. Through the years he had kept this deed a secret from Ed. The signature of the major was as touching as his action; in closing, he wrote, "I am, and always affctly. Your friend and Father."

From the rented home on 646 Washington Boulevard that George and Mary Evaline had occupied for so many years they had finally moved to 493 Jackson Boulevard (later renumbered 1418). A brief biography of the major was printed on the occasion of his birthday, Wednesday, October 13, 1909: "George T. Burroughs Sr. of 1418 West Jackson boulevard, president of the American Battery company and a native of Massachusetts, is 76 today. He carried a gun throughout the civil war and came to Chicago in 1868."[3]

For Ed the year 1909 brought an added responsibility. The family, now at 2008 Park Avenue, was increased to a total of four, with the birth of a son on August 12. He was named Hulbert, after Emma's side of the family.[4] Meanwhile, Ed had accepted a position as office manager for the Physicians Co-Operative Association at 1006 South Michigan Boulevard in Chicago. The firm, under the ownership of Dr. Stace, sold a nostrum called Alcola, publicized as a cure for alcoholism.

Stace, whom Ed found very likable, had grown ashamed of the patent medicine business and was casting about for a more reputable type of livelihood. His qualms may have been reinforced by the dubious attitude of the United States Government: "Alcola cured alcoholism all right, but the Federal Pure Food and Drug people took the position that there were worse things than alcoholism, and forbade the sale of Alcola."[5] Soon a new organization was formed, the Stace-Burroughs Company, with Ed listed as secretary-treasurer and with the office at the same address on Michigan Boulevard.

Although his failure in his own business, a recent occurrence, must have been fresh in his mind, he was unable to resist the temptations of this new get-rich-quick scheme. Stace had conceived of a partnership project and Ed blithely and eagerly acceded.

The ingenious nature of the enterprise seemed to indicate that it was an inspired product of Ed's imagination. The partner's first task, quickly completed, was to devise a course on "scientific salesmanship." It was writing, Ed confessed, "which I should have been eminently fitted to do since I knew about everything that a salesman should not do."[6] The twenty-one booklet course was sold to prospective salesmen at a reasonable price, actually less than similar courses being sold elsewhere, but in about the third or fourth lesson the catch appeared. Salesmen needed practice, which could only be obtained, of course, through selling the company's products; from these sales Stace-Burroughs would naturally make a generous profit. The trainees could choose from a wide variety of items, ranging from aluminum pots to pianos, these to be sold in door-to-door fashion. Ed did not overlook the firm and explicit reminders that the money should be remitted to the home office in Chicago.

Shortly after he started to work for Dr. Stace, Ed received a summons from Sears, Roebuck; he was offered the position of assistant manager of one of the merchandising departments. "If I had accepted it," he wrote in his *Autobiography,* "I would probably have been fixed for life with a good living salary, yet if I had, the chances are that I should never have written a story, which proves that occasionally it is better to do the wrong thing than the right thing."

The partnership scheme with Stace, which closely resembled Ed's project with Dentzer, was doomed. Its collapse, caused again by the lack of enthusiasm on the part of the student-trainees, was inevitable. Ed's comment in his *Autobiography* about the depressing outcome was brief: "The Stace-Burroughs Company sank without a trace and I was again out of a job." In these recollections of the period Ed states that he had reached the lowest depths of discouragement, a condition bordering on desperation:

I had worked steadily for six years without a vacation and for fully half of my working hours of that time I had suffered tortures from headaches. Economize as we could, the expenses of our little family were far beyond my income.

"Three cents worth of ginger snaps constituted my daily lunches for months," he wrote. "At this time I approached as near financial nadir as one may reach. I had no job and no money. I had to pawn Mrs. Burroughs' jewelry and my watch to buy food." It was a period that remained painfully sharp in his memory, one that shaped his often-quoted philosophy about poverty:

I loathed poverty and I should have liked to have gotten my hands on the party who said that poverty is an honorable estate.

It is an indication of inefficiency, and nothing more. There is nothing honorable and nothing fine about it.

To be poor is quite bad enough, but to be poor and without hope—well, the only way to understand it is to be it.[7]

His equating of poverty with "inefficiency" is based upon the success-in-business goal that had ruled his life. In this competitive world the individual rises above poverty through efficiency.

A more intense condemnation of poverty is contained in a brief poem he had written, presumably several years earlier. In its extreme bitterness the poem becomes even more representative of his feelings during this period of his most acute struggles. The poem, marked "Written about 1908," succeeds, despite its heavy, stilted language, in depicting poverty with hatred and disgust:

POVERTY!
Accurst and cursing.
Thou Drab of Sin and Vice and Misery;
Thou spur to Fortune.
From thy shrunk womb a Lincoln springs.
Engulfest thou a thousand who might have Lincolns been.
Seducer, thou, of Health and Happiness and Love;
Murdress of countless children, wan and pinched.
Honor in thee? Forefend us God!
Who lies with thee reeks of thy filth,
The butt of Ridicule the jest of Fate,
Loathing and loathed to a dishonored grave.

From an analysis of Burroughs' early career in a wide variety of jobs and business enterprises, two basic facts emerge. Although frequently on the verge of bankruptcy he was not afraid to abandon a comparatively well-paying job such as that at Sears for the exciting prospects of a new enterprise offering quicker riches. Furthermore, because of his restless and highly imaginative nature he seemed to know he could never be content in a routine and uninspiring job. Had he been imbued with the same fears that stifle so many of us, he would have pursued the safe and secure course and remained at Sears. And so, despite his frequent and periodic totterings on the brink of disaster and the consequent feelings of hopelessness and frustration, he never gave up in his continuing search for success. It was this same indomitable will to succeed that he was soon to write into his fictional hero, John Carter of Mars. When Carter faced such in-

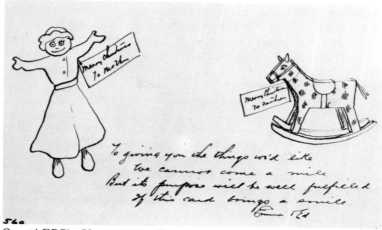

One of ERB's Christmas cards.

surmountable odds that death seemed certain, his defiant exclamation was "I still live!"

A list typed by Ed and dated September 1909 illustrates his
struggles to make ends meet on the small salary he earned with
the Stace organization:

Salary per week		*$30.00*
Grocery & Market	*10.00*	
Gas	*1.75*	
Girl	*5.00*	
Laundry	*.75*	
Milk	*1.85*	
Telephone	*.70*	
Jno. M. Smythe & Co.	*5.00*	
Car fare (*ERB*)	*.60*	
Interest	*.47*	
	Total	*26.12*
	Balance	*3.88*

*This balance of $3.88 is mostly required for clothing, medi-
cine and incidentals for a family of four.*

*Next month when I have to commence buying coal I shall have
a weekly deficit of $1.12.*[8]

The end of the year brought no change in his financial problems. He had no money to purchase the few Christmas cards he
wished to send to his family and friends, and in these circum-

stances decided to use his own imagination and skill. Ed drew the cards in ink and created his own verses. Even those somber times could not repress his sense of humor. His Christmas card to F.C.B. (Frank Coleman Burroughs) read:

Please accept this little token
It would be more were I not broken.

In the drawings of two men on the card, one man is presenting the other with a paper containing the words, "Lease to 25th floor of any 24 floor bldg." This was Ed's comical idea of the only "little token" he could afford. On another card he printed "Merry Christmas to Mother" and in one corner drew a picture of a woman in joyous pose, while in the opposite corner, next to a "Merry Christmas to Father," Ed outlined a child's speckled rocking horse. His verse reads:

To giving you the things we'd like
  We cannot come a mile
But its purpose will be well fulfilled
  If this card brings a smile.

It is signed "Emma & Ed."

A card addressed to his nephew Studley Oldham Burroughs at 1418 Jackson Boulevard is dated December 25, 1909, and Ed's verse is headed in large capitals "St.O.B." Again, he jokes about his financial state:

Please accept from Edgar Rice
The best he's got to give—advice.

In the illustration the "advice" being handed out is simple: "Start a Bank Account."[9]

The immediate day-to-day pressure of providing for his growing family left him little time or energy to implement his other creative thoughts and ideas. In his *Autobiography* he recorded:

Evidently there was not a job to be had in Chicago. I got writer's cramp answering blind ads and wore out my shoes chasing after the others. Then, somehow, I got hold of a few dollars and took an agency for the sale of a lead pencil sharpener and borrowed office space from a friend of mine, Bert Ball, who was a corset

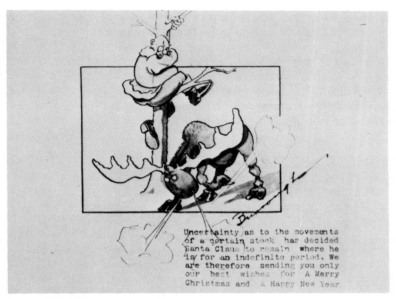

Uncertainty as to the movements
of a certain stock has decided
Santa Claus to remain where he
is for an indefinite period. We
are therefore sending you only
our best wishes for A Merry
Christmas and A Happy New Year

One of ERB's Christmas cards.

jobber with an establishment at the corner of Market and Monroe Streets in Chicago.

I would not try to sell the lead pencil sharpeners myself, but I advertised for agents and sent them out. They did not sell any sharpeners, but in the leisure moments, while I was waiting for them to come back to tell me that they had not sold any, I started writing "A Princess of Mars," my first story.

The incredible plot concerning a certain princess on a far-off planet had probably passed through a long period of gestation. In July 1911 he started writing. The words flowed swiftly, the details clear and vivid in his mind.

As the story progressed, the pencil sharpener business ground to a halt and then expired. Ed went to work for his brother Coleman, who now owned the Champlain-Yardley Company, a firm that in Ed's words "might be grandiloquently described as manufacturing stationers—we made scratch pads." In the company's office at 222 West Kinzie Street he continued his writing and completed the first half of the story. On August 14, 1911, he mailed the manuscript, together with an explanatory letter, to *Argosy Magazine,* New York, preferring to use his business address rather than that of his home on 2008 Park Avenue.

Of his first story and its submission Ed recalled that at the age of thirty-five (he was within a few weeks of thirty-six) he knew nothing about writing technique, and remarked:

I had never met an editor, or an author or a publisher. I had no idea how to submit a story or what I could expect to get in payment. Had I known anything about it at all I would not have thought of submitting half a novel. I do not know that any writer has ever done it successfully before or since.[10]

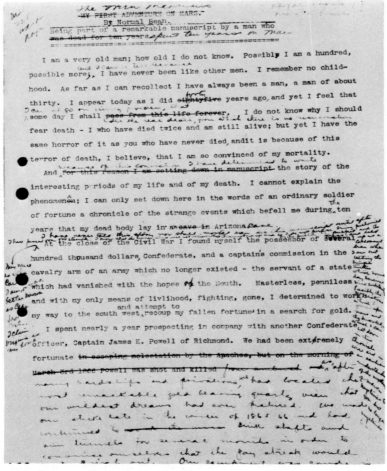

First page of manuscript of "Under the Moons of Mars;" original manuscript was written longhand.

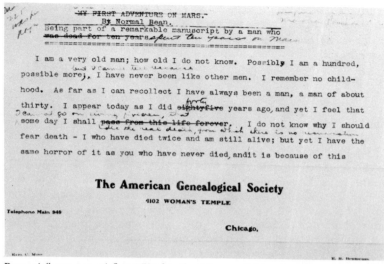

Part of first page of first "Under the Moons of Mars" manuscript and business stationery on which ERB wrote the story.

With the sale of "Under the Moons of Mars" Ed arrived at a decision: he would make writing his career. He started at once on a second story, a romantic serial, its setting suggested by Metcalf. But in spite of his first, promising success, his financial situation was unchanged. Coleman's business would not support two families, and Ed once more began a search for work. The year 1912 found him working for *System,* the magazine of business, as manager of the System Service Bureau. The offices were at Wabash and Madison Avenues in Chicago, but the magazine also maintained offices in New York and London.[11]

System had achieved great respect and popularity in the world of commerce. Termed "The Magazine of Efficiency" by its publisher, it was sometimes described as "the businessman's bible." A writer explains the reasons for its astonishing success: "It was a pioneer in introducing charts and graphs. Many businessmen worshipped charts and graphs as religious symbols. It was their belief that, if they stared long enough at these mystic curves and angles, red ink would turn into black."[12]

Ed, as manager of the Service Bureau, was assigned the task of giving business advice to the subscribers. He viewed this as somewhat unbelievable, noting in his *Autobiography:*

I knew little or nothing about business, had failed in every en-

*terprise I had ever attempted and could not have given valuable
advice to a peanut vendor; yet I was supposed to solve all the
problems of our subscribers, among which were some very big
concerns.*

The inquiries were numerous, for upon payment of fifty dollars
a year, a businessman could write to *System's* Bureau as often
as he liked and demand detailed advice on his business dilem-
mas.

Ed especially remembered a milling company in Minneapolis
or St. Paul that sent him intricate problems to be solved. "Had
God asked me to tell Him how to run heaven," he wrote, "I
would have known just as much about it as I did about the
milling business."[13] But he was not the only member of the
staff who had this type of responsibility. He could recall with
amusement that a young man of about nineteen was hired to
give advice to bankers. His sole banking experience "consisted
in his having beaten his way around the world."[14]

In one version, Ed is depicted as a counselor who used great
care to avoid any statements of a specific nature—statements
that might be clearly interpreted:

*Burroughs sat at his desk from morning until night, writing
counsel to merchant princes and captains. He used words that
rumbled with portentous business wisdom, but were too vague to
enable any industrial baron to act on them. Burroughs had a
conscience, and it was always his fear that, if his advice ever
became understandable, it would land his clients in the bankruptcy courts. With his letters he would enclose some of the awe-
inspiring hieroglyphics now known as "barometries."*[15]

The writer insists that Ed's advice never brought a complaint,
and that "he may have been as good as anybody else in this
field"; concerning the science of "barometries" it is humorously
noted that "nothing is definitely known on the subject today except that the more the charts and graphs flourish, the faster the
business decays."[16]

About the magazine *System,* its service bureau, and its owner,
A. W. Shaw, Ed, in his *Autobiography,* offered some severely
critical comments:

*Ethically it was about two steps below the patent medicine busi-
ness. One of the many differences between Stace and Shaw was
that Stace was ashamed of what he did, notwithstanding the fact
that he was constantly showered with unsolicited testimonials
evidencing the fact that his treatment cured drunkenness.*

Of Shaw himself, Ed wrote, "I never so thoroughly disliked any employer. He was an overbearing, egotistical ass with the business morality of a peep show proprietor."

Possibly during the period of varied business enterprises, Ed turned once more to his nom de plume of Normal Bean in writing a brief anecdote. Titled "Selling Satisfaction—an Anecdote," it presents, in its three pages, pointed advice on the businessman's obligations to his customers. The article, undated, was evidently not submitted to any commercial publications, although Ed, at the time he wrote it, may have contemplated offering it for sale to a magazine or sending it to a business "house organ." The emphasis upon "Selling Satisfaction" brings up the familiar Sears, Roebuck guarantee and could indicate that the article was written during his employment there or some time afterward.

He chose the anecdotal form with the entire article constructed in dialogue: "We had been discussing the failure of a competitor; the general manager and I. . . ." The competitor had been Lounsbury, head of a one-man concern. The company had failed in spite of the fact that "their goods were right, their prices right and they had an excellent organization, both sales and executive." The General Manager knew the reason for Lounsbury's failure; the policy he had followed "would wreck any house in this day of satisfaction-guaranteed-merchandising, where competition is as keen as in our line."

As Normal Bean, Ed recounts, in conversation, how he had run a general store in Montana, competing with Lounsbury. At the start, Lounsbury with his old established store had the bulk of the trade, but soon Ed acquired most of his customers. One important account, however, that of a wealthy miner and cattleman, Ed was unable to get. As the anecdote develops, a customer returns to Ed's store to complain about a pick handle that had broken. The customer does not expect any adjustment since the purchase was three months old, but Ed at once offers him a choice of selecting a new handle or getting his money back. The wealthy miner, who has witnessed the scene, is so impressed by Ed's business methods that he orders one hundred dollars worth of goods; he explains that he is quitting Lounsbury who has refused to do anything about a broken harness. Lounsbury's policy was that a purchased item belongs to the customer, and if it is defective, the storekeeper, who has not made it, cannot be responsible. "I reckon," the miner said, "that his logic is O.K., but I like your way of doing *business*."

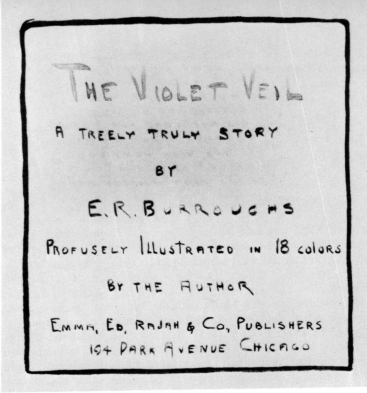

Title page of ERB's "The Violet Veil."

A page from "The Violet Veil;" ERB gave the book to Johnny and Danton Burroughs in 1944.

Ed explained that this incident had given him a permanent understanding: ". . . from that day to this I have studied to perfect a policy which I had unconsciously adopted without realizing its immense value as a business builder." This was the "satisfaction-guaranteed-policy," in which the businessman is saying to any customer, "I am as much responsible for the *value* of the goods I sell you, after you buy them as I was before."

During the years of poverty, of irregular employment, and of an equally irregular income, Ed, before he turned to writing fiction, had, as in the past, found time for whimsical and humorous expression through poetry. He had shown that he loved to create children's poems; these allowed his imagination a further outlet—the poems lent themselves naturally to his colorful illustrations and cartoons. The narrative style of poetry, similar to the verses he had inserted in "Minidoka 937th Earl of One Mile Series M.," appeared to be his favorite, and he evidently enjoyed devising wildly improbable fairy-tale plots with nonsensical ideas and phrases reminiscent of Edward Lear and Lewis Carroll. As in "Minidoka," he sensed that children's interest lay mainly in animals—that to them, the concept of animals personified, talking and acting like humans (ridiculous ones), was joy-provoking.

A sixteen-page booklet titled "The Violet Veil" is a remarkable example of Ed's talent in creating a unified work of art. Here he integrates a lengthy children's poem with watercolor drawings of animals. Ed, in a note following the title page, has written in his typical self-deprecating style, "This thing was committed prior to 1913." Within an inked rectangle drawn on the third page he presents an amusing description of the work:

THE VIOLET VEIL

A Treely Truly Story
by
E. R. Burroughs
Profusely Illustrated in 18 colors
By the Author

Emma, Ed, Rajah & Co. Publishers
194 Park Avenue Chicago

Since the address listed is at 194 Park Avenue, this might indicate that the booklet was completed some time between 1904 and 1907; Emma's maroon leather postcard album is inscribed "194 Park Avenue From 1904 to 1907."[17]

The *Rajah* listed as one of the publishers is the collie dog Ed and Emma took with them on their trips to Idaho and Salt Lake City.

Page two contains a dedication to Ed's two grandsons, obviously written many years later, "To Johnnie and Danton Burroughs with love from their grandfather Edgar Rice Burroughs, Tarzana 25 Nov. 1944." John Ralston and Danton are the children of Ed's youngest son, John Coleman Burroughs.

In "The Violet Veil" Ed returns to his favorite theme of kindness to animals, and the moral may possibly be interpreted as a warning against altering nature's perfect creations and changing their accustomed environments. Man's cruelties, often based upon whims, and his irrationally destructive acts toward the animals are being censured. The poem, in its simple objective, offers this moral lesson for children, stressing kindness to animals and revealing that nature's creatures are not to be tampered with by man.

PART 3

FROM MEDIEVALISM TO THE JUNGLE

CHAPTER 7

THE OUTLAW OF TORN

The sale of "Under the Moons of Mars" to *All-Story* Magazine was the stimulus that Ed needed to revive suppressed dreams of success. The sequence of misfortunes through the years had sobered him somewhat, given him a cautious viewpoint on life and its occurrences; but past failures in themselves had little effect in altering the basic impulsiveness of his nature—they could only temper it. A powerful influence was his conditioning in the business world, an emphasis upon dollars-and-cents practicality that had been started in the earliest years of his childhood and reinforced during his later employment experiences. This acquired habit, or quality, now seemed to act in an advisory or appraising manner to balance Ed's more imaginative tendencies.

In his letter of November 6, 1911, to Thomas Metcalf, the E. R. Burroughs of Sears, Roebuck, of hours of labor as against output, takes charge. The influence extends to his use of stiff business phrases: "While the remuneration is not exactly in proportion to the time and effort expended, I realize that for a first story it is considerably above the average, were one to include the rejected manuscripts."

In the same letter of November 6, succumbing once more to the pragmatic side of his nature, Ed advanced a skeptical view of writing as an occupation. "Does the price at which I have sold you this first manuscript establish the rate for future stories?" he inquired. His comment was made in a grumbling tone:

ERB in 1912 when Tarzan *was first published.*

This story business is all new to me, but I like the work provided I can make it pay. However, I know that it would not be worth my while to devote all my time to it at this rate, as I started this story in July, which makes the remuneration equivalent to about $100.00 per month.[1]

Upon receipt of the $400 check Ed noted that the form of endorsement did not guarantee him the stipulated book rights, and on November 17 he reminded Metcalf of this agreement. The editor replied to assure him that the omission of book rights was a technical error, and that *these* did belong to him.

Before filing the carbon of the November 6 letter, Ed wrote across the top, "Check $400 recd Nov 17—1911 ERB." He was initiating a system of meticulous care in noting pertinent data and keeping records of transactions, a method that he would maintain throughout the years.

Metcalf had asked for references, presumably to offer some assurance that the story was original, and Ed pointed out that since it was his first story, he could not give any publishers as references. "I do not know any," he wrote, adding, "The story is absolutely original and I believe the best proof to you must be the fact that I wrote the ending along lines of your own suggestion."[2] Ed did offer three personal references: Robert D. Lay, his friend and classmate from Michigan Military Academy, now with the National Life Insurance Company; Arch O. Burdick and Charles E. Rollins of a Chicago insurance firm; and two Sears, Roebuck officials, O.C. Doering, general superintendent, and Maurice D. Lynch, director of correspondence.[3]

In his acceptance letter of November 4 Metcalf laid down some conditions:

. . . I should like to stipulate that I might change the title and that I shall very likely do some cutting especially at the very beginning of the story, and also very likely entirely eliminate Solar's story, as the latter does not seem to me to be necessary to the rest of the story.

It was Metcalf, in the same letter, who persuaded Ed to create his next story in a different setting, a world almost as remote as that of the red and green Martians. Somewhat unhappily, Ed found himself returning to the thirteenth century to write a pseudo-historical romance about a gallant outlaw. To Ed, an anxious beginner, a suggestion from so distinguished an editor as Metcalf was both a challenge and a command. Metcalf wrote:

I was thinking last night, considering with how much vividness you described the various fights, whether you might not be able to do a serial of the regular romantic type, something like, say "Ivanhoe", or at least of the period when everybody wore armor and dashed about rescuing fair ladies. If you have in mind any serials, or anything of that sort, and if you think it worth your while, I should be very glad indeed to hear from you in regard to them.

Ed's response was to offer the first demonstration of his amazing ability to write at a feverish pace. Approximately three weeks after receiving Metcalf's suggestion, he had completed the story. In his letter of November 29, sent from the Champlin-Yardley Company at 222 West Kinzie Street, Ed reported the dispatch, by United States Express, of "The Outlaw of Torn"; again, only the serial rights were for sale. He explained that the story was set in medieval England, and described it by repeating Metcalf's phrase, "when everybody wore armor and dashed about on horseback rescuing fair ladies."

Ed could not refrain from presenting the same type of sales pitch he had used with his Martian story. About his hero, the fictitious second son of Henry III, he wrote glowingly, "The story of his adventurous life, and his love for a daughter of the historic Simon de Montfort, Earl of Leicester, gives ample opportunity for thrilling situations, and hair raising encounters." His obvious awareness of the limited nature of his research as well as his apprehension about any story that might require strong realism gave him a feeling of insecurity. As a result, he preferred to joke about the matter, pointing out that "while the story hinges, in a way, upon certain historic facts in connection with The Barons' War of that period, I have not infused enough history, scenery or weather in it to in any way detract from the interest of the narrative." He signed the letter, in parentheses, "Normal Bean."[4]

The plot, quite ingenious, and with no actual basis in fact, concerns the incredible revenge of Sir Jules de Vac, French fencing master in the household of Henry III, for the insult he has suffered from the English King. But if Ed had assumed that a quick first sale would put him on the easy road to success, he was doomed to disappointment. To a critical reader, "The Outlaw of Torn" was nothing more than a ragged patchwork of assorted characters and incidents, hastily conceived and ineffectively bundled together. Even as a picaresque romance with the customary string of loosely related adventures it was a failure. The semblance of a medieval atmosphere, which Ed attempted to create through brief descriptions and bits of historical reference, was completely unconvincing. Metcalf, on December 19, 1911, offered a summary of the novel's defects:

I am very doubtful about the story. The plot is excellent, but I think you worked it out all together too hurriedly. You really didn't get the effect of the picturesqueness of Torne. Opportunities for color and pageantry you have entirely missed. The worth of some of the figures of which you might make a great deal, you do not seem to realize. As, for instance, the old fencer whom you use for about three chapters and then ignore entirely until the very end of the story. In him you have a kind of malevolent spirit who might pervade the whole book.

The criticism simply revealed that Ed, a novice writer, lacked the experience and understanding to attempt a work of this nature. Metcalf termed this letter as "cursory," promising to send a more detailed one. Ed showed no discouragement in his reply of December 21; in fact, his attitude was aggressive, and he devoted much of the letter to defending his concept of what the novel required. His belief had been that *All-Story* would want something with a good plot and "as rapid action as possible, so as to not entail too much matter." He conceded that since this story was completed so soon after his first one, a reader might receive an impression that it was hurriedly written; this was clearly not the case, he insisted. "I work all day and late into the night studying my references and writing alternately. An experienced writer would doubtless cover much more ground in the same time." A period of some twenty-five days to complete a novel did not seem exceptionally brief to Burroughs.

In his reply to Metcalf he exhibited a supreme confidence that was close to cockiness. The flaws in "The Outlaw of Torn," ones that Metcalf rated as quite serious, were of minor consequence —"errors" subject to speedy correction. He was inclined to pooh-pooh them: "I can see no reason why I cannot make the story satisfactory to you, for the errors you cite are purely of omission, and they can easily be remedied."

Ed's confidence was shaken somewhat when Metcalf, keeping his promise, devoted his two-page letter of December 21 to a devastating analysis of the novel. His opening statement set the tone: "I think you have neglected great opportunities." He believed that Ed's first chapter should have been "full of color and excitement." After a brief summary of the plot, Metcalf referred to the ending: "I am not sure that there is any particular value in the happy ending. It seems to be more legitimate to have both De Vac and the outlaw die in the end, leaving the lady dissolved in tears, possibly on her way to become a nun."

To Metcalf, who obviously disagreed with Ed, the story's weaknesses were the result of excessive haste in writing: "It would almost seem that you were in such a hurry to get the story done that you muddled and underplayed many of the situations. . . ." About the development of so colorful a character as de Vac, Metcalf maintained that Ed had "fallen down very badly," noting that de Vac had been dropped entirely for almost ninety pages. In this connection Metcalf offered good advice to a beginning author:

I think this is a shortcoming in your work. When you are not using any one or any number of your characters you sort of lay them away in a drawer, so to speak, and seem apparently to forget all about them. I think it is necessary in a good story for the author always to keep in the reader's mind the fact that no matter which of the characters is in the limelight, the others are all drawing breath somewhere else out of sight or across the ocean, or wherever they may be.

A series of specific suggestions followed; and further in the letter Metcalf stressed that Ed ought to take time "to give the impression of the gorgeous barbarity of the times." He urged Ed to read Maurice Hewlett's *Forest Lovers* and Howard Pyle's *Men of Iron,* among other romantic novels, to acquire a stronger background. He presumed that Ed was acquainted with *Ivanhoe.*[5] ". . . I would not find it worth my while to be so explicit if I did not believe in your ability," Metcalf remarked, and stressing Ed's meager writing experience, added: ". . . you cannot, having been so short a time in the writing game, turn out wholly available stuff by working at a great rush, because I do not believe that you are as yet thoroughly sure of yourself."

Metcalf's appraisal of the manuscript evidently convinced Ed of the necessity for careful, studied revision, for he now worked slowly, not returning "The Outlaw of Torn" until February 2, 1912. A letter written from 2008 Park Avenue on this date was the one in which he notified Metcalf that he planned to use his real name from then on, since the compositor who had altered his pseudonym of "Normal Bean" had destroyed its future value. He was taking no chances and explained that he had devised two separate endings for the story, "one happy and the other tending toward the opposite, but leaving the matter somewhat in the reader's hands." His own preference was made plain:

For business reasons I lean to the "happy" one, because as all classes read fiction purely for relaxation and enjoyment, I imagine they do not care particularly for stories which leave a bad taste. However, I leave it to your greater experience.

Ed received no response from Metcalf during the month of February. The editor was suffering his own mental agonies as he tried to decide the fate of the novel. He later confessed, "I have been rather distraught as to exactly what my decision in regard to the story might be." Whether impatient of the delay, or already convinced that Metcalf would not accept the story, Ed sent an inquiry elsewhere, making his first contact with a book publisher. In his letter of February 29, which offered *two* stories for sale, he included a description of "Under the Moons of Mars." On March 4 a response came from Houghton Mifflin Company in Boston; it was not encouraging, and the letter, in its tone and wording, gave the impression that this staid firm viewed a novel of adventure on Mars as something so fantastic as to be detached from any world of either belief or consideration:

We thank you for your letter of the 29th ult in regard to two manuscripts that you wish to dispose of. It is not at all probable, we think, that we can make use of the story of a Virginia soldier of fortune miraculously transported to Mars, but the historical novel of the time of Henry III might be available for us. We ought to say, however, that it is almost certain that we could not use it this year, as our fiction engagements are already quite as numerous as we think desirable for next fall.

On the same date Ed received Metcalf's decision: the editor rejected "The Outlaw of Torn." "With the exception of one or two places," he wrote, "I do not feel that your rewritten version is very much of an improvement over the first copy of 'The Outlaw' which you sent me. The incidents, as a rule, seem rather wooden, and the color which you now introduce seems rather perfunctory, and you have not successfully concealed your artistry."

Metcalf, at whose instigation Ed had attempted this historical romance, now confessed, as though first aware of the idea, that "it must be a rather difficult thing to write a medieval story, unless one is pretty well steeped and interested in the period." But he then went on to make the kind of offer that Ed had never anticipated. Because he believed "so thoroughly" in the plot, Metcalf proposed to buy it and turn it over to a man in New York who had an extensive background in medieval history. The editor offered $100 for the plot and promised that when the story appeared, Ed would be listed as one of the authors.

Although Ed's financial situation, as in the past, was far from satisfactory, and the $100 offer must have been tempting, he had no intention of surrendering his plot to Metcalf. His refusal, somewhat curt and impatient, was based upon a businessman's evaluation of the amount of work and of the total hours expended. His letter of March 6 firmly closed the door on any suggestion of this sort: "I am very sorry that you do not find 'The Outlaw of Torn' available in its present form; but I thank you for your alternative offer, which, however, in view of the time I have put on the story, I cannot see my way to accept."

Even at this early period, and as a novice writer striving for acceptance, Ed exhibited the two qualities of self-confidence and unyielding independence that characterized him throughout his career. These qualities, developed mainly through his conditioning and business environment, provided a simple but explicit guide for his actions: a writer's work, plainly no different from any commodity that was placed on the market, deserved a fair price, and its value, in at least one respect, was determined by the number of hours required to complete the work.

Concerning Metcalf's suggestion for a new story, Ed explained that he had been considering a Martian sequel; however, business had picked up lately and he was finding less time for writing. Metcalf may have persuaded himself with deep feelings of relief that "The Outlaw of Torn" was now consigned to whatever place an author reserved for his rejected manuscripts. But in the correspondence of succeeding months, this belief was revealed as an illusion. The first hint came in Ed's letter of March 14:

I really think your readers would have liked that story. I am not prone to be prejudiced in favor of my own stuff, in fact it all sounds like rot to me, but I tried the Mss on some young people; extremely superior, hypercritical young people, and some of them sat up all night reading it.

Warming up, Ed became doggedly argumentative. His study of the medieval period had convinced him "that nobody *knows* anything about the manners, customs or speech of 13th century England. . . . So who may say that one story fairly represents the times and that another does not?"

If I had written into The Outlaw of Torn my real conception of the knights of the time of Henry III you would have taken the Mss with a pair of tongs and dropped it in the furnace. I made my hero everything that I thought the men of the time were not.

Metcalf, it appears, could not be goaded into a response, but on April 3, 1912, he wrote to Ed requesting material; and explained that *All-Story* was changing its policy and was again in the market for full-length novels of from 60,000 to about 80,000 words.

Ed's eager reply, fired back two days later, was what Metcalf should have expected. ". . . I have 'The Outlaw of Torn' on hand —What will you give me for the serial rights?" His scrawled postscript read: "By the way—do you suppose The Cavalier could use The Outlaw Mss? Provided of course that Allstory don't want it, or do you decide on the stories for both publications?"

In mentioning the story, Ed's use of the phrase "on hand" may have been subject to interpretation. On March 18, more than two weeks earlier, despite only the faintest encouragement, he had sent it to Houghton Mifflin Company, and he had not yet received any response from them. Whether he planned to forward another copy of the novel to Metcalf, or whether he believed there was little danger of the editor wanting it, is a moot point. But as Ed had probably anticipated, Metcalf's rejection was firm and prompt, and on April 9 he also made it plain that the manuscript had no chance for acceptance by *The Cavalier,* a weekly Munsey publication. Disappointment piled on top of disappointment. On May 7 Houghton Mifflin sent a letter of rejection which stressed the weakness of the story, but gave no details:

A careful consideration of the story left us with so much doubt of practical success that we do not think it expedient to make you an offer for the manuscript. The amount of fiction of all kinds that is constantly issuing from the press nowadays is very great and the natural competition is correspondingly large. We have doubted whether your historical romance will win out in the contest, and hence the decision we have stated above.

Much of the optimism raised by a first sale had vanished when the months of writing brought no further success. Ed continued his struggle to make a living, working as manager of the System Service Bureau for *System* magazine. He revealed his discontent in a letter of May 30 to Metcalf: "I wish that there was enough in fiction writing for me so that I could devote all my time to it for I like it. My specialties; advertising and business methods and selling command a bully salary, but they give me a highly localized pain."

Dust jacket for A. C. Mc-Clurg and Company's first edition of The Outlaw of Torn, *1927, J. Allen St. John, illustrator.*

The subject of "The Outlaw of Torn" remained quiescent for several months, but despite this fact, Metcalf must have understood that he was dealing with a man who would never give up. On October 30, while discussing other matters, Ed noted, "Am working on The Outlaw of Torn and think that I am whipping a good story out of it. Do you really think it worth while submitting it to you or would you suggest that I fire it to some other magazine?" He jokingly referred to Metcalf's frank discussion of editors in *All-Story's* column, "The Table Talks," in what amounted to an admission that editors "are but human after all" and given to mistakes.

"It is my job, you know, to read manuscripts as many times as authors see fit to chuck them my way," Metcalf replied, "and I am perfectly willing to do this so long as I have the enthusiasm I have had and always shall have for your work."

However, in sending the story to him on November 19, Ed indicated in his cover letter he had little hope for its acceptance, saying, "Please don't return it to me. When you are through with it let me know and I will send you a shipping paster and the coin to forward it elsewhere." He offered a positive prediction:

"I know that you will not like it any better than you did before," and as though baffled, added, "It's funny too, for everyone who has read it except yourself has thought it by far the most interesting story I have written."

The rejection was inevitable, even though Metcalf waited until December 18 to inform Ed; then, undoubtedly torn with guilt and regret, Metcalf said in his letter, "I should like to have sent you some kind of a check around Christmas time. . . ." Ed refused to voice any unhappiness, sending Metcalf instead what resembled an announcement of determination, or a proclamation of defiance: "I am going to do it over again when I have time— I shall stick to The Outlaw of Torn until it is published—I come of a very long lived family."[6]

Ed's struggle with the novel the year before from November 1911 through January 1912 had resulted in three versions: an original long-hand story of 215 pages; a typed manuscript, quite similar but with small corrections; and the expanded, detailed form, dated February 2, 1912, which he had submitted to Metcalf. In the first longhand version, Ed, with methodical care, began his system of recording the dates of manuscripts. The starting date on page one is noted as "Nov. 7, 1911 1:25 p.m.," and at the end Ed has written "Finished Nov. 23, 1911."[7]

In both the original longhand and typed forms the opening section thrusts the reader abruptly into the action *(in medias res),* focusing at once upon the wily, villainous De Vac and the incident leading to his terrible revenge. This opening differs from later ones:

De Vac had grown old in the service of the Kings of England, but he hated all things English, and all Englishmen. The dead King he had loved, but with the dead king's bones De Vac's loyalty to the house he served had been buried in Westminister.[8]

The revised manuscript of 1912, a collection of handwritten and typed pages, and even of odd pieces pasted in as corrections, offers evidence of what must have been exhausting writing. Some of the changes were probably based upon additional research—Ed's hasty hunt for information about the medieval period in order to give his work an authentic atmosphere. A box typed in an outline on the title page contains Ed's pen name and a statement of the theme.[9]

Ed's first two openings were discarded, and in the final published version of "The Outlaw of Torn" a more leisurely introductive section appeared. Leading into the quarrel between King Henry III and Simon de Montfort, this section substitutes an informal approach for the taut, compressed style of the other openings. It is the one familiar to Burroughs readers:

Here is a story that has lain dormant for seven hundred years. At first it was suppressed by one of the Plantagenet kings of England. Later it was forgotten. I happened to dig it up by accident. The accident being the relationship of my wife's cousin to a certain Father Superior in a very ancient monastery in Europe.[10]

Because it had the advantage of bringing the author directly into the story, this type of personalized introduction was popular with writers of the day. Having previously used it in "Under the Moons of Mars" (where it had become quite lengthy) Ed, perplexed over the various choices of openings, may have returned to it as a kind of refuge and as the easiest way to solve the problem.

At the close of 1912 "The Outlaw of Torn" remained unsold. Discouraged but not defeated, Ed had vowed to Metcalf, "I am going to do it over again when I have time." His most noticeable revision was in the introductory paragraphs; these took the final, personalized form. It was not until eight months later, after some dickering with A. L. Sessions, Editor of the *New Story* magazine, that Ed's obstinacy paid off. Sessions, in a letter of August 18, 1913, agreed to take "The Outlaw of Torn" for $500 for the first serial rights, and to pay two cents a word more if the story, according to reader response, proved to be successful.[11]

From a businessman's standpoint, as he balanced the long hours of revision and research against the net return, Ed undoubtedly considered "The Outlaw of Torn" to be a poor investment. Still, he had gained the satisfaction of another sale and had demonstrated the power of sheer stubbornness. Above all, through his unhappy experience with medieval times, castles and knighthood, he had learned that the historical romance, with its emphasis upon realistic atmosphere, was not the best outlet for his talents.

Ed's problems with "The Outlaw of Torn" during 1912 turned out to be of minor importance, however, for late in 1911 he had become engrossed in an astonishing plot, the wildest that his imagination had so far projected. As he wrote, the story, fully shaped in his mind, flowed across the pages with ease and certainty.

CHAPTER 8

TARZAN
OF THE APES

"I have been working at odd moments on another of the 'improbable' variety of tale. . . ."[1] In this modest, somewhat apologetic report to Thomas Newell Metcalf, Ed made his first reference to a *most* "improbable" tale, one launched in pathos and depicting the tragedy of a young English nobleman, initially named John Clayton, Lord Bloomstoke, but by page six of the manuscript retitled Lord Greystoke, a name that sounded more aristocratic. The tale—its ingredients consisting of a crew of mutineers, an unfortunate Lord and Lady Greystoke set ashore on an African coast, and the events that happened after their death—was called "Tarzan of the Apes." Derived from a language Burroughs had invented for his fictional tribe of anthropoid apes, the name *Tarzan* meant "white-skin." It was a product of his fascination with odd syllables and strange sounding names which he repeated aloud in varying combinations until, with the approval of both his ears and intuition, he made a final choice.

Ed's tone, in his statement to Metcalf, reflected sensations new to him, those of hesitancy and doubt, a reversal of the confidence he had felt after his sale of "Under the Moons of Mars." His elation and his dreams of a successful career had been shaken by Metcalf's blunt rejection of the revised "Outlaw of Torn." Now, Ed was a man driven back to reality—back to the dreary but practical haven of business. His attitude displayed unemotional acceptance of the situation. To Metcalf he mentioned that business "has picked up" and that "the time and necessity for writing stories are much less than of a few months ago."

"Tarzan of the Apes" cover of All-Story *Magazine, October 1912.*

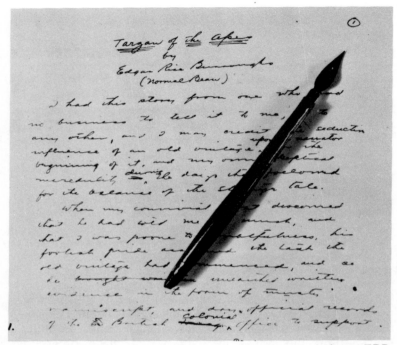

Part of first page of "Tarzan of the Apes" manuscript and pen ERB used to write it and "Under the Moons of Mars."

In this same letter of March 6, 1912, he proceeds to tell Metcalf about his latest tale, maintaining a precise, formal English so that no hint of his own feelings would emerge:

The story I am on now is of the scion of a noble English house —of the present time—who was born in tropical Africa where his parents died when he was about a year old. The infant was found and adopted by a huge she-ape, and was brought up among a band of fierce anthropoids.

The mental development of this ape-man in spite of every handicap, of how he learned to read English without knowledge of the spoken language, of the way in which his inherent reasoning faculties lifted him high above his savage jungle friends and enemies, of his meeting with a white girl, how he came at last to civilization and to his own makes most fascinating writing and I think will prove interesting reading, as I seem especially adapted to the building of the "damphool" species of narrative.

Ed's phrase "the 'damphool' species of narrative" is an early

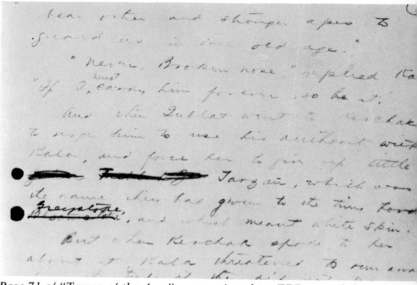

Page 71 of "Tarzan of the Apes" manuscript where ERB created the name Tarzan; *on the eighth line the first name he used appears to have been* Zantar; *next he tried* Tublat-Zan—*Tublat was Kala's mate and Tarzan's foster father—referring to the white child as* white Tublat; *finally he created* Tarzan; *in the language of the great apes of the tribe of Kerchak,* Zan *means skin and* Tar *means white; in line 10 ERB changed the name* Bloomstoke *to* Greystoke.

example of his humorous self-deprecation and an expression of his life-long feelings of inferiority. Although he has still used a "sales pitch," he finishes by stating, "If it sounds good to you let me know and I will send on a copy when it is completed."

He had commented about "working at odd moments" on the story without offering any hint of when he started it, but on the original, a thick longhand manuscript of 504 pages, Ed had noted, "Commenced Dec. 1, 1911 8:00 p.m."[2] Thus, approximately one week after he had completed the first version of "The Outlaw of Torn," he had turned to the creation of "Tarzan of the Apes." Story ideas, of course, may be spontaneous, the result of sudden inspiration; story plots, however, as in the case of "Tarzan," so neatly and logically worked out, appear to require more time for pondering, testing and rejecting, and seasoning. That the plot of "Tarzan" may have been retained somewhere deep in Ed's imagination and summoned up in his fantasies to be reshaped and even relived at various times is entirely conceivable. The "Tarzan" embryo may have gestated for long years in Ed's mind before he scratched the first story lines on paper.[3]

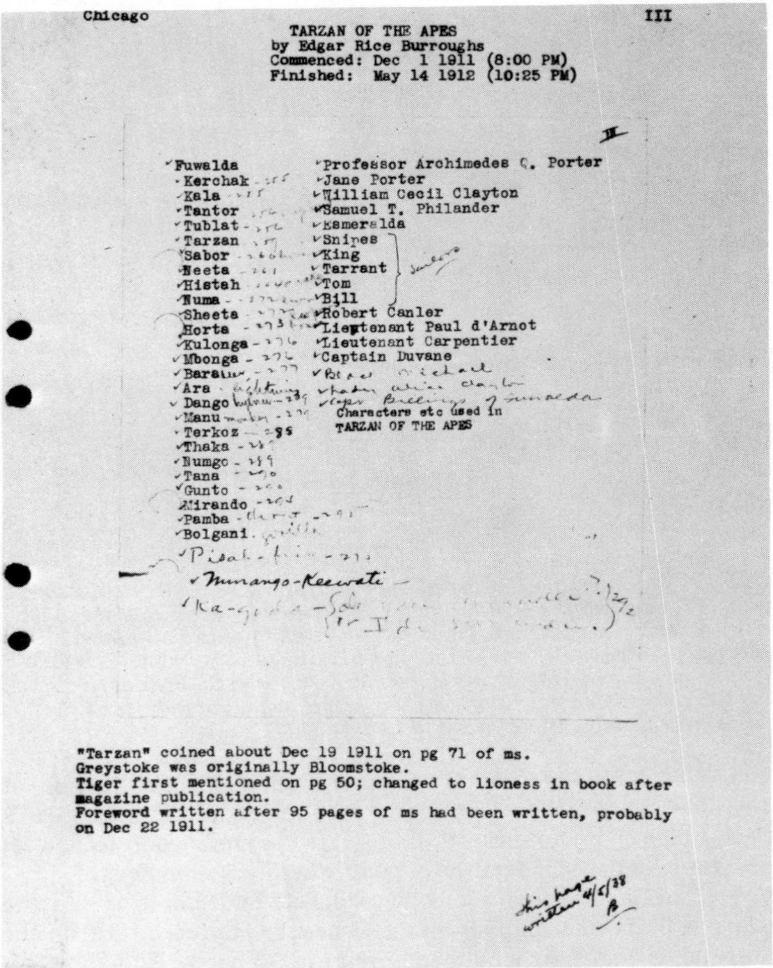

Chicago III

TARZAN OF THE APES
by Edgar Rice Burroughs
Commenced: Dec 1 1911 (8:00 PM)
Finished: May 14 1912 (10:25 PM)

Fuwalda	Professor Archimedes Q. Porter
Kerchak	Jane Porter
Kala	William Cecil Clayton
Tantor	Samuel T. Philander
Tublat	Esmeralda
Tarzan	Snipes
Sabor	King
Neeta	Tarrant
Histah	Tom
Numa	Bill
Sheeta	Robert Canler
Horta	Lieutenant Paul d'Arnot
Kulonga	Lieutenant Carpentier
Mbonga	Captain Duvane
Bara	
Ara	
Dango	
Manu	
Terkoz	
Thaka	
Numgo	
Tana	
Gunto	
Mirando	
Pamba	
Bolgani	
Munango-Keewati	

Characters etc used in
TARZAN OF THE APES

"Tarzan" coined about Dec 19 1911 on pg 71 of ms.
Greystoke was originally Bloomstoke.
Tiger first mentioned on pg 50; changed to lioness in book after magazine publication.
Foreword written after 95 pages of ms had been written, probably on Dec 22 1911.

ERB's notebook page, prepared April 5, 1938, for "Tarzan of the Apes"; center portion, pasted on, is from earlier notebook.

Metcalf, in his letter of March 11, 1912, displayed an immediate enthusiasm for Ed's theme: "I think your idea for a new serial is a crackerjack and I shall be very anxious to have a look at it." The editor must have condemned himself many times for having urged Ed to write a historical romance. Highly sensitive, he could imagine, with all the accompanying guilt feelings, Ed's intense struggles that led only to failure; in addition, he could not easily forget his own agonies in making a final decision to reject the story. From this unhappy experience he emerged with a perception and conviction: Ed's talents were best expressed through his own wildly imaginative creations. Metcalf's letter included an appreciation and an implied apology:

You certainly have the most remarkable imagination of anybody whom I have run up against for some time, and I have come to the conclusion that I had very likely better not butt in on any of your schemes, but let you go ahead as you and your imagination see fit.

Ed had no intention of allowing anyone to come between him and his imagination. Still employed by *System* magazine, he was writing furiously in his spare time, racing to complete "Tarzan of the Apes."[4] In the correspondence that followed, Ed's letters resembled progress reports, while Metcalf's displayed an uncontrollable eagerness to read the story:

Glad you like scheme of new serial.
[Ed, March 14, 1912]

Will try to finish up "Tarzan of the Apes" in the next few weeks.
[Ed, April 5]

I cannot tell you how keen I am to see your story "Tarzan of the Apes", when you get it done.
[Metcalf, April 9]

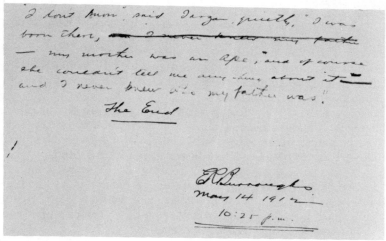

Last page of "Tarzan of the Apes" manuscript, with date and time referring to completion.

*How are you getting along with that serial? I am very anxious
to see it.*

[Metcalf, May 27]

*In about a week I should be able to send on the serial you ask
about in yours of the 27th.*

*Have had but little time to work on the story as I am managing
the System Service Bureau for The System Company, publishers
of the System magazine. Am also writing a course in salesmanship
for them and a new "How" book.*

[Ed, May 30]

*By United States Express I am sending you manuscript of Tarzan
of the Apes.*

May I have an early decision?

[Ed, June 11]

Although spurred on by Metcalf's inquiries to write "evenings
and holidays,"[5] Ed was not working with any strong feeling of
elation or optimism. With the rejection of "The Outlaw of Torn"
he had become dubious about his writing ability. As a result, he
now had little faith that "Tarzan" would be accepted. ". . . When
I finished it I knew that it was not as good a story as 'The Outlaw
of Torn'," he commented, "and that, therefore, it would not
sell. . . ."[6] The actual completion date, marked at the top of the
original manuscript, read: "May 14, 1912 (10:25 p.m.)."

The sequence of correspondence, like one of Ed's stories,
rose naturally to its climax—Metcalf's acceptance of "Tarzan of
the Apes" and his payment—truly an unexpected climax, one that
Ed had not dared hope for. (Unfortunately, this most important
letter, listing the amount of the check, with a probable statement
about the story, has vanished.)

On June 26, 1912, Metcalf wrote, "I suppose by this time you
have got a small souvenir from us to remind you of our attitude
toward 'Tarzan of the Apes'." Evidently, normal procedures were
followed in a separate mailing of the check by the Munsey business office, also under the date of June 26. The payment for
"Tarzan of the Apes"—established through other sources and records—was $700.[7] Ed's acknowledgement two days later read,
"Your check and letter came together on this morning's mail and
I thank you for both. The endorsement on the reverse of check
covered all rights, though I assume that it was as before but an
error, as I only sold you the serial rights."

The question of Ed's nom de plume of *Norman Bean* was brought up by Metcalf, who explained that the readers had been demanding more stories by the author of "Under the Moons of Mars." In apologizing for the change from *Normal* to *Norman,* Metcalf inquired, "Do you think it would be advisable to run this story ["Tarzan of the Apes"] under the name *Norman Bean,* or shall I ignore my requests for some of that gentleman's work and run it under *Normal Bean,* or your own name?"[8]

Ed's response of June 28 revealed that the printer's alteration of his name was still a touchy subject:

In the matter of the pen name, why not run this story as by Norman Bean (Edgar Rice Burroughs) and then, should I write another one run that as by Edgar Rice Burroughs (Norman Bean), thereafter dropping the pen name entirely?

This may not accord with your policy, but I think you will agree that you owe me a concession in the matter of names, for you sure did smear up the original.

It seems to me that it would be unwise to attempt to revive Norman Bean now.

At the end of the letter he asked, "By the way, when will Tarzan of the Apes happen?"

The *All-Story* of October 1912 featured "Tarzan of the Apes" as a "book," marked "complete in this issue." Metcalf accepted Ed's second suggestion, listing the author as *Edgar Rice Burroughs (Norman Bean),* the last time that Ed's pen name would appear on a printed story.

Various theories have been advanced that Ed found his inspiration both for his stories of other planets and for the Tarzan idea in fictional works by well-known authors. He often insisted that in his adult years fiction held little interest for him, but had conceded that "as a boy and as a young man I read practically nothing else."[9] The question of where he *might* have obtained his themes, especially for his earliest works, deserves examination.

In referring to an author whose novel features elements common to many stories of strange civilizations, Ed again stressed his reading habits: "I did read a part of Sir Arthur Conan Doyle's Lost World several years ago but never finished it for as a matter of fact I read practically no fiction although I remember that I was much impressed with the possibilities suggested by the story."[10] Ed's "Under the Moons of Mars" (1911) predated "The

Lost World" (1912) by one year; this very fact precluded any possibility of Ed's using Doyle's novel as a source. Moreover, any comparison of the two works reveals them as completely dissimilar.

The first claim that one of Ed's stories resembled a work of another author did appear, however, in connection with *A Princess of Mars*. Ed expressed his concern in a letter to Joseph Bray, A. C. McClurg & Company editor, on May 31, 1918:

Will you tell me, please, when H. G. Wells wrote his Martian stuff or rather when it appeared? One critic calls attention to the fact that this story of Wells' and another story which I never heard of, suggested my Princess of Mars. As a matter of fact, I never read Wells' story and as mine was written in 1911, it is possible that it anticipated Wells'. Just for curiosity I should like to know.

In this case Ed's concept of the dates is inaccurate. Presumably, the reference is to Wells' main Martian novel, *The War of the Worlds,* published in 1898, far ahead of *A Princess of Mars*. Eleven of Wells' science-fiction or fantasy novels appeared before 1911, and Wells continued to produce a steady flow of similar works through 1937. But any theory that *The War of the Worlds* even "suggested" *The Princess of Mars* is without logical evidence. Wells' novel, written in his coldly precise style in an attempt to create scientific realism, bears no resemblance to Ed's freely imaginative work with its fantastic characters and setting.

In Wells' plot, centered about an invasion of our planet *from Mars,* the Martians become grotesque monsters; he makes no effort to develop them as individuals or to characterize them. Ed creates a bizarre civilization *on Mars;* in doing so, he was concerned with neither reality nor with scientific plausibility, although he did supply sufficient and ingenious details to give some semblance of reality. Students of Burroughs attribute much of his success as a storyteller to his knack of making the impossible seem as if it could really happen. His characters, surprisingly, were projected with vividness despite the fact that they were not individualized; actually, they were stereotypes. Yet, in a way not easily explained, they became unforgettable. Beyond all this, Ed's concept of a story, in contrast to Wells', was exaggeratedly romantic; he utilized all the popular ingredients—a beautiful lady, a dashing hero, a warped, sadistic villain, and, of course, a love that surmounted all obstacles.

In his most spectacular work, *Tarzan of the Apes*, Burroughs had to face a far heavier barrage of speculations, theories, and accusations concerning the possible sources for his famous theme. *Tarzan* may have been written, according to one explanation, with the aid only of "a 50c Sears dictionary and Stanley's *In Darkest Africa. . . ,*"[11] but Ed on several occasions explained that the ancient tale of the founding of Rome had provided his first stimulus:

As a child I was always fascinated by the legend of Romulus and Remus, who were supposed to have been suckled and raised by a she-wolf. This interest, I presume, led to conjecture as to just what sort of an individual would develop if the child of a highly civilized, intelligent and cultured couple were to be raised by a wild beast without any intercourse whatsoever with members of the human race. It was because that I had played with this idea on my mind at various times, I presume, that I naturally embodied it in the story after I started writing.[12]

I started my thoughts on the legend of Romulus and Remus who had been suckled by a wolf and founded Rome, but in the jungle I had my little Lord Greystoke suckled by an ape.[13]

While the story of Romulus and Remus may have been an important source for the Tarzan idea, Ed was apparently drawing a more direct inspiration from a work by a master storyteller—Rudyard Kipling. The link is found in the *Jungle Books*, fiction that Ed recalled reading in his early years:

As a boy I loved the story of Romulus and Remus, who founded Rome, and I loved too, the boy Mowgli in Kipling's "Jungle Books". I suppose Tarzan was the result of those early loves.[14]

. . . I presume that I got the idea for Tarzan from the fable of Romulus and Remus who were suckled by a she-wolf, and who later founded Rome; and also from the works of Rudyard Kipling, which I greatly enjoyed as a young man. . . .[15]

On February 13, 1931, in a letter to the editor of *The Bristol Times,* Bristol, England, Ed replied to a statement accusing him of stealing his themes from the British writers Kipling, Wells, and Haggard. Ed tempered his reaction to the accusation by adding the phrase "unintentionally perhaps." After noting that "for some reason English reviewers have always been particularly unkind to me," Ed proceeded to a frank discussion of the auth-

ors: "To Mr. Kipling as to Mr. Haggard I owe a debt of gratitude for having stimulated my youthful imagination and this I
gladly acknowledge, but Mr. Wells I have never read and consequently his stories of Mars could not have influenced me in any
way."

In denying that he took Kipling's original idea and exploited
it to his own profit, Ed wrote:

*The Mowgli theme is several years older than Mr. Kipling. It is
older than books. Doubtless it is older than the first attempts of
man to evolve a written language. It is found in the myths and
legends of many peoples, the most notable, possibly, being the
legend of Romulus and Remus, which stimulated my imagination
long before Mowgli's creation.*

Ed again acknowledged that Kipling may have influenced
him, adding, "but I am also indebted to many other masters as,
doubtless, Mr. Kipling would acknowledge his debt to the vast
literature that preceded him. . . ." He reiterated firmly, ". . . to
Mr. Wells, whom I have never read, I owe nothing."[16]

In a lengthy correspondence Ed tried to explain the
origins of the Tarzan idea to Professor Rudolph Altrocchi of the
University of California at Berkeley. Altrocchi, in the Department
of Italian, first wrote to Ed on March 29, 1937, stressing that he
was *"not at all* a fan-writer" but one interested in "folkloristic
and narrative motifs." Curious about "the mysterious processes
of literary creation," he had previously communicated with such
famous authors as Mary Roberts Rinehart, George Santayana,
Richard Le Gallienne, and Edgar Lee Masters.

Ed made it plain that he could only speculate, or search his
memory "for some clue to the suggestions that gave me the
idea," as he had often done for the numerous people who made
inquiries during "the past twenty years":

*. . . As close as I can come to it I believe that it may have
originated in my interest in Mythology and the story of Romulus
and Remus. I also recall having read many years ago the story of
the sailor who was shipwrecked on the Coast of Africa and who
was adopted by and consorted with great apes to such an extent that when he was rescued a she-ape followed him into the
surf and threw a baby after him.*

*Then, of course, I read Kipling; so that it probably was a
combination of all of these that suggested the Tarzan idea to me.*

The fundamental idea is, of course, much older than Mowgli, or even the story of the sailor; and probably antedates even Romulus and Remus; so that after all there is nothing either new or remarkable about it.

I am sorry that I cannot tell a more interesting story concerning the origin of Tarzan. . . .[17]

The story of the shipwrecked sailor, one that Altrocchi was unfamiliar with, aroused his excitement. Eager to discover where Ed had found it, he wrote again, apologetic, offering a pun that deprecated his own accomplishments, ". . . the distinction should be made . . . between one who *is* Burroughs and one who just burrows in literary motifs."[18]

Ed replied, "The story of the shipwrecked sailor was not the basis of any book, as I recall it, but merely an anecdote that was supposed to be authentic; but where it originated or where I saw it, I cannot now recall. Anyway, it is probably not true. . . ."[19]

The determined Altrocchi embarked upon a six months' search for the anecdote, without success, and in a further inquiry posed a series of questions in the hope that they might stimulate Ed's memory. "I shall not have peace,—at least literary peace," Altrocchi wrote, "until I have located this confoundedly elusive tale."[20] Ed again had no recollection, but in his response he offered an amused reaction to Altrocchi's feverish search: "I may say, however, that you have me started now, and that life will seem quite worthless unless I can recall further details. Possibly I shall be able to do so, and if I am successful I shall communicate with you immediately."[21]

Any belief Ed might have entertained that the matter was ended proved to be illusory. Two years later, on June 13, 1939, the dedicated Altrocchi revealed that his mission—the hunt for the shipwrecked sailor story—was continuing. The professor, assuming that Ed must have read the story in some 1912 publication, had done exhaustive research within this period but had found nothing. However, he did unearth two old sources involving relationships between humans and apes. These, he noted, "are in such inaccessible books that I do not see how they could have been read by you. In fact both were then inaccessible to anybody, or almost so." The two works he identified as Guazzo's *Compendium Maleficarum,* written in Latin in the seventeenth century and "only recently translated," and an unnamed adventure novel published in 1635. He summarized the themes:

In the first a woman who had committed a crime is relegated to an uninhabited island where she is seduced by an ape and has two babies from him before she is rescued; in the second, with a similar situation, the ape-husband follows her into the surf and throws the baby after her, when she is rescued.

Altrocchi hoped that these folk-tales might revive some dormant memory of the magazine where Ed supposedly had read about the sailor. "Otherwise," he announced resignedly, "I'll have to continue my search." Ed again had no recollection, but, anxious to help, he speculated, ". . . I may have found it in some book in the Chicago Public Library at the time I was searching for material for a Tarzan book. . . ."[22] This brought an eager reply from Altrocchi who was suddenly struck with a new idea: could Ed have done research in other languages, and if so, what languages?[23]

Ed quickly understood that his reference to the Chicago library had created a mistaken impression: ". . . I am afraid that I have misled you if I have suggested that I ever made any research for a source for Tarzan. My research was for data concerning the fauna and flora of Africa and the customs of native tribes." He emphasized the important point: "I had already found Tarzan in my own imagination."[24]

Altrocchi's literary investigations and his correspondence finally culminated with a letter to Ed, on November 13, 1939, containing an announcement of his plan to read a paper at the annual meeting of the Philological Association of the Pacific Coast, the subject being, "Ancestors of Tarzan." The paper, an abbreviated version of the original fifty-four typewritten sheets, was to be read at the University of Southern California on November 24. Ed, of course, was invited.

The invitation had to be declined. Ed wrote to explain that he was leaving for New York on the twenty-first. He hoped that if the paper were printed Altrocchi might send him a copy. The more than two years Altrocchi had spent in tracing the sources of the Tarzan theme had produced little that was directly related to the Burroughs novel. Altrocchi, however, as in the two seventeenth-century references to humans and apes, demonstrated that the theme had roots deep in the past, and in his total research assembled information of high interest to folklorists, historians, and the general reader.[25] Unhappily, the source that the incredibly persistent professor had hoped to discover—the tale of the shipwrecked sailor—was never found. His letter to Ed containing an invitation to the reading expressed the hope "to have, at last, the pleasure of meeting you personally." During the two years of correspondence Altrocchi, the scholar, engrossed in his musty documents, displayed no interest in making the acquaintance of the living man—the author whose creation, *Tarzan,* had driven him into an obsessive search. Altrocchi, as in his finished work, an essay titled "The Ancestors of Tarzan," remained in the remote past, never attempting to bridge his abstract paper world with the world of human reality. The two men never met.

The claim that Ed, in *Tarzan of the Apes,* had taken his theme from Kipling's *Jungle Books,* works that he freely admitted reading as a child, was one that occasionally drew Ed's ire. But while responding in annoyance to the *Bristol Times* writer who had hinted at plagiarism, Ed also acknowledged his indebtedness to the man, saying, "He has reawakened my interest in my set of Kipling, which I have not opened for many years, and which I may still enjoy above the works of later writers, despite the disparaging remarks that I understand Mr. Kipling has made relative to my deathless contributions to the classics."[26]

Kipling's references to *Tarzan* and its author, appearing in the autobiographical *Something of Myself,* offers actual praise of Ed's creation; but through the use of the word "imitators," and the avoidance of mentioning the name "Burroughs," as though one could not bother to recall the writer of a work so superficial as *Tarzan,* Kipling achieves an air of condescension and lofty tolerance:

. . . *If it be in your power, bear serenely with imitators. My* Jungle Book *begot Zoos of them. But the genius of all genii was the one who wrote a series called* Tarzan of the Apes. *I read it, but regret I never saw it on the films, where it rages most successfully. He had jazzed the motif of the* Jungle Books, *and I imagine had thoroughly enjoyed himself. . . .*[27]

Kipling made this final comment about Ed: "He was reported to have said that he wanted to find out how bad a book he could write and 'get away with,' which is a legitimate ambition."

While not addressing himself directly to Kipling, Ed noted that one could offer a different interpretation of plagiarism if the ancient legend of Romulus and Remus were accepted as the first and original source for all the variations that followed:

That Mr. Kipling selected a she-wolf to mother a man-child might more reasonably subject him to charges of plagiarism than the fact that I chose a she-ape should condemn me on a similar count.

It is all very silly, and perhaps noticing such charges is sillier yet, but no man enjoys being branded a thief.[28]

Ed had shown himself quite willing to answer questions about the possible sources of *Tarzan* and to conjecture as to how the idea came to him. But one point should be emphasized: he was responding to those who had already formulated theories concerning *Tarzan*'s origin. In other words, these theories *were not his.* Until the critics began to analyze his works, he made no attempt to search his mind or probe his memory in the hope of recalling some source from the dim past. Once the discussions began, he agreed readily that elements of the Romulus and Remus tale and of Kipling's *Jungle Books* could have provided him with his original inspiration. This theory was logical and possible. However, an awareness of the various qualifying phrases Ed used in his answers—"I presume," "I suppose," "as close as I can come to it," and others—makes it plain he was only conjecturing. He could not identify *any source* with certainty.

Ed knew only that the Tarzan idea came from somewhere deep in his imagination. He was willing to concede that the imagination is stimulated by what one reads, but he understood that beyond this, the creative process worked in mysterious ways that often defied analysis. ERB's son Hulbert, in an interview at Tarzana, commented: "I am frequently amused and sometimes irritated by those who constantly seek to prove that there are no new ideas, that ERB *had* to have direct sources for the Tarzan and Mars themes, that he stole his ideas from other writers. I am probably biased, but it seems to me that Ed Burroughs' remarkable imagination, demonstrated in many stories over the years, was certainly capable of developing a *new* idea and that perhaps Tarzan and John Carter *were* original with him. Nobody accuses Edison of stealing a light bulb."

The answer Ed preferred to give in later years to the inevitable question, "How did you happen to write Tarzan?" exhibited his familiar uncertainty, but offered a simple, commonsense explanation:

I've been asked that hundreds of times and ought to have a good answer thought up by now, but haven't. I suppose it was just because my daily life was full of business, system, and I wanted to get as far from that as possible. My mind, in relaxation, preferred to roam in scenes and situations I'd never known. I find

I can write better about places I've never seen than those I have seen.[29]

Aside from his efforts to explain the origins of the Tarzan idea, Ed was at times drawn into a discussion of the theories or philosophies he was trying to develop in his story, or those that others believed were inherent in his story. In relation to this, the question was also asked, "what does Tarzan, as a human in an animal environment, represent or symbolize?"

The philosophic themes that were generally associated with *Tarzan of the Apes* may be listed as follows: the conflict of heredity and environment; the lone man pitted against the forces of nature; the search for individual freedom; escapism—flight from the boring routines of daily life; a destructive civilization, with man, its representative, displaying all its vices, as opposed to the simple virtues of nature's creatures.

Regarding the basic scientific controversy of heredity vs. environment, Ed stated, "I liked to speculate as to the relative values of heredity, environment, and training in the mental, moral, and physical development of such a child, and so in Tarzan I was playing with this idea."[30] At present, environment is viewed as the decisive force in shaping or conditioning the individual. Possibly without being aware of it, Ed, in *Tarzan of the Apes,* created a unique situation in which heredity, within a civilized setting the lesser influence, now emerged as the greater. Clearly, heredity's victory in the conflict was inevitable. Tarzan, even the infant Tarzan, could not repress his human attributes, his intelligence. These led to his curiosity about his surroundings and about his parents, his observation of differences between the apes and him, his discovery of weapons, his motivation to learn to read, and eventually his rejection of the jungle life and a return to civilization. The outcome might be interpreted in another way: Tarzan and his circumstances represent abnormality; within this strange situation nature's irresistible pressure for a righting, a balance, forces heredity to assume its proper place.

An early analysis of the Tarzan theme describes it as "the Robinson Crusoe idea over again" and explains:

The lone man or boy fighting for his existence single-handed against nature always attracts readers when it is well done. This interest comes doubtless from something within us which goes back to the time when our ancestors were doing this kind of thing themselves.[31]

The lone man is of course ourselves, the ever-triumphant hero of our daydreams. This Ed understood instinctively, assuming that as he lived vicariously in the role of John Carter or Tarzan, so did others live in their own illusory roles.

Associated with the concept of man versus nature is his search for individual freedom, stemming from society's restrictions and man's rebellion against the "social contract." Although we yield to civilization's controls, we yearn to break out of our confines: "Tarzan always represents individual freedom . . . which is always present with us. There is not a man or woman who occasionally does not like to get away into a more or less primitive wilderness where he is 'monarch of all he surveys.' "[32]

Viewed with differing emphasis is the concept of escapism; Ed related this to the monotony of existence:

Perhaps the fact that I lived in Chicago and yet hated cities and crowds of people made me write my first Tarzan story. . . . Tarzan was, in a sense, my escape from unpleasant reality. Perhaps that is the reason for his success with modern readers. Maybe he takes them, too, away from humdrum reality.[33]

The escapism, according to another writer, was Ed's personal release from a dreary environment: "He was nearing forty; his life was still monotonous and insecure. It was perhaps natural that he should imagine a young demigod of superhuman strength and agility, living a life of freedom in the jungle. . . ."[34]

Man's numerous vices, his greed, hypocrisy, and deceit, as well as his irrational and cruel behavior, opposed to the instinctive order and justice of nature—this theme has become familiar to most readers of the Tarzan stories. In *Tarzan of the Apes* elements of the theme are stressed in connection with Tarzan's human inheritance:

He (Tarzan) killed for food most often, but being a man he sometimes killed for pleasure, a thing which no other animal does; for it has remained for man alone among all creatures to kill senselessly and wantonly for the mere pleasure of inflicting suffering and death.

The natives' sadistic treatment of a prisoner is both a shock and a revelation to Tarzan:

As he was dragged, still resisting, into the village street, the

Cover of All-Story *Magazine, October 1912; first publication of "Tarzan."*

readers. Among them was, however, at least one who struck a sour note. He was a reader who demanded accuracy and authenticity, and he may have been the first to note the existence of an animal character who was out of context. In the "Table-Talk" of December 1912, "G. T. M." of Springfield, Massachusetts, launched a spirited controversy:

In "Tarzan of the Apes" the author stumbled into what has often proved an effective trap for the unwary. One of his principal quadruped characters is Sabor, the tiger, who is thoughtlessly placed on the continent of Africa, where he does not belong.

The tiger is not and never has been included in the fauna of the African continent. Neither history, science, nor the personal experience of the explorer or hunter records the tiger as being indigenous to Africa.

The newspaper cartoonists blundered into the same pitfall at the time of Colonel Roosevelt's hunting trip, and the surprising thing is that no one seemed to care enough about the matter to correct them.

Ed was mortified over his blunder, realizing he should have done his research more carefully. Other letters followed, with a number of readers hastening to defend Ed's creation of Sabor the tiger. Several produced convincing data:

It seems to me that it is about time that some one came to the rescue of our friend Mr. Burroughs and his much belabored African tiger, "Sabor."

. . . I quote from the introduction to Mr. Jekyll's very interesting book, "Jamaican Song and Story."

"All over South Africa leopards are called 'tigers' by Dutch, English and Germans. 'Tiger' is used in the same sense in German Kamerun and probably elsewhere in West Africa."[42]

The writer directed scathing comment at those who had complained: "Mr. Burroughs undoubtedly knows all this, but probably like some others of us, he is too busy wearing out the point of his fountain-pen to start a primary school class 'for critics only.' " At the end of the letter the writer proposed a solution, tongue-in-cheek, to the entire problem: ". . . why doesn't Mr. Burroughs gather together all his 'tiger' critics in that little hut on the edge of the African jungle, get old 'Sabor' headed in the right direction, and—let go of his tail?"

A second letter in "Table-Talk" contained other facts to support Ed's use of the word "tiger." The writer, from Cape Town, South Africa, stated:

From the Cape to the Zambezi you can scarcely pick up a newspaper but the chances are that a record is there of a "tiger" hunt, or of a "tiger" having destroyed sheep, et cetera.

Colonials all call it a "tiger" over here; scientifically it may be known as a leopard or a panther, but to South Africans—Dutch or English speaking—it is a tiger.[43]

EDITORIAL ROOMS

August 20, 1913.

Dear Sir:

We are returning under separate
cover The All-Story magazine (Oct.1912)
containing your story, "Tarzan of the Apes."
We have given the work careful consideration and while interesting we find
it does not fit in with our plans for the
present year.
Thanking you for submitting the story
to us, we are

Yours very truly,
Rand McNally & Co.
₃₄

Mr. Edgar Rice Burroughs,
2008 Park Avenue,
Chicago.

Letter of rejection typical of those ERB received from book publishers regarding "Tarzan of the Apes."

These letters mention the South African custom in using the word "tiger" rather generally and loosely to apply to a number of members of the cat family. But Ed unfortunately described Sabor as a tiger in his magazine story, referring to the animal's "beautiful skin of black and yellow." He made careful corrections and deletions before the book was published. Sabor received both a new gender and identity; the male tiger became a female—now Sabor the lioness. Her skin was merely described as beautiful, with the colors "black and yellow" omitted.

In one other important respect Sabor, as a representative of the tigers, received a character change and an exoneration. The magazine story had stated, "Sabor, the tiger, alone of all the jungle folk, tortured his prey." In the book version this calumny against the race of tigers was rectified. The bloodthirsty villain became Sheeta the leopard. Ed made certain that the tiger never again appeared in his African stories.

The publication of "Tarzan of the Apes" brought an admiring letter from Ed's old friend Bert Weston, who on September 28, 1912, wrote:

I was in the western part of the state about 2 wks ago, and thinking that I was going to have 3 hrs of day train with nothing to do, bought an All Story, *having got the habit from the Moons of Mars. It was a very pleasant shock to find that that naked young hero of a Lion-Killer on the cover was a child of your fertile brain. That is a great tale. Better I think than the Moons. . . . I hope that you combed them down good and strong for the sous for that tale, and that you are very prosperous and that your literary prosperity has only commenced. . . .*

In a previous letter of March 16, Weston had commented about "Under the Moons of Mars," making it clear that his assumptions about Ed's writing had changed after he read the story:

. . . Speaking further of babies, that is a very ingenious idea to have the Martians lay eggs and hatch them. . . . I am fain to confess that the style of your tale (Moons of Mars) was very surprising to me. I had an idea someway that your stories would be like your drawings. This one isn't. You are mighty versatile, and this is mightily to your credit. . . .

Among the many letters of praise for "Tarzan of the Apes" were those including comments on Ed's "unfinished" ending—his scheme of deserting the reader in the midst of unresolved suspense. The readers who had expressed dismay over the same type of ending in "Under the Moons of Mars" now believed they were confronted with an author who was going to make it a habit. Remarks ranged from humorous jibes and entreaties for a sequel to indignant or even disgusted statements about a writer who would dare construct disappointing endings of this nature.[44]

In "Under the Moons of Mars" Ed's ending device, somewhat different, had been a real cliff-hanger: John Carter sinks unconscious before the opening door of the atmosphere plant and awakens in the cave on the planet Earth; both he and the reader are left in anxiety and doubt concerning Mars' survival. Here, Ed's suspenseful ending, worked out with some hesitation, was a daring device—in every sense an inspiration.[45] (Actually, it was in the best tradition of the old-time storyteller who kept his circle of eager listeners on tenterhooks awaiting the next episode.)

After the success of his Mars story Ed was quite willing to undertake a sequel. In response to Metcalf's suggestion that he write another John Carter romance, he replied, "I have had in mind a sequel to the Martian story. . . ."[46] This, he made plain, would be his next task upon the completion of "Tarzan." From his statements it would appear likely that in "Under the Moons of Mars" Ed was planning a sequel at the time he created his ending.

However, with "Tarzan of the Apes," he exhibited an uncertainty. While dangling the possibility of a sequel before the tantalized reader, Ed was really dubious, not at all convinced that it would be either desirable or successful. Metcalf had first brought the matter up, mentioning the approving letters being received at *All-Story*. He added a qualifying remark, gleefully predicting Ed's response, ". . . everyone has cursed out the end, which, of course will do your soul good," and continued, "Most everybody now is talking about a sequel."[47] Admitting he had no definite suggestion, Metcalf wrote, ". . . but the jungle is still there and I suppose that Tarzan having become generally disgusted with human nature could go back and try to lord it once more over the apes. Keep your hyperbolic imagination at work on this and see if you can do anything."[48]

Ed, in his answer to Metcalf, displayed the attitude of a man seeking to be persuaded: "About a sequel to Tarzan. Candidly I don't think it would be a go, although I have a really bully foundation in mind for one. These sequel things usually fall flat. I'll be glad to think it over, however, and later if you decide that it will be wise to try it I'll tackle it. . . ."[49] Some of this hesitancy was to be expected with a beginning writer. But the frustrating failure of "The Outlaw of Torn" was still affecting him. Despite a second sale, Burroughs was wary; he would not be lured by glittering visions of the future. Nevertheless, stubborn reserves of confidence that neither doubt nor caution could destroy remained within him. The very fact that he could be considering a sequel was in itself an indication of his faith in his ability.

He sought encouragement. On October 2 he wrote, "About a score of readers have threatened my life unless I promised a sequel to Tarzan—shall I?" Metcalf's response was tactfully affirmative:

I have been thinking over the necessity of a sequel to "Tarzan" and it certainly looks as though we ought to have one, don't you think so? Of course, as you say, sequels are never quite as good as the originals, but with such a howling mob demanding further adventures of your young hero, it looks to me as though it would be a very good move to bring him again to the notice of the great public.[50]

Metcalf, meanwhile, found it good business practice to keep his readers in a state of anticipation through regular comments about a possible sequel. These appeared in consecutive issues of *All-Story* in the "Table-Talk" section:

. . . Lots of folks don't seem to like the finish and are sitting round and barking for a sequel.

It would seem that no editorial comment were necessary. But we are tempted to say—oh, why should we? [A note about Ed's letter and his query about a sequel follows.]

[December 1912]

We have a good deal of correspondence with Mr. Burroughs in re a follow-up story for Tarzan.

We believe we can persuade Mr. Burroughs to frame up a few more stunts for Tarzan.

[January 1913]

Letters still come in about "Tarzan." Also about the proposed sequel. We have done our best with Mr. Burroughs, and now we can only lie down and wait. He is a good-humored man, however, and we should not be surprised if at some odd moment he would flash something on us.

[February 1913]

The pleas and demands of the readers, and Metcalf's urgings, had little effect upon Ed's plans. His imagination and pen were working at high speed on the project he had given priority—a sequel to "Under the Moons of Mars." (On October 2, 1912, he completed the story, "The Gods of Mars," and sent it to Metcalf.) But it was evident that in the midst of all this furious writing, the next step, a most important one, had already occurred to him. "Am glad your readers liked Tarzan," he had remarked to Metcalf. "One of them wrote me a very nice letter. In this connection I am wondering if you destroy letters of this kind when you are through with them. If so might I have them instead?"[51] Considered practically and from a businessman's viewpoint, the letters were forms of references or testimonials. He explained, "I have an idea that I could show them to publishers to whom I might wish to submit my Mss for the Book part of it. . . ." Then he joked with Metcalf about the printed confession that "editors can make mistakes." Ed wrote, "Let me thank you for the very acceptable bull con you handed me via the Table Talks— you are a real artist."[52]

His mind made up, on October 5, 1912, he chose A. C. Mc-Clurg & Company, Chicago publishers, for his first inquiry. The letter in his precise business style was written from 2008 Park Avenue:

Herewith magazine copy of a story, Tarzan of the Apes, which I submit for your consideration.

I have received several letters from readers in different parts of the country indicating that the story made a hit with them at

230

least, and the Editor of All Story writes me that the magazine has had a great quantity of laudatory letters relative to this story.

These facts suggested that if published in book form the story might be successful.

The acknowledgment of the receipt of his letter and the magazine copy came three days later, bearing a signature that would become quite familiar to Ed Burroughs in the future—that of editor Joseph Bray. On October 31 a full response followed; the letter offered no concrete evaluation of the story, contenting itself with praise—and polite rejection:

You have written a very exciting yarn in "Tarzan of the Apes" and we think it deserved all the success you say it had as a Magazine story.

Although there are many points in its favor and it is quite possible that it might sell fairly well in book form, yet we are unable to convince ourselves altogether of its availability.

We hope to have the privilege of seeing more of your work. . . .

The perfunctory wording of the letter, its tone of kindly encouragement to a writer assumed to be a novice, and its choice of so vague a term as "availability" as an excuse for rejection, make clear that Bray was decidedly unimpressed by both the story and Ed's sales points.

Undiscouraged, Ed expanded his letter to include more details of the popularity of "Tarzan of the Apes" with *All-Story* readers. He explained that the approving comments came not only from the United States, but from Panama, Canada, and England, thus demonstrating that "the story appealed to sufficiently widely distributed and varied classes of readers to warrant the belief that it would make a successful book." He offered to send the readers' letters to the book publisher.

On November 3, 1912, he sent this form, with a copy of the magazine, to The Bobbs-Merrill Company of Indianapolis, Indiana, and Reilly & Britton of 1006-8 South Michigan Avenue in Chicago. Bobbs-Merrill's rejection, received about two weeks later, resembled the ones sent automatically to thousands of aspiring authors:

We are sorry to have to send you an adverse decision in regard to the manuscript, Tarzan of the Apes, *but after careful consideration on the part of our editorial readers, we can not feel that it makes a place for itself on our list.*

We are grateful for the privilege of seeing this story and only regret that we have not more favorable news to send you. . . .[53]

The firm of Reilly & Britton, early in 1913, was still struggling to arrive at a decision. The same letter, sent to Dodd, Mead and Company in New York, brought a note of rejection.[54]

At this stage Ed wrote again to the man he idolized, his old commandant of Michigan Military Academy. On January 15, 1913, in a letter to Charles King at Milwaukee, Wisconsin, he asked the general for advice; Ed, optimistic, chose to believe that Reilly & Britton's delay was a good sign, an indication that a book contract might be in the offing. To the general he explained, "I am threatened with a book, and as it is my first I want to ask what royalty I should expect, or if I sold the book rights, about what would be a fair cash price?"

He mentioned his sales of "three short novels" to the Munsey Company, adding, "This of course has been in addition to my regular work." In connection with Reilly & Britton he noted that he had seen Reilly that day, and "he seems very keen for the story. From what he said I think they will make me a proposition shortly, and of course I should like to know what I am talking about when they do—*if* they do." He sent Charles King a copy of *Tarzan of the Apes*.[55]

Ed's hopes were not to be realized—his persistent search for a publisher would not yet be successful. The debut of "Tarzan" in book form was still more than a year away.

WRITING AS A PROFESSION

New terms, names, characters, places etc mentioned in 2nd John Carter Mss

Old Ben or Uncle Ben - the writer's body servant (colored)

Holy Therns - a martian religious cult.

Otz Mountains - surrounding the Valley Dor and the Lost Sea of Korus.

plant man of Barsoom - a strange race inhabiting the Valley Dor.

Golden Cliffs - walls of Otz mountains facing the Valley Dor.

Issus - Goddess of Death, whose abode is upon the banks of the Lost Sea

of Korus.

banth - Barsoomian lion -see Chap III pg 36 orig mss
silian - slimy reptiles inhabiting the sea of Korus
Sator Throg - a Holy Thern of the Tenth Cycle 55
Tenth Cycle - a sphere or plane of eminence among the holy therns 55
Thuvia - a red Martian girl - prisoner of the holy therns 55
Father of Therns - 55
Matai Shang, Father of Therns - 55
thorian - chief of the Lesser Therns 57
Black Pirates of Barsoom 63
pimalia - a gorgeous flowering plant 65
Dator- Chief or Prince among the First Born 70
First Born - black race - the Black Pirates
Phaidor - daughter of Matai Shang
hekkador - title of Father of Therns
Thuria - the nearer moon
skeel - a Martian hard wood 86
sorapus (same) 86
Xodar - Dator among the First Born
Shador - island in Omean
Omean - the buried sea
Thurid - another black Dator 107
Thabis - Issus' chef 123
Zithad - another Dator 134
Torith - officer of the guards at submarine pool
Yersted - commander of sub-marine
Tan Gama - Warhoon warrior
Kab Kadja - Jeddak of the Warhoons of the South 159
Hor Vastus - padwar in navy of Helium 174
Xavarian - a Helium war ship
Zat Arrras - Jed of Zodanga
Temple of Reward - 182
Avenue of Ancestors 183
Gate of Jeddaks 183
tal - second)
zat - minute) see table
zode - hour)
Aisle of Hope
Throne of Righteousness
Pedestal of Truth 186
Ptarth - Thuvia's country
Hastor - a city of Helium 198
Parthak - the Zodangan who brought food to Carter in the pits of Zat Arrras 200
dwar - captain
utan - a company of 100 men (military)
Gur Tus - dwar of 10th Utan 231

1st zode   6 am (accurate
2   —   8:24 am
3   —   10:48
4   —   1:12 Pm
5   —   3:36
6   —   6:00
7   —   8:24
8   —   10:48
9   —   1:12 am
10   —   2nd 3:36 am

TABLE of TIME (MARTIAN)
200 tals — 1 xat
50 xats - 1 zode
10 zodes - 1 revolution of
     Mars upon its axis

67 PADANS = 1 TEEAN (MONTH)
10 TEEANS = 1 ORO(YEAR)

10 zodes - 88,620 Earth seconds
          1,477 "   minutes
          24 hrs 37 min Earth time

1 zode = 2 hrs 27 min 42 sec or 2.

1 xat = 2 min 57.3 sec

687 days = 1 Martian year (Ea
670 " in the
669 "

Parthak - the Zodangan who brought food to Carter in the pits of Zat Arrras 200

CHAPTER 9

THE
PROLIFIC PERIOD

In the fall of 1912, encouraged by Metcalf's acceptance of three of his stories, Ed embarked with determination upon a writing schedule that would demonstrate his ability to produce a variety of works in an unbelievably short period. Metcalf, by now convinced of Ed's talent, had suggested the sequel which became "The Gods of Mars"—a story idea which appears to have stimulated Ed's imagination. On March 4, 1912, Metcalf's letter contained this idea:

. . . I was wondering if you could not write another romance about John Carter, introducing the Valley Dorr, the River Iss and the Sea of Korus, or those other semi-religious semi-mystical regions which you mentioned, but I believe never used in "Under the Moons of Mars." You could pretend that the adventures you would be writing about in this romance occurred between the time of Carter's marriage to the Martian Princess and the catastrophe you relate in the serial now running in The All-Story.

Metcalf's view of the logical theme for the new work, proceeding naturally from Ed's references in "Under the Moons of Mars," was one that may have already occurred to Ed—the false religion of the Martians. Metcalf explained:

Carter might get into some terrific rows, apropos of religion, with some of the Martian priests. You might cook up some kind of a story showing that all this section of Mars where Carter finally lands is governed by a hierarchy of dissolute religionists, and

ERB's notebook page for "The Gods of Mars."

Carter might go to work and smash the superstition into a thousand pieces and readjust the running of the country.

Metcalf was obviously intrigued by Ed's geographical inventions: "The mystical appeal of all these rivers, valleys and seas, which you mentioned only casually in 'Under the Moons of Mars' I believe would be very strong. . . ."

During this period Ed had been involved with his first revision of "The Outlaw of Torn"; his efforts to persuade Metcalf to accept the story would continue until the end of 1912. But that was only a small portion of his writing. In response to Metcalf's request for a "Mars" sequel, he had informed the editor that the Tarzan story was in progress—"another of the 'improbable' variety of tale." Ed wrote, ". . . if I ever finish it I shall see what I can do in the way of a John Carter sequel." "Tarzan of the Apes," of course, was completed by the end of June.

The astonishing writing pace continued. On September 20 he reported, "Speaking of sequels. I have the second John Carter tale nearly completed. I can't tell you anything about it because I am no judge. I think it will prove as readable as the first."[1]

Perhaps still meditating over Metcalf's original suggestion for an ending that led to the death of the Martian Princess, Ed added, "I doubt if I can kill Dejah Thoris though." He revealed his basic sentimentality, in contradiction to the stoical attitude and dollars-and-cents practicality he liked to assume, by stating, "You know I told you that I was purely mercenary insofar as my work is concerned, but when it comes to the characters I find that I develop a real affection for them—funny, isn't it?"

With its theme established, the new Martian work could have only one title—"The Gods of Mars." In its finished form, sent to Metcalf on October 2, Ed proved again the power of his imaginative vision to project far beyond Metcalf's basic idea. To him the entire Martian religion became a sham, a hoax created for the gratification of sadistic gods—a hoax accepted with blind devotion by all the races of Mars. Around this concept Ed devised a remarkable structure, a stratum of Martian life that included the plant men, the great white apes, the Holy Therns, and the black men. Again, he developed his geographical inventions, the River Iss, Valley Dorr, Lost Sea of Korus, mountains and valley of Otz, and Sea of Omean. The elements of conflict and suspense, which Ed instinctively understood as vital to any story, are at once apparent, not only in John Carter's opposition to the Martian religion, but in the hostility between the various races.

236

In "The Gods of Mars" the Burroughs device of a foreword in which he establishes the personal relationship to "Uncle Jack" (John Carter) is again used, with the story opening after a lapse of twelve years. Carter returns to earth, and at a meeting with his nephew informs him that he now has learned the secret of journeying through space between the two planets. In presenting the written story of his adventures, he says, "Give them what you wish of it, what you think will not harm them, but do not feel aggrieved if they laugh at you."

Carter implies that this will be his last visit to the earth, stating, "I doubt that I shall ever again leave.the dying world that is my life." Ed, as his nephew, comments, "I have never seen Captain John Carter, of Virginia, since." But in later works, Ed, as the author, found the original situation too tempting to resist, and in *The Chessmen of Mars* (1922) and *The Swords of Mars* (1934) uncle and nephew meet once more on earth. Ed revives the foreword (or prelude) that he has not used in intervening Mars novels.

In creating a super-race, the First Born of Barsoom (Mars), Ed chose the black men. This may have been his way of satirizing the earthly white man's treatment of the Negro as he had done in his parody of Kipling's poem.[2] In "The Gods of Mars" Xodar, a black man, explains proudly to John Carter:

The First Born of Barsoom are the race of black men of which I am a Dator, or, as the lesser Barsoomians would say, Prince. My race is the oldest on the planet. We trace our lineage, unbroken, directly to the Tree of Life which flourished in the centre of the Valley Dorr twenty-three million years ago.

Ed's evolutionary scheme for the development of the First Born and the lesser races of Mars is both ingenious and amusing. The buds on The Tree of Life were like large nuts, about a foot in diameter, and divided into four sections. "In one section grew the plant man, in another a sixteen-legged worm, in the third the progenitor of the white ape and in the fourth the primaeval black man of Barsoom." When the buds burst, the plant man remained attached to his stem, but the other three sections fell to the ground. The "imprisoned occupants," unsuccessful in their attempts to escape, had to content themselves, through countless ages, with merely hopping about in their shells. It was the black man, however, whose initiative and adventurous spirit led to the freeing of the "imprisoned occupants":

Countless billions died before the first black man broke through his prison walls into the light of day. Prompted by curiosity, he broke open other shells and the peopling of Barsoom commenced.

Ed has Xodar explain that the black man is the only *pure* man on Mars:

The pure strain of the blood of this first black man has remained untainted by admixture with other creatures in the race of which I am a member; but from the sixteen-legged worm, the first ape, and renegade black man has sprung every other form of animal life on Barsoom.

In a later section of "The Gods of Mars" the black men are described as a type of aristocracy: "We are a non-productive race, priding ourselves upon our non-productiveness. It is criminal for a First Born to labour or invent. That is the work of the lower orders, who live merely that the First Born may enjoy long lives of luxury and idleness."

Ed had not as yet finished with his structuring of the races. The First Born, who live in an inner world beneath the surface of Mars, maintain a system of slavery. "The places of the outer world and the temples of the therns have been robbed of their princesses and goddesses that the blacks might have their slaves." Ed goes into detail:

The First Born are all "noble." There is no peasantry among them. Even the lowest soldier is a god, and has his slaves to wait upon him.

The First Born do no work. The men fight—that is a sacred privilege and duty; to fight and die for Issus. The women do nothing, absolutely nothing. Slaves wash them, slaves dress them, slaves feed them. . . .

Other than the races of the First Born and therns, Ed, in "The Gods of Mars," created the plant men who learned to detach themselves from The Tree of Life before it died. They are bisexual like true plants and move about guided purely by instinct: ". . . The brain of a plant man is but a trifle larger than the end of your smallest finger." Curiously, the plant men's diet consists of both vegetation and the blood of animals: ". . . Their brain is just large enough to direct their movements in the direction of food, and to translate the food sensations which are carried to it from their eyes and ears. They have no sense of self-preservation and so are entirely without fear in the face of danger. That is why they are such terrible antagonists in combat."

Ed's invention of the Martian gods included the supreme deity, Issus. When John Carter is commanded to turn and gaze upon the "holy vision" of Issus' "radiant face," the sight is not at all what he had anticipated:

On this bench, or throne, squatted a female black. She was evidently very old. Not a hair remained upon her wrinkled skull. With the exception of two yellow fangs she was entirely toothless. On either side of her thin, hawklike nose her eyes burned from the depths of horribly sunken sockets. The skin of her face was seamed and creased with a million deepcut furrows. Her body was as wrinkled as her face, and as repulsive.

Emaciated arms and legs attached to a torso which seemed to be mostly distorted abdomen completed the "holy vision of her radiant beauty."

The name Issus obviously calls to mind the Egyptian deity Isis, also worshipped by the Greeks and Romans. (Ed's acquaintance with mythology has been previously mentioned. His "Lost Sea of Korus" may have resulted from some recollection of the son of Isis, by coincidence named Horus.)

Xodar, the First Born, convinced at last that he has been deceived, gives an evaluation of the false religion that may approximate Ed's philosophy:

The whole fabric of our religion is based upon superstitious belief in lies that have been foisted upon us for ages by those directly above us, to whose personal profit and aggrandizement it was to have us continue to believe as they wished us to believe.

Beyond the exciting plot and the invention of a complex civilization, Ed displayed an ability for vivid description; that he was able to construct colorful passages in a story written so quickly is quite remarkable. A number of these depict the bizarre Martian environment:

There is no twilight on Mars. When the great orb of day disappears beneath the horizon the effect is precisely as that of the extinguishing of a single lamp within a chamber. From brilliant light you are plunged without warning into utter darkness. Then the moons come; the mysterious, magic moons of Mars, hurtling like monster meteors low across the face of the planet.

His imaginative use of military tactics, based possibly upon his readings while at military school, and his descriptions of the massive forces engaged in battle at the climax of the story give "The Gods of Mars" a convincing reality. John Carter offers precise instructions for the deployment of the huge fleet of battleships of the air:

Form the balance of the battleships into a great V with the apex pointing directly south-south-east. Order the transports, surrounded by their convoys, to follow closely in the wake of the battleships until the point of the V has entered the enemies' line, then the V must open outward at the apex, the battleships of each leg engage the enemy fiercely and drive him back to form a lane through his line into which the transports with their convoys must race at top speed that they may gain a position above the temples and gardens of the therns.

The appeals and complaints of readers concerning the Burroughs proclivity for "suspended" endings could not persuade him to change this practice. The cliff-hanger fitted his particular sense of humor, and of course it was a commercial device planned for a sequel that was certain to follow. In "The Gods of Mars" he left his readers in suspense once more, creating an ending that in a few pages turned a glorious victory into a temporary defeat.

On October 9, 1912, he inquired about the story and admitted that he had forgotten to title the chapters, a task that he dreaded.[3] Metcalf, in accepting "The Gods of Mars" two days later, made it plain that he also viewed the job "with considerable sinking of heart," and on October 15 Ed obliged by sending a list of titles for twenty-two chapters, commenting, "Never again. I'd rather write a whole story."

At this early period in his writing career Burroughs had his first disappointing and annoying experience with an editor in the matter of the promised payment. He viewed his writing, in one sense, as no different from any job that required an investment in time and work; he was insistent upon fair payment, even as a beginner. Upon receiving Metcalf's check for "The Gods of Mars," he sent a blunt complaint:

You promised me at least 1c a word and the Lord knows that is little enough, by comparison with what other magazines pay. As I remember it there were 245 pages of Mss. It averaged from what I counted 12 words to the line and 30 lines to the page. Allowing ample deduction for chapter heads and ends I figured that 86,000 words was giving you good measure, but if you will send me a check for another $100.00 I shall be satisfied.[4]

He thanked Metcalf for sending him a number of readers' letters that had been published in "Table-Talk" and added, "Don't forget the balance of the letters when you are through with them. My father and mother fairly gloat over them. I think they may help with some publisher; am going to try it anyway."

Metcalf's reply contained an apology for having "forgotten" his word "in regard to that one cent a word stuff." He asked Ed's permission to "make up the deficit" on the next manuscript, promising to pay one cent a word for it and add $100 to that amount.

The *All-Story* for December 1912 followed its usual custom of publicizing the next issue. A box beneath the table of contents announced new works by William Patterson White and Edgar Rice Burroughs, explaining that "the latter has written a sequel to 'Under the Moons of Mars' and has called it 'The Gods of Mars.' " In "Table-Talk," Metcalf, using his informal chatty style and florid vocabulary, described Ed as "Battling" Burroughs and wrote enthusiastically of the forthcoming Martian serial: "The author's imagination again riots over the periphery of our terrestrial neighbor. Once more we play with thoats and snarks and so forth, and six-legged gents, and the scientific paraphernalia that can exist nowhere except on Mars, where, as we learn from our savants, 'they do those things better.' " Beginning in the January 1913 issue of *All-Story,* "The Gods of Mars" ran as a five-part serial and was completed in the May 1913 issue.[5]

During 1912, with all of Ed's intensive writing done in his spare time—he was still working for Shaw's *System* organization—he could not resist an experiment with another type of fiction, the short story. So far, his imagination had found its best outlet in the longer works; his interest in creating full settings, complex scientific details, and a large gallery of characters seemed to exclude him from more condensed writing. Early in the year he wrote a story of some 3,500 words titled "The Avenger," and followed this in the fall with "For the Fool's Mother," of about the same length and written in only two days. Ed, probably having become aware of the short story market, chose to avoid his fantasy themes and attempt to construct "down-to-earth" plots.

However, in "The Avenger" he devises a plot which at its climax becomes grim and repellent, and the actions of the main character have not been developed so as to make them logical or convincing.

In February 1912, probably for the first time, "The Avenger" was submitted to The Associated Sunday Magazines, a group that handled a feature section for various newspapers. An editor's letter of February 20 commented, " 'The Avenger' is both interesting and strong, but too gruesome to make a commendable feature of our Sunday Magazine. . . ." Sent out later in the year, the story was again rejected.[6]

Ed's second attempt at short story writing, a Western drama titled "For the Fool's Mother," was completed on October 5, 1912.[7] In a letter to Donald Kenicott of the Story-Press Corporation, Ed, on October 6, appeared undecided about the title, referring to his submission as "For the Mother of a Fool, or, For a Fool's Mother." He stated, "I have in mind a series of short stories, each complete in itself, with The Prospector as the principal character. I hope that you find this one in good form. . . ."

"For the Fool's Mother" is the first of Ed's stories to make actual reference to persons he had known, in this case to acquaintances of his Idaho cattle ranch days.[8]

Once more Ed returns to a feature he had reserved for several of his heroic characters. The Prospector is described as "straight, grey-eyed," and having "keen grey eyes"; of course the picture is familiar, recalling John Carter's "keen grey eyes," "undimmed" by time, and the steely *gray* eyes of Tarzan, Lord *Grey*stoke.[9]

In this period of feverish writing Burroughs was stretching his imagination to devise a plot for his sequel to *Tarzan of the Apes*. Again, a germ of the idea came from Metcalf, who on October 11, 1912, wrote:

I have been wondering whether it would not be possible to have him (Tarzan) after receiving his congé from the girl, make a stagger at being highly civilized in some effete metropolis, like London, Paris or New York, where he very quickly finds the alleged diversions of civilization to be only as ashes in his mouth.

After this, Metcalf suggested, Tarzan then returns to the jungle and tries unsuccessfully to find happiness there. As a result of frustration, he becomes erratic, even "develops extreme cruelty and runs the gamut of doing all kinds of almost insane things with the various animals and also with the blacks." Metcalf conceived of the idea of introducing a young woman who had been "marooned in the wilderness" and like Tarzan, had grown up to be a savage.

Apologetically, Metcalf remarked, "I don't offer this line of guff as anything more than a suggestion. It may be that you may find in it something which your superior ability might whip into shape. . . ."

242

On October 30 Ed submitted a rough outline of his sequel. Metcalf's idea about "some effete metropolis" had evidently taken root, for Ed referred to his sequel as "Monsieur Tarzan," a name he had already used in *Tarzan of the Apes,* and indicated that some of the action would take place in Paris. He had shown an interest in France and the French language in *Tarzan.* Lord Greystoke's diary, the only book Tarzan had been unable to read, was written in French. Lieutenant D'Arnot, of course, is given an important role, and, as a result, Tarzan's first spoken language is French; under D'Arnot's tutelage he takes on the polish of a French gentleman, and at a later period the full name on his personal card is *M. Jean C. Tarzan.*[10]

Concerning Ed's outline of the sequel, Metcalf was critical of the shipwreck or mutiny incidents. In "Tarzan" Ed twice devised mutinies to get his characters to an African shore. Now he proposed in his latest work to have two more similar incidents, one centered about Tarzan and Hazel Strong, and the other about Jane and Clayton. Metcalf referred tactfully to this device as being "overdone."[11]

Another of Ed's ideas received a firm rejection. "I am afraid that I must definitely taboo your suggestion concerning the cannibalism of the people in the boat where Jane and Clayton are," Metcalf wrote. "Really, now, that is going a little bit too far."[12] Worried that Ed was not giving the right emphasis to the "jungle" aspects of his sequel, Metcalf sent a follow-up letter with detailed instructions. He noted that the most popular incidents were those involving Tarzan's jungle adventures and commented, ". . . you ought to have no more actual civilization in the new story than you had in the old," adding farther on, ". . . the best thing to do would be to exactly reverse the main thread of the first story and instead of having the animal become civilized, have your plot deal very largely with the unhappy and necessarily unsatisfactory attempts of Tarzan to renounce his lately won civilization."[13]

Ed was quick to agree with Metcalf's analysis and on December 5 offered an outline of the sequel that was far more precise and detailed than his previous one. His intention was to develop one of his favorite ideas—an encounter with a "strange race" who inhabit the heart of Africa, living in the ruins of a former great city.[14]

At the close of the letter he wrote, "I have two other bully stories mulling around in my head. One of them has possibilities far beyond any I have yet written—I don't mean literary possibilities, but damphool possibilities. It will be based on an experiment in biology the result of which will be a real man and a real woman—not monsters. I have it practically all planned out in my head."[15]

Metcalf had continued to send him the readers' letters that poured in, most of them containing comments about "Tarzan." Concerning these, the editor remarked, "They come in so often and ask for more of your work that I am tempted to believe we had better call the magazine the 'All-Burroughs Magazine.' "[16]

The letters, especially those with protests about Ed's unfinished ending to "Tarzan," amused him and also stimulated the mischievous side of his nature. He viewed them with glee as a challenge for further teasing or tantalizing of the impatient readers. On December 20 he wrote:

There is so much reference to the "punk ending" that I am inclined to think that that is the very feature of the story that really clinched their interest. For two cents I'd give them another surprise in the sequel. I have a bully little Arab girl, daughter of a sheik, who is the only logical mate for a savage like Tarzan. I am just "thinking," however, and probably shall not do it, though it would be quite artistic.

He reported to Metcalf that the sequel was "progressing finely" and would soon be finished: "The result is that I am working about 25 hours a day, approximately."[17]

Through December 1912 and the first part of January Ed had worked hard on the long sequel. With its completion on January 8 he remained uncertain about the title. In his correspondence with Metcalf he had called the manuscript "Monsieur Tarzan"; now he titled it "The Ape-Man."[18] To the editor a day later he wrote, "The Ape-Man goes forward to you by express tomorrow. As you will see I have changed the name from what I at first purposed calling it—I never did like the other." He was not at all reticent about reminding Metcalf of the rates he had promised to pay and of the money that was still owed him from "The Gods of Mars."

He spoke of another "bully" letter he had received, one that praised "Tarzan" highly, and he commented, "Mrs. B. says I never will write another such story—cheerful, isn't it, for one who has only just started?"

In the remainder of the letter Ed turned to a problem which, even at this early period, loomed large in his mind and would contribute to the feeling of inadequacy that plagued him throughout his writing career. Oversensitive about what he conceived to be his deficiencies in English grammar, he was inclined to view this supposed weakness as a serious handicap to his writing. To Metcalf he wrote, "That reminds me of something that I have wanted to ask you about a number of times—I refer to my English. I imagine it is pretty rotten, and I wish that you would tell me frankly if you agree with me."

Ed then gave a resumé of what had happened in his school days; this was a topic that he would discuss again, often jokingly, in the future. The very fact that it kept recurring, even with a humorous emphasis, is an indication that it troubled him.

I never studied English grammar but a month in my life—while I was cramming for West Point. I was taken out of public school before I got that far, and sent to a private school here—the old Harvard School on Indiana avenue; you may recall it—where they had a theory that a boy should learn Greek and Latin grammar before he took up English grammar. Then before I got to English grammar I was sent to Andover, where I was supposed to have had English before I came, and started in on Greek and Latin again.

As a result, Ed noted, he had studied Latin for eight years and had never learned English. He described this process as "my notion of a bum way to educate a boy" and then inquired, "I have been thinking of getting hold of an English tutor. What do you think about it?"[19]

Metcalf, who could see no reason for Ed's concern, responded that there was nothing wrong with Ed's grammar; he didn't think it was worthwhile for Ed to find a tutor, stating, ". . . you did become a little too involved every once in a while when you tried to use archaic terms in 'The Outlaw of Torn,' but otherwise —no." He suggested that if Ed were to get a good rhetoric "like Sherman Adam Hill's," this might prove valuable; but he didn't believe that "anything more serious" was necessary.[20]

Ed found Metcalf's answer reassuring. He had expected that the editor's opinion "would not be colored by any fear of offending." In noting that a person naturally assumes his English to be good, Ed remarked, ". . . my trouble is that I don't *know*." In the same letter he sought Metcalf's advice about possible dealings with a book publisher; it appeared that a firm was about to offer him a contract for "Tarzan of the Apes." The firm was Reilly & Britton in Chicago, and Ed had just stopped into their offices to deliver some readers' letters.[21] Metcalf, on January 17, gave him information about royalties and publishers' contracts, but said nothing about the "Tarzan" sequel. Ed, who had previously described himself as a "bum waiter," could contain himself no longer. "Have you finished The Ape-Man?" he queried. "How do you like it? I am rapidly choking to death with curiosity."[22]

The bad news—what might have been described as a prelude to a rejection—came a few days later. On January 22 Metcalf wrote, ". . . I have read a great deal of 'The Ape-man' and I am very sorry to say that I am pretty doubtful so far. What I feel more than anything else is a kind of lack of balance. . . ." Ed was stunned. He had felt more certain of acceptance of "The Ape-Man" than anything else he had previously submitted. The editor's disapproval, equivalent to outright rejection, was sufficient to thrust him into the deepest gloom and depression. In his letter of January 24 his emotions vary from frustration and pessimism about the future to bitterness and self-condemnation:

Sorry you don't like the Ape-Man. I put a lot of work on it. Mapped it out carefully so that I was quite sure that it would be smooth and consistent. You approved of the plans, and I did not deviate from them except in such minor details as seemed necessary. I don't understand what you mean by "lack of balance".

There is so much uncertainty about the writing game—the constant feeling, for me at least, that I don't know how my stuff is going to hit you that I am entirely discouraged. I certainly can not afford to put months of work into a story thinking it the best work that I had ever done only to find that it doesn't connect. I can make money easier some other way.

In continuing, he referred to a letter from John S. Phillips of *The American Magazine* expressing interest in his work. Ed commented gloomily, "I presume that if I worked a couple of months on something for him he would come back with the 'not convincing' or 'lack of balance' dose." He concluded by blaming himself and rejecting the entire writing game:

That's the trouble, I can't tell that what I am writing is what the other fellow wants. I probably lack balance myself—a well balanced mind would not turn out my kind of stuff. As long as I can't market it as it comes out it is altogether too much of a gamble, so I think I'll chuck it.

As though the matter were all settled and his writing days were ended, Burroughs wrote in ironic humor, "Let me thank you once again for your many courtesies during the period of my incursion into litrachoor."[23]

The letter of John S. Phillips, Editor of *American Magazine,* dated January 21, had been quite complimentary; Ed was offered an opportunity in a publication of prestige whose payment rates were much higher than *All-Story:* "I have been interested for a long time in your stories. If you ever write any short stories or a short novelette of anywhere from 12 to 30,000 words. . . . You have a wonderful imagination. I would like to get some of it into the American magazine."

Ed of course hastened to reply to him. Meanwhile, Metcalf had sent a final rejection of "The Ape-Man," stating that after careful consideration he was "very much afraid" that he could not use it. "This makes me feel very bad," he wrote, "because of course I was very keen indeed, both for your sake, for mine and for the sake of all those insistent readers who wanted a sequel to 'Tarzan' . . ." On the same day, January 27, alarmed by Ed's complete pessimism and his intention to abandon his writing career, he dispatched another letter, brief and urgent, typed in capitals: "For the love of Mike! Don't get discouraged!"

Ed may have plunged into depths of discouragement for a short period, but it was not his nature to brood over misfortune or failure. Although he possessed all of the basic uncertainties of a beginning writer, he still managed to preserve elements of confidence in his ability and judgement. To him the only response to discouragement was to find some sort of positive action. As far as he was concerned, Metcalf had been given a chance, had refused it, and now the time had come to try a new market. On January 24 he wrote to Street & Smith, describing the enthusiastic reception *Tarzan of the Apes* had received, and offering them the sequel. He added frankly, "Another consideration which prompts me to write you is that I understand that your rates are higher than those paid by the *All-Story.*"

Street & Smith showed an immediate interest. Their letter of February 8, sent shortly after they received "The Ape-Man," was one that justified Ed's faith in his sequel. The price they proposed to pay, an indication of the story's value, was far in excess of any amount he had dreamed of. From A. L. Sessions, Editor of Street & Smith's *New Story Magazine,* came an offer of $1000 for first serial rights. Ed accepted two days later.

"The Return of Tarzan" opens with a skillful use of the *in medias res* device: unintroduced characters, the Count and Countess de Coude, are conversing aboard an ocean liner that is three days out from New York and en route to Paris. ERB launches immediately into the development of Paris as the "effete metropolis" that Metcalf had suggested. The story contains the first of the foreign villains to appear in Burroughs' works; in this case they are the Russians, Nikolas Rokoff and Alexis Paulvitch, villains, without any redeeming features.

The indictment of the civilized society is resumed, with Tarzan, the simple jungle creature, baffled by the peculiarities of human behavior. Later, Tarzan encounters the Arab tribal chief, Sheik Kadour ben Saden, and in the Sheik and his "stern and dignified warriors" he discovers people he deeply admires.

In a criticism of society, Ed took the occasion to express his philosophy about hunting and to reveal his intense feelings about the indiscriminate killing of animals: "The ape-man could see no sport in slaughtering the most harmless and defenseless of God's creatures for the mere pleasure of killing." Tarzan pretended to hunt, but allowed the gazelles to escape: ". . . to come out of a town filled with food to shoot down a soft-eyed, pretty gazelle —ah, that was crueller than the deliberate and cold-blooded murder of a fellow man."

In the tentative outline of "The Return of Tarzan" Metcalf had disapproved of the incident involving cannibalism. Nevertheless, Ed created a lengthy section (later titled "The Lottery of Death") in which Jane and Clayton, adrift in a lifeboat with the villainous Rokoff and sailors from the *Lady Alice,* await the prospect of cannibalism in helpless horror as each day brings it nearer. The cannibalism is fortunately averted, and the two are saved with the arrival of rain and the discovery of land.

The plot of "The Return of Tarzan" posed a special problem, previously discussed by Metcalf, in what might be described as "civilization-to-jungle logistics." The perplexing question was how to get both Tarzan and Jane back to the coast of Africa and do it without reverting to the old ship's mutiny device. A temporary sojourn in Paris was necessary, but Tarzan must be returned to his primitive surroundings. The public demanded it; the ape-man without his jungle became nonfunctional and, more importantly, unsalable. It was at once obvious that the most fertile imagination could not create anything original: Tarzan and Jane must board ships in order to arrive in Africa. The best Ed could do was to have the *Lady Alice,* carrying Jane and Clayton, wrecked in a collision with a derelict. And Tarzan, en route from Algiers to Capetown by steamer, is tumbled overboard by the villains Rokoff and Paulvitch.

Retitled "The Return of Tarzan," the story was typical, fast-moving Burroughs. According to some critics it was marred by several instances of Burroughs' use of improbable coincidences. While these coincidental devices, exhibited also in Ed's later works, are weak links in his plots and are subject to criticism, they should be viewed with a consideration of his writing practices and the philosophy he chose to adopt. Possibly, a slower writing pace might have led to longer reflection and resulted in plotting that was more ingenious and convincing. But this is idle speculation; it was not Ed's nature to write slowly. In the matter of his philosophy, or attitude toward writing, his earliest published story, "Under the Moons of Mars," provides a good basis for deductions. The opening events—John Carter's mystic, unscientific, and unexplained journey or transmigration through space—are an indication of Ed's belief that the reader of his works would be entirely capable of accepting certain events *without explanation,* especially within the context or framework that Ed constructed. The reader received sufficient reward and stimulation from the amazingly imaginative plots and settings to compensate for any lapses into repetition, contrived devices, and coincidences.

On one occasion Ed preferred to view these illogical story elements humorously, commenting to his brother Harry about the supposedly scientific environment of Mars:

I had already read Dr. Abbot's pathetic theory relative to the inhabitability of Mars. If you will kindly compare his sources of information with mine you will readily see that there is no argument whatsoever.

He guesses *that Mars is nearly one hundred degrees colder than earth; he* guesses *that there is practically no water vapor in the atmosphere; he* guesses *therefore that Mars cannot support either vegetable or animal life. On the other hand, I have not had to guess, having had presented to me in manuscript form the unquestioned evidence of an actual observer of Martian conditions.*

If this statement does not entirely clear away your doubts, permit me to very respectfully refer you to His Royal Highness, John Carter, Prince of Helium and War Lord of Mars.[24]

For "The Return of Tarzan" Ed prepared his customary work sheet; in this case he did not include a glossary but merely listed characters not appearing in "Tarzan of the Apes" and matched the chapters and their headings with the manuscript page numbers. An unusual addition, attached to the work sheet, is Ed's "Sketch Map of Eastern Algeria for use with The Ape-Man." His source was apparently a relief map of Algeria, and Ed reproduced the northeast corner of the country with its cities,

George Tyler Burroughs,
Sr., October 13, 1903.

villages, and mountains. This marked the first of many maps Burroughs drew in his working notebook to assist him in his desire for accuracy, believability, and consistency in his stories. His maps of both hemispheres of Barsoom (Mars) demonstrate the care and detail involved. For some stories he sketched the bizarre animals he had created; in others he invented the languages, alphabets, and numbers. He dotted in the course of the railway from Constantine to Biskra. Towns mentioned in the story, including Bouira, Aumale, Bou Saada, and Djelfa are shown on his map, and Ed even entered the names of the hotels at which Tarzan stopped—the Hotel Grossat in Aumale and the Hotel du Petit Sahara in Bou Saada, both of these hotels marked as being in "garrison towns." With his usual meticulousness Ed noted the completion date as "Jan. 8 1913—9 P.M."

Metcalf, in rejecting "The Ape-Man," had commented about its "lack of balance"; his use of this vague phrase had baffled Ed, since in writing the story he had twice submitted outlines, making changes to incorporate the editor's ideas, and had finally in a letter of December 10, 1912, received Metcalf's unqualified approval of the plot.[25] However, the "lack of balance" may have been a justifiable evaluation by Metcalf if, as appears probable, he was referring to the abrupt introduction of a new setting and series of episodes late in the story. The Waziri's description of a "ruined city of gold" spurs Tarzan into a journey to Opar, but the adventures that follow, the encounters with the crooked-legged, hairy Oparians and the meeting with the Priestess La, do not relate to the theme already established. They give the appearance of a subplot, in this case one that departs too widely from the preceding actions and characters and tends to create an effect of disunity. This brief new section, inserted toward the end of the story, might better have been saved for the opening of another novel.[26]

Circumstances at home were altered during the month of February 1913 as a result of two important occurrences—one happy and the other tragic. On February 28 the Burroughs' third child, a boy, was born. There could be no doubt about the choice of a name. *John* was the name Ed most admired; he had made that clear in his creation of John Carter of Mars and in his famous John Clayton, Lord Greystoke. He had often expressed regret at not having been named John instead of Edgar. Even in later years, on January 10, 1939, he mentioned this to his brother Harry: ". . . I don't blame you for dropping the Henry. I should like to drop Edgar; but it is too late now. I always wanted to be named John, which is one reason why I named one of my boys John. . . ." Also chosen from an ancestral line, Coleman became the child's middle name.

The $1,000 windfall for the sale of "The Return of Tarzan" to *New Story Magazine* was opportune; certainly, now, more than ever, Ed, convinced that he must soon leave Shaw's *System,* could use money.

Earlier in the month, on February 15, George Tyler Burroughs, age seventy-nine, had died. About his death, Evelyn Burroughs, Harry's daughter, commented:

I will always believe that he died of a broken heart. He was nearly eighty—had seen one fortune go after many years of prosperity, but pulled himself out of that failure and was doing well with the American Battery Company. There, at the last he found that one of the distillery company partners had been over a number of years bilking him out of what should have been his, if he hadn't been so trusting. He went to bed, refused to eat, and just died. His doctor told us later he had put "heart failure" on the death certificate because there wasn't a thing organically wrong with him, and he didn't want to falsify the record.

Ed's fond recollections of his father, and the appreciation and understanding of a parent that time and maturity often bring to a son, were evidenced in a practice that Ed later followed. An October 13 entry in his diary was made regularly; it might read, "Father's birthday today," or, as noted in a 1940 entry, "My father was born in Warren, Mass. 107 years ago today."

Major Burroughs, once doubtful that his son Ed would amount to anything, had lived to witness the launching of his writing career. The sale of "Under the Moons of Mars," followed by the spectacular success of "Tarzan of the Apes," made apparent by the furor it caused and the flood of readers' letters—Ed's statement that "My father and mother fairly gloat over them" indicated that George had read the letters avidly—surely swept away much of the Major's pessimism and gave him hope for his son's future.

Ed's jubilance over the sale of "The Return of Tarzan" was countered by an unexpected reaction from Metcalf, one that appeared to have no reasonable basis. The editor's letter was indignant and accusing:

I must say that I was nonplussed upon first hearing that Street and Smith had bought the Tarzan sequel. It struck me as fairly incredible, but then your letter came and settled the matter. I realise, of course, that you were quite justified in disposing of the manuscript, wherever you may have chosen, but somehow your course of action doesn't strike me as having been more than friendly.[27]

Metcalf displayed petulance and an inclination to take the matter personally: "I wonder if you weren't a little disgruntled at what you considered my unkind criticism and determined to show me. Well, you did." The sale of the "Tarzan" sequel, as far as he was concerned, did not indicate it was a well-constructed story: "I am also pretty certain that I did your literary reputation more good by rejecting the story than Street and Smith will have done by publishing it. I don't mean to be nasty, I really believe this."

At the close of the letter Metcalf returned again to his concept of fair dealings and friendship:

I suppose it was my appreciation of your real ability that made me what you doubtless consider commercially stupid. But it is too bad you couldn't see your way to working the story over and giving us—and me incidentally—not alone a square deal, but even more than a square deal. That's what friendly relationships amount to, anyway.

If Metcalf was "nonplussed" and "struck fairly incredible" over the sale, Ed was, in turn, astounded and bewildered over the editor's response. In his letter of March 1 he displayed far more tact than Metcalf had, and in fact, attempted to be conciliatory:

. . . It is so difficult to put things on paper and make them sound just as we would really say them face to face that I am trying to pound it in my thick skull that you actually had no intention of really making that letter carry the impression to me that the first reading did.

If you had said that I was a dummy, and a boob, and a plain damn fool, and didn't know when I was well off, or what was best for me, I might have been mad; but I shouldn't have been hurt.

Ed then proceeded with cold logic, point by point, to demonstrate to Metcalf that there was no reasonable basis for his attitude. To begin with, it was only because of his friendship for the editor that he submitted "The Ape-Man" to *All-Story*—otherwise it would have been sent to a different magazine. "I know that you have paid me a very low rate for my stories," Ed stated, and it would have been "only good business" for him to have tried another magazine, but he had not done so because he believed that in all fairness, Metcalf should have "first crack" at the story.

Ed was no doubt thinking of the exhausting hours of work he had spent on *The Outlaw of Torn,* to no avail, when he demanded:

Isn't it rather unjust to accuse me of unfriendliness because I sold to another magazine a story that you had refused, and criticized as ruthlessly as you did The Ape-Man? As a matter of fact wouldn't you think a man crazy who spent a month or more in rewriting a story for you without the slightest guarantee that you would like the second version any better than the first, when he could sell the original mss for more than he could get from you for the rewritten story?

As a further point Ed stressed the fact that Street & Smith was satisfied to buy the first serial rights only and that inquiries had already been made about syndication of the story. "I should hate to lose your friendship," Ed wrote, "and I don't think I shall. You were a bit sore when you wrote that letter, and you hadn't done very much thinking about the matter *from my side.*" Ed noted an obvious fact, one Metcalf must have recognized, concerning the line of separation between friendship and business: "You don't take my stories because of friendship—you take them because you think they are good buys. I am not writing stories because of friendship—I am writing because I have a wife and three children."

Metcalf's letter conveyed an impression that the editor believed Ed was gloating over his sale. Ed denied this, pointing out that although he had received an offer from Street & Smith for "The Ape-Man" on February 10, he had not told Metcalf about it until twelve days later. This was hardly the action of a "gloating" man.[28]

In Ed's dealings with Metcalf and the Munsey Company his future problems would be similar to the ones he had already encountered, mainly relating to amounts or rates of payment. He had determined to search for other markets. Responding on January 23 to the interest shown by John S. Phillips, editor of the *American Magazine,* Ed sought more definite information. Concerning possible submissions to the magazine, he explained that he had written only long novelettes of from seventy to a hundred thousand words. He felt he knew pretty well now what his readers liked: ". . . it is as easy for me to write one of these long stories as it would be to write half as many words in a number of short stories." Phillips had inquired about stories of less than thirty-thousand words.

Ed admitted that he wished to "enlarge" his market and "graduate into the better grade magazines," but he was not clear as to the type of story Phillips wanted. "For example—was it one of the Martian Stories or the ape-man story which struck your fancy?" he inquired. He described his latest work, even more apologetic than usual about its fantastic theme:

I happen to be working now on a very improbable type of yarn along the line of the Martian stuff. It is so wildly ridiculous that I am quite sure you would not care for it—yet I have worked it out so in accordance with known scientific facts that it sounds reasonable.

If there was a chance that it might appeal to *American* readers, Ed noted, he might be able to condense it to the desired length.

In his reply Phillips stated, "I don't know that I liked your ape-man story any more than your Martian stories. I have simply been taken with the imagination you show. I would like to see anything you do."[29] A few days later Ed sent a section of "The Inner World" that he had just completed and included an explanation:

The drawings which accompany it I made before I commenced the story—while I was thinking it out. I had in mind what they would prove helpful to the artist who did the illustrating, and I am including them with what I send you that the creatures in the text may seem more real.

I can complete the story inside of 30,000 words, or less. I should prefer to do it in less, if possible.[30]

From the start of the correspondence it is doubtful that Phillips was giving serious consideration to Ed's writings. Nothing of this type had ever appeared in the conservative *American,* and its readers would have reacted with shock or bewilderment if they had discovered "The Inner World" in their magazine. Phillips took only a few days to return the story, stating, in his letter of February 4, "I am hurrying back to you your story. It's got all the wonderful imagination in it that you show in your others. . . . It is just a little unbridled for us for a serial. . . . Won't you let me see the next thing you do?" Ed had not allowed himself to be over-expectant. "It was no surprise to me that you found it unavailable," he wrote, "though of course I hoped that you *might* decide in its favor."[31]

Ed's blunt answer to Metcalf had a salutary effect, for in a letter of March 7 the editor displayed a cautious and diplomatic attitude. "Let us allow this matter to drop and start all over again," he said. His proposal now was that he was willing to accept a payment plan which Ed might suggest, a plan that would guarantee Metcalf a first refusal on Ed's novels and would provide for a reasonable amount of revision. Ed replied promptly, referring to other demands for his work—those from Street & Smith, and the *American Magazine,* and also requests for syndication. "Under these circumstances," he wrote, "I should think that 5c a word for the first refusal on my novels, with the right to one reasonable revision, would be fair. This to give you the serial rights and leave the other rights in my hands. The arrangement to be in force for one year from the date of your acceptance."[32]

Metcalf's return offer was two cents a word for first serial rights only. Ed, surprisingly, compromised at once, writing, "I accept your proposition under date of March 14th for my 1913 crop." He reported another matter of interest to him: "Mr. Reilly, of Reilly & Britton, has asked me to compete in their ten thousand dollar prize novel contest. Of course there isn't one chance in ten million that I could win out in it, but I should like to have your permission to enter a mss. . . ."[33]

While Metcalf had no objection to his entering the novel contest, Ed very quickly lost his enthusiasm. At a later date he commented to Metcalf, "Quit in the middle of my $10,000.00 prize story. Realized the futility of attempting to compete in a field so far removed from my own as is Mr. Reilly's ideal. Have been writing one of my own kind of stories since, and expect to send it on for your amiable consideration soon."[34]

Ed's awareness of money-making opportunities in another area—that of newspaper syndication—was sharpened by events that occurred early in 1913. In the sale of his stories he had at first relinquished all serial rights to the Munsey Company. This included "Tarzan of the Apes," "A Princess of Mars," and "The Gods of Mars." At a later date, through an unexplained oversight, he sold all serial rights to "The Inner World."

The Munsey Company had arranged with the New York *Evening World* for the serialization of "Tarzan of the Apes," and with the appearance of successive installments, beginning on January 6, 1913, the popularity of Tarzan created an eager market in other newspapers.[35] To Ed the possibilities for syndication of his future works became quickly apparent. An opportunity first came in a letter of inquiry, dated February 25, from Albert Payson Terhune, editor of the *Evening World*:

We have been running your "Tarzan of the Apes" as a serial. It has been extremely popular with our readers; and we would like to make arrangements for newspaper serial publication of its sequel, after its appearance in a magazine.

If you have in mind any story of similar vein to "Tarzan"—with the scene laid in the jungle or possessing some equally unusual interest—please send such story or scenario of it for our consideration. . . .[36]

In the resulting correspondence Terhune agreed to purchase the New York City newspaper serial rights for "The Ape-Man." On March 15 he wrote, "For these, Mr. Tennant, the managing editor, commissions me to offer you $300. This is just six times the sum we paid the Munsey Company for 'Tarzan of the Apes'. . . ." Ed's acceptance of course was prompt. The vision of a nationwide syndicated outlet for his stories led to his insistence upon one type of sales contract: magazine editors could purchase *first serial rights only*.[37] Through inexperience he had surrendered the lucrative rights to "Tarzan of the Apes." There had been no demand for the syndication of his "Mars" stories, but he intended to take the necessary precautions with future works.

With syndication on his mind, it occurred to him that perhaps the serial rights to *Tarzan* had not been sold to a Chicago newspaper. His attempts to obtain these rights from the Munsey Company were unsuccessful, but not at all deterred he proceeded with his plan to syndicate "The Ape-Man" and other works, using the list of "Tarzan" newspapers he had obtained from Metcalf.[38] Terhune and the *Evening World* were his most important contacts. In May he wrote to Terhune to request his check for "The Ape-Man," commenting, "I see that The New Story is running it as The Return of Tarzan, which I think is very good. . . ."[39] The story ran as a seven-part serial from June through December 1913. But in the same month he also contacted the *Cleveland Press,* explaining:

"The Return of Tarzan" will be ready for newspaper publication about the first of August. . . . I am getting about six times as much for The Return of Tarzan as was paid for Tarzan of the Apes; but those who have read the mss think it a better story; and there is unquestionably a very considerable demand for it. . . .[40]

Other sales to the *Evening World* would follow. Unfortunately, in the case of "The Inner World," which Ed sent to Metcalf on February 6, he wrote, ". . . the magazine rights which I wish to sell." The payment of $420 covered all rights. About a week earlier Metcalf had rejected "The Ape-Man," and this rejection had thrust Ed into a state of insecurity and depression. This may have weakened his confidence in "The Inner World" and made him hesitant about insisting upon first serial rights only.[41]

Continuing reader comments about his story endings were a source of amusement and stimulation to Ed, but in his letter of February 22, 1913, to Metcalf he made an astute observation clearly based upon his analysis of these endings. That he believed they had a significant value was revealed in his statement that ". . . the unsatisfactory ending left much to the readers imagination—it forced him to create a story after his own liking—it made him think more about the story than as though the ending had been satisfactory and commonplace, and so it made the story its own press agent."

In the same letter he reported to the editor that for his next story he was "having a little fun with higher education," and then followed with a brief summary of the plot:

A young man from Bosting is cast ashore somewhere. He is all intellect. Falls in with a bunch of cliff dwellers—aboriginal men and women. Accident throws him with a young female. She is strong, husky and intellectual as a she ape. He is a physical weakling filled with the knowledge of an encyclopaedia. Yet circumstances, environment and the laws of sex find her the brains and him the brawn of the combination. I am having a lot of fun with it.

It is worth noting that the plot does not follow the expected and unoriginal path but rather takes a surprising and ingenious direction.

Now able to joke about Metcalf's rejection of "The Ape-Man" —he had sold it for a good price in spite of the editor's diagnosis that it "lacked balance"—Ed offered to submit this latest work if Metcalf would "promise not to say that 'it is not convincing,' or 'lacks balance.' " Ed wrote, "Just fire it back quick if you don't like it."[42]

On March 22, the story titled "The Cave Girl," was sent to Metcalf. It was a novelette, about the same length as "The Inner World," and in his letter Ed stipulated, "If you take it please see that the endorsement on check covers no more than 1st serial rights." A few months later, after publication, he forwarded "The Cave Girl" to Terhune, who commented, "I have read it with considerable interest. In parts it is *almost* as good as 'Tarzan of the Apes'. . . ."[43]

For some time Ed had been struggling to arrive at a decision about his future. He had been dubious about the writing field as a full-time occupation and as a source of regular income, but the successive sales led him to change his mind. On a number of occasions he had asked his brother Harry to read his stories and had also sought Harry's advice. His brother had been enthusiastic about the stories, but in the consideration of whether Ed should quit his job and concentrate on writing, Harry advised against this step; to him it seemed too much of a gamble. But there never had been any question of Ed's willingness to gamble.[44]

In his *Autobiography* Ed noted that with the birth of his third child, John Coleman, he had decided to give up his job with Shaw's *System* and devote himself to writing. "Everyone, including myself, thought I was an idiot," he wrote, "but I had written five stories and sold four, which I felt was a good average, and I knew that I could write a great many more stories."

Further correspondence with Terhune of the *Evening World* brought Ed an understanding of the difficulties he would encounter in an effort to syndicate his stories nationally. Business matters involving one newspaper only, *The World,* made a steady exchange of letters necessary. All of this consumed Ed's writing time. In addition, the inquiries that came from all parts of the country included requests for quotations of charges. Here, Ed was at a loss; he had no idea what an acceptable charge should be. The greatest newspaper demands were for the serialization of "The Return of Tarzan." In this connection he sought Terhune's advice, writing:

I have been asked to quote on the newspaper serial rights for Cleveland, Cincinnati, Toledo, Akron, Columbus, Des Moines, Oklahoma City, Denver, Memphis, and Los Angeles; and I have no idea what to ask. I presume that the price would be governed largely by either the population of the city in question or the circulation of the newspaper. Can't you help me out—I shall certainly appreciate it.[45]

Ed, overambitious, had maneuvered himself into an impossible position. To even imagine the difficulties he now faced, one should remember that he had no office, was operating out of a crowded apartment on 2008 Park Avenue shared by his wife and three small children, and that, at the same time, he was attempting to maintain his incredible output of stories. Both "The Inner World" and "The Cave Girl" had been completed in the period between January 9, and March 22, 1913. Recognizing that the situation was beyond him, he decided to find an agency to handle the newspaper syndication. On May 26 he informed Terhune of this decision:

I have turned the handling of the newspaper syndicating over to the International Press Bureau, after a talk with Mr. W. G. Chapman, their president. This for The Return of Tarzan exclusive of New York City. At first he wouldn't consider it when he learned that I had personally handled the sale of the New York City newspaper rights.

Terhune had indicated an interest in "The Cave Girl," recently purchased by Metcalf, and in the same letter Ed wrote, "The Cave Girl mss will go forward to you as soon as I get it back from my mother who has been reading it." He also requested information about Ralph Danenhower of the Associated Publishers Syndicate Service, who had offered to handle "The Return of Tarzan."[46]

For some time Ed had been keeping a close count of the number of words in each story, in some cases actually listing the page numbers and totaling the words on the page. This was undoubtedly caused by the rate of payment problem he had already experienced with Metcalf. Payment, of course, was by the word, and Ed's care in counting obviously indicated his suspicion of an "under-count." In his letter to April 4 to Metcalf he acknowledged receipt of $600 for "The Cave Girl" and then demanded, "Howinel do you figure the number of words? By the most conservative estimate I cannot make it as little as 30,000. What's to be done about it? . . ."

Metcalf replied that he had totaled the word count by the same method he had used for "The Inner World," allowing an average of 320 words to a page, thus making for 89 pages, "not very much over 30,000 words."[47] Concerning the entire matter of counting, Ed, a month later commented to Metcalf that it had not been fair for him to assign the task of computing words entirely to the editor and then complain when the tallies did not agree. He indicated his future plan to list the exact number of words at the time the story was submitted.[48] Ed's meticulous work sheets, containing lists and descriptions of characters, tables, maps, and glossaries of terms, often included page-by-page word counts.

The agreement with William G. Chapman of the International Press Bureau in Chicago was finalized in Chapman's letter of June 3, 1913. Ed retained his responsibility for operations in New York and for the syndication of "The Return of Tarzan" in all other areas; Chapman's organization was to pay Ed a royalty each month of sixty percent of the gross sales. The next work for syndication, handled by Chapman later that year, was "The Cave Girl."[49]

In the midst of Ed's heavy writing schedule he still found time to aid Metcalf in a scheme the editor had devised for his "Table Talk" column. Metcalf had often referred to the cheerful and carefree manner in which his *All-Story* authors promised him the stories he requested, as though the writing of these stories was a simple and easy task. In reality, of course, the editor wrote, the writer was "sweating blood over a typewriter and hoping to goodness that he was going to be able to get this story to me." Metcalf proposed that his writers send in humorous letters refuting his cheerful account and "explaining how really sad is an author's life and how cruel an editor."[50] Ed, on February 26, sent in his humorous letter; headed "From the Man Who Knows

Mars," it appeared in "Table-Talk" of May 1913. He joked about the "natural inference . . . that writers associate, on terms of equality, with editors," exaggerating the relationship to make it seem just the opposite—that writers occupy a lofty position which editors find unapproachable. In the "Table-Talk" letter Ed complains about the treatment of his man James who delivers the manuscripts to the editor and is kept waiting for the check "as long as ten minutes." Ed adds, "I do not wish to appear harsh, but I must insist that this must not occur again—James' time is very valuable."[51]

The cover designs of the October 1912 *All-Story* containing "Tarzan of the Apes" and of the June 1913 *New Story* with "The Return of Tarzan" had drawn Ed's interest and admiration. On June 1 he wrote to Metcalf to inquire whether he could purchase the original of the *All-Story* cover from the artist, Clinton Pettee: "I am to get the one illustrating the sequel and I thought I should like to have them both. If you will find out the price that is wanted, and let me know, I'll be thankful."

At the same time he addressed a letter to A. L. Sessions, Editor of *New Story,* concerning the purchase of N. C. Wyeth's illustration. Metcalf, in his response of June 10, wrote in bold ink across the top of the page, "This is absolutely unofficial," and went on to explain that after consulting the Art Editor, he had learned that it was "the custom of the house" to sell these originals for fifty percent of the cost. In this case the asking price would be fifty dollars:

I believe, however, and of course this is strictly entre nous, that we would entertain an offer of $25.00, so if you feel at all interested you might write me a letter, very ingenuously pretending that I have not written to you, as I am now doing, and suggest that you would like to buy the cover in question if you could have it for $25.00.

My methods may seem peculiar, but I have adopted them only after considerable cogitation and discussion.

Ed's hope of purchasing the *New Story* original was not, however, to be realized. Wyeth's price, stated by Sessions on June 4, was $100, more than Ed could afford. He responded to Sessions, "I want to thank you for the trouble you have taken relative to the cover design by Mr. Wyeth. I am afraid, however, that Mr. Wyeth wants it worse than I do, so I shall be generous and let him keep it."[52] His inability to buy the Wyeth design appeared to discourage Ed, for on June 14 he wrote to Metcalf explaining that he had wanted the two cover illustrations as

"The Return of Tarzan" cover of New Story Magazine, *August 1913; illustrated by N. C. Wyeth, father of A. Wyeth.*

"companion pictures," and since he could not pay Wyeth's price, he had decided "to let the matter drop entirely."

Ed would have needed mystic powers as fantastic as any of those possessed by his creatures of other worlds to even dream that the matter of the Wyeth illustration, seemingly buried and forgotten, would rise from the past. Some fifty-two years later an astonishing postscript was to be written to the Wyeth affair.[53]

Ed's success in selling his stories had stimulated the ambitions of Ella (Nellie) Burroughs, Harry's wife. Her creative interest had been known to the family for some time, and she had shown both imagination and ability in her poems and stories. Her fictional themes were not of any world of fantasy comparable to Ed's, but dealt rather with human relationships, simple characterizations, and realistic settings. In her long story, "The Bride," appearing in 1913 in the popular magazine *The Metropolitan,* she creates a situation in which a delicate, protected Southern girl finds herself, as a young wife, abruptly transferred to a ranch in a rough frontier area. Here, Ella may have been recalling her own Southern background and her unanticipated experiences after she had married Harry and moved with him to Idaho where she faced a difficult adjustment to life in a primitive country.

As a writer Ella displays a skill in description and in the development of atmosphere, but beyond this she reveals an unusual sensitivity in painting the intense feelings, the inner struggle, of the bewildered young bride. For the bride's artist son, Ella's model was obviously her son Studley and in this creation she was expressing all her hopes for his future. Studley was then displaying an interest in drawing and painting and would later illustrate some of the Burroughs books.

In the summer of 1913, possibly at her request, Ed sent a group of her stories to Thomas Metcalf. While there is no record of his evaluation, it is possible that Ella's stories did not contain sufficient elements of action and of excitement or adventure to meet *All-Story*'s requirements.[54]

Ed's relationship with Metcalf had developed through the constant correspondence into a warm association, almost as though the two were personal friends. Much of this feeling had resulted from a mutual informality of their natures which was expressed in the free-and-easy style used by both in their letters. A first meeting took place when Ed spent two days in New York—July 30 and 31 of 1913. Burroughs' purpose in making the trip, in addition to meeting Metcalf, was to confer with the editor about future stories.[55]

Continuing his intensive writing schedule, Ed had completed an unusual story which had been stored in a corner of his mind for some time; months before, in writing to Metcalf, he had spoken of it as based upon a biological experiment.[56] On May 20, in mailing it to the editor, he titled the story "Number Thirteen." His work sheet listed the starting and completion dates as March 31 and May 10, 1913.[57] Almost immediately he set to work on a sequel to "The Gods of Mars" which both Metcalf and the *All-Story* readers had been demanding. He titled it "The Prince of Helium" and in sending it to Metcalf on July 6, described it as "the last of the John Carter Martian stories."

I hope the ending will suit everybody—especially you.
. . . Am not sure that you will find the title commercially fit. I had difficulty in finding one to suit me. First I called it The Yellow Men of Barsoom; but that didn't describe the story. I also thought of The Fighting Prince of Mars, and The War Lord of Barsoom. How would something like Across Savage Mars do?
Well, if you like the story, and I hope you will, you can dope out your own title—my think tank is exhausted.[58]

Metcalf himself was responsible for Ed's undertaking an additional writing chore. The editor felt that "The Inner World" deserved expansion; he commented to Ed that "the reptilian part

. . . could stand a lot of alteration and the whole story could be made very much more interesting . . ." He wondered whether Ed "might not add 10,000 or 15,000 more words to the middle of that story and deal with these peculiar over-sensitized lizards so that the great reading public might satisfactorily shudder. . . ." Ed quickly agreed to make the changes.[59]

During the spring and summer of 1913 Ed's efforts to find a book publisher for "Tarzan of the Apes" continued, but without success. Reilly & Britton of Chicago had held the story since November 1912, and Ed had remained hopeful because of Reilly's encouraging attitude. But this lengthy period of consideration brought no result. Ed's brief comment, written beneath the Reilly & Britton letter acknowledging receipt of the story, supplies the details: "March 4 1913—By phone Mr. Reilly explained that the syndication of Tarzan of the Apes by the N.Y. World had killed it for their purposes." The lack of vision displayed by this firm and others who had viewed "Tarzan" as a poor risk is difficult to understand. It is also difficult to understand how the syndication of "Tarzan" which created a nationwide demand for the story could have destroyed its value. On May 23 Ed left a copy of the story at Rand McNally & Company in Chicago. His memorandum read, "Submitted Tarzan of the Apes to Mr. Clow. . . . Was to have decision in about ten days." Worried about whether the company was aware of the growing demand for "Tarzan," Ed four days later sent a follow-up letter with a lengthy sales talk. Addressed to H. B. Clow, the letter first described the intense interest in the "Tarzan" sequel:

The newspaper syndicating of the sequel ("The Return of Tarzan") has been placed with the International Press Bureau, 1st National Bank bldg., and two other syndicating companies have also asked me for these rights although the story will not be available for them before November 15th. Over three months ago the New York Evening World solicited the New York City rights, and I sold them these for $300.00 (their own figure), which I understand is a rather good figure.

Neither *The World* nor the syndicating companies had read "The Return of Tarzan," Ed pointed out, and the fact that they were eager to take it sight unseen was ample evidence of "Tarzan's" popularity. In closing Ed wrote, "If you would care to see the letters of comment from readers, and the correspondence relative to the newspaper rights to the sequel I shall be glad to bring them down at any time you suggest."

Clow responded briefly on June 3, "I have read your story 'Tarzan of the Apes.' Will be pleased to talk with you on the subject at your leisure." Once again a publisher had no confidence in "Tarzan's" success as a novel. On August 20, 1913, Rand McNally & Company returned the story, offering nothing more than a conventional statement of rejection: "We have given the work careful consideration and while interesting we find it does not fit in with our plans for the present year."

In another area, that of sales of stories to Albert Payson Terhune and the *New York World,* Ed was having some success. Terhune explained that both he and the general manager, J. H. Tennant, liked "The Cave Girl," adding, ". . . we like all your stuff that we've read. Mr. Tennant wants to keep on using your stories and to see any new ones you may turn out." The *World*'s offer for "The Cave Girl" was $200, and Terhune wrote, "Unofficially, let me say that $200 is the largest sum we have paid for any serial, except 'The Return of Tarzan,' for a long time."[60] Ed, in accepting, commented, ". . . I feel that I owe you a great deal for the bully treatment you accorded me when I was entirely new to the game."[61]

During July and August he began two new stories, "The Girl from Harris's" and "The Mucker." In what appeared to be a change of pace and setting, he temporarily left the world of fantasy to deal with earth-bound characters in familiar situations. Probably for material needed in "The Girl from Harris's" he contacted John McWeeny, the general superintendent of the Chicago Police Department, who in turn gave him a letter of introduction to Lieutenant W. R. Darrow of the 2nd District: "This will introduce Mr. Edgar Rice Burroughs who desires certain information concerning methods of handling prisoners. You will kindly favor him with all the information and assistance he requires."[62]

In the first half of 1913, from January to July, Ed had completed four long novelettes or serials, "The Inner World," "The Cave Girl," "Number Thirteen" ("A Man Without a Soul"), and "The Warlord of Mars." These four totaled more than 186,000 words.

With "The Inner World," retitled "At the Earth's Core" when it appeared in *All-Story,* he returned to his favorite "frame" structure, devising a brief prologue in which Ed, as the writer or story-teller, encounters the main character, David Innes, in the Sahara Desert. Innes has passed ten years in the fantastic inner world of Pellucidar, deep beneath the earth's crust, with an old inventor named Perry who had constructed the "iron mole" that transported them there. Innes's strange adventures occur in a land in which humans are helpless creatures who duplicate the condition of animals on earth; in this inner world great reptiles, the Mahars, who communicate with each other by means of a "sixth-sense fourth-dimension language," rule sadistically over their human chattels. Here Ed, who had previously invented the settings for his dying planet of Mars and had created his own weird animals, for the first time devises a prehistoric setting— that of the Stone Age—and offers paleontological classifications for the monsters that Innes meets.[63]

At the story's end he created a "mystery" which in its reference to a count and countess who had vanished, and the finding of their locket on a deserted island, used familiar elements from "Tarzan of the Apes." By this time convinced that the ire of a small group of readers was hardly significant when compared to the large number who eagerly awaited his next story, Ed contrived the most indefinite of suspended endings, naturally with the inevitable sequel in mind.[64]

"Number Thirteen," published as "A Man Without a Soul," appears to have been thoroughly plotted by Ed before the end of 1912. In this early year of his writing he was already exhibiting the remarkable flexibility of an imagination able to shape several complicated stories at the same time. In his letter of December 5 to Metcalf he spoke of "bully stories mulling around in my head" and used his favorite phrase "damphool possibilities" in referring to "Number Thirteen."

Ed's unsuccessful venture into the short story field, as evidenced in "For the Fool's Mother" and "The Avenger," had provided convincing proof that his creative ideas were not designed for compression. On the contrary, they needed expansion— expansion of details, settings, incidents, and characters. As his writing progressed from story to story, his gallery of characters became larger and larger. In "Number Thirteen" the main characters, Professor Maxon, his daughter Virginia, Dr. Van Horn, and the Chinese Sing, are supplemented by a large variety of lesser ones and a cast of "extras" that would gladden the heart of a Hollywood producer. Included among minor characters are a Malay first mate, a Malay rajah, and a head warrior of a Dyak tribe. The participants in a succession of bloody battles are groups of Dyak warriors or pirates and an astonishing aggregation of thirteen "soulless" monsters. Ed had created a temporarily mad scientist who made Frankenstein's performance appear tame.

The professor, in his attempt to create life in his laboratory, has unfortunately overstressed physical perfection; his twelve experiments have resulted in twelve deformed monsters of superhuman strength. "You have overdone it," his assistant von Horn tells him, "with the result that the court of mystery is peopled by a dozen brutes of awful muscularity, and scarcely enough brain among the dozen to equip three properly." Bulan, who emerges as the hero of the story, is supposedly the product of Professor Maxon's thirteenth experiment. He is "a handsome giant, physically perfect," but he is soon revealed as the possessor of a high intelligence and of such virtues as courtesy, bravery, and unselfishness. In the story Ed naturally reserved a surprise for the end, and what was a greater surprise to his readers—a completely finished ending, with no possibility of the prolonged waiting for a sequel.[65]

Ed's major work during this period, completed within one month, from June 7 to July 8, 1913, was "The Warlord of Mars," at first titled "The Prince of Helium." The narrative is resumed after the suspenseful ending of "The Gods of Mars," with Dejah Thoris "entombed" in the Temple of the Sun and John Carter awaiting in agony the moment when the revolving shaft will permit the cell door to be opened so that he can learn whether his wife is alive or dead. The familiar characters of Ed's preceding Martian stories appear again, but of course there are additions, including Salensus Oll, Jeddak of Okar, and Kulan Tith, Jeddak of Kaol. Ed's imagination was especially given to the devising of new civilizations, races, and geographical settings that were unique. As though determined to achieve a variety of skin colors, he now added to his red, green, black, and white Martians, a race of yellow men, "fierce, black-bearded fellows with skins the color of a ripe lemon," who inhabit the forbidding arctic region of Mars near the North Pole. A spectacular Burroughs invention is "The Carrion Caves," the only route "through the ice-barrier of the north to a fertile valley at the pole." He describes the yellow men's fight for survival against the other races and how, fleeing, they discovered the caves:

At the opening to the subterranean passage that led to their haven of refuge a mighty battle was fought in which yellow men were victorious, and within the caves that gave ingress to their new home they piled the bodies of the dead, both yellow and green, that the stench might warn away their enemies from further pursuit.

And ever since that long-gone day have the dead of this fabled land been carried to the Carrion Caves, that in death and decay they might serve their country and warn away invading enemies. Here, too, is brought, so the fable runs, all the waste stuff of the nation—everything that is subject to rot, and that can add to the foul stench that assails our nostrils.

Ed is also adept at creating new hideous animals. In "The Warlord of Mars" John Carter encounters the huge sith and the terrifying apt. The sith, a "bald-faced hornet . . . grown to the size of a prize Hereford bull" has a poisoned sting and "myriad facet eyes" that cover most of its grotesque head. The apt is presented in graphic detail:

It is a huge, white-furred creature with six limbs, four of which, short and heavy, carry it swiftly over the snow and ice; while the other two, growing forward from its shoulders on either side of its powerful neck, terminate in white, hairless hands, with which it seizes its prey.

The creature has two great horns that protrude from its lower jawbone, and its most astonishing feature is the eyes that extend "in two vast, oval patches from the center of the top of the cranium down either side of the head to below the roots of the horns, so that these weapons really grow out from the lower part of the eyes, which are composed of several thousand ocelli each."

Apparently feeling it necessary to provide a scientific explanation for the apt's bizarre features, Ed wrote:

This eye structure seemed remarkable in a beast whose haunts were upon a glaring field of ice and snow, and though I found upon minute examination of several that we killed that each ocellus is furnished with its own lid, and that the animal can at will close as many of the facets of his huge eyes as he chooses, yet I was positive that nature had thus equipped him because much of his life was to be spent in dark, subterranean recesses.

"The Warlord of Mars," ending happily with John Carter and his beloved Dejah Thoris united, was accepted by Metcalf for *All-Story*.[66] As Ed had previously stated, this novel was "the last of the John Carter Martian stories"—at least, for the time being.

The Martian trilogy of *A Princess of Mars, The Gods of Mars,* and *The Warlord of Mars* is considered by many people, including science-fiction authorities and Burroughs afficionados, as a classic in the field of fiction. In a truly remarkable feat of creativity Burroughs not only told a gripping tale, but invented on the planet Mars entire multiracial civilizations complete with nations, religions, gods, and science.

Before the summer was over, Ed succeeded in making a sale which may have provided him with a greater satisfaction than any of the other ones. At the close of 1912 "The Outlaw of Torn" remained unsold. Discouraged but not defeated, Burroughs had vowed to Metcalf, "I am going to do it over again when I have time."

An observation about writing, contained in the Burroughs *Autobiography,* was one that other authors have noted: "The stories that are easiest to write usually sell easy." From this it may be assumed that the converse is often true. "The Outlaw of Torn," which Ed described as "the story I had worked the hardest on," appeared unsalable. On February 24 A. L. Sessions, editor of *New Story,* wrote, "I hope, now that we have established communication with you, you are going to give us a chance to read many more of your stories." Ed hastened to reply, referring to "The Outlaw of Torn" and explaining that it had been previously submitted.[67]

When Sessions stated, "I have no recollection of seeing the story," and showed an interest in reading it, Ed sent it to him. A month later the manuscript was returned with a brief statement of rejection.[68] Ed made no further overtures to Sessions, but by the summer of 1913, the growing furor over *Tarzan,* created mainly through its widespread syndication, was a factor in prompting the editor to seek another story, no matter what type, as long as it bore the Burroughs name. On July 19 he wrote, "If you have not disposed of the serial rights of your story 'The Outlaw of Torn,' I would like to consider it again for the New Story Magazine."

Ed rushed the story to him; however, on July 30, the best offer Sessions would make was $350 for first serial rights. He had some apprehensions regarding Ed's response to an offer so low and was careful to explain his reasons:

Anticipating what will probably be your feeling, that this is a rather modest sum for a story of this length, I ought to say that the reason is because we have not hitherto used anything approaching historical romance, or, indeed, any sort of material that is not what is popularly known as "up-to-date" in plot, characters, and action. So "The Outlaw of Torn" will be more or less of an experiment with us. If you are willing to accept this sum, I will see that you receive a check promptly.

As a result of Sessions' purchase of "The Return of Tarzan" Ed had promised him first refusal on the next "Tarzan" story. There appears little doubt that this opportunity to acquire a valuable Tarzan serial was dominating Sessions' thoughts and actions. The editor, eager to prod Ed into starting this new serial, offered a plot suggestion:

Another matter that I wish to bring to your attention is the question of another story of Tarzan. It has occurred to us that Tarzan's adventures might be continued still further, and if the idea appeals to you, would like to suggest that he could be taken back to Africa once more as the authorized agent of the Smithsonian Institution, heading an expedition to investigate the talking apes and possibly to bring back specimens. Doubtless you have heard of Prof. Garner's reports that monkeys have a language of their own, and possibly have read accounts of his alleged researches. . . .

Sessions believed that this idea, taken as a theme, might lead to an exciting adventure story. Despite his difficulties in marketing "The Outlaw of Torn," and the fact that this was the first offer *anybody* had made, Ed had no intention of accepting the $350. With a dogged determination, he persisted in valuing the story according to the long hours of work he had devoted to it. On July 31, while in New York to visit Metcalf, he had a conference with Sessions. Later, across the top of Sessions' letter containing the offer, Ed noted:

Saw Sessions in N.Y. 7/31 asked $1000 for Outlaw of Torn & $3000 contract for sequel to Ret of Tarzan Feb 1914 delivery.

For a while it appeared that the negotiations would reach an impasse and Ed would again be left with the manuscript on his hands. But the dickering continued, with Sessions raising his offer to $500. Ed, on August 15, accepted, with the proposal previously referred to,[69] in which Ed had stipulated, "After the story has appeared in your magazine, if you find from the comments of your readers that it has proven successful you are to pay me a further sum of 2c per word, less the $500.00 previously paid."[70] On August 18 Sessions sent a prompt agreement to these conditions.

From a businessman's standpoint, as he balanced the long hours of revision and research against the net return, Ed undoubtedly considered "The Outlaw of Torn" as a poor investment. Still, he had gained the satisfaction of another sale and had demonstrated his power of determination. Above all, through this unhappy experience with medieval times, castles, and knighthood, he had learned that the historical romance, with its emphasis upon realistic atmosphere, was not the best outlet for his talents. He would, however, later return to ancient history as the setting for a fantastic novel.

Thus, the summer's end in 1913 found Ed with a future unquestionably committed to the field of writing, the thoughts of returning to the business world thrust firmly aside. His successes had given him the confidence of a man who knows his worth. With this confidence he even dared to estimate the beginning dates of new stories and the approximate dates of completion. In a letter of August 21 he wrote to A. L. Sessions, "As to the next Tarzan story. . . . I intend starting it the first of the year, and shall have a considerable part of it ready by the first of February. . . ."[71]

In negotiations with Burroughs, editors and publishers soon realized they were encountering a type of writer they had not previously known. Shrewd and demanding, aware he was marketing a product everybody wanted, Ed sought the highest bidder. The editors who were accustomed to viewing authors' stories as so much merchandise, purchasable in a buyer's market in which they set the prices, now received a rude awakening. By their rules the acquisition of stories was a straightforward business transaction. If these were to be the rules, Ed proposed a logical extension—selling stories was also a business transaction. And the author of "Tarzan" intended to make an important change in the rules: within the limits of his powers, *he* would set the prices for his stories. The editors for the first time were confronted by a man whose shrewd business instincts and perception more than matched their own. They had no choice but to bargain with him.

Ed, in his future dealings, established himself as an unusual combination, a kind of dual personality. Seldom had a writer joined a soaring imagination with a cold dollars-and-cents practicality. He became the businessman-writer par excellence.

June 10 191

My dear wife:

Do you recall how we waited in fear and trembling the coming of the post man for weary days after we sent the Tarzan Mss to Metcalf?

And will you ever forget THE morning, that he finally came.

Not even this, our first book, can quite equal that unparalleled moment.

That we may never have cause for another such is the wish of your devoted husband

E R Burroughs

CHAPTER 10

A CALIFORNIA SOJOURN

Ed's impulsive nature, restrained awhile by family responsibilities and by the discipline of his self-imposed writing goals, once more drove him to seek change and a touch of adventure. His first concession to success, a decidedly daring one for the times, was to buy an automobile—a used Velie. He recalled the matter with amusement in his *Autobiography:* "My stories were now selling as fast as I could write them and I could write them pretty rapidly, so I bought a second-hand automobile and became a plutocrat."

This festive mood demanded a greater and more impulsive gesture. Although family duties required that he control his restless or whimsical nature, he was still, as always, prepared to gamble in a surprising and unpredictable way. On September 6, 1913, Metcalf, who might have believed he had seen the end of Ed's unexpected actions, discovered he was wrong. The letter offered an abrupt announcement: "Am leaving for California tonight. My address until further notice will be General Delivery, San Diego. When we're located I'll send you permanent address."

Ed's own comment about the sudden move was humorous: ". . . I had decided that I was too rich to spend my winters in Chicago so I packed my family, all my furniture, my second-hand automobile and bought transportation for Los Angeles."[1] Emma, who from the moment of her marriage to Ed had known little stability, and had been transported to the wilds of Idaho, may have by this time been conditioned to his whimsical decisions. Though she loved and trusted Ed, she must have been

---

ERB's autograph in Emma's copy of Tarzan of the Apes, *June 10, 1914.*

House ERB and Emma rented in Coronado, California, at 550 A Avenue, September 25, 1913; auto is old Velie Ed took on the train with him; Emma and the three children are on porch.

concerned by the difficulties of making a cross-country trip with three small children—Joan, age five, Hulbert, four, and John, an infant of not quite six months—and by the plan that included a repetition of past events—the shipping of all household belongings, the relocation, and the setting up of housekeeping in strange surroundings.

Of this California expedition, Ed wrote in his *Autobiography:*

From Los Angeles we drove to San Diego and spent the winter in Coronado and San Diego. We were a long way from home. My income depended solely upon the sale of magazine rights. I had not had a book published at that time and, therefore, no book royalties were coming in. Had I failed to sell a single story during these months it would have been over the hills to the poorhouse for us, but I did not fail. That I had to work is evidenced by a graph that I keep on my desk showing my word output from year to year since 1911. In 1913 it reached its peak with something like four hundred and thirteen thousand words for the year. By glancing at this graph I can always tell when the sheriff has been camping on my coat-tails.

Metcalf wrote to inquire, "Are you going to stay definitely in California or are you going to be there for the winter? I hope you have a very fine time anyway, and I hope that literature flourishes

*Emma and the children on visit to Tijuana, Mexico, in the old
Velie, 1914.*

like a streak out there. . . ."[2] Ed responded, "I think it is going
to be great here. We came on the children's account. We have
three, and the Chicago winters have always meant a round of
sickness and worry. We have taken a house at Coronado—I do
not know the street number, nor does anyone else; but if you
will address me as follows I shall get your letters all right: A
avenue, bet. 7th & 8th, Coronado, California."[3]

On business matters Ed noted, "The two short stories ["The
Avenger" and "For the Fool's Mother"] came the other day. I
did not cry myself to sleep over them. I told you they were
rotten, but you asked to see them anyway." These had been rejected with the briefest of comments by Metcalf. Ed, neither
surprised nor disappointed, considered the editor's opinion as a
confirmation of his own belief—that he was not destined to be a
short story writer.[4]

He hastened to maintain his other business correspondence.
William G. Chapman of the International Press Bureau, who had
already received a notification of the change of address, wrote to
discuss the syndication of "The Cave Girl." As Ed had discovered earlier, the process of serializing stories in newspapers was a
complicated one that seldom ran smoothly. Chapman was willing
to handle "The Cave Girl" on the same basis as "The Return of
Tarzan," his guarantee to be forty percent of the gross amount,
but Sessions, editor of *New Story*, had not as yet sent the needed

proofs of "The Return of Tarzan," and Chapman was inquiring if Ed was prepared to bear half the costs of printing the story so that it could be distributed.[5]

The syndication problems and the request for money were sufficient to revive Ed's worries about finances. Far from home and completely on his own, he had risked supporting his family and household solely through his writings; his concern was understandable. On October 3 he wrote to Chapman, "I find that one can use money to advantage in this neck of the woods," and later, in an inquiry about the syndication, he asked, ". . . is there any money coming in? I am starving to death among strangers."[6]

On October 7 Chapman finally had some good news to present: Sessions had sent fifty copies of each issue of *New Story* containing "The Return of Tarzan," and Chapman was now negotiating with the American Press Association and the Scripps MacRae newspapers.[7] Chapman's letter of December 20 offered a more substantial encouragement—a check for $150, Ed's sixty percent of the money paid by Scripps MacRae for "The Return of Tarzan."

Metcalf of course wrote to discuss matters of importance or of interest to Ed. On October 2 he commented, "I think 'The Man Without a Soul' ought to go pretty well." Presumably the November *All-Story* in which it would appear, complete in one issue, was out or about to come out. Metcalf reported also that "The Warlord of Mars" would begin in installments the following month, and then added one of his promotional suggestions which usually resulted in extra work for Ed: "It has just occurred to me that we could get some entertainment by publishing a line cut of the geography of Mars. Could you fake up something, seeing that you have traveled so thoroughly over that globe, which we could run?"[8]

Ed wrote, ". . . shall also see what I can do with a map of Mars —you will recall that I showed you my working map when I was in New York; but it was too meager for your purposes."[9] Again, with the payment foremost in his mind he remarked, "It is such a deuce of a way out here, and takes so long to get word back and forth that I am hoping you will favor me (again) with one of your early decisions."[10] (By this time Ed's California address had been established as 550 A. Avenue, Coronado.)

Ed's map of Mars (Barsoom), evidently drawn in response to the request, presents the planet in spherical views from two sides—first the exposed half of the eastern hemisphere progressing to one half of the western hemisphere, and then the other side of the globe with the hemispheres in reverse. He has drawn the lines of latitude and longitude and has entered important surface features and cities, including The Atolian Hills, Toonolian Marshes, Greater and Lesser Helium, Zodanga, Ptarth, and even the location of "The Hordes of Torquas."

The map contains a table of Martian measurements and a scale based upon "haads." In devising, as usual, his special terminology, he lists a "sofad" as equal to 11.69 plus earth inches, an "ad" as 9.75 minus earth feet, and a "haad" as 1949.05 earth feet. He notes that there are about 2.709 haads to an English mile and estimates the "speed of fast fliers" to be about 450 haads or 166.1 earth miles per hour.[11]

For the *All-Story* "Table-Talk" of October 1913, Metcalf, on his own initiative, arranged a glossary of Martian terms. In the column he commented, "Mr. Burroughs had all the terms at hand and we simply put them in alphabetical order and are printing them hereinafter, so that all who read the Martian stories may know exactly what is what." His glossary was divided into categories of "Proper Names" and "Common Names."[12]

The confusion over the use of Ed's pen name, "Norman Bean," for "Under the Moons of Mars" led to an amusing complaint from an *All-Story* reader. In the October "Table-Talk," writing from Hawaii, the reader commented about "The Gods of Mars":

The sequel, I notice, is written by "Burroughs" and the original tale by "Norman Bean." How is this?

Burroughs is undoubtedly one of your best writers, and the sequel is well written, but I do not think he has continued the story in the way the original author would have done, which makes it, to my idea, far less interesting. Another thing—he leaves the tale in an unfinished condition.

The reader explained, "My wife says had she known the abrupt finish of the story she would rather not have read it." Again, he urged Metcalf, "in the interest of all your readers," to induce "Norman Bean" to write "the continuation of this otherwise splendid story and finish it in a way satisfactory to all," later repeating the statement to "Try and get the finish to 'Under the Gods of Mars' " and to afterward "induce the same author—or one equally good" to write stories of life on other planets.

Ed's amusement over this suggestion must have been heightened by the blundering note from a reader in the Philippines whose letter of "heartfelt sympathy to the friends and relatives of Mr. E. R. Burroughs" appeared in the December 1913 *All-Story*. "His death must have been very sudden," the reader

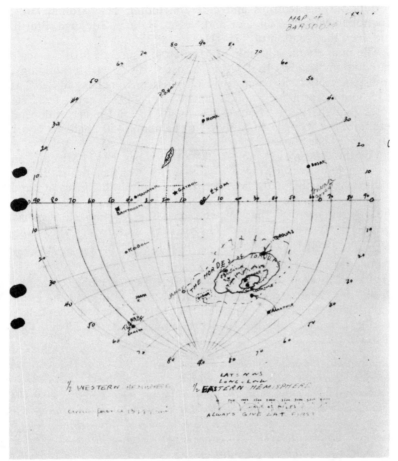

ERB's map of Barsoom (Mars), which he drew to help him maintain accuracy and realism in his geographical locations.

stated. "I liked his stories very much. It is too bad he could not have finished 'The Gods of Mars.' "

In this busy California period Ed continued to have many irons in the fire. Arrangements for serialization of his stories in the *New York Evening World,* a project he was handling personally, occupied part of his time. About "The Man Without a Soul," scheduled to appear in the newspaper after publication in the October *All-Story,* Ed wrote to Terhune somewhat over-optimistically, "I sort of have an idea that this story is going to take almost as well as Tarzan of the Apes . . . "[13]

He was working speedily on the addition to "The Inner World" that he had promised Metcalf, and in sending the completed section to the editor he wrote, "At the time Mr. Innes recounted his adventures to me he presented me with several rough pencil drawings he had made before he left Pellucidar. Believing that you may be interested in seeing these I am sending them along with the mss."[14] He noted that the addition totaled forty-nine pages or about 16,170 words.[15]

Only two weeks earlier he had finished "The Mucker," a long story he had begun in Chicago on August 16, according to his workbook, and sent it to Metcalf. Now, with only a brief period allowed for the editor's evaluation, he sent a reminder: "Let me know about *The Mucker*. I am just as childishly impatient as when I sent my first story to you."[16]

In the midst of all this feverish writing he was making plans for new sequels and commented to Metcalf, "If your readers do not tire of Mars I should like to write another story of Helium around Carthoris—Carter's son, you know."[17] Concerning the question of a sequel to "The Cave Girl," he inquired, "Has there been any considerable demand for one?" and went on in detail to discuss the story:

I noticed in a letter from a reader a comment on the "rottenness" of the ending. Do [you] imagine this referred to the fact that the principals were not brought back to civilization, or to the suggestion of the rather unconventional (as it were) relations which may have marked their companionship after they went back into the forest together? To my mind a return to civilization and the snobs I pictured his friends and relatives as being would have meant the shattering of a pretty romance.[18]

"I hated to do it—" he commented, "and then, there is always the sequel!"

Letters referring to "The Mucker" may have crossed, because Metcalf's, dated a day earlier than the inquiry from Ed, contained the editor's verdict: it was an outright rejection. He used the expression Ed had objected to previously—"I might say that I don't think the story balances." Metcalf presented a long analysis of "The Mucker's" defects, concentrating first on the section describing Billy Byrne's activities aboard the *Halfmoon*:

Ninety-nine pages, pretty nearly half the story, were spent on the ship in circumstances that are not highly original. . . . it seems to me that you have resorted altogether too much to very lengthy conversations. The effect is one of repetition and slowness.[19]

In the last half of the story, Metcalf noted, Ed erred in taking an exactly opposite approach:

. . . When you get them ashore on the island, and introduce the decadent Japanese race and situations, which at least in color are more or less unusual, you hurry through it with great speed. The whole latter part of the story is so condensed and so hastily worked up that your effects are not always gained. . . .[20]

Metcalf added some penetrating and accurate remarks about Ed's failure to achieve a convincing characterization of Billy Byrne, the "Mucker," and commented, "I have a feeling that you started to write this story without having doped it out very carefully. . . ."[21]

Ed's response had a tone of gloom and dejection, although he made it plain he appreciated Metcalf's patience in taking the time "to point out the weak spots." Ed wrote:

I think that maybe I have been falling into that thing of dragging out the openings of late and I shall certainly try to guard against it in the future. I did not intend to hasten the ending, but toward the close I recalled one of your letters in which you stated that you were not particularly keen for stories of over seventy thousand words.[22]

Metcalf's criticism of overlong introductions or opening sections recalls, of course, his analysis of Ed's first story, "Under the Moons of Mars," with its original four-page foreword, which was finally reduced to several paragraphs of summary and placed on the title page.

While in "The Mucker" Ed departed from the fantasy or other world settings he often used, he nevertheless returned to a favorite theme, similar to the one he had developed in "The Cave Girl." It was based upon the regeneration of a weak or dissolute character following his removal from a physically and/or morally destructive environment to a rugged and somewhat primitive environment of nature. Here, while he is being forced to battle for survival, two strong influences operate to transform him into a healthy, moralistic individual: one is the result of a rigorous outdoor life and the other develops from his encounter with a particularly wholesome specimen of womanhood whose approval and love he desperately wants.

In "The Mucker" Ed used another story element upon which

he would depend even more heavily in the future—that of a strange lost or misplaced race. On the island the passengers from the wrecked ship are being watched by "a little brown man with beady, black eyes set in narrow fleshy slits." The man, who wore "strange medieval armor" and carried "two wicked-looking swords," was described as "Oda Yorimoto, descendant of a powerful daimio of the Ashikaga Dynasty of shoguns who had fled Japan with his faithful samurai nearly three hundred and fifty years before upon the overthrow of the Ashikaga Dynasty."

Ed's concept of a lost race, as with the Oparians in "The Return of Tarzan," led him to create a people who were decadent and sadistically warped:

Upon this unfrequented and distant Japanese isle the exiles had retained all of their medieval military savagery, to which had been added the aboriginal ferocity of the head-hunting natives they had found there and with whom they had intermarried. The little colony, far from making any advances in arts or letters had, on the contrary, relapsed into primeval ignorance as deep as that of the natives with whom they had cast their lot—only in their arms and armor, their military training and discipline did they show any of the influence of their civilized progenitors.

The inhabitants of the island, the samurai, "cruel, crafty, resourceful wild men trapped in the habiliments of a dead past," represented Ed's favorite version of the "lost race" theme; later variations involved a race (or races) reverting to primitive life or savagery and surviving on the ruins and remnants of an ancient civilization which, in some cases, was far more advanced than theirs. The anachronism—the idea of a group of people living in isolation and clinging to odd customs and fearful rites of a remote period—was evidently intriguing to Ed.

In the development of "The Mucker" with its rather loose-knit structure, Ed for the first time used a variety of "earth-bound" settings. Billy Byrne flees from Chicago to San Francisco, is shanghaied, and then shipwrecked on a Malaysian island, and at the story's end turns up in New York, where he meets Barbara Harding, the girl he loves, and gallantly renounces her and tells of his plans to return to Chicago and his "own kind."

Although Ed may have expressed his gratitude for Metcalf's criticism of "The Mucker," he had no intention of getting involved in extensive revisions until he had tried the story elsewhere. However, his submission of "The Mucker" to Sessions at

New Story brought a firm rejection.[23] Resigned to the inevitable, he then began revisions, shortening the story to about 58,000 words.[24] Past experiences with rejections by Metcalf made him dubious about "The Mucker's" chances at *All-Story,* and on December 22 he chose instead to submit it to *Adventure.* His letter to Arthur S. Hoffman, the editor, revealed his doubts that the story would be accepted: ". . . If 'The Mucker' doesn't meet your requirements I'll be glad if you will let me know wherein it falls short, so that I may have another try later. . . ." Within weeks "The Mucker" was once more brought to Metcalf's attention:

Have rewritten The Mucker cutting out those parts you did not like, lopping off several closing chapters, changing the ending, and shortening the whole thing by some ten or eleven thousand words. It is out now with a magazine for which it is totally unfitted so I am expecting it back daily. Would you care to see it?[25]

At the same time Ed announced a change of address; he was now at 4036 3rd Street in San Diego:

. . . I have again been in the throes of moving. Coronado was too low and damp and we are now situated in a rose bowered (!) bungalow on the hills of S. D. By standing on tip toe we can peek over the mountains to the east and see almost to Schenectady.[26]

As expected, "The Mucker" was returned by *Adventure,* but Ed, continuing the intensive California writing schedule begun in early fall, had little inclination to brood over this failure. On October 26, he had turned again to royal adventure in "The Mad King of Lutha," completing it within a month. Continuing his rapid writing pace, Ed launched at once into "Nu of the Neocene," a shorter 25,000-word story that he finished in only twenty days.[27]

In "The Mad King of Lutha" Ed assembles familiar elements found in pseudo-historical romances of the day—a young king deprived of his rightful position, a villainous regent, a beautiful princess, and a courageous young American, Barney Custer of Beatrice, Nebraska, who is merely a tourist in the kingdom of Lutha, his mother's native land. Barney, because of a lost election bet is not permitted to shave for a year; his full red beard gives him a superficial resemblance to the escaped "mad" king, and as a result becomes embroiled in danger and intrigue. Ed, in imitation of the settings adopted by other historical novelists, chooses to give his kingdom of Lutha an Austrian or German flavor, creating such characters as Peter of Blentz, Prince Ludwig von der Tann, Lieutenant Otto Butzow, and others. The heroine, Princess Emma von der Tann, is of course named after Ed's wife. The selection of Beatrice, Nebraska, as Barney's home town, and the emphasis this small town receives, is explained by Ed's close friendship with Herbert (Bert) T. Weston who had been his classmate at Michigan Military Academy. Weston, with his wife, Margaret, and their children, lived in Beatrice, Nebraska, and from there maintained a lifelong correspondence with Ed.[28]

Instead of establishing a historical period of the past, as he had done in "The Outlaw of Torn," Ed preferred to modernize "The Mad King" and in the story makes his first use of the automobile. Barney Custer drives into Lutha in a gray roadster and soon afterward maneuvers the car daringly to rescue Emma, the heroine, from a runaway horse. The presence of the automobile at once removes the story from the customary Victorian setting and places it in the twentieth century.

"The Mad King of Lutha," a melange of unoriginal devices and incidents, is hardly an example of Burroughs' imaginative best. Its plot, based upon the chance circumstances that force a visitor to a tiny kingdom to impersonate its king, closely resembles that of *The Prisoner of Zenda,* by Anthony Hope, published in 1894.

In accepting "The Mad King" Metcalf commented that it was "a pretty fair yarn," [29] and on December 8 Ed replied to thank him for the early check that came in "mighty fine for Christmas."[30] The main subject of concern to Ed was the coming expiration of his agreement with the Munsey Company; in this, for the past year, he had granted them first refusal on all stories. Ed explained his views diplomatically:

I am anxious to try for other magazines for purely business reasons. Personally I should rather write for you than any of them, for no one could have accorded me more courteous treatment than I have received at the hands of The Munsey Company. I feel, however, that though I may never receive as decent treatment from others I should be making some effort to discover what other magazines want, and, if I can, enlarge the market for my stories.[31]

On December 17 Metcalf replied with an offer for first refusal on all of Ed's 1914 output: the Munsey Company would agree to pay two and one-half cents a word. Metcalf pointed out that Ed's market would not be limited, since "whatever we feel we cannot use you will be able to send immediately to other magazines, and you will thus learn what their needs are. . . ."

Ed, evidently weighing Metcalf's proposal, was in no hurry to commit himself, responding only after a second query from the editor,[32] and then making a terse counter-proposal: "As to the 2½c proposition, 3½c would be infinitely more interesting."[33] This offer included certain reservations, specifically in the matter of the third Tarzan story which Ed had promised to submit to Sessions for *New Story Magazine.* Ed wrote:

I do not see that it would be right to do otherwise, though I am not bound to accept his offer for it, nor is there any reason why you should not see it and make me an offer for it if you choose; but if we reach a mutually satisfactory arrangement for 1914 this story will, of course, have to be excepted.[34]

Ed then inquired, "How would an arrangement covering each alternate story that I write strike you?"[35]

ERB and lifelong friend, Bert Weston, about 1901.

284

During the exchange of letters Metcalf revealed the new plans to transform *All-Story* into a weekly and noted, "This means that I can use all manner to stuff, novels 30,000 to 40,000 words long, serials and short stories. This is the chance of a life time for a brilliant young author."[36]

He also included critical comments about one of Ed's favorite practices: ". . . I would like to suggest that you do *not* use the present tense in writing at any time. There is no particular advantage to it. It has gone out of fashion nowadays and it is pretty awkward to the average reader."[37] In replying, Ed expressed a willingness to accept the suggestion: "Thanks for the present tense criticism. Will try to dodge it in future. I'll appreciate it if you'll tip me off to any other little oddities of style that my stuff would be better off without. . . ."[38]

The negotiations over a new agreement with Munsey revealed that Ed's worries and uncertainties over his writing future, although temporarily thrust aside during this successful period, could easily return. On January 19, 1914, he wrote:

Am still up in the air about the $.025 stunt,—or was it three and a half? I feel that it would result in selling all my best stuff at two and a half cents and not being able to sell what you didn't like at any price, even though it was not entirely rotten, and so I wouldn't have any chance to break into a wider field, and then when I have shot my wad as far as the All-Story readers are concerned I shall be just where I was when I first started to write, as far as other magazines are concerned. . . .

His strongest fear, the one that plagued many writers, was the fear of running out of ideas, of being *written out*. To Metcalf he explained:

. . . I cannot forget what you once told me about the majority of writers playing out after a couple of years. I imagine they play out with readers who have followed them for that long, as in two years a fellow pretty nearly exhausts his stock of situations, phrases and the like.[39]

"I feel that most of mine are already worn to a frazzle," Ed remarked gloomily. "If I knew that you were going to take it all it might make a difference; but of course neither of us can know that."[40]

His comment about writers whose ideas were exhausted, and especially his mention of "a couple of years" as a time limit, when considered in the light and length of his future career, of course seem incongruous. But to Ed's personal insecurity at the time were added his doubts about writing as a permanent profession with an assured income. These combined factors account for the fears that were further sharpened by Metcalf's statement.

Ed thus revealed a painful awareness of the limited nature of the themes, incidents, and devices he had been repeating. It undoubtedly appeared inconceivable to him that he could build a successful writing career on this slim stock-in-trade—continuing variations of "Tarzan," discoveries of lost races and primitive societies, sequels to "Mars" and other-world stories, and occasional "historical" romances. In later years Ed referred with caustic amusement, and some satisfaction, to the dire predictions of critics that his popularity could not last.

His final remark to Metcalf indicated his concern about the future: "Wish that I might talk to you about it—writing is most unsatisfactory."[41]

On January 29 Metcalf's reply urged Ed to accept an agreement for 1914 based upon the offer of two and one-half cents a word; the editor emphasized that with *All-Story* now a weekly, "we very likely could use 50,000 words of yours a month which, at the rate of 2½ cents a word would mean practically an income from us alone of something considerably over $10,000 a year. That's a pretty good proposition, it seems to me."

Metcalf noted that based upon past occurrences Ed would have no difficulty in marketing any stories that were rejected by the Munsey Company. Accordingly, a year's contract would in no way harm his chances for sales. "I pay you, as it is, the highest rate I pay anybody, which, of course is a matter between you and me alone . . . ," Metcalf wrote.[42]

Surprisingly, as in the past year, Ed capitulated without further argument; perhaps Metcalf's logic had proved convincing. "I'll accept your 2½c per word offer for my 1914 output—first serial rights only—with the exception of the Tarzan story I am now finishing," he replied.[43] This was the story on which he had promised first refusal to Sessions at *New Story Magazine*. However, he restated his plan to send copies of the new *Tarzan* story to both magazines at the same time with the understanding that the best offer would be accepted. The agreement with Metcalf presented an opportunity which Ed was prompt to seize. With his usual persistence he hastened to advise the editor that he was sending a copy of the "revised Mucker," explaining once more that the revisions accorded with Metcalf's suggestions. Ed had eliminated "useless conversations, shortening it considerably more than ten thousand words."[44]

Undoubtedly influenced by the readers' clamor for more stories bearing the Burroughs name, as well as by the improved structure of "The Mucker," Metcalf now agreed to purchase it. On March 3, 1914, Ed received the largest amount he had so far been paid for any of his works—$1,450.00.[45]

Two months earlier Metcalf had taken "Nu of the Neocene," a story involving a double passage in time, first to the future and then to the past. Nu, a stone age man, after being buried in a cave for one hundred thousand years, awakens in modern times; later, accompanied by an American girl of the twentieth century, he is transported back to the prehistoric period. The story, titled "The Eternal Lover" when it appeared in *All-Story,* depends upon familiar names for its sequence of adventures. The heroine Victoria, from Beatrice, Nebraska, is the sister of Barney Custer, leading character of "The Mad King." Since the setting is in Africa on the vast estate of Lord and Lady Greystoke, where Victoria and Barney are guests at a hunt, brief parts are provided for Tarzan and Jane. This is the first reference to the estate and to the fact that the Greystokes are making their permanent home in equatorial Africa.[46]

From the restrictive and imitative plot and characters of "The Mad King" Ed must have returned to the fantasy world with a feeling of relief. His favorite subjects—the primitive life, the savage and his mate, fierce combat in the jungle, and of course the creation of Nu of the Neocene, mighty-muscled hunter of Oo, the saber-toothed tiger, as another version of Tarzan—allowed him to be freely imaginative and to devise situations amid familiar backgrounds.

In "The Eternal Lover," possibly as a result of hasty writing, Ed runs into occasional problems of appropriate language and style. At the beginning, in what appears to be an unnecessary explanation and a peculiar viewpoint intrusion by the author, he refers to Barney Custer as having come to the Greystoke estate "to hunt big game—and forget," and then adds:

But all that has nothing to do with this story; nor has John Clayton, Lord Greystoke, who was, once upon a time, Tarzan of the Apes, except that my having chanced to be a guest of his at the same time as the Custers makes it possible for me to give you a story that otherwise might never have been told.

Strangely, this author's viewpoint has no further development; no mention is again made of Burroughs as a guest or observer at the Greystoke estate, he offers no personal comment and he does not play a part in any of the scenes that follow.

An awkward writing practice, probably the one that provoked Metcalf's disapproving remarks about the use of the present tense, is demonstrated in Ed's shifts in verbs from the past to the present. In doing this he may have felt he was making the action more vivid and dramatic. After such uses of the past tense as "the hunter loosened the stone knife . . ." or he "drove his heavy spear deep. . . ," Ed then in other paragraphs changes to the present and writes, "Oo is creeping upon him now. The grinning jaws drip saliva. . ." or ". . . the beast succeeds. The paw closes upon the spear. . . ."

During this intensive writing period, with a succession of stories being completed and dispatched to Metcalf, the editor may have felt like a man buried beneath a deluge of words. He gave understandable indications of being both stunned and confused. Concerning Ed's gallery of characters, especially in stories that had been purchased but not yet published, he seemed, on one occasion, to have lost track of both identifications and relationships. In sending a check for "Nu of the Neocene" he evidently displayed uncertainty about Barney Custer, who is assigned a limited role in the story.[47] Ed explained in detail:

Barney Custer appears first in The Mad King of Lutha. His mother was Victoria Rubinroth. I created a sister for him—Victoria Custer—to use as leading lady in Nu of the Neocene. I also used Barney in the latter story, as well as Lieutenant Butzow from The Mad King, and Tarzan and some of his characters. As I needed several minor characters I thought I might as well call upon old friends to give the tale additional human interest to those of your readers who happen to be familiar with these various characters. Those who have never heard of them before will find the story no less interesting because of them.[48]

He commented that he planned to use Barney again in another Lutha story; stressing his intention to include Butzow also "as the principal of a future yarn," he remarked, "I liked him exceedingly."[49]

On January 7, 1914, he turned his creative energy to the writing of the story awaited by his readers and both Metcalf and Sessions—the third Tarzan story. He had mentioned to Metcalf on February 3 that it was near completion, and a week later he wrote to announce it was en route and to reveal the title he had selected: "The Beasts of Tarzan." He was careful to again emphasize the conditions:

> . . . *This is the one I am forced to withhold from our 1914 arrangement owing to my promise to submit it to another publisher, as previously explained.*
>
> *I can however entertain other offers for the first serial rights to it, and if you like the story I hope you get it.*[50]

Months earlier, in writing to Sessions, he had discussed plans for the new Tarzan story, obviously attempting to gauge the extent of Sessions' interest and even predicting that the story would be started by the first of the year, with "a considerable part of it ready by the first of February. . . ."[51] That he should make a prediction of such astonishing accuracy—"The Beasts of Tarzan" was completed within the period of January 7 to February 9—is an indication of the remarkable efficiency and discipline Ed Burroughs maintained in his work. Although Sessions, during the summer of 1913, had displayed an eagerness to obtain a Tarzan story and had been not at all perturbed by Ed's advance price tag of $3,000, his later correspondence appeared to show a lessening of interest, or so Ed interpreted the matter. Ed had written, "As to the next Tarzan story. I took it from your last letter that you desired to do nothing about cinching this for New Story, and so did not mention it further."[52] Ed chose to become idealistic about his objectives:

> *Whether you make a contract with me or not I am going to try to make this as nearly as good as Tarzan of the Apes and The Return of Tarzan as a sequel can be, with the hope of improving on both stories if it's in me. I realize that the Tarzan stuff is what put me on the map, and that if I fall down on the next Tarzan story it would have been better for me never to have written it at all.*[53]

With the forwarding of "The Beasts of Tarzan" to Metcalf and Sessions at the same time, Ed inaugurated the kind of brazen bidding that no author had ever before attempted with an editor. It was a record "first" in the annals of story marketing. His opening maneuver, a week later, consisted of a follow-up letter to Metcalf in which, after explaining that he had written "The Beasts of Tarzan" entirely with the editor's "needs and desires in mind," he continued with an amusingly exaggerated sales pitch about "Tarzan's" popularity: "The other two Tarzan stories have been read by some eighty nine million English speaking peoples, each of whom sat up all night to finish them. The entire civilized world is lying awake waiting for this sequel. I think, under these circumstances, that it might increase Munsey's circulation. Don't you?"[54] (The reference is to *Munsey's Magazine,* the top publication of the Munsey Company. It rated far above *All Story* in prestige and paid higher rates; as a result, Ed had for some time hoped to place a story in the magazine.)

More seriously, Ed proceeded to the financial details:

I hope this tale will net me about twice what my best previous effort has brought. I refused a bona fide offer of $1500.00 for a contract for it before it was written, and have been told since that my request for $3000.00 would be no bar to its purchase.

With the popularity of its predecessors, which not even my blushing modesty prevents me from realizing, I think the story worth all of the latter sum, if not considerably more. . . .[55]

The competitive bidding between Metcalf and Sessions was conducted mainly through a series of telegrams between San Diego and New York. Metcalf initiated the contest with an offering price, one he must have realized would not be accepted: "Feb. 17, 1914. Two thousand for Tarzan. If yes wire. Check immediately."

Ed promptly wired Sessions that he awaited his offer. But a complication had arisen; the manuscript sent to *New Story* had not arrived and was apparently lost in transit. The dickering was temporarily delayed while Wells Fargo was asked to trace the manuscript. On February 18 Ed wrote to Metcalf, "Did not think it worth while wiring you until I had something definite to say. I thank you for the offer, though, and hope you get the story—at a higher figure."

Too impatient to wait, and apprehensive that the bargaining might come to a halt, Ed sent a telegram to Metcalf: "Feb. 24, 1914: Sessions Tarzan manuscript lost. Kindly loan him yours on request." In his determination to keep the contest going, Ed appeared unconcerned about his astonishing request that one bidder share his copy of the manuscript with his competitor. Whatever Metcalf's initial reaction may have been, he nevertheless acceded to this unheard-of request. Negotiations reached a climax on February 28 in a rapid-fire sequence of telegrams:

A. L. Sessions
79 Seventh Ave
New York City
   Will consider three thousand or more. Wire best to-day.

                                                        E R Burroughs
      Collect

Thomas Newell Metcalf
175 Fifth Ave
New York City
   If can increase Tarzan offer materially wire best to-day.

                                                        E R Burroughs
      Paid

Edgar R Burroughs
4036 Third St San Diego Cal
   Very sorry cannot offer more than two thousand

                                                          A L Sessions

E R Burroughs
4036 Third St San Diego
   Do not want to be party to dickering name price will accept or reject immediately have a heart

                                                              Metcalf

Thomas Newell Metcalf
New York City
   You can have for twenty five hundred. Wire.

                                                        E R Burroughs
      Paid

Ed's eagerness to complete the sale the same day, now that only one prospective buyer remained, was not matched by any haste on Metcalf's part. $2,500 was probably the largest amount of money that *All-Story* had ever considered paying for a manuscript, and the editor obviously intended to weigh his decision with care.

Several days passed, and on March 3, nervous over the silence from Metcalf's office, Ed wrote:

. . . I don't know whether you have decided to take the story or not. Since last August I had fixed the price in my mind at $3000.00. That is what I asked them [Sessions]. The concession to you was to demonstrate that I have a heart.

If you don't take it I shall wait until I get my $3000—someone

291

will give it. I really think you should have been glad to in consideration of the small sum the first Tarzan story cost you. Anyhow, I hope to beat the band that you get it even if I lose $500. . . .

On the same day the letter was mailed, a telegram came from Metcalf. The purchase of "The Beasts of Tarzan" for $2,500 was confirmed in two words: "All right."[56]

About the use of the same manuscript, Ed, on March 3, commented, "Probably I shattered all the age old ethics of the publishing business by suggesting that you loan Sessions yours. Howsomeever I saw no other way, and when there is but one and that requires shattering there is nothing to do but shatter."

The plot of "The Beasts of Tarzan" is centered once more around the schemes of the two Russians, Rukoff and Paulvitch, the villains of "The Return of Tarzan." Their plan for revenge leads to the kidnapping of the Greystokes' infant son Jack and the luring of both Tarzan and Jane aboard the steamer Kincaid, where they are made prisoners. Tarzan is set ashore on a jungle island and there, through a note written by Rokoff, learns the details of "the hideous plot of revenge":

You were born an ape. You lived naked in the jungles—to your own we have returned you; but your son shall rise a step above his sire. It is the immutable law of evolution.

The father was a beast, but the son shall be a man—he shall take the next ascending step in the scale of progress. He shall be no naked beast of the jungle, but shall wear a loin-cloth and copper anklets, and, perchance, a ring in his nose, for he is to be reared by men—a tribe of savage cannibals.

Tarzan is also informed of the terrible fate reserved for his wife.

The jungle setting, with Tarzan returning to his savage life, and the favorite technique of maintaining suspense through alternating scenes, unresolved, in which Tarzan or Jane face new terrors, are of course familiar Burroughs fare. But Ed gives an original twist to his story with the introduction of an amazing crew composed of Sheeta the panther, a native named Mugambi, and a dozen huge apes led by the superintelligent Akut; all are trained by Tarzan to work as a unit and to respond to his summons for help. In endowing his beasts with almost-human attributes, Ed far exceeds the animal development he had devised in "Tarzan of the Apes," and equips the savage pack with an intelligence, discipline, and esprit de corps that strain the bounds of all belief. Among other accomplishments the "Beasts of Tar-

SATURDAY   MAY 16   TEN CENTS

ALL-STORY
CAVALIER
WEEKLY

The
Beasts
of
Tarzan
by
Edgar
Rice
Burroughs

ANOTHER ROMANCE OF THE "APE-MAN"

"The Beasts of Tarzan" cover of All-Story Cavalier Weekly,
May 16, 1914.

zan"—the panther, apes, and Mugambi, the native—become the most awe-inspiring crew to ever occupy a dugout or canoe; these seasoned mariners make hasty forays across the waters when Tarzan or Jane need rescuing.

In the exchange of letters with Metcalf, Ed brought up a new topic in regard to the ability of his young nephew Studley Burroughs. The son of Harry and Ella, Studley had from an early age shown unusual skill in drawing and illustrating and had chosen to make art his field of study. Ed wrote to inquire about possible opportunities:

By the way, if my nephew cared to submit a cover design with one of my future stories would it receive consideration? He's a mighty clever young chap, and I don't know of anyone I'd rather see him get a start with than you. He's doing fairly well now, but nothing very steady, and his work is improving wonderfully. . . .[57]

About his latest writing, Ed remarked, "Am finishing up a story that Mrs. Burroughs says you will like. She has called the turn on all of them so far. So I have hopes. . . ."[58] He also disclosed his plans to leave California on March 28, returning to Chicago and his old address at 2005 Park Avenue. The new story, identified in his next letter, was called "The Lad and the Lion." Ed was somewhat dissatisfied with the title: "If you take it you may wish to change the title, and as several suggested themselves to me I'll pass them along to you for what they are worth: The Lord of the Lions. The Lion-Man. The Brother of the Lion. The Lion's Brother. Azìz-El-Adrea. The Prince and the Lion."[59]

To Ed's inquiry about the possible acceptance of art work by his nephew Studley, Metcalf replied that a cover design might be submitted. Ed wrote, "When I get home I'm going to get my nephew to try for one."[60] In the same letter he explained, "It will be some time now before I shall be able to send you another story as from now until the middle of May we shall be all muddled up with moving, house hunting and settling, though I may find a way to knock out another in the mean time."[61]

In commenting humorously about Metcalf's purchase of "The Beasts of Tarzan" after the frenzied round of bargaining, Ed noted, "Was glad to have your 'All right' telegram, and to know once more the w.k. solar system could continue on its accustomed trail, breathing regularly."[62] Ed included a reference to the $10,000 prize short story contest sponsored by Reilly & Britton.

He had contemplated submitting a work in the contest but had changed his mind during the summer of 1913 and had "abandoned" the story after the completion of some sixty-seven pages. To Metcalf he remarked, "It is about half done—provided I cut it down to a short novelette, so I think that I shall finish it up now and let you have a look at it."[63] The story was revealed to be "The Girl from Harris's," and Ed required only thirteen more days to finish it, sending the manuscript to Metcalf on March 20.[64]

Continuous correspondence with Metcalf covered matters of writing and publication. Concerning "The Eternal Lover," about to appear in the March 7, 1914, All-Story (the first issue as a weekly), Ed, upon re-reading the story, noted that it wasn't "half bad." When it was first completed, he had been disgusted with it and had begun a revision, but changing his mind had decided, "Oh Hell, let's wait 'til Metcalf makes me." He showed his dependence upon Emma and the importance he placed upon her opinions: "Mrs. Burroughs hadn't been able to read it ["The Eternal Lover"] before I sent it away, or I should have known that it was all right, for she has read it now and likes it immensely."[65]

Some months earlier he had indicated an interest in doing another Mars story, one centered about Carthoris, John Carter's son. Now Metcalf urged him to write the sequel and offered suggestions. On March 13 Ed wrote, ". . . I don't know about bringing Carthoris down to earth. But I might take Tarzan up to Mars, although with two such remarkable personalities in the same story I might find difficulty in doing credit to either. . . ." In continuing, he noted, "My plan for a Carthoris story centered principally about a little love affair between that young hybrid and Thuvia of Ptarth." A subject of further discussion was "The Mucker," and both Ed and Metcalf agreed that a better ending was needed. Ed commented, "The present close is beautifully artistic, but it's rotten at that. . . ." Of the editor, who had agreed to pay for revisions, Ed inquired, "How many more thousand words will you stand for? And, how soon do you want them?"[66]

Once more, an apparent misunderstanding on the part of Metcalf, relating to serial rights, this time hardly believable, caused strained relationships. In a postscript to his letter of March 13, Ed complained, "They made the old mistake on the Beasts of Tarzan check that they used to at first—the endorsement covered all rights, whereas I only offered you the first serial rights. Please have the proper formal letter of release sent me."

Metcalf, in his response, freely admitted that the fault lay with him; because of the large amount ($2,500) Munsey had paid for "The Beasts of Tarzan," the editor had assumed that all serial rights were included. He described the situation at the time of the purchase:

. . . We were discussing whether or not we could afford to buy this story. I was talking with Mr. Munsey about it, and he said: "If we pay him this sum, which will be considerably more than four cents a word, we will, of course, get all serial rights." And I said, "Why, yes, certainly." I explained very carefully to the clerical end of our manuscript department that when the cards were made out for our filing system it should be distinctly noted that we owned all serial rights on this latest Tarzan story.[67]

In a personal appeal to Ed, Metcalf wrote, ". . . I find myself very uncomfortably placed, because I am having a cover made for the yarn, which I suppose by this time is practically finished, and the story is entirely scheduled, and all that sort of thing. So you can see I am pretty much up a tree."[68]

As the disagreement over serial rights grew more intense, with Ed's impatience and annoyance growing, certain shifts and changes were taking place at the Munsey Company. In the previous month Metcalf had written to hint about these: ". . . it may be that I shall be given control of some other magazine in the house. I cannot speak in any way definitely. . . . Please don't say anything about this matter. . . . I am sure I may rely on your discretion."[69]

Ed viewed this possible change as a chance to improve his own fortunes. He wrote, "About the thing you suggested in your last. There is nothing I'd like better than following you where ever your rising star of fortune leads. I know that if the change should put me in line for a publication which payed more than *All-Story* that you would look after my interests."[70]

With the shift of positions Metcalf now became the editor of *Argosy Magazine* and Robert H. Davis was given the editorship of the amalgamated *All-Story-Cavalier* weekly. Not directly informed of the changes, Ed heard about them from William G. Chapman, his agent for newspaper syndications. A concern about his future writing agreement with Munsey and uncertainty over other matters drove Ed into a state of agitation. His hasty inquiry to Metcalf echoed all his worries: he wanted to know if the "successor" on *All-Story* still cared to have "The Mucker" changed, and if so, in how many words; and what about the words in the Carthoris story? Or did the new editor *want* the story?[71] From these lesser problems Ed progressed to a more serious subject, one that aroused his familiar fears of wasting his writing efforts:

I was just thinking that possibly this change might put some one in who isn't keen for my brand of litrachoor, and if such is the case won't you use your good offices to obtain a release from my arrangement with Munsey. Otherwise I might write my head off on stuff that wouldn't do for any other magazine only to have it turned down. Take sequels, for instance. I knew pretty well what you wanted, but I don't know what the other fellow wants, so I don't want to write any sequels until I hear something definite.[72]

Notwithstanding the confidence Ed had expressed in Metcalf, and his willingness to follow the editor wherever his "rising star of fortune leads," he had no intention of relinquishing the serial rights to "The Beasts of Tarzan." That newspaper serialization of his stories would prove highly profitable had already been demonstrated, especially in the *New York Evening World;* through Chapman's International Press Bureau Ed was currently distributing "The Return of Tarzan," and he planned to follow the same procedure with "The Beasts. . . ." His letter to Metcalf contained a cold rejection of the editor's plea:

. . . I cannot see how there can be any chance for a misunderstanding. Months ago I distinctly stated that I only wished to offer the first serial rights to my stories. There was nothing said to the contrary about this story. I should have been mad to have sold you all the rights for $2500.00. The newspaper rights to the Return of Tarzan have already brought in $950.00 and are still selling.[73]

A comparison of the returns from his own newspaper sales with those of the Munsey Company was highly revealing. It was clear that Ed, with his acute business and bargaining instincts, could give a lesson in salesmanship to the magazine's syndication department. His comment was bluntly critical:

Another thing, and the most important to me; if the newspaper rights are sold by your syndicating department at anything like their usual rates it will tend to ruin the market for my future stories as I will have been getting much more all along the line than your syndicating department sells mss for;—as much as six times what they sold Tarzan of the Apes for in one instance.[74]

His letter contained a threat to take an action that could lead to a complete break with the Munsey Company: "If Mr. Munsey insists upon holding me to the technicality of the check endorsement the only thing that I can see to do is to buy the story back from you. I hope that this will not be necessary for I wish you to have it. . . ."[75] He stressed his hopes for a satisfactory agreement, noting that one of his greatest pleasures in writing for the Munsey Company would disappear if he felt he might be "similarly misunderstood at any moment in the future," and that his interests "were not unquestionably safer" in their hands than in those of other publishers.[76]

With the changes in the editorial staff and the resulting confusion the matter remained unsettled. Ed's protests were unanswered, but with a bulldog tenacity he continued his one-sided campaign to acquire a clear ownership of his serial rights to "The Beasts of Tarzan." His succession of letters in the following months, written to both Metcalf and Davis, contained repeated references to the subject. To Metcalf he forwarded a personal appeal:

. . . The present policy of ignoring me does not set very well. I asked several questions that should have been answered, which, you advise me, you relayed to the Proper authority; but I've heard nothing.

And about the Beast of Tarzan rights: I can understand that you made an honest mistake in perfectly good faith; but I can less well afford to suffer by it than The Frank A Munsey Company.

They got a story that their readers wanted for what they paid, while I will get nothing at all for a loss of several thousand dollars.

It would mean very little to The Munsey Company either way, but a great deal to me, and I shall never let my rights to this story go without contesting it to the utmost.[77]

"So keenly do I feel the injustice of it," he wrote, "that I am seriously considering writing nothing more until my arrangement with The Munsey Company is up the 31st of December."[78] In a second letter of the same date to Metcalf he stated, "I have heard nothing further about the several rights to The Beasts of Tarzan, and as a matter of form I should be very glad if the formal release such as was sent me in previous instances should be sent to me, releasing all but first serial rights. . . ."[79]

By this time the Munsey Company could entertain no illusions that Ed would forget the matter. In fact, it appeared plain that he would never allow *them* to forget it. To Robert Davis, the new editor of *All-Story Cavalier,* he wrote, ". . . Just at present I am particularly concerned with the matter of the several rights to The Beasts of Tarzan, relative to which I have written Mr. Metcalf in the letters which you mention. . . . I state specifically that I can entertain offers for the first serial rights, nor anywhere in any letter have I even remotely suggested that I sought to dispose of any other rights."[80]

The battle may have been protracted, but the Munsey Company, at an early stage, might have perceived that in dealing with a man of Burroughs' dogged determination their chances were nil. The inevitable surrender came in a letter from Davis: "This shall be your authority to exercise for your own account all rights in your story entitled 'The Beasts of Tarzan,' which ran serially in The All-Story Cavalier Weekly from May 16 to June 13, 1914, save the first serial rights."[81]

Ed continued to expend his unlimited energies in other directions. Syndication was very much on his mind, and an inquiry from the *Tacoma Tribune* prompted him, on February 26, to write to Chapman, who agreed to contact the newspaper concerning the two available Tarzan stories. Chapman revealed that the Munsey Company had granted him "the privilege" of making sales of "Tarzan of the Apes"; because of the small payments received by the syndication department, the company had evidently lost interest in marketing the story. Chapman's report that he had offered to release both "Tarzan of the Apes" and "The Return of Tarzan" to the *Tribune* for a mere $75 was hardly cause for elation. But the *Tribune* was one of the lesser outlets; newspapers of this type all over the country were included in Ed's ambitious plan to find some type of mass market for serialization of his stories.[82]

Ed was still plagued by a regret that he had relinquished the serial rights of "Tarzan of the Apes." His past attempt to repurchase these rights had been unsuccessful, and now, in an inquiry to Chapman, he again discussed the possibility of obtaining them. Chapman's reply was discouraging; about the story he wrote, "Nothing can be done. . . . They won't let go of it."[83]

Ed continued to conduct his own negotiations with Terhune at the *Evening World.* His telegram of March 11, 1914, to the editor read: "You may have New York City newspaper rights Eternal Lover for one cent per word. Immediate payment." Terhune, on the same date, wired a protest:

One cent a word for "Eternal Lover" would be three times as much pro rata as we paid for "Return of Tarzan" and nearly ten times prorata price of "Tarzan of Apes." We want the story but not at so prohibitive a price. Won't you reconsider terms and telegraph. We consent to immediate payment as you propose.

In a letter of March 13 Ed presented a lengthy exposition of his sales philosophy. His statements were again based upon a businesslike analysis of the market value of his wares:

If the prices I asked for the New York City newspaper rights to The Eternal Lover seem high it must be remembered that my stories are worth more now than at first.

I am not viewing the matter from an egotistical standpoint. I have always tried, and I think succeeded in eliminating ego from my business consideration of my work—otherwise I might be prompted to give my yarns away.

He offered a logical comparison of past and present values:

. . . My last story brought six times what Tarzan of the Apes brought, and over ten times that which I received for the story that preceded it—my first. I only asked you three times as much as you paid for the first story you bought of me, which I think you will admit was very generous of me.

Ed brought up a further point, which he felt was "the most potent":

. . . Two large publishing houses shied at Tarzan solely on account of the fact that it had run in the newspapers. Some day someone will put my stories into books; but in the mean time I am losing just that much by allowing them to be syndicated, so I do not feel that I can afford the luxury without ample remuneration.

His final comment to Terhune was that "$300.00 is not an exorbitant price for such a story as The Eternal Lover if your readers like it. Of course, by the yard, it may seem a high price, but who would purchase works of art by the yard!"[84]

In answering on March 20, Terhune again stressed that the terms were prohibitive, adding, "I'm sorry, on my own account; and chiefly because of the thousands of Evening World readers who love Tarzan and are so eager to read every word about him." He offered $200 for "The Eternal Lover" and pointed out that this was a record fiction price for his "twenty years of service" at the *World*. The magnetism of the Burroughs name *on any story* and its power to lure readers was already demonstrated, even at this early period. As a result of this popular demand Ed had altered, or to a certain extent reversed, the normal author-editor relationship with the editor dictating the terms. That Ed was the dominant party, negotiating from a position of strength, was revealed in Terhune's personal plea, most unusual in that it came from the editor of one of the country's greatest news-papers. In continuing his letter Terhune implored, "Won't you reconsider on that basis? We should be your debtors and so should our readers. Telegraph in such event; and a check for $200 will be sent you by the next mail."

Concerning the rejection of "Tarzan" by book publishers, Ter-hune wrote, "If you will refer any future publishers to us, we shall be only too glad to testify to the tremendous interest the story has aroused among our readers. . . ."[85] Before the com-bined appeal of the editor's plea and his praise of "Tarzan," Ed's resistance collapsed. On March 25 he wired, "Two hundred dollars . . . Eternal Lover acceptable. Remit to Chicago address."

The two stories that signaled the end of the prolific California writing period were entirely dissimilar in their plots, settings, and styles. "The Girl from Harris's" (when finally published, the name Harris was changed to Farris), begun in Chicago a year earlier, depicted big city corruption, creating at times the ef-fect of an exposé. It established some elements of realism, while, in contrast, the second work, "The Lad and the Lion," returned to fantasy and to a transparent repetition of situations and de-vices that had given "Tarzan" its popularity.

In "The Girl from Harris's" Ed adopts the role of a social reformer, commenting bluntly and witheringly about the alliance, in Chicago, between certain vice interests, scheming politicians, and powerful real estate groups and property owners. In addition, through his portrait of a hypocritical clergyman he offers a caustic view of religious do-gooders and of society's narrowly puritanical standards. Ed's characters are created with a sentimentality that weakens the story's realistic effect. The hero-ine, first introduced as "Maggie Lynch," is revealed to be a prostitute, an employee of Abe Harris, described as "the most notorious dive keeper in the city." Later events show that the sup-posed connection with a man's death has enabled Harris to black-mail her and keep her in his establishment against her will.

Maggie, aided by Ogden Secord, a handsome young businessman, and inspired by his faith in her, attempts to start a new life and takes a position as a typist, now using her real name—June Lathrop. Another character, the Reverend Theodore Pursen, exemplifies, as a minister, the worst qualities of false piety.

Ed, in developing the plot, devises an ironic twist or reversal of the roles of the two main characters. Ogden Secord receives a blow on the head during a robbery in his office and as a result, his memory and his power to think clearly are impaired. With the loss of his prosperous business he deteriorates, in the end becoming an alcoholic. The changing situations allow June Lathrop, now leading a respectable life, an opportunity to assist the man who had given her needed encouragement.

In the last few chapters the setting is abruptly shifted, and both Ogden and June are transported from Chicago to Idaho. June turns up as a waitress, hundreds of miles from Chicago, in the town of Goliath, the very same town where Ogden, a down-and-out drunk, has wandered. Once more Ed returns to his theme of a man's regeneration through a combination of a healthful outdoor life and a woman's faith and love. Ogden works as a miner, washing gold as Ed and his brothers had done. Actual towns are referred to: Ketchum on the Salmon River near Sun Valley, and Shoshone, farther south.[86]

As he had done in "The Mucker," Ed attempted to give his dialogue a realistic flavor through the use of the argot of the lower or criminal classes. The heroine, in her first role as Maggie, slips into the coarse slang of the times.[87] From the extremes of the vernacular Ed moves, in other sections, to the use of dialogue which is stilted, unnatural, and which gives a melodramatic effect: "You can't help being kind and sweet, for your soul is pure and true—I can read it in your eyes; but even that can't blind you to the bald and brutal fact of what I am—a drunken bum."

The Lad and the Lion" presents an opening deliberately made vague, with brief, mysterious hints of the Lad's noble birth. The fourteen-year-old boy aboard the ship is summoned by "Old Jagst," a faithful attendant, when a shipwreck is imminent. Jagst says, "Quick, Your Highness," and later there is a reference to "royal blood"; but the Lad receives no name and the kingdom is not identified. The boy reveals his courage by refusing to enter a lifeboat, insisting that the place be given to a woman. As the ship goes down, he is struck on the head by a piece of timber, finds himself in the water and then climbs into a drifting lifeboat. The blow on his head has destroyed his memory.

Later the story develops bizarre elements. The Lad is taken aboard a derelict ship whose only occupant is an odd creature, a half-mad epileptic, an old man who is also a deaf-mute. On the same ship is a young lion in a cage. The old man, who has derived a sadistic pleasure from teasing and torturing the animal, now begins to mistreat the boy, and in the passing months subjects him to threats and beatings. The Lad is required to learn the sign language of the deaf-mute. He shows kindness and sympathy toward the lion, and the two develop a strong bond of affection.

Four years of this life continue, until the lion kills the old man. The ship then drifts ashore on the coast of northern Africa, and the pair enter the desert together. A romance emerges between the Lad and Nakhla, the exotic daughter of Sheik Ali-Es-Hadji, complicated by the customary evil schemes of a villain, Ben Saada. From Nakhla the Lad finally receives a name, Aziz, meaning "beloved" in Arabic. With the introduction of Marie, the daughter of Colonel Joseph Vivier, commander of the French garrison, Ed devises the typical conflict of a love triangle.

The familiar device of a loss of memory is accompanied by its equally familiar solution: clubbed on the head in a battle with the Arabs, Aziz regains his memory. In the very last section of the story, the past returns to him. He recalls the ship and the "gray old man" who had cried, "Quick, Your Highness!" Beyond the ship he also sees, as in a vision, "a stately pile of ancient masonry," and a scene returns to him of a little boy being saluted by soldiers. He realizes that he is a royal prince and that a throne awaits him.

In its final love scene between the Lad and Nakhla, the story remains somewhat cryptic and inconclusive. The Sheik, when informed by Aziz that he would wed Nakhla and the two would then dwell in the family douar, had only accepted because he appeared to have no choice. As a foreigner, Aziz had been viewed with contempt by the Arabs, and had been called a "dog" and a "pig" by them. Now, with a realization of his royal birth, the Lad's feelings of inferiority are replaced by a sudden pride: "No longer was he a dog, or a pig. Now he knew precisely what he was and what awaited his coming upon another continent. . . ." He gazed into the eyes of Nakhla, "and then with all the ease and grace of centuries of breeding behind him, he dropped to one knee before her, lifting her slim brown hand to his lips. 'My Queen,' he said. 'My Queen—forever!' "

Whether the Lad intended to marry Nakhla and live in the Arab douar with her, or whether he planned to return with her to his unnamed kingdom is uncertain. The story is without a definite resolution. The typical Burroughs stratagem must be suspected: the possibility of a sequel was being held in abeyance.[88]

Ed was to achieve one more success, valued by him above all, before his return to Chicago. In February 1914 events began moving rapidly toward his long-desired goal—the acceptance of "Tarzan of the Apes" for book publication. The serial installments of the story, especially in the New York *Evening World,* had spread its fame and popularity. In the passing months the public's response had grown until it could be better described as a fascination with the very idea of Tarzan and his jungle environment. But Ed was not depending solely upon newspapers and public interest to promote the book possibilities. According to one report, for a period of several months he had made daily trips to A. C. McClurg & Company's store on South Wabash Avenue in Chicago to talk to Herbert Gould, McClurg editor and an old friend, and to others at the publishing company. Ed was a single-minded man, and the sole topic of discussion was the appearances of Tarzan stories in magazines and newspapers and how they were causing "Tarzan's" popularity to soar. Ed's dogged campaign was almost sufficient in itself to overcome the resistance.[89]

The Tarzan fame prompted John G. Kidd of Stewart & Kidd Company, Cincinnati, Ohio, on February 20, to express an interest in acquiring "Tarzan of the Apes" for publication. In his response Ed displayed a confident attitude. He knew there was a public demand for "Tarzan" in book form and that this demand would increase when "The Beasts of Tarzan" appeared in *All-Story.* The struggles and uncertainties of 1912 were long gone. He could afford to wait now until he received an attractive offer.[90] Nevertheless, he was curious about Stewart & Kidd and he sought information from Herbert Gould. His main concern was whether the firm had enough experience and capital to handle the book successfully. ". . . Have they a reputation for square dealing?" he also inquired.[91] Gould, on March 13, rated Stewart & Kidd as "first class," explaining that they had been in the book business and were "ambitious" to turn to publishing. "I have my doubts," he confessed. ". . . They certainly do not have the facilities for handling a novel as it should be handled." Undoubtedly to Ed's surprise and elation, Gould made a counter offer: "If you have not gone too far, it might be possible for you to again submit to us the manuscript of your story 'Tarzan

Rare first edition of Tarzan of the Apes *(hardback).*

of the Apes.' I will be glad to have our publishing department reconsider their decision of last Fall about publishing it."[92]

Acceptance of "Tarzan of the Apes" by A. C. McClurg & Company was now a certainty. However, as negotiations continued, Ed preferred to let his agent William Chapman handle them. The sale of "Tarzan of the Apes" to a book publisher was the climax of two years of struggles and a sign of personal and creative triumph. But if Ed considered it so, his actions at this moment of success defy all explanation. With Europe in a turmoil and events moving rapidly toward declarations of war by the various powers, he arrived at a rather surprising decision: he wanted to be a war correspondent. Toward the end of April 1914 he sent his request to Albert Payson Terhune at the *Evening World.* Terhune was clearly incredulous:

I've turned over your war correspondent application to Mr. Tennant, the Managing Editor. Though why a man who can write such fiction as you write should want to do press work, is beyond my understanding. In any case, I wish you all the luck there is.[93]

On April 25, with the "Tarzan" sale assured, Ed dispatched instructions to Chapman. The matter was one quite obviously dear to his heart:

I wish to have appear on the fly leaf of Tarzan of the Apes:

To
Emma Hulbert Burroughs

Or,

Emma Hulbert Burroughs
Her Book

The latter is rather irregular, but it fits the case—Mrs. Burroughs has always had a partiality for Tarzan, calling it her story from the first.

Will you please see to this for me.

Thanks.

Chapman, on May 1, notified Ed that the final agreement with McClurg had been reached.[94] A day later in a letter to Terhune Ed indicated that his desire to be a war correspondent was a mere impulse, subsiding as quickly as it had arisen. He wrote, ". . . I guess that war correspondent job will have to lie over until Teddy comes in again in 1916. . . ."[95]

Seldom did Burroughs display in his business correspondence the warm sensitivity and emotions that were so much a part of his private nature. His feelings about Emma and "Tarzan of the Apes"—Her Book—were touchingly revealed in the autograph he penned to Emma in a first edition copy of the book, published on June 17, 1914, at this milestone in his career:

June 10, 1914

My dear wife:

Do you recall how we waited in fear and trembling the coming of the postman for many days after we sent the Tarzan Mss to Metcalf?

And will you ever forget the morning that he finally came?

Not even this, our first book, can quite equal that unparalleled moment.

That we may never have cause for another such is the wish of your devoted husband

Ed R Burroughs

Delighted by the Fred J. Arting illustration of Tarzan in moonlit silhouette on the title page of the book, Ed pasted a miniature sticker of the drawing onto the letter of July 20 that he wrote to Bob Davis. Beneath the tiny rectangle showing Tarzan poised on a tree branch, Ed typed, "Ain't this a cute little sticker?"

The end of the California period and the return to Chicago brought this comment from Ed in the final lines of his *Autobiography:*

Before we left San Diego for the East I must have been feeling flush again for I ordered a new automobile for delivery in Chicago when we arrived.

Once again we auctioned our belongings, including the old second-hand Velie.

His earnings, collected during the summer of 1913 before he

307

left California, totaled more than $4,600 from sales of stories and from the *Evening World* syndication. In California, from October payments from Chapman had brought him approximately $6,000.[96] He had written approximately 413,000 words. He was hardly in danger of going "over the hills to the poorhouse" and was well ahead of the sheriff.

PART 5

FROM STORIES TO MOVIES

CHAPTER 11

THE WRITER AT HOME

With his return to Chicago at the end of March 1914, Ed, his financial situation now secure, planned to purchase his own home in a neighborhood suitable for the raising of his three children, Joan, six, Hulbert, five, and Jack, barely one year old. Ed had stayed temporarily at the Hulbert home at 2005 Park Avenue, renumbered from its original 194. He directed his mail to be forwarded there, but intended to remain there for only a brief period. He decided to buy a home in the upper middle-class suburb of Oak Park, at 414 Augusta Street, near Ridgeland, and on May 11 he moved his family into the large five-bedroom home which was advertised as having "the best hot-water heating plant in Oak Park."[1]

In the productive schedule of writing that he continued to maintain, Ed certainly demonstrated himself to be the least temperamental of writers. He had approached his story creations in the past with a businesslike, matter-of-fact attitude, and success had not changed him. Noises or distractions had little effect upon the flow of his ideas; he required neither complete silence nor isolation. While at work in his study, he permitted the children to enter and leave at will, and even had no objection to stopping in the middle of a passage to answer questions or play with them. As Ed typed a story, it was not unusual for Jack, then three or four, to climb up and perch himself on his father's knee.[2] A writer of the period reported:

Burroughs family at 414 Augusta Street, Oak Park, Illinois, 1915; left to right: Joan, Ed, Hulbert, Jack, and Emma.

Three beautiful children, Joan, Hulbert and Jack, the oldest six, clamber over Mr. Burroughs' anatomy, and desk and typewriter while he is turning out the tales you all clamor for. "Were I literary," he says, "and afflicted with temperament I should have a devil of a time writing stories. . . ."[3]

In these early Oak Park days Ed's office was in his home. He had already adopted a schedule that would become a habit with him, one that he would adhere to for the remainder of his writing career. Finding the morning hours most productive, he was at his typewriter at seven or seven thirty, worked until noon, and after a pause for lunch, perhaps continued for an hour or so longer. In later years he wrote only in the morning. He followed this schedule five or six days a week, and on occasion worked in the evenings, especially when he corrected the pages he had written during the day. The corrections, though brief, sometimes involved typing errors or the substitution of one word for another, but Ed seldom rewrote or did lengthy revisions unless these were requested by a publisher.[4]

He was unaffected by the kind of temperament often evidenced in writers who went through agonizing struggles in a search for ideas and who claimed that they had to wait for the inspiration to arrive. His later philosophy revealed an impatience with these writers; he did not understand their inspirational requirements—he simply sat down to write and the ideas came.

At this time he typed all his stories himself, and having no training in the touch system, he used a two-finger method, pecking away rapidly with an accuracy that was quite remarkable. His daily output averaged from ten to twelve pages, double-spaced. His approach did not include rough drafts, a practice followed by many authors who then revise or polish their material. Instead, he reflected upon each sentence, carefully working away rapidly and with an accuracy that was quite remarkable. while, meditating, head down, in intense concentration, before turning to type the complete sentence. With this method he seldom found it necessary to make changes.

Ed maintained that often, as he wrote, and the fantastic characters and actions sprang from his imagination, he had no idea of what was coming next. This was clearly a humorous exaggeration; the plot and its general direction were already established in his mind. However, he would never depend upon a strict, detailed outline, claiming that this would restrict him, tie him down in a way that would hamper his imaginative flights. The closest thing to an outline might be a summary of several sentences in which the theme or essence of a forthcoming chapter was briefly stated. Ed admitted, with amusement, that because of his spur-of-the-moment writing or improvising, he would sometimes get his character into a seemingly impossible situation and not know how to extricate him. Nevertheless he always did.

While in his writing he was freely imaginative, preferring to devise incidents as he went along, in his record keeping, as previously explained, he was thoroughly businesslike and methodical. (His card index of sales and payments has already been referred to.) With his first published story, "Under the Moons of Mars," he began his worksheets, using Roman numerals. On these sheets he noted beginning and completion dates, chapter headings, and page numbers, often with word counts, and listed his characters—later, because of his sequels, consisting only of new characters not involved in the previous stories.[5]

At this stage Emma was the first to read his stories, and she became his most valued critic. In seeking the opinions of his brothers, however, he naturally turned to Harry, who had been closest to him and had helped him through many difficult situations in the past. Earlier, when his first Martian story was in progress (then titled "Dejah Thoris, Martian Princess"), he had brought sections to Harry and his wife Ella (always addressed as Nell or Nellie) for their reading and reactions. They had of course been enthusiastic about the story and, at a later reading, about "Tarzan of the Apes." Their children, Evelyn and Studley, through family discussions and their own reading, became familiar with Ed's creations.[6] When, with these successes, Ed had considered quitting his job, he sought Harry's advice. Cautious, and without very much confidence in writing as a career, Harry advised Ed to stay where he was, reminding him of his responsibilities to his wife and children. He urged Ed to view the writing merely as a part-time occupation.

Ed's family and friends had often commented about the names he devised for the strange characters in his stories. His ability to create exotic civilizations and races and surround them with an other-world atmosphere that appeared scientifically plausible and realistically convincing was matched, and necessarily so, by his adeptness in inventing names that fitted naturally into his bizarre settings. He formed his names, at times, by combining odd syllables, selecting and sounding them while he listened for the odd, foreign effect he was seeking. On occasion he chose or modified words from foreign languages, especially Latin. His ear,

A PRINCESS OF MARS
(Under the Moons of Mars)

-Iss - River of Death.
-Tars Tarkas - a chieftan; 2nd to Lorquas Ptomel.
-sak - jump.
-Sola - young green-martian woman.
-Lorquas Ptomel - Jed among the Tharks.
-Woola - a Barsoomian calot.
-Sarkoja - a green-martian woman.
-Thark - city and name of a green martian horde.
-Tal Hajus - Jeddak of Thark.
-Dejah Thoris - Princess of Helium.
-Mors Kajak - a jed of helium, her father.
-Helium - the empire of the grandfather of Dejah Thoris.
-Barsoom - Mars.
-Jeddak - Emperer.
-Jed - King.
-Dor - Valley of Heaven.
-Korus - lost sea of Dor.
-Korad - a dead city of ancient Mars.
-thoat - green martian "horse".
-Tardos Mors - grandfather of Dejah Thoris.
-Zad - Tharkian warrior.
-o mad - man with one name.
-Dotar Sojat - Captain Carter's Martian name, from the surnames of the
        two warrior-chieftans he first killed.
-sorak - a little pet animal among the red martian women; about the
        size of a cat.
-Warhoon - another community of green men; enemies of Thark.
-zitidars - mastaionian draught animals.
-calot - dog.

A Community:(figures are approximate only)
                500 warriors
                 20 chieftans
                250 women
                250 youths
                500 children (immediately after a hatching)
                250 chariots
               1000 thoats
                300 zitidars
                500 calots

July 14 1912 - commenced sequel to "Under the Moons of Mars" GODS OF MARS   IV
Bar Comas - Jeddak of Warhoon.
Dak Kova - Jed among the Warhoon (later Jeddak)
kaor - greeting
Kantos Kan - padwar of Helium navy.
padwar - lieutenant.
Zodanga - Martian city of red men, at war with Helium.
Ptor - family name of three brothers - Zodangans.
darseen - chameleon.
Sab Than - prince of Zodanga.
Than Kosis - Jeddak of Zodanga.
Notan - royal psychologist of Zodanga.
Gozava - Tar Tarkas' dead wife.
                (Above Martian names and words used in Under the Moons of Mars)

*ERB's notebook page for "A Princess of Mars"; ERB recorded
information included in each of his stories which, when he started
writing sequels, helped him keep characters and other facts in order.*

the final judge, told him when the sound was right. Above all, the name must fit the character. *Tars Tarkas* seemed natural for a brave Martian chief, and *Tal Hajus* for a cruel, villainous ruler (the sound was hard and cacophonic enough), while *Dejah Thoris* was perfect for a beautiful Martian princess. The name *Tarzan* itself appeared uniquely chosen—as though no other name could have possibly been accepted.

In devising names for his animal characters Ed was equally skillful. Somehow *Tantor* seems appropriate for a towering, majestic, and kindly elephant, *Sheeta* menacing enough for a leopard, and *Akut* just right for a protective ape companion. While many names were formed through the combining of syllables, Ed freely admitted he may have used actual names that somehow remained in his memory. In a letter of July 2, 1923, to his brother Harry who had inquired about his methods, Ed wrote:

. . . I try to originate all the peculiar names for people, places and animals in my stories. Sometimes I must unconsciously use a word or name that I have read and forgotten, as for instance Numa the lion. There was a Roman emperor, Numa, of whom I had forgotten until I was recently rereading Plutarch's Lives. The name must have been retained in my sub-conscious brain, later popping out as original. . . .

The other-world effect was also evident in the geographical names he invented. Such words as *Barsoom* for Mars, the *Otz Mountains, Ptarth, Phutra, Zodanga,* and others, through their strange, alien sounds, helped achieve a natural atmosphere for Ed's fantastic civilizations.

On a number of occasions Ed had expressed his preferences among his own writings, revealing that he liked his Martian stories better than the Tarzan stories; he had also been quite explicit about his choice of reading, his favorite authors—and his aversions. He liked Kipling's poetry but found his stories boring. He detested Dickens; according to one biographer this feeling may have resulted from Major Burroughs' habit of reading aloud to his young son:

When, for example, his father read Dombey and Son, Edgar hated Dombey and had the impression that Dombey and Dickens were one and the same person. When he learned the difference, it was too late for him to overcome his ingrained prejudice against Dickens. . . .[7]

Hulbert, Emma, Jack, and Joan Burroughs, about 1915.

At some period during his early years Ed had developed a dislike for Shakespeare which he could never overcome. On the
other hand, his school studies and readings in Latin, including
Caesar's *Commentaries* and the works of Gibbon, had given him
a permanent interest in the Romans. This led to an intense admiration for Thomas Babington Macauley's *Lays of Ancient
Rome;* in the vigorous style of these ballads, their regular meter,
stirring narration, and martial tone Ed found pleasure and excitement.[8]

His early readings in fiction had made certain authors his favorites. These included Jack London, George Barr McCutcheon
with his *Graustark* novels, Anthony Hope with his *Prisoner of
Zenda,* and Zane Grey with his stories of the West. Much of his
later nonfiction reading was done for research, but he had found
the adventurous works of Richard Halliburton highly enjoyable.[9]

In the home life of the Burroughs family Ed naturally turned
his vivid imagination loose to create the most fantastic of stories
for his three children. Storytelling, which he first practiced as a
child, reversing the normal procedure by telling his mother the
stories he made up, had always been his special delight. For his
children he invented such characters as Grandpa Kazink, an old
man with a flowing white beard who embarked in his own flying
machine for the wildest of escapades. Accompanying him, and
sharing in the hair-breadth escapes was a little girl named Saphronia.[10] In later years Ed invented Arabella the Coyote who

was involved in animal adventures that might include pursuits by lions or tigers.[11] Ed's procedure in telling his stories to the children at bedtime was a duplicate of the to-be-continued, cliff-hanging style he adopted in his published stories. Grandpa Kazink, as well as the others, went on and on with continuing new sequences:

When the children were very small, it was Burroughs' job to tell them bedtime stories and, after a hard day's writing, pacing in the corridor outside their rooms, he broadcast improvisations wholesale. Characteristically, he had several serials going at the same time. In one of them "Grandpa Kazink and his Flying Machine," Grandpa, something of an interplanetary superman on a child's level, was constantly rescuing his girl friend Saphronia from otherworld savages. After Burroughs had worked the kids up to an unbearable pitch, with Grandpa hanging on to the edge of Mars while six-legged Moaks hacked away at his tiring fingers, he would call, "That's all, children. Now go to sleep." . . .[12]

The Burroughs' Augusta Street home in Oak Park was typical of any home where three children were being raised. Included in its activity and excitement were the noises of children at play, the barking of dogs, and the sounds of music—singing and piano playing. Ed had always liked children, enjoyed playing with them and devising games for them, and Emma had her heart and interest centered in her home and family. As a result, the relationships of parents and children were warm and close. In their childhood Ed and Emma had developed a lasting fondness for dogs, and they soon acquired two Airedale terriers. The male, naturally named Tarzan, became a permanent pet who would also, in the future, become a traveler, journeying with them to California.[13]

While Ed often made joking references to his voice, his inability to carry a tune, and freely admitted that his musical tastes were limited—he liked only marches, martial music, and hymns, claiming they were the only kind of music he understood—he nevertheless regretted his lack of musical background. As a result, he was pleased to have music become an important activity in his home. Emma, who had studied voice in the hope of becoming an operatic singer, entertained the family and friends. They encouraged all the children to take piano or singing lessons.

The Burroughs family early became aware of the strange and often frightening nature of their father's dreams. Throughout his adult years Ed was subject to nightmares. These occurred regularly and involved the kind of situation, familiar to many dreamers, where some fearful creature or unidentified peril was

The Burroughs children in front of home at 414 Augusta Street, Oak Park, Illinois, 1915; auto is ERB's Mitchell.

approaching the room, and the individual, aware of his danger, tried desperately to move but found himself paralyzed. Ed would twist about, moan and cry out loudly and awaken the family. Sometimes Emma soothed him until he became calm. Statements or suppositions that these nightmares contained fantasy scenes of other worlds or dangerous encounters with creatures of the type created by Ed in his stories, and that he would draw upon these nocturnal adventures for his plots, are unfounded. His nightmares should not be confused with his daydreams during which he might devise characters and situations for his stories.[14]

At the time when he first turned to writing, Ed developed an illness that became troublesome. The sharp pain in his left shoulder was diagnosed as "neuritis." His most acute suffering occurred at night. The Burroughs children sometimes awakened in the middle of the night to see their father pacing the floor, unable to sleep because of the pain.[15] After a number of years the "neuritis" apparently vanished, or so Ed believed; on June 22, 1918, in a letter to his friend Bert Weston concerning the illness of Weston's wife, he discussed the matter:

I was mighty sorry to learn from your letter received today that Margaret is afflicted with neuritis. It is a mighty painful disease as I know from seven years experience with it. I am pretty well shut of it now and it may interest Margaret to know that my improvement immediately followed the taking of a medicine which I obtained while in Coldwater [Michigan] the 1st of March.

I do not take much stock in patent medicines but after a fellow has had neuritis for seven years he would take almost anything to be rid of it.—I even tried Christian Science once. This dope which I obtained is put up by a druggist in Coldwater from a prescription given to one of the Coldwater plutes by a traveling salesman—but where the traveling salesman got the prescription, deponent sayeth not. Anyhow, it costs one and a half bucks per bottle and is absolutely guaranteed to be harmless.[16]

Noting that Dr. Earle had scoffed at the idea of the medicine having any effect, Ed wrote, ". . . it was a remarkable coincidence that immediately after commencing to take it the pain left me for the first time in years and I have been steadily improving since."[17]

Whatever relief Ed may have obtained, real or imaginary, it was evident that the medicine did not provide a permanent cure. A year later he revealed that the pain had not disappeared:

For a considerable part of the past seven or eight years I have suffered the tortures of the damned with neuritis; but I have studiously avoided the use of drugs, preferring the pain to the possibility of acquiring a habit that always had seemed peculiarly revolting to me. . . .[18]

Again, in a letter to his brother Harry three years later concerning Nellie's (Ella's) illness, Ed also discussed his troublesome neuritis:

. . . Was very sorry to learn that Nellie had been suffering so from neuritis. Mine has come back again, after leaving me for two or three years, though it is not as bad as it used to be. I learned yesterday of a theory that acids aggravate it; therefore let us leave acids alone.[19]

Whether by modern diagnostic methods the illness would be called "neuritis" is doubtful. To his nephew Studley, who many years afterward complained about arthritis, Ed responded, ". . . It hurts like hell. I know. But I am over mine. I also had bursitis. . . ."[20] The entire problem may have simply resulted from inaccurate diagnosis and treatment.

Despite his periodic suffering from neuritis, Ed continued to indulge in a recreation that was one of his greatest sources of pleasure. He had always loved automobiles and driving. The 1914 biographical sketch written for William G. Chapman (author unknown) comments about this:

Next to Mr. Burroughs' devotion to his family comes his love of motoring. Rain or shine, summer or winter, you may see him every afternoon with his family upon the Chicago boulevards or far out on some delightful country road beyond the city's limits. . . .

The author writes jokingly about Ed's ability in sports:

His tennis is about the funniest thing I ever saw, and his golf is absolutely pathetic, yet he loves them both, and baseball too, though he couldn't hit a flock of balloons with the side of a barn door, and if he did probably he would be as likely to run for third base as first.

Even at this early period, the fact that Ed was not a good social mixer was evident:

. . . . Whatever Edgar Rice Burroughs may be he is unquestionably the world's poorest conversationalist, nor does that fact cause him the slightest concern. Unlike most people who cannot talk he is an equally poor listener. He believes that the average man or woman has little or nothing worth saying and that they spend so much of their waking lives in saying it that they have no time to think—they exercise their vocal organs while their brains atrophy.

Much of this attitude toward people at social affairs, and his impatience with the type of light chatter that went on in groups, remained with him in later years. He commented, on a number of occasions, that most people bored him, and at times, in crowds, he made little attempt to conceal this boredom. (According to his son Hulbert, this reaction to large social gatherings was largely due to a natural shyness. Among close friends he was at ease.)

With the passing of the years, circumstances had of course changed for the remaining members of the Burroughs family. After the death of her husband, Major George Tyler Burroughs, in 1913, Mary Evaline continued an active life. She especially enjoyed traveling and visiting her sons, and at a later period adopted a custom of spending three months of the year with each son and his family.

The failure of their gold-dredging enterprise in the Stanley Basin of Idaho forced George and Harry Burroughs to seek new occupations.[21] After returning to Chicago, where he was unable to find satisfactory employment, George again succumbed to the lure of Idaho and in 1904 went to the small town of Burley, not far from his old location at Minidoka. George tried various occupations, finally establishing himself in the Burley Hardware Company, in later years adding a garage and car agency to the business.[22]

At the time the two brothers were attempting to wind up the affairs of the Sweetser-Burroughs Mining Company and to salvage whatever they could, Harry had an unfortunate accident. He was chopping some kindling for the stove and was struck in the eye by a piece of wood. His eye was severely injured and his vision impaired. With regular medical treatment he appeared to be recovering, but there were complications; a bad inflammation of the optic nerve developed and soon spread to the other eye.[23] For a year he was virtually blind. Medical treatment continued, with Harry traveling back and forth from Parma, Idaho, where the family lived, to Boise to see the specialist, Dr. Buffem.[24] His condition remained unchanged, and as a result he decided to return to Chicago to seek new medical help. After a year of treatment, he began to improve, and regained partial vision.[25]

Harry found employment of various types, including a position as office manager for the Physicians Co-Operative Association, the same organization for which Ed had worked. Harry entered the new field of the automatic telephone, taking a job with the Automatic Electric Company. He became a telephone installer, and at the time his two children Evelyn and Studley were in high school, he was struggling to make an adequate living. Ella had even taken an office job—an almost unheard-of thing for a gentlewoman of the times.[26]

Frank Coleman Burroughs, closest in age to Ed, had remained in Minidoka, Idaho, after the others left, later returning to Chicago. Evelyn, Harry's daughter, recalled his activities:

He had seen the need for a general store where the people living there and on ranches for miles around could order staples and yard goods etc. from Eastern cities. So he built a house near the railroad and after his marriage brought his bride there to try the experiment of running a general store. It was quite successful, but difficult, and eventually fire destroyed most of the store and its contents—after the fire Uncle Coleman and Auntie Grace went back to Chicago.[27]

Katherine Burroughs Konkle, in recollections of her father Frank, noted:

After growing up in Chicago and attending school in Massachusetts, (Andover) he fell in love with the West and loved the small town life. However, after being twice burned out—both business and home—in a town where water was at a premium and there was no fire department, he brought his little family back to Chicago.[28]

Upon his return to Chicago sometime between 1906 and 1908, Frank and his wife Grace finally settled in the suburb of Wilmette. At this time he was working for the Champlin-Yardley Company, dealers in stationery. Ed had worked there also and had used the office and the mailing address in his early writing period. Frank later took a position with the Pullman Company.[29]

Burroughs family on a Sunday drive, Illinois, 1914; auto is ERB's Hudson.

The association between Harry and George and their Yale classmate Lewis Hobart Sweetser had been close and continuous. With the collapse of the gold-dredging project, Sweetser remained in Idaho. In 1901 he had started a new venture, sheep ranching, but met with only limited success; he ceased operating it three years later.[30]

Sweetser next decided to try his fortunes in politics. He achieved a steady success, serving two terms in the Idaho legislature, following which he was twice elected lieutenant governor, in 1908 and again in 1910. As Republican candidate for governor in 1912 his chances for election seemed excellent, but unfortunate personal circumstances forced him to withdraw from the race.[31] He continued in a variety of business activities in Idaho.

Through the years 1913-15 Ed devoted spare moments to what might be described as his only creative hobby—the writing of light verse. Here, in sharp contrast to the practical money-making attitude he had adopted for his story writing, he chose to write, often humorously, for plain enjoyment. A number of these poems were submitted to two columns in the *Chicago Tribune,* first to "In the Wake of the News" by Hugh E. Keogh (HEK) and then to "A Line-O'-Type Or Two" by Bert Leston Taylor. Many of these appeared in print, mainly from 1914 to 1915, but several had been published earlier, possibly as early as 1909. In these newspaper contributions Ed maintained the only use of the pen name he had devised years before—Normal Bean.[32]

In these poems Ed had on occasion shown a strong interest in the Chicago Cubs baseball team, revealing himself to be a staunch fan. One of the earliest poems, saved in his collection, dated September 16, 1911, appeared in "In the Wake of the News" and was titled "O, Yes; It's Getting Thick"; its humorous subject is about the differing effects of the Cubs' losses and victories:

> *My dear, he said at breakfast time,*
> *The Cubs have lost some more;*
> *But as a loser I'm sublime,*
> *'A Good Game Loser,' that is I'm;*
> *List' not, you'll hear no roar.*
>
> *Say, what in———is this———stuff?*
> *It tastes to me like slops;*
> *As coffee it's a rotten bluff.*
> *This steak is raw and awful tough;*
> *Those market guys are wops.*
>
> *Then at the office: "Say, how much*
> *Do you folks think I'll stand?*
> *That straight front blonde'll get in Dutch*
> *If she ain't here on time. Lord, such*
> *A bunch should all be canned.*
>
> *"Say, boy, you ain't no brickybrack,*
> *You're paid to do some work.*
> *Hike out o' here, and don't come back.*
> *Who wrote these credits here in black?*
> *Where's that———billing clerk?*
>
> *"My sweet," he said, at eats that night,*
> *"Although it's naught to me,*
> *I note the Cubs played outosight*
> *Today. They'll nail that pennant right.*
> *This is delicious tea."*

On the "In the Wake of the News" world series staff, jokingly appointed by Hugh E. Keogh, Normal Bean occupied a prominent spot. The group of "correspondents" was announced in the column:

To cover the world's series, The Wake of the News *has come to an understanding with the fetchingest staff ever turned loose on a sporting event. We have gathered and enshrined under this roundtop the greatest collection of literary pinch hitters unpinched and the finest bunch of mot makers that ever fed sweetmeats to a gaping populace. . . .*[33]

Ed's letter, addressed to HEK from Austin, Illinois, and printed in the column, announced his readiness for the assignment: "Arrived at Fifty-second avenue at 7:10 a.m. Expect to reach Chicago, via Oak Park limited, by Saturday to cover assignment. Normal Bean."[34]

In his poem "Must Fight or Run Out" Ed offers a philosophical defense of prizefighting and sportsmanship. He is critical of the highbrows' view that Rome declined because the gladiators took to fighting each other, or that the fighting bulls caused Spain's downfall. He reminds these highbrows that "The fact that Caesar loved a scrap/Was what put Rome upon the map;" and ends by stating:

> *To those who say the fighter's worst*
> *I might remark: "He's also first*
> *Because some ancient guy could fight*
> *You owe the fact you're here tonight."*[35]

In answering the charges of brutality leveled at the prizefighting game—charges that Ed seemed unusually concerned about—he took the side of the supposed "lowbrow" who attended the fights, as opposed to the highbrow who went to auto races. Ed's opinion is expressed in a poem printed in "In the Wake of the News" and titled "Look on This Picture, Then on That." An introductory description of the poem is offered by HEK:

A study in contrasts shuffled up and presented by Dr. Normal Bean of Oak Park, an adept with the physical and metaphysical speculum, a man of broad and deep perspective and withal some pinch hitter at making verses. Cut the cards.[36]

The lowbrows, who "reek of stables and of bars" are pictured watching "two husky guys" pound each other until one is knocked out.

In Canto II he depicts the highbrows "attired like clowns on circus day" attending the auto races with their wives and children. He creates a scene of havoc and death:

> *A punctured tire—a deadly curve—*
> *A mangled heap of blood and nerve—*
> *A broken gear—a lost control—*
> *A dead man mussing up the goal*

After the tragedy which includes "a dying son—a sweetheart dead," Ed develops his contrast in a short stanza titled "The Wind Up":

> *The highbrowed gent, it seems to me,*
> *Who takes his wife and kids to see*
> *The mangled entrails, tortured bones,*
> *And hear the shrieks and moans and groans,*
> *Can learn a lesson from the dope*
> *Of lowbrow's game, of "white man's hope"*
> *He may not have a massive dome,*
> *But—wife and kids he left at home.*

Ed's defense of the lowbrow and the supposed lower-class sport of prizefighting, and his derision for the highbrow are revelatory of his identification with the common man. This had been evidenced in his almost defiant choice of Normal Bean as his pen name. With his insistence on being considered ordinary and his championing of ordinary tastes and attitudes, he was announcing belligerently that he belonged with the masses. But this self-relegation to the ranks of the ordinary was also an indication of something else—the feelings of inferiority he had long possessed. This inferiority was to be intensified with the poor reception his stories would receive in literary circles and from highbrow critics, along with his own understanding of his limitations and of the fact that he was not a "literary" writer. In the future he would continue to class himself with the common man and as the writer for the average or ordinary person—with repeated emphasis upon his philosophy that entertainment, not literary style, was the purpose of writing.

From San Diego Ed sent two poems to Bert Leston Taylor's "A Line-O'-Type Or Two." These poems represented a Chicagoan's critical appraisal of Southern California and the treatment the tourist received. The first one, later titled "Nay, It Hath Not Gone" by Taylor and reduced to four stanzas, was mailed by Ed on January 24, 1914, in its original six-stanza form:

I've missed The Wailing Place of Late,
And glean it hath been swiped.
I'm full of rails and eke of wails—
With sorrow I am piped.

Oh, who hath copped The Wailing Place?
I ask you, dear old pal.
No Place they keep where one may weep
In sunny southern Cal.

And if The Wailing Place hath gone
Forever and for keeps
What shall we do (whom all do do)
For where to spill our weeps?

The butcher man he robs me blind;
Robs me, the grocer deft;
The brigand cruel who sells me fuel
He taketh what is left.

The garage man (accent the gar),
Unmindful of my groans,
He wrecks my car with loud Har! Har!
And later picks my bones.

And now The Wailing Place is gone
Where shall we find us rest?
Unless you say: "Come hither, pray,
"And weep upon my vest."

Normal Bean[37]

Other poems by Ed appeared in "A Line-O'-Type Or Two" from 1914 and 1915. His poetry scrapbook contains poems of various types: these include printed poems with his pen name, Normal Bean, but updated; printed poems with both column or source and name missing; and typed poems which may or may not have been printed in a newspaper. Pasted on a page in his scrapbook are five printed poems, four of these from "A Line-O'-Type Or Two," but without an author's name. They appear to be in Ed's humorous, satirical style. Two of the four contain the earliest printed dates of any poems so far discovered—August 21, 1909, and October 23, 1909.[38]

Possibly in the period of 1908-09, Ed had also written a song-poem, not intended for submission to the newspaper. Titled "Joan's Pick-Me-Up Song," it was composed for his daughter born January 12, 1908. The three-stanza poem imaginatively represents the crooning song of an infant who wishes to be picked up:

> *I am not crying 'cause anything's wrong;*
> *I am just singing my Pick-me-up song.*
> *Pick me up, mamma, and then if you do*
> *I'll show you how nicely I gurgle and coo.*
> *I have been sleeping so all the day long*
> *That now I will sing you my Pick-me-up song.*

After a changing second stanza, the third becomes a repetition of the first. Ed's penchant for writing on the backs of old letterheads from defunct businesses is again demonstrated in this typed poem. The letterhead, with *Burroughs* printed at the top and beneath it a listing of eight different titles, carries an address of 82 Sherman Street in Chicago.

Ed's past, as with the past of many famous individuals, had a way of returning. Letters from old acquaintances and friends often stirred his memories and caused him to reminisce. A letter from Edward H. Doughtery, Sales Manager for Foster & McDonnell, Chicago publishers, referred to the early days when Ed was sending his poems to the *Chicago Tribune:*

A copy of the "War Chief" by Edgar Rice Burroughs, was just laid on my desk, with a letter asking for a review of this book as soon after September 15th., as possible. It struck me as a coincidence and will appreciate your advising Mr. Burroughs of my receipt of same.

It was my privilege to be his office boy some fifteen years ago, when his chief effort was in "making" The Line, and my main duty as office boy, was carrying these efforts to the office of B. L. T. . . .[39]

Ed, in his response, chose to joke about the lethal effects of both his poetry and prose:

. . . How many changes have occurred since the days when you carried my immortal lines to B. L. T.!

H. E. K., who conducted "In the Wake of the News," on the sporting page of the Tribune, died after publishing several of my gems. It took me longer to kill B. L. T., and I was nearly ten years disposing of Frank A. Munsey, and then there was Ogden McClurg, who succumbed after publishing more than twenty of my novels. The man who made my first motion picture died shortly after it was released, and so I cut my bloody swath across the literary fields of the twentieth century, but fortunately for me a few of my readers still survive. . . .[40]

The California sojourn being over, Ed resumed his intensive writing schedule; in mid-April 1914 he began what he had described as "a Carthoris story" (later titled "Thuvia, Maid of Mars").[41] Robert H. Davis, who had replaced Metcalf as the editor of the amalgamated *All-Story Cavalier*, wrote to Ed on May 29 to state that he would soon offer suggestions about future writing plans. These came in a letter of June 12:

I have read "The Mucker" and "The Girl from Harris's" . . . familiarized myself with Tarzan. . . .

. . . my opinion that you and I ought to have a conference and that at an early date . . . five things I want to talk with you about.

1. . . . rehabilitation of Tarzan. 2. . . . plan to lengthen "The Girl from Harris's." . . . 3. "The Mucker" should be concluded. . . . 4. . . . sequel to perhaps "The Mad King" or "At the Earth's Core." 5. . . . the pleasure of seeing you.

If you are on for this suggestion, we will supply you with transportation both ways, and a one day's conference will be sufficient. . . .

In his reply Ed displayed a cooperative attitude, discussing Davis' points in order. Concerning the "rehabilitation" of Tarzan he was somewhat dubious: ". . . I may as well tell you frankly that I have never written anything in accordance with another's suggestions that has proved satisfactory to the other, although I am perfectly aware that the other fellow's ideas are probably much better than mine—the thing is that I can't ever seem to grasp what is wanted."[42] Ed was willing to accept the remaining suggestions: he could "easily" lengthen "The Girl from Harris's"; at the start he had intended to make it a full-length novel. In the story a problem had arisen about the elder Secor; Davis believed he should be eliminated. Ed commented, ". . . we can talk of that when I see you; but it seems to me that whatever plot the tale has hinges on the old gent."[43]

In the matter of a conclusion for "The Mucker" Ed explained he had previously written a different ending and was now forwarding it to Davis. He groaned at the mention of "sequels," commenting, "I am sick of writing sequels; but I appear to be doomed. The Mad King sequel seems less appalling than that to The Eternal Lover. However, I can write sequels for both if they are wanted."[44] He expressed pleasure at Davis' invitation to a conference, volunteering to travel to New York within the following two weeks, but preferably in the early part of the next week. He actually arrived in New York on June 23.[45] He had hastened to mail the ending of "The Mucker" to Davis, and about it noted, ". . . I tried to make him do a big thing simply. I hope the readers will get it. . . ."[46]

Writing at a furious pace, he had only a few days before he notified Davis of the mailing of the story he still titled "Carthoris." His letter mentioned "another Martian story, the first serial rights to which I wish to sell for use in the *All-Story Cavalier Weekly*."[47] He proceeded methodically to another task. Davis' remarks about "The Girl from Harris's" had included a disapproval of the role of John Secor, the wealthy old man who dupes the heroine, June Lathrop, into a false marriage. After Secor's death June and the old man's son Ogden fall in love and at the story's end are planning to get married. Davis had commented, "It's hell for a man to wind up as the husband of his father's mistress."[48]

Aware of this odd situation, Ed nevertheless had no intention of eliminating John Secor from the story; this would have required extensive revision. He searched for the easiest way out of the dilemma, and on July 11 wrote to Davis "about The Girl from Farris's." (Note the title had now been changed.) "If I make the old man his uncle or foster father will he cease to offend you? I think I could do it better that way than another. Please let me know by return mail as I am all set." From Davis came a prompt agreement. He preferred the foster father and remarked, "Anything to eliminate the blood relationship. . . ."[49]

Ed's labor-saving approach resulted in brief revisions centered about two pages, plus minor changes throughout the story. In sending the new version to Davis on July 21, Ed explained, ". . . have substituted 'Abe' Farris for 'Al' Harris wherever the latter appeared. However, it might be well to warn proof readers, or whoever do such stunts, to look out for any instance where I may have neglected to make the change. It is a tiresome job—I wouldn't have done it for anybody but you. . . ."[50]

Thuvia, Maid of Mars *frontispiece by St. John, 1920.*

To solve the problem, Ed had contrived the simplest and most abrupt device. The nonplussed reader, arriving at the story's end, encounters a sudden, amazing revelation that John Secor is not Ogden's father. The explanation is given by Ogden to June: "I was the foster son of John Secor's brother. When he died I went to live with the John Secors, and after the death of their only son I entered Mr. Secor's office, taking the place of the son he had lost, later inheriting his business."[51]

"The Girl from Farris's," with Ed's creation of Maggie Lynch (June Lathrop) as a prostitute and an occupant of a house of ill-repute owned by Abe Farris, "the most notorious dive keeper in the city," constituted a surprising departure from his usual fantasy and adventure stories. Whatever prompted him to make this abrupt turn from "Tarzan" and "Mars" and the "Inner World" to the subject of vice in Chicago—a subject that in 1914 would have to be handled with discretion—is difficult to tell. That Ed himself felt uncomfortable with the theme, or even doubtful that he had been wise in developing it, is indicated in his letter of September 19, 1914, to Davis:

In this connection, though it is none of my business, I am wondering if it might not be a good plan to run The Girl from Farris's *in something other than* The All-Story Cavalier *whose readers appear to have a considerable antipathy for smut. I should hate to offend them as they have been very kind to me.*

"Smut" is a strong word, and Ed's use of it to characterize his own writing reveals his sensitivity to the supposedly sordid theme he had chosen. But the word is also revealing of limitations of Ed's moral attitude and conditioning. Bob Davis, an experienced editor who would have certainly rejected any material that might have been offensive to his readers, had offered no criticism of the theme. Obviously, he had found nothing wrong with it and the manner in which it was developed. His only objection had been to the relationship of the two Secors.

In the short period of contact with Davis, including the personal conference in New York, Ed's relationship with the editor had reached a pleasant, informal level. The correspondence of both men carried a friendly and jesting tone, similar to the one maintained by Metcalf and Ed. On June 29, 1914, Davis wrote to thank Ed for "one handsome copy of 'Tarzan of the Apes'" and referred to the autographed note: "Those flippant lines in 'Tarzan' in which you take a wallop at my parlor English are delightful. You and I alone understand what it means."[52] Davis acknowledged the additions to "The Mucker" and remarked:

I have performed the laparotomy and Wednesday will send you a check for the additional 5,400 words. You've got old Euclid tied in a clove hitch when it comes to mathematics. But I forgive you because the brand of words you spill seems to please a large number of readers, and those are the people we are after. . . .

Prompted by the request of Joseph Bray, McClurg editor, for publicity in connection with the publication of Tarzan in book form, Ed had written several times to suggest that a notice be inserted in *All-Story Cavalier*. On July 2 Davis forwarded a page proof from the forthcoming July 18 issue of the magazine; the "Heart to Heart Talks" contained an announcement about the Tarzan novel.[53] Davis continued to be cooperative, and a month later sent a copy of *All-Story Cavalier* in which Ed's letter discussing sequels was featured.[54]

In the months that followed, the flow of correspondence was steady, while the writing, because of requests for revisions, became more intensive and exhausting. But even though he had grown tired of the interminable sequels, he was still able to joke about them to Davis and to reveal, at the same time, the formidable writing tasks he had set for himself:

In reply to your recent query relative to The Cave Girl, The Mad King, The Eternal Lover, *and* At the Earth's Core, *let me assure you that but half of each of these stories has yet been told.*

You see I couldn't know that any of them would interest the All-Story Cavalier *readers sufficiently to warrant prolonging them, and in the case of the Pellucidar narrative the fate of David Innes was not cleared up until quite recently, so that I couldn't have gone on with that one, anyway.*

In the near future I rather expect I'll have all the data complete on each of these, when I shall be very glad to submit all the evidence to my bully friends of the All-Story Cavalier.[55]

With the changes in the Munsey staff and the assignment of Bob Davis as editor, the status of Metcalf had become uncertain.[56] On June 28 Ed received a card from Metcalf, mailed from the Harvard Club at 27 West 44th Street, New York, explaining the situation:

The Munsey Co. and I have split. It has been brewing—if splits may be said to "brew"—for some time. I have nothing definite in mind as yet, but when I do—if it is a business in which we may deal together I shall, of course let you know.

I am sure that your relations with Davis will be wholly satisfactory so don't worry about that end of it. If there is anything I may undertake for you, don't hesitate to write me. You may always address me here.

Ed responded, ". . . Cannot tell you how badly I felt to hear that you are no longer with Munsey. I hope that when you connect up again it will be in a way that will permit us to work together as in the past. . . ."[57]

Thousands of words produced, stories dispatched, revisions demanded, word counts disputed—this was the pattern of the last half of 1914. On August 17 "The Cave Man," a sequel to "The Cave Girl," was mailed to Davis. In the bickering that ensued, Ed first conceded that he had overestimated the word total, but nevertheless accused the Munsey Company of under-counting:

I made a bull in my word count of The Cave Man. Before I started it I figured the number of pages that should be necessary to give 40,000 words, and then I gave you what I thought a couple of thousand words for good measure. When the check came, for which by the way I thank you, I was surprised to see that it was for less than $1000. So I got busy and counted the words—suffering a second surprise when I discovered that there were less than 40,000, though at that whoever counted them at the other end short-changed me still further.[58]

With the forwarding of his next story, "Sweetheart Primeval," Ed explained that he had used the same method for his word count, and as a result of this inaccuracy the total was below the 50,000 words requested by Davis. "I am very sorry," Ed wrote, "but if you take the story, please plead with the Appollonius Pergasus who computes the remuneration to be generous upon my side this time."[59] He was hardly exaggerating when he added, "I am working like a wall-eyed part-horse, and hope to complete all your commissions this year."[60]

He had enclosed a check for $6.00 for two subscriptions to *The All-Story Cavalier,* one of these intended for his mother.[61] Davis evidently had decided by this time that the only safe and effective way of dealing with Ed was to kid him and to respond with the same type of humorous insults that Ed hurled at him. Upon receipt of Ed's check, Davis addressed him as "My dear

Colonel Burroughs" and commented, "A letter from you containing real money is such a startling proposition that I dare not tarry acknowledgement. . . ."[62]

Concerning the word counts, Davis somewhat despairingly suggested that Ed should list the exact number of words in his manuscript. "God knows," Davis said, "everybody in this shop tries to count your manuscripts so that there will be no argument. Life is too short to rush every issue to the Supreme Court. . . ."[63] About "Sweetheart Primeval" Davis asked, "What, in your opinion, is the exact number of words. . . ? Disregard everything else and deal only with this particular manuscript. Let us strike a basis for reckoning that will be permanent."[64]

At the close of the letter Davis again became humorously insulting:

Sorry you weren't with me this summer. I could have made it very pleasant for you at times and disagreeable at others. I think the only way to get good results out of you is to hand you the four seasons—spring, summer, autumn and winter. Continuous perfect weather is a bad thing for Burroughs. Somebody must step up and bite you or hit you with a stone axe or push you into a bottomless pit or clamp an abyss on you before you really begin to get human.[65]

Although appreciative of Davis' good-natured sarcasm, Ed could not be sidetracked and clung doggedly to the issue of the

INCOME from stories		
Under the Moons of Mars	1911	400.00
The Outlaw of Torn	1913	500.00
Tarzan of the Apes	1912	700.00
The Gods of Mars	1912	750.00
The Return of Tarzan	Feb 1913	1000.00
The Inner World	9th	400.00
The Cave Girl	Apr	600.00
A Man Without a Soul		1165.00
War Lord of Mars		1141.00
The Return of Tarzan (N Y World)		300.00
The Cave Girl (N Y World)		200.00
The Ret of Tzn(Am Prss Assn)$200-60%		120.00
Inner World (addition to)		320.00
OVER		

First of ERB's many file cards on which he entered income from story sales and book royalties.

word count in "Sweetheart Primeval." He replied with his own brand of humor:

You have been so good to me always that it tears my heartstrings to haggle over this business, but every time a heartstring starts to tear, up comes a word at 2½c per and bleats in its ear. The result is that I am immediately "torn by conflicting emotions." . . .[66]

As Davis had requested, Ed enclosed his exact count of "Sweetheart Primeval," at the same time pointing out that this could not be used as a permanent standard since the length of lines varied in different stories. Unable to repress his business instincts —an almost obsessive fear of being underpaid—he explained, "The Cave Man ran 11.44 words per line, while this one shows 11.9."[67] He added:

If it will be of service to you I am perfectly willing to submit a similar word count for each story—it would require but a couple of minutes each day to keep it up as I write.

I don't want to ask anything out of the ordinary, though, so if you would rather do it your way, why go ahead—though I must reserve my inalienable right to howl. . . .[68]

A week later, on September 29, Davis conceded that Ed's method was "pretty nearly exact," and urged him to continue his word counts. Davis remarked humorously, "I want to remove any possibility of your howling at my conclusions, because, believe me, Burroughs, you are one hell of a howler and the uttermost confines of the world are not sufficiently remote to escape the tremendous reverberations of your throaty protests." In noting that he planned to eliminate about 2,000 words or more, Davis wrote, "I am going to tie a can to some of those deep-sea reptiles and chase a little slime off the page."

Concerning these prehistoric monsters, Ed replied, "Of course the pterodactyles, plesiosaurs, ichthyosaurs, and the like are perfectly all right in a pre-glacial dream, but if you don't like them, why can them. Sir Conan got away with them, though, in a tale of the 20th Century—hold on now, I know I aint."[69] Reflecting over the shortened manuscript, Ed commented, "I suppose I really ought to howl, so that you won't find it too easy to fall into the habit of slicing great hunks of hard earned mazuma out of my mss. My artistic temperament writhes in contemplation of those fifty-odd bucks going into your waste basket; but possibly, were you to rush along the check for the balance, it might survive the shock. . . ."[70]

Ed, like a runner leaping over obstacles at a breakneck speed, continued his writing schedule of one sequel after another. "Barney Custer of Beatrice," the sequel to "The Mad King," was sent to Davis on November 2. Ed would not permit himself a breather, writing, "I shall immediately start in on the sequel to At the Earth's Core, and after that will come, in order, The Son of Tarzan. . . ."[71] Contemplating 1914, past and future, he added, ". . . subsequent to which I think shall lie me doon an' dee, for I sure have put in one hell of a year at hard labor—and all for you. I wouldn't have done it for anyone else on earth."[72]

The "hard labor" was compounded by further demands for revisions; Davis was far more difficult to please than Metcalf. The tone of his letters remained lightly ironic, but his criticisms were blunt and scathing. Upon receipt of "Barney Custer of Beatrice" he wrote, "In all your previous work you have established a reputation for speed and plot and movement. That is why you are getting large money these days. Also, you are A-1 for originality."[73] Then he proceeded to aim devastating blows at Ed's fictional cliches:

I will forgive you for having the King and Barney look alike, although it is the oldest device in modern fiction. But it isn't fair for Barney to make his escape by stealing two automobiles in Chapter V and Chapter VI hard-running. There is no art to that, Burroughs, and no ingenuity. A man can go on writing sequels for the balance of his lifetime if he is permitted to resort to these time-worn stunts.[74]

Davis' criticism continued with reference to page 27 of the manuscript in which the way the hero escaped the firing squad was "nothing short of preposterous." Davis commented, "Falling forward on one's face goes on skating rinks and in the presence of district leaders, but it is beneath you to pull it in fiction."[75] The reactions of the magazine's readers were his main concern: ". . . I do not want the sequel to be so much worse than the first part that the reader is dissatisfied. 'The Mad King' made considerable of an impression and a large number of readers are waiting for this sequel, which I have announced."[76] Davis exclaimed, "But great international God, Burroughs, don't hand them a hack story."[77]

Speaking frankly, Davis stressed the point that he would accept the story "even in its present form," but urged Ed to consider the criticisms and see if he couldn't "do better by the reader and the publication." He noted Ed's complaint about "one hell of a year at hard labor." As a new editor, Davis had made suggestions for sequels which, to a man as ambitious and hard-driving as Ed, were equivalent to orders. Ed's furious writing pace was the result of his own compulsiveness, his need to demonstrate that he could do the seemingly impossible; it was not caused by unreasonable demands on the part of Davis. Actually, the editor advised caution and a slow-down:

If you are already exhausted, after writing " 'Barney' Custer," what kind of a sequel will you turn out to "At the Earth's Core"? And where, oh where, will "The Son of Tarzan" wind up for the grand finish? I don't ask you to break your neck or wear yourself out with this thing. I would much prefer you to take your time and do something you are proud of. Any man who starts out as tired as you say you are ought to be seated somewhere along the line of march and take a little rest.[78]

Davis' joking tone at the end—"You may consider, under all circumstances, old Tarzan, that I am yours to a cinder. . . ."— may have helped to soften the severe criticisms. On November 13, 1914, in a night letter to Davis, Ed stated, "Feelings not lacerated. Will at once make changes you suggest; but as you accept the story for the love of Mike send a check. Five Hundred bucks advance will help a lot. Spare coin tied up in real estate and need money for current bills."

The money, dispatched at once by telegram, arrived the next day. Ed wrote again to explain that he had devised changes for "Barney Custer." He planned to complete them and return the manuscript quickly. "Have taken a two weeks rest," he said, "and shall start on sequel to At the Earth's Core today or Wednesday— Tuesdays I play golf with increasingly pitiful results."[79] It was clear that Davis' admonitions would have little effect in diverting him from his hectic schedule. On November 16 the "Barney Custer" manuscript was sent to Davis, the changes indicated in Ed's letter:

Instead of having Barney dodge the bullet, I let it go as a bum shot which merely creased his head, which of course is quite reasonable.

And I changed the stealing of the second auto, which so grated upon your artistic temperament, so that he didn't have to steal one after all.

By this time Davis must have realized that any Burroughs revisions would cost the Munsey Company money. Ed appeared constitutionally unable to revise by eliminating or condensing. Ed wrote, "These changes have added 900 words to the mss."[80] Concerning Davis' worried remarks about overwork, Ed responded:

Who said I was tired? Can't a fellow lie down and die if he wants to without being tired? Nay, I am not, and furthermore I have seldom worked more enthusiastically upon a story than upon this last one. I enjoyed it and really thought that it was better than most of them—so you can see what a shock your letter was. I wish that you would be more careful what you eat before you pass on my stuff.[81]

Flabbergasted at Ed's ingenious method of revision, Davis, on November 24, after noting that a check for the $825.00 balance due on " 'Barney' Custer of Beatrice" was en route, remarked, "I swear to God, old man, I can't see how you got in 900 extra words without increasing the number of pages. I am figuring the whole thing out now at 53,000 flat, which I trust will pacify your tempestuous soul. . . ."

During the latter part of 1914 Ed continued his newspaper syndications, maintaining his personal contact with Terhune at the New York *Evening World*. Answering Terhune's request, Ed, on November 14, sent him "The Beasts of Tarzan"; and to open price negotiations, pointed out that although the story was shorter than "The Return of Tarzan," the payment for it had been two and one-half times as much. Ed explained that he would not ask for any such increase from Terhune. He wrote, "I will be perfectly satisfied with the same price for the New York City newspaper rights as you paid for The Return of Tarzan; namely, $300.00." Ed attempted to dicker, but Terhune remained firm at $200, a price that Ed finally accepted.[82] In the same period there was regular correspondence with Chapman about national syndications, and the dealings with his agent revealed that at this time he turned to a new and unexpected type of writing.

The outbreak of World War I in Europe in 1914 had revived his interest in military matters and his patriotic concern about the state of the U. S. Army. In a letter of September 24 to Chapman, he asked the agent to examine the "enclosed" and let him know whether it might be syndicated in the papers that had printed *Tarzan* stories. He remarked:

It struck me that owing to the interest in martial stuff it might take on, my idea being primarily that it would be good general publicity stuff for the Tarzan stories. It could be run as, by Edgar Rice Burroughs, author of Tarzan of the Apes.

If you could get real money for it—fine! If not the publicity would be our reward.

Chapman responded on the 25th, referring to the "Army MS" Ed had sent and indicating that it would be forwarded to the Journal. The *Journal* was presumably the *Army-Navy Journal,* because four years later another Burroughs article titled "A National Reserve Army," was published in that service magazine on August 31, 1918. Chapman wrote, ". . . I hardly think that papers would be inclined to pay money for it; I believe it will have to be considered publicity stuff."

The "Army MS" was an article of approximately 2,200 words, titled "What Is the Matter with the United States Army?" It was Ed's first professional article, and in writing it he drew upon his own military background and made specific proposals for the creation of an army with a "new purpose." His unrewarding experiences at Fort Grant, where he had not found the "real soldiering" he had sought, remained vivid in his memory, and drove him to view the army's methods with contempt and disgust. He recalled his commander at Fort Grant as a "pick and shovel man" and bitterly described his assignments under this commander. Ed noted that he had become "one of the loveliest little ditch diggers in the army," had proceeded from there to a "coffee-cooling" job, and then to being a stableboy, his task consisting of "chamber work for fourteen horses." He described the situation graphically (and with some guilt): "My comrades poked fun at me—and were envious. Mine was a sinecure. I was a gentleman of leisure. They—poor devils—had to work. They had to *soldier* while I loafed. I carried and fed and watered fourteen horses. I hauled hay and oats for them. I made their beds at night and unmade them in the morning, and as I rode luxuriously across the parade ground on top of a load of manure I saw my fellows sweatingly engaged in plucking house-size boulders out of the virgin soil of Arizona."

In introducing his plan, he offered some statistics about the army of his times:

We are spending nearly $100,000,000.00 each and every year to maintain our standing army—an army that half a dozen of the new Krupp guns would wipe out of existence in about forty-seven minutes.

We spend one hundred million dollars, then, to train eighty-five thousand recruits, and six hundred million to board and lodge them for the remaining six years of their enlistment. To my mind we are throwing away the six hundred millions.[83]

"How much better it would be," he said, "were we to turn eighty-five thousand trained men into private life every year and spend their board and lodging money in training eighty-five thousand more!" His familiar businessman's efficiency was now at work. He conceded that a yearly eighty-five thousand enlistment under present conditions would be impossible, and proposed to change these conditions, the first target being the seven years enlistment law—four years active service and three in the reserve. His indignation stirred him to rhetorical extremes:

Seven years! What grey-beard conceived such an eternity of time for a young man? Or was it suggested by a jealous foreign power that wished to see our little army dwindle to nothingness? Were you ever young? Then you will recall that seven years was a mighty long time. Would you enlist in any man's army in times of peace for seven long, weary years? Neither would I.

As a first step, service in the regular army would be set at one year, but not the kind of service he had suffered—"that wouldn't make a soldier in seven years or seventy." After emphasizing that the young men, in whom "the spirit of Romance and Adventure breathes strong," do not want to dig ditches all day long, Ed turned to specific suggestions for the army with a "new purpose." Ditch digging should be done by hired laborers; soldiers and officers should devote an eight-hour day to military theory and practice. Under this program a recruit would not need a year for training—three months would be sufficient. A further result would be an increase in the soldier's pride; he would acquire an "esprit de corps which is so essential in a military organization, and which you seldom see among ditch diggers."

Under Ed's plan, the year in the army would be part of a total three-year requirement, the remainder, at the soldier's option, to be served either in the regular army or in any state militia. This would provide the National Guard with a steady reserve of trained men.[84]

There is no record of any publication of the article "What is the Matter with the United States Army?" or of further communications with Chapman on the matter.

An early statement of Ed's philosophy concerning "Tarzan of the Apes" was contained in a letter addressed to M. N. Bunker, publisher of *The Naturopath*, Salina, Kansas. Bunker's inquiry about the *Tarzan* novel had been forwarded to Ed by Joseph E. Bray, McClurg Editor. On August 24, 1914, Bray wrote:

. . . I take it you will have a peach of a time explaining just why you wrote Tarzan, *because as I understand it, you did it because you hoped to make money out of it. Writers, however, are not supposed to compose their masterpieces for this sordid reason.*

Mr. Bunker (whose name, by the way, has a rather suspicious sound) evidently wants to get an argument for Physical Culture out of Tarzan. *. . .*

In noting that he had answered Bunker's letter, Ed, on August 26, wrote to Bray:

Had I more time I could give him quite a spiel on the physical culture possibilities of Tarzan; but I am in the midst of another story and way behind my schedule. However, I imagine Mr. B. to be much better qualified to get the physical culture germs out of the book than I. . . .

To Bunker, on the same date, Ed explained,

Of course the primary motive of a story like Tarzan of the Apes is to entertain, yet in writing this and other stories I have been considerably influenced by the hope that they might carry a beneficial suggestion of the value of physical perfection and morality.[85]

Because Tarzan led a clean, active, outdoor life he was able to accomplish mental as well as physical feats that are so beyond the average man that he cannot believe in their possibility, and if that idea takes root in the mind of but a single young man, to the end that he endeavors through similar means to rise above his environment, then Tarzan of the Apes will not have lived in vain.

Ed's statement of his primary writing motive as entertainment was of course the one he later preferred to stress. Perhaps the idealistic purposes he offers in the letter had influenced him in the creation of "Tarzan of the Apes"; perhaps they were ideas he had produced on the moment's inspiration purely for Bunker's benefit. Similar ideas—themes, motifs—may always be discovered through analysis after a work is completed. Nevertheless, the philosophy of physical perfection that is so vital to the idea of a Tarzan relates closely to the Burroughs family's early goals of fitness, exercise and sports, and vigorous outdoor living. The transference to the "Tarzan" story came as part of a natural expression of belief.

Bunker had also inquired about the origin of the "Tarzan" plot. Ed responded:

In answer to your second question, the story is not founded on fact, though in greater part the life of the apes is more or less true to nature. The earthen drums of the anthropoids have been found and described by reputable travellers and explorers, and the natives of certain central African tribes insist that there is a race of apes of immense size and of much greater intelligence than the gorilla.

Upon publication of his review of *Tarzan of the Apes,* Bunker sent Ed the page from *The Naturopath* containing the review. At the bottom of the page Ed typed the notation "Ackd Nov. 14, 1914." The review appeared in the Physical Culture section, and Bunker glowingly summarized the book as "Natural Healing gotten up in a splendid fiction form." Important points are copied from Ed's letter: the primary function of books such as Tarzan of course was to entertain. But stories of this type carry a "beneficial suggestion of the value of physical perfection and morality." The novel, Bunker explained, provides a moral lesson "because Tarzan led a clean, active outdoor life. . . ."

In another review of *Tarzan of the Apes* appearing a month later, the writer offered some precise criticism and made an amusing analysis of the Burroughs style. The review in the Chicago Press Club's *The Scoop* of December 12, 1914, referred to Ed's writing as "uneven" and commented on his "occasional habit of writing excessively long sentences." A particularly elongated sentence that became a paragraph was quoted. Introducing the "fierce, mad, intoxicating revel of the Dum-Dum," and comparing this ritual of the apes to our modern functions, the sentence begins, "From this primitive function has arisen, unquestionably, all the forms and ceremonials of modern church and state, for through all the countless ages, back beyond the last, uttermost ramparts of a dawning humanity. . . ."

The writer chose to compare the Burroughs style to that of

Thomas Macauley, noting pungently, "In his preface to the *History of England* (fifty thousand words) Macauley wrote one perfectly limpid sentence of over two hundred words. Burroughs runs Macauley a prosperous second with a paragraph of a hundred and eleven words." The Burroughs paragraph, consisting of one sentence, utilizes commas, but remarkably does not contain a single semicolon. That the reviewer should have mentioned Macauley is oddly coincidental, since Ed, from his earliest studies in Latin, had become acquainted with Macauley's writings and had developed a deep admiration for them. In later years he could, on occasion, recall *The Lays of Ancient Rome,* with its stirring poem "Horatius."[86]

The 1914 Chicago writing period—the nine months that followed Ed's return from California—brought the completion of four stories and the near-completion of another. "Pellucidar," a sequel to "At the Earth's Core," was begun on November 23 but not finished until January 11, 1915.[87]

"Thuvia, Maid of Mars," the fourth of the Martian series, was completed on June 20, 1914, after two months of writing. It contains familiar plot elements; its action is launched with the abduction of the beautiful princess of Ptarth and a scheme to implicate Carthoris, John Carter's son, in Thuvia's disappearance. Although there is little freshness in the plot, Ed, as usual, produces some original devices. Anticipating an invention of modern times, the automatic pilot, Ed has Carthoris contrive an instrument for blindflying, described as "a clever improvement of the ordinary Martian air compass, which when set for a certain destination will remain constantly fixed thereon, making it only necessary to keep a vessel's prow always in the direction of the compass needle to reach any given point upon Barsoom by the shortest route." This was supplemented by an auxiliary steering device that upon arrival at the destination "brought the craft to a standstill and lowered it, also automatically, to the ground."

To avoid the possibility of collision with another craft, Ed has Carthoris invent an "obstruction evader," a type of "radium generator diffusing radio-activity in all directions to a distance of a hundred yards or so from the flier." Carthoris, in the story, explains the "evader's" workings in detail:

Should this enveloping force be interrupted in any direction a delicate instrument immediately apprehends the irregularity, at the same time imparting an impulse to a magnetic device which in turn actuates the steering mechanism, diverting the bow of the flyer away from the obstacle until the craft's radio-activity sphere is no longer in contact with the obstruction, then she falls once more into her normal course.

If an aircraft should approach from the rear, both the speed control and the steering gear are actuated, and as a result Carthoris' flyer either shoots ahead or moves evasively up or down. Other contingencies have been anticipated:

In aggravated cases, that is when the obstructions are many, or of such a nature as to deflect the bow more than forty-five degrees in any direction, or when the craft has reached its destination and dropped to within a hundred yards of the ground, the mechanism brings her to a full stop, at the same time sounding a loud alarm which will instantly awaken the pilot. . . .

In "Thuvia, Maid of Mars," Ed's most imaginative feat, startlingly original, is the creation of the Phantom Bowmen of Lothar. Seeking a safe haven from the green hordes, the last of the race of Lotharians had retreated to an impregnable fortress. Only men had arrived—some twenty thousand of them, the women and children having died en route. Faced with extinction of their race, the Lotharians, after realizing the Great Truth—that mind is all—developed superhuman mental powers. Through these they overcame death, which, after all, was "merely a state of mind."

The next step was to create their "mind-people," described as "the materialization of imaginings." These are the Phantom Bowmen who are summoned from nothingness to battle the enemy. To Carthoris, Jav, the Lotharian, explains:

We send out our deathless archers—deathless because they are lifeless, existing only in the imaginations of our enemies. It is really our giant minds that defend us, sending out legions of imaginary warriors to materialize before the mind's eye of the foe.

They see them—they see their bows drawn back—they see their slender arrows speed with unerring precision toward their hearts. And they die—killed by the power of suggestion.

In order that the enemy, the Torquasians, not suspect that they are fighting imaginary creatures, the Lotharians arrange for some of the bowmen to "die" on the battlefield. They are "pictured" as being killed, "to lend reality to the scene." If the Torquasians once learned the truth, "no longer would they fall prey to the suggestion of the deadly arrows, for greater would be the suggestion of the truth, and the more powerful suggestion would prevail—it is law."

Since there is neither food nor water in Lothar, those who call themselves "realists" create these substances through their imaginations. By "materializing food-thoughts" and then eating, they cause digestion and assimilation. The argument advanced by the "etherealists" among the Lotharians is that substance is non-existent. However, the others believe that "mind has the power to maintain substance even though it may not be able to create substance." Thus Jav, a realist, explains, "We chew, we swallow, we digest. All our organs function precisely as if we had partaken of material food. And what is the result? What must be the result? The chemical changes take place through both direct and indirect suggestion, and we live and thrive."[88]

Next in order on Ed's list of sequels was "The Cave Man"; completed in less than a month, on August 17, 1914, it continued the exploits of Waldo Emerson Smith-Jones in his transformation from a skinny weakling to a powerfully muscled fighting man renamed Thandar, "the brave one." The plot weaves about his love for Nadara, the half-savage cave girl, and his plans to return to civilization with her. Waldo cannot bring himself to take Nadara as his mate according to the primitive customs of the cave people: "She—his wonderful Nadara—must become his through the most solemn and dignified ceremony that civilized man has devised." Waldo's thoughts, expressed in this stuffy language, reveal his prudish attitude, and place him in contrast to Nadara, child of nature, who can find no need for a ceremony and wishes simply to mate with the man she loves.

Nadara's father, himself baffled by Waldo's strange behavior, describes how he took his wife many years before by dragging her to his cave and beating her. No argument, however, can budge Waldo from his noble determination to give Nadara a civilized wedding, and through numerous hair-breadth escapes he clings unwaveringly to this goal, until, at the end, the two are transported back to Boston on the Smith-Joneses' yacht, the *Priscilla*. Waldo's blue-blood snobbery is satirized by Ed, and before the story is finished both Waldo and his mother appear to have overcome this snobbery. Ed seems also, on first impression, to be satirizing Waldo's and society's conventional morality, but the emphasis upon marriage as the only possible solution, and the ending with the triumph of legality and respectability, indicate an acceptance of society's standards. That Ed might have been opportunistic, catering to what he believed his moralistic readers would expect, must of course be considered. However, in "The Cave Man" this seems doubtful. This story, as with many stories, offers some revelations about the author: Ed's moral convictions—at least of circa 1914—are clearly evident.

Curiously, while approving the convention of marriage, Ed, in this early work, vigorously rejected the funeral ceremony. His attitude emerges from the description of the death of Nadara's foster-father, following which the body was deposited at the top of a cliff. "There was no ceremony. In it, though, Waldo Emerson saw what might have been the first human funeral cortege —simple, sensible and utilitarian—from which the human race has retrograded to the ostentatious, ridiculous, pestilent burials of present day civilization." Through this indignant and almost violent criticism, Ed's philosophy of death and modern funerals is revealed. It would remain unchanged throughout his life.

Once more, in his plot devices, Ed falls into repetition, this time returning to a "Tarzan of the Apes" incident. A man and woman float ashore on the island of the cave people. The man is dead, but the woman lives long enough to give birth to a little girl, who of course turns out to be Nadara. Apparently reluctant to give his blessing to a union between the aristocratic Waldo Emerson and a savage cave girl, Ed, at the end of the story, makes the marriage more palatable by producing one of his predictable "surprises": the cave girl's mother is identified as Eugenie Marie Celeste de la Valois, Countess of Crecy, and so, happily, when the wedding takes place, the minister is able to enter another aristocratic name on the certificate—Nadara de la Valois.[89]

"Sweetheart Primeval," a sequel to "The Eternal Lover," was also completed in less than a month, on September 14, 1914.[90] To continue the adventures of the time travelers, Victoria Custer and her "troglodyte" lover Nu, Ed again reverts to his needed device—the earthquake. In the cave when the earthquake occurs, Victoria awakens as the primitive Nat-ul, making her journey "Back to the Stone Age." The entire story takes place in the prehistoric past and includes encounters with other savage races— the Boat Builders and the Lake Dwellers. At the end, after another earthquake tremor, Victoria is transported to modern times, finding herself in the familiar surroundings of Lord Greystoke's bungalow on his African estate. With her are brother Barney, William Curtiss, the suitor she can never accept because of her love for Nu, and Lieutenant Butzow, who had left Lutha to accompany Barney to Beatrice, Nebraska.

Davis' revisions of "Sweetheart Primeval," to which Ed had grudgingly acceded, had undoubtedly eliminated certain prehistoric monsters—plesiosaurs, ichthyosaurs, and others—but some, including a pterodactyl and several unidentified mammoth reptiles, remained in the story.[91] For orientation Ed drew a brief map. The points of the compass are shown at the top, and to the east he has marked "The Restless Sea." A river winds away to the north, and just south and west of it, the habitation of the cave-dwellers, "The Barren Cliffs," is entered on the map. Far south Ed shows "The Cliffs of Nu" and "The Cave of Oo." At the extreme southern end of the map the area of "The Boat Builders" is marked, and near it Ed has drawn the "Mysterious Country (Islands)."[92]

In the sequel to "The Mad King," titled " 'Barney' Custer of Beatrice," the story opens in staid Nebraska surroundings, with sister Victoria present at the start, but only in a minor role. As a tribute to his friend Bert Weston, Ed had selected the town of Beatrice to be the setting for the original story, and now in continuing he even makes reference to Bert and his wife Margaret. Victoria, at the beginning of the story, wants to go motoring with Lieutenant Butzow and regrets her promise to Margaret to play bridge.[93]

Barney, in whose veins the royal blood of Rubinroth flows (his mother, the Princess Victoria, having fled from the kingdom of Lutha to marry Barney's father), is "stagnating" in Beatrice; he still dreams of Emma von der Tann, the woman he loves, and recalls the exciting days in Lutha, when, because of his close resemblance to Leopold, he had been mistaken for the king. Mysterious bombings in Beatrice are revealed to be the work of Captain Ernest Maenck, and in pursuit of the captain, Barney travels to Austria and then to Lutha.

The adventures that follow are similar to those created in "The Mad King," and Ed depends upon coincidence for a number of his plot devices. On two separate occasions Barney finds himself situated so that he can overhear important conversations coming from adjoining rooms. Lined up against a wall with a group of others fated for execution by a firing squad, Barney once more finds chance on his side. He is the only one to emerge alive, his skull merely creased when the volley of bullets is fired.

However, in " 'Barney' Custer of Beatrice," Ed displays ingenuity; for the first time he uses a real earth-type airplane. Lutha's sole plane is assigned a lookout post high above the battlefield and hovers there while its occupant scans the horizon for signs of the approaching allies, the Serbians. Barney's eyes "were fixed upon the soaring aeroplane"; he could wait only fifteen minutes for the vital signal. Then it came:

. . . there fluttered from the tiny monoplane a paper parachute.

348

It dropped for several hundred feet before it spread to the air pressure and floated more gently toward the earth and a moment later there burst from its basket a puff of white smoke. Two more parachutes followed the first and two more puffs of smoke. Then the machine darted rapidly off toward the northeast.

Ed uses another imaginative device so that Barney can gain entrance to a garage. Unable to smash a window because the sounds would be heard, Barney recalls how a thief had cut a "neat little hole" in the window of a jeweler's shop on State Street in Chicago. The thief used a diamond. Barney borrows Princess Emma's diamond ring, scratches a "rough deep circle" close to the lock, and then taps the glass out.

Ed makes even greater use of the rather typical coincidence he had adopted for "The Mad King of Lutha"—the similarity in appearance of Barney and the cowardly King Leopold. The two men change roles, and their identities are confused several times. But Ed, with no sequel in mind, avoided his familiar "open" ending and provided a firm and happy finish for Barney and Emma.[94]

" 'Barney' Custer of Beatrice" was written between September 26 and November 1, 1914. His next story, "Pellucidar," revealed elements of Burroughs' philosophies. His longheld belief in the rejuvenating effects of vigorous outdoor living are demonstrated in Abner Perry's physical condition:

. . . instead of appearing ten years older than he really was, as he had when he left the outer world, he now appeared about ten years younger. The wild, free life of Pellucidar had worked wonders for him.

Ed's dubious view of religion is illustrated through Perry's fears and what follows:

Perry was almost overcome by the hopelessness of our situation. He flopped down on his knees and began to pray.

It was the first time I had heard him at his old habit since my return to Pellucidar, and I had thought that he had given up his little idiosyncrasy; but he hadn't. Far from it.

Beyond this lies the characterization of Innes and, for that matter, of all of ERB's heroes who face dangers and seemingly hopeless situations undauntedly and with a refusal to yield to discouragement. With these men the solution always is found in action, not in "flopping down" to pray. This rejection of passivity—a resignation to fate or quietism—was part of Burroughs' practical view of life, that when a difficult situation arises, a man must do something to solve it on his own.

His antiwar philosophy is revealed in this comment by David Innes:

What we have given them (the Pellucidarians) so far has been the worst. We have given war and the munitions of war. In a single day we have made their wars infinitely more terrible and bloody than in all their past ages they have been able to make them with their crude, primitive weapons.

Through David Innes, Burroughs revealed his own love of animals. To him a man's life was not complete without a dog. Concerning the primitive tribes of the inner world, Innes, as ERB's spokesman, stated:

. . . I had never guessed what it was that was lacking to life in Pellucidar, but now I knew that it was the total absence of domestic animals.
Man had not yet reached the point where he might take time from slaughter and escaping slaughter to make friends with any of the brute creations. . . .

On impulse David Innes is driven to saving the life of a fierce wolf-dog, a hyaenodon, injured when it plunged after him from the top of a sheer cliff into the sea. Watching the animal as it seemed on the verge of drowning, Innes was seized by pity: "The look of dumb misery in his eyes struck a chord in my breast, for I love dogs. I forgot he was a vicious, primordial wolf-thing—a man-eater, a scourge and a terror. I saw only the sad eyes that looked like the eyes of Raja, my dead collie of the outer world."

In gratitude, the wolf-dog later saved Innes' life, and with a bond of affection and trust established, the animal was given the name *Raja*. "Somehow all sense of loneliness vanished," Innes said. "I had a dog!"

As in his other stories of fantasy worlds, "Pellucidar" rises toward Ed's favorite climax—a furious battle scene on a grand scale. Abner Perry has succeeded in building the navy of the empire of Pellucidar. Against this fleet and an army supplied with guns and gunpowder, the forces of Hooja and the evil Mahars are helpless.

Innes' goal of moving Pellucidar into the twentieth century leads to the establishment of a political and economic system that modern scientists would have scrutinized in disbelief. The monarchy with David I as emperor depends for its support on various chieftains and naval officers who have been given the titles of king and duke. It is like a medieval empire. Ed's choice of a super-ruler is revealing of the philosophy he accepted—that somehow a benevolent dictator was needed to direct the lives and affairs of the lower groups and to transform a primitive country into an ideal nation.

The economic system of Pellucidar is reduced to its simplest level through an elimination of money. Commerce, restricted by unusual regulations, becomes a matter of bartering:

A man may exchange that which he produces for something which he desires that another has produced; but he cannot dispose of the thing he thus acquires. In other words, a commodity ceases to have pecuniary value the instant that it passes out of the hands of its producer. All excess reverts to government; and, as this represents the production of the people as a government, government may dispose of it to other peoples in exchange for that which they produce. Thus we are establishing a trade between kingdoms, the profits from which go to the betterment of the people—to building factories for the manufacture of agricultural implements, and machinery for the various trades we are gradually teaching the people.

Thus the Empire of Pellucidar became a combination of opposites, truly strange bedfellows: rampant special-privileged royalty and nobility were assigned the task of developing a system of economic socialism.

"Pellucidar" offers examples of Ed's ingenuity in his creation of the "Brute-Men," skilled rope-throwers who dispatch their foes by lassoing them and hauling them to the top of the cliff.

The light and sometimes jesting tone, the loose style, and the rambling plot structure do not allow for sufficient development of excitement, suspense and conflict. These vital elements, normally Ed's stock-in-trade, are weak and unsustained in "Pellucidar."[95]

Among the items outlined for his *Autobiography* Ed had noted, "In 1914 I write 400,000 words, everything sells." Ed's 1914 production, exclusive of revisions or additions, consisted of eight stories, the shortest, "The Lad and the Lion," containing 40,000 words, and the longest, "Pellucidar," totaling more than 60,000 words.[96]

CHAPTER 12

FILM FRUSTRATION

Early in 1914, through an initial step taken by Albert Payson Terhune of the *New York Evening World,* Ed began a new search for success—this time in the motion picture field. On March 20 Terhune had written, "By the way, I gave Stern & Co. [playbrokers and moving picture managers], your address today; and advised them to try at once to secure from you the dramatic rights on Tarzan."

From Edna Williams of Joseph W. Stern & Company of New York came an inquiry about *Tarzan of the Apes* and any other works with dramatic possibilities.[1] In his reply Ed explained that he had so far made no attempt to do anything with the motion picture rights of Tarzan, adding, "Am open to suggestions and an offer. If this story should succeed as a picture play I have others which might then be open for consideration."[2]

This contact brought no tangible result, but Ed's interest had now been aroused, and several months later, through the efforts of Bob Davis, Munsey editor, Ed communicated with Cora C. Wilkening of the Authors Photo-Play Agency of New York. He had sent her a copy of *Tarzan of the Apes,* and in his letter of June 24 presented his usual sales talk about *Tarzan* and *The Return of Tarzan* having appeared in newspapers from coast to coast, and asked, "Won't you please write me at your convenience confirming the conditions under which you undertake to place Tarzan with a moving picture producing company. . . ."

Mrs. Wilkening, apparently eager to handle Ed's work, wrote, "I think I know the company who will be delighted to put on

Vivian Reed, who played the part of Nakhla in The Lad and the Lion, *1916.*

your 'Tarzan.' I will submit all offers to you first for your approval."[3]

On July 10, upon returning from "a little vacation in the country," Ed responded, mentioning his file of letters from magazine readers "from nearly every English speaking corner of the globe and from every state in the Union." He voiced his main concern humorously:

By the way, still in the role of the modest violet by the mossy stone: I wish, in case you make a deal with a producer, that you would stipulate that my full name as author appears at the beginning of each reel—if that is what you call them. . . .

The passing weeks brought no word from Mrs. Wilkening. Impatient, Ed, on August 20, queried, "What's the matter?" The reply was glowingly optimistic: "I am now negotiating with two concerns who are considering the book on a royal basis with cash advance. . . . It will make a splendid feature—something absolutely original, and I am confident of being able to secure an excellent offer. . . ."

Ed was pleased to hear that things were going well, but noted that he was puzzled over the word "royal." He assumed it was intended to be "royalty" and commented, ". . . it sounds so much like a king's ransom that I get quite excited whenever I think of it. Anyhow, let's hope that the results will be 'royal'."[4]
On August 31 he asked Joseph Bray at McClurg to forward three copies of *Tarzan* to Mrs. Wilkening and on the same date cautioned her, "In closing with anyone for the moving picture rights to Tarzan I hope you will be guided even more by the ability of the purchaser to produce properly and by his reputation for square dealing than by the size of the royalty or advance offered."

Ed's next contact with an agent was truly a comedy of errors. On November 9, 1914, a letter from the Frank Henry Rice Agency of New York referred to the subject of motion picture rights. Howard A. Archer, with whom Ed had previously communicated, explained that upon his return to New York he had found an inquiry concerning "The Cave Man" (seemingly a confusion in title for "The Cave Girl"). Archer wrote, "Please let me know if you will accept five percent on gross royalties with an advance of not less than five hundred dollars. It may be possible to obtain one thousand dollars advance against ten percent." An agency contract was forwarded for Ed's signature.

Ed was quite willing to allow the Rice Agency to handle "The

Cave Girl"; with the signed agreement he noted, "I think The Cave Girl as good as any for photo-play purposes, and really a better story than its sequel."[5] Once more he requested that his full name be displayed as the author at the beginning of each reel; he also insisted that in any contract with a producer, a clause should be added stating this requirement.[6]

However, whatever hopes Ed may have had were quickly shattered. On November 18 Frank Henry Rice wrote, ". . . I have found that the play for which I have an inquiry is entitled 'The Cave Man' which is an adaptation of 'Lady Mechante' by Gelett Burgess, and not 'The Cave Girl' which is written by yourself." Rice, however, promised to seek offers for any other Burroughs stories suitable for motion pictures, and on November 21 Ed sent him a copy of "A Man Without a Soul."

Earlier, Ed had again written to Mrs. Wilkening to inform her that three agencies were interested in Tarzan. "I have been holding them off hoping to hear something favorable from you," he said. "I wish that you would let me know just what is wrong. If the producers don't want the story I should like to know it, so that I can get it out of my system and forget it. If they do want it, please tell me why they don't take it."[7] He emphasized that his interest in motion picture possibilities was "greater than formerly." Mrs. Wilkening responded that *Tarzan* was being considered by several companies. "I will do my utmost to close the matter during the coming week. . . ." she wrote.[8] But Ed's patience was running out. On November 28 he sent a succinct order to Mrs. Wilkening: "Please yank Tarzan off the movie market. I thank you for your efforts in his behalf." However, several days later, through Mrs. Wilkening's efforts, a new and hopeful prospect appeared.

William N. Selig of the Selig Polyscope Company was searching for material suitable for motion picture production. That Selig was an important contact was evidenced by the fact that Mrs. Wilkening hastened to journey from New York to meet him in Chicago for a conference.[9] On December 3 Ed wrote to Selig at the Chicago studios: "At Mrs. Wilkening's suggestion I am asking McClurg to send you a copy of Tarzan of the Apes. And herewith I am handing you a copy of The Lad and the Lion in mss. . . ."

He explained that although the Munsey Company had purchased the story, it had not yet appeared in magazine form, and under the circumstances no production could be begun without Munsey's agreement.[10] Ed added, "Mrs. Wilkening also suggested that you might wish to talk with me relative to these stories, and to this end I asked her to arrange with you to take lunch with me at your convenience—say Monday or Tuesday of next week, or later if you prefer."[11]

From William G. Chapman of the International Press Bureau, who was still acting as Ed's syndication agent, came an inquiry about *Tarzan of the Apes.* Chapman, on December 22, sought permission to submit the story to the Universal Film Manufacturing Company. Ed replied in a letter, sent a day later, and explained the situation, "One of the largest and best equipped producers in the country is now considering Tarzan of the Apes, favorably. However, they have no option on it. If you care to go ahead with the Universal people I have no objection."

Stressing his terms—"a good sized cash advance and a generous royalty," Ed stated, "Whoever makes me the best offer first can have it. It might be well to quote me liberally in writing to your prospect."

Chapman's request to act as a Burroughs agent in this new field made Ed aware that some explicit agreement was needed. In his response of December 23 he restated the terms, "I do not recall that we ever had any understanding about your commission in event of your placing Tarzan as a movie. 10% is customary. All the agents that have written me have mentioned this same commission. If this is satisfactory to you it is to me."

To Chapman Ed presented an attitude of indifference about the difficulties of finding a producer for *Tarzan.* It was of course an attitude assumed by him to conceal his disappointment. "To be perfectly candid," he remarked, "I am no longer 'het up' about placing Tarzan. I do not believe that any of the first class producers will be crazy about tackling it, or that they will want to pay enough for it to interest me. In other words, so far as Tarzan of the Movies is concerned, I am as independent as a hog on ice."

He commented to Chapman that Selig's company was his choice to make the movie—they have "the best zoo equipment of any of them." He explained the past situation: "Several weeks ago I yanked Tarzan off the movie market, but a New York agency wanted to submit it to one more prospect and they are the people who are now considering it." His annoyance was indicated in a final statement: "I shall close with some one by the first of January or I shall again grab it off and keep it off," to which he added, "I am getting bored by it."

Universal displayed no serious interest in *Tarzan,* but as a result of the contract that Chapman had made, Ed would later begin a submission of other works to them.

Meanwhile, with the end of 1914 came the first inquiry about a foreign language translation of *Tarzan of the Apes*. In December Joseph Bray forwarded a letter from Dr. Ralph Julian Sachers of New York requesting German rights to the famous story. Ed was inclined to view the whole matter with skepticism. The European situation, with World War I in full swing, made a request for terms on German translation rights appear particularly inappropriate. On December 22, Ed wrote to Bray, "It seems to me that if there is anything in this at all that the time is most inopportune for anything of the sort."

Aware of the strong animosities of the opposing sides, England and France vs. Germany, Ed commented, "In the first place it is doubtful if Germany would prove a profitable field at this time even for a novel of the first magnitude; and in the second the popular interest in a novel featuring an English lordling and a French Officer in heroic roles would be notable for its absence."

However, he stressed that if Dr. Sachers could obtain a "bona-fide cash offer for the rights from a reputable German Publisher" who would also handle the translation, the matter might be considered more seriously.[12]

With the negotiations for "The Lad and the Lion" continuing, Mrs. Wilkening had telegraphed Ed to inquire about a price that would be acceptable to him. Ed could offer nothing definite: "I have less idea of the value of The Lad & the Lion than you. I do not know how many reels it will make, and if I did I shouldn't be much better off. I am sure that Mr. Selig is very keen for it, from what he has said to me, on the several occasions we have spoken of it."[13] Upon Selig's return to Chicago, Ed planned to discuss the price with him, but he urged Mrs. Wilkening, in the meantime, to suggest what she thought a fair price might be.

In this short period of his first contacts with the motion picture field and the use of scenarios, Ed had already acquired a skeptical attitude, made evident in his remark to Mrs. Wilkening: "As I told you once before, for the labor involved and the plots wasted I don't think much of the prices paid for scenarios that I have heard of at least; but of course I can tell more about it when I know what they will give me for The Lad & the Lion."[14] In the same letter he noted that he "liked Mr. Selig immensely and should be glad to write for him regularly."[15]

Toward the end of January 1915, Ed reached an agreement

with Selig for the sale of the movie rights to "The Lad and the Lion" and a story in synopsis form titled "Ben, King of Beasts." Ed's pessimism about the payments received for film material was clearly justified. The price was $100 a reel, with "The Lad and the Lion" figured at five reels and "Ben, King of Beasts" at three, for a total of $800. Mrs. Wilkening's commission was fifty dollars.[16]

Plagued by the problem of inadequate payment for film stories, and worried about the forthcoming royalties from McClurg for *Tarzan,* Ed turned to The Authors' League of America for advice. Located in New York, the League displayed an impressive roster of officers with Winston Churchill as president and Theodore Roosevelt, vice-president. (Its British agent, Curtis Brown, in London, later became Burroughs' agent.) Ed applied for membership in January 1915 and was accepted a month later. In correspondence with Eric Schuler, secretary of the League, Ed at once brought up the matters that were troubling him. His first concern was with the McClurg royalties; he noted that the League's publication in its March *Bulletin* of an article titled "No Business-Man" had "raised a ghost that has been haunting me for a long time."[17]

Ed described his background in the business world, mentioning his practical education in "the school of experience" and explaining:

I even took an expert accountant job once, and "brought home the bacon"; but I am free to admit that I have quailed before the idea of demanding from McClurg an examination of their books, though I have fully realized that it was the proper thing to do.[18]

In seeking information about a point headed "Number 2," Ed wrote:

I recently sold the motion picture rights of two stories to The Selig Polyscope Company, and I wish to know if I received a fair and reasonable price for them.

It is my first experience in this line, of which I know less than nothing.[19]

He provided the details:

One story I submitted in mss form just as it had been accepted by a New York magazine that has not yet published it. Mr. Selig liked this story very much. He is the only member of his company who has read it, and until it came to making me an offer for it I dealt with no one else. He also read the other and accepted it—it was simply a synopsis.[20]

Ed, after listing the amounts received, noted that he was to be paid, in addition, $100 per reel for each extra reel that might be made in production. His appeal to the League for information brought little of consequence. It was clear that in this new field of motion picture writing, the League had nothing specific or practical to offer. Obviously, any stimulating or innovative ideas on the marketing of manuscripts would come from Burroughs, not from the League.

On the subject of second serial rights and the necessity for authors not to relinquish them, Ed could become eloquent. He had never forgiven himself for his early ignorance about these rights. The article "No Business-Man" in *The Bulletin* was concerned with syndication, and this was sufficient to arouse Ed's interest and cause him to express his own ideas on the matter. In sending a "communication" to *The Bulletin* on March 9, 1915, he commented: "If you feel that the subject merits the space necessary to give it publicity I only ask that you do not publish it over my name—the initial Z will do unless another uses Z, in which case the alphabet is at your disposal."[21]

The ideas contained in Ed's brief article "Syndication" were part of a philosophy he had discussed on previous occasions. He was anxious to awaken writers "to the possibilities for profit which they are throwing away—and worse than throwing away—when they permit the second serial rights to their manuscripts to pass out of their hands without receiving for them, in real money, what they are worth."

Jabbing in humorous disparagement his attitude, as a new writer, in feeling "fully qualified to spill advice promiscuously among my betters," he nevertheless pointed out, "I am making more real money out of the second serial rights to my stories than some famous authors whose work is of infinitely greater value than mine." Ed explained:

I sold three stories to magazines before I discovered that second serial rights had a value. [Actually the total is four if his first story, "Under the Moons of Mars," is included.] From then I have retained these rights and the fourth story has already brought in $729.00 in cash and is still selling. I have received as high as $300.00 for the newspaper rights to a story for a single city. I have repeatedly sold to publishers who maintain a syndicating

*bureau of their own without the slightest demur on their part
as to the retention of my second serial rights by me. I have sold
for use in a single city to a newspaper that maintains a syndicating service covering many cities.*[22]

Ed's most important suggestion was that the League should
form a syndicating bureau which would be allowed a "reasonable
commission" for its services. This, he maintained, could not only
make the bureau self-supporting, but could also "reimburse the
League for the loss of literary agents advertising in *The Bulletin.*"
If a bureau were created, Ed indicated he would submit a list
of the newspapers that had purchased his stories, together with
the prices they had paid. Other writers might then do the same,
and the collected information would establish a price basis suitable for all syndication dealings between authors and newspapers.[23]

The appearance of the article in *The Bulletin* of April
1915 brought a response and inquiry from author Walter Prichard Eaton. The signature of "Z" had proved to be no secret, since
secretary Schuler had identified Burroughs to Eaton. Seeking
further details, Eaton wrote:

*. . . Your letter interested me strangely, seeing's how I never
get a red cent out of any second rights of a single story of mine.
It's only lately that I've had intelligence enough to hang on to
the 2nd rights, anyhow. And now that I've got 'em, what am I
goin' to do with 'em? Your letter gives me a glimmering hope
that maybe you are a sort of Moses, to lead us sheep-like authors into the promised land. Why don't you organize a little 2nd
rights bureau, and handle stuff for some of the rest of us, and let
us pay you a commish or something? Have you got a scheme?
If so, for Heavens sake, let's hear it!*[24]

Ed, in his response of May 20, noted, "Yes, I had a lovely
scheme, but Schuler blue pencilled it. It was to have the League
establish a syndicating bureau." He then restated the paragraph
that Schuler had deleted from the article before it was printed.
This contained the reference about a League bureau supported
by commissions from newspaper sales. Schuler's reason for removing this paragraph was obvious: he was fearful of antagonizing
the literary agents who might then withdraw their ads from
The Bulletin. Ed's contention that the commissions would "more
than reimburse" the League for loss of revenue from agents' ads

was apparently unconvincing to Schuler. In the long letter to Walter Prichard Eaton, Ed presented other ideas:

There is, however, an alternative; but, to be perfectly candid, I don't know that it would work. It is for a few of us to organize a bureau, pay regular commissions to it for placing our work and depend upon the profits for the reduction of our personal commissions.

By this means we could do a regular agency business including book, magazine, newspaper and photo-play rights for the general writing public, and have a medium of our own for marketing such of our own rights as we did not care to handle ourselves.[25]

Concerning Eaton's suggestion that Ed organize and direct the bureau, he replied, ". . . it is out of the question—I am too dinged lazy; but I could easily find a manager who could devote all his time to it." Ed commented about the problem of raising capital, but believed that it should not be too difficult to get a contribution from each author. The man he had in mind for manager of the projected bureau was his brother Harry.

I was talking with my brother about it last evening, seeing if I could interest him in it. He has considerable mail order experience, which is just what a man would need to handle this work successfully, and the idea rather appealed to him. I think he might be willing to manage a bureau, though I am not sure.[26]

Ed demonstrated that in the business world his ideas possessed the same imagination and originality that he displayed in his stories. He envisioned the future—a plan only in the dream stage: "Way in the backs of our heads we could harbor the hope that some day the bureau could develop into that ideal (for the writer) organization—an author's publishing house, by means of which we could not only get our royalties, but also a share of the profits from our books," and added, "I *know* that there are great possibilities in such a hope. I have even dreamed of a magazine, but as 999.9 of all magazines fail there is a legitimate doubt as to the feasibility of the latter."

In this letter of May 20 to Eaton, Ed recalled his position as department manager for the A. W. Shaw Company, publishers of *System,* The Magazine of Business, and commented, ". . . accept it from me, there is money in a sanely conducted magazine and publishing business combined."

Ed's visions of the future were not merely the vague and

stimulating illusions that drift beyond the grasp of individuals; they were based upon practical business instincts. They resulted from his characteristic impatience with those who could not appreciate the value of his stories, or those who were handicapped by overcaution and limited imagination. He had exhibited both this business confidence and impatience in the past. When book publishers were reluctant to gamble on "Tarzan of the Apes," he seriously considered publishing the story himself. And when *All-Story*'s syndication bureau appeared satisfied to settle for meager payments, Ed, contemptuous, proceeded to prove that newspaper sales could be highly profitable.

The differences between Burroughs, the man of action, and writers such as Eaton, were clearly emphasized in Eaton's response of May 23, in which he deplored Ed's refusal to direct the proposed bureau. Eaton, lost in business matters, spoke of his "abysmal ignorance" of the whole subject and confessed helplessly that he had not the faintest idea as to what to do with his second serial rights. Representative of the average writer, Eaton, richly imaginative, lived in his world of creativity, concentrated as did the others on producing his characters and situations, and was willing to leave business dealings to editors and agents. Through custom and convention the artist, whether a painter, musician, or writer, had always been pictured as a creative but wholly impractical individual. Burroughs, the paradox, now shattered this old-fashioned concept. He demonstrated that an author not only could, but should combine a business acuity and determination with his writing imagination.

That his visions *were* practical would be proved in the future. With Burroughs an idea was appraised, gripped firmly—and then made inevitable. When the time was right, he would accomplish two objectives: establish his own publishing company and arrange for the production of his own motion pictures.

1915 brought a succession of dealings or contacts with agents and individuals about varied writing projects. All of these proved time-consuming and fruitless. On January 29 Ed wrote to Frank Henry Rice, "If you haven't done anything by this time with A Man Without a Soul, kindly let it drop, as I have decided to withdraw it. I enclose 4c for return of copy." Ed's faith in agents was rapidly vanishing, and Rice's response offered nothing to strengthen it: "Your magazine story, 'A Man Without a Soul' has been submitted to a producer for reading. . . ."[27] It was a typical agent's report—one that had brought no result in the past. Searching for new outlets, Ed on January 29 queried the Universal Film Corporation in New York, mentioning that his stories in magazine form possessed "photoplay possibilities." He noted, "One that I have in mind has a panther in it, but there are others in which no wild animals figure, so, if you care to see one, please let me know which class you prefer. . . ." On February 4 a reply from Anthony P. Kelly, editor of the scenario department, indicated that Universal was interested. Kelly, who signed his letter "Yours for Universal Peace", wrote, "Only please, Mr. Burroughs, enclose a brief concise synopsis with each one of the stories submitted. . . ."

The hope of establishing a syndication bureau to handle all types of story and photoplay rights was soon abandoned. Whether insufficient interest was displayed by other authors, or whether the entire matter was impractical is difficult to ascertain. However, Ed still placed reliance upon The Author's League and turned to it for assistance. A letter from Alec Lorimore, president of the National Movement Motion Picture Bureau of New York, contained a proposal that Ed should novelize "a serial photo drama," evidently for submission in a contest. Ed doubted that he could afford "the expenditure of time," but added:

If Bob Davis, after reading the scenario, were to say that he believed I could write a novelization that would be acceptable to him, I should not hesitate to attempt it provided of course that my net remuneration was satisfactory.

As to the title of authorship, in case I wrote the novelization, I have very decided convictions on that subject, and should expect credit for the novelization only.[28]

Ed had been in communication with Eric Schuler of The Author's League, this time seeking information about copyrights. Schuler had sent details, but Ed, as in the past, was ready with one of his own imaginative schemes. He wrote, "There should be some way that an author could copyright his work before sending it to a publisher. Has any plan ever been suggested or considered? It seems to me that one might copyright the first and last pages of a mss., sending duplicate copies of each with fee in accordance with the regular procedure, or, perhaps, copyright a synopsis of the story, which would cover the plot and title. I wonder if it would be legal."[29] In the same letter he included an inquiry about the reputation of Lorimore and his company and remarked, "If I am becoming a pest you must thank yourself, for I recall that we are urged to make use of The League. Anyway, I thank you from the bottom of my heart for your patience and kindness, and when I can reciprocate shall be delighted to do so." Concerning Lorimore, Schuler could discover nothing: ". . . I found it difficult to get any information . . . and when I did finally . . . the information . . . was certainly not such as to warrant my recommending it to you."[30]

Although Selig had purchased "The Lad and The Lion" and "Ben, King of Beasts" for motion picture production he apparently showed no real interest in *Tarzan of the Apes*. Ed had discussed the story with him in a conference in December 1914. Perhaps Selig believed that the difficulties of producing such a jungle epic would be insurmountable. However, an inquiry from H. Morris Friedman of Ottumwa, Iowa, led to a reply from Ed revealing that Selig still had *Tarzan* under tentative consideration. Friedman, whose letter of March 11, 1915, was forwarded by McClurg, sought the photoplay rights to *Tarzan*. Ed replied, ". . . I rather doubt if I should care to close with a producer at this time, as one company already has a man in Africa trying to get bona fide ape-life pictures for an elaborate production of Tarzan. . . ."[31]

This unusual action of Selig was mentioned in Ed's letter of January 13, 1915, addressed to Terhune at the *Evening World*:

Mr. Selig, who is considering Tarzan of the Apes, is sending a man to Africa next week. A part of his equipment is a copy of the Tarzan book, and included in his instructions are orders to take moving pictures of ape life in the jungle. When that is released Tarzan should boom.[32]

To Ed the whole idea of a cameraman attempting to locate the African apes in the jungle, and to creep up on them and take moving pictures, appeared hilarious. He could readily imagine the difficulties the man was going to encounter. His humorous report of this near impossible feat, addressed to Mrs. Wilkening at the Authors Photo-Play Agency, led her, on February 8, to comment appreciatively:

I am very much amused in regard to your remarks concerning the success of the man who thinks he is going to take pictures of the apes in the African jungles. You have given this subject considerable study and I imagine you know the lively time the poor man will have.

A steady flow of communications with Selig about "The Lad and the Lion" and other matters followed. On March 12 Selig noted, "We expect to shortly start work on the scenario . . . find we are in need of another copy of the book. . . ." A day later, in sending his only copy, Ed requested its return, explaining that "as the magazine often makes changes which I do not care for, I like to have a copy of the original against the possibility of book publication."

On behalf of his sister-in-law Ella, who displayed writing ability, Ed wrote to Selig to ask that she be given a tryout as an actress. "It is not the emotional notoriety-longing of a young girl," he said, "but the desire of a mature woman to utilize her talents and training for purposes of bread winning. . . . It is with a full realization of the fact that you must be bored to death with similar requests from people who have a right to ask favors of you, which I have not, that I ask this of you."[33] Selig's reply, sent from Los Angeles, was courteous: ". . . upon my return will be pleased to give your sister-in-law a fair trial. Will keep you posted as to the exact time of my return to Chicago."[34]

Eager to write material for the motion pictures or to adapt his own stories for film use, Ed found himself baffled and frustrated by the scenario form. He called a story outline a "synopsis," while Selig, in his letters, preferred the term "scenario." This type of explicit characterization plus a plot or action summary was contrary to the full and detailed novel style that had become second nature to him. In this new writing area he once again had all the sensations of a beginner, his old doubts and insecurities returning. He viewed the synopses he completed with disapproval or evaluated them as outright failures; it was plain to him that he did not, as yet, understand this special writing form.

He had written to John F. Pribyl of the Selig Polyscope Company to request a copy of a scenario to be used as a model. Pribyl had forwarded a copy of "In the Tentacles of the North" by James Oliver Curwood, and in a letter of January 9, 1915, had given valuable advice on motion picture writing:

The script will give you a general idea of the construction of a scenario. The importance of your story will determine the number of reels, whether one, two, three, four, or even five. The chief purpose in writing a scenario is to get as much action in each reel as possible and each reel is to contain a strong punch, all leading up to a final climax. If a two reel story can not have a big incident in each reel it is better to crowd all of the incidents in one reel.

Pribyl brought up the matter of expense. "If a photoplay is in one reel," he wrote, "it will not justify an expensive production, but if the production runs into three or more reels there is a possibility of economy in one or more reels to offset an expensive construction in the balance of the story, thus the general average of cost will be the same as if we were making single reel productions."

Pribyl expressed the belief that in discussions with Selig Ed had acquired "a general idea as to what is feasible for a camera." He stressed the point that a writer must look at all situations through the camera, commenting that, "anything that can not be photographed should not be written. Unfortunately, the camera has not the advantages of printers' type in this respect." Pribyl's succinct summary of instructions for film writing would be as relevant today as in 1915. On January 11 Ed thanked him for "loan of scenario," stating, "I'll get it back to you in good order in a few days. I want to keep it at hand while I experiment on one of my own."

Despite Pribyl's advice and the use of a scenario, Ed continued to have difficulties. To Selig, in seeking an offer for photoplay rights, he wrote, ". . . I am sending a rather bum synopsis of The Mad King . . . ," and by way of apology added, "The scenario would, I think have to be written from the magazine copy, as I have omitted many details and situations from the synopsis which are necessary to the interest and continuity of the story. I am not exactly hep to the writing of a synopsis. . . ."[35] And to Pribyl a few days later, he wrote, "Am sending you herewith synopsis of a comedy. Even though it may not be adapted to your uses it may help me to discover just what you can use, so do me the kindness to look it over."[36] Ed's pencil notation on the letter identified the comedy as "His Majesty: The Janitor"; it was Ed's first venture into a comedy synopsis designed for the movies.

His uncertainty about film writing was illustrated in his letter to Anthony P. Kelly of the Universal Film Manufacturing Company of New York. Kelly had earlier suggested that he submit one of his stories in synopsis form, and on August 28 Ed replied, "The trouble is that I haven't an idea as to how to go about it—whether merely the bare argument of the story is all that is necessary, or a summary showing all the principal situations and carrying the plot throughout. . . ."

However baffled he may have felt over motion picture writing, Ed, determined to enter this new field, displayed the same dogged persistence that had marked his past efforts in story selling. Unaffected by rejections, he dispatched queries and a stream of stories and synopses to various film companies. The summer and fall of 1915 was an especially hectic period. On August 19, Pribyl acknowledged "His Majesty: The Janitor," remarking, "Yes, it's funny, but don't know if the balloon stuff can be made. Have passed the script along to Colonel Selig. He knows things I don't know—and that's a hell-uva lot! You'll hear about this later. . . ." In the synopsis, Jerry, the janitor, fleeing from a policeman, escapes in a balloon. Later, he falls out of the balloon and crashes through the ceiling of the royal palace.

Selig quickly rejected the comedy and other material Ed had sent him, and on August 27 wrote, ". . . returning your two scenarios, a western story and a comedy. The western story contains a theme which has been done over and over again and is not new. The comedy is not just suitable for our purpose, but we believe should be good for others. The other one I am still reading and expect to give you an answer within a day or two." The western story was evidently "For the Fool's Mother," written in 1912, or possibly a synopsis expansion of it, "The Prospector," completed later.[37] The "other one" referred to by Selig was Ed's synopsis of "The Mad King."

These rejections caused Ed to remark gloomily to Selig, "As a photoplay writer I'm a fine little chauffeur. Am enclosing another, which is even rottener than those you returned. It's mighty good of you to read them, and I appreciate it."[38] The enclosed material, Ed's second comedy synopsis, was titled "The Lion Hunter." On August 31, J. A. Berst, Vice-President of the Selig Company referred to Ed's synopsis of "The Mad King" and explained that the two books would make a five-reel picture. Evidently the "synopsis" was not suitable for motion picture production; Berst inquired how much Ed wanted for his story and also if he intended to write the "scenario." Concerning the comedy "The Lion Hunter," Berst advised that it would make a one-reel picture. ". . . We offer you $60.00 for same, as that is what it is worth to us," he wrote. An assignment of rights was enclosed for Ed's signature.

Having had only limited contacts with writer Burroughs, the Selig Company could not know, as both Metcalf and Davis had learned, that they were dealing with a man who was adamantly stubborn about what constituted a fair price for his stories. Of course, the company's piddling offer had confirmed the dubious view he already had of the motion picture business, but that did not prevent him from trying elsewhere. He at once sent "The Lion Hunter" and "The Mad King" to the Universal Film Manufacturing Company in Universal City, California.[39] To Kelly, Universal's scenario editor, he had, on August 28, sent "His Majesty: The Janitor." With no reply received, he tried to dicker with Selig, requesting a higher offer for "The Lion Hunter" and $100 a reel for "The Mad King."[40] Berst, in his reply, was unresponsive to both proposals:

> . . . $100 a reel for "The Mad King" is too high, as we have to write the scenario and this is going to cost us also quite some money.
>
> It is well-known by me that many of your novels have been published by newspapers and magazines, but it is not much of an asset for picture work as the public does not care so much who wrote the scenario. They are looking for a good story properly acted.
>
> "The Mad King" is worth to us at a maximum $80 per reel. Of course, if it was in scenario form, ready to produce, we would be willing to pay more. . . .[41]

It appeared that Ed's customary references to the popularity of his printed works had made no impression upon Berst. In his letter of September 21 Ed apologized for a delay in answering the Selig offer; he had been ill. The illness was undoubtedly a recurrence of the neuritis that had troubled him for a number of years. The periodic flare-ups seemed to result from overwork and anxiety or tension, and more specifically, to be caused also by the many hours of storywriting or typing, in which the arm, shoulder, and neck may be held in a rigid position.

A further attempt by Ed to persuade Universal to purchase "The Lion Hunter" and "The Mad King" was unsuccessful.[42] The prospects of turning these into motion pictures were hardly encouraging. However, as demonstrated in the past, Ed had a constitutional resistance to wasting any of the material he had labored on. Possibly a comment of Berst—that a scenario form would be worth more money—may have motivated him. More than a month later he again sent "The Mad King" to Selig, this time as a scenario. But the work had been in vain. On November 30, Selig replied, "I have read your scenario 'The Mad King' and regret to state that we will not be able to use it for the reason that we already own three or four plays of that kind. . . ."

Among minor business matters that occupied Ed's time was a connection with a newspaper clipping bureau, that of Henry Romeike, Inc., of New York; Ed had subscribed to the service in June 1914, paying five dollars for one hundred clippings. When later billed for renewal, he wrote to Romeike with some asperity:

I have kept an accurate record of all clippings received from you, and including the last batch which came subsequent to your letter I have received but ninety five all told. These include a number of worthless cuttings such as publisher's notices like the attached.

Of course if you think it right to include these, go to it; but I really should have the full one hundred clippings that I have paid for.

Another thing. Under the contract, I believe, I was to receive clippings for a year. My advance payment was for the first one hundred. The balance up to the expiration of the contract were to be charged to me at 5c each, and the contract still has about three months to run.

The entire matter is trivial. If you say so, I'll send you another five; but I wish you would tell me: Why is an agreement?[43]

Tarzan's popularity continued to bring inquiries from agents, among them Edna Williams, now with the International Theatrical Play Bureau of New York; she had written Ed several times about film possibilities and on April 16 explained that "a very large manufacturer" was seeking a scenario which would use some trained animals. It occurred to her that *Tarzan* would allow him to plan outside scenes for these animals; she was thinking of a serial which might combine *Tarzan* and *The Return of Tarzan*. Ed, unimpressed by agents' projects, replied that *Tarzan* was being considered by a producer. ". . . And so I should not care to submit it to another," he said, adding, "To be perfectly candid, I am not much excited about the movie end of my writing—there is not enough in it."[44]

Miss Williams was stubbornly persistent, and her letters finally wore Ed down. On May 25 he wearily responded:

If you wish to submit Tarzan of the Apes and The Return of Tarzan to some one producer other than The Selig Polyscope Company I do not know that I have any particular objections, other than a natural desire to obviate useless effort on your part, for, in the first place, it is impossible to produce these stories properly, and, in the second place, I would want more for my rights than anyone would pay me.

He authorized her only "to receive and transmit" offers. His statement that the *Tarzan* stories could not be produced "properly" was both surprising and unexpected. Selig's hesitancy led to an obvious interpretation—a huge jungle film of this type posed too many production difficulties and was, in fact, unfeasible. Such doubts would of course have contributed to Ed's negative attitude. Selig selected "The Lad and the Lion" as a motion picture vehicle because the story had fewer complications of plot and setting.

Ed's dubious view of *Tarzan of the Apes* as a suitable story for movie production did not change in the months that followed. However, evidenced in a letter of September 2, 1915, to Kelly at the Universal Film Company in Los Angeles, he had modified his doubts about the second *Tarzan* story. In planning to meet Kelly, he wrote, "Among other things, I want to talk over the movie possibilities of *The Return of Tarzan,* which could be much more easily produced than *Tarzan of the Apes,* which I have always considered unproducable."

Once more the question of translating *Tarzan* into German arose, this time in a proposal by Dr. Arthur Meyer of Paterson, New Jersey.[45] Ed was unenthusiastic, indicating on November 8 that he was not sure what advantages would "accrue" to him through this translation, and was equally uncertain that Meyer could translate the work "in a style that would insure it a place among the best fiction in the German language. . . ." Again, with the war in mind, he wrote, "The hero is an Englishman, his best friend is a Frenchman, and the author is an American— do you think Germans would wax very enthusiastic over such a combination, especially at such a time as this?"

In a letter describing his qualifications, Meyer noted that since a German copyright for *Tarzan* had not been obtained, anybody would be free to translate the book. He stressed, however, his desire to work with the author. He proposed that Ed pay him $150 for translating *Tarzan* and for securing a German publisher.[46] Now worried about the German copyright situation, Ed wrote to Schuler of the Author's League, inquiring whether the best procedure might be to contact a reputable German publisher directly.[47] Without sufficient information about existing copyrights on *Tarzan of the Apes,* Schuler could give no definite advice.[48]

The Selig Polyscope Company was having its difficulties with "The Lad and the Lion." Plans had been made to schedule the motion picture release to coincide with the publication of the story in *All-Story* magazine. On March 28 Ed remarked to Bob Davis, "Selig tells me you and he are going to pull off The Lad

& the Lion simultaneously. He is all het up about the story and is figuring on making a big feature production of it with the great Kathlyn in the lead. It should be of a lot of benefit to both the play and the magazine to have them come together, and incidentally to that modest violet, the author."[49] On April 26 Davis wrote:

I had a talk with Mr. Selig a few weeks ago about "The Lad and the Lion". I shall schedule it so that it will terminate in the issue of October 30, simultaneous with its appearance on the screen throughout the United States. I am going to make some noise about this thing and give it lots of publicity. . . .

Because of delays at the studio, Davis's schedule could not be followed. Months later the production of "The Lad and the Lion" was still in a state of uncertainty and Ed, in contact with Berst, learned that "the scenario . . . was not satisfactory to him. . . ." To Davis Ed explained, ". . . he (Berst) expected to get busy on it himself very soon; but he did not mention any other difficulty, and spoke as though the obstacles might be easily overcome. I gathered from what he said that production would be completed early this winter, though he stated nothing definite as to time. . . ."[50] On December 1 Ed confessed to Davis, "I can't learn anything from Selig, and as the only other man there I was well acquainted with has left them, my sources of info in that quarter are nil. . . ."

1915 drew to a close with all of Ed's strenuous efforts to find a motion picture producer for *Tarzan* proving futile. Except for "The Lad and the Lion" and "Ben, King of Beasts," described as a "wild animal scenario," dealings with Selig had brought no result. In acknowledging the return of the scenario for "The Mad King," Ed wrote, "You also have another of mine, The Lion Hunter, which Mr. Berst made me an unsatisfactory offer on. Will you kindly return that, as well. . . ."[51]

"His Majesty, the Janitor," Ed's first experiment with the comedy-synopsis form, is constructed around a series of wildly slapstick incidents that rival those contained in a Mack Sennett comedy. In fact, many of Jerry the Janitor's brash and insolent actions appear Chaplinesque. For his concept of Jerry as a character, Ed adopted and exaggerated a prototype—that of the old-time apartment building janitor who ruled his domain and his tenants with the supreme authority of a king.[52]

In a second comedy-synopsis, "The Lion Hunter," Ed devises a situation of mistaken identity involving Algernon D. Simpson, an inept ribbon counter clerk who has just been fired, and the great French explorer and lion hunter, Alphonse de Sachet. At a boarding house where he is about to apply for a job as a porter, Algernon, because of the initials A.D.S. on his suitcase, is assumed to be de Sachet. Influenced by the adoring glances of a pretty girl, Algernon decides to continue his impersonation of the famous lion hunter.

The series of escapades that develops is clearly slapstick, giving "The Lion Hunter" the appearance of a Chaplin or Laurel and Hardy comedy. When de Sachet finally arrives at the boarding house, Algernon, who has even arranged for a circus photographer to fake a picture of him with one foot on a lion's carcass, is exposed as a fraud and scorned by the pretty girl. His chance to redeem himself comes with the entry of an unexpected visitor to the boarding house—a lion that has escaped from the circus. De Sachet, the intrepid hunter, flees in panic and hides under a sofa, while Algernon emerges as a hero, routing the lion with a broom. The predictable romantic ending occurs.[53]

"Ben, King of Beasts," purchased by Selig for $300, is a fourteen-page synopsis with highly complicated plot elements. The characters travel from the original setting in Virginia to the wilds of Africa and back. The theme—one of Ed's favorites—centers about the close bonds between Dick Gordon, the hero, and Ben, a huge African lion.[54]

Burroughs' frustrated struggles with the movie synopsis form—a type of writing he felt he could never master—led him, about 1914-15, to scrawl in despair on the front of an unfinished work, "Synopsis of a bum photoplay." The plot of the handwritten, fourteen-page synopsis centers about the hazards faced by Hiram Huston, inventor of a highly explosive powder and a wireless detonator, and his daughter Deodora, the only one who knows where her father's notes and data are concealed. Other characters include Carter Colfax, Deodora's fiancé, whose father owns a large powder plant; Borsted, Covalla, and Klein, secret agents of a foreign government, Covalla having special powers as a hypnotist; Horta, an alluring female spy working with the trio; and Smith, Huston's secretary, a young man of weak character.

Huston, in an effort to interest the government in his invention, journeys to Washington. When Congress refuses to appropriate funds to purchase the invention, Huston visits Theodore Roosevelt at Oyster Bay; at Roosevelt's request Huston promises not to dispose of his invention to any foreign power.

The four agents, determined to steal the invention, concentrate first on Smith, Huston's secretary, and through the wiles of the lovely Horta, persuade him to join them and to spy on his employer. The plot develops complicated twists, with Burroughs reverting to one of his favorite and most convenient devices— that of switched identities. Colfax is drugged, and Borsted, who closely resembles him, takes his place; the conspirators also capture Huston. They set off an explosion at the experimental field, arrange for bits of Huston's clothing to be found, and convince Colfax, who has been hypnotized by Covalla, that he is responsible for the inventor's death.

The succession of incidents includes the police hunt for Huston's "murderer," the hypnotizing of Deodora, Colfax's awakening realization that he is not guilty, based upon such clues as the bloodless shreds of clothes and a duplicate walking stick, and, quite unbelievably, a reverse switch with Colfax now assuming the identity of the villainous Borsted.

Ed's persistent attempts during 1915 to break into the motion picture field had been severely disappointing. The minor sales of "The Lad and the Lion" and "Ben, King of Beasts" to Selig were hardly impressive when balanced against the producer's rejection of *Tarzan of the Apes*. The delay in production of "The Lad and the Lion" was exasperating, and as far as "Ben, King of Beasts" was concerned, Selig was making no plans at all to turn the story into a motion picture.

Various queries to Selig concerning "The Lad and the Lion" produced no definite information. Selig was evidently having production difficulties. In an exchange of letters between Ed and Bob Davis of the Munsey Company, both revealed their frustration:

Have you learned anything definite about the production of The Lad & the Lion? I imagine not. I am told that it will be useless to wait on Selig. . . .

[*Ed to Davis, April 27, 1916*]

I think I will notify Selig that I am going to put "The Lad and the Lion" to press without any further delay from them. At least it will have the effect of flashing an answer. Then I will let you know what they say.

[*Davis to Ed, May 4, 1916*]

"The Lad and the Lion" I am withholding until I hear from the Selig people. If they don't come across soon, I shall print it regardless of them.

[*Davis to Ed, October 25, 1916*]

Motion picture set of The Lad and the Lion; *Joan Burroughs at age eight took photo with her Kodak Brownie camera.*

I think you are a nut to wait . . . for The Lad and the Lion Production. . . .

[*Ed to Davis, November 21, 1916*]

I think I will let Selig go over the dam on the "Lad and the Lion."

[*Davis to Ed, November 27, 1916*]

I note that you are going to let Selig slide. . . .

[*Ed to Davis, December 3, 1916*]

I was out at Selig's Zoo the other day and learned that they expect to start on The Lad and the Lion soon; but. . . .

[*Ed to Davis, February 10, 1917*]

Davis, who had purchased "The Lad and the Lion" on April 2, 1914, first serial rights only, had withheld publication, acceding to Ed's request that the appearance in *All-Story* be timed so as to coincide with the movie release. To Davis's astonishment, without prior consultation, Selig, on April 21, 1917, informed the editor of a planned prerelease of the film, to "take place in New York, Chicago and one or two more of the larger cities," and of a general release scheduled for June. Davis, irked, hastened to reply: ". . . These dates make it impossible for us to present this story in the proper manner in the *All-Story Weekly* and we do not feel justified in permitting a pre-release to come out before we can give the story publication."[55]

Los Angeles set of Selig Polyscope Company during filming of ERB's story The Lad and the Lion, *1916.*

Davis reminded Selig of Munsey's purchase of the story in 1914, commenting, ". . . in 1915 when we were about ready to put this story to press, Mr. Burroughs asked us to hold it back until the Selig Polyscope Co. could present it on the screen. We have been carrying it now as you will see, for nearly three years, during which time you have been unable to make your production. Our rights come first. . . ."[56]

Nevertheless, in a conciliatory approach, Davis noted that the "issue" was "purely reciprocal" and assumed that Selig would not wish "to depreciate the value of a property . . . held exclusively by us." He offered a compromise proposal: Selig was to hold the prerelease until June 13 so as to allow *All-Story* sufficient time to publish "The Lad and the Lion"; in this way the cooperative plan could still be followed.[57]

On May 14, 1917, in a note to Ed marked "Confidential," the editor described the outcome of the situation:

Yes, Mr. Selig has settled the matter, and the "Lad and the Lion" will appear in the films May 14th.

Davis added, "So far as you are concerned, Edgar, not a cloud hovers in the sky between us and you can crack my safe or my ice-box for all it contains. I am going to see that 'The Lad and the Lion' by Edgar Rice Burroughs gets a good square deal in all our publications. I know you will like the cover. Will send you one as soon as it is ready." Davis signed his letter, "Yours to a cinder."[58] In his reply Ed expressed appreciation to Davis, saying, "You are the best scout I ever did business with and if the time comes when I feel that I must pick pockets for a living you may feel perfectly secure."

Davis, despite his anger at Selig, allowed the movie reasonable publicity when the story, the first of three parts, appeared in the *All-Story Weekly* of June 30, 1917. The magazine featured a colorful cover illustration of the Lad and his lion companion. A motion picture announcement was printed at the bottom edge of the cover. It stated briefly, "On the Screen Selig Polyscope Company."

In the movie, Selig's departure from the original story was evident from the beginning. He had removed Burroughs' hints that the Lad was of royal birth and had made him William Bankington, son of a millionaire, played by Will Machin. Others in the cast were Vivian Reed as the Arab girl Nakhla; Charles Le Moyne as Dan Saada; Al W. Filson as Sheik Ali-Es-Hadji; and Lafayette McKee as James Bankington.[59]

Selig also removed from the story the half-crazed old epileptic who mistreats both the boy and the lion, the years aboard the drifting ship, and the odd scenes with the old man, a deaf-mute, instructing the boy in sign language; he replaced the old man with a brutal stowaway, Broot. Thus, the opening incidents are drastically revised:

James Bankington, a millionaire, consents to his only son, William, making a trip to Africa. The boy takes passage with Captain Tagst. . . . They pass a sailing vessel carrying a caged lion to America. In the hold is a stowaway named Broot, and the pipe he smokes starts a fire. Knowing there is a consignment of powder the captain and the crew abandon the ship. The stowaway extinguishes the blaze and discovers the lion.

Captain Tagst's ship is wrecked and William is left alone on a raft. The stowaway rescues the lad. Fright and exposure have robbed him of his memory. Time passes and the lad has made friends with the lion, for both are kicked and cuffed by Broot, the stowaway. Later the lion escapes and Broot springs overboard.[60]

The major action takes place in a North African Arab village where the Lad falls in love with Nakhla. A band of brigands, whose chief falls in love with Nakhla, is introduced; a love triangle develops; the Lad has his memory restored by a blow on the head in a fight with the brigand chief; and the lion springs upon the

"The Lad and the Lion" cover of All-Story Weekly, *June 30, 1917.*

chief and kills him. Aware of his identity, the Lad still proclaims his love for the simple Arab girl. Ed's original story complications are followed in the major action.

During the 1915 period, when ERB's interest in screen writing had been stimulated, he devised two other synopses. The first of these, an eleven-page manuscript, "The Prospector," develops the plot of "For a Fool's Mother" (1912), but expands the story with additional action. "For a Fool's Mother" has no romantic interest, so Ed introduces two suitors for the seventeen-year-old Mary Turner. He also indicates familiarity with the scenario form, with emphasis on the visual, and such cues as: "Show Kid Turner, ragged, coughing, and weak, tramping along railway through desert country."

The plot includes many popular ingredients of the Western story—the escape from the sheriff, the recapture, a mob storming the jail and preparing to lynch the Prospector, and the nick-of-time testimony by a wastrel which saves the Prospector's life.

The synopsis ends with a happy future promised the lovers and Cole, the rival for the girl's hand, making a heroic sacrifice. Shaking the Prospector's hand, he says: "I'm going back east tomorrow but I'd like to leave a good superintendent in charge of the camp. Will you take my job—my secretary goes with it."[61]

A brief handwritten synopsis, completed on August 31, 1915, and titled "The Zealots," may be described as the original medical or doctors story. There is no record of its ever having been submitted to a motion picture producer. The love interest between an "M.D. Allopath," and his hometown sweetheart become minor as the story emphasizes conflicts based upon the opposing theories and practices of two doctors, and, in addition, the beliefs of Christian Science. Ed's paradoxical theme with its opposing elements of condemnation and approval for different healing practices is best explained at the end with a statement by one doctor that "there is good in all men and in all schools." The title unifies the theme well and offers symbolic interpretation: all three major characters, as exponents of certain healing methods, are zealots. In the end, zealotry is defeated, and balance and moderation triumph.[62]

PART 6

TRAVELS AND WORLD WAR I

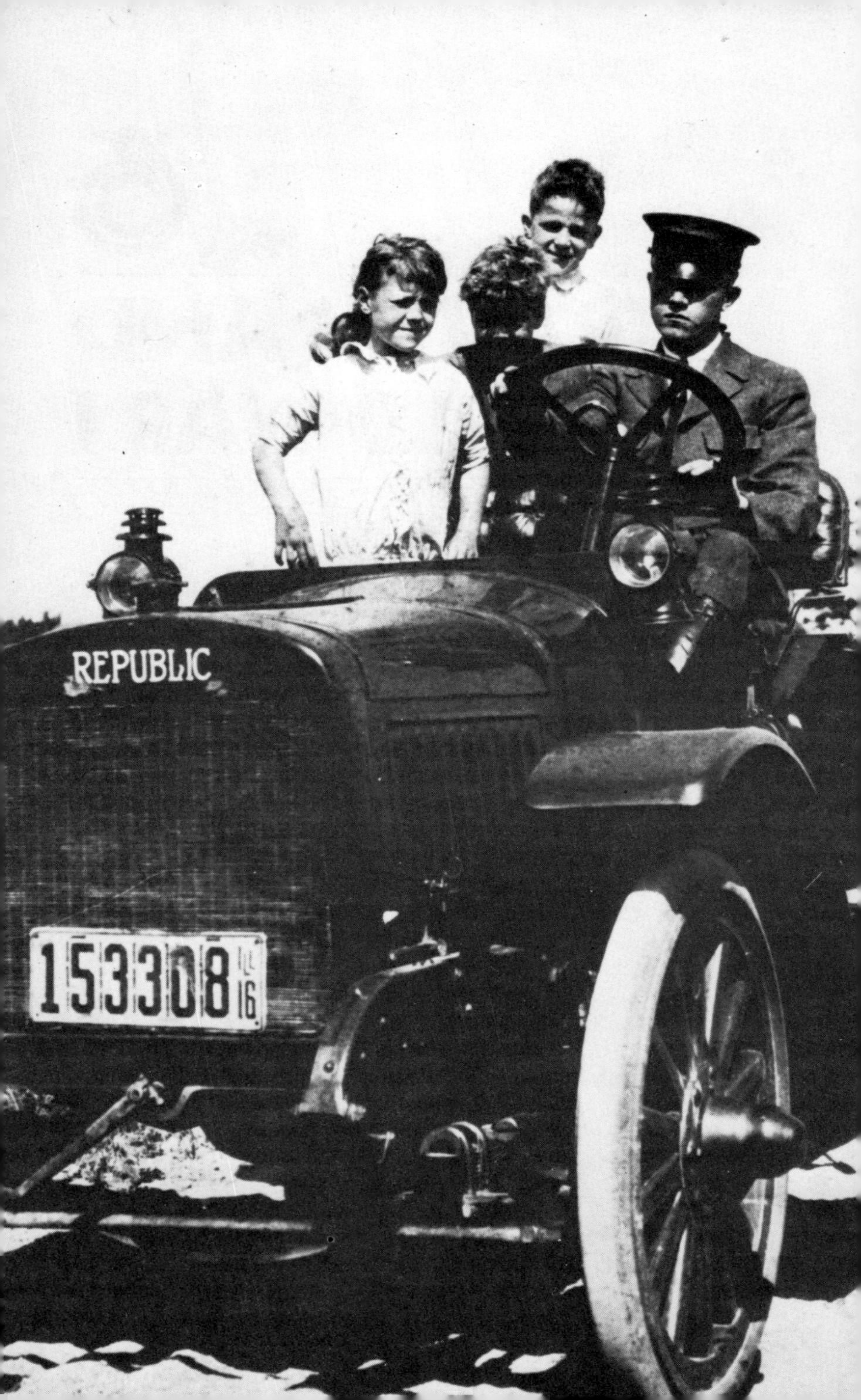
REPUBLIC
153308 ILL 16

CHAPTER 13

AUTO-GYPSYING

Before the arrival of summer 1916, Ed, plagued by severe neuritis pains in his shoulder, and exhausted by months of intensive writing, was devising plans for a long vacation. His fascination with automobiles and driving would allow him to consider only one type of vacation as desirable: he and the family must embark upon an extended motoring and camping trip. The destination was the Maine woods, specifically Moosehead Lake, and afterward they would visit Portland, where his father and mother had lived for two years, and where his brothers George and Harry had been born. An automobile trip of this type, in some respects daringly "pioneer" for 1916, required careful preparation; first of all, information was needed, and Ed sent an inquiry to *Camp and Trail* magazine concerning campsites in the eastern states. His letter was forwarded to another author, Raymond S. Spears of Little Falls, New York, who on May 21 sent details of eastern routes and campsites. Sears, explaining that there would be no difficulty in finding these sites, wrote, ". . . I met dozens of camping parties last summer, running a motorcycle from this city (Little Falls) to South Dakota. . . ."[1]

Commenting about the Adirondack region, which contained the only "wild country," Spears noted humorously, "I suppose, from Tarzan, that you want primitive conditions, and the Adirondacks will give you a kind of 'wilderness.' " To Spears, the purpose of traveling was mainly to find materials and sources for

Republic truck ERB purchased in Alma, Michigan, for California trip; left to right: Joan, Hulbert, Judson Branch, and Louis J. Ziebs, July 2, 1916.

writing—the rich regional and native color, picturesque characters and settings, and elements preserved in Americana. About other areas, again through a writer's eyes, he remarked, ". . . Thoreau, for example, at Cambridge, camped just out of town—and around there are still to be had camping grounds. . . . On Chesapeake Bay, west side, you will find countless places of interest—Potomac River is the sailing land of the Maryland Oyster Pirates to this day, and they used to shanghai preachers, lawyers and poets—if they could catch them—to work oyster boats." Spears spoke of Warm Springs, Virginia, where Ed would find "moonshiner country." Spears' fascination with the people of the isolated "closed-off" regions and their unique cultures was evident:

Somewhere in that territory is a colony of Irish immigrants, with a brogue as broad as Cork, who never heard of Ireland, except by ancient tradition and fairy lore. Most of the Hill Billies are of English descent, however—primitive—and you can hardly go amiss, so far as material is concerned. The stories would come to your camp, in blue poke sunbonnets, figures unrestrained by stays and blue-eyed amazement. Don't fail to attend Mountain Preachin'.

He also advised that in the foothills of Kentucky Ed could find the "feud and night rider country," adding that if he were to camp on the Ohio Bottoms "almost anywhere, but especially at a loquacious ferryman's site," he could discover "endless material and river lore."[2]

Ed's letter to *Camp and Trail* had given Spears the impression that Ed planned to collect material and to write while on his camping trip. But the acquisition of material from real-life sources had never been one of Ed's prime objectives. Here the differences between the two writers were obvious. Spears was an author who delighted in the discovery of colorful characters, people with odd customs or traditions, and all the richness of folklore. On the other hand, Ed drew his characters and events of fantasy worlds from his imagination. A summary of his writing approach was made in the *Detroit Journal* at the time of his vacation trip: ". . . he has found that he can't write about anything he is thoroughly familiar with. . . ." And to this jesting statement with its basis of truth, Ed himself added, "The less I know about a thing, the better I can write about it."[3]

Several weeks earlier Ed had ordered some camping equipment, listing items on a familiar form, headed (naturally) Sears, Roebuck and Company, Chicago. The list included folding camp beds and chairs, a kerosene oil-gas stove, fifty yards of canvas, and four pieces of mosquito netting.[4]

Spears urged Ed to stop off at Westfield where Jay Brown, Spears' cousin, had a farm. "Speaking of Gypsying," Spears wrote, "have you read The Romany Rye, the Bible in Spain and The Zincali by George Borrow? . . . While they may not help much in camping lore, yet they give zest to the meeting of Gypsies whom you are certain to meet or pass along the way."[5] He added, "I've never had any trouble on the road—no one is more cordial to a note-book man than feud fighters, bad men (particularly a Sears-Roebuck bad man) and river pirates."[6] Spears' previous invitation to Ed to visit the Spears' home at Little Falls was followed later with a hasty dispatch—"I thought I ought to let you know that measles have become epidemic in this city. . . ."[7]

The itinerary for the trip listed distances between cities, route numbers, and projected campsites. Familiar places were included: Coldwater, Michigan, the site of the Hulbert Sunnyside Farm; Orchard Lake, where Michigan Military Academy was located; Portland, Maine; and of course Warren, Massachusetts, noted "Father's birthplace." Moosehead Lake was marked "Terminal Camp Turn Back," and after one more northern stop at Bangor, the plan was to head south to Portland and then proceed to New Hampshire, to other eastern states en route to New York City, and finally to Washington, D.C.[8]

Ed was naturally prepared to keep a detailed account of the trip. Headed "Auto Gypsying," it opened, "June 14, 1916. Left Oak Park, Illinois, 5:30 P.M. Wednesday. Odom. 7664." This meticulous approach, so typical of his nature, had been illustrated also in his painstaking records of story sales and payments. The remainder of the trip diary is thick with minute details. The camping tour members were humorously introduced:

The party leaving 414 Augusta street, Oak Park, upon this fateful day consisted of Emma Hulbert Burroughs, Joan Burroughs (8½), Hulbert Burroughs (6½), 'Jack' Burroughs (3¼), Theresa Witzmann, maid, Louis J. Ziebs, chauffeur; Edgar Rice Burroughs, Emma Hulbert's husband; Dickie, canary bird; and the Jinx.

The Jinx, who made himself evident at the very start when Ed slammed the front door and then discovered he had locked all his keys inside, was to be very prominent during the journey and at times would dominate it. Also included, and described as

Title page of ERB's diary of 1916 trip.

"the most important member of the party" was Tarzan, the Airedale terrier pup.

The "rolling stock" was listed as a Packard Twin Six 1-35 motor carriage, "vulgarly" known as a touring car; an Overland delivery car named *Happy Thought,* and a trailer, fittingly titled *Calamity Jane.* The machinations of The Jinx were undoubtedly aided at the start by the Burroughs' plans to carry an immense amount of supplies and baggage. Ed explained:

Had planned to leave in the morning but it took longer to load than we had anticipated. Louis could not help me much as he had two flat tires to attend to on the Overland. After we had crammed the Overland full and still had a mountain of equipment left on the garage floor we discovered that the rear fenders were resting on the tires—she seemed tiring rather early in the game. It was then that the use of a trailer occurred to me as an easy escape from our dilemma, and I bought one that is made by an Oak Park concern. It was assigned to trail a Ford and carry pianos. Unfortunately about the only thing we had neglected to include in our equipment was a piano.

At the first stop, in Chicago, the travelers picked up Emma's mother and a little later dropped the canary bird Dickie at brother Harry's house. The peculiar Burroughs caravan, unparalleled for the times, at once attracted attention and throughout the trip continued to draw amazed and disbelieving onlookers. But the chronicle of the tour was one of misfortunes, of heavy rains and muddy, almost impassable roads, of constant car trouble and regular breakdowns. Each day brought new and exasperating obstacles:

June 14: Happy Thought, the trailer . . . illuminating gas gone . . . no headlights, tail lamp broken. . . . I ran behind it shining my headlights on it . . . quite an interesting pastime. . . .

June 15: Near Gary . . . pole of the trailer stuck its nose into the road . . . a sheaf of tent poles did the same, breaking three of them and ramming a hole in the bottom of the steamer trunk . . . decided to go in camp . . . commenced to rain . . . Louis and I had never put up the tent together . . . I had had a canvas floor sewed to it . . . The poor egg who had done the work had started to sew with a twelve foot end of the floor against a twenty foot side wall, and gone merrily around until he met his starting point. The result was appalling . . . occurred to me that we might rip out the floor . . . we got the tent up . . . it was a frightful job driving those enormous two foot wooden stakes into the ground in the dark. . . . We have named this Camp Despair. *. . .*

June 17: . . . got our usual early start about 11 a.m. . . . a questionable road. . . . Happy Thought and Calamity Jane stopped in the heaviest part of it—to rest, presumably . . . backed up and hitched the Packard to them . . . road gang called something . . . trying to tell me that Calamity Jane had broken off—diplomatic relations I was about to say but there was about as much diplomacy in a mule as there was in Calamity Jane. . . . Hired a scraper team to tow Calamity Jane to camp. This is Camp Disaster. *. . . It rained hard during the evening. . . .*[9]

June 19: Reached South Bend, Indiana. . . . We towed Happy Thought and Calamity Jane up nearly every hill and at one railroad crossing we pushed them across by hand, much to the amusement of a carload of tourists. I think Happy was on her last legs. At South Bend I bought a new ¾ ton Republic Truck that had just been brought down from the factory at Alma, Michigan, for an ice man. I beat the ice man to it, probably the first time an ice man ever got the worse of it. . . . Left the old transport at South Bend to be sold on commission and started off once more about 6 p.m. We are perfect gluttons for this evening start stuff. . . . located a camp site with my spot light. In driving in through tall grass Louis hit a hidden stump and bent the steering rod of the nice, new truck into a U. . . .

1.

June 14, 1916 - Left Oak Park, Illinois, 5:30 P.M. Wednesday. Odom 7664. Had planned to leave in the morning but it took longer to load than we had anticipated. Louis could not help much as he had two flat tires to attend to - on the Overland. After we had filled the Overland and still had a mountain of equipment left on the garage floor, we discovered that the rear fenders were resting on the tires - she seemed tiring rather early in the game. It was then that the use of a trailer occurred to me as an easy escape from our dilemma, and I bought one which is made by an Oak Park concern. It was designed to trail a Ford and carry pianos. Unfortunately we had not thought to bring a piano. The afternoon was consumed in having the couplings altered so that the trailer could be attached to the Overland. It seemed a little thing at the time that it became necessary to invert the coupling clasps; but that was before we had to do it on a hot, dusty country road with a heavy load on the trailer. Just as we were ready to leave I discovered that I had forgotten something and went back into the house, laying the garage key and front door key on the billiard table. Then I came out and locked the front door after me - just a playful antic of the Jinx which had already attached itself to us. Mr. Whitaker, my neighbor, promised to send for a locksmith to rescue the keys.

The party leaving 414 Augusta street consisted of Emma Hulbert Burroughs, Joan Burroughs (8-1/2), Hulbert Burroughs (6-1/2), "Jack" Burroughs (3-1/4), Theresa Witzmann (maid), Louis J. Ziebs (chauffeur), Edgar Rice Burroughs (Emma Hulbert's husband), Dickie (canary bird), and the Jinx. The rolling

First page of diary of 1916 trip.

386

Entire Burroughs expedition on road through Indiana, 1916.

June 20: . . . Had steering rod straightened at Mishawaka. . . . Reached Coldwater 3 p.m. Just inside city limits truck motor commenced to pound and Louis stopped her . . . found we had burned out a connecting rod bearing. Made about 90 miles today. Much better than Happy Thought and Calamity Jane could make in five days.

June 26: . . . Louis and I started for Alma, Michigan, about 1 p.m. in the truck, as we found while replacing one bearing that others were in bad shape . . . damage due to running without oil in crank case . . . oil gauge had shown Full. *. . . started out again about 1:30 a.m. Driving a new road on a cloudy night without headlights . . . the barn lantern was all that saved us. Reached Alma about 9:30 a.m. . . . take two days to repair the truck . . . started back for camp by R.R. . . . about 140 miles from Alma to Morrisons Lake by auto; but it took us twelve hours to make it by train, taking four different lines of road. . . . Michigan is a great state but it is through no fault of the railroads—they are doing and have done, always, their best to keep people out of Michigan. As far back as I can recall, Michigan has had the poorest train service of any state in the Union. . . .*[10]

At Morrison's Lake, near Coldwater, the travelers set up Camp Branch,[11] so named because it was the lakeside vacation cottage of Roy and Julia Branch, Emma's sister. From there they

"Camp Disaster" near Rolling Prairie, Indiana, June 18, 1916.

went on to Detroit. About the city that he had not seen in some time, Ed commented:

Detroit is a night-mare of a place to drive a car—narrow, winding streets, packed solid on both sides with cars where ever the law permits them to park. . . . Detroit has grown like a weed since I last visited it. . . . To me it has lost much of its charm and beauty in the last twenty five years, and I regretted the days when they used to stop the street cars to watch a dog fight, as I have seen done in the past. . . .[12]

As demonstrated by his past actions, the unexpected was on occasion to be expected from Ed Burroughs. In a sudden decision, all of the detailed plans and itinerary for the tour of eastern states, all of the information furnished by Spears, and the destination of Moosehead Lake, Maine, were discarded. On July 15 Ed recorded the decision in his diary: "Emma and I have decided to give up the eastern trip and head for Los Angeles instead. The prevalence of infantile paralysis in the east has frightened us. . . ." This decision would shape and change the entire course of his life. "We are pretty nearly ready to start," Ed claimed, but they remained at Camp Branch until July 27, spending a total of thirty-seven days there before launching the caravan on the road. The first destination was Oak Park and home, and on the twenty-eighth they were at 414 Augusta Street, back where they had started.[13]

Departure was scheduled for August 7, and on that day Ed wrote:

Have all the furniture in storage after nine days at home, and to-day we set out for Los Angeles at 10:15 a.m. Odometer 10145.0. . . . Got a new chauffeur while in Chicago. Ray [Hebert] is his name. Lewis was afraid to attempt the trip west owing to the return of an old trouble for which he was once operated on. Truck almost stalled on steep grade out of Starved Rock Park. Weighed the truck at Sandwich—5965 lbs. gross, or about 2700 for the load. Some *camp equipment. Those who doubt this statement should unload it after a long day's drive and load it again in the morning after a rotten night. . . . camp at school house about seven miles east of Ottawa, Illinois. The flies were awful. We call this* Camp Fly.

On August 8 Ed noted, "Joan is ailing—another of her bilious attacks, I think," but on the next day, after a dosage of calomel and a cathartic she was much better, and Ed recorded proudly, "Joan and Hulbert drove the Packard all day to-day. They steered and used the foot accelerator. . . . All that I did was to sit ready to save us from sudden death. . . . Joan is eight and a half and Hulbert will be seven Saturday."[14]

Although the Burroughs travelers had reversed their destination to the western side of the continent, the weather remained the same—unalterably bad. The account was repetitive: "Storm brewing. Put side curtains on Packard. . . . commenced to pour about 1:30 . . . came down in torrents for a long time. . . ." On August 11, at Camp Point, Illinois, Ed recorded what had become a type of normal catastrophe:

. . . commenced to rain . . . roads became suddenly frightful. . . . We skidded from the verge of one ditch to the brink of the opposite for a mile . . . futile to go on, so we turned around, which was quite some stunt in itself, and started back for Camp Point. In half a mile the truck went into a ditch. I couldn't get traction to pull it out, though I tried. Ray and I were in mud to our hips. Finally I left him and drove on for help. Just inside town I went into the ditch myself, worse than the truck had gone in.[15]

In the midst of the struggles and hardships Ed forgot about

Ed Burroughs at Morrison Lake, Michigan, June 1916.

the neuritis in his shoulder and the fact that he was traveling for his health. After pushing the truck uphill, he commented, "Last winter Elsie or Theresa had to help me on with my overcoat. Now I run about the country with loaded motor trucks on my shoulder. There is nothing like the simple life for invalids."

On August 12 the Republic truck was towed into Hannibal, Missouri, while the vacationers took rooms at the Mark Twain Hotel. The rain continued as did repair work on the truck, and the Burroughs family took the opportunity to visit Twain's boyhood home in Hannibal. The fifteenth found them still in town, with work being done on the Packard—Tarzan had "knocked out" the glass from three rear windows. A group of Hannibal's bankers and businessmen welcomed the Burroughs and volunteered to take them on a tour of Mark Twain's famous cave. Ed described the experience:

Joan, Hulbert and I went, the others not caring to. Mr. Main-
land fastened candles on the ends of sticks and after he had
smashed the padlock which secures the door of the cave we filed
in. . . . The corridors are quite narrow and winding and seem to
be myriad, running in all directions through the hill. They say
that some even wind down beneath the river, and that the cave
never has been fully explored. I am quite sure that I should not
care to explore it in company with a little girl of eight and a little
boy of seven, each armed with a lighted candle at the end of a
long stick, and each gazing in every possible direction except at
the business end of their candle. . . . This is the cave in which
Tom Sawyer hid, or was lost; or was it Huckleberry Finn?

About the atmosphere Ed wrote, "It was cold and damp, silent
and inky dark. To be left there without a light must be a trying
experience. Three minutes after we entered I could not have
found my way out alone, even with a battery of arc lights. How
the characters in some of my stories get along so well in 'Stygian
blackness' is beyond me, yet they do it. . . ."[16]

The hectic journey through Missouri and Kansas continued
with the familiar succession of bad weather, breakdowns and re-
pairs.[17] On August 28 at Emporia, Kansas, Ed visited an author
whose poems he had admired very much, noting, "Called on
Walt Mason this afternoon, and found him a real human being,

ERB's yacht, Morrison Lake, "Camp Branch"; left to right: Judson
Branch, Joan Burroughs, Theresa Witzmann, Hulbert Burroughs,
Emma Burroughs, Jack Burroughs, and Julia Branch.

ERB in front of Mark Twain's boyhood home, Hannibal, Missouri, August 15, 1916.

whom no one could help but like. . . . Lying hospitably he said that he had read all the Tarzan stories and liked them. . . ."[18] Two days later, at Newton, Kansas, the travelers encountered some unanticipated danger:

Ray [Hebert] placed his cot some distance from the tent under thick trees. . . . Something woke him and he saw two grim beasts sneaking about him in the darkness. . . . Together we searched for the intruders. . . . All night someone not far distant was firing a rifle . . . sat up until 2:45 waiting for the wild beasts to return. . . . We were told the next day that our prowling visitors were coyotes; but I doubt it. Coyotes howl. These beasts did not. . . . We named yesterday's camp Camp Coyote.

At the dinner table in Larned, Kansas, the Burroughs family was surprised to discover that the distinguished William Jennings Bryan was seated near them; he had come to open a chautauqua series. Ed, disapproving of Bryan's pacifist philosophy, commented disparagingly about him: "He is not as large a man, physically, as I had thought. His face belies his peace-at-any-price character. I have no admiration for him; but I imagine he would fight as well as the next man if necessity arose. It is sad to see one of his ability striving to paint a whole nation yellow and making them like it. . . ."[19]

392

The arrival of September 1, his birthday, found Ed twelve miles west of Dodge City, and caused him to reminisce: "Am 41 today. Twenty years ago this Sept. 1st I rode south from Fort Grant, Arizona, with 'B' Troop of the 7th Cavalry after the Apache Kid and his band, and I was about as uncomfortable as I have been on this trip. . . ."[20] As the caravan entered Colorado the hardships and difficulties increased; the succeeding days were filled with troubles and problems:

September 6: . . . Started to search for a camp site in the mountains above Manitou. . . . Drove the Packard up Ute Pass in search of a camp site. Could find nothing. Went as far as Cascade . . . turned back toward Colorado Springs. . . . Tried to reach Bear Creek. . . . Pushed truck by hand up 20% grade and discovered another, a down grade, even steeper . . . turned back again. . . . Joan has been sick. We are all discouraged and 1403 miles from Los Angeles. Since we left Oak Park August 7th we have driven 1365 miles by the Blue Book, so have come less than half way. . . .

September 7: Joan sick all day. After supper she stiffened out as though dying . . . drove into town . . . got Dr. Tucker to come out . . . doctor said it was merely reflex action following a bilious attack. . . .[21]

Joan's illness and the problems with the other children brought Ed and Emma to a decision: they would abandon camping out. Ed wrote, "NEVER AGAIN! At least not with three little children. It is impossible to keep the flies away from them, the food is improperly cooked, the meals are irregular, cold and unpalatable . . . if one of them should be taken sick in a camp a long way from a big town I do not know what we could do. And I don't intend to find out. . . ."

The hazards also included poisonous snakes. Ed described his encounters with these:

Ray found a snake near camp today and I went out with my automatic to slay it. It was a copperhead, three feet long. A few days ago, in Kansas, I shot one, hitting it in the neck the first shot; but this last one was not so accommodating. Emptied the magazine and did not hit him at all. . . . This is our third copperhead in a week . . . glad we are quitting the camping business, as the children wouldn't have a chance in the world against one of them. . . .

Breaking camp for last time.

With the camping definitely finished, Ed, on September 9, re-marked, "Have shipped the bulk of equipment by freight to lighten load. Shall drive through to Los Angeles over the Santa Fe Trail as rapidly as possible, Ray following with truck more slowly. . . ." The unexpected hardships of the camping tour had made writing impossible. As a result, concerning his decision to hasten to Los Angeles, he noted, "It is just as well as I am close to being behind in my contract with The Blue Book Magazine, and find that I cannot, or at least do not write on the road. In fact I have to be at the threshold of the poor house with the sheriff levying on my coattails before I can really buckle down to work properly. . . ."

About the two Kansas farmers who had inspected the caravan with all its paraphernalia, with one remarking, "This, by hen, is a mighty inexpensive way to travel," Ed wrote, "Sure it is. I could only have taken my family around the world three or four times, with side trips to Mars and Orion, for what it has cost—and the end is not yet." The entire Los Angeles trip had of course resulted from an impulsive decision, and Ed's tendency to yield to these impulses was clearly demonstrated in his actions in Colorado, involving one particular excursion of September 10:

It was a cloudy, threatening day, so, with my w.k. acumen I selected it to drive up to the top of Pikes Peak. . . . We all went —Ray, Theresa, Tarzan. It is a long pull—about ten miles from Colorado Springs to the foot of the Pikes Peak Road, and all up grade, then eighteen miles to the summit. . . . It rained, hailed, snowed and fogged—principally fogged. It was a cold, dispiriting, uncomfortable, frightful trip—a regular pleasure exertion. The children wore socks, while I disported myself in a summer suit,

394

Rare photo of ERB and his camera.

B.V.D.'s, and no overcoat. . . . At the top there was nothing but fog and outhouses. When the fog blew around a bit we had fleeting glimpses of the out-houses. It was a wonderful view from the top of Pikes Peak.

On September 12 Ed noted that he had shipped two trunks and seven suitcases to Los Angeles, and on that day, according to plan, Ray Hebert started off early with the truck. Ed followed later with the Packard, and about passing Hebert on the road commented, "We each experienced a strange sensation as we saw the truck ahead and again as we left it for the last time. It is odd that we can grow fond of inanimate objects, yet we do. I remember when we sold our first car the day before we left San Diego, the old Velie. When the poor egg who bought it wobbled down the street in it a lump rose in our throats. It was like parting with an old friend—an old friend who was about to experience four blowouts. . . ."

With the rains of Kansas and Colorado behind him, Ed was happy to drive through Arizona and New Mexico, covering distances of from 140 to 200 miles daily on roads that were at least temporarily dry.[22] However, there was little improvement in the quality of the roads. Of the one from Holbrook to Winslow, Arizona, described by Ed as "a sad, uncanny, practical joke," he reported having heard that in the rainy season as many as fourteen cars had piled up on this one stretch of road. He thought one story deserved repeating:

A young woman with her elderly aunt were touring alone. They left Winslow and running into this mud hole were unable to get out, so they camped in the ruts. The young lady slept in the car, her aunt in a cot attached to the running board and covered by one of those tents which attach to the top of a car. Probably they did not light their tail lamp; for after dark, while they were both asleep, another car came along and hit the old lady's cot. She must have been a nimble old lady and a light sleeper, for while the cot was demolished she herself escaped by leaping. After that some nine or ten more cars came along and stuck all around them, trying to pass them, I imagine, so that by the next noon there was quite a company. They stayed there two or three days, getting out at last only by placing boards in front of the cars, one at a time, and placing them in front again.[23]

On September 20, en route through Arizona, the Burroughs family saw the wreck of the Santa Fe California Limited. It had been derailed at a sharp curve and in the accident four or five people were killed. "At Yucca," Ed wrote, "we struck the Mojave Desert and from there to Topock the road was hideous. There was no road—merely wheel tracks where other damn fools had come or gone. . . . Was so tired that I dozed at the wheel several times. . . ." The difficult late-night driving continued the next day with the travelers reaching Barstow at eleven p.m. and Ed again dozing at the wheel and during one period, even falling asleep and dreaming. About the area and the matter of desert driving, Ed, in making a prediction, offered an amusing account of his mistaken beliefs:

Some day a paved boulevard will connect Kingman and San Bernardino, and when that day comes the desert will cease to exist in so far as it is of any concern to motorists. So much had been told us of the dangers of the desert crossing that we were prepared to discover the landscape dotted with the bleached bones of motorists who had died of thirst there, and to see poor wretches crawling on hands and knees, raving for water, while every few yards some thirst-crazed Forder turned his Henry upside down to drain between his parched and swollen lips the seven drops of water remaining in the radiator. As a matter of fact the desert is monotonously devoid of danger, if one can keep awake—I mean the one who is driving.[24]

§aturday September 23 saw the Burroughs caravan leaving San Bernardino for the last brief lap of the trip. Ed re-

*"At the Summit of Cajon Pass our troubles ended" (ERB's caption),
September 22, 1916.*

ported, "We arrived in Los Angeles a little after noon, terminating
three months and nine days of touring and camping with a total
of 6008 miles recorded by the odometer. All are here and all are
well. The odometer also shows that I have driven the Packard
3527 miles between Oak Park and Los Angeles."

About the supposed motive for the cross-country journey, he
wrote, "The trip, which was undertaken in the hope that it would
rid me of neuritis, has not been entirely successful in this; but
my general health is much better. Last winter I had to have assistance in putting on an overcoat; now I can lift a trunk to my
shoulder and perform other Herculean stunts—that is I could if I
were not so lazy."

On this final day, in meditating over the hardships of these past
months, Ed conceded that neither he nor Emma would care to
undertake such a trip again, nor would they, on the other hand,
wish to "part with the memory of the summer's experiences."
If the 1916 tour were ever again to be attempted, he might suggest only one change in equipment: the bathtub and the typewriter could be eliminated, "as neither seem to have been in
great demand." He would also suggest the addition of another
driver for the Packard and a "general roustabout or camp boy"
for the truck. He closed his diary of the trip with a sentimental
observation:

However, if I had the choice of three children from all the chil-

dren in the world, and one or more wives from all the wives in the world, for another similar trip, I could not find any better than those with which God has blessed me.

Now I lay me down to sleep.[25]

Hulbert Burroughs, who was only seven years old at the time, has some vivid memories of the trip:

To me as a child, and with none of the responsibilities, the 1916 trip from Chicago to California was an exciting adventure. Memories that come to mind are the occasions when we drove at night and the car's headlights illumined the glowing eyes of mysterious wild animals fleetingly visible on the road ahead. Through parts of Colorado, New Mexico, and Arizona there were still thousands of prairie dogs and jackrabbits. I recall how my Dad would let our dog, Tarzan, out of the car for exercise, and how the big Airedale took out after the jackrabbits. There were so many that he was never on the trail of the same one for more than a few seconds at a time. I can still recall hearing his frustrated hunting yelps as he sought vainly to catch one.

It is difficult today in this era of the great transcontinental freeway system, to envision the primitive condition of most of the roads along what was then rather grandiloquently called the Lincoln Highway. They can best be compared to the tortuous Mexican Baja California road, scene of the famous Baja 1000 road race, prior to the recent completion of the newly paved "Trans-peninsular Highway."

I recall with vivid clarity a particularly horrible section of road through the Glorietta Mountains of New Mexico west of Santa Fe. It was called La Bajada Grade—where the route west descended out of the mountains down the cliffs in a series of steep and tight hairpin curves. By tight, I mean the radius of the arc of each curve was such that the big Packard Twin-Six could not negotiate them in one pass. My Dad had to extend the front wheels as far as possible to the brink of the abyss, then set the large emergency hand brake while he laboriously turned the steering wheel preparatory to backing up the few feet necessary to finally round the curve. My poor mother was so terrified of these steep grades that she would insist on leaving the car with us three children while Ed wrestled the car to safety. I don't know what she planned to do if Ed and the car had hurtled into the void.

The only pavement we encountered was in some of the more affluent cities and towns. Such pavement usually consisted of red bricks and in some cases four-by-four wooden blocks. One of the most interesting stretches of roadway was across the vast California desert sand dunes west of Yuma, Arizona. Because of the soft, shifting sands, a one-lane wooden plank road was constructed with occasional wider turnout sections for passing oncoming cars. Remnants of that old plank road can still be seen in a few places near the present high-speed freeway on Interstate 8.

Travel with three young children necessitated frequent stops. To minimize such delays to his westward progress, Ed partially solved the problem by inserting a funnel in the wooden floorboard of the tonneau.

During the camping tour Ed had maintained some correspondence with Bob Davis at the Munsey Company, sending him several Kodak photos which Davis, on August 28, described as "the Burroughs family ravaging the Michigan frontier," and adding, "the picture taken near Rolling Prairie, where Calamity Jane laid down and spit out such life as happened to be in her, interests me greatly because it shows Burroughs sitting down while the balance of his family stands up. . . ."

After a brief stay at the Hollenbeck Hotel, Ed had moved to a rented house at 355 South Hoover Street in Los Angeles, and from there he wrote to Davis, offering to send the editor the lengthy diary of the trip. Davis indicated willingness to read the diary and remarked, "What a devil of a time you must have had on that tour. You ought now to wear epaulets and a medal on your left breast with the following inscription: 'Bill Burroughs, the peace maker of the Piute Indians.' Any guy that can slip across a continent with a lot of his own female relatives in the same tent is not an enemy to society. . . ."[26]

Davis's comment that he had lived in Los Angeles himself, on Pico Street (now Boulevard), off Figueroa, brought a reply from Ed on November 21 in which he claimed he had driven around those streets but could find "no monument commemorating the historic fact. . . ."

To Ray Long, editor of *Blue Book Magazine,* who had contracted for a series of *Tarzan* short stories, Ed confided his fondness for Los Angeles and his approval of the Hoover Street home he had rented:

You ask when we expect to return. Have rented this house until June 4 and shall probably stay the limit. To my surprise I like it here very much. I do not know when I have been more contented. We have a very pretty little place with many flowers

End of trip; house at 355 South Hoover Street, Los Angeles, September 1916.

and trees, and a good lawn. . . . The children are playing out in front now with no wraps, and wearing sox. . . .[27]

He suggested that the editor and his wife might live in Los Angeles, pointing out that Long could edit just as well there "as in a snowstorm." Ed also wrote, "There are oodles of writers here, too, so that you would be close to a supply. Am trying to get Walt Mason out here. If I could establish a colony of human beings it would be a nice place to live permanently."[28]

In letters of November 21 to both Long and Davis he spoke of the diary of his trip, informing Long that he had completed the manuscript—a total of 37,000 words, and reminding Davis of his promise to read it:

I am going to send it to you; but you don't have to read it. I just finished typing it from notes made on everything from Old Hampshire Bond to toilet paper at ten cents the roll. I thought that it was going to be interesting; but it is not. Please send it back to me when you have kept it long enough to make believe you have read it.

His hesitancy and his apologies about the diary reveal that, as in the past, he had little confidence in any writings that departed from his fictional style. This was more strongly demonstrated by his decision, a week later, not to send the diary at all; he explained to Davis:

. . . when Mrs. Burroughs had read it she opined that it was so dinged uninteresting that it would be a crime to inflict it on anyone outside the family. No one else on earth could cross a continent, spending three months and nine days in touring and camping, run off six thousand and eight miles on the odometer and fail to encounter a single thing that would interest anyone outside his own kitchenette. This is my unique record.[29]

It was not until two years later that Ed gathered sufficient courage to send the diary to Bob Davis.[30] In his humorous analysis of the thirty-six page "Diary of an Automobile Camping Tour," Davis noted that "it ought to be divided into three installments, as follows: Rain, Mud, Curtain," and remarked, "It is perfectly plain to me now, Edgar, that you could move Ringling Brothers circus across the continent and not lose a single elephant."[31]

Concerning Tarzan, the Airedale pup, Davis said, ". . . he is as near to the saber-tooth tiger as any animal you ever came upon." About Ed's difficulties Davis wrote, "It is perfectly absurd that the man who wrote Tarzan and the Martian stories, and who has turned pain and bloodshed and a diet of grasshoppers into a small fortune, would be perfectly helpless in a jungle covering more than a single acre."

Davis' banter was directed at various happenings on the trip:

You carefully neglected throughout the entire story to tell us what became of the canary bird. Was he eaten by The Jinx?

As a ditcher you appear to be the world's champion. If you were touring Italy through the Appian Way you would probably back yourself into the Tiber three times a day. . . .

Of course you pensioned the chauffeur, having ruined him for life. The next time I see a shattered old veteran holding out his hand asking for alms, I will ask him if he isn't the guy who made the transcontinental drive with Edgar Rice Burroughs in 1916.

Sorry your neuritis didn't entirely depart away from you. You speak of assistance to put on your overcoat. The last time you were in New York City it kept me busy seeing that you didn't put on some other fellow's overcoat when you left the restaurant.[32]

The cross-country trip caused Ed to digress briefly for an unanticipated type of writing, a promotional article done at the

ERB and children, Jack, Joan, and Hulbert, en route to San Diego from Los Angeles, 1916.

request of the Republic Motor Truck Company of Alma, Michigan. In his diary, early in the trip, on July 1, Ed had commented enthusiastically about the helpfulness of the "Republic Truck people" and of the assistance given by T. F. Bates of the service department in attempting to repair the Packard Twin-Six. In a letter of July 21 from Bates, sent to Ed at Coldwater, Michigan, after his return from the aborted eastern tour, the service manager was pleased to note that "the truck came through in good shape" and that it was being equipped with a "Prairie Schooner" top. In his diary Ed referred to *Kodak* No. 12 which "shows *Camp Branch* from rear with Packard, and Republic fitted with prairie schooner top made by W. H. Schmedlen of Coldwater." Later, Ed jokingly titled the outfit the Burroughs Yacht. Bates wrote, "I think you will enjoy the trip West much more than if you had decided to go East," adding a hope that Ed might find some way to "boost" the Republic truck, and thanking him for a copy of *The Beasts of Tarzan*.[33]

On December 9, W. A. Somerville, Republic advertising manager, wrote Ed in Los Angeles to offer a writing proposition:

We would like to get out, in De Luxe form, a little book, detailing your experiences with your Republic truck, on your recent transcontinental journey. We would like to have you give us this information in the form of a story; say about 1000 to 1500 words in length. We would also like you to furnish us your photograph, so that we may use it as a frontispiece in this little book.

Somerville explained that in return for this courtesy, the company would publicize Burroughs in these booklets as the author of four Tarzan novels, and stressed that since the small book would have a circulation of about a quarter of a million, it would be as valuable to him as to the Republic Company.

In his reply Ed made clear that he was quite willing to accept the assignment: "It will be a pleasure to me to partially reciprocate the kindness shown me by yourself and my other friends at Alma, and if a little story of the truck on the hike is what you want I'll do the best I can."[34]

The completed article of approximately 1900 words was titled "An Auto-Biography," and Ed wrote it in a whimsical vein, creating the truck as a first-person character recounting the story of the adventurous journey. Ed's personality comes through, as does his penchant for ridiculing his own actions and viewing himself as the most illogical and blundering of travelers. The Republic truck establishes its own character from the start:

Without undue vanity and with no intention of boasting I think I am warranted in saying that I have probably crowded more real living into the first four months of my life than the majority of my brothers and cousins experience in all the years which intervene between the factory and their ultimate burial ground—the junk pile.

How little did I imagine in my brief childhood as I purred through the quiet streets of Alma or rolled along the shady country roads beyond, what lay in store for me! Ah, but those were clean and happy days! The testing and the tuning were my playtimes, and always then were they careful of me. They never took me out without plenty of oil in my crank case and water in my radiator, and one would have thought me a petted child of luxury designed to transport nothing less ethereal than a Parisian gowned debutante to her first ball so careful were they of my paint and varnish. . . .[35]

The truck, "born" in the early days of June, told of a score or more of brothers and cousins who were "delivered daily from the womb of our mother, The Factory"[36] and who were allowed very little time at home before being "hustled out into the world." The truck had dreamed of "nothing less than Chicago" where many other Republic trucks had gone; it had hoped to be purchased by a large packing company, and, in this case, would be

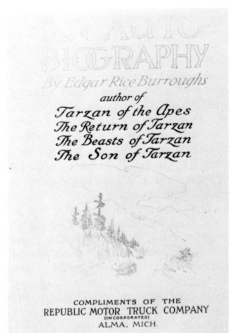

AUTO-
BIOGRAPHY
By Edgar Rice Burroughs
author of
Tarzan of the Apes
The Return of Tarzan
The Beasts of Tarzan
The Son of Tarzan

COMPLIMENTS OF THE
REPUBLIC MOTOR TRUCK COMPANY
(INCORPORATED)
ALMA, MICH.

Title page of ERB's "Auto-Biography," story of 1916 trip as told by Republic truck.

envied by "less fortunate fellows." But fate had determined otherwise: "It was in the midst of one of these day dreams that I was sold to an ice-man in South Bend. I wept bitterly."

Arriving on June 18, the truck waited unhappily for its new owner: "I was still sobbing when The Agent brought a man to look at me. At first I thought it was the ice-man and made up my mind that I would run over him the first time he cranked me; but when I saw his garb I commenced to doubt, for I had seen the ice-man at Alma and he, I recalled distinctly, did not wear corduroy riding breeches, tan leather puttees or a deer skin coat. . . ."

The Man and a uniformed chauffeur both peeked under the bonnet and "looked wise," and after the purchase the truck was backed up to "a disreputable looking outfit consisting of a delivery car and a trailer, both heavily laden." The truck, its "side lamps opened pretty wide" stared disbelievingly at the objects as they were transferred: "There was an enormous refrigerator, a cook stove, a fireless cooker, a hat box, galvanized iron tanks, a phonograph, folding cots, stools, tables, a bath tub, two trunks, countless suit cases and bags, seven rolls of bedding, toys, a flag, tent poles and stakes, a great tent. . . ."

The truck could not comprehend why anyone would want to transport "all this junk clear to the Atlantic Ocean" until it learned that The Boss was "one of these writer fellows, for whose mental functionings there is no accounting." Overloaded with a ton and a half of equipment, the truck joined in the wild journey that followed, "up and down the sides of mountains, through sand, through mud, through rivers. . . ." Despite its suffering, the truck had periods of contentment when The Boss bragged about its performance. It was especially pleased at night when they went into camp: ". . . they used to hoist Old Glory at the end of a staff that fitted into a socket at the front end of the top. I liked that, and I can tell you that I was mighty proud, and happy, too."[37]

After the travels through nine states and the arrival in California, the truck's odyssey was at an end; it now had a new assignment, but could not forget its glorious past: "It is all over now and I am hauling boxes for a new Boss in Los Angeles; but to the day I am junked I shall carry the pride and the memory of my Fame ever uppermost in my mind, and strive to be what I always have been and what my brothers and my cousins are—the best motor trucks for the money that ever were built—a *Republic*."[38]

At the beginning of 1915, Davis, while pleased with the steady flow of stories from the Burroughs pen, waited impatiently for the *Tarzan* sequel Ed had promised. On January 20, after noting that "Sweetheart Primeval" had been given the cover illustration on *All-Story Cavalier,* Davis wrote, "I am very good to you, Edgar. Now, young feller, sit down and write 'Tarzan's Son', or God have mercy on your soul."[39] Ed sent a progress report:

Yes, I am working on The Son of Tarzan, *and I have been working on him for several months. I have written but little, but I've thought a lot. I am going to give you a good Tarzan story. Almost all of it will be in the jungle. But it will, if I can make it so, be entirely different from the other Tarzan stories. I shall base it on the fundamental suggestion that you made while I was in New York—that is of the boy and the ape running away together from London to Africa. The difficult part is to keep from a tiresome repetition of stunts that I have pulled in the three other Tarzan Tales, but I believe that I can fairly well succeed.*[40]

Ed's fear of repetition brought some joking repartee from

Davis: "Come now, Burroughs, for God's sake don't cramp your correspondence like this, because when it comes to pulling duplicate dope and getting away with it, you hold the Charles K. Fox diamond belt."[41]

The completion of "The Son of Tarzan" obviously posed more problems than Ed had anticipated; the manuscript was not mailed until May 12. During the intensive writing, a period of four months, Ed was ill. He informed Davis, "It has taken me two months longer to write it than I expected, and so it has cost me already three times what it should have—due to the fact that I have had to devote a lot of time trying to get well—treatments here and a couple of weeks away. . . ."[42] Davis' acceptance came quickly, although minor changes were later suggested.[43]

Earlier, on May 1, the first installment of "Pellucidar" had appeared in *All-Story Cavalier;* and printed with it, in four of the five issues, was Ed's map of the strange inner world. Ed joked about the map: "It should prove quite instructive. If The National Geographic Magazine wishes to reproduce it I have no objection. . . ."[44]

The hasty acceptance of "The Son of Tarzan" was contrasted with an equally hasty rejection of "Ben, King of Beasts." Ed, on June 10, described the manuscript as "the novelization of a wild animal scenario I recently sold to the Selig people," adding, "I understand that they do not expect to release it until after The Lad & the Lion. . . ." Davis, who had reached a stage where he had misgivings about turning down *any* Burroughs story, and had always regretted Metcalf's failure to buy "The Return of Tarzan," had been careful to use group evaluation on "Ben, King of Beasts." On June 17 he wrote:

I have no doubt it will make a corking movie, but it does not seem to have the proportions of Burroughs' regular novels. Four of us tried our durndest to get interested in it, but it did not hook any of us. . . . Kneel down and pray for me. I know I'm crazy. But there are four other nuts here who feel the same about this as I do.[45]

Later in the summer Ed experienced his second rejection in a row, this time with a story that differed startlingly from his familiar other-worlds creations. "Beyond Thirty," set in the year 2137 on our earth, but with a Europe and Asia that had reverted to a primitive, savage existence, is one of only two Burroughs stories of the future.[46] About it, Davis commented:

"Beyond Thirty" reminds me of a magnificent piece of scenery

with no play. You have drawn an extraordinary picture and set the stage for a stupendous thing. Then the curtain falls.

You must not, however, regard this criticism as a protest against your style, for it is full of the "Burroughs" quality, and I have not any doubt that some people will like to read this story. However, I am trying to escape war, rumors of war and themes kindred to war. That is the particular reason why I pass "Beyond Thirty" back to you. . . .[47]

In this 1915 period Ed was in contact with A. L. Sessions, editor of Street & Smith's *New Story,* and had queried him about "Ben, King of Beasts." When Sessions expressed an interest, Ed, on June 10, sent the manuscript to him, but the result was only a noncommittal rejection. Attempts in August to sell "Beyond Thirty" to the higher-paying markets were similarly unsuccessful. Rejections came from the *Saturday Evening Post, Colliers* and *American Magazine,* whose editor remarked, "I'm mighty sorry but this story of Europe's reversion to savagery two hundred years hence doesn't get me. . . ."[48]

Having exhausted the prestige markets, Ed now turned to Sessions. The editor had been previously involved in the Burroughs dickering and was cautious, laying down conditions in advance: ". . . 'Beyond Thirty' . . . will be glad to retain it if we can agree upon a price. The circumstances being what they are in the magazine business at the present, I do not feel justified in offering you more than $400.00. . . ."[49] Ed's procedure could have been predicted; he would never succumb to a first offer. He reminded Sessions that the editor had purchased "The Outlaw of Torn" for only $500, one of the lowest prices ever paid for a Burroughs story. This was the compromise amount for "Beyond Thirty," a "dinged low" figure, which Sessions could not afford to turn down.[50]

Ed, as usual, was keeping all of his varied irons in the fire. Payments for newspaper syndications came in steadily, both through his own negotiations with Terhune at *The New York World,* and through the dealings of Chapman, his syndication agent. On January 11, 1915, Terhune inquired about any unpublished Tarzan stories, while at the same time commenting enthusiastically about the readers' response to "The Eternal Lover," previously sold to *The World.* Ed suggested that Terhune might consider "Sweetheart Primeval," then appearing in *All-Story Cavalier.*[51] Terhune, who was also well acquainted with

"Pellucidar" cover of All-Story Cavalier Weekly, *May 1, 1915.*

Ed's bargaining tactics, on March 15 queried him about "The Mucker" and "Sweetheart Primeval," adding a somewhat stern note of warning:

May I suggest, unofficially, that war times are not flush times and that the most rigid economy governs every newspaper today? If you can see your way to letting us have this story at a low rate, we shall be gratified; and you will find that no other New York paper is prepared, just now, to offer more.

I hope for our readers' sakes and for ours that you will quote Mr. Tennant a price he can accept.

After some protestations, Ed explained that he would not do any haggling; he was evidently impressed by Terhune's severe attitude. He offered a concession if Terhune would accept both stories—five hundred dollars for the two. He added, "I didn't intend to come down any when I started this letter; but now you see I've gone and done it after all—I suppose it was that sob stuff about the war; though why the devil Mr. Tennant should hold me responsible for the great European conflict is beyond me."[52] Terhune sent a prompt acceptance.

In response to one of Chapman's misguided marketing attempts, Ed wrote a letter whose tone was both panicky and humorous. "For the love of Mike," he exclaimed, "have I been letting you sell newspaper rights to *At the Earth's Core?* I don't own the serial rights to this story—I sold them all to Munsey. . . ." At the end he stated, "I am enclosing a list of my stories, showing ownership of serial rights, and you had better paste it in your hat, or we'll both be breaking rock at Leavenworth."[53]

Ed had also maintained a steady flow of communications with Joseph Bray at McClurg, as preparations were being made for book publications. *The Return of Tarzan,* contracted for on December 5, 1914, appeared on March 10, 1915, with a dust jacket illustration by the distinguished American artist Newell C. Wyeth, the same picture that had been drawn for the *New Story Magazine* cover. Next to be accepted by McClurg was "The Beasts of Tarzan," contracted for on October 1, 1915; it would not appear in print until March 4, 1916.[54]

Ed's shrewd business instincts, as always, drove him to search for new marketing opportunities. In the past he had dealt with newspapers on second serial rights only, after the first rights to his stories had been sold to magazines. Now he conceived the idea of selling the first rights directly to the newspapers, in other words, allowing them the privilege of printing a *new* Burroughs story. He tentatively experimented with the plan, making up a form which he sent to various newspapers and syndicates, and in this case concentrating upon one story, "Ben, King of Beasts," based upon the scenario still retained by the Selig Polyscope Company. The responses were not encouraging. A number of rejections followed, but on October 18, 1915, the *New York Evening World* purchased all newspaper rights to the story, now retitled "The Man-Eater" by Ed—the price, $350. The sale of the 37,000-word "novelization" established a first and only instance of a Burroughs story going directly to a newspaper.[55]

This first experience did not, however, cause Ed to abandon his plan. In a letter of October 8 in which he had accepted Terhune's offer for "The Man-Eater" and "The Man Without a Soul,"[56] Ed brought up the subject of direct newspaper sales, urging the editor to read an article in the September *Bulletin* of The Author's League. The article, titled "A Crying Need," contained an interview with George D. Smith, Editor of the *Newark Star,* which Ed summarized:

. . . *he states that newspapers would prefer to purchase first serial rights to stories, and pay a much higher price for them than for the "stale" fiction which they now pay $35 to $50 for. He says that an original novel by a well known writer would bring $100 and up in five hundred newspapers throughout the country, and that sooner or later someone is going to form a syndicate for this purpose.*

Ed appeared quite excited over the prospect of receiving money in this amount from more than five hundred newspapers. To Terhune he presented a comparison of the total payments from a magazine plus syndications vs. newspaper sales only, and explained that he would be willing to experiment with an original *Tarzan* story, certain to have the highest nationwide appeal, for direct sale to the newspapers.[57] On first sight the scheme offered great possibilities. Ed's past was filled with schemes eagerly conceived and quickly abandoned, and this one followed the same pattern. The main reasons may have been physical. Even his astonishing energy had its limitations—perhaps his illnesses and neuritis resulted from states of exhaustion. And of course there were the limitations of time.

During the years Burroughs received a number of queries about the correct pronunciation of "Tarzan." The first, on

The Return of Tarzan *book cover, 1915; N. C. Wyeth, illustrator (same illustration used on magazine cover, June 1913).*

October 19, 1915, came from Davis: ". . . Many readers have made the inquiry. I'll leave it entirely to you. He is your off-spring, not mine. This is a case where a man's monkeyshines shine brilliantly. . . ."

Ed's reply was in the same humorous vein: "It should be pronounced in low, barking gutturals, after the manner peculiar to huge, hairy anthropoids. I have heard a termangani pronounce it with the o silent, as in mice. Personally, I never pronounce it—I merely think it; but since you have forced the issue upon me, I should say that Tär'-zan is about right."

To a fan who later raised the question, Ed wrote, ". . . My conception of the word Tarzan was originally that neither syllable should be accented, but, as a matter of fact, I find that in using the word I always accent the first and rather slur the second, in accordance with the American lazy method of speech. However, pronounce it the way it sounds best to you and you will have it as correct as anyone."[58]

An inquiry from Charles E. Funk of *The Literary Digest* brought a response that Tarzan was pronounced with the accent on the first syllable, "the first *a* as in *arm,* the second *a* as in *ask."* Ed noted that this was supposed to be the correct pronunciation, but added, "I and my family have always slurred the second syllable, pronouncing it as though it were spelled *zn."*[59]

The question finally came up in a letter from G. & C. Merriam Company, received by Ralph Rothmund, Burroughs' secretary, and forwarded by him to Ed who was then in Hawaii. Rothmund commented, ". . . will you please give me a copy of your reply for permanent filing here at the office. After being around here for more than thirteen years, I too, would like to know how to pronounce the damn name!"[60] To the Merriam Company Ed responded:

The pronunciation of Tarzan (tär'zăn) given in the 1934 edition of Webster's is the correct official pronunciation.

The word derives from the simian tar, *meaning white, and* zan, *meaning skin. It is, therefore, wholly descriptive; and both syllables should be pronounced.*

The fact that I, personally, slur the last syllable merely reflects my sloppy diction.

With this weighty matter now permanently settled, I trust that the planets will return to their orbits.[61]

Perhaps influenced by a differing pronunciation he heard in later years, Ed, on occasion, accented the last syllable and pronounced it fully, not slurring it. This is revealed on a dictaphone cylinder in which the *zan* is drawn out, with the "a" pronounced as in *man*.[62]

Once more, although on a more limited scale, Ed attempted to set up a competitive bidding situation between *All-Story* and *New Story* magazines for his latest *Tarzan* story. Completed on October 19, 1915, it was titled "Tarzan and the Jewels of Opar." Editor Sessions at *New Story* had always been eager for a Tarzan story to increase the circulation of his magazine; after his purchase of "The Return of Tarzan" in 1913, he had been promised a "refusal" on the next one, but in the bidding that followed he had lost the story "The Beasts of Tarzan" to Metcalf. Later, without very much enthusiasm, Sessions had accepted "The Outlaw of Torn," but as a result of Ed's price demands, the atmosphere between the two men had become quite strained.

Later, in negotiating with Sessions for the purchase of "Beyond Thirty," Ed mentioned his new *Tarzan* story, again indicating that the editor would be given a chance to make an offer for it. This was probably Ed's way of dangling a reward if Sessions would buy the lesser work, "Beyond Thirty." On October 20, 1915, to signal the start of a hoped-for competition, "Tarzan and the Jewels of Opar" was mailed to both Sessions and Davis. Ed commented to Davis, ". . . I imagine you won't want another Tarzan story so soon; and I shouldn't have written one so soon had I known that I was going to be able to dispose of *The Man Eater* and *Beyond Thirty;* but for a time it looked as though these two were doomed never to sell."[63]

Sessions pondered over the story for more than a month before explaining his reactions. The value of the story, he contended, had become somewhat speculative because another Burroughs work, "The Son of Tarzan," was about to appear in *All-Story.* Sessions referred to an announcement that advertised Jack Clayton, Tarzan's son, as the hero, and remarked:

The purpose of the announcement is, of course, to transfer the interest of the reader from father to son, the assumption being, I suppose, that the reading public has become more or less indifferent to Tarzan, or if not actually indifferent, it is at least in a mood to welcome a change. . . . If this turns out to be the case you will doubtless agree that "Tarzan & the Jewels of Opar" will hardly have the same value for our magazine as the other.[64]

Based upon this reasoning, Sessions was prepared to offer only $1,000 for the story.[65] Indignant, Ed wired that he would not accept less than $2,500. He annoyedly refuted the editor's argument about the reduced value of the story, stressing that "the conclusion of The Son of Tarzan leaves Tarzan of the Apes still the dominant figure in the cast." He noted, "I was unable to arouse in myself any such enthusiasm for the son as I had conceived for the father, and I think the same will be true of the readers. The public is not tiring of Tarzan."[66] He urged Sessions to consult Terhune and Bray about the public demand for Tarzan. Anger spurred him to an insulting accusation: "I am not asking an exorbitant figure for this story, and I feel that you have tried to take advantage of me by offering what you did for it."[67]

Meanwhile, Davis, having read "Tarzan and the Jewels of Opar," was fairly critical of it, expressing the opinion that it was weaker than the previous Tarzan stories. "It contains nothing new," he wrote on November 20. "You have introduced the old wallop-on-the-bean idea for the purpose of side-tracking Tarzan's intelligence. A good deal of stuff where the ferocious guy breakfasts on caterpillars, grasshoppers, etc., will have to be cut." Although he felt that the story was not worth what he had paid for the last one, nevertheless he believed that all of Burroughs' work belonged in the Munsey magazines.[68] Ed, now worried, departed for New York on the 22nd to see Davis. After a two-day get-together, Ed wrote a memo: "He will take story at satisfactory price to be decided on later." Shortly afterward, Ed telegraphed to specify that the payment must be $2,500.

Upon receiving Ed's accusation, Sessions, irate, ended all dealings and returned the story. He stated icily, "I have had a long and somewhat varied editorial experience, but this is the first time that an author has ever interpreted my offer to buy his story as an attempt to take advantage of him."[69] Although the sale was apparently completed with Davis, Ed did not notify Sessions, and made it appear that the proper offer would be accepted. On December 9 Davis bought the story at Ed's price.[70]

In the midst of all the bargaining and correspondence, Ed still found time to finish his latest, a 40,000-word royal romance titled "H. R. H. The Rider." Rejected by Redbook, it was sent to Davis, who ushered in the new year of 1916 by purchasing it, on January 2, for $800.[71]

An incident involving the actions of an imposter, the first of its type, was experienced by Ed in the passing year. A letter addressed to *All-Story* from Ithaca, New York, inquired whether or not Edgar Rice Burroughs was in the city, and explained that a man was "masquerading" under that name and "claiming the 'Tarzan' stories as his." The writer said, "This person is indebted for room rent and it is in the interest of his landlady that I am writing this."[72] The events that followed were amusing. The imposter, evidently alerted to the fact that inquiries were being made, moved hastily to a new location in Ithaca, but still maintained his false identity. A week later the same type of letter about a "certain Edgar Rice Burroughs" was received from a concerned occupant of the second house. In this case the imposter, described as an "author," was using the name of Frank Davis, but claimed he was really Burroughs. However, in his second try he apparently had as little success convincing people as on the first occasion.[73]

On November 8 Ed notified *All-Story* that he had twice written to the chief of police at Ithaca, and remarked, "I realize that in a college town hoaxes are often pulled off, and this may be a hoax. If so, I am hectic to discover upon whom rests the joke." On the seventeenth Ed noted "the termination of The Imposter of Ithaca case." His attitude, in writing to Bob Davis, was without resentment and exhibited a kindly tolerance and a tendency to poke fun at himself:

In my first letter to the Chief I told him that I did not care to prosecute the man. As a matter of fact anyone who is simple enough to try to get anything on my name has my sincerest sympathy.

If you vindicate me in The Heart-to-Heart Talks you won't, of course, publish the poor gink's name?—that's a dear.

During 1915 Ed's creative energies had been partially directed to the writing of motion picture synopses, a diversion that resulted only in frustration and disillusionment. His output of stories had been smaller than the previous year. Upon completion of "Pellucidar" on January 11, he turned to "The Son of Tarzan," a work in which elements of the plot were carefully planned and woven together. Jack, Lord Greystoke's son, has been kept ignorant of his father's jungle background. However, through the arrival in London of Akut, Tarzan's former ape companion who has been placed on exhibition by Paulvitch, a vengeful enemy of Tarzan, and events that follow, he learns of his father's upbringing. Akut and Jack become close friends, and in his defense the ape is forced to kill two men—Paulvitch and a thief named

Condon. Certain that he will be charged with murder, Jack, accompanied by the ape, flees to Africa. There, as he duplicates the jungle feats of his father, he is named Korak—meaning "Killer"—by Akut.

Aware, as always, of romantic necessities, Ed introduces ten-year-old Meriem, supposedly an Arab girl who is cruelly mistreated by Sheik Amor ben Khatour. In reality she is Jeanne Jacot, the abducted daughter of Captain Armand Jacot of the French Foreign Legion. Inevitably, the story's plot calls for her to join Korak in his free jungle life and to become almost as adept as he in swinging through the trees.

Other characters include two new villains, this time Swedes named Jenssen and Malbihn, and the "Hon." Morison Baynes, freshly transplanted from England to the Greystoke's African estate. Baynes becomes a familiar Burroughs type, the handsome, effete young man, not inherently bad, whose weakness leads him to take part in villainies involving the lovely heroine—in this case Meriem, who is being temporarily sheltered by Tarzan and Jane. Before the story's end Baynes repents of his evil deeds and cowardice, redeems himself in heroic actions, and dies of his wounds. When little Meriem's true identity is finally revealed, Ed cannot resist inserting one of his favorite devices: Armand Jacot, a man of modesty, is disclosed to have the title of Prince de Cadrenet, and this of course makes his daughter Jeanne, the former "Arab waif," a princess in her own right.

Ed, producing some new ideas and incidents, limits the attributes that Korak has inherited from his famous father. The son, after killing Sheeta the panther, has a "strange desire," raises his face toward heaven, and opens his mouth "to voice a strange, weird cry." But the victory cry of the bull ape does not come from his lips. Unlike his father Tarzan, Korak, despite a powerful emotion, will remain silent after all future kills.

In "The Son of Tarzan" animal behavior, as in other stories, is both interesting and amusing. Hordes of baboons, for the first time, are enlisted for an organized rescue effort. Placing faith in the theory about the elephant's indelible memory, Ed has Tantor recognize Malbihn as the evil ivory poacher who many years before had killed the elephant's mate. Tantor takes his just revenge, stamping out the life of the villain.[74]

"The Man-Eater," a Burroughs-expanded development of the synopsis "Ben, King of Beasts," utilizes a prologue for exposition of a tragic drama that occurred in the African jungle nineteen years before the main story opens. The coming of Jefferson Scott, Jr., and his friend Robert Gordon to the Methodist mission; the marriage of Scott to Ruth Morton, the missionary's daughter; and the deaths of the older Mortons and Scott at the hands of the savage Wakandas are all detailed. With the passing of years, the story then shifts to the Virginia home of Jefferson Scott, Sr., his death, and the matter of the will and the inheritance of the property. The heroine Virginia Scott, hero Richard Gordon, and dissolute villain Scott Taylor remain the same, and the story closely follows and fills in the plot outlined in the synopsis.

Devoid of originality, "The Man-Eater" becomes a mixture of overused devices. The action of course must be set in the African jungle; there are the usual natives, and the situation involving the Man-Eater, the familiar "huge, black-maned lion," is a repetition of the idea presented in "The Lad and the Lion." This time the beast acquires a gratitude and affection for Richard Gordon, the man who rescued him from a lion pit. The unabashed use of coincidence in having the lion turn up at the Virginia home after a conveniently planned railroad wreck nearby produces a rather unconvincing effect.

The scenes involving Negroes in "The Man-Eater" are of course not the first created by Burroughs; his other works contain unflattering characterizations of blacks as individuals and demeaning views of them in groups or tribes—the natives. The obvious criticisms can be made; it is no longer possible to accept the false picture of the Negro as servile, treacherous, fiendishly sadistic, cowardly, and without loyalty or honor. But viewing him understandingly in modern times and depicting him according to assumptions, distorted and prejudiced, of earlier periods are two different matters. Burroughs, forced to devise African jungle settings continuously, accepted the popular concept of the black native, considering him as a customary stage prop to accompany a jungle drama. There was neither malice nor prejudice in his attitude; in fact, he often created noble blacks—witness the faithful and courageous Waziri, Tarzan's retainers—and his worst villains were depraved whites who were shown as inhuman in their mistreatment and torture of innocent natives.

Burroughs' action in adopting the Negro as primitive or savage in order to utilize him for jungle setting or atmosphere was, as part of the times, a mere writing device. In real life, during his army career at Fort Grant, he had praised the colored regiment as "wonderful soldiers and as hard as nails," noted that they were held in high esteem, and recalled that in doing menial tasks under a black sergeant, he had found the man to be fair and considerate. Burroughs had also shown sympathy and com-

SATURDAY   DECEMBER 4   TEN CENT

ALL-STORY WEEKLY

The Son of Tarzan

A Sequel to all the Tarzan Tales by Edgar Rice Burroughs

"The Son of Tarzan" cover of All-Story Weekly, December 4, 1915.

418

passion for the Negro. In his Pocatello days he had saved Kipling's poem "The White Man's Burden," pierced through its hypocrisy, and written his own version of "The Black Man's Burden," exposing how the white man's culture had ruined the helpless Negro. It should be stressed that in his earliest writing years, with the creation of "The Gods of Mars," he established the black men as the "First Born," the aristocracy and rulers of the planet Mars.[75]

In "Beyond Thirty," begun while he was vacationing at the Hulbert family farm in Coldwater, Michigan, and completed at Oak Park, Ed devised a plot of unusual originality. For some two hundred years after a devastating "Great War," the Western Hemisphere had lived in complete isolation from the belligerent, ever-warring Eastern Hemisphere. All relationships between the two halves of the world had been permanently severed. As a result of a Pan-American Federation, the Western Hemisphere was linked "from pole to pole under a single flag." Young Jefferson Turck, the protagonist and commander of the *Coldwater*, an aero-submarine, notes that since the world division, "peace had reigned from the western shores of the Azores to the western shores of the Hawaiian Islands, nor has any man of either hemisphere dared cross 3OW. or 175W. From 30 to 175 is ours —from 30 to 175 is peace, prosperity and happiness."

As a child he had been brought up to regard "beyond thirty" as the "great unknown." The Eastern Hemisphere did not even exist on the maps or in the histories of Pan-America. All mention of it was forbidden. To travel "beyond thirty" or cross 175W. was high treason, with death as a possible punishment.

In the early section, well launched, the story appears to have interesting possibilities. But presumably as a result of hasty writing, Ed did not give sufficient care to the development and structure of the story and to the many ingenious situations that could have been devised. The provocative plot of "Beyond Thirty" deserved a full, imaginative development; it was unfortunate that Ed did not devote the time and thought that might have made this one of his best stories.[76]

Another of Ed's 1915 works, "Tarzan and the Jewels of Opar," opens with Tarzan's enforced return to the treasure vaults of the ruined city in search of ingots—the cause being the failure of a British company in which all his money was invested. The villain of "Opar" is Belgian Lieutenant Albert

Werper, who after murdering his commanding officer, joins the outlaw band of Achmet Zek, Congo slave trader and ivory poacher. The ingredients of the story are familiar. Tarzan is deep in the rocky vaults of the Oparians when an earthquake occurs. Struck on the head by a jagged fragment that tumbles from the roof, he becomes unconscious; he awakes to a loss of all memory of his identity as Tarzan and as Lord Greystoke. The repetition of this old device brought a disapproving comment from Davis. Both the treasure ingots and a bag of jewels motivate the evil deeds of Werper, Zek, and others. Inevitably, Jane, Lady Greystoke, is kidnapped, escapes and faces peril in various forms. In Werper, Ed creates a man who reveals some remnants of honor in his behavior toward Jane, but does not, as in previous stories, become the villain or weakling who redeems himself and makes the supreme sacrifice. Werper's misdeeds continue to the end and contribute to his death.

Interestingly, in "Tarzan and the Jewels of Opar," Ed establishes the specific origin of High Priestess La and the Oparians, originally described in "The Return of Tarzan" as a lost race of whites who were the survivors of a kingdom that had sunk into the sea. The kingdom was the legendary Atlantis, first mentioned by Plato; Ed explains, "When Atlantis, with all her mighty cities and her cultivated fields and her great commerce and culture and riches sank into the sea long ages since, she took with her all but a handful of her colonists working the vast gold mines of Central Africa." The race of "gnarled men of Opar" was bred from these and their "degraded slaves and a later intermixture of the blood of the anthropoids," but in La, the old Atlantean strain of females had been passed down in its purest form.[77]

"H.R.H. the Rider," completed December 5, 1915, resumes the fascination with miniature kingdoms and lovely princesses that Ed had displayed in "The Mad King." In the story Ed also repeats a plot element he had used in "The Mad King"—the introduction of an American, this time a certain Hemmington Main, into the royal complications that follow. The plans for an arranged marriage, one deemed necessary to assure friendly relationships between two royal houses, require that Princess Mary of Margoth and Prince Boris of Karlov, who have never seen each other, accept the union obediently. However, both of them rebel, and as the plot develops, Ed reverts again to a favorite device—the exchange of identities. In this case not two, but four individuals are involved in the exchanges. Prince Boris and a notorious bandit, "The Rider," trade roles, while Princess Mary is mistaken for Gwendolyn Bass, the daughter of an

American millionaire. Gwendolyn's desire to wed Hemmington Main, the man she loves, is frustrated by her socially conscious mother who has "higher ambitions" for the future of her daughter. The typical incidents occur, many of them involving conflict, dangerous encounters and shootings, but in the expected happy ending the loving couples are properly and finally joined.[78]

Although Davis purchased "H.R.H. the Rider," he was frank in discussing its weaknesses, noting the situations in the story that "strain the probabilities" but admitting, "I do not suppose anybody is justified in analyzing this type of yarn too closely."[79] With 1915 drawing to a close, Davis was more concerned about marketing plans for next year's crop of Tarzan stories. During Ed's sales efforts for "Tarzan and the Jewels of Opar," Davis had stressed, "I am not going to make this a bidding contest by any means, and regardless of what conclusion we may arrive at, I am to be acquitted of juggling rates with you. . . ."[80] On December 11 Davis demanded, "Would you mind giving us some idea as to future rates for this particular simian hero? We do not seem to be in unity at all on tariff. I cannot help but feel that Tarzan belongs to us; and that we should not be obliged to bid against other magazines. . . ."

Concerning Ed's temporary concentration on a new character, Korak, son of Tarzan, and the confusion caused by his return to Tarzan in ". . . the Jewels of Opar," Davis doubted that "we ought to ball the family up by pulling the son and then harking back to the father," and joked, "I suppose old grandpop will come along some day and pop at me like a jack-in-a-box. If he does, Edgar, I'll bean him as sure as you are born."[81]

Ed, in response, exhibited uncertainty as to what proposition to offer Munsey for the year 1916. He stated bluntly that he could not refuse to sell stories elsewhere if the payment were higher. "From all I hear," he wrote, "I am the only boob in the country who gets less than 5c a word, and were it not for my excessive modesty I should remark right here that there's lots of 5c stuff that isn't pulling as well as our old friend Tarzan."[82] The two men finally agreed to follow the past procedure. A copy of every Burroughs story would be submitted to Davis. Ed promised not to ask him to bid against a competitor, but would reserve the right to accept or reject the Munsey price.[83]

CHAPTER **14**

WRITER-PATRIOT

His first attempt to enter the motion picture field, based mainly on the hope of finding a producer for *Tarzan of the Apes,* had left Ed in a state of deep frustration. The distrust he acquired for producers, because of this experience, would undergo very little change in the future. On one occasion he wrote to Chapman, "You have several of my scripts (?) which are of no earthly use to anyone, so, if you will please return them to me, I will see if I can't sell them for a few hundred thousand dollars,"[1] and Chapman requested permission to continue marketing them. Ed's answer was bitter: "No, I'd rather you'd send the photo-play stuff back to me. I shall never again peddle any of that stuff around. The majority of producers are petty crooks and when I deal with any of them I wish to personally select my own crook."[2]

The disappointments of this early motion picture period brought a response that was typical of Ed's character. As in the past when his goals were blocked, the unsatisfying circumstances aroused his impatience and drove him to action. He usually turned to schemes of his own. On March 4, 1916, he informed Davis:

There are tangible indications that a company will shortly be formed to film Tarzan. The men back of it number several who have backed other features that have made their millions. I won't let it go ahead unless I am assured of success, and that it will be a ripping big thing.

ERB, Chicago, 1916.

423

In carrying out his plan to reserve stock for his friends, he offered Davis an opportunity to join the venture, but urged, "Keep this under your hat until it is ripe. . . ."

When Davis expressed an interest, Ed promised to supply more details later, and explained, about *Tarzan,* "There are four outfits after it now, so I am waiting for the best proposition. My hope is to form a company of my own and produce not only my own stuff, but a lot of the other that is now unavailable because of the suspicions which many writers harbor concerning the present-day producers."[3] He could see no reason why a producing company should not operate in as organized and legitimate a fashion as a publisher, so that authors would receive a "perfectly square deal devoid of even a suspicion of sharp practice."[4]

On April 12, Davis, after some consideration, revealed a change of attitude toward the proposition; because of his connection with the Munsey Company, he believed it inadvisable to become involved in the project, either as a stockholder or director.[5] And a week later, in an abrupt decision caused by his agonies with neuritis, Ed announced, ". . . I have about decided to abandon my venture for the time at least. . . ." Instead, he was making plans for the summer 1916 "gypsying" tour.[6] At the same time, however, he contacted David H. Watkins, a friend who was acting as a negotiator between him and the National Film Corporation of America, to indicate he was now "willing to entertain an offer for the photo-play rights to Tarzan of the Apes—cash and a royalty."[7]

Only two days before his departure from Oak Park on the camping tour, and in the midst of the feverish preparations for the trip, he still found time to complete arrangements with William Parsons, president of the National Film Corporation, for the production of *Tarzan of the Apes.* The agreement for the project stipulated that Ed was to be given $5,000 in cash, $50,000 in capital stock, and five percent of the gross receipts.[8]

With the creation of a new board of directors, Parsons, on July 7, notified Ed that his old boyhood friend, Robert Lay, secretary of the National Life Insurance Company in Chicago, had been elected vice-president, and Henry Carr, another Chicagoan, assistant treasurer. Parsons later moved his office to the Steger Building in Chicago.[9] The plans called for Ed to assume the presidency of the company, and upon Lay's advice—"I rather think it is to your interest to do so," he accepted the position.[10] Little action was expected in the summer months, but Parsons predicted that in the fall, with Watkins in charge of the campaign (he was described as "the father of 'Tarzan of the Apes' motion picture" by Parsons), the company would raise the required capital without difficulty. However, money problems arose at once. Unable to pay Ed the promised $5,000, Parsons stalled by paying $1,000 for extensions until December 1916.[11] Discouraged, he wrote to Ed, then in Los Angeles, "I had about made up my mind that I cannot count on Watkins. . . ." On the verge of dropping the project, he decided to go ahead with it, because "at the last moment things looked so bright."[12]

Ed's suggestion, upon accepting the presidency, was that an assistant be selected to serve as his representative in dealings with Parsons; the man he had in mind was his brother Frank. Past unhappy experiences with producers had firmly conditioned the attitude of pessimism and suspicion which Ed continued to display. The beginning difficulties made him expect the worst; in a letter of October 7 to Parsons he remained dubious, waiting to be convinced. A most important provision had not been carried out. Ed mentioned that "the transfer of the $50,000.00 worth of stock to me is called for in our agreement," adding, "This, I think, you have overlooked."[13] He had struggled so far to express his disappointment tactfully and with some attempt to be patient; however, on October 18, his restraint vanishing, he wrote bluntly to Parsons to reveal his displeasure: ". . . Am as anxious as you that the company succeeds; but am in no position to know just what the prospects of success are. Up to date I cannot say that I have been much encouraged." He reminded Parsons that both he and Watkins had been "extremely sanguine and enthusiastic," and that Watkins had claimed he could easily raise money for the Tarzan picture "in Chicago, in Wyoming, in Tampa, in Jacksonville." Both of them, Ed conceded, were salesmen of "high ability"; yet, in four months they had raised "something like two thousand dollars on a proposition which should have at least fifty thousand in the bank before a wheel turns."

Parsons himself had stated a dissatisfaction with Ed's failure to cooperate, especially in the matter of seeking subscriptions from his friends. Ed, by this time, had made it clear that he had not sufficient faith in the company to ask his friends for money, noting he still had not received his capital stock and other monies due him. He resented Parsons' implication that he had not lived up to his part of the agreement and commented, "As a matter of fact I did not agree to ask my friends to subscribe. Once, many years ago, I did a thing like that, with disastrous results, and since, I have not ever done it—nor shall I."[14] Ed stressed, in addition, that he did not want the presidency of National Film Corporation—he had taken it only because his friend Robert Lay had advised him to do so.

One of Parsons' first acts had been to print new stationery for the film corporation. The Arting silhouette of Tarzan poised on a tree limb, drawn for the book's dust jacket, was reduced to a rectangle three inches high by one and three-fourths inches wide and placed in the center of the sheet. In bold type, divided above and below the illustration, was the phrase, "The Wonder Story of the Age."[15]

Ed's rejection of the presidency, and other problems in finding officers for the corporation, led to changes. He now accepted the position of director general; the stationery, reprinted, showed Parsons as president, Robert D. Lay as vice-president, and Sherman L. Smith as secretary and treasurer.[16] Plans to include Frank (Coleman) Burroughs in the corporation had not materialized. Eager to placate Ed, Parsons again offered him the presidency, volunteering to step down to the office of vice-president and general manager and then go out into the field as a salesman.[17]

Frustrated by the difficulty of communicating caused by the distance between Chicago and Los Angeles, and also by Ed's aloof attitude of noninvolvement, Parsons appealed to him to grant the power of attorney to brother Frank so the two could work together in making plans and decisions. Parsons wrote plaintively, "I am willing to do more than my share but I would like some help and you were to give me that and you ran away to Gods Country and left me to do it all alone. . . ."[18]

Ed continued to view both Parsons and the project with little confidence. Once more he refused the presidency—"I do not believe it sound business practice for a company to have any but *active* officers."[19] He noted coldly that he could see no reason why his brother Frank should be given the power of attorney. Concerning Parsons' appeal for help, he replied that he would be happy to assist in the production of the film, as he had promised, but not in the promotion, of which he wrote, "I know nothing and care less."[20]

Corporation matters and Burroughs-Parsons relationships deteriorated steadily. Robert Lay, the vice-president, while conceding that Parsons would be able to raise the needed money, expressed doubt that he had sufficient financial background to administer the corporation's funds. Possibly infected by Burroughs' suspicions, Lay resigned his position.[21] Even the dispatching of 10,000 shares of corporation stock to Los Angeles, in fulfillment of the contract, could not dissipate Ed's pessimism about the venture. Desperate in his search for a president, Parsons urged Ed to suggest somebody. While doubtful that he knew anybody who had "the time, money and ability," Ed mentioned his old friend Watterson Rothacker, head of a film company, and also enclosed a letter of introduction to Carl Meyer of the law firm of Mayer, Meyer, Austrian & Platt in Chicago.[22]

On January 9, 1917, Ed informed Parsons, "This is my first day at work since coming out of the hospital where I was laid up for a short time by a minor operation."[23] Ed discussed his meetings with William E. Wing, the man chosen by Parsons to write the scenario of *Tarzan,* noting that he liked him "immensely," but that the two did not agree on one point:

He has the dyed-in-the-wool movie conviction that every story has to be altered before it can be filmed; while I am still firmly convinced that to change Tarzan, even though the change made a better story of it, would be to ruin it for the million or so people who have read the story. I have also called his attention to the fact that you have secured the rights to but one story and the moment you change the ending of that story you take something from the second book which you have not purchased and at the same time ruin the moving picture possibilities of the second story.

About these contemplated changes in *Tarzan,* Ed's idea was to get "an expression of opinion from a large number of readers throughout the country." This would also serve as publicity for the motion picture. "Possibly a circular letter to the several hundred names I have would do it," he wrote.[24] He had always taken pride in his fan letters, had answered them zealously, and had used them to promote his sales to newspapers. The letters, in a bound volume, were sent to Parsons, and accompanying them was his own sample draft of a circular letter for the group of readers. Cautious, as always, he instructed Parsons to send him a copy before the form was printed—"inasmuch as it is going out over my signature I wish to know precisely what is going to be said—my bloomin' signature being one of my assets."[25] On March 12, 1917, Parsons noted that Ed's files had contained only a hundred letters, enclosed a copy of the form letter to be circulated, and inquired, "When do you expect to be back in Chicago?"

The letter, addressed to a Chicago reader, pointed out that the screen has "certain limitations which the novel has not" and mentioned "a few slight changes and contractions" that "are absolutely imperative." Questions were then posed for the reader to consider:

Shall we adhere to the rather unpopular ending of the first Tarzan story in which Tarzan renounces his birthright and the woman he loves, or shall we take something from the second story and have a happy ending? And shall we confine the entire production to the jungle, which is the natural setting for Tarzan's life and romance? Or, shall we follow the story verbatim?

The forthcoming film was termed *"The* animal classic of motion photography"; the animals, actions, and jungle settings were vividly described:

. . . the largest and finest specimens of apes to be found . . . not two or three lions, but a herd of twenty or thirty . . . lions will be actually roped and killed by Tarzan . . . two or three thousand cannibals will take part in the battle and village scenes under Mbonga, the chief . . . hyenas, wild boar, leopards, antelope, and all the other numerous fauna of Central Africa will appear. . . .

In closing, the circular stressed that "the advice of every friend of Tarzan" was being sought, and urged the reader to respond.[26]

In the summer of 1917 Parsons' National Film Corporation acquired a studio in Los Angeles at Santa Monica Boulevard and Gower Street for the production of "The Wonder Story of the Age." The distances were the same, although reversed—Ed returned to Oak Park on April 3 of that year, and the communication gap remained unchanged.[27] His desire to purchase a larger and more elaborate home had prompted Ed to correspond with W. H. Gardner; a sale was quickly arranged, with Ed taking the two-story residence at 700 Linden Avenue in Oak Park.[28]

Ed apparently had no objection to Parsons' subscription forms and newspaper advertisements offering the film corporation's stock at five dollars a share. Notices in the *Oak Leaves* of May 5 and 12 were obviously inserted because Ed had become Oak Park's most celebrated citizen, and the paper may even have been chosen at his suggestion.[29]

Because of Ed's almost violent dislike of Wing's scenario, and his suspicion that he was not receiving an accurate financial accounting, the relationships between him and Parsons neared the breaking point. Upon his return to Chicago Ed had not tried to see Parsons, even though he knew the producer was at his office there. In July Ed took his family to Coldwater, Michigan, for a summer vacation, and on the twenty-eighth of the month wrote a bitter and threatening letter to Parsons. With this, much of Parsons' restraint came to end; in two letters, as he struggled to control himself, he broke forth into angry comments about Burroughs' behavior:

Aug. 2: I am really quite upset over your letter and I don't feel that I am in a frame of mind to answer it. We never agreed to submit anything to you, but for your edification will say, that Mr. Wing's scenario was not used. We have had one written that is rather a composite of five different men. I am quite certain that it is your "ignorance of what is being done" that has caused you to write a letter of that kind. Considering the foolish price that was paid for this story I certainly don't like that part where you say "you will take means to prevent the coupling of your name or that of Tarzan with any film produced in accordance with Mr. Wing's story."

If I get in a better frame of mind regarding this letter I'll write you.

Aug. 3: After a night's thought . . . I am still as peeved as ever . . . have been working night and day on this proposition . . . many of the things you promised to do you have been unable to do. . . .

. . . you, yourself, stated that you had no desire to have anything to do with the production because of your complete ignorance of that phase of the business. . . . I still cannot understand how you dare to threaten me and it still rankles. . . . I suggest that you read it (your letter) and then ask yourself how you would like to get one from a person who has been getting all the best of it.

. . . this morning finds me provoked beyond measure at your daring to offer a threat such as was contained in your note, and I certainly feel that unless an explanation or apology is forthcoming that it will be useless for us to correspond.[30]

At National Film's Los Angeles studio, as reported in *The Moving Picture World* of August 11, unusual preparations were being made for the production of *Tarzan of the Apes*. The work of E. M. Jahraus, chief property man, was described. He and a corps of assistants were engaged in making costumes to simulate the apes; presumably, the costumes were for those "ape" companions of Tarzan who had roles to play, while the real apes were to be used as jungle setting. The costumes consisted of a hairy covering for the body, and a head and face cleverly devised to be lifelike: "By the use of a peculiar spongy material and ingenious arrangement of wires, opening the mouth pulls back the lips from the teeth of the mask, and wrinkles the skin of the cheeks." The brown goatskins used for these outfits were prepared at a special studio tannery.

The *New York Times* of February 3, 1918, in addition to reporting that "sixty tailored ape suits were made from specifications supplied by Darwinian students," presented colorful details of the production:

Trips were made to Manaos, Brazil; Iquitos, Peru; New Iberia, La.; Great Bear Lake, Cal. and Banff, Canada. . . . In all 12,000 miles were traveled by train and over 6,000 miles by steamer. . . . Three hundred native huts were built in the Brazilian jungles. Two thousand native Negroes de Costa (Amazon River Negroes intermarried with Peruvian Indians), twenty principals, a working crew, directors and supervisors were transported from New York to Manaos on the steamer Madeirense and then a nine-car train chartered for the trip to New Iberia and thence to the studios at Los Angeles.

The *Times* account included other information:

Eleven hundred natives were used in the production. . . . Forty high priced aerial acrobats were engaged and paid for an entire season's work, although required but one month. Four lions, six tigers, several elephants, eighteen living apes (all that exist in this country) . . . were purchased and transported to the various locations. Wooden huts, similar to those at our army cantonments, fully screened against insect invasion, were built in the jungle at a small place called Itejuca, sixty miles inland from the Amazon River. . . .

Among the unusual happenings, as part of the plot, the three hundred native huts were built, burned to the ground, re-built and burned again. During the three-month period in this location near the equator, the company experienced fourteen serious accidents, one death and a delay of two weeks caused by "an outbreak of ulcers from which almost all the white players suffered great agony."[31]

Parsons, in his determined efforts to raise capital, had gone as far afield as Wyoming, and there secured the support of J. M. Rumsey, president of The Stock Growers National Bank in Rawlins. The roster of officers of the film corporation, with Parsons still president, now included Robert Middlewood of the Rawlins bank as vice-president, Fred L. Porter of Los Angeles as treasurer and secretary, and Rumsey himself as director.[32]

Ed's dissatisfaction was aggravated by a magazine report which caused him to demand of a friend in Culver City, "Can you tell me what the Parsons person is doing with, or to, Tarzan? Jimmie Quirk says he is producing it in a backyard. . . ."[33] In a letter that was a combination of inquiry, complaint and accusation, Ed wrote to Rumsey concerning Parsons' activities; Rumsey responded in defense of Parsons and chided Burroughs:

We here in Wyoming invested because the chief feature was your production and that you were connected with it. We had every faith in Mr. Parsons and we believe that if you handle him right that you will have no trouble in having him do whatever you desire. . . .[34]

Rumsey scolded Ed as though he were a misbehaving child: "Now, I urge that you handle Parsons diplomatically and I believe everything will come out all right."[35]

These fatherly attempts at mediation did little to alter Ed's impatience and his distrust of Parsons. He could muster no faith in the corporation, and on December 12, 1917, seized the opportunity to sell his ten thousand shares of capital stock, valued at $50,000, to David H. Watkins for a mere $5,000.[36] He remained bitter about the motion picture industry, and in a letter to E.V. Durling of the Los Angeles *Morning Telegraph,* who had sought suggestions about forming a film company, commented, "As far as my own work is concerned there is very little of it adapted to the screen. In fact, of late, I have made it a point to write things which could not be produced, and which, therefore, could not be stolen. . . ."[37]

On January 16, 1918, with *Tarzan of the Apes* scheduled to open at the Broadway Theatre in New York on the 27th, Harry L. Reichenbach, publicity manager for the National Film Corporation, advised Ed that a box was being held for him. The Burroughs reply was frosty and succinct: "Thank you for your invitation to the opening of the Tarzan picture, which I shall have to decline."[38] Throughout the years of waiting, Ed had experienced rebuffs and rejections in his numerous attempts to have *Tarzan* produced, and the repeated statements about the difficulties of adapting the jungle story to the screen had almost convinced him that a *Tarzan* film was impossible. Yet, it was produced, and was advertised in *The New York Times* of the twenty-seventh as "from the original story by Edgar Rice Burroughs," while its author, as a result of petty quarrels and irritation over a scenario he could not approve, refused to attend its premiere.

Tarzan of the Apes, directed by Scott Sidney, was an eight-reel film that followed the Burroughs story in most respects but discarded or changed certain incidents in the plot. In the book, Tarzan's transition to a spoken human language had been in French, with Lieutenant D'Arnot as his tutor; the film, for very practical reasons, eliminated both D'Arnot and the French instruction sequences. These scenes involving the two men would not have been of sufficient importance to justify the introduction of a French character and a foreign language, and they might have proved confusing to American viewers. Instead, Tarzan learns English directly from a sailor named Binns. The original ending, with Tarzan's "noble act of self-renunciation," now became less definite. To satisfy the movie-goers' demand for a resolution with happier possibilities, a closing scene showed Tarzan and Jane embracing, indicated plans for them to return to England together, and implied that somehow their love would finally triumph.

Tarzan, the boy, was played by Gordon Griffith, a well-known child star, while for the role of the adult Tarzan, Elmo Lincoln, whose real name was Otto Elmo Linkenhelt, was chosen. Lincoln replaced a New York actor originally assigned the part. The powerful, twenty-eight-year-old Lincoln had been given his screen name by D. W. Griffith, and the famous director had used him in a number of movies, including *Birth of a Nation, The Kaiser,* and *Intolerance.* The role of the heroine, Jane Porter, was taken by Enid Markey.[39]

With the passing months of 1918, Ed's anger at Parsons, and his belief that the National Film Corporation was not paying him the royalties to which he was entitled, led him to consult his friend Carl Meyer, a Chicago attorney. The argument had now become technical, the question being whether National, under the Burroughs contract, was allowed to sell the distribution rights of *Tarzan;* this action, because of payments to the distributing company, resulted in smaller royalties.[40] Meanwhile,

Ed, feeling that he needed a Los Angeles attorney, had engaged the services of Harry C. Levey. The issue of distribution rights was soon eclipsed by a larger one. In May 1918, a small item in Kitty Kelly's *Chicago Examiner* column alerted Ed to a situation which at first seemed incredible: Parsons was making *another* Tarzan film.[41] On May 29 Levey reported a rumor he had heard: ". . . from what I can gather there is another copy or film of your story that someone back in Wyoming has. Parsons had a hand in it. . . . you had better have things looked after to determine whether you are getting your proper share. They look like a bad bunch. . . ."[42]

Parsons' explanation was simple and ingenious. He was *not* producing an unauthorized film; he had bought the complete *Tarzan of the Apes* novel and was now adapting the last half of the book as a movie sequel. Ed's shocked protest to attorney Carl Meyer brought a discouraging response: "If . . . the new film is really the second half of your book . . . there may be some difficulty in stopping its production. . . ."[43] In a letter to Levey of June 17, Meyer explained that the First National Exhibitors Circuit of New York was now distributing *Tarzan of the Apes:*

This company advanced the National Film Corporation of America the sum of $125,000. when they took over the distribution of the picture. The information which Mr. Burroughs has received is to the effect that the picture is making big money, and that the pictures which have been the biggest money makers for the last six months are the Charlie Chaplin Film, Gerard's Four Years in Germany, and Tarzan of the Apes. . . .

With Parsons apparently unperturbed by threats of legal action, Ed, unable to receive any accurate information on the corporation's earnings, sought the services of his friend Watterson Rothacker, head of an industrial film company, to act as his representative and to confer with Parsons. Changes in National Film had brought in Harry M. Rubey as president, with Parsons shifted to treasurer. In a conciliatory tone Parsons emphasized that the new picture would not affect "The Return of Tarzan," should Ed decide to sell it for film production. For the second Tarzan movie Parsons had selected the title "The Romance of Tarzan"; he believed that this title would lure a large audience to the box office. Urging Ed to arrange with him for the filming of "The Return of Tarzan," Parsons boasted, "No company in existence can do more justice to the 'Return of Tarzan' than we, because we have learned something from each picture."[44] About their personal conflicts, he wrote:

I have come to the conclusion, Mr. Burroughs, that our trouble has been that we have done business through other people. I think most of the stories told me as coming from you have been lies, and undoubtedly, same has taken place in stories told you. In the future, if I have anything to say, or you have anything to say, let's say it to each other.[45]

Ed now adopted a conciliatory attitude, maintained that he liked the title "The Romance of Tarzan," and through the mediation of Rothacker, agreed to accept an advance of $2,500 on the new film.[46] He even advised he was "looking forward with pleasure to seeing this film" and hoped that if it were shown privately in Chicago, he would be notified.[47] After refusing to attend the premiere of *Tarzan of the Apes*, he had seen a later performance, and even made the admission that he "thoroughly enjoyed it."[48]

Released in September 1918, *The Romance of Tarzan,* directed by Wilfred Lucas, again starred Elmo Lincoln and Enid Markey. In the film, which was hastily improvised and had little relationship to the book, Tarzan is wrongly suspected by Jane of having an affair with another woman, played by Cleo Madison. The scenario, written by Bess Meredyth, established the Porter home in San Francisco, and Tarzan, deserting his jungle environment, follows Jane there. In the big city scenes he not only discards his loincloth, but dons a tuxedo. Viewers who had found Lincoln highly stimulating as the bare-chested ape-man were critical of his transformation to a gentleman in dress suit. They had become accustomed to thinking of Elmo and Tarzan as the primitive, half-clad savage. It became obvious that in *The Romance of Tarzan* too many scenes had been cast in a civilized setting; Tarzan out of his jungle surroundings for lengthy periods was like a fish out of water.

During the course of the years the tremendous popularity of the *Tarzan* stories, especially among the young readers, led to the formation of a number of Tarzan clubs. The first of these appeared in the fall of 1916. On November 21 Ed wrote to Bob Davis, "There is a very enthusiastic boy down in Virginia at Staunton who is forming a Tribe of Tarzan. He says Tarzan has made a man of him. If he writes you be good to him and encourage him. His name is Herman Newman." Ed was honored with membership card number one, dated 1916, and signed by Acting Chief Newman and Secretary Gilbert Wheat. Davis replied jokingly, "More strength to Herman Newman, Emperor of the Tribe of Tarzan . . ." and added a hope that all the members would subscribe to *All-Story* for twenty years in advance.[49] Ed, not amused, rated the project as worthwhile, noting that the boys were "in real earnest" and that their interest was undoubtedly shared by other young readers. He offered two reasons why *All-Story* should become the official organ of The Tribe of Tarzan: the obvious one was for circulation-building purposes, but more important was the opportunity to "accomplish something for the good of the boys. . . ."[50] Davis remained reluctant about sponsoring the group, but agreed to run an announcement which Ed had written:

The boys of Staunton, Virginia, have organized the first Tribe of Tarzan. They would like to hear from boys in other cities and towns who are interested in forming tribes in their own jungles. The men of Staunton are helping the boys of Staunton. The latter have a Tribe Room where they hold their meetings; they have grass ropes, bows and arrows, hunting knives, and the author of Tarzan of the Apes is having medallions struck for them symbolic of Tarzan's diamond studded golden locket. Boys who are interested are invited to write to Herman Newman, Acting Chief of The First Tribe of Tarzan, 113 N. Jefferson street, Staunton, Va.[51]

The announcement appeared in the Heart to Heart Talks of *All-Story* on January 20, 1917. About it, Ed remarked:

I rather imagine that Herman Newman, Esq. will be swamped by mail. I hope so. He has kept me busy for months; but when I think of Frank Baum I realize that I should not complain. He gets about a hundred and fifty letters a week from kids and answers them all long-hand. . . . all Los Angeles loves him. . . .[52]

At a later date, Ed wrote to urge the *Chicago Herald* to promote the Tribe of Tarzan through a special department in the newspaper, but the *Herald's* response was negative.[53] Through Ed's contacts with Joseph Bray, McClurg undertook to give the Tribe some publicity, and in their *Bulletin* of August-September 1918, in the section "Literary Items of Interest," a column was devoted to the organization, its founder, Herman Newman, now heading another Tribe in Covington, Virginia.

McClurg's *Bulletin* provided details of the rules that had been established for members of the Tribe of Tarzan. The purposes of the organization were idealistic—health, courage, and chiv-

PITTSBURGH JUNGLE

CRIBE of TARZAN

This is to Certify That_____

OF_____

IS A MEMBER IN GOOD STANDING IN

THE _____TRIBE

_____   _____
        SCRIBE   CHIEF

TARZAN CODE

A Tarzan Tribesman will always be truthful, honest, manly and courageous.

He will obey the laws of health and cleanliness.

He will smile in defeat and will be modest in victory.

He will do unto others as he would have others do unto him.

One of the cards, front and back, issued to members of the Tribe of Tarzan, founded in honor of ERB by Herman Newman of Staunton, Virginia.

alry—and members were required to take an oath to be honest and truthful; to "think clean thoughts"; and to protect the weak.[54] The bronze medal that members still wore about their necks "symbolized the studded locket that Tarzan wore." With the United States at war, it was noted that the Tribe at Covington had sold $28,000 worth of Liberty Bonds and was now "working in the Thrift Stamp Campaign and for the Red Cross."[55]

The problems and irritations of film controversies in 1916 did not stifle the flow of Burroughs' story imagination. In two cases he mulled over ideas for unusual works, based upon subjects that departed from his customary patterns. On January 3, in writing to Davis, he appeared intrigued by an odd theme:

Another thing I have had in mind is The Autobiography of Cain, a monkey-man story of our revered ancestors who chewed upon one end of a ripe caterpillar while the green juice ran out at the other upon their hairy chests. Of course you could emasculate the mss later. I would reveal to a waiting and eager world the long hidden secret that Cain has been a much maligned party, and was, really, rather a decent sort.

Davis found the idea amusing but offered a cautious warning that it might be "a pretty hot proposition," which could result in his being entangled "with the Presbyterian Synod, the Methodist Conference and the Episcopalian Bishop. . . ."[56] Ed explained that his idea was to create the story of Cain's childhood and develop the family life outside the garden of Eden. He would not overlook the opportunity to "drag in" a few prehistoric animals, and in succeeding episodes would "tell of the quarrel between Cain and Abel and give the real facts which led up to the killing, then follow Cain on his wanderings which led to the Land of Nod, his finding and fighting for a mate there."[57]

Ed noted frankly, "I want to be irreverent; but I know that you wouldn't stand for it, so I'll just hover around the verge without offending anyone." He joked, "There are a number of things in that part of Genesis which need explaining, and as Cain and I know all about them we'll clear matters up a bit. . . ."[58] He was blunt about the religious aspects: "Because I am not religious don't think that I couldn't write a religious story. It's just a matter of imagination, and I can easily imagine myself a religious bigot; and anyway I wouldn't make it too damn religious."[59] Possibly because Davis was not overly enthusiastic about the theme, and because of motion picture and other involvements, Ed allowed the idea of a Cain autobiography to fade away; he made no efforts to revive it.[60]

A second topic of an even more unusual nature, in a serious nonfiction area that Ed had never before contemplated, occurred to him late in 1916. In December he queried Bruce Barton of *Every Week* and the *Associated* of New York, expressing an interest in writing a biography of Jack London. With his entire success lying in his freely improvised fiction, that he should consider a severely structured form, such as a biography, is surprising. However, he had always admired London and his works. London had died that year. On December 19 Barton replied:

I happen to know that Mr. Sterling has already begun work on the life of Jack London, which is being offered in New York at this time. I don't see how we could use the life of Mr. London. Whether one of the other magazines would have a place for it I cannot tell, but I should think there was a sufficiently good chance to justify you in writing to some of the editors.

ERB also wrote to Davis, the indication being that in this case Ed was thinking of an article about London rather than a full biography. Davis answered, "Just between you and me, I don't give a whoop about Jack London's 'rough neck days on San Francisco Bay.' " But he offered advice and encouragement: "The people who will be interested are those who have been printing his stuff, notably Hearst's, Cosmopolitan and the Saturday Evening Post. I don't think you will have any trouble selling your dope."[61] Whether Ed made any further inquiries is not known. The plan to write about Jack London became another of his discarded projects.

Once more there was a return to the never-ending Burroughs catalog of "unfinished business"—the list of stories that had been left dangling for the inevitable sequels. "The Mucker," mentioned to Davis, brought the editor's response: "Yes, the poor wretch seems to demand rehabilitation of some sort," and a strong hint about any future plans for "The Mucker": ". . . conclude his career so that the scalawags who like your sort of fiction will regard the curtain as down for all time on that classic personality."[62] From the start, Davis had been lukewarm about "The Mucker."

On March 16, 1916, Ed sent the sequel, titled "Out There Somewhere" to Davis, along with a customary word count. The adventures of Billy Byrne, falsely accused of the murder of old man Schneider and still sought by the Chicago police, are continued, with Billy captured, sentenced to life imprisonment, and then escaping. He travels west and south, and for the first time there is a Burroughs setting in Mexico; Billy, happy in the midst of excitement and danger, is pleased to accept a captaincy under General Pesita, a Mexican bandit. His love for Barbara Harding and her faith in him had led to his reform, and the thought of her still served to control his actions. But curiously, in the sequel, Burroughs introduces a new inspirational force to affect

All Around Magazine

Formerly "New Story Magazine"

| Vol. XI | FEBRUARY, 1916 | No. 4 |

Beyond Thirty.

By Edgar Rice Burroughs.

CHAPTER I.

SINCE earliest childhood I have been strangely fascinated by the mystery surrounding the history of the last days of twentieth-century Europe. My interest is keenest, perhaps, not so much in relation to known facts as to speculation upon the unknowable of the two centuries that have rolled by since human intercourse between the Western and Eastern Hemispheres ceased—the mystery of Europe's state following the termination of the Great War—provided, of course, that the war had been terminated.

From out the meagerness of our censored histories we learned that for fifteen years after the cessation of diplomatic relations between the United States of North America and the belligerent nations of the Old World, news of more or less doubtful authenticity filtered, from time to time, into the Western Hemisphere from the Eastern.

Then came the fruition of that historic propaganda which is best described by its own slogan: "The East for the East—the West for the West," and all further intercourse was stopped by statute.

Even prior to this, transoceanic commerce had practically ceased, owing to the perils and hazards of the mine-strewn waters of both the Atlantic and Pacific Oceans. Just when submarine activities ended we do not know; but the last vessel of this type sighted by a Pan-American merchantman was the huge Q 138, which discharged twenty-nine torpedoes at a Brazilian tank steamer off the Bermudas in the fall of 1922. A heavy sea and the excellent seamanship of the master of the Brazilian permitted the Pan-American to escape and report this last of a long series of outrages upon our commerce. God alone knows how many hundreds of our ancient ships fell prey to the roving steel sharks of blood-frenzied Europe. Countless were the vessels and men that passed over our eastern and western horizons never to return; but whether they met their fates before the belching tubes of submarines or among the aimlessly drifting mine fields, no man lived to tell.

"Beyond Thirty" cover of All Around Magazine, *February 1916.*

Billy—almost incredibly it is the force of poetry. To Billy, poetry now becomes a revelation; its impact is powerful, and about the poets he says, "I always had an idea they was sissy fellows, but a guy can't be a sissy and think the thoughts they musta thought to write stuff that sends the blood chasin' through a feller like he'd had a drink on an empty stomach."

The particular poem which provides the greatest inspiration is Henry Herbert Knibbs' "Out There Somewhere," a favorite of Ed's and one that became both the title of his story and an interwoven romantic theme. Concerning the poem, Ed later explained to a fan, "I saw it first in a magazine many years ago and was so greatly taken by it that I could not resist the temptation of using it in my book."[63] In the story, lines from the poem are chanted often by the character Bridge, a hobo who is paradoxically a man of sensitivity and refinement. This unusual man-of-the-road arouses in Billy a new appreciation of a culture he had once derided. The most compelling lines are about the woman who is waiting, in a sense, for every lonely, wandering man: "And you, my sweet Penelope, out there somewhere you wait for me,/With buds of roses in your hair and kisses on your mouth." Bridge, the personable vagabond, also displays a fondness for Kipling and Robert Service, and in "Out There Somewhere" quotes passages from Service's poems.[64]

The publication of "Out There Somewhere," carrying the magazine title of "The Return of the Mucker," brought a letter from Knibbs, a Los Angeles resident, who had not known that Burroughs was staying temporarily in the same city. On October 18, 1916, Ed replied sentimentally:

I, too, dreamed of a Penelope. On night herd beneath the brilliant stars along the Snake, I dreamed of her, and amidst the dark, nocturnal shadows of the cottonwoods beside the Gila, while the troop slept and I stood guard, I dreamed of her. For ten long years I dreamed, and then my dream came true.

Penelope and I are here, and we'd like mighty well to have you come and see us.

We are old and bald-headed now, and have eight or eleven children and very few teeth; but the spirit of romance still burns brightly in our withered hearts. . . .[65]

When the book later appeared in 1921 as *The Mucker,* it combined both stories, and Knibbs' poem drew numerous reader queries that led to responses by Burroughs.[66]

Since 1916 was the year of the "Auto Gypsying" tour and the extended California vacation, Burroughs' remaining literary output consisted of the first eight of twelve stories in "The New Stories of Tarzan," a series of short stories purchased by Ray Long, editor of *The Blue Book Magazine*. Davis had been uninterested in these brief *Tarzan* tales, and had even inquired, "Who was so foolish as to take . . . the series?" To this Ed answered, "It was Ray Long, but for the luvomike, don't tell him he was foolish."[67]

Previous attempts to write short fiction with the characters and settings drawn from ordinary life had resulted in stories that were mawkish and trite. Examples of these are "For the Fool's Mother" and "The Avenger." But when Burroughs dealt with the purely imaginative and with material that interested and stimulated him, his writing, as demonstrated in "The New Stories," could emerge with a sensitivity and philosophical subtlety not present in his longer works. These stories, flashbacks to Tarzan's early years and his growth to manhood in a jungle environment, portray his learning-through-experience and, beyond that, his gropings toward the unknown and his struggles to penetrate the primitive world of superstition that enclosed him.

One facet of his human intellect, man's most persistent and prodding impulse—curiosity—lifted him high above his animal associates. It allowed Tarzan no rest, drove him to search and inquire. So began his search for an understanding of nature, of the baffling behavior of the sun and moon, and above all, for an explanation of the word *God* he had found in his dictionary, a word identifying a Being whose awesomeness, mystery, and power he both reasoned and sensed.

Among the twelve short tales that compose "The New Stories," one, "The God of Tarzan," develops young Tarzan's attempt to discover some definite meaning behind the vague concept of God. His ape friends' superstitious belief that Goro, the Moon, is the all-powerful force causes Tarzan to hurl a challenge at the moon, but this brings no result and drives him to hunt elsewhere. In the native village he sees a grotesque figure with the head of a buffalo, a long tail, and the legs of a man. Tarzan does not know of the witch doctor's disguise and is ready to believe that this strange creature, half-man, half-animal, is the god he seeks. Once again, however, he is disappointed; he finds that the buffalo hide conceals a black man who cringes in terror before him. In a rage he kills the man. But later, as he is about to kill Mbonga, the native chief, he sees that he is clutching a helpless old man who "seemed to wither and shrink to a bag of puny bones beneath his eyes." Tarzan, for the first time, is seized by the sensation of pity; he leaves Mbonga unharmed.

Through this episode Burroughs creates a beginning of Tarzan's vision of God: some "strange power" had "stayed his hand. . . . It was as though someone greater than he had commanded him to spare the life of the old man." Was this the mysterious force behind everything, he wonders, the God associated with the word "create," the God who made all things different, the ape unlike the deer, the panther unlike the rhinoceros, and Tarzan himself unlike the others? The rescue of Teeka, the female ape, and her baby from the grip of Histah, the snake, an instinctive act done at the risk of his own life, brings the final revelation to Tarzan. Teeka herself, despite her fears, had leaped "into the embrace of death" to save her baby. Why did she do it, and what made him do such things? The answer comes, "Somebody more powerful than he must force him to act at times." He recalls the word he had read: "all-powerful."

These involuntary acts were commanded by God because they were right and good. This was proved by what had occurred. And from these he reasons further:

The flowers and trees were good and beautiful. God had made them. He made the other creatures, too, that each might have food upon which to live. He had made Sheeta, the panther, with his beautiful coat; and Numa, the lion, with his noble head and his shaggy mane. He had made Bara, the deer, lovely and graceful.

To Tarzan, unaware of the limitations of human reasoning, it appears for a time that he has solved the mystery of God. But Burroughs confronts him abruptly with the gap in his neat pattern of logic. An inconsistency becomes suddenly apparent. Stunned, Tarzan hurls the question: "Who made Histah, the snake?" In a powerful climax Burroughs thrusts Tarzan back into humanity's constant puzzlement about God and His actions. Tarzan cannot be granted escape; like any other human, he cannot be given assurance. He must remain, still questioning, in his world of uncertainty. And in Tarzan's dilemma, Burroughs poses the familiar, age-old philosopher's problem: Why did God, the Creator of all things good and beautiful, also create Evil?

The development, in a short story, of certain interpretations of God's role, raises the question of Burroughs' personal attitude toward religion. In one of his earliest fantasy works, "The Gods of Mars," while exposing the Martian "Heaven," the priesthood, and the entire concept of the established church as a cruel and sadistic hoax, he was giving more than a hint about his own religious convictions. To begin with, here and in other works he made plain his distrust and rejection of organized religion. But the indirect presentation of his religious views, the inferences drawn from the statements or thoughts of his fictional characters, does not constitute the only evidence. Burroughs, as always, was not hesitant about stating his opinions bluntly and directly. A letter to Hulbert, written later, contained a severe condemnation of the church:

I was pained to discover how sadly you misinterpreted my attitude toward religion. I have no quarrel with religion, but I do not like the historic attitude of any of the established churches. Their enthusiasms and sincerity never ring true to me and I think that there has been no great change in them all down the ages, insofar as the fundamentals are concerned. There is just as much intolerance and hypocrisy as there ever was, and if any church were able to obtain political power today I believe that you would see all the tyranny and injustice and oppression which has marked the political ascendancy of the church in all times.[68]

This criticism of the established church, he stressed, "does not mean that I am not religious. I am a very religious man, but I do not subscribe to any of the narrow, childish superstitions of any creed."[69] In his letter he spoke of "the disgusting lust for publicity, which animates many divines." But Burroughs, as a man of science and a staunch believer in Darwin's theories, reserved his greatest contempt for the church in its attitude toward scientific progress and "toward the promulgation of the truth in art and literature. . . ." Between the established religions and their narrow beliefs, and the rationality of science, there was an irreconcilable conflict:

A man can be highly religious, he can believe in a God and in an omnipotent creator and still square his belief with advanced scientific discoveries, but he cannot have absolute faith in the teachings and belief of any church, of which I have knowledge, and also believe in the accepted scientific theories of the origin of the earth, of animal and vegetable life upon it, or the age of the human race; all of which matters are considered as basic truth according to the teachings of the several churches as interpreted from their inspired scriptures.[70]

Burroughs, in expressing his views on God, could at times become jokingly irreverent. In a letter of October 28, 1920, to Father Dom Cyprian, a priest with whom he had previously corresponded, Burroughs' comments about the Lord's actions had a humorous tinge:

I was very sorry to know that rheumatism has been bothering you. It seems to me that the Lord should look after you better than he does as you certainly must have earned more of his gratitude than a poor pagan such as I; yet, notwithstanding my ungodliness my neuritis has almost left me. Inscrutable indeed are the ways of Providence.

Father Cyprian's quoting of a remark by Dr. Barton brought a pointed reply: "I do not understand your reference to Dr. Barton and his belief that I am a godless man. You have aroused my curiosity and now you must relieve it. My daughter is in a Catholic convent and I am smiled upon by the Reverend Mother and a number of the Sisters which would never be true were I so godless as your remark suggests."

In his stories Ed's depiction of nature as the all-wise creator of living things, the Great Perfectionist who demonstrated her perfection in her scheme of things—the animals, plants, and their environments—indicated that his religious philosophy tended toward pantheism. His further statement to Father Cyprian supports this view: "Really, I think I have a more satisfactory God than Dr. Barton for I am not afraid of my God and I enjoy His company every day in the sunshine and flowers and the beautiful hills and I do not have to crawl into a dark closet to pray to him."[71] Ed's skepticism about the church did not affect his attitude of good-humored tolerance and helpfulness; beneath his letter to Father Cyprian is his scrawled note: "$1.00 bill enclosed with this letter."

Through the years his comments about God continued to be in a jesting tone. To his brother Harry Ed revealed his happiness about his Tarzana ranch and wrote, "It took God millions of years to get Tarzana and me together but I can see now that He was evidently working to that end since it occurred to Him to create Earth, and I have to give Him credit for pulling off at least one very successful job."[72]

His reply to the Reverend L. Eugene Wettling of Religious Films, Inc., New York, June 14, 1928, made clear his disapproval of the church:

Permit me to assure you of my appreciation of the honor con-
ferred upon me by election to your Honorary Advisory Board.

My religious convictions are such, however, as to make such
a connection incongruous, and as it might cause embarrassment
to all concerned I sincerely hope that you will withdraw my
name. . . .

His remarks, while of a joking nature, implied, on occasion, some acceptance of God's role as Creator. To a fan who had commented about the absence of snakes from his stories, Ed conceded that he had "fought more or less shy of them" because he felt they were "anathema" to his readers and editors, but added, "However, I may be able to invent something better than a snake, to try and put an extra thrill into my stories, as I have already created almost as many strange creatures as God; though He remains one up on me with the creation of Man."[73]

Burroughs, attempting to be open-minded on matters of religion, was particularly careful to avoid influencing his children or dictating to them. He advised his son Hulbert, then at school, in this manner: "You will be wise if you attend church occasionally, at least, if not regularly. It is a very necessary part of the education of all cultured men and women. Your own good judgment will tell you what to accept and what to reject."[74]

However, individual rights in a religious choice were quite different from any plan to introduce compulsory religion on a mass basis. In response to the query of Henry Goddard Leach, editor of *The Forum,* "Shall We Force Religion into the Schools?," Ed was vehemently on the negative side: "Compulsory religious training in any form in schools supported by taxpayers seems to me to be contrary to the highest ideals of American democracy."[75] He noted that even in endowed colleges religious subjects should be electives, and about the Bible, could see no practical way of using it in the public schools. He conceded that the "historical and literary phases" might be of value for study, but insisted that if the Bible were used, equal time should then be devoted to the Talmud, the Koran, and other works. Since, in his opinion, the material was not needed, and the school hours were insufficient for all these religious works, it was best that these subjects should be excluded from the public school curricula.[76]

In discussions with his sons Hulbert and Jack, Burroughs stated his religious attitude clearly: he did not believe in the Bible, Christ, the Immaculate Conception, or God. He called himself an atheist. To his sons, Burroughs, who did not attend church, had often expressed his dislike for any form of organized or sectarian religion. At times, especially because of his efforts to be tolerant about other people's religious views, he gave the impression of being an agnostic. On occasion when he termed himself a "religious" man, he was referring to his objectives of following the moral or ethical precepts taught by Christ or found in the philosophies of the Greeks and the Romans. Concerning the typical religious attitudes displayed by characters in his stories, both of his sons have maintained that these should not be interpreted as representing Burroughs' beliefs—they are merely inserted as necessary elements in the story, or to create the particular effect he was seeking.[77]

For a period of exactly one year, from March 17, 1916, to March 18, 1917, Burroughs worked on his series of "The New Stories of Tarzan," dispatching them individually to *The Blue Book Magazine* and receiving a prompt $350 for each. They appeared in *Blue Book* one each month in issues dated September 1916 through August 1917. On March 29, 1919, they were published in book form by A. C. McClurg & Co. under the title *Jungle Tales of Tarzan*. In *Blue Book* the first story bore only the series title, but as Chapter One of the book it was titled "Tarzan's First Love." The remaining eleven had subtitles in the magazine, which later became chapter titles two to twelve in the book.

The series had been launched in Oak Park, one story even completed on the camping tour and the remainder finished in Los Angeles.[78] The stories, containing some of Burroughs' best writing, were highly praised by Ray Long; however, there were exceptions, one being number six, "The Witch-Doctor Seeks Vengeance." Here, the opening scene establishes a satirical comparison between the "civilized" Lord Greystoke, William Cecil Clayton, who had assumed the title and lands of Tarzan, and the real Lord Greystoke, the young savage of the jungle. Burroughs had used this same comparison in *Tarzan of the Apes*. His satire, again stressing one of his strongest aversions, the hunting and killing of animals, described how the British Lord Greystoke had shot "many more birds than he could eat in a year," while Tarzan in the African jungle killed only what he needed for food. Burroughs had also repeated another device—Tibo, the native child, seized by Tarzan in the previous story, is now stolen again by the witch doctor. About story number six Long noted:

I don't care for those references to the Lord Greystoke in Eng-

446

Burroughs home at 700 Linden Avenue, Oak Park, Illinois, 1917.

land. Unless you object very heartily, we will take those refer-
ences out. I also felt it was a mistake to return to that child. He
was all right for one story, but he was not a good character for
two. . . .[79]

Ed offered no serious objection: "The references to Lord
Greystoke in England were made for artistic contrast. Something
similar in the first Tarzan novel has been commented upon very
favorably. I thought they were real cute; but if you prefer, however, you may cut them out. I am seldom so hectic about the
children of my brain but that I can see them murdered without
a sigh—if they are going to be paid for. . . ."[80]
Early in 1917, still in Los Angeles, Ed had taken time from
his writing chores to join the Uplifters, a purely social group,
described by him to Davis as "a select bunch of millionaires,
clerks, and other celebrities, all members of the Los Angeles
Athletic Club, who meet weekly for luncheon and occasionally
evenings for dinner and have a heck of a good time. Frank
Baum, the fairy tale man, introduced me to them."[81] But these
pleasant occasions were more than offset by personal health
problems and illnesses in the family. On January 22, in correspondence with Joseph Bray about plans for a British edition of
Tarzan of the Apes, Ed reported his troubles with his tendency,
as usual, to exaggerate financial difficulties:

I may need some money before pay day. I have recently come
out of the hospital after a minor operation performed by a sur-

geon who has no superior in his specialty. I have not yet had his bill. God alone knows what it will be. My oldest boy has been under the care of another high priced specialist for a month. My littlest boy has diphtheria. He has it mildly and is about well; but the bills will presently materialize.[82]

However, the world situation was drawing his attention away from these personal problems. The United States' policy of neutrality in the European War could not conceal the country's strong anti-German sentiment. Undoubtedly, to Ed, an entrance into the war on the Allies' side appeared inevitable. Driven, as in the past, by an intense patriotism, he had already begun preparations for some type of military service. Because of his army experience, he naturally thought of the cavalry and in the fall of 1916 enrolled in the Los Angeles Riding Academy for a brush-up course in horsemanship. Here, in contrast to the free, rough-and-tumble riding he had learned at Michigan Military Academy, he was drilled in the formal English style of riding.[83]

The war situation had both aroused his patriotism and created apprehensions about continued story sales. Of Davis he inquired, "What will a war with Germany do to poor boobs who write fiction?" and he then followed with the familiar request: "If you have a pull get me a commission, . . ." mentioning his army career but admitting "that was in the days of crossbows and catapults."[84] Meanwhile, deciding that the most practical approach would be to seek a commission in the reserves, he reverted to past habits and wrote to his old mentor, General Charles King, who advised him to apply for a captaincy in the cavalry—Officers Reserve Corps—and to get various letters of recommendation. "I will add a corker," said King, "and War or no War we'll have you on the List. . . ."[85] A reply from another former Michigan Military Academy commandant, Frederick Strong, now a major general in the army's Hawaiian headquarters, noted Ed's inability to enter active service because of his age and suggested that he join the Quartermaster Officers' Reserve Corps.[86]

In the past, when seeking military appointments, Ed had gone all out to acquire letters of recommendation from his friends and associates, but on this occasion he far exceeded all previous records, amassing a total of thirteen letters or statements. Included in these were recommendations from Brigadier General Fred Smith; W. H. Butts, his former teacher, now at the University of Michigan; Isaac K. Friedman of Wilmette, Illinois; Joseph Bray of McClurg; Robert D. Lay of the National Life Insurance Company; and Jacob Vogt of the Los Angeles Riding School. Ed also forwarded a copy of his March 15, 1897, army discharge, signed by Colonel Simmons with a character reference by Lieutenant Tompkins.[87] Under these circumstances it was not at all surprising that his commission was granted. The United States declaration of war against Germany came on April 6, 1917, and after his return to Oak Park, where he purchased a home at 700 Linden Avenue, Ed received the official notification from the state of Illinois; his appointment as captain in the reserves was issued as of July 19, 1917, Company A, Second Infantry.

Until the appointment came through, Ed had continued to seek a war correspondent's job. Davis confessed that he had no idea how to get him an assignment covering the war front, explained that there were "a thousand applications to every job," and added that "on our three newspapers we receive at least fifty appeals per diem. . . ."[88] He offered some typical raillery about Ed's qualifications:

You would make all previous war correspondents look like a lot of lame ducks tied in a coop. You know more about blood and trouble and pain and anguish than any other five scribes in the business. I don't know that it would improve your style any to go to the front, but it is a certainty you would improve the war.

. . . Between pronging a Hun and getting his opinion as to how well you executed the job, you could easily subtract enough material to write three serials and then three sequels to those serials.[89]

Despite all these inquiries, Ed, in the summer of 1917, managed to complete another story, "Bridge and the Oskaloosa Kid," and to indulge in his usual vacation at Coldwater, Michigan.[90] In the fall he turned to the first of his patriotic writings, undertaken at the request of John N. Willys of the War Camp Community Fund, who in a circular of October 9 requested that authors contribute articles to help the war effort. The specific need was for articles "advocating the opening of American homes to boys in the uniform of the army or navy." Ed had agreed promptly to write articles and to offer one each week to newspapers that had printed his stories. About the opening of homes to soldiers, on October 16 he suggested to John Willys that "after proper investigation and under proper authority" a flag be issued to each private home or public facility willing to accept soldiers; this flag would serve as a kind of beacon to the man "walking the streets of a strange city" and call his attention to a place where he might find a "ready welcome."

Ed sent three articles of four hundred words each to Jerle

ERB as a captain in Illinois Reserve Militia, Oak Park, Illinois, 1918.

Davis of the Western Newspaper Union in Chicago and asked that he print fifty proofs to distribute to other newspapers, to which Davis agreed.[91] The three articles, titled "To the Mother," "To the Home Girl," and "To the Woman on the Town" (asking prostitutes to stay away from soldiers) were all on the same theme—aiding the lonely soldier adrift on the streets of the big city.[92]

Toward the end of April or the first part of May 1918, Ed took an office in a small brick building at 1020 North Boulevard, Oak Park; although the office was to function as a study and permanent business address, Ed, at times, was quite willing to use it for one of his favorite projects—the recruiting of men for the reserve militia. Summer activities were mainly of a military nature. From August 12 to 25 Ed joined his Oak Park company in training at Camp Steever, Geneva Lake, Illinois, under Commandant F. L. Beals. After his return in September came the announcement of his promotion to major and to the command of the First Battalion, Second Infantry of the Illinois Reserves. But he was convinced that a further contribution was necessary: his writing skill must be dedicated to the war effort. As a result, in 1918 a stream of patriotic articles poured from the Burroughs pen. These included the following:

Do Boys Make Good Soldiers?
Patriotism by Proxy and Who's Who in Oak Park, both published in *Oak Leaves*.
Home Guarding for the Liberty Loan, a speech delivered at Flag Day exercises, Oak Park, June 14, 1918.
A National Reserve Army Proposed.
Go to Pershing.
Peace and the Militia.[93]

Despite his past censure of the army for its bungling and inefficiency, and curiously, despite the fact that in his own youthful army career he had been unable to adjust to the discipline, had been a rebel, and had implored his father to get him out of the cavalry as quickly as possible, the arrival of a national emergency aroused his pride in the military and stimulated an intensely chauvinistic attitude. In common with many other Americans he blindly accepted the vicious anti-German propaganda. An illustration of this is found in "Home Guarding for the Liberty Loan," with its bloodthirsty references to the "Hun" and "Boche":

Front cover of The Oak Parker *magazine with photo of ERB as a major, September 28, 1918.*

Each and every one of us pines to go over the top and spear a Hun. . . . Next to sticking a bayonet through a Hun's gizzard, you can inflict the greatest pain upon him by jabbing him in the pocket-book. . . . watching the home Boche wriggle when you get his purse pinned down.

In this and other articles Ed revealed how he had been influenced by the wave of public suspicion directed at German-Americans. He admitted that his methods for selling Liberty Bonds may not have been ethical: "We went out in selected groups decked out in all the panoply of war and armed with a bunch of yellow cards each of which bore the name of some suspected German sympathizer, included in which were those who had subscribed for no liberty bonds or to the Red Cross or to the Y.M.C.A. fund." He endorsed this as a way to "spear a Hun right here at home."

These bitter attacks on those who did not conform to his rigid standards of patriotism were also illustrated in articles about the reserve militia. In "Patriotism by Proxy" Ed used a combined approach of lecturing, scolding, and hurling invective at men who had not joined the reserve: "Are you in the service of your country? If you are not and might be, you are either a traitor or a slacker. . . ." He referred to various kinds of patriotism.

"Patriotism of the head" prompted a man to buy Liberty Bonds; this was laudable, but only a beginning. The highest form of patriotism was in service. Those able-bodied men who have contented themselves with lesser contributions to the war effort and have not enlisted in either the armed forces or the reserves, are "patriots by proxy."[94]

Concerning "Who's Who in Oak Park," Ed explained that the title, like the big guns at the war front, was camouflaged. In the article he commented scathingly about the men who had not joined the reserves. "The real title should be 'Who Ain't in Oak Park' for it deals with alibi artists and other lizards, as well as some well-meaning people who rear up on their hind legs and paw the air if anyone suggests that they are not rabid patriots."

Some of the opposition to the militia was displayed by labor union members who, because of the past actions of the national guard, were convinced that one of its main functions was strikebreaking. The contemptuous description of a union member, in the article, revealed unfortunately that Ed had insufficient background in labor history:

I recall one narrow chested, pimple-faced, chinless, anthropoid creature who met me at the door in his bare feet. I wouldn't have had him in my company if he'd been the only male thing in the world; but we put the question to him in the hope that there might be a human being around the place whom we did want. It seemed there was not; but he explained that the reason he couldn't join was that the militia was organized to shoot workingmen! I regret that my vocabulary is too limited to allow me to comment adequately upon this statement. . . .

About the man who had signed an application and then changed his mind because he had heard that the militia was used for strikebreaking, Ed noted, ". . . this man must have been deliberately misinformed by some disloyal acquaintance. . . ."

Ed was equally intemperate in his comments about churchgoers who chose to attend Sunday morning services rather than drill, and about ministers who have been opposed to these drills. Members of the militia, he maintained, were "performing a religious duty" and in defending the churches and homes against "the forces of disloyalty, disorder and lawlessness" were being far more positive than those persons who went to church and "prayed to God to do it for us." He supported the practical reasoning of "The Lord helps him who helps himself": "We are showing Him that we believe that these institutions for which He stands are worth fighting for. . . ." His attacks on the clergy were violent:

To those who have preached against our drills let me say that I consider you a menace to the cause and welfare of the state; I believe you to be as disloyal at heart as any other pro-German and I am very far from being alone in that belief. . . . Let me tell you that Oak Park's loyal clergy should start a thorough house cleaning. Beside the men who preach against enlistment in the reserve militia there is at least one who has preached against enlistment in the federal forces, and he has a German name that smells to heaven.[95]

In his article "Do Boys Make Good Soldiers?" Ed's answer was in the affirmative; as evidence he cited his training at Camp Steever, where young instructors, all under twenty-one, showed remarkable ability, poise and efficiency in handling men, many of whom were far older than they.[96] His Flag Day speech of June 14 was highly emotional in tone: it had been a fad among "so-called intellectuals," he remarked, "to scoff at the puerile sentimentality of flag worship," and he used to believe that something was wrong with him, "some taint of mental weakness," when tears came to his eyes as the colors passed by. Now he knew that "the trouble was with the scoffers"; we should be glad that we can "choke up" when soldiers march past.

His article "A National Reserve Army Proposal," published in the Army and Navy Journal, August 31, 1918, contained an explanation of the weaknesses of a volunteer reserve militia and a demand for the formation of a compulsory national reserve army. ". . . Every man should be compelled to serve in some capacity. . . ." and the enforced training of these men, in addition to furnishing recruits for the regular army, would provide the states with "protection against internal disorders."

"Go to Pershing," written as the war neared its end, again extolled the virtues of military training and predicted that civilian training camps would be continued in peace time. Indications were, the article pointed out, that the new Camp Pershing, to be situated in Kentucky, would be the greatest of its kind. Ed's support of these camps was not primarily for military reasons; he believed other factors were more important. For the older man especially, after years of sedentary life, the program of exercise, drills, and vigorous outdoor activities would restore some physical fitness and bring back "the fire of youth." Other values of military training were the creation of friendships and the development of efficiency, tact, and resourcefulness—qualities, Ed stressed, that would be particularly useful to the businessman and employer. In "Peace and the Militia," published November 16, 1918, after the armistice was declared, Ed repeated his familiar demand for a continuation of the Illinois Reserve Militia, needed in peacetime to suppress certain elements at home that he conceived to be dangerous or disloyal:

. . . it is very possible that we shall see loosed upon the community a raft of street-corner orators of the I.W.W. and Bolshevik types.

The events of the last few days have clearly demonstrated that German propagandists are still among us.

We have thrashed the trouble makers of Europe and it is within the range of possibilities that we may have to deal with similar cattle here.[97]

The harsh attitude he displayed toward those who did not meet his exacting standards of patriotism and service to the country were no more severe than his assessment of his own contributions. His desire, above all, had been to enter active service at the war front; this could not be realized because of his age—almost forty-two when war was declared. The reserves were a compromise that did not at all satisfy him. He had been forced also to yield to Emma's opposition; to his friend Bert Weston, on September 17, 1918, he complained that militia work was "the only military activity which Emma will permit me to indulge in. . . ."

This combination of superpatriotism and disappointment in his own war performance led to feelings of guilt which drove him to resigning from the Military Order of the Loyal Legion of the United States, an organization which he had esteemed because his father had belonged to it. On January 15, 1919, in a letter to Lieutenant Colonel George V. Lauman, he explained the reasons for his resignation:

I applied for membership in the order out of respect for the memory of my father who had answered the call in his day in defense of the flag. When my opportunity came with the present war unfortunate circumstances prevented me from going and I now feel that to wear the insignia of the legion or claim membership is equivalent to assuming as my own the honors that were worn by another man. I did not have this feeling prior to the recent war as I felt that I had not had my chance and therefore I was warranted in showing a just pride in my father's service.

Though undeserved, he accepted the blame for a war record that he considered inadequate:

I feel very keenly the unfortunate circumstances which prevented me from entering active service and I cannot ever again wear the button of the legion without a sense of humiliation, for even though it was through no fault of my own that I did not serve, the fact, however, remains that I did not. . . .

Ed stated that if Colonel Lauman believed he should continue to be a member, he would pay dues but would not wear the legion button.

During 1917-18 Ed maintained his association with William G. Chapman, who continued to be his syndicating agent. On February 10, 1917, Ed reported with obvious satisfaction to Chapman, ". . . they sold only 30,000 copies of Tarzan of the Apes during the six months ending Dec. 31; which seems pretty good for the third year of something what aint literatoor. If it had been the chances are it would have been dead long since." Chapman, representing the Burroughs stories for all newspapers except those in New York City, forwarded inquiries from Henry M. Eaton, managing editor of the Philadelphia *Evening Ledger* concerning "Tarzan and the Jewels of Opar" and "The Jungle Tales of Tarzan." The numerous requests from readers who wished to get in touch with Burroughs personally were forwarded by Eaton to Chapman's press bureau in Chicago.

In the summer of 1918, while authorizing Chapman to accept newspaper offers for the Tarzan stories he had been handling, Ed insisted that he now planned to take over all syndication himself. On May 14, he wrote to Chapman that this was caused "by the necessity for increasing my income to take care of a part of the additional expenses I am bearing on account of my connection with the reserve militia." He maintained that the syndication could not produce enough money for two persons. Two days later Ed notified Davis that he was arranging to handle his own syndicating and requested that Chapman's agreement with the Munsey fiction syndicate be transferred to him. To Joseph Bray at McClurg, on May 27, he sent information of the change and commented in frank disapproval of Chapman as an agent:

Confidentially, I have been very much disappointed in Chapman's handling of all my work. He seems to lack pep and force and he certainly has not only brought me practically no new accounts, but has lost one or two of the profitable ones which I turned over to him.

In further correspondence with Davis, Ed suggested a plan for mutual cooperation in marketing the stories, but, on May 25, commented pessimistically about those works whose rights belonged to Munsey—"Tarzan of the Apes," "Under the Moons of Mars," "The Gods of Mars," and "At the Earth's Core"—stating, ". . . as a matter of fact I do not think that what are left of the syndicate rights of those stories which you own are worth a tinker's dam." Davis did not agree, noting on May 29 that these stories were "salable for an indefinite period" and explaining that the Munsey business department "intends to make another drive" to sell the stories. Discussions on the matter continued into the fall, with little result. A. T. Locke of the Munsey Bureau on October 31, 1918, rejected Ed's plan to issue a combined circular to be distributed to newspapers and to contain a brief description of all the Burroughs stories. Locke's opinion was that *Tarzan of the Apes* had been syndicated "just about the limit" and was "practically a dead issue anyway because it has been picturized." He believed it would be best for Ed to adopt an individual plan "featuring Edgar Rice Burroughs only." Thus, with 1918 drawing to a close, Ed, already overburdened with other activities, had added the personal handling of his newspaper sales.

To answer the public demand for more books by Burroughs, McClurg, beginning in the fall of 1914, had arranged for the publication of the second Tarzan novel—*The Return of Tarzan.* With its appearance on March 10, 1915, others were scheduled to follow. They included *The Beasts of Tarzan,* March 4, 1916; *The Son of Tarzan,* March 10, 1917; *A Princess of Mars,* October 10, 1917; *Tarzan and the Jewels of Opar,* April 20, 1918; and *The Gods of Mars,* September 28, 1918.

Tarzan of the Apes had been dedicated by Ed to his wife, and continuing this practice, he dedicated succeeding novels to members of his family: *The Return of Tarzan* to Mrs. George Tyler Burroughs, his mother; *The Beasts of Tarzan* to daughter Joan; *The Son of Tarzan* to his oldest son Hulbert; and *A Princess of Mars* to his son Jack. Because Bray had overlooked Ed's instructions concerning the dedication of *The Son of Tarzan,* none appeared in the first edition. On December 3, 1916, Ed had written, "Please see that this book is dedicated to Hulbert Burroughs and win my undying regards." Ed expressed disappointment over the omission, noting on March 12, 1917, "I wanted a book dedicated to each of my children. . . ." In later printings the dedication was added.

During the publication of the various novels, interesting matters were developed in the correspondence. In connection with

The Gods of Mars, Bray, recalling Burroughs' remark that the *All-Story* version was somewhat abbreviated, requested the original manuscript. Ed's notation of April 24, 1918, read "Del'd mss of 'Gods of Mars' to Bray . . . in person."

The assignment of illustrating the first two of the *Mars* series, *A Princess of Mars* and *The Gods of Mars,* was given to Frank E. Schoonover by Joseph Bray. Schoonover, whose dust jacket and illustrations appeared in both the McClurg and British Methuen editions of *A Princess of Mars,* made a careful analysis of the Burroughs stories and extracted details of the costumes, ornaments, and weapons of the varied Martian races. The meticulous nature of his preparation for the drawings in *A Princess of Mars* is revealed in his letter of July 27, 1917, to Bray; Schoonover enclosed a copy of the notes he had made for his own use—notes based upon the galley proofs and containing a list of information drawn from Burroughs' statements and descriptions. To Bray, Schoonover wrote:

You will find recorded all that the author has to say regarding costume. . . . you will observe in galley 11 that mention is made of ornaments strapped upon the head. If the Tharks had decorations upon their ugly top pieces, how much easier it would be for the people of Helium to wear them. So I imagine that Dejah Thoris had just about what I have painted, plus the diamonds as mentioned in galley 50. Also there is ample authority for the scabbard—see galley 42—"drawing long sword"—and gal. 71 —"sheathing my bloody blade."

Schoonover's determination to faithfully portray the Burroughs costumes and to make the illustrations as authentic as possible is demonstrated in further comments to Bray, with reference to the guiding notes he had made:

These few notes were written after two or three days study and after making dozens of sketches. There has been worked out a sort of sliding scale of design for body decorations for the hordes of Barsoom. Their costumes can be made brutal and rough or refined to suit the Martian tribe under depictment. This, it seems to me, is absolutely necessary if there is to be a series of Martian books. . . . I am thoroughly at heart in the matter and I believe I have gotten some real originality in the make of the "metal". For example, in the picture that you have in hand now, there are some true Tharkian touches. The pistol butt is absolutely correct: it is true Thark. The belts are also common to the same tribe and can only be found upon the green men

Frontispiece and cover illustration of A Princess of Mars, *1917; Frank Schoonover, illustrator.*

*that roam the dead sea bottoms. You can depend upon it—
that is correct. The white metal is a mark of a true Tharkian:
silver is common to the Zodangans while the people of Helium
love the finely wrought ornaments of gold.*

Schoonover, convinced that *A Princess of Mars* had been written "with an idea of a sequel or even a third volume," insisted
that "it would be well to establish a foundation of costume that
can be elaborated and refined or brought to the level of the dead
sea bottom according to the custom of the tribe pictured." In
adhering to this plan, he had invented a collection of belts and
guns that could be altered "to suit the locality to be portrayed."

The "artist's visualization," Schoonover stressed, must be based
upon "solid reasoning"; in creating his costumes he had made
notes of all Burroughs' descriptions of "body adornment."
Schoonover's fascination with the story was evident: ". . . my
imagination has been aroused to such an extent that I hardly see
how Mr. Burroughs can drop the Martian curtain without telling
us a little more." Schoonover posed questions that needed answers:

*What, for example, is at the mouth (?) of the river Iss. Men
or beasts or nothing.
What happens under ground.
What goes on at the source of the water supply.
What eventually happens to Carter, Dejah Thoris and the egg.
Is the egg saved. (It is)
And so on.*

With the publication of the second of the *Tarzan* series, *The
Return of Tarzan,* McClurg employed J. Allen St. John as the
illustrator; St. John's association with the Burroughs books would
continue for many years, and his colorful and exciting drawings
would bring him fame. For *The Return of Tarzan* McClurg
created a dust jacket using the picture drawn by N. C. Wyeth
for the August 1913 cover of *New Story Magazine;* St. John's
contribution consisted only of twenty-six small sketches placed as
chapter headings. However, in the remaining novels of the
1917-18 period, *The Beasts of Tarzan, The Son of Tarzan,* and
Tarzan and the Jewels of Opar; the dust jackets and all illustrations were done by St. John.

Ed, in his 1917 output, completed varied stories designed for
magazine publication. Among these, "Bridge and the Oskaloosa
Kid" received an incredulous reception and firm rejection from
Davis. Ed had returned to his hobo favorite, the brave and gallant

Bridge (who continued to quote poetry by Henry Herbert Knibbs), and involved the vagabond with a strange and diverse aggregation of characters. There were Abigail Prim, daughter of Jonas Prim, Oakdale's wealthiest citizen; no less than six hoboes, all either criminals or murderers; Giova, a gypsy girl, and Beppo, her trained bear; the Cases, a farm couple, and their son Willie, an amateur detective; and a long list of others.

Burroughs' scenes, devised for the slender Oskaloosa Kid, who had apparently burglarized the Prim home, and the suave Bridge, take place in a "haunted" house, the terrifying apparition being "The Thing," a creature that drags a clanking chain along with it. The Thing turns out, unbelievably, to be Beppo the bear. A surprise ending is the disclosure that the Oskaloosa Kid, who has traveled about with Bridge and with the gang of hoboes, is really the charming Abigail Prim, disguised in men's clothes. This was too much for Davis; his protest combined indignation with disgust:

None of us can swallow the fact that the "Oskaloosa Kid" is a pullet. Lord! Edgar, how do you expect people who love and worship you, to stand for anything like that. And the bear stuff, and the clanking of chains! . . .[98]

Confident of other outlets for his material, Ed displayed indifference about the Munsey rejection, commenting on July 28, 1917, ". . . sorry you couldn't see the Bridge story because I think it belonged in All-Story; but otherwise it cuts no figure as I sold it immediately." The purchaser, Ray Long of *Blue Book,* paid $600, and upon its publication in the March 1918 issue, the story was retitled "The Oakdale Affair."

In two other novelettes of the 1917 period, "The Lost U-Boat" and "Cor-Sva-Jo," Burroughs returns once more to a familiar theme—the discovery of a primitive world teeming with prehistoric monsters and peopled with a hierarchy of strange races. However, he made it plain from the start that he was planning a trilogy. On October 15 he wrote to Long, "Saturday I brought down the first of the three novelettes—The Lost U-Boat; but missed you by a few minutes. Laid the manuscript on your desk. . . ." The master of "withholding," Burroughs deliberately provided an atmosphere of mystery in the first two works concerning the evolutionary process in Caspak, the interior region of the lost island of Caprona. This mystery was resolved in the third story, "Out of Time's Abyss," completed by midsummer of 1918.[99]

"The Lost U-Boat," re-named "The Land that Time Forgot"

With naked hands he faced the maddened Tantor

Cover of Tarzan and the Jewels of Opar, *1919; J. Allen St. John, illustrator.*

Illustration of Korak, the son of Tarzan, and Tantor, the elephant, *1918; J. Allen St. John, illustrator.*

by Ray Long, is the first of Ed's fictional works to contain a strong condemnation of the Germans; they are painted as subhumans —men without any redeeming qualities. The adventures of Bowen J. Tyler, Jr., (the name is a Burroughs ancestral one, passed down to George Tyler Burroughs, Ed's father) supposedly described in a manuscript found in a thermos bottle floating near the southern tip of Greenland, are launched with the torpedoing of an American liner by a German U-Boat. The succeeding incidents depict the German brutality.

Burroughs, again exhibiting the influence of World War I propaganda, depicted an American traitor almost as despicable as the Baron. The creation of Benson, a sailor who sabotages the submarine, illustrates the wartime attitude of contempt and distrust toward the IWW's.

In "The Lost U-Boat" Ed departs briefly from the story form to present dated reports from the journal prepared by Bowen Tyler. After the manuscript, placed in a bottle, is found (the discovery is made by Burroughs, who as first-person narrator takes part in some of the action), a rescue mission is planned by a new character, Tom Billings, the protagonist in "Cor-Sva-Jo," the second of the trilogy. And the last work, "Out of Time's Abyss," concentrates upon the adventures of Bradley, one of the

"The Land That Time Forgot" cover of Amazing Stories, *February 1927; J. Allen St. John, illustrator.*

British sailors, in his encounters with the ghastly winged Wieroos, the dominant race of Caspak. Here the mystery of the Caspakian seven-cycle scheme of evolution is finally explained. The trilogy appeared in rapid sequence in the *Blue Books* of August, October and December of 1918, under the titles "The Land That Time Forgot," "The People That Time Forgot" ("Cor-Sva-Jo"), and "Out of Time's Abyss."[100]

"The Little Door," a short story written November 17 to 23, 1917, again developed a theme of hatred and revenge against the Germans. It is Burroughs' most violent and bloodthirsty story of the anti-German type. The victorious Germans, invading a small French village, force their way into a home where the young girl Jeanne and her father live. Innocent and childlike, "her life had been one of kindliness and love," and she had no knowledge of evil. It remained for the Germans to teach her about terror and death. Aurele, the family's tottering old servant, and her father are viciously killed.

A Prussian officer seizes Jeanne and makes clear what she must consent to if she wishes to live. Strangely composed, and now apparently unmoved by the sight of her dead father "lying in a great pool of blood upon the floor," Jeanne urges the officer to send his men away, responds warmly to his kisses, and says, "You know nothing of love, you Germans." She leads him to the "little door" of a small room. Once he is inside, she slips out and slams the door behind him. There she pulls upon a silken cord and then drags down upon a heavy manila rope. ". . . From beyond the door came muffled sounds which sent her shrinking against the wall, her palms tight pressed against her ears; but only for a moment. . . ."

Jeanne uses the same tactics to lure, in succession, a lieutenant and then another German officer through the little door into the chamber of doom. Now the terrible shrieks do not affect her and she does not cover her ears. With her dagger she scratches crosses on the door frame of the small room, one for each German.

From then on she stands at the doorway of her home, smiling invitingly at the German officers who pass by, and luring them inside. The German forces are now retreating and the French soldiers are approaching the village. Jules, the man Jeanne loves, has returned secretly and from the house across the street is watching her actions with "burning eyes." Bitter at what he believes to be her wanton behavior, he enters her home, knife in hand, determined to kill her. He pursues her into the room beyond the little door and there an angry growl brings him to a sudden halt. The mystery of the room from which no German ever emerges is finally solved:

In the dim light of the single gas jet in the chamber Jules saw a huge black-maned lion rise, snarling, from the dead body of a German captain. About the floor were strewn helmets and side arms, torn pieces of blood stained, grey cloth and human bones.

The lion, at first menacing toward Jules, recognizes his voice and yields to the command of "Down, Brutus!" The two lovers lock the beast in the room and go to the window where they witness the victorious entry of the French troops.

On December 15, after "The Little Door" had been rejected by *Collier's,* Ed sought Davis' advice: "I am going to send it to you and ask you to tell me what in hell is wrong with it if you don't want it."[101] Once more Ed commented irritably that he "should like to be able to write a salable short story occasionally," but didn't seem to know how. Davis' answer of the eighteenth pinpointed, as usual, the story's weaknesses: "There is nothing the matter with 'The Little Door,' except that behind it is a tidal-wave of bloodshed, horror, and suggestion. There has been so much written about the terrible Boche and his evil impulses that there is nothing more left to the imagination."

Davis' final bit of advice was significant: "Can the war, Edgar, and believe that I am still your peaceful friend and ally."

Despite this sound analysis, Ed stubbornly persisted in sending "The Little Door" out again, this time to *The People's Home Journal,* where it received a firm rejection.[102] The story was never published.

The war situation also encouraged Ed to express his patriotism in verse. In "Little Ol' Buck Private," which at the start announces, "We're marching on Berlin/We'll stop around at Potsdam/And please to let us in," Ed concedes that the officers are doing their share, but asks, ". . . who would win the battles/if 'tweren't for me and you?" The "little old buck private," whether Smith, Schwartz or Murphy, is the one on whom the country depends. In the poem Ed resorts to stereotyped anti-German statements of the period:

We'll get the Kaiser's nanny,
We'll get the Kaiser's goat,
We'll get the Kaiser's army
And his damned U-boat.

A second poem, written shortly after the war, is titled "For

the Victory Loan," and in it Ed develops a patriotic and sentimental appeal for support of this 1919 loan. With the war over,
and people tired of sacrificing, the poem stresses the rebellious
attitudes of Americans; in this case, Ed was probably depicting
a real-life resistance to appeals for money. The miser is first
shown with his "glittering hoard" whining, "I can give no more.
Four times I've given. . . ." But the dancer, pausing "on the
ballroom floor," also refuses, crying, "You here again? . . .
Away! and let me enjoy life;/I'm tired of hearing of war and
strife." The next two stanzas contain similar responses:

A fat man wheeled in his swivel chair.
   "Just look," he cried, "at that window there!
" 'Tis thick with posters and flags galore.
   "I've got to live—I can loan no more."

A workman held up a grimy hand.
   "With this," he said, "have I served my land.
"Four times I've loaned of my savings, too.
   The war is over and I am through."

But Ed reserves his last, climactic stanza to emphasize why Americans must still be willing to sacrifice:

A mother gazed on a star of gold,
   "I gave my best and I'm growing old;
"But God be praised that I still may give
   "That the Peace he died to win may live!"

In contrast to his patriotic exhortations and violent
anti-German propaganda of 1918, Ed, almost as though the end
of the war had suddenly dispelled the somber atmosphere, allowed his humorous instincts to be released. At the year's end
he contributed a piece of burlesque writing to the Coldwater,
Michigan, *Daily Reporter,* whose editor was Emma's sister, Leila
Hulbert Westendarp. It was a fictitious foreign correspondent's
account of a visit to Paris, where a "Local Mystery" received an
explanation. Dated December 30, 1918, the article opens:

*I arrived in Paris early yesterday morning and found the city not
much changed since my last visit notwithstanding the fact that I
am assured by trustworthy informants that France has been at
war. With the true news instinct that marks the successful correspondent I immediately set forth to run this rumor to earth and,*

*with the assistance of a scoop shovel, I am now able to present
to the readers of The Reporter the startling announcement that
France has been at war with Germany for four years.*

Ed joked about the difficulty of traveling about Paris; the
problem was that "this village has no streets, the place being a
mess of avenues, places, boulevards and rues, especially rues."
He was on the verge of grasping "the meaning and purpose of
a rue" when an incident occurred which plunged him into confusion. While dining at a sidewalk cafe he noticed a dissolute
old man causing a scene at a nearby table. An inquiry of a
French friend as to who the man was, produced an answer—
and a planned pun. The French woman replied, "Rue A, mong-
sewer." ("Roué, monsieur.")

Although our "foreign correspondent" is in Paris and would
be expected to discuss events, in the French capital, he discon-
certingly shifts to a report of the discovery of a huge mastodon's
tooth in the river near Coldwater, Michigan,—a discovery blared
forth in the Paris newspapers. Burroughs describes the mastodon as "a species of preglacial mouse which lived in trees and
fed upon flying fishes. . . ." The creature "had but one tooth, not
having room in his mouth for any more, which I think that anyone who has seen this tooth will admit is entirely reasonable."
Logical reasoning leads to the belief that when the mastodon ate,
"it was necessary to remove the tooth in order to get food into
his mouth. . . ."

To solve the question as to how the enormous tooth
came to be deposited in a river near Coldwater, Michigan, Burroughs explained he had consulted two professors in the Department of Paleontology at the University of Paris. From Professors
L'Ostete and Tapebaton he received two different theories.
L'Ostete maintained that "M. giganteus" was perched in a tree
when he saw a large flying fish approaching; he removed his
tooth and laid it carefully upon a branch, then launched into a
ferocious attack upon the fish. In the fierce battle that ensued,
M. giganteus was carried some distance away. A terrific hurri-
cane arose, and after he had conquered the fish, eaten it, and
returned to his tree, he could not find his tooth; it had fallen
into the river.

Professor Tapebaton disagreed heatedly with this theory, insisting that M. giganteus was asleep under a tree and was awakened by "the growling of a winged, saber-tooth blue gill." He
attacked the animal "without remembering to remove his tooth

and . . . while devouring his kill, he swallowed his tooth and choked to death."

For his closing statement Ed saved the one news item that could be considered an "accomplished fact"; he wrote, "I have it upon reasonably good authority that the war is over."[103]

PART 7

A CALIFORNIA SETTING

CHAPTER 15

GENTLEMAN FARMER

Ed's return to Oak Park, Illinois, had been caused by patriotic motives and his involvement with the reserve militia, but he had no intention of making his permanent home in the Midwest. On December 4, 1918, he wrote to his Los Angeles physician, Dr. W. H. Kiger, "Mrs. Burroughs and I are both very anxious to get back to California. This climate is simply abominable. We had a more or less rotten Summer and entirely rotten Fall and from where I sit it looks as though it is going to be a rotten Winter. . . ." His main concern, as expressed to Kiger, was the flu situation in Los Angeles; he wanted to know whether it would be safe to come there with the children in January: "I wouldn't want to run into another epidemic . . . especially as we would have to go to a hotel and live for a month or so where it would be difficult to keep the children from being exposed. . . ."[1]

On December 11, in a letter to his old friend Howard Platt, who had gotten him the job as railroad policeman in Salt Lake City, Ed revealed a plan that appeared incongruous for a successful author: "We expect to go to California about February next and I wish to get a ranch and raise swine. . . ." He noted that he would need alfalfa land, and explained that this surprising ambition "to raise stock and live on a farm" was partially motivated by his affection for his brother Harry; Ed hoped they "might be together some day," but stressed that he had not discussed the matter with Harry and did not intend to until something definite materialized.[2]

ERB and Colonel, about 1927.

A week earlier, to Bob Davis, he had also mentioned his plan to leave for California around the first of the year, and to buy a small ranch where he would raise "purebred Berkshire swine." At the same time he commented with aversion about the prospect of further Tarzan novels:

I feel now that I can never write another Tarzan story and I am not posing when I say that I do not see how the reading public can stand for any more of them if they are as fed up on Tarzan as I am. Of course I suppose that it is much harder work writing these stories than it is reading them since I feel that I have said and re-said a dozen times everything that there is to say about Tarzan—this is why the work is so hard, I suppose.[3]

His attitude, later in the letter, was less adamant: "The chances are that I will not write another Tarzan story until I am convinced that it is absolutely wanted by someone, and I have been away from Tarzan long enough to approach him again with a refreshed mind."[4]

Ed's opinion of Southern California, expressed satirically in his 1914 poem "The Climate and the View," and nothing else, had not changed. In trying to persuade his close friend Bert Weston to join him in California, he wrote, "You will not like it at first. It is the experience of a great many people that they

ERB's advertisement to sell his property in Oak Park, Illinois, in preparation for move to California.

472

return to California a second and often a third time before they finally decide that they wish to live there permanently."[5] His added remarks about California were far from complimentary:

You will soon be disillusioned as to the "perfection" of California's climate. It can be just as rotten there as anywhere and really during the rainy season it is abominable. . . . it has been over-touted and a man goes there for the first time with the expectation of dropping into the Garden of Eden whereas the fact is that southern California is nothing more than desert land, certain spots in which have been reclaimed. The soil is enough to make a man from the Mississippi Valley laugh himself to death, but on the other hand it has for me the advantage of a longer period of sunshine than this climate and the lure of mountains and ocean.

"I would never go to California to make a fortune," he explained, "although I expect to make money out of hog-raising."[6]

To Colonel Charles S. McEntee, his Uncle Charles, who was staying at the Hotel Alvarado in Los Angeles, Ed sent details of the departure:

We expect to land in Los Angeles Monday, February 3rd, having made reservations on the Santa Fe for January 31st and were figuring on stopping at the Alvarado if we can get accommodations. As I understand that you are there again this year am imposing on your generosity to ask you to speak to the management to see if they can reserve us three adjoining rooms. . . . P.S. Party will consist of my family and maid—Theresa, whom you may recall. Shall bring chauffeur, too; but thought of getting him a room in a private family.[7]

The permanence of this removal to Los Angeles was without question; included in the traveling assemblage were two canary birds and the Airedale terrier Tarzan, and on January 14, 1919, Ed informed Arch Burdick, his insurance agent, that he was shipping the household furniture and the Packard automobile.[8] In trying to allay the concern of his mother about the separation, Ed wrote, "You must not feel that you are not going to see us again as we have been planning on having you and Mrs. Hulbert out as soon as we are located in California."[9]

Ed's departure required a special farewell ceremony by his numerous friends—all sharing with him a membership in

Tarzan's Feast
of Departure

The White Paper Club
of Chicago
to Major Edgar Rice Burroughs
Hotel La Salle, Tuesday Evening, January 28, 1919

*Special program of White
Paper Club of Chicago
honoring ERB; J. Allen
St. John, illustrator.*

The White Paper Club of Chicago. The club, composed of journalists and authors, and dedicated to promoting "friendly intercourse between those engaged in the transformation of white paper into art in any of its printed forms," had adopted its constitution and by-laws on April 11, 1917, and elected its officers and board of governors at that time. The president was Emerson Hough; secretary-treasurer, Ray Long; and on the board of governors, in addition to these two, were Frank Reilly, James R. Quirk, and Charles D. Frey.[10]

At the banquet held in Chicago's La Salle Hotel on January 28, 1919, Ed was subjected to the banter and practical jokes that the occasion called for. A brochure, titled "Tarzan's Feast of Departure," with cover illustration by J. Allen St. John, contained "The Blackest Page in White Paper History," presumably from the secretary's minutes, reporting a supposed speech of Ed's:

Mr. Burroughs requested the floor, and, on being recognized, spoke as follows: "Mr. President: It seems to me that our club is of such size that 'treating' is out of the question. I move, therefore, that it be out of order for a member to purchase any drinks other than for his own consumption, except in case of a guest or a guest of the club." The motion was seconded and carried. Mr. Burroughs then concluded, with force and feeling: "Gentlemen, I thank you! Waiter, bring me a stein of beer."

1919 aerial photo of part of Tarzana Ranch, which Ed purchased from estate of General Harrison Gray Otis; shows main residence, to which Ed added other rooms; ERB's stables, dairy barn, creamery, and chicken coop are visible to left of main house; trees surrounding hill on which house is located were mostly rare species imported by General Otis.

In the same brochure was a "night letter" from William Parsons, devised by someone who knew of the dispute that had raged between Burroughs and Parsons about the royalties from *Tarzan of the Apes,* and the production of *The Romance of Tarzan:* "Delighted to hear you are coming to California. Trust that I may continue to produce your stories in motion pictures. I did so enjoy Tarzan and my young lady friends equally enjoyed the parties I gave out of the profits. Bill Parsons." Burroughs' reply, by direct wire to Hollywood, and also someone's invention, was a blunt "Go to hell."

Newspaper accounts of the farewell banquet noted that about thirty members were present, that Hiram Moe Greene, editor of *Woman's World,* was toastmaster, and that Joseph Bray "voiced the sentiment of appreciation to Mr. Burroughs who responded with a promise 'not to forget any of you'." It was reported that Ed "will shortly leave for California, where he will devote his time to an ostrich farm and writing."

A membership list attached to the brochure and headed, "Society for the Prevention of Waste of White Paper," contained the names of such distinguished authors and editors as Howard Vincent O'Brien, Edwin Balmer, Oliver M. Gale, Randall Parrish, and William McHarg. To pay tribute to Ed, an unidentified author had composed a sonnet; titled "Burroughs," the sonnet eulogized Ed as the man who sings "of Nature's voice" with his "wild words."[11]

Upon arriving in Los Angeles in February 1919, Ed at once began his search for the ranch he so strongly desired. During that period the Burroughs moved from the Alvarado Hotel, renting a furnished home at 1729 North Wilton Avenue in Los Angeles.[12] In the last week of February Ed found what he was seeking, but it was a far cry from the "small ranch" he had mentioned in his letters. On March 1 he purchased the country estate of the late General Harrison Gray Otis, founder and publisher of the *Los Angeles Times* newspaper. The estate, called Mil Flores, was located in the San Fernando Valley in the foothills of the Santa Monica Mountains. Details of the purchase were reported in the *Sunday Times* of March 2, 1919: "The estate, created by Gen. Otis near the close of his life, and occupied by him immediately following his presentation to Los Angeles county for a public museum of his Wilshire boulevard home, the Bivouac, was used by him as a place of residence much of the time in the year prior to his death in 1917. . . . The holding comprises approximately 540 acres lying along the south side of the State highway (Ventura road) and toward the western end of the San Fernando Valley."[13]

Concerning the estate house, the article notes that the hill on which it stands "comprises about fifteen acres and is set out to a great variety of rare shrubbery and plants. The world was combed for the greenery on this knoll, hundreds of the plants coming from Asia and Africa." Ed, at the time of the purchase, had explained his intention to rechristen the estate Tarzana, a name which he planned to adopt also as a trade name for any products that were offered for sale. With the estate Ed acquired a small herd of registered Angora goats, living in the hills and deeper canyons. This herd was a project of General Otis, who had been convinced that much of the foothill land, then standing idle, would afford good range for goats. Ed's plans were to continue raising goats in these upper areas, increasing the size of the herds, while using the lower ground for his Berkshire hogs.

Problems beyond the ordinary arose during the moving from Oak Park to Los Angeles and then to the Tarzana Ranch. On March 21, 1919, Ed commented on "the frightful job of installing our furniture which had been shipped from Oak Park, arriving a few days before I closed the deal for a ranch," and added, "On top of this I have had the responsibilities of a going ranch of 540 acres and 500 head of livestock (mostly the goats) with all the help quarreling and everything going wrong. My secretary only arrived from the East Monday and we are now digging into six weeks accumulation of correspondence."[14] The problems with the help, involving disagreements over salaries and working conditions, became quite serious. A number of employees, including the maid Theresa, left Tarzana and returned to Oak Park; the secretary Grace Onthank and her husband Fred, a member of the Oak Park police department who had left his job to accept a position at Tarzana, both departed in a huff, claiming that Ed had reduced their promised salaries and not paid the agreed-upon moving expenses. They especially resented their treatment by Emma, referring in a letter of January 20, 1920, to "the actions of Mrs. Burroughs which you know was the real reason for us leaving." Noting that the situation Ed had "pictured so wonderful . . . had not materialized in the least," Fred Onthank wrote: "We would not have cared, and could have put up with all these things, if you, and especially *yours* had been congenial and treated us at least like white servants should be treated and not niggers."[15] At a later period, the hard feelings apparently dissipated, the Onthanks returned to Los Angeles, and were given letters of reference by Burroughs.

In spite of these troubles Ed was beginning to relish the things

477

North side of Burroughs home at Tarzana Ranch, about 1921.

he valued most and had dreamed of for years—the invigorating outdoor life, the pioneer or western environment, and the sense of ownership as he gazed from the knoll of his home to see the valley, the groves and canyons, and the mountain peaks in the distance. In trying to persuade his friend Bert Weston to bring his family and settle in California, Ed wrote in detail about the ranch activities:

The range into which Tarzana runs is very wild. It stretches south of us to the Pacific. We have already seen coyote and deer on the place and the foreman trapped a bob-cat a few weeks ago. Things come down and carry the kids out of the corrals in broad daylight. Deeper in there are mountain lion. I think Collins and Jeff would like it here. I have bought a couple of .22 cal. rifles for Hulbert and myself beside my .25 Remington and automatics, so we are going to do some hunting. Jack has an air rifle with which he expects to hunt kangaroo-rats and lions and I am going to get them each a pony.

. . . There is plenty of room for a golf course and a mighty sporty one too. Also expect to put in a swimming pool and tennis court.[16]

He described his problems wryly and humorously to Joseph Bray, while making it plain that nothing could lessen his enthusiasm for Tarzana:

My secretary and her husband threw up the sponge and departed hence for Illinois last week. I am now my own secretary, hog expert and goat impresario. Also both my goat herders quit

478

*ERB, Emma, and Hulbert
with .22 rifles, 1921.*

*Saturday, a coyote killed a kid yesterday, three other kids died,
I fired the ranch cook, it rained all over my freshly mown hay
and the starter on the Chandler won't work. Otherwise we are
having a heluva nice time. (I just glanced out the front window
to discover that the pole on the rake has broken and that two
men have stopped work to look at it, leaving a team and a
tractor idle.) But somehow I can't help liking it—I never loved
any place in my life as I do this and if anything happens that I
don't make a go of it I believe that it would about break my
heart.*[17]

It is interesting to note that in 1923 Burroughs read and
gave to his eldest son a remarkable book entitled *Mother Nature*
by William J. Long. Long expressed views about animals that
were some fifty years ahead of the current ecological movements.
He stressed love of all wild things which he felt have an inherent right to life and should be protected by man rather than
slaughtered for the sport. From that time on, Burroughs would
not permit hunters on his ranch. He even became a deputy
sheriff so he could more easily enforce his no-hunting rules.

While attempting to establish the Tarzana Ranch on a
paying basis, Ed was at the same time arranging with his Oak

479

ERB on patio at Tarzana Ranch, wearing a toupee that he finally threw away, May 31, 1922.

Park real estate agent for the sale of the two homes and a lot.[18] The ranch problems were far from being solved, and to Douglas Rothacker Ed had commented, ". . . God knows I have had enough trouble since I took it. . . . Everything seems to be conspiring to make it difficult for me. . . ."[19] However, he remained optimistic, especially about the success of his livestock project. This abrupt transformation to a gentleman farmer and pig and goat breeder, even if viewed as a temporary situation, appeared strange indeed; the mind and imagination that had created fantastic worlds in outer space was now involved in petty details of animal breeding:

. . . we now have over 250 kids and have only had four die which I think is a mighty good record . . . the goat is a mighty hardy animal. I have seen them born on a cold morning after a rain, on a cold, damp ground and in a few minutes they would be up wagging their tails and trying to nurse. If pigs are any-where near as hardy as these goats we ought to make a fortune in Berkshires. . . . just with the natural increase we could start with one sow and at the end of five years have a million pigs but inasmuch as we are going at it slowly, we intend to start with only five sows and at the end of five years God knows how many we will have.[20]

*ERB and sons with their Shetland ponies "Bud" and "Buster,"
about 1921.*

His practicality did not prevent him from responding to the
beauty of the ranch setting: ". . . as I sit in my office I am
looking out across green fields and a tree dotted valley to the
mountains ten miles away on the opposite side. The roses are in
bloom in a long winding border on either side of my driveway
down the hill to the county road, and in my orchard the fruit
trees are in full blossom. 250 Angora kids are kicking their heels
in the corral up the canyon while their mothers are out on the
grassy slopes in the mountains at the farthest end of the
ranch. . . ."[21]

The first signs of the Tarzana Ranch's potential seemed highly
encouraging. To Bray Ed wrote, "We started shearing yesterday
noon and the fleece from the first' hundred goats now commences
to look like real money, the first that I have seen with the exception of 34c which somebody paid for a cash meal at the
ranch house. . . ."[22] The fertility of the land was already
demonstrated: "My beans are up, baby limas; my corn is up,
Orange County Prolific; my apricots are heavy on the limbs; my
new alfalfa is also up, Hairy Peruvian. I thought some of drilling
in safety razors with it. My barley is nearly all out and the
binders have started on it. . . ."[23]

The ranch also provided the opportunity for Ed to return to
horseback riding—an activity he had loved ever since his school

ERB's series of fish ponds or water gardens; building at top left is chicken house; beyond to right is dairy barn and creamery, where Ed had cream separator and butter churn.

days in Chicago and at Michigan Military Academy. Before departing for California he had hoped to acquire a saddle horse; in August 1918 he had met Harry M. Rubey, the new president of the National Film Corporation, who was passing through Chicago on his way to Camp Johnston in Florida for army service. Rubey offered his horse King to Ed as a present and arrangements were made to ship the animal from Fort Collins, Colorado. Rubey stressed that King "is not what I consider a 'show' horse, but a perfect type of cavalry horse. . . ."[24] Although eager to receive the animal, Ed was unwilling to expose it to injury or "unnecessary discomfort" and insisted that if it could not be shipped without danger, the whole matter should be dropped. To Rubey he wrote:

. . . I certainly have had my heart set on him ever since you told me about him, as I have never owned a thoroughly broken horse . . . write me everything that will be of interest about him . . . I should also like to know just how I should handle him, especially in regard to the proper way to put him through his various gaits. If we succeed in getting him here, I am going to try to get Jimmy Quirk to run his picture in the Photo-Play magazine with a little story. . . .[25]

Ed's love of horses and enthusiasm for riding had been passed on to his family. On October 10, 1918, in receiving with delight the news that King had been shipped, he informed Rubey, "I have just bought a polo pony for my children and am looking forward with a great deal of pleasure to being able to ride with them. All three down to five year old Jack have been taking riding lessons and appear to take to horsemanship as a duck takes to water. . . ."

The anticipated joy in owning the saddle horse King was not to be realized; the bad news arrived a week later. King had disappeared, apparently stolen. Rubey later wrote, ". . . we have located him and will try very hard to have him shipped as soon as we can get possession of him. . . ."[26] Possibly because of the confusion of the war period, the horse was never sent to Tarzana.

By the following year riding had become an important part of the family life. The children had their own saddle ponies, and even Emma had taken up the sport. Ed offered his friend Robert Lay details of the activities: "Emma rode yesterday for the first time in the morning and again after supper at night, and did very well indeed. I managed by accident to get just the sort of a horse for her—a well-broken, gentle, easy-gaited mare and yet who has plenty of pep or rather, plenty of willingness to go. Emma's horse and mine would not win any blue ribbons at the New York horse show but they are very much what we want out here."[27]

Ed's happiness with the ranch, and his view that his whole life now seemed under a kind of Tarzan "spell," was expressed in his letter of May 8, 1919, to Bert Weston: ". . . We eat and sleep Tarzan. . . . The dog is named Tarzan, the place is Tarzana. . . ." But an unnamed man, mentioned in the same letter, appeared to have the mystic qualities of a soothsayer who was envisioning the shape of things to come: ". . . a guy bobbed up day before yesterday with the plan of a whole village he wished to plant in my front yard—school, city hall, banks, business houses, motion picture theater—and it was labelled City of Tarzana, which sounds like a steamboat."[28]

In the summer of 1919 Ed acquired a new secretary, John A. Shea, a man on whom Ed would depend and whose advice he would seek. Also in this summer the family group was augmented by the arrival of Ed's nephew, Studley Burroughs. The son of Harry and Ella, Studley, who had exhibited artistic talent from his earliest days, had been working in the field

ERB riding with western, or stock, saddle and bridle with curb and snaffle bit with four reins.

484

of commercial design and illustration. The visit to Tarzana resulted from tragic circumstances; Mary Becker, his wife of only two years, had died in childbirth on April 22, 1919. On the verge of a breakdown, Studley, leaving his infant daughter in the care of his parents, accepted Ed's invitation to stay temporarily at the Tarzana Ranch. Golfing was his favorite hobby, and at the ranch he aided Ed in laying out a nine-hole golf course; Studley also designed a special golf scorecard.[29] He spent less than a year at Tarzana. In March 1920 he received the news that his daughter Margaret Mary, only a year old, was seriously ill with spinal meningitis. His hasty return to Chicago was too late—the child had died.[30]

Studley, who in later years was to illustrate a number of the Burroughs novels, used his artistic skill to create an unusual ex libris (bookplate), devised especially for Ed's personal books. Designed in the period of 1916-20, the bookplate attracted a great deal of attention from Burroughs readers and collectors. The ex libris, quite large (4 inches high by 2¼ inches wide), was described by Studley Burroughs in a letter to Ed:

The central figure is Tarzan, embraced by one of his apes (Kala perhaps) and upholding the Planet Mars, which can be easily identified by its two moons, the Greater and the Lesser. (Not being a landscape artist I omitted the canals. They are the only things I think I have omitted.)

The pen crossed with the sword indicate what I believe to be your two chief interests at this date. The laurel wreath, of course, depicts a degree of fame.

In the crest below I have symbolized the four most pronounced epics of your career, starting with your days in the Cavalry, and following, in order, your life in the West, your return to the more civilized East, and lastly, your advent in the world of books, magazines, et al. (If anything of moment occurred before this, it was prior to our acquaintance.)

In the panel behind Tarzan may be found my conception of the characters in some of your other bully-good stories.[31]

Ed, who became a bookplate collector at a future period, was pleased to send copies of his own ex libris to those who had the same hobby. He was careful to interpret his bookplate and to provide details about the four objects contained in the crest: "The shield in the lower left hand corner represents what my nephew conceived to be four important epochs of my life—my interest in military affairs being symbolized by the cavalry boot and spur, the cow's skull representing my experience as a cowboy, the automobile wheel my interest in motoring, and the open volume my love of books."[32]

In the winter of 1918, concerned about the Bolshevik revolution in Russia, Ed considered using a fictional approach to alert the public to the menace of communism. It was his first demonstration of the intense dislike and fear of communism that he would display for many years. On December 4, in an inquiry to the Department of Justice, Ed spoke of "the Bolschevik movement . . . an organized effort to spread these doctrines throughout the world for the disruption of existing forms of government." He maintained that if the Bolsheviks were successful, the result would be an end to "all commercial and social progress" with the world being precipitated into "a period similar to that which followed the decadence of Greek and Roman civilization." He then explained the fiction he was planning:

I have in mind a novel of the future showing conditions one or two hundred years from now, presupposing a world-wide adoption of Bolshevikism. It is not my expectation to write anything that will revolutionize public opinion as my stories are primarily for entertainment, but if I could obtain information on the I.W.W. movement here and also Bolshevik literature which would permit me to write more intelligently on the aims and practices of these parties, it might be that my story would be of value in setting people to thinking of the results which must follow the continued dissemination of this type of propaganda.[33]

On December 6 a response came from a Mr. Clabaugh of the Department of Justice: ". . . Personally, I seriously question the advisability of confining an article, or series of articles, to the subject to which you refer, as it may do more harm than good. . . ." but Ed, a day later, irked by the rejection, offered a frosty reply: ". . . I doubt if my fiction would be taken seriously enough to do any harm and the only possible value it could have outside of entertainment might be to suggest a line of thought inimical to anarchistic tendencies."

Obviously, Clabaugh's negative attitude could have no effect in dissuading Ed from his project; his alarm over the events in Russia and the actions of the IWW's at home drove him to the task. In a sense, he felt that he was fulfilling a patriotic duty. The story, written April 30 to May 21, 1919, was titled "Under

ERB's ex-libris, designed by nephew Studley O. Burroughs, depicting main elements of ERB's interests and life work.

the Red Flag." Its record was a dismal one: during 1919-20 it received a string of rejections from various magazines including *Cosmopolitan, All-Story, Saturday Evening Post,* and *Red Book.* Differing reasons were given; Editor Harriman of *Red Book* referred to "the difficulty . . . of 'Under the Red Flag' . . . which goes far into the future in defining the reaction at that time from a present condition. Somehow, we feel we are serving the country best by allowing our anti-Bolshevik fiction to be reflective sharply of the present instant."[34] Ray Long, on the other hand, noted that the story sounded "too confoundedly impossible" and added, "It was not because of the writing so much as it was because of the subject. In spite of all we know about what Bolshevism does and has done, it seems incredible that anything of this sort could happen to America. . . . plausibility. . . . That's what it seemed to me to lack."[35]

From Bob Davis came another reason for rejection; he contended that the "chief difficulty with 'Under the Red Flag' was its appalling justification." His opinion was that people would benefit by the story, but that "the Pharasees would raise hell with any magazine that resorted to fiction designed to point out the obvious truths." Stirring up the populace, he explained, wasn't either good ethics or good business for magazines; this was the job of the daily press.[36] None of these reasons proved convincing to Ed. In fact, he believed that the editors were reluctant to reveal the truth and were offering subterfuges instead. It was almost as though there were a tacit conspiracy to prevent the publication of a story that was too controversial, too hot to handle. On September 24, 1919, he commented in exasperation to Joseph Bray, "I managed to get an expression from two well known editors and I find that it was not the fact that they didn't like the story but that they were afraid of the effect it would have on the public mind. Personally I think it is ridiculous to believe that a story showing the unpleasant consequences of Bolshevist rule would do any harm." He added, ". . . I intend to try and find somebody to publish it even if I have to publish it at my own expense, as I am personally sore that none of the magazines would take it for such a silly reason."[37]

The past dealings with William Parsons in the production of *Tarzan of the Apes* and the unauthorized second film *The Romance of Tarzan* had increased the caution and skepticism that Burroughs exhibited in responding to all proposals from producers. Yet, in this early period of the film industry, the producers who contacted him were mainly men operating on a shoestring, whose schemes were always the same: they hoped to acquire a Tarzan story, form a company, and then seek capital. Although aware of this procedure, Ed could do little but resign himself to it.

Beginning in May 1918 and continuing for several years, Ed found himself the middle man in a complicated series of film transactions that for manipulation and connivance made all past motion picture projects seem simple and straightforward. Under a barrage of letters from Pliny P. Craft of Monopol Pictures, New York, who was eager to produce *The Return of Tarzan,* Ed's resistance finally weakened. Nevertheless, he was super-cautious in clarifying every detail and requirement. On August 5, 1918, he stressed the existing situation, that two films had been made from *Tarzan of the Apes,* the second one ready for September release. Then he stipulated what the contract must contain: a clause confining production to *The Return of Tarzan* only; a financial arrangement similar to that made with Parsons —$50,000 worth of stock, five percent of the gross receipts and a $5,000 cash advance on royalties; and "some voice in the direction of the production." Other provisions, added on August 11, included a request that Ed be employed as co-director, that a maximum of about thirty percent be paid for distribution, and that if two pictures were to be made from *The Return of Tarzan,* the contract must so state, and "reasonable time limits" must be established for the second picture.

With all this agreed upon, and with his salary as assistant director set at $5,000, Ed signed the contract on September 21. Craft's new company was to be called the Apex Picture Corporation. His attempt to change this to Tarzan Pictures Corporation was firmly rejected by Burroughs who noted, ". . . this name is worth more to me than the picture rights to any of the Tarzan stories."[38]

Seemingly all problems had been anticipated; Ed had taken extreme care to avoid any of the difficulties he had encountered with Parsons. But trouble began at once. With the showing of *The Romance of Tarzan* in theaters, Craft dispatched a threatening letter to the First National Distributors claiming that this picture infringed upon the rights contained in his contract for *The Return of Tarzan.* Craft's claim was that the movie duplicated scenes found in this book. Parsons, upon notification of the supposed conflict, and apparently frightened, arranged for a payment of $3,000 to Craft. Ed's first awareness of the situation was when Parsons, incredibly, wrote to demand that this money be repaid to him.

With Ed now receiving angry demands and accusations from Craft—". . . how you became induced to authorize the release of the picture, [*The Romance of Tarzan*] under the circumstances, is more than I can understand," the quarrel became increasingly bitter. Inevitably, the lawyers entered the dispute, Harry G. Kosch of New York representing Craft, and Ed using his old firm of Mayer, Meyer, Austrian & Platt in Chicago. Craft's compromise suggestion, based upon his claim that *The Return of Tarzan,* because of Parsons' infringement on the plot, had lost most of its movie value, was that Ed should offer him a contract for the balance of the Tarzan stories.[39] On January 6, 1919, Ed proposed his own compromise which Craft reluctantly accepted. Ed wrote: "If you produce a successful Tarzan picture and otherwise fulfill the terms of our present agreement I agree not to dispose of the picture rights to subsequent Tarzan stories until you have had a reasonable opportunity to accept or reject them."

Concerning *The Beasts of Tarzan*, Craft's opinion was that the story could not be produced as a film, but that some of the incidents might be combined with scenes from *The Return of Tarzan* to make an additional movie. To this Ed did not agree. Surprisingly, however, he was amenable to the plan to discard the title *The Return of Tarzan*, and suggested, Tarzan of the Jungle would make a good title and could be used in connection with a subtitle stating that it was a picturization of *The Return of Tarzan*.[10]

At an earlier period (September 13, 1918) Elmo Lincoln, who had taken the role of Tarzan in both of the Parsons films, had written to urge Ed to join with him in forming a company to produce the remaining *Tarzan* stories. Ed rejected the proposal. Lincoln later became the subject of a discussion between Craft and Burroughs. On January 25, 1919, Craft wrote, "I have made tentative arrangements with T. Hayes Hunter to direct the first picture. . . . He made the *Border Legion* which he has just released through Goldwyn Pictures Corp. I wish you would see this picture and tell me what you think of Hunter as a director. . . . Also let me know if you think Eugene Strong, who plays the lead in 'The Border Legion' would make a good 'Tarzan.' He is handsome and a real actor, but is he big enough for the part? Will the public expect to see a man as big as Elmo Lincoln? Lincoln is now working in some serial picture at the coast. I don't think he is the right man anyway."

In response, on January 28, Burroughs explained how he envisioned Tarzan as a movie character:

In the matter of a man for Tarzan, it may help you some to know that Elmo Lincoln was . . . far from my conception of the character. . . . Tarzan was not beefy but was light and graceful and well muscled. The people who could see Tarzan of the Apes and the Blacksmith of Louvain as identical characters had just about as much conception of my story and of the character as one might expect after seeing some of the atrocious things they did to the picture and the story.

He presented an image of Tarzan that was clear and definite:

In the first place Tarzan must be young and handsome with an extremely masculine face and manner. Then he must be the epitome of grace. It may be difficult to get such a man but please do not try to get a giant or a man with over-developed muscles. It is true that in the stories I often speak of Tarzan as the "giant Ape-man" but that is because I am rather prone to use superlatives. My conception of him is a man a little over six feet tall and built more like a panther than an elephant. I can give you some facial types that will give you an idea of about what I conceive Tarzan to look like though of course it is impossible to explain an ideal. I should say that his face was more the type of Tom Meighan's or Tom Forman's but not like Wallace Reid. In other words, I conceive him of having a very strong masculine face and far from a pretty one.

Burroughs' opinion of Elmo Lincoln was more forcefully stated in a letter of March 27, 1922, to his brother Harry:

. . . I have told producers and directors of Tarzan pictures the very same thing that you mentioned in relation to Elmo Lincoln, in fact I have told Elmo himself upon numerous occasions that he was not my conception of Tarzan. . . .

In the letter Burroughs also commented discouragedly about the way his stories were adapted for the Tarzan movies:

The producers never read the stories, and it is only occasionally, I imagine, that the director reads them. In fact, in the making of Tarzan of the Apes, it was forbidden that anyone connected with it read the story, for fear it might influence their work and make it more difficult for the director. Little wonder then that such asinine methods produce such asinine results. As far as I know, no one connected with the making of a single Tarzan picture has had the remotest conception of either the story or the character, as I conceived it. Whatever beauty there was in the character of Tarzan or in the stories themselves, was not brought out, but the pictures paid well in box office receipts, and really that is all that counts.

He matched his criticism of Elmo Lincoln with an equally

disparaging opinion of the actress chosen to play Jane Porter: "Miss Markey is not the type at all. When the time comes if you have several girls in mind and care to do so, you might send me their pictures from which I could give you an idea of the type that really most nearly represents the character as I see it."[41]

Hoping that the dispute with Craft was now settled, Ed wrote to suggest that the Tarzana Ranch could provide an ideal location for a studio. He referred to a friend, Walter Beckwith, who owned "twenty-three of the finest lions you ever saw in your life"; Beckwith was willing to bring the pride of lions to Tarzana if Ed would furnish the cages. Ed explained, ". . . with very little expense we would have a corner on the most expensive part of wild animal production . . . we would have the best lions in the world and could make more or less of a specialty of wild animal stuff."[42]

Any illusion that Craft's grievances were forgotten or, for that matter, that Burroughs was satisfied with the progress of *The Return of Tarzan,* was abruptly dispelled. Burroughs, upon reading the scenario, complained irritably that it bore little resemblance to his story. As in the past, the reasons scenario writers made these drastic changes and deletions baffled him; this familiar practice, which he viewed as outright mutilation of an author's work, was followed because of purely selfish motives: ". . . the only explanation is that unless they do make changes there would be no reason for their employment at a high salary. . . . they have kidded some of you producers into believing that these changes are necessary. . . ."[43]

Unexpectedly, Craft abandoned all attempts at reconciliation, returned angrily to the supposed infringement of *The Romance of Tarzan,* demanded that Burroughs waive his salary of $5,000 as assistant director, and as further compensation, give him a contract for *The Son of Tarzan.*[44] Burroughs' response to Craft, then in Los Angeles, was curt: ". . . talk with my attorney, Mr. Oscar Lawler, for I have had about all the trouble and annoyance on account of motion picture producing that I care to have."[45]

From June 1919 on, the Burroughs-Craft relationship continued in an unbelievable sequence of bickerings, wild threats by Craft, and lawyers' communications. It was only fitting that in the midst of the confusion, Craft should perform the most astonishing action of all. On September 23 he notified Burroughs that he had assigned *The Return of Tarzan* to Numa Film Corporation, a New York outfit headed by Louis Weiss; the corporation was newly formed for the purpose of producing a *Tarzan* movie.[46] Burroughs' exasperation with Craft was further extended into a lesser area. In a moment of mistaken confidence he had given Craft the die which was used for making The Tribe of Tarzan medals. The indignant Burroughs discovered that Craft was freely distributing the medals to boys, contrary to the tribal rules that these medals must be earned. To Burroughs, the idealistic, high-minded purpose of the organization was important. About the boys, on June 9 he wrote to Craft, "They have to win a membership in the Tribe before they are entitled to a medal, and why I should have been so thoughtless as to let you have the die without explaining this to you, I do not know."[47] The value Burroughs placed upon the Tribe was more than matched by the devotion of its founder, Herman Newman of Staunton, Virginia. Upon returning from the war in France, Newman went to Oak Park to look for Burroughs, and not finding him there, traveled to California to Tarzana Ranch.[48]

The sudden death of William Parsons on September 28, 1919, ended the three-way squabble about the conflict between *The Romance of Tarzan* and the projected *Return of Tarzan*.[49] But this did nothing to change the altercation between Craft and Burroughs. Upon the precondition that he "satisfactorily" complete *The Return of Tarzan,* Craft had been given an option on *The Son of Tarzan* until July 1, 1919. With the failure to fulfill the terms, Ed sold *The Son of Tarzan* to The National Film Corporation. From then on Craft continued his harassing actions, dispatching a series of threats to both Burroughs and National Film, attempting to interfere with movie production, and trying to sell his "rights" to D. W. Griffith in Hollywood; his contact there was Elmo Lincoln.[50] Unsuccessful in this effort, he filed a lawsuit against Burroughs, and soon after publicized his plan to form the Tantor Picture Corporation, with its first production to be a fifteen-episode serial titled *The Adventures of Tarzan*. An announcement read, "The new serial . . . will contain new features of unusual interest, chief among these, the casting of Bull Montana as chief of the ape clan. Production will be on the coast."[51]

Craft's lawsuit prompted Ed to hire New York attorney Benjamin H. Stern (Stern & Rubens), but it shortly became apparent that Craft's daring had no limit. On March 10, 1921, *Wid's Daily,* a New York publication, broadcast a full-page ad announcing, in huge black print, "The Real Tarzan is Coming." The film was listed as "The Adventures of Tarzan," and at the bottom of the page, in equally bold type, appeared the amazing affront: "Tarzan Film Company." Traced to a small office in New York through the efforts of a detective, Craft was evasive, but it became evident that these were his latest harassing tactics; the records revealed that no company of this name had been organized.[52]

The legal preparations by Stern & Rubens for the forthcoming court trial brought further contention to the existing film disputes. On December 29, 1921, Ed reacted with anger and outrage to the bill for $1,000 sent him by the law firm. He wrote bluntly, "I think you have charged me a great deal too much and I am frank in saying that I cannot afford you. I hope it will develop that a mistake was made in this charge, which seems to me fully four times what it ought to be." In reply, Stern & Rubens insisted their charge was reasonable in view of the fact that Craft was suing for $100,000 and that the defense had involved considerable labor and time.[53] Unmollified, Ed noted, "I am no better off than I would have been had I not retained you"; he at once severed his connection with the firm.[54] Actually, Ed's dissatisfaction with Stern & Rubens may have developed during a long series of communications with Craft and his attorney. In a letter Stern & Rubens had hinted that Ed might settle for a few hundred dollars in order to save the trouble and expense of a New York trial. Ed had been adamant in stating that he would not pay Craft a cent.[55]

The legal affairs were now transferred to Clarence E. Pitts, with the New York law firm of Clark, Prentice & Roulstone, and through their intercession, Ruben & Stern's fee was settled for $500. From then on matters moved quickly. Notified on January 13, 1923, that the case had been placed on the calendar, and that he should plan to be in New York in February, Ed, on the sixteenth, asked for a postponement until spring: ". . . physician advises against my going before April or May." When his lawyers indicated that a doctor's affidavit would be needed, Ed, anxious to have the case ended, changed his mind, arriving in New York on February 18. The action was decidedly anti-climactic. On February 28 the case was dismissed "on merits." Thus the almost four years of charges, threats, and demands were finally halted.

Other film negotiations, while not as complex, followed a similar pattern of bickerings, extensions of time, production failures, and transferences of contracts. The assignment of *The Return of Tarzan* to Numa Pictures Corporation, headed by

Louis Weiss, with the attorney Harry Kosch as secretary, September 1919, brought no tangible result until the spring of 1920. On April 28 Weiss notified Burroughs that the world rights to the completed film had been sold to Goldwyn Distributing Corporation, with the agreement calling for a $100,000 advance and a percentage basis. Numa Pictures, previously granted the privilege of making a second film from *The Return of Tarzan,* now began dickering with Burroughs on this one. For the fifteen-episode serial the titles of "Adventures of Tarzan" and "Exploits of Tarzan" were suggested; Burroughs preferred the first title.[56]

The matter of a title for the full-length movie to be distributed by Goldwyn, and assumed to be *The Return of Tarzan,* became a subject of dispute. On June 15, 1920, Numa Pictures wired, "Exhibitors throughout Country under impression Return of Tarzan is re-issue. Upon consultation with Goldwyn executives have found it advisable to change title to Revenge of Tarzan. Wire immediately your approval or whether you have better suggestion." Burroughs' refusal was prompt: "Cannot approve change of title Return of Tarzan. If McClurg's estimate ten million (10,000,000) Tarzan book readers correct, it would be poor policy to ignore this advantage and the greater millions of newspapers and magazine Tarzan readers." In response, Numa Pictures stressed that the change was "for financial benefit of all concerned," explained that they wanted to attract both the movie public and the book public, and stated firmly, "Using title Revenge of Tarzan adapted from Edgar Rice Burroughs' famous book Return of Tarzan."[57]

Burroughs, equally adamant, wired back, on June 18, "Regret must insist title Return of Tarzan stand unchanged. My professional and financial interests demand this. Suggest you use title 'Return of Tarzan, a New Tarzan Story by Edgar Rice Burroughs, Author of Tarzan of the Apes.'" In the actions that followed, his objection to the new title was ignored. Although Numa Pictures had earlier taken a full-page ad in *The Moving Picture World* (December 6, 1919), extolling the new film *The Return of Tarzan,* a later ad informed the trade that "All posters, mats, cuts and other accessories have been changed to read The Revenge of Tarzan," and on July 20, 1920, the film was released under that title.

The Revenge of Tarzan, directed by Harry Revier, featured Gene Pollar, a brawny, 200-pound New York City fireman as Tarzan, and Karla Schramm as Jane. Other roles from the novel included D'Arnot, Franklin Coates; Clayton, Walter Miller; Paul-

ERB and children visiting set of The Son of Tarzan, *1920.*

vitch, Louis Stearns; and Countess de Coude, Estelle Taylor. Burroughs again experienced the discouragement of having the movie bear little resemblance to the story.

In dealings with The National Film Corporation through its president Harry M. Rubey, Ed, on September 6, 1919, had agreed to write the synopsis of a fifteen-episode serial based upon *The Son of Tarzan.* After the customary wrangling during which National Film cancelled its option to purchase four of the Burroughs books and decided to concentrate upon *The Son of Tarzan,* Rubey, on November 14, signed the agreement requiring completion of the film in one year. At the end of the year Rubey formed a financial partnership with distributor David P. Howells. Ed had been paid a total of $20,000, but in the arrangements that followed, the plan to have him write the scenario was apparently dropped. Upon reading the synopses of episodes in progress, Ed, as usual, protested the unwarranted changes and made specific suggestions which, also as usual, received little attention.

A further protest by Ed related to the failure to provide the personal publicity that had been promised. In viewing the "leader" for *The Son of Tarzan,* he was dubious about its publicity value, reminding Rubey, on June 14, 1920, of the paragraph in the contract which stated, ". . . the name 'Edgar Rice Burroughs' to appear as author, in letters as large as the letters of any other printed matter therein, and immediately beneath said name shall cause the words, 'Author of Tarzan of the Apes, A Princess of Mars, etc.' . . ." A week later, Ed, irritated, wrote again to protest the content and make-up of the two-page ad in *The Moving Picture World* of June 15. He objected both to the unauthorized statement that world rights to *The Son of Tarzan* were controlled by David P. Howells and also to the fact that, once more, his name was not appearing in print as the agreement stipulated. Howells quickly forwarded an apology and a promise to see that future publicity would provide the proper emphasis to the Burroughs name.

Produced in the west coast studios of National Film, with Revier once more directing, *The Son of Tarzan,* a fifteen-episode serial, was a long time in the making, not completed until January 1921. Publicity releases stressed that the film had been very costly because two sets of players were used, one to appear in a prologue which depicted important past events from Tarzan's life. His romance was portrayed, and the prologue contains a scene in which Tarzan and Jane, in England, are married by a minister. The story then continues with Tarzan's son, Korak, then assuming the main role. His part was taken by Kamuela C. Searle, a Hawaiian actor, and others in the cast included P. Dempsey Tabler, Tarzan; Karla Schramm, Jane; Eugene Burr, Paulvitch; Mae Giraci, Meriem as a girl; Manilla Martin, Meriem as a woman; and Gordon Griffith, who had played the young *Tarzan of the Apes* in the 1918 film, now cast in a brief role as ten-year-old Jack.

During the production of *The Son of Tarzan* the actors faced unusual dangers. Tabler and Burr received broken ribs when a rowboat capsized; Mae Giraci was bruised when attacked by an ape; Roy Somerville, who had adapted the story for the screen, had a narrow escape from death; and with the filming of the serial almost at end, an unfortunate accident led to a tragedy. Kamuela Searle, handled too roughly by the elephant that was carrying him, sustained injuries which resulted in his death.

Roy Somerville, script writer, and ERB on movie set of The Son of Tarzan, *1920.*

Ed, who was present often on the set while the movie was in production, found himself included in a special scene. In a letter of August 29, 1921, Enzo Archetti, a fan from New Jersey, commented on seeing Burroughs on a "wild horse," explaining, ". . . before they began the serial from where it left off the week before, it showed you on a wild, bucking broncho. I think you were 'breaking' it. Am I right?" On September 9 Ed responded:

You are quite wrong in assuming that I have a wild horse. As a matter of fact the director and cameraman played rather a mean trick on me. The Colonel is a very beautiful horse in action, but the cameraman turned the camera so slowly that when the picture is shown on the screen it makes the horse appear to be going up and down very rapidly like a rocking horse or a jumping jack. I tried to insist that they take it out of the picture and they promised to do so but failed to keep their promise. . . .

In the fall of 1920 Ed once more experienced the familiar experiences of working with a film company—this time Numa Pictures. The Weiss brothers, Louis and Adolph, were now in control, with attorney Harry Kosch still retained as treasurer. The maneuvers led to arrangements for Great Western Producing Company, a west coast organization, to produce the next scheduled movie—*The Adventures of Tarzan,* with Elmo Lincoln assigned the major role.[58] Publicity for the film, completed in August 1921, advertised it as "picturized" from the concluding chapters of *The Return of Tarzan.* With Robert F. Hill as director, the cast included Louise Lorraine, only sixteen years old, as Jane; Lillian Worth as Queen La of Opar; and Frank Whitson as the villainous Rokoff.

Probably within the period of 1920-22 Burroughs wrote a scenario titled "The Savage Breast"; it remained unsold, but two years later he forwarded it to his former secretary John Shea, then associated with William Sistrom at the Hollywood Studios. Sistrom was looking for inexpensive story material for film purposes. At that time, May 1924, Shea returned "The Savage Breast," and on the eighth Burroughs remarked:

You probably remember when I wrote it, and why, and realize as well as I that it is a hackneyed subject and none too well done at that, a fact which I knew Mr. Sistrom would realize as soon as he read it, but it was something that I could sell cheap, and that was what I figured you wanted for these four program pictures. . . .

On set of Adventures of Tarzan, *1921; left to right: Emma
Burroughs, Frank Merrill (who played the role of Tarzan in two later
pictures), Elmo Lincoln (who played Tarzan), ERB, and Louise
Lorraine (who played Jane).*

The scenario "The Savage Breast" has apparently disappeared,
and there is no information about its plot or characterization.

In March 1920 Ed's dealings with Curtis Brown Ltd.,
his British agent, brought a new offer, one to dramatize *Tarzan
of the Apes* for stage presentation in England. After correspondence with C. B. Fernald of Curtis Brown's London office, Ed,
on May 10, signed a contract with Arthur Gibbons for the production of *Tarzan.* Gibbons and Arthur Carlton were both involved in the enterprise, with Major Herbert Woodgate assigned
the task of adapting the novel for the stage. Ed accepted the
contract reluctantly, influenced by Curtis Brown's recommendation, and noted that it was against his "better judgment" since
he knew nothing about Gibbons or his plans. He also agreed,

with some hesitation, to allow the dramatist to use several incidents from *The Return of Tarzan*. The financial arrangements required a $1,000 payment and royalties of ten percent, but problems at once arose with Gibbons seeking a reduction in royalties in the event the play was presented at the Lyceum in London. This request Ed rejected.

The plans called for *Tarzan of the Apes* to be given a trial run in the provinces before the play was brought to London, and on October 4 it opened for a two-week stay at Brixton. Gibbons had ten weeks' bookings to follow at other suburban theaters. At the Brixton opening, as reported by Curtis Brown, the audience was highly enthusiastic: "The jungle scenes were effective and proved distinctly to the taste of the audience. The parts of Tarzan and Kala were both played extremely well, Kala being particularly good."

In the play, with its prologue and four acts, the background and early events of the novel were developed. Surprisingly, Tarzan, age ten, was played by a young girl—Gwen Evans. Actors took the ape roles, Leon Du Bois playing Kerchak, the bull ape, and Edward Sillward in the part of Kala, the she-ape. They both continued their roles when the prologue ended, and the major section of the play presented Ronald Adair as Tarzan and Ivy Carlton as Jane. Adair appeared to be well-chosen for the difficult enactment of a live "stage" Tarzan.

On December 14 Ed was notified that the tour of *Tarzan of the Apes* in England would end that week, but that one performance of the play had been scheduled for London on Boxing Day, the day following Christmas. However, arrangements for this performance fell through, and *Tarzan* was never staged in London. The limited success of the play did not discourage Gibbons from proposing a contract for the production of *The Son of Tarzan;* the financial terms were the same, and Ed, on February 4, 1921, cabled his agreement.

Meanwhile, confusing on-again, off-again notices concerning *Tarzan of the Apes* were being dispatched. The play continued irregularly until June and was then halted because of the "industrial unrest . . . strikes and restricted transport" which hampered business and theatrical activities in England. Gibbons and Carlton still had plans to produce the play in London in the fall of 1921. At that time *Tarzan* made its debut on the New York stage, opening September 1 at the Broadhurst Theater, Forty-fourth street and Broadway in New York. The advertised "Dramatic Version" presented by George Broadhurst was in four acts and ten episodes, with British authors Woodgate and Gibbons listed, and with staging by Mrs. Trimble Bradley. Members of the original British cast included Ronald Adair as Tarzan and Edward Sillward as Kala. Lady Greystoke was played by Alice Mosely, and Ethel Dwyer took the part of Jane. The play became more daring than the British version; Broadhurst had real lions on stage—two of them. Jim, the original Tarzan lion, and Beauty, the lioness, were noted as playing "silent but active parts."

The play, in its New York performance, found the public and critics unenthusiastic; its run was brief. To Bray, on September 20, Ed commented about the telegram he had received from George Broadhurst, which stated "the stage version of Tarzan of the Apes is a complete failure and that they are withdrawing it." Ed wrote:

From the newspaper criticisms which I received today I judge that there was no reflection upon the story and that it will do the books no harm. Most of the critics seem to think that the impossible has been attempted and I rather imagine they are right. However, it has been well received in England although it has never played in the West End of London. Broadhurst tells me that he believes he can send out a condensed version on the vaudeville circuit and personally I think it is better adapted to that than to the drama.

Astonishingly, for an author who had set high standards for a serious film production of *Tarzan,* Ed added, "My idea of a paying proposition for the stage based on Tarzan would be a real, honest-to-God Burlesque."

On October 19, in reporting that *Tarzan* was a failure in New York, the Curtis Brown office sent an evaluation:

From the accounts we have had of the production, it seems that it was an adequate one and the play was well cast, but in spite of that the play only ran a short time and all the returns have been sent to you. I am afraid there is little chance of the play going on the road as George Broadhurst feels that the production has shown it is not likely to appeal to American audiences. . . .

Ed's suggestion and apparent approval of an "honest-to-God Burlesque" was hardly an idea that the British producers would have endorsed. In an amusing 1921 sidelight in England, Gibbons and Carlton brought a court action against Dick Mortimer for his sketch, obviously a burlesque or parody of Tarzan, presented at the Victoria Palace in London. The sketch, titled "Warzan and his Apes," featured a cast of a man with a loin cloth, two actors dressed as apes, a pseudo-lion and a "property" baby. The jungle setting consisted of artificial trees and shrubbery. Certain scenes, copied from Tarzan, were done in "dumb show."

Lawton, the attorney for the defendant Dick Mortimer, maintained that the sketch had first been produced in Paris in 1914 and had been running in various music halls since then. Mortimer, an acrobatic gymnast for twenty years, had played the "Tarzan" role in the original Paris sketch. Unbelievably for a British trial, which is expected to be dignified and sedate, this trial, with Justice Avery presiding, was transformed into a burlesque more hilarious than the *Tarzan* sketch. The jokes of Lawton about Tarzan and apes brought rounds of laughter from the spectators, and Justice Avery appeared to enjoy the comic atmosphere. An example of this type of humor was displayed in the cross-examination of the actor who played the role of the she-ape. When the counsel for the plaintiff asked him if he had read the original story, Lawton interposed, "How could he read the manuscript if he is an ape?"

During discussions of the story, a number of references were made to "niggers," and it was revealed that in certain performances of the music hall sketch the "niggers" had been changed in color from black to red because of rumored dangers of race riots. Justice Avery, who had commented that a burlesque might be helpful to the *Tarzan* drama and might "improve the reputation of the original," finally made a decision, to nobody's surprise, in favor of the defendant with no order as to costs. His ruling was based mainly upon the evidence that the sketch had been playing in music halls for at least six years prior to the stage presentation.

In the same years, from 1919 on, legal problems based upon Ed's relationship with William G. Chapman and his International Press Bureau provided additional complications. Chapman had handled some Burroughs newspaper syndications and had also been involved in the submission of *Tarzan of the Apes* to McClurg for publication. The book had been sold entirely through Ed's efforts and through his dealings with Joseph Bray. However, because Chapman had been consulted, Ed agreed to pay him commissions on the royalties of *Tarzan of the Apes* books sold in the United States. Now, Chapmain claimed he was entitled to the newly opened foreign rights; to Bray he had insisted that all rights belonged to him and that all arrangements should be handled through him. On May 12, 1919, Bray commented to Ed about Chapman's limited assistance in the past: "It seems to me that he has done pretty well out of 'Tarzan of the Apes.' He has made considerably over one thousand dollars for bringing the manuscript here one morning which we had already practically expressed our willingness to publish."

Ed, noting that he was already paying commissions to Curtis Brown Ltd. on all foreign sales and to McClurg for British sales, refused to pay a further commission to Chapman. There was confusion as to whether Chapman had actually been promised or given some commissions by McClurg's before December 1920. The quarrel inevitably wound up in the hands of lawyers, with Mayer, Meyer, Austrian & Platt defending Burroughs, and Beach & Beach representing Chapman. During years of claims and counterclaims nothing was resolved. Ed, never one to yield or compromise when a principle was involved, refused to settle for a sum of $1800. The trial was finally set for June 1, 1926, in Chicago. Reluctant to appear, Burroughs wrote gloomily to Cary Meyer, "In the first place, I am an extremely poor witness. My memory is very faulty, and I have been in an extremely nervous condition for so long that I am inclined to be rather excitable, so that I make as much of a botch as a witness as I do a dinner speaker, which I can assure you is some botch."[59]

Resigned to the trial, Ed arrived in Chicago on May 29. He had indicated that he might consider a settlement if Chapman relinquished past and future rights to all *Tarzan* enterprises, including drama, films, and newspapers. This was agreed to, and since compromise was inevitable, Chapman's claims were satisfied through a moderate payment, with the trial ended in its preliminary stages.

A life crowded with business activities—moving his family to California, running the ranch at Tarzana, raising livestock, negotiating with movie producers, and facing legal entanglements —still could not prevent Burroughs from working on new stories. In May 1918, while still in Oak Park, with the war almost ended, he conceived of a Tarzan story based upon the campaign against the Germans in Africa. The influence of anti-German propaganda upon him was strong; his view of German behavior as subhuman and his belief in the atrocity reports were unchanged. With the story in mind he sought information from Bray about published works describing the war in Africa, and at the same time he made contemptuous reference to the Germans' colonial record.

On May 29 Bray replied that he could find only one book,

Marching on Tanga, which he was sending, and noted that official accounts of the British government might be available. Concerning the African hostilities, Bray noted, ". . . it would be rather difficult to make much of the campaign, for the Germans were outnumbered I think in every engagement and I do not know of any dramatic happenings. Should you write such a story it seems to me I would use the war merely as a background, and not make too much of it." Bray revealed his calm objectivity in countering Ed's low opinion of the Germans: "My impression is that, except for that excessive veneration for the Fatherland which seems to obsess most Germans, the German colonies in Africa have a pretty good record. Their neighbors did not like them because a German colony simply means the transporting of a bit of Germany to another land. . . ."

Ed, not at all persuaded, disagreed about the "pretty good record" of the Germans and wrote, with some attempt at humor:

> . . . *although I know nothing about the Germans in Africa, I have learned enough about the Germans in the last four years to know that there aint no such thing as a good German record. Having reveled in hate for the last four years, I should dislike to give up the pleasure derived therefrom by thinking any good thoughts whatever about Germans. Therefore if I write this story, I shall put the wickedest kind of Germans into it and let Tarzan chew their hearts out.*[60]

As future events would demonstrate, Ed made a mistake in not adopting Bray's more moderate attitude toward the Germans.

Influenced by the success of the *Tarzan* short stories he had sold to *Red Book,* and the good prices he had obtained, Ed decided to produce the African war stories in a similar sequence. On October 7, 1918, Ray Long tentatively agreed to a series of twelve Tarzan stories, with payment of $450 each for the first six and $500 each for the rest. The story total was later reduced to ten, and at a conference Long suggested that the war background be eliminated. Ed was reluctant to make the change to ten stories; his goal of about 100,000 words was of course based upon plans for a future novel. Nevertheless, he agreed to the reduction, while refusing to accede to the request for a different setting. On October 18 he wrote to Long, ". . . sending you the first of the Tarzan and the Huns stories." He completed five in 1918, and by January 1919 before leaving for California, had sent six stories to *Red Book* Magazine. These appeared serially in *Red Book* in the issues of March to August 1919. The goal of ten stories was never attained. The seventh story, finished at Tarzana Ranch on September 10, 1919, titled "Tarzan and the Valley of Luna," was rejected by *Red Book* and *Cosmopolitan* and wound up in the pages of *All-Story,* appearing serially in the five weekly issues of March 20 through April 17, 1920. All seven of the stories were combined as the book "Tarzan the Untamed," published by McClurg on April 30, 1920.[61]

In the first story, "An Eye for an Eye," Ed disconcerted his readers by creating the apparent murder of Jane by the sadistic German officer Hauptman Fritz Schneider. The scene at the Greystokes' African estate is one of death and destruction, with burned buildings and slaughtered blacks. Here Tarzan recognizes the body of his beloved Jane with the familiar rings still on her fingers. Ed's plan had actually been to have Jane killed, but protests from Bray and Long, and particularly from his wife Emma, forced him to change his mind. To Bert Weston, on May 10, 1920, he wrote:

. . . I left Jane dead up to the last gasp and then my publisher and the magazine editor rose up on their hind legs and roared. They said the public would not stand for it as I was having Tarzan fall in love with Bertha, so I had to resurrect the dear lady. After seeing Enid Markey take the part of Jane in the first Tarzan picture I was very glad to kill her.

It appeared that Ed followed Bray's suggestion on sparing Jane; Bray had urged, "Have her apparently dead if you want to and let Tarzan think that she is dead; however, bring her back in the last chapter and have Tarzan go home and find her in the old place. . . ."[62] In response to Ed's query about the fate of Jane, Bob Davis wired, "Think Bray right" and then wrote, "I think it a good idea to let Mrs. Tarzan survive"; he joked about Ed's creation of the ape-man: "You unchained this damned monkey in a thoughtless moment and now the organ-grinding-son-of-a-gun climbs in the window and chews the rag on the foot-board. When you die and go to hell a delegation of pithecanthropus erectus will greet you at the gate and pick the cooties from your low receding brow."[63]

In *Tarzan the Untamed,* from the very beginning, Burroughs reveals his detestation of the Germans and their "Kultur" as he describes the "cruel wounds and bruises" upon the bodies of the helpless native porters. After the supposed death of Jane, Tarzan embarks upon a spree of revenge against the Germans; imprisoning a lion in a narrow gulch, he confines a German major in the same spot, where he will be devoured by the starved beast. He also accomplishes the feat of forcing a huge lion into the German trenches, and as the trapped soldiers fight madly to escape, "Numa, a terrific incarnation of ferocity and ravenous hunger," leaps upon them, "rending with talons and fangs." Later, Tarzan kills both the men he blames for his wife's death—Underlieutenant von Goss and Hauptman Schneider. The remainder of the novel then departs from the anti-German revenge theme and presents typical Burroughs devices—encounters with hostile blacks and the discovery of a walled city peopled by maniacs whose main deity is the parrot. A romance develops between British Lieutenant Smith-Oldwick and Bertha Kircher, whom Tarzan is forced to protect, although he believes her to be a German spy.

In "The Black Flyer," published in *Red Book,* August 1919, Ed had contrived a scene in which the savage Usanga is taught to fly an aeroplane by Smith-Oldwick. This scene brought a severely critical letter from First Lieutenant Karl de V. Fastenau, stationed with the Air Forces at Wilbur Wright Depot in Dayton, Ohio. On July 31 Fastenau remarked about the "absolute absurdity of Tarzan's latest 'stunt,' " and wrote:

Let me say that I am myself a pilot with some two years experience so am fairly well qualified to criticize this last story from that viewpoint. How can you attempt to foist upon a reading public such ludicrously absurd "stuff" as, for instance, having an absolutely ignorant savage from an African jungle take off a plane after two days of "instruction" (assuming that such an aborigine were capable of receiving it), flying the plane while a man was swaying back and forth on the end of a rope attached to it, having the girl pilot the machine (again assuming that the feat of changing from the rear seat to the front seat while the poor savage was still flying the machine were at all possible), and then to cap it all to have them make a landing and "as it struck among them and mowed through them, a veritable juggernaut of destruction" still have the machine in perfect condition . . . so that the other two characters could fly off.

Fastenau implored, "For God's sake, man, have a heart. It is all so ridiculous that it is really amusing. . . . Your practical knowledge of airplanes and flying is a little less than nil. Stick to your jungle stuff of which you seem to really know but for 'the love of Mike' if you must spring anything so clearly out of your line go out and get a little rudimentary information on the subject first." Fastenau commented, "You are 'getting by' with quite a lot as it is, don't you think?" He added, "I suppose you really are put to it grinding out a new Tarzan story every month so that you have to fill up with such stuff as that referred to for want of new material." The brief reply of August 9, sent by secretary John Shea, offered thanks to Fastenau and an assurance that Burroughs "always welcomes constructive criticism."

Another of the *Tarzan* short stories, "The Golden Locket," appearing in *Red Book,* May 1919, brought a request from William R. Kane, of *The Editor,* for an account of the genesis and development of the story. Kane, on April 25, explained his need for information that would inspire other writers, and in replying to him, rather than focusing upon "The Golden Locket," Burroughs chose to offer general suggestions about writing. He spoke of two methods he had tried, the first one based upon a "very broad and general plot" around which he extemporized, letting "one situation suggest the next." He stated, "I did not know what my characters were going to do or where the plot was heading in the next paragraph; as I was writing merely to entertain I sought to put action or the suggestion of future action into each paragraph."

The second method, in which he plotted his stories more carefully, involved a chart "covering the principal situation and action in each chapter." However, he found the chart difficult to follow, and his writing "became tedious labor" by comparison with his former method. As a result, he returned to the old plan and used it in most of his stories. Interestingly, Burroughs maintained that this system would not work if the story depended upon an "intricate" plot; he believed that in his writing, the action was of most importance and the plot was "merely . . . a simple clothes-horse upon which to hang the action." A consideration of the intricacies of some of his stories, not necessarily in plot, but especially in the lengthy gallery of characters, the complex details of equipment, and the various customs and backgrounds, indicates that this evaluation of his stories as mere improvised sequences of actions is far too limited. Both plot and content could be intricate—for example, in the Martian works, where on occasion the stories were unified around a central theme, and the fact that Burroughs could produce these complicated plots from a general idea, with very little outlining or planning, is quite remarkable.

For the Kane article, Burroughs' advice to young writers related first to their attitude; they were not to take themselves or their work "seriously." He stressed that each writer had his own

Illustrations by J. Allen St. John, ERB's favorite illustrator.

method of expressing himself—his style. Here Burroughs revealed his own distrust of style, perhaps because of the criticisms of his works as being superficial or nonliterary and his suspicions that style was associated with lofty literary creations, often written for a select audience:

If you take yourself and your work too seriously you will devote too much effort to mastering a style which you believe will insure your success. Forget style while you are writing. Write in the way that interests you most, tell the stories that you are interested in and if you cannot succeed in this way it is because nature never intended you for a writer.

Through his own experiences he viewed the best writer as the natural or untrained one. He rejected the concept of writing as a craft that required an apprenticeship period, like any other profession, a period in which the writer would develop through careful study, practice, and analysis of other authors' stories. This, Burroughs, a natural storyteller, had never done. A conflict of goals was also involved; he could conceive only of writing to entertain. The subtler and more refined uses of language—those that he might regard as a kind of stylistic pretense—were of course integral to the story's aims and the demands it made upon the reader. If the challenge were intellectual and the goals included a psychological probing of the characters or a perception of social issues, the language and style of the story were not separable from its content. These goals, often associated with realistic or "literary" stories, were beyond Burroughs' scope.

The years from 1918 on brought various events and interests. During August 1918 Ed assigned an option to Red Book Corporation (Story-Book Press) for the motion picture rights to "The Oakdale Affair," receiving $1,000 in payment. The movie, produced a year later by the World Film Company, was a five-reeler starring Evelyn Greeley. In another area, the popularity of *Tarzan* led to a humorous eulogy of the ape-man in a poem in "The Periscope," a column by Keith Preston:

Heroes of Fiction

How many thousand readers greet
Tarzan, half ape, but incomplete.
And wait, with interest never stale,
For sequels to complete his tail!
If sales a trusty index be,
Of vogue and popularity—

510

A fact you simply can't escape—
The apex goes to this ex-ape.[64]

In correspondence with Paul R. Reynolds, a New York agent who sought to handle his stories, Ed stressed his opinions about illustrators, writing, "There is one man who has absorbed the spirit of the Tarzan stories and who visualizes the characters and scenes almost precisely as I visualize them when I wrote the stories. I refer to Mr. J. Allen St. John of Chicago. . . ." At the same time he remarked, "I have been very much disappointed with the illustrations in the *Red Book* series. . . ." The artist, Charles Livingston Bull, had drawn Tarzan with a full beard; Ed spoke of this as "entirely ruining the character. . . ."[65]

On occasion he did not hesitate to express disapproval of some aspects of St. John's work. To Bray, who on August 21, 1919, sent him a postal card proof of *The Warlord of Mars,* Ed commented:

I like everything except the man's face and I suppose if you are going to use this for the jacket of the book it's too late to change it, though I hope not. It is not a fighting face, but more the face of a dreamer. . . . His eyebrows are arched too much for one thing and his mouth is not strong enough, nor am I stuck on the dimple in his chin.

Interesting to note, Burroughs' own knowledge of drawing enabled him to pinpoint the features—the eyebrows, mouth, and chin—that had created the objectionable "dreamer" or non-masculine effect. He added:

I think I can make these criticisms safely for it is the first adverse criticism I have ever had to make of any of St. John's work which, as you know, has always more than satisfied me. The girl is a pippin, although she has too many clothes on for the part. You will recall that Dejah was naked except for the harness. However, I suppose for the sake of the public morality you had to robe her. . . .

Bray agreed with Ed that the man in the illustration, John Carter, did not look like a fighter; he remarked, "Unfortunately, these artists are about the craziest loons the world contains at present. With a few exceptions they are all interested in making pictures rather than illustrating a story. . . . I have an awful time in impressing upon him (St. John) that the illustration on the paper jacket of a book is an advertisement and not a picture for the walls of an art dealer." In Bray's opinion, Frank Schoonover would have done a better job.[66]

Upon returning with his family to Tarzana, after a motor trip through Yosemite to San Francisco, Ed was disappointed to hear of St. John's refusal to change Carter's face; the picture, Ed believed, might harm the book sales. Nevertheless, St. John continued to be his favorite illustrator. On May 18, 1920, Ed wrote to compliment him on his drawings in the *Tarzan* books: ". . . If I could do the sort of work you do I would not change a line in any of the drawings. I think your work for Tarzan The Untamed is the finest I have ever seen in any book. Each picture reflects the thought and interest and labor that were expended upon it. . . ."

With the completion of two stories in September and October 1919, "Tarzan and the Valley of Luna" and "The Efficiency Expert," Burroughs continued his dealings with Munsey and Bob Davis. On October 14, in sending "Tarzan and the Valley of Luna" to the editor, he inquired about the readers' attitudes toward Indian stories and explained an idea he had in mind: "I believe I could make another character similar to Tarzan using a young Apache warrior. There never was a more warlike people. They fought every human from Kansas to Mexico; they could travel on foot all day with mounted men and be fresh at night; their senses were as acute as those of wild beasts; physically they were perfect and many of them were handsome even by our standards. . . ." He eulogized the Apaches, noting that before their wars with the white men, they had committed no atrocities; he considered them to be the "he-race of the Western Hemisphere" and thought he should write about them "before their power and glory waned."[67]

In the same period, responding to a letter from *The American Boy*, Ed indicated he would like to write juvenile stories and mentioned his custom of telling bedtime stories to his own children; these he kept humorous, noting, ". . . it was unwise to send them to bed with their heads full of raging lions and sudden death." He brought up an idea of "writing a series of stories around an Apache Indian boy during a period before the Indian country had been encroached upon by the whites," and explained, "I think I could make of the boy almost as interesting a character as Tarzan, because I have lived for a while among the Apaches . . . and found . . . great abundance of material in their exploits. . . ."[68]

"The Efficiency Expert," written between September 22 and

October 22, 1919, was a 50,000-word story centered about the adventures of Jimmy Torrance in the business and social world of Chicago. In creating Torrance, Burroughs obviously drew upon his own experiences, the years of erratic business ventures, the shifting occupations, and the periods of poverty and unemployment. Torrance in rapid succession becomes a clerk in a hosiery department, a sparring partner for a well-known fighter, a waiter in a cabaret, a milkwagon driver and finally an "efficiency expert." In the last-named role Torrance, who without any previous experience or training is hired to improve the operations of the International Machine Company, duplicates a period in Burroughs' past when, with a combination of effrontery and desperation, he took the position of "expert accountant" for a Chicago firm.

Torrance's success in "efficiently" straightening out the machine company is, in many respects, a dramatic portrayal of Burroughs' own efficiency in the business world, first in his job as a department head for Sears, Roebuck, and then as an adviser for Shaw's System Bureau—where some dubious "efficiency" was demonstrated. The dependence Torrance places upon the small book "How to Get More out of Your Factory," and his amusing glibness in reciting nonsensical jargon from the book, is Burroughs' way of ridiculing the impractical sales books he had read and the slick salesmanship courses he had written.

The autobiographical elements in "The Efficiency Expert" are also evident in the creation of Torrance as a college graduate with a poor educational record, who had concentrated mainly on football, baseball, and boxing. The ultimatum by the college president that he should either start studying or leave school brings to mind Burroughs' expulsion from Phillips Academy and his later problems at Michigan Military Academy. In "The Efficiency Expert" Burroughs disparages the college diploma as a piece of paper of no practical use, or even as a detriment in the business world. Jimmy Torrance discovers, in the story, "that rather than being an aid to his securing employment, his college education was a drawback, several men telling him bluntly that they had no vacancies for rah-rah boys." This was perhaps a defensive reaction resulting from a sensitivity about his own failure to attend college. He may also be flaunting, with an understandable satisfaction, the remarkable success he had made despite his limited education. In a way he *is* Jimmy Torrance; the father of the fictional Jimmy accepts his immature behavior with a resigned amusement—"Well, son. . . it is what I expected"—while, in a comparable response, Ed's father showed disappointment at his son's actions, but also became resigned, making plain his belief that his son would never amount to anything. In returning to this past situation, Ed, as Jimmy Torrance, is redeeming himself, proving that through simple practicality and other qualities superior to education, he had risen to meet his father's expectations.

Sold to *All-Story* on November 17, 1919, "The Efficiency Expert" appeared as a four-part serial in October 1921.

In April 1919, Ed once more launched plans to form his own company. He mentioned his project at the same time in letters to Joseph Bray, Bob Davis, Eric Schuler of the Authors' League, and Ray Long of *Cosmopolitan*. If a production company were formed, the Tarzana Ranch would provide an ideal location for a studio. To Bray, Ed described the existence of a small canyon that was "almost a natural amphitheater," and spoke of his two-part plan to "make a specialty of wild animal productions" and to "attract writers of repute whose stuff is now unavailable." He referred to his friend Walter Beckwith again and his big lion Jimmy "who pulls some of the most hair-raising stuff you ever saw." The idea was to interest a group of well-known authors in joining the company. "I have been jipped, insulted and robbed by motion picture producers. . . ." Ed wrote to Davis, insisting that authors must band together to get a "square deal."

Schuler, in commenting on the plan to form a company that would preserve authors' rights and the integrity of their works, referred to Rex Beach, the president of The Authors' League, who had achieved some success in the motion picture field. Beach's first advice was not to have an "authors only" company, but to include business and technical experts. Ed had written to an old family friend, Judge Adelor J. Petit, about the project; Petit, in the past, had attempted to interest some of his associates in financing the production of *Tarzan of the Apes*. Reminding Petit of the money-making opportunity he had missed, Ed suggested that the judge find backers for this new venture. However, Petit, recovering from a serious illness, explained that he was unable to offer any active aid to Ed. He took the occasion to resurrect the past, and while remarking about Burroughs' fantastic stories, noted jokingly, ". . . I am very much disappointed to think that you have not written the story we talked about some years ago in which you were to weave some romantic tale in which the old Phoenix Distillery would play a part. I think we decided we would have the hero rescue his sweetheart from the old chimney. . . ."[69]

Ed determinedly pursued his correspondence with various individuals and companies from 1920 to 1924, including contacts with the First National Exhibitors' Circuit and the W. W. Hodkinson Corporation. He had abandoned his plan to form a company of authors and sought only to find definite outlets for the distribution of the films based upon his own stories that he hoped to produce. However, because of financial difficulties and other problems the project floundered. More years were to pass before a Burroughs production company finally went into operation.

CHAPTER 16

TARZANA— FAMILY, BUSINESS, CREATIVITY

To the busy and happy days at Tarzana Ranch, the invigorating days of outdoor living, came a somber touch. On April 5, 1920, Mary Evaline Burroughs died. She had been staying at Tarzana for a month prior to her death, and for a time had been under the treatment of a Christian Science practitioner. As her condition worsened, Mary Evaline asked that she be examined by Ed's physician, Dr. Egerton Crispin. The doctor found that her heart was badly affected and, in addition, discovered a tumorous growth on her kidney. Her death, at age seventy-nine, came shortly afterward. The Burroughs family had shown a preference for cremation, and this practice was to be followed with Ed's mother. The first plan had been to scatter her ashes, but it was decided to place them in a receptacle at the Los Angeles Crematory.[1]

Other family matters during these years included attempts to sell the old Phoenix Distillery property in Chicago. The search for a buyer was being handled by Adelor Petit, with contacts being maintained by Ed's two brothers, Harry, now employed by the National Life Insurance Company in Chicago, and Coleman, residing nearby in Wilmette, Illinois. On April 17, 1920, as a sale failed to materialize, Ed commented gloomily to Harry, ". . . I don't care very much one way or another as the distillery property has always been a hoodoo. It helped to kill Father and I am inclined to think it also helped to kill Mother. . . ." The sales efforts dragged on until 1923 when, in January, Petit succeeded in selling the property for $88,000.

Completed ballroom-garage building, August 12, 1921; Hulbert and Jack in right foreground.

ERB's mother, Mrs. George Tyler Burroughs, at Tarzana Ranch, about March 15, 1920.

At Tarzana the family life exhibited the typical activities and concerns. Joan and Hulbert for a time attended the only elementary school in the area, located about three and one-half miles from the ranch in Marion, a village named after General Otis's daughter; its name was later changed to Reseda. In this early schooling period Ed also created a classroom at the ranch, using the quarters above the garage; there, for several years, the children were instructed by tutors. Ed coached Jack in various school subjects, with emphasis upon spelling and arithmetic, and as the two worked in the study Ed would interrupt his writing to check his son's answers. For a while Joan and Hulbert were given piano lessons by John Shea, the Burroughs' secretary.

Ed's and Emma's method of raising the children appeared on the surface to be one of over-protection, of reluctance to expose them to the rough-and-tumble of ordinary life. However, Ed and Emma were strongly influenced by a deep fear of serious illness. Ed had lost two infant brothers. He himself had been frail as a child. Emma's only brother, Alvin, Jr., had died of appendicitis in his teens. Their son, Jack, nearly died of diphtheria shortly after coming to Los Angeles in 1919. Thus, rightly or wrongly, Ed's and Emma's concern was fear that in the larger public schools their children would run a greater risk of exposure to disease. And there were no wonder drugs at that time. Ironically, despite these precautions, both Hulbert and Jack apparently contracted mild cases of polio about 1921, but these were not diagnosed as such until years later.

Joan, age twelve, in August 1920 entered the Ramona Convent in West Alhambra, California, not for reasons of religion but to join a friend who was attending there. At the same time, Hulbert and Jack were enrolled in the Page Military Academy. Before the Christmas holidays Joan was withdrawn from the convent; Ed noted in a letter that, because of her "extreme nervous condition" and "physical frailty," she would not return. Her education was continued at the Hollywood School for Girls; on January 4, 1921, Ed reported to Harry that Joan was delighted with the school and that the atmosphere there was much more pleasant than at the convent.[2]

Ed's first approval of the Academy with its military organization underwent rapid change. Jack, age seven, a sensitive and timid child, was unhappy in the disciplined environment. He was soon removed, and Ed, perplexed as to what procedure to follow, commented:

I suppose we are bringing them up all wrong and that they will go to the damnation bow-wows because we don't beat them with sticks and make them go to the schools where they are unhappy, but I have an idea that if a child doesn't get a great deal of happiness during its childhood it never will get it, and they are certainly entitled to all that Nature allows.[3]

He noted his sons' complaints that the boys at the academy were "a bunch of little roughnecks," placed there because of discipline problems at home. While concerned that his sons might be "effeminate," he was not inclined to believe so, explaining that the boys at the military academy were without adequate supervision and did not know how to play, "their idea of a good time being in running around and pushing each other down and fighting." Hulbert, age eleven, would finish out the year at the academy; Ed described his oldest son as possessing "a more phlegmatic temperament" which allowed him to adjust to the school circumstances.[4]

Ed and Emma soon recognized the need for alterations and additions to the old Otis residence to suit their life-style. The heating facilities of the house were inadequate for a family of five. Ed contracted for the installation of a central steam heating system which necessitated extensive tunneling beneath the house to bring heat to each room.

The most ambitious project was a building to be constructed

ERB's two new Packards—a sedan and a sports roadster—and a Hudson roadster, with consecutively numbered license plates; bumper on Packard at left includes chrome-plated semicurved ends that could be moved to trip front wheels.

about one hundred feet west of the main house. This new addition comprised a three-car garage on the ground level and a second story containing rooms for two servants, a photographic darkroom, a workshop, and a study which later was used as a schoolroom where the children were tutored. Later, Ed used it for his writing.

The lowest level of this three-storied building was a combination ballroom and movie theater with a small balcony at one end that served as a projection booth. This large playroom became the center of much weekend social activity. Because of the prohibitive distance to the nearest motion picture houses in those years, Ed brought the movies to his own little theater. Every Friday evening Burroughs and his Tarzana Ranch theater played friendly host not only to his own family and friends but to neighbors of the area. Burroughs was both host and projectionist, screening the popular comedies and features of the day. He particularly enjoyed Charlie Chaplin, Buster Keaton, and Douglas Fairbanks. Following the production of *The Son of Tarzan* as a serial, he personally edited and cut the 15 episodes to a feature length picture in this ballroom-theater. Jack Burroughs recalls the many lines of string in the tiny projection room on which Ed hung the labeled film clips ready for splicing. (Ironically, it was this very Tarzan film, printed on hazardous nitrate base, that spontaneously ignited 38 years later and nearly destroyed the Burroughs office building.)

ERB's secretary, John A. Shea.

In that same year, 1920, Burroughs decided to install a swimming pool adjacent to the house. He designed the pool and personally supervised the construction. Recalls Hulbert Burroughs:

In the early 1920's there were no swimming pool contractors in the Valley. My Dad simply determined what size he wanted and instructed a crew of his ranch employees to start digging. Most of the excavation was done with a team of horses and a Fresno scraper with final digging and shaping a pick and shovel operation. It was before the days of Gunite, so wooden forms were built and the cement poured from a wheelbarrow. No filtering equipment was then available so the plan was to periodically gravity-drain the water, clean the pool, and refill.

The pool was a great success as far as we kids and our friends were concerned. We all learned to swim well and it became the natural focal point for many parties for family and friends. However, compared to modern pools with crystal clear filtered water, ours was a mess. No one today would think of swimming in such murky water. Between drainings, the walls and bottom of the pool became green and slippery with algae. Despite the use of copper sulphate, we could never see the bottom. During the mating season, innumerable toads used the pool as a breeding ground. Frequently, luckless rabbits, gophers, and ground squirrels drowned in the dark waters at night. We all should have contracted horrible diseases, but we managed to survive. My Dad had the ridiculous notion that arising early on a cold winter morning for a dip in the pool would, in some mysterious way, prove beneficial. We would line up at the deep end of the pool, Jack and I shivering and trying to muster the nerve for the ordeal. With the exclamation "He who hesitates is lost!" Ed would plunge in, with Jack and I reluctantly following, flailing over those 50 feet of icy waters for dear life.

By the fall of 1921 all of the children had been withdrawn from school; Jack had temporarily been enrolled in the Hollywood School for Girls. Arrangements were now made to have them tutored at home. Thus, in handling his own children Ed had shown an indecisiveness and an obvious tendency to overprotect them. His actions, in many respects, were the result of *his* conditioning; certainly, as the youngest of four brothers, raised by a father at times stern and domineering, and on other occasions overindulgent, Ed's problems with his own children were clearly predictable.

For Christmas of 1920 Hulbert and Jack received unusual presents from Harry Rubey of the National Film Corporation. They were each given a lion cub, and Joan was presented with two monkeys, described by Ed in one caustic phrase "as tractable as a pair of rattlesnakes. . . ." About the lions, Ed, on December 27 supplied details to his brother George:

They are not very big lions although each of them is capable of devouring three pounds of raw meat a day and tearing it from the bone in a truly lion-like fashion. The children go in the cage and play with them . . . They were brought up with a little female puppy who lives with them in the cage and they are a never ending source of amusement to the children. The monkeys are vicious things and as far as I can see are utterly useless.

Not exactly pleased at the menagerie set up behind the house, Ed remarked, "The only thing that I can imagine that would have been less acceptable would have been an elephant." Burroughs lost little time in finding a more suitable home for the animals.

After taking his first airplane flight, Ed's unenthusiastic com-

Enjoying pool are Hulbert on left, Emma under umbrella, ERB, Jack, and David Ohrland, Emma's driver, on right, 1921.

ments about it had caused Emma and the children to change their minds about flying. He described the event as a "great disappointment," noting there was "only a knowledge of the danger incurred without any compensating thrill." His main complaint was that "the speed sensation was about what you derive from riding in an automobile at the rate of ten or twelve miles an hour." Although the speed was seventy miles an hour, the plane seemed to be standing still. Used to the excitement of auto driving, he found the plane ride both dull and disagreeable. He was also pessimistic about the safety factors, quoting statistics to George: "for every engine driver killed, one thousand pilots would be killed." Ed's attitude toward flying would be reversed in later years.

Contacts with old friends remained unbroken; in June 1920, Walt Mason, whose poems Ed had long admired, visited the Tarzana Ranch. In 1920-21 Ed corresponded with General Charles King, then living in Milwaukee, describing the ranch and the surrounding hills abounding with quail, deer, and coyotes. Ed noted the presence of mountain lions and spoke of the family's enjoyment in riding along the "many beautiful trails." A letter to King, of course, evoked the past: ". . . I always associate you in my mind with saddle horses, remembering as I do your horsemanship and your love of horses. Mrs. Burroughs and I each have our saddle horse and the children each a Shetland pony, besides which we have a couple of extra saddle horses, so if you do come out I can assure you of a good

Jack Burroughs in lion's den of short-lived Tarzana zoo, December 1920.

mount. . . ." When Ed later received a photo of King on horseback, he wrote, ". . . it is really the way I always think of you. I have been bragging for nearly thirty years now of the fact that I once rode under your instruction. . . ."[5]

Ed's political views during the election year of 1920 were forcefully stated in a letter to Bert Weston. Denying any preference for California Senator Hiram Johnson as a presidential candidate, Ed claimed he knew little about politics, but stressed, ". . . I hope to God I never see another Democratic president." Theodore Roosevelt had always been one of his favorites, and because of this he admitted that he "leaned" toward General Leonard Wood as a Republican candidate: ". . . I think he must have imbibed a great many Rooseveltian ideas and ideals and he looks ugly enough to railroad his views through." He became vituperative in expressing his opinion of Woodrow Wilson: "Of one thing I am positive: Johnson, Wood, Lowden, Pershing, or some congenital idiot from a county poorhouse could be no worse than the ass we have had for the last seven or eight years."[6]

Hard reality was shattering Ed's dream of becoming a gentleman rancher—at a profit. In his diary on January 7, 1921, he noted a report made by his secretary: "Shea closed books for 1920. Says loss on ranching $17,000 for last year. . . ." The $1,000 cost for a new henhouse was hard to believe. Ed wrote, "those hens will have to work overtime to pay for it . . . resembles a castle . . . the first building of its kind in the world. Concrete slabs or panels nailed to frame studding . . . a better house than most Hollywood bungalows. . . ." The hog-breeding project had turned into a disaster; on March 27 the *Los Angeles Times* announced an auction at the Tarzana Ranch, with the entire herd of pure-bred Hampshire hogs being closed out. The auction, to be held four days later, would include "the aged sow, Floreine 2nd, the sow that was given championship honors last fall at the Los Angeles Livestock Show. . . ."

The attempts to grow crops were equally unsuccessful. Years later, to his friend Charles K. Miller, who had described him as "author and film playwright," Ed responded in wry humor, "you forgot to mention my particular claim to fame—that of Farmer DeLuxe and World's Champion Potato Grower. About twelve years ago I planted an acre of potatoes and, as none of them has ever come up, I am inclined to think that they were planted upside down and are probably making their way slowly toward the Antipodes. . . ."[7]

In 1922 Ed arranged to offer for rent the agricultural and stockraising facilities at the ranch; he was finding it impossible to

One of ERB's Berkshire hogs, champion Marimoor Peer, July 1921, and Peter Putz, ERB's pig foreman.

concentrate upon his writing because of the pressure of numerous duties at Tarzana. To his nephew Studley, on July 26, he wrote gloomily, "Our golf course is only a memory, except for a few tees upon which we sweated so three years ago," and about the ranch, "Still have the hogs. Am trying to sell them. . . . We will have nothing left but the dairy cows and saddle horses and the necessary barns and corrals for them. . . ."

In applying for a loan on August 24, 1922, Ed confessed that he did not expect to meet the payments through any ranch income, but at the same time revealed that his earnings as an author, in 1921, had totaled $98,238.28. He noted that the land around him had been selling for subdivision purposes at more than $1,000 an acre, but stated hopefully that he had no plans to dispose of his property: ". . . I wish to retain it intact for my children." However, within a few months he changed his mind; Burroughs' business instincts would not allow him to accept a losing investment or to overlook any money-making possibility. Although he could not afford to expend the time and energy, he soon became involved in an attempt to sell residential and business lots.

In 1922 he formally subdivided approximately fifty acres of his ranch land extending from Tarzana Drive at the foot of the main ranch house hill north to Ventura Boulevard (El Camino Real), bounded on the east by Avenida Oriente and on the west by Mecca Ave. The City of Los Angeles assigned to the subdivision the official designation of Tract 5475. The land consisted of sixty-three commercial lots on Ventura Blvd. and 139 residential lots, many of which were an acre in size and dividable into smaller one-third acre parcels.

The advertising featured the concept of Tarzana as a milieu for artists and writers; this approach Burroughs believed to be a mistake which hampered the sale of lots for homes. On November 8 he commented to Bert Weston, "We rather overdid the high brow stuff in the first advertising. I did not mean it in the way people seemed to choose to interpret it. I wanted decent people in here, not a bunch of roughnecks, and as for an artistic colony, that was a little advertising come-on bunk that didn't pan out very well, possibly because the majority of people are just about as crazy to live with a bunch of authors and artists as I should be. . . ."

Although he was able to sell a few lots, the project languished until the following year. In the interim he decided to intensify efforts to have the ranch used by motion picture companies for location purposes. The ranch had provided a setting for occasional pictures, one of these being described by Ed to Irene Ettrick, a young fan from London, on January 10, 1922: "My children are having a great deal of excitement now because the Universal people are making a picture of the days of Buffalo Bill in the canyon on the back of the ranch. . . ." However, a year later Ed followed a plan to contact the various studios and to advertise the Tarzana Ranch as an ideal location for filmmaking. A circular, headed "A New Location," was mailed to the studios in January 1923; it mentioned the "Koonskin Kabin" situated on the ranch, an "artistic log cabin," a permanent set which could be used for dressing rooms or other purposes. Rates were listed at $15.00 per day, $75.00 a week. In a letter to Goldwyn Studios, Ed urged the location manager to use the ranch for scenes in *Ben Hur*.

Ed soon acquired film location rights for 3,000 acres adjoining the Tarzana Ranch and made tentative plans, never realized, to build his own movie sets which would be available for all companies. During 1923 and later, various studios, including Vitagraph and Metro, brought crews and actors to Tarzana; the picturesque setting near the Koonskin Kabin was a favorite spot. Despite these uses, the income derived from movie locations was insufficient to make the ranch a financial success.

Although his income from the sale of stories and book royalties was substantial, his expenses as a gentleman farmer of 540 acres had hurt him. Subdivision costs had been a burden and lot sales disappointing. Property taxes had been on the rise. Additionally, federal income taxes were beginning to take a bigger bite. By his very nature, Burroughs was not a money saver.

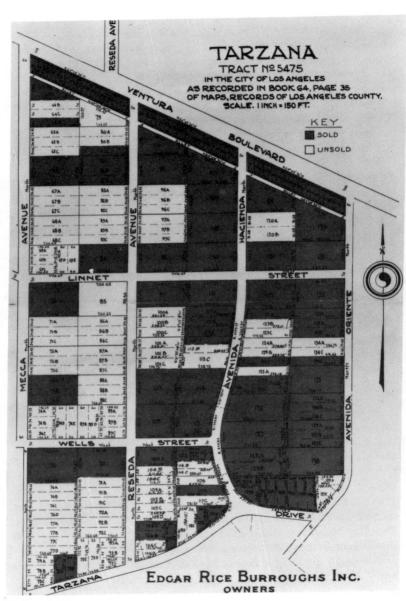

Map of Tarzana.

How could he cut expenses and realize a higher net income? After long consultations with his tax accountants and attorneys, he was advised that he should become a corporation!

In 1922 this was a unique concept. Certainly, so far as is known, no other author at that time had incorporated himself. And so, on March 26, 1923, Edgar Rice Burroughs, Inc., a California corporation, came into being. One week later, in a document dated April 2, 1923, Edgar Rice Burroughs, the author, granted to the new Edgar Rice Burroughs, Inc., all of his rights, title, and interest in his current and future literary rights. In exchange for these assets, he and his family received shares of stock in Edgar Rice Burroughs, Inc., with Ed having controlling interest by virtue of owning one share more than Emma. The three children were given token shares, with their father as trustee. Shortly thereafter Burroughs also granted to the new company the remaining real estate in his Tract 5475 subdivision.

From that time until his death in 1950, Burroughs was a salaried employee of ERB Inc. with all of his literary output becoming the property of the company. Although nothing immediately spectacular resulted from this change, there were decided tax advantages to a corporation as opposed to Burroughs as an individual. The advantages would become apparent in the years to come with the remarkable proliferation of the business into new fields.

With the development of small businesses along Ventura Blvd., and the subdivision of adjacent land by a number of other owners, Ed felt the time was ripe for a further step. On September 7, 1922, in anticipation of his already planned incorporation move and the expected greater sales efforts in lots in Tract 5475, he disclosed to his brother Harry, ". . . I am going to start a town and call it Tarzana. . . ." This unofficial creation and naming of a new town—the nearest post office was Reseda, California—was announced in the *Los Angeles Examiner* of October 15. The existence of an adjacent subdivision called Runnymede led to some confusion and conflict. The next Burroughs plan was to get official sanction through the establishment of a post office at Tarzana. After making application, on December 12, 1923, he wrote to Representative Walter F. Lineberger in Washington, D.C., to request his assistance:

Tarzana is a name that is associated with this locality and is not only well known locally, but nationally, and even internationally, while Runnymede has absolutely no local significance. . . .

Since writing the enclosed, I find that there is a Runnymede post-office in Kansas, and . . . in New Jersey, while so far as I know there would not be another Tarzana in the world. . . .

The reply of John H. Bartlett, first assistant postmaster general, on April 28, 1924, revealed that unmentioned complications and hidden motives had now emerged. The competition between Burroughs and Melvin S. Daniel, the proprietor of the Runnymede subdivision, who had applied both for the post office and the job of postmaster, was discussed: "The inspector says that within this tract [Runnymede] are 75 very small houses, a small grocery store, three small lunch rooms and a filling station. This section is devoted principally to poultry raising." As limited as Runnymede was, it appeared large in comparison with Tarzana, which was described by Bartlett as "a residential section, consisting of but five homes, including the residence of Edgar Rice Burroughs, who is the promoter of the Tarzana tract."

Bartlett noted that Ed had been frank: "Mr. Burroughs informed the inspector that he concurred on his opinion that there is no necessity for the office and that his chief interest in the proposition, which was advanced by the owners of the Runnymede tract, was to prevent the office being called Runnymede inasmuch as he had been there longer and the community is known as Tarzana." The final recommendation by Bartlett was that no new post office be established; he indicated that both areas, Tarzana and Runnymede, would receive the best service if the mail were handled through a rural route from Van Nuys, a larger adjacent district.

The community itself did not approve the name "Tarzana" until four years later, when on July 20, 1928, at a meeting of the Tarzana Civic League, the resolution was passed; four names had been proposed, and of the 400 members who voted, approximately ninety-five percent preferred "Tarzana." The Civic League next campaigned vigorously for a post office, and on December 11, 1930, Washington sent an official notice of its establishment in Tarzana.

Burroughs' hopes for success in farming had long since dissipated. Soon to become a reality was his planned incorporation and the end of farming. At a well-advertised auction sale on January 15, 1923, most of the livestock and all of the farm tools and equipment were disposed of. Seven saddle mares bred to the famous pedigreed Arabian stallions Letan and Harara were sold, but Ed still retained a number of other horses, including Colonel, his favorite saddle gelding, and Brigadier Rex, a registered saddle stallion. Other livestock at the auction were the dairy cattle and the herd of Berkshire swine, totaling more than one hundred, all registered or subject to registry. Two days later Ed commented to Bert Weston, ". . . it is over and I am through with farming, which is worth the loss, and I believe I could write a book on Gentlemanly Agriculture that would more than compensate me for all that I have dropped in this line of endeavor. . . ."

The Ghostly Script," a work of unusual complexity in which Burroughs devised a bizarre theory and philosophy of the afterlife, was begun on March 16, 1920, discontinued after the completion of five pages that included a foreword and chapter one, and not resumed until ten years later in October 1930. The manuscript at that time reached a total of some thirty-one pages, mainly in rough draft, handwritten form, and it was never finished. Allegorical in its effect, with the events in a supernatural environment clearly applicable to man's behavior on earth, the story opens with a foreword again in Burroughs' favorite style, with him as the narrator of happenings communicated to him by another person.[8]

Some eight years after he had started "The Ghostly Script" and allowed it to remain half-forgotten in his files, an inquiry from a fan brought the story theme to life again. On

---

ANNOUNCING THE ESTABLISHMENT OF AN INDEPENDENT

POST OFFICE AT TARZANA, CALIFORNIA, AND OUR

CONSEQUENT CHANGE OF ADDRESS FROM RESEDA, CALIFORNIA

TO

TARZANA, CALIFORNIA

EDGAR RICE BURROUGHS
EDGAR RICE BURROUGHS, INC.

TARZANA RANCH,
TARZANA, CALIFORNIA
DECEMBER 16, 1930

Announcement of Tarzana post office, December 16, 1930.

December 27, 1927, Leo Baker of Port George, Nova Scotia, Canada, revealed a vision and perception of a remarkable nature. In an erudite expression of his ideas, he spoke of "the possibility of other forms and modes of life which our limited intelligence would not permit us to appreciate even if they were explained to us," and insisted, "There must be other worlds and other intelligent, living beings. . . ." He confessed having similar thoughts to Burroughs', thoughts "unuttered because of lack of coherent descriptive power. . . ." They had lain "latent" in his brain for years. Then, possibly as "a presumptuous interloper," he offered a tentative suggestion: "Why do you not write a story describing a world within our world. That is to say, suppose there were another world of living beings, inhabiting the same space which we occupy, but on account of being on a different plane, so to speak, not appreciable to us, nor to them. . . ." By way of analogy, Baker noted that before the invention of radio we were not aware of "the countless sounds and noises" that were in the air. Through science we were able to capture and record these. Similarly, could there not be certain elements in "our immediate vicinity" that remain unnoticed because we have not the proper means to detect them?

Highly intrigued, Burroughs, on January 11, 1928, mentioned "the rather remarkable coincidence of your suggestion that I write a story describing a world within our world." He proceeded to explain the theme of "The Ghostly Script," according to the brief section he had written in 1920:

I started a story along similar lines based on a supposed theory of angles rather than planes: If we viewed our surroundings from our own "angle of existence," the aspect of the vibrations which are supposed to constitute both matter and thought were practically identical with those conceived by all the creatures of the world that we know; whereas, should our existence have been cast in another angle, everything would be different, including the flora and fauna and the physical topography of the world.

Thus, Baker's ideas centered about an invisible world existing on a different *plane,* while Burroughs conjured up one based on a newly viewed *"angle* of existence." He wrote to Baker:

The thought underlying the story was that death was merely a change to a new "angle of existence," wherefrom, viewed thus from a different angle, the vibrations that are matter took on an entirely different semblance, so that where before we had seen oceans, we might now see mountains, plains and rivers inhabited by creatures that might be identical with those with which we had hitherto been familiar or might vary diametrically.

Ed confessed that it was a "crazy story," commenting, "There was a reason why I did not finish it, though some day I may do so." Baker, in his letter, urged Ed to read Einstein's "theory of relativity," and noted that "Time, Space, Matter, are all purely relative and are simply artificial factors which we have adopted to suit our orthodox conditions of existence."

With the writing of "Tarzan the Terrible," from August 14 to December 16, 1920, and the customary contacts with the Munsey Company, Burroughs found himself confronted by a changing situation. The story, accepted by Munsey with only a short section completed, was sent to Davis at various times in installments. To Ed's surprise, while the story was still in progress, on December 7 he received a note from Elliot Balestier of *Argosy All-Story* announcing that Davis was no longer with the Munsey Company. He had gone into business for himself, forming the Robert H. Davis Corporation, a New York agency organized to handle the work of a group of well-known authors. By arrangement with Munsey he was assigned all of their syndication dealings and was allowed to represent them in the book and motion picture areas. In responding to Ed's good luck message, Davis wrote, "I thought I had better try my hand uptown among the merchants. I got rather tired of the editorial and reading game. . . ." On January 12, 1921, Ed noted, "You have a lovely letterhead. Every once in a while I used to go into business for myself, the only result, however, being a new letterhead. . . ." He conceded that since Davis's letterhead was more impressive than any he had used, the editor would probably be more successful.

As a sequel to *Tarzan the Untamed,* a novel whose ending revealed that Lady Jane Greystoke, supposedly killed by the Germans, was still alive, *Tarzan the Terrible* continues Tarzan's search for his mate and takes him to one of the strangest of lands, Pal-ul-don, where creatures walk erect like men but have long sinuous tails. A familiar theme, first used in the Martian series, centers about the willingness of intelligent beings to change, and even in a savage world to realize that a life of peace and amity with other beings is preferable to one of constant hatred and warfare. The odd creatures of Pal-ul-don, the pithecanthropi, especially in the clash of black against white, represent similar enmity on earth, and in the story's solution

Tarzana Ranch
Van Nuys California
1920

TARZAN THE TERRIBLE

was finished Dec.16,1920 by Edgar Rice Burroughs

words: 94325

pithecanthropus 1, 2, 8, 11
jato - hybrid lion, black and yellow striped, sabre tooth 4
ja - leopard spotted lion - 4
titanic reptiles first mentioned 8, 9
Ta-den - (Tall-tree) white, hairless warrior. Tarzan's first acquaintance-15
Om-at (Long-tail) black, hairy warrior. Tarzan's second acquaintance-15
A-lur (City of Light) Capitol of Pal-ul-don-16   INSERTS
Bu - the moon - 16   A - 7
Waz-don (Black-men)-16.   B - 10
Ho-don (White-men)-16   C - 155
Ko-tan (Mighty-warrior) king of the Ho-don - 16   *Killed 149*
O-lo-a (Like-star-light) Ko-tan's daughter - 16
Dak-at (Fat-tail) chief of a Ho-don village - 17
Ja-don (Lion-man) chief of a Ho-don village and father of Ta-den-17
Bu-lot (Moon-face) a Ho-don, son of Chief Mo-sar(Short-nose)-17
Mo-sar (Short-nose) Chief and pretender to Ho-don throne-17
Es-sat (Rough-skin) chief of Om-at's tribe of Waz-don-18.Killed-33
Pan-at-lee (Soft-tail-doe) Om-at's sweetheart-18
Pastar-ul-ved - Father of Mountains - a peak-19
Jad-ben-Otho- The Great God -19
Jad pele ul Jad-ben-Otho - The valley of The Great God-19
Pal-ul-don (Land-of-man) name of the entire country-20
Kor-ul-ja (Gorge-of-lions) Es-sat's gorge and tribe-22
Kor-ul-lul (Gorge-of-water) Waz-don tribe in next gorge S.E.of Kor-ul-ja-25
Kor-ul-gryf (Gorge-of-triceratops) lair of gryfs-27
Tarzan-jad-guru (Tarzan-the-Terrible)-31
gund bar - chief battle-31
Ab-on - acting gund of Kor-ul-ja during Om-at's absence-35
In-sad() Two Kor-ul-ja warriors who accompanied Om-at,Ta-den & Tarzan in
O-dan) search of Pan-at-lee -.36
An-un (Spear-eye) father of Pan-at-lee -41
Id-an (Silver-spear) One of Pan-at-lee's two brothers-41
In-tan (Dark-warrior) Kor-ul-lul left to guard Tarzan-51. Killed-52.
tor-o-don (beast-like-man)· true pithecanthropus, or anthropoid ape of Pal-ul-don.56
Mention of stranger 22,33,44,60,77,99,116
gryf-27 description-66
dor-son - 87
Dak-lot - one of Ko-tan's palace warriors- 87
Dor-ul-Otho (Son-of-God) -87
Lu-don (Fierce-man) High priest of the temple at A-lur
Jar-don (stranger-man) stranger - name given Korak by Om-at 119
U-ja - lion city - Ja-don's Capital - 145
Jad-ben-lul (Big great water) name of lake at A-lur - 145
Bu-lur (Bright city) mosaic city
pal-e-don-so-(place where men eat) - banquet hall - 151
an-aat (soft skin) a prisoner - creature of Lu-don - 154
jad-in-lul - the dark lake
Lt.Erich Obergatz - Jane's escort into interior
jad-bal-lul - an golden lake - 174
Bu-lur (moon city) City of waz-ho-don - (Brown-white-men) half breeds
iron - 196
waz-ho-don - 189

NOTE:

Names of male hairless pithecanthropus (Ho-don) begin with consonant, have even number of syllables and end with consonant.

Female Ho-don - begin with vowel, have odd number os syllables and end with vowel.

Male hairy pithecanthropus (Waz-don) - begin with vowel, have even number of syllables and end with consonant.

Female Waz-don - begin with consonant, have odd number of syllables and end with vowel.

Numerals
1-en
2-enen
3-ad
4-aden
5-adenen
6-adad
7-adaden
8-adenaden
9-adadad
10-on
11-onen
20-ton
30-fur
40-ged
50-het
60-og
70-ed
80-et
90-od
100-san
1000-xot

Application:
sanen-101
sanenen-162
enensan-200
xotsantonen-1121
tonxot-20,000

XXXVIII
Pithecanthropus
MALE
AND
FEMALE
HO-DON

Back of notebook page for "Tarzan the Terrible," showing Ed's pen and ink sketch of male and female pithecanthropus as he conceived them for mysterious land Pal-ul-don.

535

demonstrate that the hostility caused by mere differences in color or appearance and customs, no matter where it occurs, can be eliminated through honest efforts at friendship and understanding. The concept of a primitive religion, one based upon superstition and fear, and one that resorts to human sacrifice, is developed within the same theme of reform or change, and the end of *Tarzan the Terrible* brings the destruction of the priests' power and the promise of a religion of love and humanity.

The oft-repeated Burroughs philosophy of the perfection of nature as demonstrated through her simple creatures, unspoiled by a degenerative civilization, is developed, with some contradictions, in the novel. Tarzan is shown as different from his "fellows of the savage jungle" since he possesses certain "spiritual" characteristics, which, precisely *because* he is a man of civilization, enable him to appreciate the beauties of nature: "The apes cared more for a grubworm in a rotten log than for all the majestic grandeur of the forest giants waving above them. The only beauties Numa acknowledged were those of his own person as he paraded them before the admiring eyes of his mate. . . ."

In his approval of carvings and handicraft of Pal-ul-donian artisans, Tarzan becomes a spokesman for another Burroughs philosophy:

A barbarian himself, the art of barbarians had always appealed to the ape-man to whom they represented a natural expression of man's love of the beautiful to even a greater extent than the studied and artificial efforts of civilization. . . .

And of course one of the greatest qualities of "the simple-minded children of nature" is illustrated in Pan-at-lee's unstinting loyalty: "It has remained for civilization to teach us to weigh the relative rewards of loyalty and its antithesis. The loyalty of the primitive is spontaneous, unreasoning, unselfish. . . ."

In one respect *Tarzan the Terrible* evidences no change— Burroughs' detestation for the Germans remains intense. Erich Obergatz is a "pig-headed Hun," and, as with all Germans, never to be trusted. Obergatz says, "What are promises? They are made to be broken—we taught the world that at Liége and Louvain. . . ." His actions are always villainous, and at the story's end he becomes demented, imagines himself to be a god, and is finally killed by young Jack Clayton.

Tarzan, with his love of nature's beauties, her "picture of

peace and harmony and quiet," anticipates modern man's guilt in the pollution of his environment; Tarzan surveys the waters, green landscape and mountains and meditates:

What a paradise! And some day civilized man would come and —spoil it! Ruthless axes would raze that age-old wood; black, sticky smoke would rise from ugly chimneys against that azure sky; grimy little boats with wheels behind or upon either side would churn the mud from the bottom of Jad-in-lul, turning its blue waters to a dirty brown; hideous piers would project into the lake from squalid buildings of corrugated iron. . . .

Burroughs, with this vivid 1920 picture and prophecy of the contamination to come, reveals himself as one who was aware of this serious problem many years before ecology became a national concern. *Tarzan the Terrible,* purchased by Munsey's for $3,000, appeared in *Argosy All-Story Weekly* as a seven-part serial, from February 12 to March 27, 1921.[9]

The writings of 1921 included "Angel's Serenade," a story outline which Burroughs would rework in 1936 and then develop into a 24,000-word story three years later. Its main character, Dick Crode, grows up in the tenement streets of a large city and progresses through early years of petty thievery to become head of a crime syndicate. The title "Angel's Serenade" refers to the song his mother had played on a violin—a song Crode could never forget. Burroughs had originally conceived the story, in outline form, as the basis for a motion picture with the main role assigned to Lon Chaney. On May 15, 1921, he sent two copies of "Angel's Serenade," described as a "rough draft," to Lewis Jacobs of the Century Film Corporation in Hollywood. A month before, Burroughs had contracted with Jacobs for the production of ten stories, five *Tarzan* and five non-*Tarzan,* to be filmed within six years. In offering "Angel's Serenade," Burroughs explained the title:

If you do not happen to recall Angel's Serenade, I may say that it is one of the beautiful old compositions that has survived the ravages of time and the onslaught of many years of popular songs and modern jazz. It was suggested by Mrs. Burroughs, who says that it makes an especially beautiful violin solo.

The story was rejected by Jacobs.[10]

During the year, Burroughs completed a remarkable work, one that for imagination and for complexity of detail and settings exceeded any of his previous writings. In "The Chessmen of Mars," written January 7 to November 12, 1921, he produced an incredible aggregation of characters and creatures and devised Martian customs and practices of unusual ingenuity. His worksheet, one of the most involved he had ever prepared, listed seventy items—people, buildings, rooms, equipment, and geographical references, all briefly identified or explained. Weaving the theme of the game of chess—called *jetan* on Mars —into the story was truly an inspiration. This Barsoomian game is normally played upon a board of a hundred alternate black and orange squares, with the two opponents each allotted twenty pieces in either black or orange. But in "The Chessmen of Mars" the climactic game becomes one of life and death, played on a huge scale. A gigantic jetan board is laid out in the arena at Manator: "Here they play at Jetan with living pieces. They play for great stakes and usually for a woman—some slave of exceptional beauty. . . . When a warrior is moved to a square occupied by an opposing piece, the two battle to the death for possession of the square. . . ." Each player is dressed according to the piece he represents.

The idea developed undoubtedly from Burroughs' knowledge of chess and his turning to the game for an occasional diversion. During this period his opponent at times had been his secretary, John Shea. In the prelude to "The Chessmen of Mars," with John Carter once more returning to earth, Burroughs, as his nephew, opens with a reference to the game he had been playing: "Shea had just beaten me at chess, as usual. . . ." Burroughs had "twitted" Shea about his skill, mentioning a theory that "phenomenal chess players are always found to be from the ranks of children under twelve, adults over seventy-two or the mentally defective. . . ." It appears, however, that Burroughs preferred to assume the role of a regular loser at chess in the story, a role not indicated in real life. A January 3, 1921, entry in his diary, written before he had begun "The Chessmen of Mars," reads: "Played one game of chess with Shea. Won. If scientific theories are correct it is more of an honor to lose at chess than win. I do not recall ever having lost a chess game— though I have played but few times. . . ." He then jokes about the fact that this ability might establish him within the three classes described in the scientific theory. In February 1922 John Shea left Burroughs' employ and was later associated with the Hollywood Studios whose general manager, William Sistrom, in 1924 accepted an offer to manage the proposed Edgar Rice Burroughs Productions, Inc. The enterprise, launched with a goal of producing stories by Burroughs and other authors, was to be

Cover of The Chessmen of Mars, 1922; J. Allen St. John, illustrator.

financed by George B. Currier in Los Angeles; however, the organizational plans never materialized.

Concerning the game jetan, Burroughs received a letter of August 6, 1922, from Elston B. Sweet, a convict in Leavenworth Prison. Sweet offered information of unusual interest. After reading "The Chessmen of Mars," he and a fellow prisoner had used the details provided in the story to carve a full set of pieces for jetan. Sweet noted, ". . . We have not only played dozens of games between us, but have succeeded in making the game a favorite among several other prisoners." He inquired whether jetan was being manufactured commercially, and if so, hoped that Burroughs would send him a set. According to Sweet, he and his friend had been sentenced to terms of fourteen and ten years; however, in 1924 Sweet's sentence, commuted to six years, expired, and he was released.

On August 16 Burroughs responded to explain that the two prisoners had made the first set of jetan and that no commercial set had been produced.[11] Reader interest in jetan remained high. Burroughs supplied a further summary of the game for publication in the appendix of the novel, and in September 1927 two young fans, Stephen Lavender and John Creighton of Thomaston, Maine, sent Burroughs a photograph of the jetan board and pieces they had made.[12] A chapter is devoted to jetan in the book *Chess Variations* by John Gollon, published in 1968.

Because of his jetan theme, Burroughs in "The Chessmen of Mars," achieves a unity and intensity not attained in other works which at times could become loosely strung sequences of adventures, battles, and escapes. In addition, the Burroughs imagination is startlingly evident with the creation of the rykors, headless bodies that are mounted by the hideous Kaldanes, living heads without bodies who manipulate the brainless flesh. As explained by Ghek, a Kaldane who later assists Tara of Helium, the heroine of the story, the Kaldanes are part of nature's evolutionary purpose, with the brain becoming larger and more powerful. This process would continue: ". . . in the far future our race shall develop into the superthing—just brain. . . . Deaf, dumb and blind it will lie sealed in its buried vault far beneath the surface of Barsoom—just a great, wonderful, beautiful brain with nothing to distract it from eternal thought."

Because of strong friendship ties with Bob Davis, Burroughs felt he should be given an opportunity, in his new agency, to market "The Chessmen of Mars." However, the price stipulated by Burroughs, as quoted by another agency, was a minimum of $7,500. On March 23, 1921, Davis agreed to contact magazine editors and to "talk about a figure around $10,000." The price, even farther beyond the bounds of realism than the story, brought no takers; the year drew to a close with "The Chessmen of Mars" unsold. On December 12, Charles MacLean of *Popular Magazine* rejected the story, commenting ". . . If he [Burroughs] were to try something not quite so extravagant, something like Jules Verne's submarine story, he would break into a new field and one I think, offering a better chance for his genuine literary ability. . . ." Resigned to the inevitable, Ed, as in the past, returned to his only available market and to a far more modest price; on January 4, 1922, Munsey's bought the story for $3,500.[13]

Davis' venture into his own corporation proved to be brief. To Ed, on November 4, 1921, he explained that while his agency had been even more successful financially than he had anticipated, the business world was not to his liking. "I prefer literature to the counting room," he remarked. "I am something of a lemon as a business man." He revealed that he would return to his old position at Munsey's on the first of the year.

The experience with "The Chessmen of Mars" plunged Ed into a state of gloom; the limited market for his type of fantasy stories was painfully evident. His depression drove him, on November 15, in a letter to Davis, to state once more, ". . . As I wrote Joe Bray today, I think I am through writing Martian and Tarzan yarns. . . ."

Burroughs had long since reached a point of weariness with the Tarzan idea and a discouragement over the clamor from editors and readers for new *Tarzan* works. He could anticipate years of unending sequels to *Tarzan,* an apparent life chore to which he must resign himself. A repeated comment had been, "I want to be known as Edgar Rice Burroughs the author, not Edgar Rice Burroughs the author of *Tarzan.*" Past periods of rebellion against this enforced single-track creativity had driven him to try other works, a number of these involving realistic characters and settings. At previous times and also in 1924 when he attempted to organize his own motion picture company, his hope had been for the production of non-Tarzan stories; included in these were *The Mucker* and a newly completed story, "The Girl from Hollywood," written from November 16, 1921, to January 7, 1922. The story, first titled "The Penningtons," demonstrated Burroughs' perception of a serious contemporary problem—that of drug addiction—and his daring, both in developing the theme and in setting his fiction in Hollywood.

CHAPTER 28

Jetan (Martian Chess)

Those who have all or part of Edgar Rice Burroughs' Martian series should recognize the name of this game. Possibly some who remember *The Chessmen of Mars* even recall some of the rules. However, most readers probably reacted as I did—they dismissed the game as another of Burroughs' strange flights of imagination, unworthy of a true chess player's attention.

When I was gathering information on the various chess games, I happened to think of Jetan, and decided to include it in the book as a novelty. I made a set of pieces and played out a game. I was surprised to find that the game is quite good—very playable and entertaining. I therefore include Jetan not as a mere novelty but as a respectable game.

The game is supposed to represent (according to Burroughs) a battle between the black race of the south and the yellow race of the north. For this reason the Jetan board is supposed to be placed so that the end with the black army is at the south, and the end with the orange army at the north.

The board itself is of ten-by-ten squares, the squares being checkered orange and black. Positions of pieces are given on Chart 32.

Page of explanation of Martian game of Jetan, *invented by ERB for* The Chessmen of Mars, *as printed in book* Chess Variations *by John Gollon, Charles F. Tuttle Co., 1968.*

542

In "The Girl from Hollywood" he did not introduce the drug theme merely as an expected background for the supposedly depraved movie colony the public so often read about in the papers; instead, he made his heroine Shannon Burke, whose professional name was Gaza de Lure, a drug victim snared by a villainous film director fittingly named Wilson Crumb. After being tricked into snuffing "snow," Shannon descends to complete addiction and is forced to become Crumb's mistress and to occupy a Hollywood bungalow where she peddles cocaine, morphine, and heroin. In contrast to the unhealthful atmosphere of Hollywood, a city painted as a glamor capital that lures naive, movie-struck girls to their downfall, Burroughs uses his Tarzana ranch for another setting—the ranch demonstrating the virtues of a simple outdoor life and the invigorating effects of horseback riding. Rancho del Ganado, so-named in the story, is owned by a Virginian, Colonel Custer Pennington, who lives there with his wife, son Custer, Jr., and daughter Eva. With the narrative placed in the prohibition era, Burroughs inserts another complication in his plot, the storing of a large quantity of stolen liquor on an adjoining ranch, and the illegal activities of Guy Evans, a suitor for the hand of Eva, who is involved in the sale of the liquor.

Burroughs clearly indicates his objections to prohibition in describing Evans' attitude: "Like many another, he considered the Volstead Act the work of an organized and meddlesome mincrity, rather than the real will of the people. There was, in his opinion, no immorality in circumventing the Eighteenth Amendment whenever and wherever possible." However, Burroughs emphasizes his disapproval of any trafficking in *stolen* liquor.

The deplorable influence of drugs in the Hollywood setting is further developed through the addiction and death of Grace Evans, young Custer's fiancée, who has rejected the pleas to remain in the idyllic surroundings of the ranch, and who insists upon seeking an actress's career in Hollywood. She also falls prey to the dissolute Wilson Crumb.

With the inclusion of certain elements—the description of life at Tarzana, the realistic details about the ranch house, and the horseback rides into the hills and canyons—the story does arouse some strong interest. In Eva, the daughter and darling of the Pennington household, whose doting parents indulged her capricious behavior, Burroughs' real-life model was probably his own daughter Joan.[14]

Although accepted by Davis for magazine publication, "The Girl from Hollywood" received an unenthusiastic appraisal from Joseph Bray of McClurg. While approving Burroughs' motives in writing it—"You pay a deserved tribute to the healthy country life as you have lived it . . ."—Bray felt that the story's appearance in book form would be a mistake. On June 23, 1922, he wrote:

. . . you do not have here a story that will interest people to an extent worth mentioning. You bring the movies into your story. You show the harm an unprincipled man can do and there is no reason to suppose you have overdrawn things. People, however, are not much interested in stories of conditions in Hollywood. . . .

Bray commented about the publication of a number of movie stories in the past months, noting that *Merton of the Movies,* by Harry Leon Wilson, although well-written, was selling poorly.

Bray was also critical of the plot complications involving both bootlegging and drugs. His view of prohibition was quite different from Burroughs':

The bootlegging business you bring in just for the sake of plot development is likewise something in which there is not much interest. I do not know what your attitude towards prohibition is; prohibition is here to stay. Any person who looks at results so far with a clear mind can not escape the conclusion that the country has benefitted greatly from the passing of the eighteenth amendment. . . .

He insisted that the drug theme was not convincing; it seemed illogical for a famous, highly paid director like Wilson Crumb to turn to drug peddling as a business enterprise.

Bray's main fear was of the effect the publication of "The Girl from Hollywood" could have on the other Burroughs books: ". . . it will react against the sale of your books in general and future books in particular." He stressed that the readers expected "lively stories of adventure" from the Burroughs pen, and that Ed should not write stories "in which very little happens." Bray added a frank comment:

. . . I think the publication of "The Girl from Hollywood" would do you a great deal of harm, but let me say in this connection if you want to take the chance, we shall not say no to its publication. My advice, however, would be to forget it as a book. . . .

544

As a McClurg editor, Bray's concern, naturally, was with sales and profits. He spoke of the decline in sales of Burroughs books recently, and noted that *The Mucker,* about which he had always been dubious, was obviously a money-loser.

Burroughs, having formed his own opinion about the story, was not in the least persuaded by Bray. He had been quite sure that the editor would reject the story, but preferred to give him the "first refusal." Burroughs was positive and impatient: ". . . I intend to have it put in book form before Christmas. It will never be timely again." His most compelling reason, his desire to achieve success in nonfantasy works, was evident: "I wish . . . to ascertain if there is a market for other than highly imaginative stuff from my pen."

Unwilling to let McClurg publish a book in which they had no confidence, Ed turned to Bob Davis. In the dealings that followed, Davis contacted Carl B. Milligan of Service for Authors, a New York agency that had taken over the Davis corporation. Through Milligan, a contract for the publication of "The Girl from Hollywood" was obtained from The Macauley Company early in 1923, and the book appeared on August 10 of that year.

The reviews of the book contained the strongest criticism ever leveled at Burroughs' writings. Much of this resulted from Macauley's unfortunate selection of a book jacket with a lurid illustration of a partially undressed woman. However, Burroughs was also castigated for the subject he had chosen. The *Chicago Daily News,* on September 5, viewed *The Girl from Hollywood* with repugnance, commenting insultingly about the book and its author:

When we find the vice and depravity of Hollywood dressed up to make a novel with no purpose other than to entertain, we get the strange feeling that something ought to be done about it. . . . In this book he (Burroughs) has taken a timely theme and served it up as so much sensational hash. The jacket on the book pictures a woman dropping a robe to expose her naked shoulders as the camera turns, while a man with leering eyes extends fingers to help take off the robe. Within the jacket is the appealing line: " 'Women are cheaper in Hollywood than in any town this side of Port Said,' said a motion-picture director not long ago."

The *News* noted that here was a situation for a great writer, such as Zola, who might present a powerful exposé of vice and realistically depict human suffering. Obviously, the review concluded with contempt, the author must be "more than an Edgar

Rice Burroughs, writing feebly for a multitude that sees in a nation's shame nothing more than a cheap diversion. The curse of Hollywood is too dangerous to be played with by men of small talents."

To L. S. Furman, Macauley editor, on October 26, 1923, Ed expressed unconcern over the critical reviews, remarking: ". . . as long as they say *something* I am satisfied." However, he bluntly placed the blame with the Macauley Company:

The illustration on the jacket was suggestive, and to me, disagreeable; while the notice printed inside would lead the book buyer to assume that he was to be regaled with a nasty sex story. Those who like that sort of thing must have been disappointed, while those who do not like it would not buy the book.

He explained that his only regret in connection with the reviews, was that "nearly all of the reviewers seem to have the idea that my book was an arraignment of Hollywood's morals, and was intended to portray a generally existing condition there." Stressing that this was *not* his purpose, he insisted that motion picture people were "clean, hard working people" and Hollywood was "a delightful home community." Whatever vice he had described, existed in all walks of society.

"I hoped that the story would deter young people who had never used narcotics from taking the first step," he wrote, "and that it might hold out hope to those who already were addicts." The reviewers who classified the book as mere sensational entertainment were clearly without perception. The contrast between the tawdry and wretched life of the drug victim in Hollywood as posed against the healthy outdoor life on the ranch was forcefully presented. Burroughs commented sadly about this:

. . . The one big thing I tried to get over, and evidently failed, was a plea for simple, natural, wholesome family life, as typified by the Penningtons. Only a few reviewers grasped this, the majority seizing upon every shred or suggestion of smut they could lay hands upon.

Another project on the 1922 writing agenda was a revision of the unsuccessful "Under the Red Flag," an anticommunist story which, through 1919-21, had suffered eleven rejections. In the original story of a twenty-first-century world under Soviet domination, Burroughs had created characters and events to match the communist setting. Julian 9th, the main character, had been born in the thirty-first Commune of the Chicago Soviet. The top officials, as listed on the Burroughs worksheets, were Lantski Petrov, president of the United States, elected in the year 2016; Otto Bergst, also shown as Comrade General Bergan, the new commander of the Red Guard at Chicago; Hoffmeyer, an agent of the Bolsheviks; Krantz, the Bolshevik coal baron; and Soord, the new tax collector.

Burroughs had become resigned to the fact that his fictional exposure of the evils of communism was unsalable. He was baffled as to the reasons why, but inclined to suspect that powerful and insidious forces were at work to intimidate editors; their unwillingness to publish the story could be viewed as cowardice or even as a lack of patriotism. His businessman's instincts would not allow him to waste the hours of writing, and since some revision was necessary, he merely changed the setting and turned to the safer and more familiar area of science-fiction. The earth's totalitarian conquerors who by the twenty-first century had reduced an advanced civilization to a primitive, agricultural society, were the Kalkars, sadistic invaders and colonizers from the moon. With this revision, "Under the Red Flag" became "The Moon Men," and with the usual planned sequels the story was shifted in order and became the second of a moon trilogy. The first, "The Moon Maid," was written later in 1922, and the third, "The Red Hawk," did not appear until 1925. All three were combined for book publication as *The Moon Maid* by McClurg in 1926.

Once more utilizing a favorite device, the prologue, to bring the main character Julian into contact with an unidentified narrator, Burroughs, in "The Moon Maid," establishes a bleak setting of a 1967 world finally at peace after a half-century of warfare. Julian and the narrator, whose only role is to be the recipient of Julian's extraordinary tale, meet on the transoceanic airship *Harding,* en route to Paris. The day is one of unusual importance—Mars Day—with the earth, after attempts that spanned twenty-two years, at last receiving a message from Mars marked Helium, Barsoom. But in one of the most richly imaginative of all his stories, Burroughs projects his events farther into the future, allowing Julian to recount, through a series of reincarnations, the sequence of happenings that would bring a terrible catastrophe to the earth.

In "The Moon Maid," as Julian tells his story, the incredulous listener learns that the man is really Julian 5th, born in the year 2000, and now returned to earth in one of his reincarna-

Cover of The Moon Maid, *1926; J. Allen St. John, illustrator.*

548

tions. Julian explains, ". . . I differ only from my fellows in that I can recall the events of many incarnations, while they can recall none of theirs other than a few important episodes of that particular one they are experiencing. . . ."

Julian reveals that after the fifty years of war ended in 1967, the world had been completely disarmed. Other than those weapons retained by the International Peace Fleet, whose duty was to prevent any preparations for war, "there wasn't a firearm in the world. . . . There was not a gas shell nor a radio bomb, nor any engine to discharge or project one; and there wasn't a big gun of any calibre in the world. . . ." Man had apparently eliminated the war threat on earth. But he had naively failed to foresee another danger, "external sources over which he had no control." Because of the scheming of a warped genius, Lieutenant Commander Orthis, whose sabotage of a flight to Mars forced the airship to make an emergency landing on the moon, an unarmed earth was to find itself helpless to resist an invasion that had never been anticipated—from the moon.

Through the science-fiction theme, Burroughs, always a supporter of the military, was expressing his alarm over our weakened armed forces and his objections to the disarmament proposals of the postwar period. His 1918 articles had stressed the need for the maintenance of a strong reserve army. In these writings and in his opinions he had left no doubt that the prime source of apprehension here on earth was the radical movement socialism or communism. The new and frightening government of Russia, the one he referred to as "Bolshevikism," he viewed as a menace to which the world must be alerted; his "Under the Red Flag," the original version of "The Moon Men," had been written for that purpose. However, Burroughs' later imaginary vision of danger and disaster coming from the moon is both startling and provocative—an idea significant in what it could portend for our future. As the result of an actual disarmament which our world might attain by the twenty-first century, could *we* face the appalling possibility of destructive invasion from another planet?

Perhaps the most remarkable aspect of the moon trilogy is displayed in Burroughs' preparation for the writing, notably in his worksheets for "The Moon Maid." His astonishing capacity for detail and for devising names and places for his exotic civilizations is evident in these pages of planning, but beyond the notes and glossary of terms, he has gone to unusual care to compile a lengthy list of all of Julian's reincarnations, with birth and death dates and other information. From Julian 1st, born in 1896 and killed in France on Armistice Day, and Julian 2nd, born in 1917 and killed in battle in Turkey in 1938, Burroughs proceeds far into the future to Julian 20th. Both Julian 3rd and 4th were killed in service as the line progressed into the twenty-first century; Julian 15th, life span 2259-2309, merits the note "Drove Kalkars from Desert 2309," and the list moves successively through the centuries of reincarnation to end with Julian 20th, born in 2409.

Burroughs' worksheets also contained his drawing of a Va-gas, a human quadruped, described as "A Marauder of the Moon" and "A Lunar Savage," and a page with two drawings, one a cross-section of the moon and the other a smaller area marked with geographical places. He notes the crater where Julian 5th entered the interior of the moon and provides locations of the airship, river, woods, and sea. Interestingly, he had fastened a newspaper clipping to a sheet; its headline read: "Radio Impulses Can Run Plane," and the article reports on the powers of remote radio control and on the instruments displayed at a convention of electrical engineers.[15]

Through his creations in the trilogy, Burroughs expounds other philosophies. In the origin of the Kalkars on the moon, they were first members of a secret society called The Thinkers, "who did more talking than thinking," but who managed to influence the people to rise up and take over the government. The implication

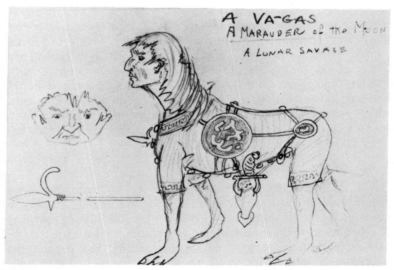

ERB's pencil sketch of a Va-Gas, *a lunar savage, for "The Moon Men."*

of similar dangers from communism is obvious. Burroughs, however, a man of action, is also exhibiting his contempt for the passive intellectuals who merely theorize. As described in "The Moon Maid," The Thinkers "would not work, and the result was that both government and commerce fell into rapid decay." Here Burroughs, in his own way, is jeering at the Communists and especially at the IWWs of World War I whom he had previously condemned; these radicals were merely idle "thinkers," who wouldn't stoop to hard work and who had impractical and dangerous political solutions for the world's problems.

At the end of "The Moon Maid," with its "frame" structure of a story told to a listener (and narrator), Julian 5th completes his tale and then promises to give an account of the adventures in a later reincarnation—that of Julian 9th. With "The Moon Men," now the second of the trilogy, the conquest of the earth occurs. Julian's bitter enemy, Lieutenant Commander Orthis, who retains his unchanging hatred through a series of reincarnations that match those of Julian, had devoted his twenty-four years on the moon to persuading the Kalkars that an unarmed world was theirs for the taking, and to directing them in the organization of a huge army equipped with new weapons of destruction. In the year 2050, with the aid of an electronic rifle which disintegrated metal through the hurling of radioactive vibrations—"the electrons of the attacked substance increased their own vibratory rate to a point that they became dissipated again into their elemental and invisible state"—Orthis was able to wipe out most of the International Peace Fleet. In the final battle, however, Julian 5th produces his own counterinvention and the two plunge to a flaming death in their airships. "The Moon Men" then tells the tale of Julian 9th, born in 2100 in Chicago, and, in a primitive world surviving on the ruins of the past civilization, governed by the Kalkars with their all-powerful Committee of the Twenty-Four.

Within this setting Burroughs angles unexpectedly for the creation of one of his characters. In "The Ghostly Script" he had exhibited sympathy for the Negroes and had made his main character a Negro sergeant; now he chose to turn to a minority group again and deal sensitively with the Jew, old Moses Samuels, who made a living tanning hides. Moses and Julian, close friends, are united also through their hatred of the Kalkars. All religious worship is forbidden, but the descendants of Protestants, Catholics, and Jews all join to hold services in a concealed church. Strangely, old Moses has saved a tiny image,

the figure of a man nailed to a cross, given to one of his ancestors by a Catholic nurse; Julian, presented with the carving by
Moses, has no idea what the figure represents, and it remains for
the Jew to tell him that the man is the Son of God. The death
of Moses is foreshadowed. After terrible torture by the Kalkars,
as he lies dying, Julian tries vainly to save him: "Tears came to
my eyes in spite of all I could do, for friends are few, and I
had loved this old Jew, as we all did who knew him." In
the violent revolt that comes at the end of the story, many of
the Kalkars are murdered, and Julian notes, "More than once I
heard the name of Samuels the Jew. Never was a man more
thoroughly avenged than he that day."

Throughout "The Moon Men" the American flag, banned by
the Kalkars, but kept hidden and almost worshipped by Julian
and his friends, serves as a symbol of their former freedom and
as a means of uniting them in readiness for resistance. At the
end, Julian 9th kills his reincarnated enemy, now named Or-tis,
and is himself killed; but once more, on the completion of his
story, he suggests to his narrator that an account of a future life
is forthcoming.

The final story of the moon trilogy is set in the year 2430,
with Julian 20th leading the struggle against the Kalkars, who
have been driven across the continent and are confined in an
area adjacent to the sea. The bitter feud between the houses of
Julian and Or-tis continues. Titled "The Red Hawk," after Julian,
who is the chief of a hundred fierce clans that swear allegiance
to his house, the story continues the warfare in a country whose
inhabitants have returned to the tribal customs and apparel of
the American Indians. Thus oddly, after four hundred years of
battles, "the wheel is come full circle," and the United States has
reverted to the nomadic civilization of its first Americans. Feath-
ers are worn in the bands that confine their hair, and Red Hawk
is so named because he displays the clan sign of his family, a
single feather from the redtailed hawk. In various other ways
these Americans duplicate Indian customs: they use ocher to
paint themselves; their clothing is made of deerskin; they are
armed with lances, swords, and bows and arrows; and they take
the scalps of their enemies.

For geographical names and places Burroughs on occasion retains those belonging to an ancient America of the twentieth
century. With the warfare raging near the Pacific Ocean, there
are references to Bear Lake, Cajon Pass, Rustic and Santa
Monica canyons, and the capital at Pasadena, near Los Angeles.
Corruptions of American names include the tribes of the Kol-
rados and Utaws, the Nipons as descendants of the Japanese,

and the flag handed down through the generations—the Flag of Argon (Argonne).

In contriving an ending for "The Red Hawk" and the trilogy, Burroughs uses a variation of the Romeo and Juliet theme, one of a happy nature. The four-hundred-year feud of the houses of Julian and Or-tis is finally resolved when the two join forces, Americans all, to drive the Kalkars into the sea, and when Julian falls in love with Bethelda, an Or-tis descendant, and takes her for his wife.[16]

Despite his diminished interest in writing further *Tarzan* novels, based both upon his belief that he had exhausted the theme, and his fear that public demand was on the wane, in 1922 he turned again to contrive adventures for the ape-man, this time in the familiar setting of Opar and with the addition of a new African country dominated by gorilla-men. Davis, at *All-Story,* had no doubts about the continuing public fascination with *Tarzan* stories; it was sufficient for him that the new story bore a *Tarzan* title and carried the Burroughs name. His acceptance of "Tarzan and the Golden Lion" was prompt.

On June 14, in thanking Davis for the $4,000 check, Ed commented, "I was not at all sure that you would find the story acceptable, as I was very much disappointed in it myself. . . ." Davis' reply a week later was in his typically bantering tone. He noted that, to him, Ed's confession revealed he was "not entirely without shame." The story, he conceded, was not the best one Ed had written; it had insufficient conflict and consisted mainly of "long treks—going away from here and coming back again." Nevertheless he planned to feature it in the Fortieth Anniversary issue of *Argosy All-Story* with a special four-color cover illustration and the announcement, "Triumphant Return of Tarzan of the Apes."

Earlier that year Ed had signed an agreement with the Munsey Company guaranteeing them the first reading of his entire output of fiction for the two years from May 1, 1922, to April 30, 1924. While he noted that his aim would be to supply them with "one hundred eighty thousand words of Tarzan manuscript," he stressed that this plan was not to be binding. He again disparaged "Tarzan and the Golden Lion" in his letter of June 28 and remarked, "My readers have been too good to me to deserve another 'Tarzan' story as rotten as this last one. . . ."

The novel, written from February 10 to May 31, 1922, served up a familiar fare, but did provide colorful sections in the creation of Jad-bal-ja, the Golden Lion, raised from a cub by Tarzan

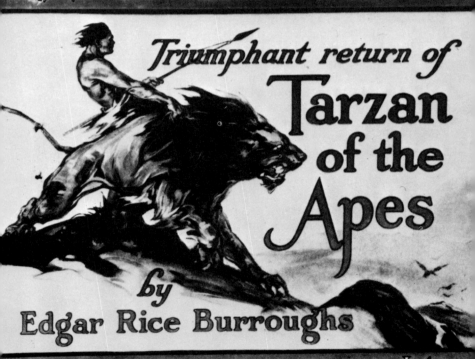

ARGOSY
ALL-STORY
WEEKLY

Triumphant return of
Tarzan
of the
Apes

by
Edgar Rice Burroughs

10¢ PER COPY   DECEMBER 9   BY THE YEAR $4.00

"Tarzan and the Golden Lion" cover of Argosy All-Story Weekly,
December 9, 1922.

554

Tarzana's baseball team, about 1922, which ERB helped sponsor; ERB, with white cap, in back row.

and trained to attack, retrieve, or kill at his command. Burroughs this time devises an entire group of villains, repeating his past tendency to make his most evil characters foreigners.

In "Tarzan and the Golden Lion" Burroughs again states his philosophy of the decadence of civilization as compared with the simple virtues of nature. The old white man who had been held prisoner by the gorilla-men for many years is advised by Tarzan not to return to civilization, but to stay and help the natives. Should he return, Tarzan says, he will find "deceit, and hypocrisy, and greed, and avarice, and cruelty." For himself, Tarzan explains that he had always been glad to come back to the jungle—"to the noble beasts that are honest in their loves and in their hates—to the freedom and genuineness of nature."[17]

On September 8, 1922, for publication in the special anniversary issue of *Argosy All-Story*, Davis requested a 400-word introduction to "Tarzan and the Golden Lion," in which the Tarzan series and characters would be traced from the first story. The article, as written by Burroughs (1,200 words), contained some interesting data:

Tarzan of the Apes had been rejected by thirteen London publishers before Metheun accepted it. The story (as of 1922) had been translated into Swedish, Norwegian, Danish, Dutch, German, Russian and Arabic, with offers pending for French, Spanish, and Italian translations.

Burroughs also provided some revelations; he was able to clarify the philosophy about Tarzan that he apparently had come to believe:

The life of Tarzan of the Apes is symbolic of the evolution of man and the rise of civilization, during which mankind gained much in its never-ending search for luxury; but not without the sacrifice of many desirable characteristics, as well as the greater part of its liberty.

Concerning *Tarzan the Terrible*, written in 1920, he noted:

A year or so before, the late Walter Winans, Esq., of London, commenced sending me clippings relative to purported encounters between white and native hunters, and some huge creatures of prehistoric appearance in the swamps of central Africa. Mr. Winans, I believe, was himself convinced of the existence of such a creature. Upon it I constructed the Gryf of Tarzan the Terrible, and wove the story of the Ho-don and the Waz-don and the land of Pal-ul-don. . . .

With "Tarzan and the Golden Lion" Burroughs adopted a new writing practice—the use of the Ediphone. On his worksheet he noted, "Commenced dictating on the Ediphone on page 9 of this mss.," and in connection with "The Moon Maid," a later story, commented that he had used the Ediphone partially and then changed to the typewriter. Finding some difficulty in adjusting to the process of direct dictation, he was inclined to attribute his supposedly inferior writing, during this period, to the new method. To Davis, on September 27, 1922, he confided that he had "discovered the reason" why "Tarzan and the Golden Lion" and "The Moon Maid" were not up to his usual quality: "These two stories I dictated to an Ediphone. I wanted to give the machine a fair trial, since there is no question but what it would have greatly reduced the actual labor of transferring my thoughts to paper, and it would have relieved me of practically all eye strain, which, with advancing years, I find to be increasing."

He added, "After finishing The Moon Maid, I abandoned the Ediphone and my last story I wrote directly on the typewriter, with the result that I think you will find considerably more action, and at the same time a better knit story." In later years, however, he returned to the use of a dictating machine, the Dictaphone.

The need for a respite from the jungle and fantasy stories prompted him to seek for ideas elsewhere, but in the new writing he resorted to an overused theme—intrigue centering about the monarchy in a miniature kingdom. "Beware," written from August 9 to 31, 1922, features the plotting of revolutionaries to seize power in Assuria. However, Burroughs does devise a new approach, shifting from the Assurian revolution, the death of the king and queen, and the flight of the infant crown prince to a resumption of events twenty-two years later in New York City. In the prologue, where the royal tragedy occurs, the newly born Prince Alexander is saved by Lieutenant Donovan, an officer of the foreign corps. Mrs. Donovan, who herself had given birth to a son two days before, pretends that twins had been born; taking the young prince, she and her husband flee. On board the ocean liner one of the infants dies.

With the passage of twenty-two years, Macklin Donovan, established as a son of the former Assurian officer, becomes the main character. The older Donovan is a police lieutenant, while Macklin, working in the United States Secret Service, is investigating the involvement of wealthy Mason Thorn with a group of Assurians. The interest in Macklin displayed by the snobbish Mrs. Glassock and her daughter Genevieve is motivated by his supposed family prestige and wealth. Macklin is really in love with the exotic Nariva, a mysterious guest.

The story now takes an unexpected direction. Messages to Macklin, printed notes containing the single word "Beware," emanate from a locked closet. The incidents that follow create an impression of a typical detective story. The mystery involves various secret panels that lead to the adjoining house where the conspirators are operating. At the ending Burroughs prefers to leave the most puzzling question unanswered. Is Macklin Donovan really the Crown Prince Alexander? Only Mrs. Donovan, gravely ill and not expected to live, can supply the answer. But she is in a coma, and whether she ever gains consciousness and makes a statement is not revealed.

In sending the 24,000-word story to Davis, Burroughs suggested that the editor read the prologue last to see what the effect would be. In this case the early events in Assuria would emerge at the end as a type of additional denouement. Davis' evaluation of "Beware," sent on September 12, 1922, was one of blunt disapproval:

. . . I think Beware is the nearest approach to mediocrity that

*ever came from your pen, and Lord, Edgar, how did you come
to fall back among the Russians, the Grand Dukes, Prince Alexander, Crown Princes, then drag them and their descendants
along with Saranov down to the present day. That whole bunch
smell to high heaven in fiction. . . .*

One rejection had never been convincing to Burroughs,
and the usual list of submissions followed. Refusals came from
Blue Book (1922) and *Detective Tales & Weird Tales* (1923).
An offer of $230 for the story by *Weird Tales* in 1929 was
turned down. Sales efforts continued, and a rejection by *Detective
Book* was received in 1938. Finally, in 1939, "Beware" was
purchased by Raymond Palmer, editor of *Fantastic Adventures,*
for $245. With some of the characters and plot elements changed
by Palmer, and the time setting projected to the year 2190,
"Beware" was now transformed from a hodgepodge royal
intrigue-detective mystery novelette to a science-fiction story
and published in the July 1939 issue of the magazine, where it
somehow acquired the incongruous title of "The Scientists Revolt."

Miscellaneous writings from the Burroughs pen, both
published and unpublished, were produced in the years 1921-25.
His article, appearing in *The American News Trade Journal,*
April 1921, was a practical one, stressing the required cooperation of the publisher, jobber, retailer, and author in the sale of
books and periodicals. But Burroughs first discussed his personal
feelings about books: "I like to handle them and to own them.
I hate to see them abused. I sometimes fancy that an adult who
habitually marks his place in a volume by turning down the
corner of a leaf would kick a dog or strike a horse without even
provocation of anger." Beyond this emotional attitude toward
books, of course, was the "stern necessity" that prompted him to
write books, and the dealers to sell them, "the ability . . . to
provide for ourselves and our families." He noted that a man
does not search for fame; this, perhaps, may come to him later.
"It is the box office receipts that really count most while we
live." As always, he had a suggestion for increasing book sales.
Recognizing the public's interest in the author, Ed proposed that
meet-the-author sessions be held each Thursday afternoon at
book shops, with selected individuals notified through mailed invitations. In later years he attended many similar sessions at
which he autographed copies of his latest book.

Through the years, Burroughs' works had been subjected to severe criticism by those who valued writings of different literary quality. Included in this group were other authors, university professors, and librarians. An article attacking the *Tarzan* stories, published in the March 1922 *Wisconsin Library Bulletin,* had come to Burroughs' attention. The author, Professor Noble, chose to condemn the books, first of all, because of their harmful effects upon children; he also offered scathing comment about certain plot devices, emphasizing their faults and improbabilities. On April 24, in his response to the "rather violent attack" on the *Tarzan* books, Ed presented a logical and convincing argument: The *Tarzan* books were not written for children, though some children were reading them; there was still no evidence that highly imaginative fiction, taken in moderation, was harmful to children. Ed agreed that his works were designed for entertainment, not instruction, adding that the "use of them for this purpose in schools is ridiculous." He had never encouraged this practice. He showed tact in agreeing with Noble that "an exclusive diet of *Tarzan* books would be harmful. . . ."

It is significant to note that in later years after Burroughs' death various schoolteachers were using his books as a means of stimulating an interest in reading. One teacher on a Navajo reservation found the *Tarzan* books to be his best tool for teaching the English language.

In his defense of the imagination Ed displayed a depth of perception: "The power of imagination is all that differentiates the human mind from that of brute creation. Without imagination there is no power to visualize what we have never experienced, and without that power there can be no progress." Although not an educator, he had sound theories on how the child's mind could be developed. Fairy tales, for example, not only stimulate the child's imagination, but "inculcate . . . the first seed of the love of books, and whatever accomplishes this, so long as it carries no harmful teachings, is well worth while." He noted that many adults today derived their first love of literature from reading the *Nick Carter* books. Thus, it was not wise to force children to read books in which they had no interest; they could develop a "subconscious abhorrence" of books. The more intelligent approach was obvious: permit the child to read any story that was not harmful, having confidence that after he had learned to love books, his taste in literature would expand and improve as the years passed. Ed pleaded that children be allowed some voice in choosing what they read—other than those books required in English classes. He remarked, "I have yet to learn of any greater harm resulting from the reading of

Tarzan than an injury sustained by an English boy who fell out of a tree while attempting to emulate him."

To Ed's astonishment, from faraway Truro, England, came a statement of support and protest from William G. Hale of the Free Public Library. Indignant over the attack on the *Tarzan* books, Hale, on May 24, addressed a four-page letter to the *Wisconsin Library Bulletin,* offering a point-by-point analysis of Noble's criticisms; Hale sent a copy of the letter to Ed. While thanking him for his advocacy, Ed, on June 20, was doubtful that the *Bulletin* would print the response, and commented, "I understand that American Librarians are laboring under the delusion that their proper duty in life is to safeguard public morals and education rather than to furnish people with reading matter they desire."

Hale, who had been a public librarian for twenty-six years, observed that "the faults found with the Tarzan stories are no worse than the speech with which Kipling endows his animals; they are the legitimate license of the novelist." Hale made specific references to four plot elements derided by Noble: Tarzan's learning to read through a picture book; the unusual strength of a grass rope; Tarzan's manufacture of a knife with the aid of a whetstone; and Tarzan's "nimble and quiet transit" through the trees. All of these, according to Hale, appeared reasonable within the setting, and moreover, they did not exceed the bounds of license allowed to a writer of romances.

Again, Hale established comparisons with Kipling, whom he admired greatly, despite his "improbable soldiers" and his jungle animals who talk "sheer fairy-like stuff." But Hale reserved his most telling blow for the end, what he termed "the real rock of offence in the Tarzan books." It was not the faults of the plot or any defects in the English. Hale confessed that in other American books he had squirmed over such rendering of good English words as "catalog," "program," "colum" and "other dock-tailed words which make one think of a Manx cat." Nor was the objection by Noble based upon the improbabilities in the *Tarzan* stories. Hale, in a brilliant insight, discloses the real cause behind Noble's distaste for Tarzan:

It is the true and close parallel which Mr. Burroughs draws between the ape and the man showing the essential relationship between the two. Such parallelism vexes the egotism which would fain keep man on a separate plane of creation by himself, disowning the crowd of animal forms from which he has sprung, and to which in moments of primal emotional stress he so plainly reverts.

Burroughs' fervent support of Darwin's theories was of course evident to Hale. To Burroughs, Tarzan's development illustrated Darwin's ideas:

The Tarzan stories constitute the epic of the great evolution of man from the ape, a process in which there were no breaks, no supernatural interventions, but just the irrepressible upward surging of the divine thought through its animal stages from ape to man.

The jungle childhood and growth of Tarzan represents a "similar resume of that evolution to the older and longer one which every animal embryo runs through. . . ." Hale summarized, "In the embryo, we get the whole course of evolution; in Tarzan the course of its mental evolution from ape to man."

Hale continued his penetrating analysis with an appeal:

Let us cast aside this ancient cant of man's separateness. We are not separate; we are close kin to all that breathes; a blood brotherhood exists that will not be denied, and that Mr. Burroughs has rightly and legitimately emphasized and made plain in Tarzan. . . .

Undoubtedly, Burroughs, without articulating it, had been aware of his "blood brotherhood" with the animals, as part of the great plan of evolution, and had demonstrated this in his love of animals, his admiration for their simple virtues, and his solicitude for their treatment by man.

In carrying his logic a step farther, Hale noted that this idea of common origin was what made the appeal of the Tarzan books "so strong and universal"; the public showed an "unconscious approval" of the idea. "Tarzan realizes the jungle life of our ancestors of long ago," Hale maintained. "If he is trash, so are we [even including the professor] for we come of the same stock. . . ." Hale referred to one of Burroughs' favorite themes —the decadence of our supposed "civilization"—in mentioning man's "thinking his way up" from the jungle to the city:

"Up," did I say? What about Upton Sinclair's Jungle, *the abysmal depths of our filthy city brothels and "society" scandals, the atrocities of war, the gaols and the asylums? Any of these in Tarzan's jungle?*

In another letter to Ed, also dated May 24, 1922, Hale turned to a different topic, this time a special interest. He had adopted geology as a hobby, had given a series of lectures on the subject, and in the course of these had done much reading and investigation of the supposed "lost" continent of Atlantis. He now urged Ed to use Atlantis as the setting for a sequence of novels, with emphasis upon the lost continent as an entity in the long chain of human evolution. Hale suggested a "plan of order" in which reincarnation of characters might be utilized to "link distant periods of time." The steps would include the following: the "sheer brute man stage" (ape land) evolving in the south polar area; the beginnings of tools and civilization as man moved westward during the Southern Glacial Period; the separation of races to the Pacific continent, to South Africa, and to South America and Atlantis.

Hale stressed his theory that "the geographical rising and sinking of the continents" had a significant effect upon human evolution. In enclosing two small maps for Burroughs, he noted that the "ghost of Atlantis" was evident in the great mass of submerged land. "Any chart shows a surprising lot of reefs and banks in N. Atlantic which the ordinary land atlases ignore, showing that old Atlantis is not so utterly gone as some might imagine." He added that "the Azores and Canary Islands seem the best existing points to anchor an Atlantis story to. . . ."

Hale also enclosed a descriptive list of books about Atlantis. The nonfiction group of course included the earliest source contained in *Timaeus,* one of Plato's *Dialogs,* and referred to Darwin's *Coral Islands* picturing a "slowly sinking sea bottom" which would provide some foundation for an old continent in the Pacific. He noted, in addition, a number of fictional works about Atlantis, and offered to send all these books to Burroughs.[18]

Hale's enthusiasm was transmitted to Burroughs who, on June 20, appeared strongly inclined to accept the suggestion to write a series about Atlantis, but not until a future period when present work was completed. Burroughs explained his intention to obtain the listed books by asking his London agent, Curtis Brown, to purchase them. On August 29 he sought Davis' opinion on the choice of Atlantis as a story subject. The editor's reply of September 8 was bluntly negative: ". . . if I were you I wouldn't monkey with that submerged continent. It has already been hit so damned hard that nobody cares whether it ever reappears again." Possibly as a result of this, Burroughs abandoned the idea. Concerning Hale's suggestion that reincarnation of characters be used (to develop the evolutionary sequence), Burroughs had already conceived of this idea in "The Moon Men," completed January 1922, but it is possible that in "The Moon Maid," written in July of that year, with the worksheets listing a lengthy series of reincarnations from 1918 to 2409, Burroughs had been stimulated by Hale, with the result being his greater emphasis upon the reincarnations. But curiously, if a comparison is to be made with Darwin's theories, the "evolution" is in reverse; mankind, on earth, *retrogresses* from an advanced, highly civilized form in the Moon trilogy to the primitive, savage level of the American Indian, as the events of the last story, "The Red Hawk," take place. Burroughs' imagination, perhaps subconsciously, found its own method of adapting Darwinism. In other works, notably his first, *A Princess of Mars,* he had pictured this backward journey, this reversal of man's natural evolution, with the planet Mars returning to barbarism, and again one might conjecture that Darwin's theories provided the inspiration.

Ed's conviction that evolution was a scientific verity, a law beyond dispute, influenced him in 1925 to issue a statement to the press at the time of the Scopes Trial at Dayton, Tennessee. Written for the International Press Bureau and Universal Service, the article appeared in various papers, including the *New York American* of July 6, where it was headed "Evolution held undeniable. Nature's law, says author." Ed's delivered opinion had a tone of impatience with those who needed to be informed of the obvious:

It really does not make much difference what Mr. Scopes thinks about evolution, or what Mr. Bryan thinks about it. They cannot change it by thinking, or talking, or by doing anything else. It is an immutable law of Nature; and when we say that, it is just the same as saying that it is an immutable law of God—that is, for those who believe in God—for one cannot think of God and Nature as separate and distinct agencies.

He went on to explain, "If we are not religious then we must accept evolution as an obvious fact. If we are religious then we must either accept the theory of evolution or admit that there is a power greater than that of God. . . ." His arguments, in the remainder of the article, were based upon the evidences all around us—"the infant into the adult . . . the seed into the plant, the bud into the flower:" these illustrate that all organisms pass through preliminary stages of development to attain a final form. The "marvelous miracle of evolution" is that everything, the entire universe, follows a natural "unfolding." Concerning the human race, a simple consideration of the succession of the Piltdown man, Neanderthal man, and Cro-Magnon man, in progress up the scale of development, makes it clear "that Nature did not produce the finished product originally, but something that was susceptible of improvement. . . ." Ed did not attempt to deny God's connection with this evolutionary plan; the individual could view it as Nature's law or God's law, but above all, mankind must accept "the proofs that God, or Nature, has left for our enlightenment." On an obvious level, those who cannot understand Darwin's theories should be able to perceive how "the entire evolution of the human race" is reproduced "within the womb of every mother."

In other writing of the period, Ed, for Arbor Day, 1922, prepared a speech for presentation to the Uplifters, a social group to which he belonged. Here again he revealed his early awareness of ecology and expressed his ardent support of conservation. Once more he took care to create a combined tone of religion and pantheism in his speech. God may be considered as "The Great Scientist" who maintains a laboratory where He "tries" new forms. All of these experiments are not successful. Evolution is referred to; God discards many forms, and "the object of His changes lies in the direction of eventual perfection." His master works are the earth with its plant life, mineral kingdom, and the great mountains. But in the animal kingdom "He has not done quite so well, if man is his ultimate conception. In fact, He is doubtless rather disappointed."

As an Arbor Day speech, the main subject then became the tree, "a living, breathing thing which in majesty, dignity, and beauty, transcends all His other works. In the tree God has attained perfection." The Uplifters' task for that day was to plant trees. Ed mentioned the eucalyptus, one of his favorites, and one of the most ancient of trees which probably existed in Eocene times, and from that offered a belief: ". . . trees will still be here after man has gone the way of all the countless forms of animal life that preceded him." To Ed it was a "tremendous" thought which suggested the greatness of Nature and the insignificance of man. After all, the saber-tooth tiger who may have stalked his prey in the Tarzana canyons was gone, "although he took very much better care of himself than we do. . . ." Obviously, man will not "persist through eternity," but the trees will. Ed noted, "I can contemplate with equanimity the thought of a manless world; but a treeless world—never!"

Those individuals who in the 1970s began to display a serious concern about the destruction of the earth's surface should appreciate the remarkable fact that Burroughs, through a unique philosophy that united him in love and respect with all of nature, had preceded them by more than fifty years in this concern. In his loving and understanding and fiercely protective attitude toward animals, trees, and plants, he truly exemplified the religious man who in his highest form is described by Coleridge: "He prayeth best who loveth best/All things both great and small. . . ." Burroughs, who as a writer was given to personifying the animals in his stories, thought of his trees in the same way. Toward the oaks, sycamores, and walnut trees on his ranch he felt not only an "affection," but "an intimate and personal touch which implies, at the least, friendship."

The value he placed upon trees was demonstrated in the unusual nature of his alfalfa fields, dotted with sycamores and walnuts. Here the trees made the harvesting more difficult and expensive and were occupying land that could be used for crops. Ed remarked about the foreman who objected to them and who thought he was a "hopeless idiot" when he (Burroughs) insisted that if driven to a matter of choice, he would do away with the alfalfa rather than the trees. He spoke with regret of the huge old oaks, located on property recently subdivided in the Tarzana area, that were now being cut down. To him this was "an odious crime," and he wondered if a law could be enacted that would place all native trees, even privately owned, under the protection of the state. In later years this became a reality in the neighboring community of Encino. Of all his trees, one that he especially cherished was an enormous walnut in his orchard: ". . . I often ride into its shade on my horse in the summer time and I am sure that twelve or fifteen horsemen could stand beneath its branches without crowding."

To the Uplifters listening to his speech Ed offered to donate Tarzana live oaks for transplanting; *Quercus Tarzania,* he noted, was "some tree." He stressed one final thought: we are planting trees for the benefit of our children and our children's children. And through our examples, they may learn to love and treasure trees and to plant them for succeeding generations.

What Ed had viewed or experienced during motion picture production involving the use of animals became the subject of his first article in this field. Titled "Wild Animals in Pictures," the article was completed on March 23, 1922, at the request of E. E. Graneman of Anchor Films in Los Angeles, and appeared in June of that year in the magazine *Hollywood Screenland*. Ed's emphasis, as might be expected, was upon the humane treatment of these animals. They were trained by "masters who have felt and demonstrated an actual affection for their charges. . . . The 'bad' lion, like the 'bad' horse, is usually the result of brutal and ignorant mishandling by a trainer." Ed mentioned watching such trainers as Walter Beckwith, Charlie Gay, and Joe Turner and being impressed by their intelligent and kindly treatment of their animals.

Although conceding that some of the animal scenes are faked, Ed explained that the really thrilling action is bona fide, and the actors, or even the trainers who double as actors, take suicidal chances. He had especially admired the courage of tiny Louise Lorraine. " I have seen a whole bevy of lionesses pass directly over her half naked body, and a full-grown lion spring upon her and throw her to the ground." He described a scene in which Charley Gay, doubling for an actress, was required to dive off a fifteen-foot cliff into a pool with a lioness in close pursuit. The terrified beast had to be driven to the cliff's edge, and as a result, the trainer and the lioness struck the water together. Ed commented that he would hardly have swapped places with Gay who rose to the surface of the small pool to face an infuriated lioness.

Ed recalled his most dangerous personal experience when, at his request, he was allowed inside the arena to witness a scene involving a "particularly vicious lion." He had presumed that the director and leading actor would accompany him but, to his consternation, found himself alone. The director had handed him a large club and said, "Do not run if he comes for you. Just stand still and use this." His actions make it appear that the whole situation was somebody's idea of a practical joke. Ed described what followed:

While I was reviewing my past life and wishing that I had been a better man, they opened the gate at the end of the runway and loosed the lion upon us. . . . I had always considered him a very beautiful lion, but as I faced him in the arena it occurred to me that he had an extremely low forehead and a bad disposition. He was the incarnation of all the devil-faced man-eaters with which I had filled the pages of the Tarzan books.

Moments later the lion was driven back into his runway, and Ed noted, "it was with a sigh of relief that I laid aside my futile war club and stood in the fresh air of the sunshine beyond the limits of the studio jungle."

In a 1,000-word article written for Thomas Ford, literary

editor of the *Los Angeles Times,* and sent to him on December 29, 1922, Ed, after reiterating that fiction should not read for purposes of instruction or enlightenment, made reference to a number of his favorite authors. First mentioned were Mary Roberts Rinehart and Booth Tarkington, but he reserved his highest praise for Owen Wister's *The Virginian,* which, along with *The Prince and the Pauper* and *Little Lord Fauntleroy,* he admitted having read five or six times. Ed wrote:

I believe The Virginian *to be one of the greatest American novels ever written, and though I have heard that Mr. Wister deplores having written it I venture that a hundred years from now it will constitute his sole link to Fame—and I am sure that* The Virginian *will live a hundred years, if the Bolshevists and the I.W.W. permit civilization to endure that long.*

Ed then launched into an attack on "literary people"—he was quite sensitive to their disparagement of his works—and remarked that he had met a few but had "never stayed awake long enough to get acquainted." About them he commented sarcastically, "Literary people do not write. They read what other people write, discuss it, criticise it, quarrel about it and altogether take it much more seriously than the people who write it." They love to meet their favorite authors, he noted, but "sometimes they are happier when they don't":

If one should meet God and find that He wore a dirty collar, ate with a knife and picked His teeth in public he would feel shocked and disillusioned—would one not? Well, of course you can not expect all authors to be better than God. There are some to be sure; but we are in the minority.

Concerning the practice of collecting, termed "a peculiar form of insanity," he recalled how he had saved stamps, coins, and postmarks in his boyhood, and reported that his two sons were now making a "weird" collection of animal bones. The "true spirit of the collector" is revealed in the acquiring of "useless, valueless, discarded things." The "most hideous form" of collecting, according to Ed, was that of uncut books; no individual who really loves books would have an uncut volume on his shelves.

He reserved his most caustic comment for those "modern writers of so called sex stories"; he was quite willing for their books to remain uncut, and to these he added "the complete works of Charles Dickens, each of which bore me to extinction."

A different type of writing, a loosely compiled account of vacation travels, was one that Ed completed during this period. His ten-page description of a 1924 fishing excursion, into California's Sierra August 22 to September 1, was headed "Notes on Trip to Mono Creek and Porpoise Lake." With his two sons, Hulbert, age fifteen, and Jack, age eleven, Ed left Los Angeles in his Packard roadster, heading north-east, his destination originally Mammoth Lakes, but changed to Mono Creek, a more remote and less crowded area where fishing would be better. As in the past, the first problem was with the car which failed to start the next morning. The handyman had forgotten to place tools in the car, but Ed, a pioneer in long auto trips under the most difficult and primitive conditions (for example, the 1916 cross-country journey), had through circumstances become a fairly skilled mechanic and troubleshooter. He succeeded in opening the carburetor with a jackknife and can opener, and within an hour the trio was on its way.

The article reported the typical vacation events and minor catastrophes:

Fished up Rock Creek . . . Jack fell in the creek and had to go back to camp and change. . . . Jack was sick all night—

Camp table of willow and quaking aspen built by ERB at Mono Creek, August 27, 1924.

up three times. Gave him cascara . . . Sunday August 24 we started for Mono Creek with Earl Proebstel as packer and guide. [All rode horses.] . . . took us 7½ hours to reach Mono Creek . . . pleasant afternoon fishing down stream . . . we passed the time until bedtime telling stories . . . the boys asked for a Timothy Twiggs story and one about Mabel, the sub-deb coyote, taking us all back to the bedtime stories I told for many years . . . Mabel; Timothy Twiggs; Arabella, Sophronia and Grandpa Kazink; Percival and Gwendolyn—night after night. . . .

In a 1974 interview at Tarzana, Hulbert recalled some occurrences of the trip:

One afternoon while resting on the bank of Mono Creek, Dad and my brother Jack were doodling in the sand with sticks. It was on this occasion that Dad devised the curious symbol that became his personal mark. He called it the Doodad. *It was later used as the now-familiar colophon on the spines of the books his company started publishing in 1930. He frequently signed personal notes and memos with it.*

The trip turned into one of illness and suffering for my father. The altitude of near 10,000 feet was the highest he had ever been for any length of time. Although we did not then understand the reasons, he was probably suffering from oxygen starvation.

Ed's main problem was his inability to sleep and shortness of breath. His complaints were repeated: "Followed another night of torture, during which I occasionally lapsed into a semi-comatose condition. . . . I do not understand . . . in perfect physical condition and so physically tired at the end of the day . . . I could swear that I'd sleep on a pile of cobble stones for twenty-four hours at a stretch. . . ."

Recalls Hulbert: "He did not complain at all, and we did not learn of his suffering until much later. He was so unselfish that he did not want to spoil the trip for Jack and me. It is obvious in retrospect that we should have left immediately for a lower altitude. This may have been an early symptom of the heart trouble that developed in later years."

On August 29 Ed noted their arrival at Porpoise Lake, the elevation of their new camp now being about 10,000 feet, and also listed the fishing tally to date: Hulbert, 43 trout; Jack, 4; Ed, 3. Clearly, as Ed commented, Hulbert was "the only dyed in the wool Isaac Walton in the family." Ed's eagerness to forget that he was forty-nine years old, and his overexertions in keep-

Burroughs family at Tarzana Ranch, about 1921; left to right: Joan, Hulbert, Emma, Jack, and ERB.

ing up with his boys brought him a bad cold. While fishing he had stripped and entered the icy cold water to rescue a fly that had become entangled in a log. He had been ill for three days, unable to eat, and on August 31, as the return trip began, he had to summon all of his strength to make the journey. Perverse fate made certain that nothing would go easily; a series of car troubles followed. The battery ceased to function and the lights became too dim to view the road. The travelers arrived at Mojave at 2:30 a.m., and near dawn they ran out of gasoline. Luckily, they were on a down grade and coasted to within two miles of Saugus; then they pushed the car the remainder of the way. More pushing followed to make the car start. In his account Ed finally reported reaching home on September 1—his birthday—and wrote, ". . . I think that in the course of three or four months, if I eat enough and sleep enough, I will approximate normalcy again."

The love of horses and horseback riding, developed from his early years in Idaho and at the military academy, still remained with him. The winding paths, hills, and canyons of Tarzana Ranch provided a unique opportunity for indulgence of this riding hobby. Ed's interest both in the saddle horse and the show horse led to his contributing an article to the *Los Angeles Times* of January 1, 1925, titled "The Saddle Horse in Southern California." Among the group of photos accompanying the article was one of Burroughs mounted upon Brigadier Rex. The article stressed the advantages possessed by the California rider, the rich beauty of nature all about him, the interesting contacts with deer or coyotes or even mountain lions, and the vast area available to the rider. But it also emphasized the healthful aspects of riding, quoting from a statement by Dr. A. J. Ochsner of Chicago who observed that no other form of exercise "so fully affects every nerve and every organ of the human body" as horseback riding does. "Nothing will bring out a healthy glow more quickly or enjoyably. . . . Nothing will more promptly put one's organs of digestion and those of elimination into the way of performing their physiologic work properly. . . ."

After discussing the expansion of horseback riding in Southern California and the growth of private and commercial stables, Ed proudly noted that interest in the horse show was now high and that this sport, especially because of the mild all-year-round climate of Los Angeles, promised to increase rapidly. He then listed prominent residents of the Los Angeles area and the five-gaited, prizewinning horses that they owned.

An unusual form of writing for ERB, a compilation of terms, is titled "Glossary of Hoodlum Language." Although undated, this five-page glossary features many expressions of the prohibition and bootlegging era; the inclusion of these indicates that the glossary was probably written in the mid-twenties. Burroughs' alphabetical list, incomplete, terminates at the "H's." Such expressions as "alky," "blind pig," "chopper," for machine gun, and "gat" are reminiscent of the prohibition-gangster period, but others in the glossary apply to differing types of disreputable activities and rackets. A number of the terms are still understood and used today: Bar flies, big house, beat the rap, broad, cop a plea, dip, fall guy, framed, grapevine. However, most of the expressions, as with the slang or argot of many periods in the past, have long since vanished from the public vocabulary. Some of these are humorous and ingenious:

Ah-ah: *Self-important, attention demanding, e.g. "Tony's broad is an ah-ah dame."*

Big cough: *Bomb containing a heavy charge of explosive.*

Block and tackle: *Watch and chain.*

Butterfly: *A worthless check.*

Caught with a biscuit: *Caught with incriminating evidence.*

Croaker: *A doctor, either physician or surgeon.*

Dance: *To die by hanging.*

Eerbay: *Beer. (Note: so-called "pig Latin" or English words turned around is commonly used among hoodlums when they want to talk in code.)*

In compiling the "Glossary of Hoodlum Language," Burroughs' intention must have been a practical one, to use the expressions in a story he was contemplating or in a series of future stories. He had done some research into the jargon or slang of the criminal classes and lowest elements of society in the past to create vocabularies for characters in "The Girl from Farris's" (1913-14) and "The Mucker" sequence (1913-16).

Always one to speak out bluntly and forcefully in protest against injustice, Ed, in the article "The Absurd Quarantine," attacked the stringent and unreasonable quarantine regulations imposed upon stock raisers and dairy owners. During the period, evidently about 1920 (reference made to the nation's income from farm products in 1919 would appear to establish this date), Southern California was in the throes of a serious epidemic of hoof-and-mouth disease. Apparently, the authorities, in a near-panic, were adopting drastic measures to prevent the spread of the disease. Although the evidence indicated that humans could not contract it, the officials had posted armed guards at various ranches and farms to prevent individuals from coming in contact with supposedly diseased animals.

The question, undetermined, was how did the disease spread? Concerning the measures being used, Ed was bitterly accusative: ". . . while they experiment, California is being ruined. . . . There never has been so widespread and strict a quarantine anywhere for anything, and yet the disease hops here and there at will. Do they know the carriers? I doubt it. Cats, dogs, birds are being destroyed ruthlessly. The destruction of bird life alone might so easily upset nature's balance as to cause material losses to the farmer and fruit raiser."

Ed had noted the huge swarms of bees migrating over the fields of the Adohr Dairy, adjacent to his Tarzana Ranch. Since these bees alight on alfalfa blossoms and the cattle are pastured in the alfalfa, could the bees be the carriers, he wondered. He

ERB in coaster made by Hulbert, 1919.

referred to the "absurd quarantine" that was presently spraying the inside of city dwellers' cars to .prevent the spread of the disease. Would it not be more logical, he demanded, to assume that insects, especially the flies, might be the guilty carriers?

To Ed, the severe measures were being enforced to protect the assets of a comparative few—those who owned $12,000 pedigreed bulls. But what aroused his strongest indignation was the statement from the quarantine board that "whoever opposed the quarantine methods . . . was in the same category as the man who, in 1917, opposed the war." An individual who protested was classed as a traitor.

Ed pointed out that rabies had been on the increase in the Los Angeles area for the past five years; this involved the safety of the entire community, and yet no regulations had been passed.

Emma Burroughs, about 1922.

To him, the reasons for this indifference were evident. Money and wealthy owners were not involved, as in the hoof-and-mouth situation. Nobody cares, Ed maintained, "if your baby or mine is bitten by a mad dog."

He closed with an angry and defiant charge, "The quarantine as now administered is unfair, unjust, un-American, unconstitutional and absurd—but mostly absurd. If this be treason, make the most of it."

During the period of 1920-25, Burroughs turned occasionally to verse, usually light or humorous, but at times sentimental. Two poems written on December 29, 1920, titled "Sweetheart Eternal" and "Sweet Rose in God's Garden Above," are love poems of a conventional nature.

I loved you when the stars were young
And when the world was new
And every song, as yet unsung,
Welled in my heart for you.

I loved your arms, your soft, brown arms
With copper bracelets bound.
The leopard skin half hid your charms—
The depths that love would sound.

The allusions to "brown arms," "copper bracelets," and "leopard skin," and to "jungle eyes" in a later stanza, indicate that Burroughs may have intended to insert the poem in one of his stories.

"Sweet Rose in God's Garden Above" is a tragic poem, its theme based upon the death of a woman, either real or imaginary:

I dwell on the crest of a mountain
Where the winds volley up from the sea
And clouds sweeping down from the heavens
Leave no one but God there and me.

In February and June 1923, Ed wrote two narrative poems with Western settings. The first, "The Passing o' my Pal, Bill," by Texas Pete (an actual character encountered by Ed in Idaho), was later inserted in "The Bandit of Hell's Bend," written March 30 to May 24, 1923. As recounted by Texas Pete, the poem re-creates a shoot-out between Bill and another cowboy hired by the sheepmen to "git" him. Pete accompanies his friend to a bar where Bill's opponent, a "raw-boned guy," is waiting—but with a girl. The poem develops an unexpected situation:

An' the raw-boned guy wheels and the girl there she squeals:
"O, fer gawds sake don't shoot, Bill, it's dad!"

Fer the thing she had saw was Bill reach fer the draw
When the guy she called dad drawed on Bill.

At his sister's cry, Bill freezes, unable to draw, but "thet damn raw-boned guy with the ornery eye" shoots Bill "dead in the door." Texas Pete narrates the end of the tragedy:

But I'm here to opine with this bazoo o' mine
Thet he wont shoot no hombres no more.

Jest a moment, an' where they'd been five o' us there,
We hed suddenly dwindled to three—
The bar-keep, he was one—the darned son-of-a-gun—
An' the others, a orphan an' me.

Ed, who through the years had found invitations to join clubs irresistible, on various occasions had composed light verse for club functions. From his earliest period in California he had belonged to the Los Angeles Athletic Club and had later become involved in an authors' group, The Writers. In 1925 he was quite active in the Breakfast Club, and, as its most creative member, was expected to contribute poetry on demand. This varied from two poems written on August 21 to eulogize Thomas E. Campbell, ex-governor of Arizona, who was being granted honorary membership in the club, to a series of verses or lyrics designed to be sung to the melody of Upidee at a Breakfast Club function, "the passing of the oil can," in tribute to the attending oil company officials. Working on the Advisory Committee with Maurice De Mond, Ed contributed a number of lyrics for group singing.

Two other poems, possibly intended for Breakfast Club affairs, were "Hollywood" and "I'm the Guy That Sowed the Sage Brush in the Hills of Hollywood," subtitled "I Knew Him When"; these were written in October and November 1925. In "Hollywood" Ed writes of the famous heroes and great nations of the past that have long since vanished—Agamemnon, the daring Genoese, Babylon, proud Rome—and comments about Hollywood:

Thy standards flaunt the breeze today
As nations flock to homage pay
To thee, the darling of a world;

Our Hollywood!

In the second poem, humorous raillery directed at various acquaintances, Ed remarks, "I could have bought an acre right at Hollywood and Vine/If I had had ten dollars back in eighteen fifty nine" and evokes other memories of the past while noting the changes that had occurred.

Ed's other light verse included "The Wampas," written for the Western Associated Motion Picture Advertisers group attending a Breakfast Club meeting on November 20, 1925. In a satirical view of the film industry, during the same year, Ed composed a poem (untitled) describing a scene in heaven with St. Peter. A "spook," evidently a Hollywood producer or promoter, approaches St. Peter with a plan to expand and glamorize heaven with "pageants and prologs" and "The Great Ten Billion Theater," with films being shown for ten dollars a seat. But upon investigation, the producer loses all enthusiasm for the project:

"There are plenty of authors in heaven
And orchestra leaders as well;
But people who act,
Directors—in fact
All the rest of the talent's in Hell."

By 1926 the overburdening pressure of business enterprises and writing projects forced Ed to relinquish his Breakfast Club activities. To DeMond, in referring to these responsibilities plus the problems of two lawsuits, Ed, on April 23, explained that he had no time to write the song requested, and in fact no time to do anything beyond his own business "for at least a year or two."[19]

Poems of a differing type, undated but probably written in the same period, were one in the prosy rhyming style of Walt Mason, whose verses in the Chicago newspapers Ed had long admired. The poem referred jokingly to glamorous movie stars of the times, including Gloria Swanson and Bebe Daniels:

'Twould joy me more than you can guess
to purchase socks for Gloria S., or
lingerie for Bebe D. In fact my sweet philanthropy
suggests I purchase all their clothes from hats to hose—
especially hose. But several things discourage me
and one of these is Mrs. B.

In 1925 Burroughs conceived of a project that would enable him to utilize his motion picture relationships. To Earle Martin of the Newspaper Enterprise Association of Cleveland, on December 17, he wrote, "I have in mind the preparation of a column or half column of studio gossip over my signature, to be furnished weekly, fortnightly or monthly. . . ." He explained that as a member of the board of directors of the Writers Club of Hollywood he heard much "inside studio gossip," noting that most of the board members were employed in the movie field. He stressed that he had "entree" to the studios and was personally acquainted with many directors, producers, and actors.

Ed's idea was to merely conduct a friendly and gossipy column, not to adopt the role of a critic or a reviewer. The column would not be used to provide publicity for individuals; he would prefer to confine himself "principally to the most prominent and widely known members of the profession." The expected question arose: would the "returns" be sufficient to warrant the amount of time he would devote to this column, including the hours he would have to spend at the principal studios? There is no record of a response from Martin; evidently Ed received no encouragement and the column idea was abandoned.

Probably no other author could match the stream of letters that Burroughs received throughout the years from readers and friends. But the constancy and loyalty of these individuals can be attributed to the care Burroughs exhibited in answering all their letters. He sincerely felt that if his loyal fans thought well enough of him and his stories to take their time to write to him, the least he could do was to show his respect and gratitude by replying. Very few of the queries, criticisms, or notes of praise remained unanswered; as though driven by some determination or feeling of pride, he responded to letters of every variety, at first writing personally and later dictating his replies. Among his most tenacious correspondents were three who began in the early 1920s and were still going strong (aided by Burroughs' persistence) from twelve to twenty-five years later. One, in the United States, was Charles K. Miller, a friend of the family and an owner of a clipping bureau in Chicago, while the other two were Burroughs readers abroad, both in England. Through dozens of letters the bond of friendship between Burroughs and Irene Ettrick and Frank Shonfeld became unbreakable, and yet, most remarkably, he never met either of them.

Miller, from about 1922 on, began reporting various comments in the press and magazines about the Burroughs books and enclosing articles or reviews and items of literary interest. On January 3, 1923, in thanking Miller for clippings, Ed wrote, "I think you must be willfully blind to see only the kindly references to my work. . . . A recent one from my clipping bureau speaks of 'that awful trash, the Tarzan stories . . .' but I manage to bear up and get three meals a day—and pay for

Irene Ettrick of England, who as a child started writing to ERB; their correspondence continued for years.

them. I hope my critics can do as well." In the passing years other letters from Ed to Miller had typical remarks:

May 17, 1927: "It always flatters my vanity when I hear of an intellectual who admits to liking Tarzan."

June 6, 1929: "Naturally, I am not particularly enthusiastic about book clubs inasmuch as they do not distribute or recommend my books."

August 16: "Inasmuch as no one would ever recommend my books, the book clubs are not particularly harmful to me. . . ."

April 29, 1932: "What success I have had is still as much of a mystery to me as it must be to many others."

April 13, 1934: (upon receipt of a clipping) "I noticed also that my name was coupled with those of Twain and Kipling. But did you notice that Tarzan of the Apes and the Bible are on the same list? We are certainly traveling in fast company. . . ."

Irene Ettrick, who at the time of her first correspondence with Ed was about twelve years old—the same age as Joan Burroughs—was the daughter of the Reverend Maughan Ettrick, Rector at Little Ilford at Essex, England. On November 9, 1920, she wrote to acknowledge the books Ed had sent her; in replying, Ed noted his hope to come to England some day. For Christmas 1923 Irene's present to the Burroughs family was some English candy, and to her, on January 17, Ed explained that relatives on his mother's side had come from Staffordshire.

In 1924 Ed regretted that he must disappoint her and confessed that he had traveled very little: "I should be able to tell you that I had walked all over Africa, Asia, Europe, and the North Pole, but as a matter of fact, I have never been off my own continent. . . ." Irene's communications with Ed had stirred her own literary ambitions, and in May 1925 she sent him a copy of her story "The Deferred Hope" for his comments. As a rule Ed had refused to evaluate stories that writers wished to forward to him, but in this case he read her story and observed, "You have a sense of dramatic values and narrative form which study and experience will unquestionably perfect. . . ."

Irene had suffered some illness, and on February 18, 1926, Ed wrote, expressing his sympathy and answering her questions about hunting: "I cannot derive any pleasure from the taking of a wild animal's life. I would rather shoot a man than a deer, and I used to spend a great deal of time during the deer season riding over my property to protect the deer from a lot of counter jumpers who would just as soon shoot a doe as a buck." In this letter he also noted with a feeling of surprise that Irene would soon be eighteen: "I always think of you as a very little girl, as you were when you first started to write to me." Irene, in May 1926, reported that she was trying to sell some of her stories, without success, and Ed, on the twentieth, suggested that she turn to American magazines and urged a submission to Bob Davis, the Munsey Editor. In December 1927 Ed was pleased to hear that Irene had become a "motion picture actress"; he hoped to have an opportunity to see her one day in a British film.

The correspondence with Irene was maintained regularly throughout the 1930s. On December 20, 1937, Ed acknowledged her Christmas card and wrote, "I wonder if you have a recent snapshot which you will send me? I have pictures of you since you were a very little girl, and I should very much like to have a later one. . . . I look for you in every English picture we see, but so far I have not been able to recognize you. . . ." In May 1938 Irene told of the death of her father, the Reverend Maughan Ettrick, and on the sixteenth Ed sent a letter of condolence. In December of that year, a card from Irene revealed that she then lived in Brighton, Sussex, England.

Frank Shonfeld, whose first correspondence with Burroughs was probably in 1923, lived in Croydon, England; his father and his grandfather, in accordance with British tradition, had followed the family trade of a tailor, and Frank, at a later period, also had his own tailor shop in Croydon. A dedicated reader of the Burroughs stories, Frank, in his letters, often asked questions about the writings or made comments and criticisms. He had literary aspirations and in 1925 sent a manuscript, without a previous inquiry, to Burroughs who tactfully explained his policy to avoid reading others' creations and returned the manuscript unread. Shonfeld, experimenting with songwriting, in 1926 forwarded a copy of his "Columbine Song" to Ed who replied, "I have absolutely no sense of music whatsoever," and refused to offer any criticism of the song.

Shonfeld undoubtedly took the honors as Ed's most continuous correspondent. In 1937, then a sergeant in the 4th Battery, Queen's Royal Regiment, he was still fascinated by the Tarzan books, and revealed, on March 15, that his tailor shop and house in Croydon were about to be demolished, because of "Town Planning," and that he was now planning to find a new occupation. In 1941, Shonfeld, still in the British army, wrote a lengthy letter describing his attitude about the crisis in England and the war. Deeply impressed by Shonfeld's exemplification of the loyalty and patriotism of the simple English soldier, Ed sent his letter to *Life* on August 1, urging that it be printed; however, the magazine found the letter unacceptable for publication.

PART 8

TROUBLED TIMES

AUCTION SALE!

Monday, Jan. 15, 1923, 9:30 A. M.
TARZANA RANCH
Ventura Boulevard at Reseda Avenue

Farm Tools *Implements* **Work Horses**
Saddle Horses *Dairy Stock* **Swine**

TOOLS AND IMPLEMENTS

The principal items offered below are practically new, many of them having been used but a single season. The Case separator, for instance, is a notably good buy, as is, also, the grain drill, the John Deere mower, the side delivery rake, the manure spreader and a number of other implements that are practically as good as new.

Catalog
No.

No.	
1	2 small galvanized iron drinking fountains.
1A	1 large galvanized iron drinking fountain.
1B	2 galvanized iron hog troughs, 10 ft. x 13 in. wide x 6 in. deep.
1C	6 hog troughs 2 ft. long, galvanized iron.
1D	1 galvanized iron tank, 2000 gal. capacity.
1E	1 galvanized iron tank, 1000 gal. capacity.
1F	1 galvanized iron tank, 7000 gal. capacity.
2	About 750 feet surface irrigation pipe, 8 1-2 inch.
3	One 1-horse walking cultivator.
4	One 1-horse plow.
5	One 2-gang 14 in. bottoms John Deere moldboard riding plow.
6	One 2-gang John Deere disc riding plow.
7	One 2-gang Emerson disc riding plow.
8	One 3-gang 12 in. bottoms Oliver moldboard riding plow.
9	One 3-section smoothing harrow.
10	One 2-section smoothing harrow.
11	One 4-section spring tooth harrow.
12	One 1-horse garden cultivator.
13	One P & O riding cultivator.
14	One Killifer chisel cultivator.
15	One clod smasher, roller type.
16	One P & O tractor disc with trailer.
17	One 4-horse Fresno scraper.
18	One Thomas hay loader .
19	One Thomas side delivery hay rake.
21	One John Deere mower.
22	One Weber wagon with hay rack.
23	One Sandusky 10-20 Tractor.
24	1 Case 20x28 thresher.
25	One 6 in. 4-ply transmission belt 200 ft. in length.
26	One Ohio No. 9 feed cutter.
27	One Wilson feed grinder.
28	One lister.
29	One P & O No. 140 2-row corn planter.
30	One Van Brunt grain drill.
31	1 John Deere self binder.
32	1 John Deere manure spreader.
33	1 steam cooker.
34	1 small cyclone weed cutter.
35	1 bean cutter.
36	1 pair light wagon shafts.
37	1 H A M M Company feed cutter and blower.
38	1 Fairbanks-Morse 15 H. P. Type "Z" Engine.
39	1 belt, 6 in., 4 ply, 50 ft. in length.

CHAPTER 17

PROBLEMS AT HOME AND ABROAD

The lifelong dream of owning land, a wide expanse of land in its natural and unspoiled state, land without the clutter of people, buildings, and paved roads, had been realized, and yet in a brief period of four years was being relinquished. Raised in the crowded environment of the big city, Ed's first experience with the open spaces and the free, outdoor life had been in Idaho as a young cowpuncher. The experience was a revelation to him. But to the urge for a return to this outdoor life was added a further drive—that of owning something. His background made this understandable. He had grown up in a rented home and had lived, after marriage, in a succession of apartments. In rebellion against the crowded quarters of Chicago he had moved to the quiet suburb of Oak Park, and there, to satisfy his craving for ownership, had purchased a home. The suburban life was a compromise, still not the realization of his suppressed dream. The opportunity had come finally—Tarzana Ranch with its hills and canyons, with all the room for a man to stretch and roam. But what had gone wrong with the dream?

The answer lies in the Burroughs personality. He had originally intended to keep the 550 acres intact, to save them for his children. The key may be revealed in his comment to Bert Weston: "They were subdividing all around me. . . ." Burroughs was never a man to stand by and watch others reap the profits. With the rise in land values and the influx of real-estate agents and homeowners, the money-making fever, always with him, became dominant, overpowering his desire for calm withdrawal and seclusion in the broad, open expanse of Tarzana Ranch.

ERB's announcement of auction sale of farm equipment and livestock.

True, he had lost money in his venture as a gentleman farmer and had complained that the taxes and expenses of running the ranch were too high. But his financial situation, at this time, was hardly critical. Payments on the ranch mortgage were of course still due, but the phenomenal sales of his books continued and his income from writing was high. For the years 1919-20 almost two million copies of his books were sold in the United States, while in England his royalties approximated two-thirds of the American receipts for the same years. *Tarzan of the Apes,* although seven years old, had sold 55,000 copies in the last half of 1920. His total income for 1921, including $20,000 paid by Numa Pictures Corporation in advance for movie rights, was close to $100,000. Additional royalties were being received from foreign sales of books translated into Norwegian, Swedish, Danish, Dutch, Russian, German, and Arabic.[1]

Achieving little success in his efforts to sell residential lots, Burroughs, in 1923, decided to assign the entire project to a land developer. As usual, he had too many irons in the fire, and the departure of his secretary John A. Shea, who accepted a position with William Sistrom at the Hollywood Studios —Sistrom was to be the general manager of the Burroughs Production Company which never got beyond the tentative stage— increased his responsibilities. Shea was replaced by G. L. Young. In the fall of 1923 H. B. Currier, a local agent, took over the subdividing of Tarzana. The advertised opening of sales to the general public was announced in the papers as of September 27, with a "great jungle barbecue" to be served by Tarzan himself —Elmo Lincoln—and with Louise Lorraine to be present to sign autographs. Concerning the Ford that was raffled off, Burroughs noted acidly, "The guy who won the Ford didn't buy a lot."[2] A photo, supposedly of Elmo, supplied by the subdivider and printed in a newspaper, was actually someone else; Elmo, irked, refused to appear, and there were threats of a lawsuit.

In 1924 Ed continued to divide his energies in miscellaneous money-making enterprises. The Tarzana Ranch with its picturesque Koonskin Kabin was occasionally being rented to film companies for production, especially of Westerns. That year the ranch was utilized by Phil Goldstone Studios for *The Bar "F" Mystery* and *Bred in the Bone,* both starring William Fairbanks; by The Vitagraph Company for *The Pioneer* and *Terrible Terry,* starring William Duncan; and by Triograph Productions for *The Squatters,* featuring Bill Patton. No possible source of revenue could be overlooked. That same year the Golden Gate

Oil Company was granted a permit to drill for oil. July 23 to 24 the company reported reaching a depth of about 1,300 feet and predicted they would soon find oil. Traces of oil were detected, but never anything in sufficient quantity, and by the fall of 1926 the company abandoned its lease and sold its equipment at auction.[3]

The financial problems were not the only ones encountered during this Tarzana Ranch period. A disturbing family situation, already too apparent, was aggravated by the intensive social life at the ranch. With Tarzana being a unique San Fernando Valley meeting place, the Burroughs family became social leaders in this somewhat isolated area; weekends at the ranch were regularly open house, the guests often including members of the film colony. At these parties the liquor, despite the prohibition law, flowed freely, and food was plentiful. This situation, while exasperating, was not as serious as the problem that centered about Emma. For some years she found it difficult to limit her dependence upon liquor, and a steady round of parties provided a temptation that was irresistible.

Ed's concern over her increased drinking brought matters to a climax. At this time, in anger and disgust, he proceeded to pour the gallons of liquor into the swimming pool and to announce that the unrestricted open houses at the Tarzana Ranch were finished. The only visitors were a small number of personal friends. The changed situation, now that the free refreshments were discontinued, caused Ed to comment bitterly that it did not take long to find out who his real friends were. Emma, however, could not control her drinking, and in the future this habit would produce a crisis in their relationship.

Early in 1924, Ed committed himself to the most ambitious of his business projects, the sale of 120 acres of the Tarzana Ranch, including the large house and other buildings, for a country club. To his brother Harry, on January 18, he confided the details:

It is to be called El Caballero Country Club, and the aim of the promoters is to make it the finest and most exclusive country club on the Pacific coast. There will be two golf courses and a polo field. Our residence will be used as the nucleus of a larger club house. . . .

He explained that the club promoters were also purchasing one hundred acres from the adjacent Woodrough property on the west, and at the end, commented, "We do not feel so badly about giving up the place . . . since we will have the use of it, without any of the responsibility, and really can enjoy it just as much, if not more than before." Ed informed his brother George, now living in Burley, Idaho, that if the sale were completed, the family would have to leave Tarzana by June 1. He offered a practical reason for the move: "It was necessary, however, that we live in town, as the children are all attending school there, and it is much too far to drive twice a day."

Ed provided a vivid account of the changes taking place in the Tarzana area:

Formerly we were way out in the country, while now everything is rapidly moving in our direction. . . . With the exception of one or two tracts, everything between us and Los Angeles has been subdivided. . . . It is nothing unusual for lots to jump in two or three resales from six thousand and eight thousand to fifteen and twenty thousand dollars. A lot that I purchased six weeks ago for $16,800 I was offered $22,500 for, while the only other similar lot on the street, which lot is a little larger than mine, is being held for $30,000. . . .

"With all these improvements and changes," Ed wrote, "five hundred and fifty acres would have been a very expensive luxury. . . ."[4]

Throughout 1924 and into 1925 Ed maintained activities at a furious pace. The business side of his dual nature now became uppermost, although he did take time to write his longest novel, *Marcia of the Doorstep,* between April 12 and October 13, 1924. As a natural organizer, one who loved to take charge of things and one who was flattered by requests to do so, he found supervisory positions irresistible. To Weston he explained that the office of managing director of El Caballero Country Club had been "wished" on him and that he was obliged to take over the downtown office and handle the membership drive, the building plans, and the club program. He wrote, "I am at the office from about nine to five thirty every day, not even going out for lunch, and when I reach home I am a total loss, being probably the world's tiredest business man."[5]

The assumption of all these responsibilities, with the enforced sacrifice of creativity—he told Harry "I am giving up my writing and practically everything else to put this club across"—resulted, as in the past, from Ed's excessive pride in his business and managerial ability. He could not overcome the tendency, stemming from his years of experience in business and the success of his shrewd bargaining practices with editors, to view himself as The Efficiency Expert. Another factor, strangely enough, was his need for recognition, a need not fully satisfied by his writing achievements. The business judgments and decisions, often hasty and emotional, could be plain miscalculations, as Ed was beginning to understand. Apparently, his vaunted business acumen applied only to his dealings with editors; the future would demonstrate even more clearly that in his financial schemes his lack of success would be paradoxical to his success in the marketing of stories and books. One other point must be emphasized: a harried man is not an efficient man. Ed's habit of undertaking too much, of working desperately under too many pressures, was self-defeating.

To account for his motives in organizing the El Caballero Country Club, one must remember that *his* land was involved, and that he was anxious to devise some scheme for making a profit from the land, after previous projects had failed. The governors and members of the advisory board of the country club, a distinguished group of civic leaders, included bankers, real estate developers, business owners and an attorney.[6] Yet, from the start, the enterprise showed no sign of fulfilling Ed's glowing hopes. A publicized clubhouse opening in July 1924 brought insufficient response; later, the clubhouse was closed, and affairs remained in a state of uncertainty. One problem may have been the membership restrictions. While the club brochure denied any intent toward a "false idea of exclusiveness," yet care was to be taken to find members with "congeniality

ERB's life membership card in El Caballero Country Club.

and harmony of tastes." In order to pay for the land—a total of 236 acres had been acquired, 116 of these purchased from R. L. Woodrough whose property adjoined Burroughs'—membership certificates were to be sold. Life membership cost a minimum of $2,500, and regular members were to pay from $600 to $1,250. To avoid overcrowding, membership was limited to 750; it was by invitation only, and all applications were passed upon by a secret committee before submission to the board of governors. The club's major attractions, obviously to Ed's taste, were to be found in its planned eighteen-hole golf course and polo field; naturally, the emphasis was upon "equestrian features" for those who loved horseback riding.

Ed welcomed the New Year, 1925, on the El Caballero golf links. *The St. Louis Globe Democrat* reported:

Edgar Rice Burroughs, novelist, won the first 1925 golf tournament played in the United States. He defeated L. W. Craig of Los Angeles, 2 up, at 2 o'clock New Year's morning over the El Caballero Country Club's eighteen hole obstacle course. The course was electrically lighted. Playing started New Year's Eve at eight o'clock and reached the finals just after midnight.

That the new year brought no improvement in the financial situation was evident in a letter to Frank Burroughs of January 22, 1925; Ed spoke of "trying to work out the salvation of the Country Club which purchased some of Tarzana. . . ." The duties he had now undertaken appeared beyond the energies of any one man:

I spend practically all of every day in a downtown office. I am also trying to gather up the loose ends of a real estate subdivision which was left in bad shape by an agent and from which I have, up to now, realized little or nothing. In addition there is the regular routine work of my profession . . . on top of it all I had wished on me the chairmanship of the Publicity Committee of the Association which put on the Animal Horse Show here. . . .

In an attempt to rescue the foundering El Caballero, Ed mortgaged his Tarzana property to the extent of $200,000. His attorneys, Lawler & Degnan, on March 4, 1925, noted that the mortgage had been arranged "in order that the bonds secured thereby may be sold for the benefit of the Club. . . . The transaction, therefore, is practically a loan by you to the Club of the proceeds of the bond issue. . . ."

A month later Ed provided a description of his activities to Harry: ". . . plans for a new home in Beverly Hills . . . put unsold lots on the market myself . . . concluding a $200,000 bond issue by Edgar Rice Burroughs, Inc. . . . completed laying eleven miles of pipe in the golf course in El Caballero . . . reopened the clubhouse the first of April . . . feeling that I have too much time on my hands I have recently taken an option on 120 acres close to the heart of town and I am arranging to promote a public golf course . . . between times I am trying to exercise five saddle horses, keep up my reading, and work for the interest of the saddle horse and bridle trail promotion here. . . ."[7]

In the midst of all this Ed had been bombarded by Davis and Bray for a sequel to *The Moon Men* and another *Tarzan* and Mars story. Overwork, as in the past, often brought him to the edge of illness or physical collapse. He had ignored Dr. Crispin's advice, months earlier, to drop everything and go away for a long rest. About this behavior he commented jokingly to Harry, "Being naturally a lazy man, there is only one explanation for my behavior—that I am what the English probably call a bit balmy."

The added project, a public golf course, launched despite the unsolved problems of the El Caballero Club, was called the Rolling Hills Golf Club. Its planned site, a 120-acre tract on El Sereno Avenue, was five miles east of the Los Angeles downtown area and distant from Tarzana.

The Rolling Hills brochure deplored the existence of the private clubs designed for the "Wealthy Few," where memberships could run as high as $2500 (an obvious barb at El Caballero). It stated, ". . . not one man in three hundred can afford to pay such prices for his golf . . . but there are thousands of ardent golfers who can and will be glad to pay from one dollar to three dollars for a game of golf on a first class course which is not overcrowded."

In the promotion of the club, Ed, weighted down with duties, had turned once more to John A. Shea, who resumed his position with Burroughs in the fall of 1924 and was then made vice-president of El Caballero Country Club. Shea was given a dual position as secretary of the Rolling Hills Golf Club, was one of the original subscribers and a stockholder, and handled much of the club business from an office in the Commercial Exchange Building in Los Angeles. Other officers of the club, in addition to Burroughs as its president, were William Sis-

Golf course at Tarzana; photo by Donald Biddle Keyes.

trom, vice-president, and William P. Bell, the architect who had designed El Caballero Country Club, also vice-president.

The Rolling Hills enterprise, reminiscent of several of Ed's first impractical ventures as an entrepreneur, staggered through a period of public indifference until it was finally abandoned. On April 5, 1926, Ed explained to a friend, "The property is to be opened as El Serrano Country Club as I learned from an article in one of the daily papers recently. I have nothing to do with it."

When their luxurious Tarzana home was adopted as a clubhouse for the El Caballero enterprise, the Burroughs family, in June 1924, moved into town, renting a home at 544 South Gramercy Place, Los Angeles. For transience the Burroughs record would be hard to match; two years earlier Ed had remarked to Harry, "If you keep on moving you will soon equal Emma's record and mine of 22 moves in 21 years. . . ." The future would continue the successive changes to homes or apartments. The financial situation involving the El Caballero Club had been steadily deteriorating. By the fall of 1925 Ed had severed all official connections with the club. Various legal maneuvers followed. The golf course, however, was opened for play in 1926. Hailed as one of the finest courses in the West, it was host to the 1927 Los Angeles Open Golf Tournament, won by Bobby Cruickshank.

The family was now living at 674 South New Hampshire in Los Angeles, but Ed decided to move back to Tarzana where he built a seven-room cottage on a level section in his Tarzana tract at 5046 Mecca Avenue. This was occupied in the fall of 1926, and in wry comment about the change from a "mansion on the hilltop," Ed observed, "The place is so small that we have to go outdoors to turn around, and if we have more than two guests for dinner the table has to be extended out in the living room. . . ."[8] The situation in which a famous author, whose income exceeded that of most other writers in the country, should have arrived at this unhappy state through his own business blunders is surprising but not unheard of; Mark Twain's financial failures are also noteworthy. In a sense Ed had duplicated impulsive actions of his earlier years, and this tendency to devise unsound money-making schemes would lead to further problems.

With the El Caballero Country Club bogged down in a financial morass, a number of years passed in legal battles. In 1929 Ed started foreclosure proceedings. The original $250,000 bond issue was secured by a mortgage on the club property and on 315 acres of adjoining land that Ed owned. In the 1930 settlement Ed received approximately thirty acres, with the club allowed to retain ninety-six acres as a golf course. Ed's property contained the clubhouse, garages, stables, and other buildings. The ninety-six acres ceded to the club constituted a loss of some $50,000. Ed had received most of the land back, including the large home on the hill, his ownings now totaling 345 acres, but his debts were heavy. To Harry, on May 21, 1930, he noted gloomily, ". . . my expense will be not under twenty thousand dollars a year . . . also, I lost some twenty-two thousand dollars last year in mistaken investments, which I made in a hectic effort to get some quick money to save the ranch." On November 17, in writing to Weston, he spoke of expenses of twenty-five thousand dollars to rehabilitate the property, and added, "I think I shall start in unloading, even if I have to take considerably less for the property than I know it to be worth. . . ."

The reference to losses in "mistaken investments" reveals that Ed's penchant for business gambles continued to lead him into trouble. In the summer of 1929 he became involved with two related enterprises, jointly promoted by three men (Heffron-McCray-St. John). One was a plan for a Los Angeles Metropolitan Airport to be constructed in the San Fernando Valley; the other was a plan for the manufacture of an airplane engine by a company to be called Apache Motors. Convinced of the tremendous future of aviation, Ed purchased 1,000 shares of the airport stock at ten dollars a share, plus additional stock in Apache Motors, and persuaded his friend Bert Weston to make the same investment.

The publicity released by the Metropolitan Development Syndicate heralded the certain expansion of the San Fernando Valley, where Tarzana was situated, but here Ed needed no persuasion. On July 3, 1929, he noted that their statements were "conservative," that he had observed the growth of the valley in the past ten years, and that Metropolitan represented one of the safest investments he had ever encountered. Actually, Ed had sold himself; it would almost appear that he was promoting the venture:

. . . What appeals to all of us to a greater or lesser extent is the speculative value of securities . . . doubt if even a wild flight of imagination today would make it possible to visualize the development of the next two or three years . . . impossible to prophecy what heights this stock may soar in view of the increasing air-mindedness of the entire nation. . . .

His most glowing predictions were about the future of the valley. He stressed the airport as a vital requirement for the valley:

Without aviation, there seems little to expect other than a community of small farms, which at best are far from profitable and in this instance almost foredoomed to failure because of the high cost of land and water. With the coming of the Metropolitan Airport, the valley is being rapidly transformed into an industrial aviation center. . . .

He predicted a development not to be attained in his own time: ". . . the center of population of the city will be on this side of the Santa Monica Mountains, and it will no longer be a question as to how far the valley is from Seventh and Broadway, but how far Seventh and Broadway is from the valley. . . ." The prophecy was to be fully realized within the decade after Burroughs' death.

In the first stages of the venture, as always, the reports were optimistic. To Weston, Ed repeated forecasts that the stock would rise to forty dollars a share and that the company was "going to make a lot of money for you." Within a few months his comments became cautious. On October 7, 1929, with the early signs of the stock market crash, Ed wrote to Weston, "The Metropolitan Airport stock went on the market just about the time that the big slump occurred." However, he felt that the good publicity given the airport project would drive the stock upward. Apache Motors had scheduled a Department of Commerce test of the airplane engine, and Ed believed that with the department's approval of the engine, there would be "sufficient orders to make the stock extremely attractive. . . ."

To the Westons, now on a vacation in Cuba, Ed boasted of the rapid growth of the southern California area, adding his opinion, on January 21, 1930, that Margaret Weston had been wise in buying two lots at Miramar. But with the country in the throes of the Great Depression, hopes for the success of the airport venture were vanishing. Concerning Apache Motors, on May 16 the worst possible news was received. From Washington came the report that the 200 H.P. Apache engine had failed the test, disqualifying itself because of supercharger trouble. Production of engines now came to a halt, and affairs of the Metropolitan Airport were tangled in financial confusion. ". . . I feel like hell about the airport and engine company investments, which you certainly would not have made had I not brought them to your attention," Ed wrote in gloom and guilt to Weston.

Because of the deficit, the stockholders had already been required to pay an assessment. Ed opposed later attempts to impose another levy; he offered more apologies to Weston for having involved him in the project, and remarked, ". . . I still think that we would have made some money had the Wall Street slump not taken place." The Metropolitan Airport, Ltd., close to collapse, staggered along into 1931. When efforts to sell shares of capital stock to meet an assessment resulted in no bidders, the only remaining course, as explained in a notice of June 4, was "to liquidate the corporation as quickly as possible and with the least possible expense." Nevertheless, it was not until March 3, 1932, that Burroughs made the final payment on his indebtedness to the corporation.

The world-wide demand for Burroughs' books had resulted in heavy sales of these in foreign translations. To the multitudes of those clamoring for *Tarzan* stories were added, of all people, the Russians. Six of the Tarzan novels—pirated, since the Soviets viewed capitalist copyright agreements with indifference—had been printed in sixty-cent paperbacks. The reading situation in Russia led to a despairing report in a Moscow journal of April 1924:

We are being defeated on the literary front. We publish books and pamphlets about Marxism and our great revolution. We encourage young authors to interpret its spirit and inspire the masses. We even issue cheap editions of the Russian classics. But the public reads—what?—"Tarzan."

Although the total printing was 250,000, the supply was insufficient. A Russian publisher commented, "We could easily sell a million. They read it in offices, read it in street cars, read it in trains, read it in factories. Go to the villages and you find the educated young soldier reading 'Tarzan' to a circle of peasants with mouths agape."

While noting that Burroughs was the Russian favorite, the Moscow newspaper also admitted that a stream of other American and British writers followed him in popularity—O. Henry, H. G. Wells, Jack London, Conan Doyle, and Upton Sinclair. The newspaper was blunt in explaining why no Russian authors were on the list: ". . . old Russian literature is out of date, and the new dry, dull, or too subtle for mass comprehension." Walter Duranty, *The New York Times* Moscow correspondent, had a different and insulting interpretation of the Soviet reading habits: ". . . the newly emancipated Russian nation represents the average cultural level of the American schoolboy between 11 and 16."[9]

A perceptive analysis of the reasons for the Tarzan fascination was given by Axionov, president of the Russian poets' "Soviet," a writer described as "the most sophisticated Russian littérateur." He referred to "the love of fairy tales instinctive in primitive peoples in general and Russians in particular":

Our revolution killed the fairies, just as education killed them in Western countries. But if you dress up Jack the Giant Killer in a sufficiently modern guise to give him at least a semblance of probability, the masses will love him as did their fathers and grandfathers. And to the fact that Tarzan takes his readers away from strenuous, complicated modern life can be attributed the secret of his success.

Axionov then drifted into some ideological ambiguity: "In my opinion this alone proves the necessity for some dictatorship over the proletariat. On the other hand it appears that 'Tarzan' is

Assortment of foreign language editions of ERB's books.

also extremely popular in America—but comparisons are odious." It should be emphasized that Axionov's point about the importance of the imagination and the delight the average individual displayed in fairy tales and other fantasy creations that transported the reader far from the routine of everyday life, is exactly the point stressed by Burroughs in defending his writings against attacks by American literary experts.

On May 8, 1924, in thanking *Time* editor Henry R. Luce for sending him the magazine's article about Russian reactions, Ed revealed his amusement over the "primitive" Soviet readers, and wrote, "The British are notoriously the worst offenders, even in view of the fact that they have been strenuously warned against me by their reviewers (one of whom recently described me as a man with the mind of a child of six). . . ." To Bob Davis, who sent him the *New York Times* report, Ed remarked, "It is evident that Tarzan is overthrowing the Soviet government. I knew when I first wrote the story that it was inspired, but for what purpose it remained for Mr. Duranty to discover."

Concerning the unobtainable Russian royalties, these alone, according to estimates, could have made Burroughs wealthy. Other royalties, however, were pouring in; after the first Tarzan story had been circulated for only six months in Germany in 1924, Burroughs had received the largest royalty check ever paid to a foreign author for a similar period. On June 6, 1925,

The Outlook of London stated that "contracts have been made for 'Tarzan of the Apes' in no fewer than seventeen languages, including Arabic and Urdu." But Burroughs' own list, sent to Edwin C. King of FBO Studios in Hollywood on December 13, 1926, contains a more accurate count. His books, in translations, were being distributed in at least twenty-one foreign countries: Arab nations, England, British Colonies, Czechoslovakia, Denmark, Norway, Holland, Finland, France, Germany, Hungary, Iceland, Italy, Poland, Roumania, Russia (also published for Russian-speaking people in Belgium), Spain, Sweden, Urdu, Canada. The number of Arab nations reading *Tarzan* was impossible to determine; the British Colonies included South Africa, Australia, and others. Ed supplied a list of all the publishers in these foreign countries.[10]

In the same letter Ed attempted to estimate his total foreign royalties, but conceded that he could not obtain accurate figures. However, based upon incomplete statements, he indicated that sales of his books in the United States and in Great Britain, Sweden, Germany, Hungary, Denmark, Norway, plus the Tauchnitz Continental English Editions, were approximately six million copies.

An inquiry from Florence, Italy, concerning the distribution of *Tarzan of the Apes,* came from the bearer of a famous musical name—Enrico Caruso, Jr. On March 3, 1925, Ed responded:

. . . I am inclined to think that my foreign agents, Messrs. Curtis Brown, Ltd. of London have made arrangements for the Italian book rights. . . . I hope you will be able to see them, or at least communicate with them, however, as I believe that a name so illustrious as yours would add greatly to the selling value of my stories in Italy.

The anti-German sentiments in America and England, aggravated by the distortions of wartime propaganda, were still strong. During the latter part of 1922 Ed had learned of the boycotting of Baron Tauchnitz and his English language paperbacks by outstanding authors. Worried, Ed on January 3, 1923, wrote to Davis, noting that he had just learned of the boycott and that he and Joseph Hergesheimer were "leaders of the opposition," since they had permitted Tauchnitz to publish their works.

Davis, in his reply of the tenth, explained that many American writers during the war "began to boycott the old boy because he was down." Davis defended the baron: ". . . Tauchnitz was about the first foreigner who took American copyrights and paid for something he could have had for nothing. He has done a great deal for literature and for book-making generally. . . ." In advising Ed to continue with Tauchnitz, Davis remarked, "England kicked up a helluva stink and spread a lot of unnecessary odor without reason. . . ." A week later Ed replied, "My mind is relieved. I thought possibly I had unwittingly become a traitor to my country."

This decision about the German publisher Tauchnitz became a minor matter, but Ed's problems with Germany, based upon his own prejudices, were only beginning. Two years earlier, in correspondence with Enid Watson of the Curtis Brown foreign department, he had revealed the intensity of his anti-German feelings and his indifference to German opinion. The letter of August 23, 1921, to Burroughs quoted a request from Dr. Curt Otto of the Tauchnitz Library:

I regret to find that Tarzan the Terrible *is written in a strongly anti-German tendency, and we shall therefore be glad if you will consent to our issuing* Jungle Tales of Tarzan *instead of it. . . . we should like to publish the third book by Mr. Burroughs as soon as possible. . . .*

On September 9 Ed gave permission for Tauchnitz to issue *Jungle Tales of Tarzan,* unaware, in his statement, that he was predicting the crisis to come: "I presume for the reasons they do not care for Tarzan the Terrible they will not want Tarzan the Untamed." His further remark was tinged with arrogance and contempt: "If they knew half what I thought of the Germans, they would not want any of my books."

The spread of *Tarzan* translations throughout the world, resulting from the remarkably persistent efforts of Enid Watson of the Curtis Brown Agency, continued. On January 23, 1923, Ed wrote to express his appreciation: "You will soon have all the foreign languages exhausted and then what will you do, unless you turn your attention to Mars. . . ." He noted that Mars should provide an unlimited field, since the written languages of all the races were different. About the foreign rights, he was unhappy that the publishers would not guarantee royalties "after they had made their profits," but expressed the hope that Ingolfur Jonsson might get rich on the Icelandic rights.

In March, Enid Watson reported the sale of *Tarzan of the Apes* to *Le Petit Parisien,* a French newspaper, and in July she wrote triumphantly, "After negotiations lasting over several years I have at last found a publisher for *Tarzan* in Germany."

Tarzan *in braille*.

She stressed the difficult conditions facing German publishers
and felt she should be congratulated for having signed an agreement with Dieck & Company that provided an advance of fifteen
British pounds for each book, on a royalty of ten percent. This
was the first contact with the Charles Dieck firm. In praise,
Ed commented jokingly, "You certainly are blanketing the world
with good literature. . . . am particularly interested in the Hot-
tentot rights. . . ."

On September 12, 1923, in response to a request from the
Curtis Brown office, Ed granted permission to the National Library
for the Blind to braille *A Princess of Mars* and *The Gods of Mars,*
with the stipulation that these works could not be sold for
profit. Ed wrote, "Some time ago they brailled 'Tarzan of the
Apes' if I am not mistaken in the title, and I am wondering
if they have brailled any other of the Tarzan books." Noting
he knew nothing about the process, he wondered if he might
ask for a brailled page of one of his books, "merely as a curiosity."

Throughout most of 1924 the German sales increased; on August 1, Charles Dieck wrote from Stuttgart, ". . . we are now at the issue of the third volume. Over 40,000 copies of Tarzan are now on advance orders. . . ." Ed, on September 2, answered to thank Dieck and suggest that the Martian series be considered. An experienced and imaginative publisher, Dieck devised various schemes to promote the sales of *Tarzan*. In a letter of October 10, he informed Burroughs of plans and occurrences in Germany:

. . . towards the end of this month the fourth Tarzan volume, that is "Tarzan's Son," will make its appearance. . . . Of late some writers and publishers are getting jealous of our successful handling of the Tarzan books . . . nearly daily appear criticisms and discussions about the value of Tarzan books. . . . Beginning 1925 we thought to start with "Jungle Tales of Tarzan" and "Tarzan and the Jewels of Opar", shortly followed by "Tarzan and the Golden Lion" and "Tarzan and the Ant Men."

He supplied newsy items: ". . . in Germany two Tarzan parodies have come out; namely 'Tarzan has dreamt' and the 'Tarzaniade'. Both volumes are the products of jealousy, and we are informing the public that these books are erratic and without leaning towards natural conditions or surroundings, but that the original Tarzan books are of good moral standard, as even severe critics could not deny. . . . We came into possession of a very good gorilla death mask and had many copies made in plaster paris, with bronze covering, with which we are supplying the book stores. . . ."

No German protests had as yet been registered about the anti-German themes emphasized in several of Burroughs' earlier stories. These were especially severe in *The Land That Time Forgot,* with references to the "Kaiserbreed" and the depiction of von Schoenvorts, the U-boat commander, as a man without scruples or conscience, and of course in *Tarzan the Untamed,* where a German major is fed to a lion and later an enraged lion is prodded into the trenches to attack the "Huns." However, by the summer of 1924, with the German market expanding, Ed was already exhibiting apprehension over some of the scenes and characterizations he had contrived. On August 8 he wrote Enid Watson:

I wish again to call your attention to the necessity for changes in the text of some of my stories for the German market. The Land That Time Forgot, for instance, is a story which I believe will be a big seller there. . . . as it was written during the height of hostilities it contains rather bitter diatribe aimed at Germans individually and collectively. As I do not write propaganda, and the sole aim of my work is to entertain, I believe it will be perfectly proper to fit the text to the public we wish to sell to.

"How would it be to make the Germans Austrians," he inquired, "or will these volumes circulate also in Austria; and in any event tone down some of the language I have used?"

Ⅰn Burroughs' type of fiction a villain was a necessity; the various twists of the plot could not have been devised without one. His standard procedure was to create one, usually of foreign extraction, like the Russians Rokoff and Paulvitch or the Belgian Werper. But at an early period, with the increase of foreign editions of *Tarzan,* Burroughs himself had sensed the general problem that could arise. On January 11, 1921, to Enid Watson he had noted:

In writing my Tarzan and Martian stories I always endeavored to avoid giving offense to any considerable proportion of my readers and therefore many of my villains were selected from the nations least likely to read my books. They were Russian, Swedish and Belgian, not because I harbor any particular dislike of these people but merely because few of my readers would be from these countries.

He observed that now, however, with the many translations, conditions were different. In a joking tone he pointed out that he would not "enjoy" an adventure story "in which the principal characters were all Russians and the dyed-in-the-wool villains American," and then stated the procedure he would prefer: ". . . so far as I am concerned there would be no objection to changing the nationality of the villains, or leaving them without nationality." These comments, four years before the German controversy exploded, in which Burroughs actually authorized the translators to change his villains, demonstrate that the villains were simply creatures of his plot; in general, no prejudice or animosity was involved.

With his war-time German characters, and in at least one other case, Burroughs deviated from his nonpersonal attitude. Here, his contention that he wrote only to entertain was not supportable. Himself an easy victim of war propaganda, he had been led by his prejudices into writing the "bitter diatribe" he mentioned. He had written propaganda, as he had also done, with a different goal, in "Under the Red Flag," published in 1919, with its violent attack on Bolshevism. Davis and other editors, in rejecting this work, had made exactly the point Ed had previously stressed and then violated—fiction was not a proper vehicle for propaganda.

As yet, Burroughs was not concerned with the moral question or the injustice of these indictments of the Germans; his only worry was that German sales might be affected. He was even willing to change his villains into Austrians. Under these circumstances he would have been condemning the Austrians collectively. Granted he needed his villain, but there was a great difference between portraying an individual sadist or murderer and in damning a whole race. This Burroughs would perceive at a later period.

Early in 1925, through the publication of Stefan Sorel's *Tarzan the German-Devourer (Tarzan der Deutschenfresser,* Carl Stephenson, Berlin), the German public became aware of the content of *Tarzan the Untamed.* Sorel, in his reading of the English edition—the book had not been published in German—had discovered the scene in which Major Schneider is fed to the lion, and other savage scenes involving the deaths of German officers or "Huns." These actions of Tarzan were in retribution for the supposed murder of Jane. Of course Sorel's exposure of the book and its violent scenes aroused indignation and anger among Germans who had been helpless to refute the wartime reports, obviously Allied propaganda, of their "atrocities," and who had not only lost the war but had been forced to accept the blame for starting it.

On January 30 Dieck wrote in agitation, "Somebody has unearthed the fact . . . that you produced 'Tarzan the Untamed' during the war and that in it the Germans are cruelly drawn. Undoubtedly he has kept silent about it, since it is treated in a volume long suppressed. . . ." Dieck made several suggestions, among them that Burroughs, in his next *Tarzan* story, "might let the Germans come into their right also?" He added, "We want no praise but we would like justice." Dieck also urged that Burroughs write an article "which might breathe of friendliness for the Germans." He promised to "hurl this article" at the press so as to quiet the critics. For incidental information he noted the translation of *A Princess of Mars,* with a frontispiece by Professor Hohlwein, and the plan to release the book about March 15. He mentioned also the scheduled publication of a special volume, *Wild Animals on the Film,* "drawn up by a manager of animal films."

The rising German furor found Ed in the midst of corrections on *The Land That Time Forgot,* soon to be published in England by Methuen & Company. On February 12, 1925, he noted receipt of the first proofs and explained to Curtis Brown that he would have to make changes in the book because of the anti-German sections. While waiting for the second proofs, on February 21 he wrote to Enid Watson, "If they are greatly delayed I wish you would take the matter up with Methuen and see that all inflammatory references to the Germans are sufficiently modified so that they will not necessarily offend. . . ." He referred to the "considerable importance" of his German royalties and the deep resentment against him in Germany because of *Tarzan the Untamed.*

In defense of the *Tarzan* publications, a German officer, Vice-Admiral Daehnhardt, had issued a statement which Dieck planned to use as a preface for one of the books. The *Tarzan* stories were described as "non-political" and Daehnhardt stressed the economic gain to the Germans of the Dieck editions: "Right here in Stuttgart there is the least inducement to turn against it, for a year and a day whole rows of Stuttgart publishers and bookhandlers, Swabian paper mills, etc. have turned running machinery and service to the Tarzan edition. Already the export dealers have protected Stuttgart workers from becoming breadless. . . ."[11]

On February 9, as Dieck realized the situation was becoming extremely serious, he dispatched a cable to Burroughs, "German Tarzan editions now much attacked by our press. Give us quickly good notices that your book 'Tarzan the Untamed' is born during war-bitterness and most of all that you are fond of German people, otherwise your German business will diminish." Burroughs at once wired back "Suggestion dislike Germans ridiculous. Am writing." In his reply to Dieck he explained that during the war he had submitted to much banter from Mrs. Burroughs because for many preceding years the Kaiser had been one of his most admired heroes. Ed wrote, ". . . even as late as the time I wrote The War Lord of Mars, the influence of my admiration for the German Emperor had a great deal to do with the stimulation of my imagination in the conception of that story. The war shattered a great many things, however, from thrones to ideals."[12] He then enclosed a four-page letter addressed, "To My German Readers." In it he recalled the bitterness that had existed between the North and the South during the American Civil War and how, in the passing years, this antagonism had gradually vanished. He predicted that the animosities created by World War I would also be dissipated in the natural friendship of the "two great republics of Germany and America."

Ed did not offer excuses for the anti-German sections in his two novels. "They reflect truly what I thought and felt at the time that I wrote them," he stated, "and because this is a fact I cannot apologize for an honest conviction however mistaken it may have been." He observed, quite logically, that the types of individuals he vilified "were the types that the German people themselves have inveighed most bitterly against . . . the cruel, ruthless, arrogant German officer." Ed noted that he had used Russian villains in two of his stories, believing that they would never be translated into Russian. But now that they were, he nevertheless had received no complaints from his Russian readers. Ed stressed, ". . . I have no hesitancy in offending those whom I consider a menace to society regardless of their nationality or of their purchasing power," and added that he would "as bitterly assail" the misconduct of Americans as he would the undesirable or evil actions of Germans, French, or English. In evidence he referred to *The Girl From Farris's* and *The Girl From Hollywood,* "in which Americans and American customs are attacked." Burroughs insisted firmly and defiantly:

. . . if I should never sell another book in Germany I should still be as bitterly antagonistic toward Hauptman Fritz Schneider, as all my German friends in this country are and as the vast majority of the German people in Germany are and, I hope, always will be.

Burroughs maintained that of most importance was the pleasure that thousands of Germans derived from his books; this could not be "lessened" because an American writer attacked a "conscienceless militarism that is to be found among certain classes in every great power in the world." In answer to those who accepted *Tarzan the Untamed* as evidence of his dislike of all Germans, Ed pointed out that he had a German brother-in-law, a native of Hamburg, whose two daughters had recently been guests at the Burroughs' home in Los Angeles, and that in America, among the great many people of German origin, he had made numerous friends. None of these had been offended by his statements in *Tarzan the Untamed.*

"I hope to visit Germany next year," Ed wrote, "and I have no doubts whatsoever as to the kindliness and cordiality of my reception, which would not be the case if I believed that Hauptman Fritz Schneider was typical of even a negligible minority of the German people."

This explanation and plea by Burroughs had little effect upon the German press which in the spring and summer of 1925 printed a series of violent denunciations of him and his *Tarzan* stories. From such newspapers as the *Berliner Tageblatt, Frankfurter Zeitung, Prager Press,* the *Berlin Lokal Anzeiger,* and others came these bitter attacks, many of them appealing to the Germans' nationalistic pride. Although Burroughs was being denounced as an individual writer, to the German mind he was representative of all the foreign powers that had defeated and humiliated the German nation:

We have learned much out of the war and who were our former foreign friends. We were not prepared, however, to learn to like the silly admiration for their outlandish literary compositions and which are of so inferior worth and such a lash in our face. It is not otherwise possible that a greater calumny of the German reading public (or insult to the German reading public) could be written than the Tarzan Romance and which is itself such a miserable "Schmierwerk" (botch job). . . .

In mentioning Burroughs' "noble and holy hate against the Germans and Germany," the article reveals the deep resentment of a defeated country against the victor: "The writing of this calumniator and liar traduces a German Vice Admiral in the innocent minds of our German youth, rather than literary counsel. When will we reach the limit of cringing and fawning upon all of this outlandish volatile foreign domination."

Other attacks were more personal. Concerning the Lion Numa who had devoured the German Major, one newspaper commented, "You will not like Tarzan's action, dear German reader, but you will understand it if Tarzan tells you that this monster of a German Major had murdered and burned the noble wife of Tarzan, the noble monkey-man." The reference is to *Tarzan the Untamed* as the "seventh Tarzan book," containing "deeds accomplished by the dear Tarzan against the overfed German beasts." Six *Tarzan* novels had been published in Germany, and Sorel's book had led the German press to believe that *Tarzan the Untamed* was the seventh in sequence, written in 1925, rather than 1918. Thus, it was the "same Burroughs who had fattened himself with the proceeds of the German translations" who "six years after the war . . . has written one of the most evil works of wartime literature to insult Germany." The article mentions

Burroughs' letter to the German readers and his insistence that he does not dislike the Germans; this is viewed derisively as entirely unbelievable. ". . . Mr. Burroughs really does not have any national sympathies or antipathies. . . ." He is only interested in attracting as many readers as possible and concerned about "hurting his pocketbook." The Germans are given concluding instructions:

Is it after what we have said still necessary, German reader, to tell you that you should hastily throw your Tarzan books into the garbage can and faithfully promise to never touch a Tarzan book again? [Immediately after the publication of Sorel, Tarzan disappeared from the German book stores.]

A book review of Stefan Sorel's *Tarzan the German-Devourer,* (Berlin *Lokal Anzeiger*) comments that the great masses of readers who "became victims" of the *Tarzan* reading fever exhibited poor taste and judgment. This "romantic journey" which increased "with as much rapidity as the prolificacy of rabbits" represents "the greatest piece of stupidity ever thrown on the book market." The author of this "colportage series," referred to as "Mr. Rice Burroughs," is one of the "basest German-devourers existing in the Anglo-Saxon countries."

A lengthy article by Felix Salten, the popular author of *Bambi* and other children's stories, offered a contemptuous estimate of Burroughs' writing ability. In "Tarzan Reflections," appearing in the *Neue Freie Presse,* Vienna, May 3, 1925, Salten, who had started a *Tarzan* book because a friend had referred to Burroughs as "a second Kipling," remarked after reading only a few pages "that the writer . . . lacked practically all the qualities of an author." Burroughs' "cold-blooded, well-calculated complications" could arouse a reader's curiosity, but if one compared his writing, for example, to Conan Doyle's in *Sherlock Holmes,* one could easily detect Doyle's superiority. His books also are "well calculated," but they reveal "a spark of imagination" and "a great many admirable qualities"; none of these are present in the *Tarzan* stories.

Salten's phrases are picturesque: the German people had been seized by a "Tarzan Epidemic"; the books "had been like a literary grippe." They had appeared in different forms, had spared almost no one, but like the grippe, they were "in the process of dying out." The Germans were recovering from "this Tarzan-fever" and they will now be "immune against the infection."[13]

To Charles Dieck, Burroughs now expressed his intention of creating "one of the typical Germans that we all respect here" in his next *Tarzan* story. He promised fervently, "I shall eschew politics forever hereafter." It was plain that the world-wide circulation of his writings made necessary the avoidance of any political viewpoints.

From Enid Watson, on March 25, had come a letter which cast an entirely new light on the virulent German press campaign against the *Tarzan* books. For some time there had been a suspicion that the attacks on Burroughs were not merely motivated by his anti-German sentiments. Miss Watson's view of the situation followed upon an extremely pessimistic statement by Theodor J. Ritter, the Curtis Brown representative in Hamburg, who reported that sale of the *Tarzan* series had come "almost to a complete standstill." Ritter commented, "The bookshops are boycotting the books and the name of Tarzan begins to stink in Germany." He repeated the newspapers' ominous predictions that Tarzan's name would be "obnoxious forever" to the German readers. Miss Watson, however, believed that Ritter's statement was highly exaggerated and overlooked one important factor. The German hostility was not based purely upon Burroughs' supposed "calumny" or his insults to the intense nationalistic pride. Another more obvious reason could be detected. Miss Watson wrote:

. . . *my personal opinion is that this is based not so much on the anti-German attitude as expressed in 'Tarzan the Untamed' but on the jealousy evinced by a certain section of the German press (and not a very important section) at the success of a foreign book in their own country.*

Charles Dieck, whose initiative and enterprise had led to the sales of a half-million Tarzan novels, had earlier noted "some writers and publishers are getting jealous of our successful handling of the Tarzan books, and trying through the Press to work against us." The furious newspaper campaign against Tarzan, seemingly organized, with its appeal to German nationalism, was deceptive. The postwar grievances were being deliberately stirred up as a pretext for destroying the sales market for Tarzan books. Of course the press had succeeded. The German people, emotionally susceptible because of the war, had turned much of their anger and hatred against Tarzan and Burroughs.

Ed had begun to suspect that the German campaign was

a subterfuge, and Enid Watson's opinion confirmed his. On April 11, 1925, he wrote her to insist that he could not "assume a spineless attitude and retract and apologize ad nauseum." He repeated her view even more forcibly: ". . . the attitude of the German press has nothing whatsoever to do with patriotism or injured German sensibilities but is quite evidently prompted by jealousy of German publishers who did not have the business foresight and sense of values possessed by Mr. Dieck." Feeling he had made a "fair and reasonable" effort at conciliation, Ed lost patience. To Enid Watson he remarked angrily that if the Germans were anything like the Americans, they would have more respect for him if he were to tell those in the press who doubted his explanation, "that they might go to—." He added, "I was going to say hell, but inasmuch as I am writing to a lady, of course I cannot use that word."

That *Tarzan the Untamed* would never appear in a German translation was obvious; but, as Enid Watson pointed out, its sale in other languages would be difficult to stop. Ed's most pressing worry was about *The Land That Time Forgot,* scheduled for British publication by Methuen. On April 26 he explained his apprehension to Charles K. Miller, noting that the story was written immediately after the sinking of the Lusitania. If the Germans ever read the book, he commented wryly, "I am afraid my life will not be safe should I ever visit Germany."

Inquiries to Dieck about the situation brought a long letter of April 16 describing not only the intense antagonism toward *Tarzan,* but also the effects of the war and Allied propaganda upon the Germans.[14] Dieck's financial position daily grew more serious: ". . . Tarzan has disappeared from the German book market . . . books are being returned to us . . . those who have not returned them do not pay and threaten to send them back. . . ." He explained that plans to publish *Tarzan and the Jewels of Opar* and *A Princess of Mars* had to be abandoned: ". . . we had to withdraw these books, which caused us further great losses. . . ." Dieck offered what was to him the only possible solution: ". . . If you are still anxious to sell your books in Germany, you will have to take some energetic steps, and will have to withdraw the seventh edition also in English speaking countries."

Ed's deepest regret now was about the harm that had been done to Dieck. On May 18, in a general statement addressed to the German press, Ed presented a defense both of his novel and of Dieck's role as publisher; he again stressed that *Tarzan the Untamed* was written "during the heat of an extremely bitter war" and not six years later as Sorel had maintained. He added:

. . . I am sorry, too, that this matter should have brought financial loss to Mr. Dieck . . . who took the stories in good faith without any knowledge whatsoever of Tarzan the Untamed. . . . but perhaps his very success has been his undoing, in the jealousy that it has aroused.

"If I have been stupid in not realizing the harm that Tarzan the Untamed might do," he stated, "I have at least tried to remedy the wrong by instructing my publishers and agents to withdraw this book from circulation as rapidly as possible throughout the world and never to offer it again. . . ." He noted that since his stories were published in twenty countries, his losses would be far greater than any income he could ever derive from German sales. Ed closed, "I know that the German press wants to be fair. I do not ask them to be fair to me but I sincerely hope that they will be fair to Mr. Dieck, a fellow German."

On the same date, in enclosing a copy of this letter to Enid Watson, Ed gave instructions to remove both *Tarzan the Untamed* and *The Land That Time Forgot* from the market in all countries, "insofar as it is possible." If she thought these stories could be rewritten without giving "unnecessary offense," he was willing to do so, after which they might be placed on sale once more. To Eric Schuler, secretary of The Authors' League of America, he sent copies of the German newspaper clippings and of other correspondence relating to the controversy. About this material he noted, "I should like to have it on file with the League in the event that it should be needed in the defense of other American writers from attack on my account."

During August 1925 Ed continued to make inquiries about the German situation, both of Dieck and of Enid Watson. Dieck had succeeded in placing favorable reviews of *Tarzan* books in the newspapers, but these had no effect in reviving the sales. On September 8 Dieck sent a detailed account of events; concerning the royalties for the first half of the year, a matter mentioned by Ed, Dieck replied that these were out of the question. He had suffered heavy losses—"the battle alone has cost me between thirty and forty thousand marks"—and the damage to the firm's reputation was serious.

The German disaster had at least produced one positive result. From here on Ed would display extreme caution in his judgment of all foreigners, both personally and in his fiction. To

H. C. Paxton, editor of *The Country Gentleman,* in discussing new works, Ed, on October 28, remarked that he would like to write a story of the Southwest some day with a Mexican as a hero. His statement indicated a new awareness:

Among the many things we have done to arouse the hostility and antagonism of Mexicans has been our treatment of them in our fiction, where they are nearly always portrayed as heartless scoundrels. I believe that a policy of consideration and fairness toward our sister republic in our literature would do much to lessen this hostility. . . .

However, his social concern was weakened by an added reference to business opportunities: the antagonism "makes it difficult for Americans to transact business profitably in Mexico, where, politicians to the contrary notwithstanding, we are most cordially hated."

On November 6, with German conditions unchanged, Ed depressedly had a suggestion to make to Enid Watson. Having received an opinion that it was he and not Tarzan whom the Germans disliked, he proposed, ". . . we might publish my books in Germany without my name, using instead a German name. . . ." This view of the German hatred as directed toward him was inaccurate, as Dieck, on November 28, pointed out in a letter to Theodor Ritter. Dieck reported that while he faced a "somewhat thankless task" in promoting the *Tarzan* books, still there were signs that some of the bookstores were again making sales. He commented, "Gradually the conviction is penetrating that the whole Tarzan campaign is on a materialistic footing, and has little to do with Idealism." Dieck explained the German enmity; they hated Tarzan, not Burroughs. "The Schoolmasters and their coterie . . . consider him as offal; . . . the National circles have hatred of Tarzan implanted in them because it has brought about attacks on Germany. Concerning the person of Mr. Burroughs they think nothing." Dieck stressed that it was *Tarzan the Untamed* that they wished to "expel from German earth," and added, "in this they are partly right."

Ed was now convinced that the popularity of Tarzan would gradually return to Germany. He expressed the belief to Enid Watson, on January 13, 1926, that once the antagonism had dissipated, the sales of the books would be as heavy as before; the press campaign could have the opposite effect from what was intended, with the publicity arousing the public's interest in reading the *Tarzan* stories. Ed continued, in future years, to reiterate his distrust and rejection of all wartime propaganda. In 1927 he recalled the anti-German reports of World War I and remarked, "I realize that much of this was exaggerated and I know that it does not do any of us any good to foster enmity and hatred. . . ."[15] A request for a statement about propaganda from Henry Goddard Leach of *The Forum,* in 1929, brought a very vehement response from Ed:

Wartime propaganda, including as it did vicious and inexcusable falsehoods sponsored by our Government, has effectively immunized me against all forms of propaganda with the result that in matters concerning which I have no personal knowledge, I believe only that which I wish to believe or that which is commended to my judgement through ordinary processes of reasoning. . . .[16]

To his brother-in-law William Westendarp, on February 28, 1933, Ed made specific references to his past mistakes: "I always regretted the anti-German tone that I permitted to enter two of my stories following the sinking of the Lusitania. I think we must have all been a little stupider than usual during the war, for how any intelligent person could have believed the propaganda stories that we swallowed hook, line and sinker is beyond me." He added, "In some of my later books I tried to atone as best I might by depicting German characters in pleasant and sympathetic roles."

Any hope possessed by Burroughs that certain segments of the German press might modify their vindictive and revengeful attitude toward him and the Tarzan books was quickly dispelled. In 1926, obviously in a further attempt to keep public enmity alive, the press launched an attack directed personally at Burroughs. On April 8, noting that "the campaign against Tarzan has again been revived," Dieck forwarded a copy of an article of April sixth from *Der Mittag,* a Dusseldorf newspaper, headed "The Author of the Sensational Novels 'Tarzan' Is a Plagiarist!" According to the article, the original accusation came from the "well-known Russian author" W. Strujski, a Paris reporter for the *Sewodnja* of Riga. The supposed author of a novel that contained the identical Tarzan theme was a French writer, a "Parisian-Bohemian" named Robida, who lived in the Montmartre section some twenty-three years earlier. Robida, a frequenter of bars, would read his works to those present, in exchange for free drinks of absinthe. The article reported, "About fifteen years ago Robida succeeded in finding a publisher who agreed to publish his fantastical novel 'The Adventures of Captain Saturnin Fernandoule.' " A summary of the plot followed:

The French Captain Fernandoule is making a trip to India accompanied by his wife and child. On the coast of Asia the ship was wrecked. The Captain and his family were saved and landed upon an uninhabited island. In fighting wild gorillas, mother and father are killed, and only the child remains alive. Little Saturnin is found by a female gorilla and taken care of. After a good many years a French man-of-war touches the island and the French marines find this half-man, half-ape, take him to the man-of-war and they take him to Paris.

In the *Der Mittag* account, Robida's novel is highly praised. He has described "how in the soul of this creature the battle between beast and human started." Robida's development of this battle is a "psychological masterpiece and the principal attraction of this book." However, Robida wrote in an early period, when a novel of this type could not be appreciated. He died, and both he and his work were forgotten. Ten years later, the article stated, "the reading public had changed its tastes which were more of a nervous, sharp and nonsensical taste." Burroughs' plagiarism is then described:

Evidently he was well acquainted with the forgotten novel of Robida. He changed in his books the names, the time, added a few more chapters, cut out a few things, and copied almost verbally the already mentioned battle of the soul of man and beast, and thus created of the unknown French novel by Robida, the famous book Tarzan, *for which he collected the nice little sum of six million-golden francs.*[17]

The article had referred sneeringly to the "smart English author, Edgard Burroughs," and later to "Mr. Englishman." To Dieck, on April 24, Ed confessed that he "scarcely knew how to reply to such a silly charge" coming from someone who did not even know his nationality or how to spell his name. He was willing enough to concede that such a story might have been written fifteen years ago or fifteen hundred years ago: ". . . there is nothing new in the idea nor have I claimed there was anything new in it. It has been used repeatedly from the time of Romulus and Remus and probably long before." Ed had never seen Robida's novel or had any knowledge of it, but he emphasized

613

that since he read no French, the book could not under any circumstances be a source of information for him. Ed offered a pungent remark: "The lion has fleas but he keeps on going about his business as a successful lion. I have Strujski, Der Mittag, and other minor irritants but I expect to keep on going about my business of being a successful author."[18]

Dieck, in response, noted that the Strujski article had been copied from its original French source by several German newspapers. His letter was encouraging, and to demonstrate that there was still some "affection" for Tarzan in Germany, two "well trained" monkeys were being exhibited under the names Tarzan I and Tarzan II. Dieck had also granted permission to the popular Bush Circus to present a Tarzan pantomime in the shows at Hamburg and Breslau.

Finding it necessary now to obtain further information about Robida and his supposed novel, Ed, on May 20, wrote to his Paris publisher, Artheme Fayard & Cie, enclosing a copy of the *Der Mittag* article (French translation by E. Muller, Burroughs' secretary). Fayard's reply of June 18 contained a surprising statement:

> *. . . as you request we have made the necessary investigation.*
> *We find, however, that Robida never wrote* The Adventures of Captain Saturnin Fernandoule. *We do not even know of any book, by Robida or any other author in which there exists a plot similar to the one you have constructed for Tarzan.*

On July 8 Ed triumphantly forwarded the Fayard letter to Dieck to be used to discredit the plagiarism charges, and at the same time sent an article reporting the controversy to Henry Gallup Paine, Editor of *The Bulletin* of The Authors' League. Titled "An Adventure in Plagiarism," the article quoted the *Der Mittag* statement verbatim and the response of Fayard. Interestingly, Ed, in referring to the numerous queries he had received as to the source of *Tarzan,* revealed that he had thought at last he was "on the right trail" when he wrote to Fayard. Perhaps, unknown to him, there was a work with the *Tarzan* theme. The Fayard reply led to the conclusion that the entire matter, including even *The Adventures of Captain Saturnin Fernandoule, a* "novel" nobody could produce, was a fabrication. In his article Ed emphasized that in addition to searching for measures to punish plagiarists, The Authors' League should find means "for protecting ourselves against those who can now with impunity bring wholly groundless charges of plagiarism against us."

The period 1923-26 became an experimental one, with Burroughs venturing beyond the customary *Tarzan* and Mars stories to utilize new themes and settings. The innovations consisted of his first Western novel; his longest romance, totaling 125,000 words; the Indian story he had contemplated for a long time, centered about the Apaches and their struggles against the white men; and a *Tarzan* juvenile. The period also included two continuing *Tarzan* and Mars adventure stories.

The writing of the Western novel, not at all a project that Burroughs initiated, came through a suggestion from a most unusual source—Sir Algernon Methuen, owner of the British publishing company. In October 1922, after Sir Algernon's suggestion had been forwarded by Curtis Brown, Ed responded, "I have never written a wild west story, although I think I could do it. . . ." He of course had his experiences in Idaho and Arizona to draw upon. The phrase "wild west," as used by Sir Algernon, gave Ed the impression that "the English readers would want the motion picture type of cowboy, which exists only in the pictures." A proposal of this kind from a member of the British nobility was highly flattering to Ed. Still, he exhibited caution, asking, "Has Sir Algernon any special offer to make me on the British book rights on such a story, which might have little or no value here, since the readers on this side seem to prefer my highly imaginative stuff?"

Replying on November 17, 1922, Sir Algernon, even wilier than Burroughs, was careful to make no commitment. He agreed that Ed had the ability to write a good "wild west" story, but added, ". . . if such a book would have little or no value in the States I fear that its success here would not be likely to give Mr. Burroughs sufficient remuneration." He emphasized that the decision lay with Ed.

As in the past, Ed turned to Bob Davis for advice; the editor gave strong encouragement: "You seem to be pretty well equipped to handle rough men, wild animals, and coarse country. I would print a western story from you in a minute. Let 'er go." While Davis' urging may have spurred Ed into the project, it appeared evident that Sir Algernon's request was irresistible. Ed knew that from a sales standpoint the book would be a dubious investment—he had already made that plain. On March 31, in notifying Curtis Brown that he had started "the Wild West story for Sir Algernon Methuen," Ed explained, ". . . I am writing this story with little likelihood of its being very enthusiastically received by my American publishers. . . ." He also felt that "for

English consumption" the "rather prosaic life of a cowpuncher will have to be speeded up a bit. . . ."

With the completion of the 81,000-word story on May 24, Ed sent some brief information to Curtis Brown: the story was titled "The Bandit of Hell's Bend"; although not mentioned in the manuscript, the time was about 1885; it contained many of the characters Ed had known in Idaho and when he was in the 7th Cavalry in Arizona; he was sure the story contained "many inaccuracies"; he had tried to use the colloquialisms and slang of the people he had actually known—a hodge-podge group from all parts of the United States; the story was decidedly not a historical novel; he had given it the love interest and happy ending Sir Algernon desired.

To Davis he noted that two other titles had occurred to him—"The Black Coyote" and "Diana of the Bar Y." He also referred to two points he should have researched more thoroughly: as a territory, did Arizona have a sheriff or a U.S. Marshal? And did Apaches circle their enemies on horseback, as the plains Indians did?[19] A unique aspect of the story was the inclusion of original poetry, constructed in ballad form. About these poems Ed commented, "It was easier to compose them than hunt up others and then get permission from the copyright owners to use them."[20]

The plot of "The Bandit of Hell's Bend" involves the competition of two men for the love of Diana Henders, daughter of wealthy ranch and mine owner Elias Henders, who early in the story is killed by the Apaches. At the ranch in Arizona, named the Bar-Y after the old ranch founded by Yale graduates George and Harry Burroughs in Idaho, the hero "Bull," whose last name is never revealed, loses his foreman's job and suffers various misfortunes, all through the connivance of Hal Colby, the devious villain. The story derives its title from the mystery surrounding an actual bandit, "The Black Coyote," an outlaw who specializes in stage holdups; his face is covered with a black handkerchief, and because "Bull" also possesses one, many of the townspeople are convinced that he is the bandit. Other complications are introduced with the arrival at the ranch of Jefferson Wainwright, Senior, and Junior, an attorney named Corson, and the sensuous Lillian Manill, all sophisticated big city people who eventually join forces to attempt to swindle Diana out of her ranch and gold mine.

A number of characters who are assigned roles in "The Bandit of Hell's Bend" are freely drawn versions of individuals mentioned in Ed's *Autobiography*. "Gum" Smith, originally "Gum" Brown, is depicted in slapstick fashion and provides comic relief as the cowardly sheriff and saloonkeeper whose favorite order, "Ah depatizes yo'-all" is greeted with derision by the cowboys. Texas Pete, sympathetically described in Ed's *Autobiography,* becomes the balladeer of the novel, singing the "song" lyrics Ed had devised; Pete, as a protector of Diana Henders, emerges as a hero second only to "Bull." In the description of Pete, "a thing of beauty and a joy forever," gaudily equipped with silver-inlaid Mexican spurs that dragged the ground when he walked, spurs that had dumbbells attached to their hubs and "tinkled merrily a gay accompaniment to his boyish heart," Ed was possibly re-creating himself as the greenest of cowhands on his first visit to the Idaho ranch.

In this 1923 novel the Mexicans are referred to as "greasers" and Gregario, an outlaw companion of "The Black Coyote," is called a "dirty greaser." But before the story's end Gregario reforms, helps to trap the villain, and is characterized as "whiter'n some white men." The Apaches appear only in the briefest of scenes, merely skirmishes with the cowboys.

Davis, who had eagerly reminded Ed about "the cowboy story," saying, ". . . that's mine as soon as it is finished," upon receipt of "The Bandit of Hell's Bend," was severely critical. On June 14 he sent three pages of comments and suggestions for revision. He wrote, "You sure have written a conventional Western story here, and drawn little upon your imaginative powers. I can't understand how a bean as active as yours could refrain from butting in and slamming a few novelties into the good old powder-burned frontier." He listed the weaknesses and errors: the dialogue was up-to-date, not typical of the period. Ed had even mentioned a checkbook and the cowboys being paid by check. There was reference to a "black" bandanna, which Davis explained as an impossibility, a bandanna having figures and being either red or yellow. Concerning the sexy scene where Colby clasps half-clad Lillian Manill in his embrace and "beats it for the bedroom," Davis viewed this with a censor's eye: "Shame on you, Edgar. You've got to stop this. You've got to stop it short outside."

The significant weakness in some of Burroughs' writing was as apparent in "The Bandit of Hell's Bend" as it had been in other hasty attempts at realism. He had inserted a few true-life details of setting or character from his background to give some strength to the story. But this superficial approach could hardly provide realism to the characters and their actions, especially within the framework of a trite plot. He had missed an opportunity to recreate the turbulent, colorful Arizona of the 1880s and to depict the exciting cowboy and ranch life of the period. Perhaps the Burroughs goal of making the story as wild and woolly as possible for a British audience may have contributed to this failure. Curiously, although the novel was tailored-to-order for Sir Algernon, it appeared first in print in *Argosy All-Story* in 1924, then in book form for McClurg, June 4, 1925, and finally in the British Methuen edition, January 28, 1926.

In August 1922 Burroughs contemplated turning his writing talents in a different direction. His proposal, sent to Curtis Brown, his British agents, was that he should undertake a series of articles about one of the most picturesque men of the period, a soldier-of-fortune named General Lee Christmas. The astonishing career of General Christmas, his exploits and precarious adventures in Central America, had created public interest and admiration. A locomotive engineer from Louisiana, Christmas, when twenty-eight years old, had fallen asleep at the throttle and crashed his train. His employment opportunities now dim, Christmas left the States, worked for a while on the Mexican railroads and then moved to Honduras. In describing him as "The Last Great Soldier of Fortune," Samuel Crowther in *The Romance and Rise of the American Tropics* provides details of his life and adventures:

There [in Honduras] he and his engine were captured by the revolutionists and he was ordered to run the train for them. He did more than that. He fitted up a flat car as a mobile fort and captured all the engines on the line! That made him a general —one does not much bother about the intermediate ranks in these armies. Also he became superintendent of the road. He organized what he called his machine gun regiment—which was a machine gun and Guy Maloney, a friend of his from the New Orleans police.

But Christmas' wild exploits were just beginning. As a fighting filibusterer he took part in battles in four Central American countries, traveling back and forth between Honduras, Salvador, Guatemala, and Nicaragua. He became bodyguard and chief of staff to a half-dozen presidents. Christmas was wounded many times and reported killed so often that the newspapers, finally skeptical, reserved a special headline for him—Lee Christmas Killed Again! In 1907 he aided President Bonilla of Honduras in a war against Nicaragua. Honduras was defeated, and once more the familiar report appeared—Christmas was dead, so stated the Encyclopaedia Britannica, eleventh edition. The indestructible general was alive and well in Salvador in 1908, and without any scruples proceeded to head an invasion of Honduras. His hectic career of war, forays, and revolutions did not hamper his personal life; he still found time to acquire four wives. His end was not violent. Lee Christmas demonstrated the accuracy of the saying "Generals die in bed." His death was caused by malaria.

Burroughs' admiration for the dashing general was so strong that he offered to go to Guatemala to interview him. On August 31, 1922, he explained to Curtis Brown, ". . . I had planned to write my articles with a view of putting them into book form after they had appeared in a magazine." He noted that the material could be considered as separate articles or as chapters of "a life story." His interest in Lee Christmas was understandable; beginning with John Carter of Mars, Burroughs' favorite heroes were adventurers, men who performed reckless acts without any fear of death. Through these soldiers-of-fortune he had lived vicariously and now the daring general appeared like a storybook warrior fresh out of the pages of a Burroughs novel. Christmas was fulfilling all the heroic actions that Burroughs had dreamed about but never performed; the exploits of Christmas, a real-life adventurer, could provide a vicarious thrill far more exciting than the deeds of imaginary characters.

Unhappily, Ed's proposal to write the series of articles was hedged about with conditions; he had insisted that he must receive a definite commitment from some suitable magazine to accept the articles. On August 25, Lida McCord of the Curtis Brown Agency replied, "We have interested the Saturday Evening Post in your work but they are not willing to make any definite promise until the manuscript is completed." Ed, not inclined to gamble with any of his valuable time, began to cool toward the project and the journey to Guatemala. He was blunt: "I doubt if I would care to undertake the trip without some more definite assurance that I can dispose of the magazine rights, and also, I shall want to know the rate that I would be paid. . . ." A further letter from Curtis Brown on September 21 explained that none of the editors they had contacted would promise to accept the articles sight unseen.

On September 29, 1922, Ed made it plain that he was abandoning the project: ". . . it commences to look as though I might not be able to do anything in this matter for the present, at least, as I understand that Gen. Christmas is expecting to come to the states, in which event it would probably be advisable to wait until I could talk the matter over with him personally." There is no record of any meeting with General Christmas or of any future plan to write the series of articles about this famous soldier-of-fortune.

Once again, with Davis' encouragement, Ed began considering various ideas for a new *Tarzan* story. From Davis in February 1923 came a suggestion: why not place Tarzan among Lilliputians or some type of tiny people? Ed was intrigued by the idea; upon returning from a trip with Emma—in driving they had encountered 24 below zero weather in Wyoming during which he slept in his overcoat and "nearly froze to death," he turned to his own imagination for an original approach to the story. On March 3 he wrote to Davis, "I am thinking of the new Tarzan story and have obtained a copy of Sir John Lubbock's work on ants." But soon afterward he became dubious about the "little men" theme, believing that while the idea might be workable for a chapter or short story, he could not "carry them through a full length novel with Tarzan." He was prepared to adopt an alternative idea: ". . . I had thought of taking Tarzan into Abyssinia where there is a real Emperor surrounded by real warriors, with a system of religious rites already well established. I should like to have your ideas on the subject, and in the meantime, I shall have to read up considerably on Abyssinia. . . ."[21]

Davis found the little men idea highly stimulating. He thought Ed was visualizing the men as "too small," like diminutive pygmies, and commented, "I think if they were two feet high they would be more negotiable." He could picture "the towering Tarzan defending these miniature men against the beasts of the jungle and the discordant elements." The little men would have "their government, their wars, their intrigues, their treasures and their cities." Naturally, the jungle animals would remain in their normal sizes. Davis could envision "a certain intimate understanding between the kings of the little peoples and the giant Tarzan." However, he was willing to settle for Tarzan in Abyssinia and the mysterious religious rites, but urged Ed not to "clutter Tarzan up with a retinue of black people."[22]

Two weeks later Ed confessed to Davis that after scanning various books on Abyssinia, his interest had waned. He thought he might return to the pygmies after all. Davis, approving, offered his ideas. "Turn the women into archers because of their accuracy and indifference to pain. . . ." The pygmies could, as a defense, have a "manufactured odor which they have discovered and perfected." He went on jokingly: "The odor need not be disagreeable as, for example, the kind you emit. I suppose editors smell just like that to authors. . . . ." Davis had other practical suggestions.[23]

Ed displayed a more serious reaction to his writing, one that had depressed him before. His feeling was that Tarzan had "shot his wad"; possibly he and everybody else was tired of the subject. Later he complained that the Tarzan story was hard work and wrote, "I think this will be the last. They are not worth the effort I have to put on them now." In the time required for one Tarzan story, he could write three others. "Instead of enjoying my work," he noted, "I am coming pretty near to loathing it. . . . If I had not promised you this one I would chuck it right where it is."[24]

Davis was both distressed and alarmed, demanding, "If you loathe the Tarzan stuff . . . why do you go on with it?" He was concerned about Ed doing a weak job that would not be fair to either of them. However, in response came a more reassuring statement. Certainly the writing was difficult, especially "after having said all there is to say about Tarzan seven or eight times." But Ed had no intention of handing Davis a lemon. Actually, he had found a new angle and was now "having some fun" out of the story.[25] Ed varied the discussions over stories to make an important announcement; to Davis on May 25, 1923, he wrote, ". . . you are doing business with a soulless corporation." The amazing tripersonality, farmer-businessman-writer was now converted to Edgar Rice Burroughs, Inc.

On November 23 Ed sent the 86,000-word story to Davis, explaining, "I was going to include an appendix and glossary, but thought better of it." He was worried that Davis might object to Tarzan being reduced to the size of the Ant Men, and wrote, "I found it impossible to have him play around with them while his stature remained normal." Davis telegraphed on December 3 to accept the story, but stated, "Esteban Miranda seems totally unnecessary from every point of view. I request his absolute elimination from this story." Davis' reasoning was that with the removal of Miranda, Tarzan's whole adventure would involve the "little people"—a better arrangement.

The editor's request brought a summary rejection from an exhausted Burroughs. Adamant about *any* revisions, he fired back, "Think Miranda Okay. If insist change buy manuscript as is and make change there. I put in five months on story and though I would do almost anything for you I would not work on it again if I never sold it or another. . . ."[26]

The complexity of "Tarzan and the Ant Men" makes it plain that Burroughs' complaint about the "hard work" was, if anything, a mild understatement. The complicated details of the Minunians' customs and social structure required the most intense planning; only a writer with Burroughs' predilection, almost an obsession, for such detail could have created a story of this type. To devise and keep track of the Minunians' names, in itself, was no mean feat. Ed's evident determination to create the longest possible names for the tiniest people, an idea perhaps arising from Swift's concoctions in *Gulliver's Travels*—Brobdingnag, Glubbdubdrib, and Luggnaggian—led him into the amusing realm of names with as many as nineteen letters. The list of "unpronounceables" included King Adendrohahkis, his son Komodoflorensal, the Veltopismakusians, King Elkomoelhago, and the Trohanadalmakusians. On his worksheets Ed had even meticulously placed accents over certain letters in the names, a procedure that was evidently too much for the printer, who chose to ignore them.

The four-page worksheets for "Tarzan and the Ant Men," complete with glossary, chapter headings, word counts, maps, measurements, and dimensions for a pigmy civilization, and drawings of Minunian hieroglyphics provide an astonishing example of Burroughs' capacity for inventive detail. Ed's drawings include a cross section of one of the gigantic dome-houses, constructed in antlike fashion by the Minunians, and Adendrohahkis' Palace, the largest building, is noted as "220 feet in diameter; 110 feet high; 36 stories. Capable of housing 80,000 people. Scale ⅛ inch equals 4 feet."[27]

Although indebted to Davis for the germ of an idea about Tarzan among the pygmies, Burroughs, once he had turned his imaginary powers loose, devised his own combination of plot, subplots and a host of characters, in all a remarkable demonstration of his ingenuity. In the five months of intense work he had transformed the basic suggestion into a complicated story of races, both giant and diminutive, that in its structure far exceeded any previous development of bizarre civilizations with their customs, equipment, and habitations. In the story Tarzan's adventures are launched through a new and foolhardy action. Under his son Korak's instruction he has been learning to pilot a plane, and despite his son's protests insists upon taking off in a solo flight. Beyond the Great Thorn Forest the plane crashes and here the unconscious Tarzan is carried away by a huge Alalus woman, a creature of a primitive race in which the females, massive and heavily muscled, are dominant over the timid males. The young males, between the ages of fifteen and seventeen, after being liberated and chased into the forest, were later hunted and captured by the females for mating purposes. This "unnatural reversal of sex dominance" is changed through Tarzan's efforts, his rescue of an Alalus lad, and his demonstration to the boy of how the brutal females can be defeated. With instruction in the use of the bow and arrow the Alalus males are able to overcome the mighty muscles and clubs of the women; thus, they assume their role of the dominant male.

From the Alalus, who occupy only a short section of the story, Tarzan moves to his main encounter with the Minunians, tiny creatures who in battle are mounted upon the miniature Royal Antelope. Davis had insisted that the "pygmies" should not be too small—they might then "have the quality of banshees and leprechauns, the habits of gnomes, and the characteristics of fairies." As a compromise, Ed made the Minunians eighteen inches in height. The antelope stood "fifteen inches at the withers." He was also careful to create them as "real pygmies," not the familiar black tribe, but a "lost white race" referred to in myth and legend.

Early in the story Ed makes clear his plan to compare the habits and activities of these little people to those of the ants. This intention had been indicated in his ant research. The movements of the tiny warriors and workers toward the openings of their domelike structures, carry "to the mind of the ape-man a suggestion of ants laboring about their hills." In addition to devoting detail to the complex social organization of the Minunians, and to including the unusual function of the slaves—their adoption as creatures for intermarriage so as to "infuse new blood" into the physically degenerating Minunians—Ed takes obvious delight, as in the past, in describing the superb military maneuvers of these tiny warriors in their combat against their enemies, the Veltopismakusians.

Ed's indignation against the war propaganda that had deceived him and led to his depiction of the Germans as subhuman, impelled him to insert a comment about the noble motives that drove the Minunians out to battle: "No chicanery of politics here, no thinly veiled ambition of some potential tyrant . . . none of these, but patriotism of purest strain energized by the powerful urge of self-preservation. . . ." He then spoke bitterly of "captains of the outer world who send unwilling men to battle for they know not what, deceived by lying propaganda, enraged by false tales of the barbarity of the foe, whose anger has been aroused against them by similar means." This pointed attack upon the "lying propaganda" and "false tales" reveals that by the fall of 1923, more than a year before the German resentment reached its climax, Burroughs was painfully aware of his prejudiced writing.

In "Tarzan and the Ant Men" unique elements of the plot include the reduction of Tarzan to the stature of a Minunian, a feat accomplished by the "wizard" Zoanthrohago; fortunately, the change is not permanent, and despite his miniature size, Tarzan conveniently retains his former strength. The ants themselves had in the past constituted a serious danger to the Minunians. At the lowest strata of the domes, where the dead had been left, the ants had at first been the scavengers; they soon began to attack the living and great battles followed in which the ants were victorious until the Minunians destroyed their nests and their queens.

On December 7 Davis notified Ed that in compliance with his instructions he had "eliminated entirely from this manuscript the person of Esteban Miranda to the extent of eleven thousand words." Miranda was the Spanish villain who had impersonated the ape-man in the previous novel, *Tarzan and the Golden Lion.* Davis maintained that this deletion improved the story "from every conceivable angle." He disapproved of Ed's ending which finds the imposter Miranda claiming to be Lord Greystoke. This obviously indicated that Ed was "setting the stage for a sequel." Davis requested a three-hundred word ending, "bringing Tarzan back to his family in a normal way," and added, "In my humble opinion the Ant People are big enough for another socking good story. Let Miranda remain among the dead."[28]

Ed responded with some mild annoyance about the revision which was costing him five hundred dollars. His failure to even mention a new ending brought a further demand from Davis who spoke coaxingly of the wonderful cover he was preparing for the "Ant People," one that looked like "a segment from 'Gulliver's Travels.' " As usual, Davis' tone was joking and he threatened, "Give me the end of this story or I'll write it myself. The best way to do an author a lot of damage is to finish a story for him."[29] Ed maintained the same humorous attitude, reminding him of the earlier telegram which had stated that "if you did not like my story you knew what you could do." Ed wrote, "If you want me to write the new ending badly enough to pay me for it say so. If not, turn the job over to the office

Cover of Tarzan and the Ant Men, *1924; J. Allen St. John, illustrator.*

Cover of Tarzan and the Golden Lion, *1923; J. Allen St. John, illustrator.*

Cover of Pellucidar, 1923;
J. Allen St. John, illustrator.

boy. It won't make any difference, for when the story appears in book form it will read as per my original version, than which there can be nothing better!"[30]

In the five-month period from November 1923 to April of the following year, Burroughs, immersed in business activities, the El Caballero Country Club, and the sale of Tarzana lots, could devote little effort to writing. Continuous agreements with McClurg had produced a steady flow of books: *At the Earth's Core* (1922); *The Chessmen of Mars* (1922); *Tarzan and the Golden Lion* (1923); *Pellucidar* (1923). For the latest publication Bray returned to an old Burroughs story "The Land That Time Forgot"; it would appear on June 14, 1924.

Burroughs' two-year contract with Munsey expired in April 1924, and the customary negotiations began. The rate had been five cents a word; Burroughs noted frankly that he could see no advantage to a contract unless Davis either agreed to take all of his work at that price or to raise the rate on the stories that were accepted. An unwritten "gentleman's agreement" was finally arrived at. For a rate of six cents a word, Davis was granted first refusal on all the stories. Concerning those that did not appear to be the type Munsey would want, Ed planned to submit only sections in progress, believing that in the event of rejection, he might not finish the story. However, he proceeded to ignore this plan at once, launching into one of his most untypical stories, and finishing it on October 13. "Marcia of the Doorstep," estimated at some 125,000 words, was the longest work he had ever written.

In his creation of this long novel, Ed was again symbolizing his protest or rebellion against the repetitive sequence of *Tarzan* and other fantasy works that he was forced to write. Although he must have been aware of the extreme difficulty he would face in marketing the novel, he was still driven to complete it. This impulsive action was contrary to the cold-blooded, dollars-and-cents attitude that had long since dictated his writing procedures. But in this case the frustration and the psychological need to be recognized as something more than "Burroughs, the author of Tarzan," were too powerful to suppress. Along with this, despite his often-repeated statements about writing only to entertain, went a hidden dream of creating something that would have a touch of the literary quality, a piece of writing, highly realistic, that might confound the critics who rated him merely as an author of superficial escapism and cause them to view him with a new respect.

The writing of "Marcia of the Doorstep" became a secretive process. In contrast to his usual method of mentioning a contemplated work, sounding out Davis or Bray about it and then discussing its progress, Ed gave no indication at all that the novel was underway. From this, the alternate assumptions could be that he was sensitive about revealing this shift to a new and impractical type of writing, one that broke sharply from his established patterns, or that he desired to keep the work secret, hoping to produce as a complete surprise a novel of unusual strength and appeal. To further insure secrecy, hiding the project even from his secretaries, he wrote the entire 125,000-word novel in longhand on lined legal-size notebook paper. At a later date he commented disparagingly about "Marcia of the Doorstep," explaining that he had written it at a time when his mind "was occupied with other things," financial and business entanglements, and that the "rottenness" of the story was "more or less" a reflection of his "mental attitude" during the period.[31] There may have been some truth in this explanation, but one must deduce that any author who devotes more than five months to a lengthy work is surely motivated by something beyond mechanical persistence—a sustained interest in the story, its characters, and its development.

In the romantic plot of "Marcia of the Doorstep" Burroughs devised involved relationships in a city-life setting and added some background references to the stage and motion picture field. At the same time, he could not resist bringing in one of his much-used shipwrecks with the inevitable mutineers and a landing on a deserted island. Burroughs' past preoccupation with the evils of socialism, Bolshevism, and his contempt for the IWWs is again evident in his occasional lapses into propaganda attacks against "agitators" and their ilk. But most significantly, in the creation of the loathsome villain Max Heimer, the basest caricature of a Jew, Burroughs reveals his susceptibility to the racial prejudice of the times and the steréotype that resulted.

The fortunes of Marcia, an infant left on the doorstep of the Sacketts and raised by them, are the main concern of the story. The story, in its 1906 opening, describes how John Hancock Chase, Jr., the son of a United States senator, is being blackmailed by Max Heimer who has convinced him that on a certain night, after the supposed consumption of too much liquor, he (Chase) had sexual relations with a disreputable woman,

Mame Myerz, resulting in the birth of an illegitimate child. Chase, a married man, is unable to pay any more money and is finally driven to suicide.

The reader, of course, is given the impression, after this scene, that the infant is Marcia, who grows up in the home presided over by Marcus Aurelius Sackett, a familiar type of old-fashioned Shakespearean actor. Other members of the household include his wife Clara and an actress, Della Maxwell. Marcus, completely impractical, is childlike in his handling of money and naive in his estimates of human nature. Because of his irregular

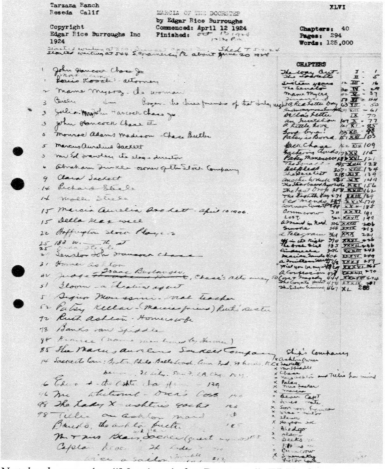

Notebook page for "Marcia of the Doorstep," ERB's longest novel, unpublished.

income, the family lives on the edge of poverty, but despite this, Marcus will never consider entering a field that he abhors —the motion pictures. The years have passed; Marcia is now sixteen and Marcus is once more unemployed; but when, in order to pay for her singing lessons, she volunteers to seek work in the movies, Marcus forbids it.

Heimer, appearing at the Sackett home on a legal matter involving Marcus' current play, discovers that Marcia is a "doorstep" baby, perceives the connection with the man he had blackmailed years before, and sees his new opportunity—to go to old Senator Chase and extort money from him. Chase, believing that Marcia is his granddaughter, establishes a trust fund for the girl, with the proviso that the two must never meet, and provides $20,000 for the Sacketts as compensation for raising Marcia. The cunning Heimer manages to swindle Marcus out of most of this money. As treasurer of a Shakespearean touring company, Heimer convinces Marcus that the tour is a financial failure, although it is actually successful, and, as a result, Marcus, believing he has foolishly wasted all of his money, attempts suicide. He is saved by his wife Clara.

Marcia had always assumed she would marry her childhood sweetheart, Dick Steele, but finds herself involved with two men who fall in love with her. Through wealthy acquaintances, the Ashtons, she meets Banks van Spiddle and later accepts an invitation to join these people on a yacht cruise in the Pacific. At Honolulu, where he is stationed, Lieutenant John Hancock Chase, III, the grandson of the old senator, becomes a member of the party. Marcia and Jack Chase fall in love, and here Burroughs creates a situation which raises the problem of incest, since, presumably, unknown to either one, they are really brother and sister.

Judge Isaac Berlanger, a trusted friend of the Chase family, had foreseen the danger of a shipboard romance and obtained the permission of the senator to reveal the relationship. Berlanger cables, but it is too late; the shipwreck has occurred and the ship is abandoned. Marcia and Jack are in a lifeboat with crew members who include a number of dangerous mutineers. Jack courageously keeps these men under control, and after the lifeboat has been adrift for some time the passengers land on a deserted island.

These adventures alternate with an account of the Sacketts' troubles at home. Financial problems have driven Marcus to accepting handouts from Heimer. In the meantime, no word is received of the shipwreck survivors. Marcia and Jack eventually are rescued from the island, but upon her return she finds the cable revealing their relationship. Distraught, she leaves without explaining matters to Jack and launches a successful career in the movies as Marian Sands. Fortunately, a letter from Della Maxwell, written on her deathbed, discloses that Marcia is really *her* daughter.

At the end Heimer receives his punishment and is required to make restitution for the money he has stolen from Marcus. Marcia's happy union with Jack is somewhat marred by the tragic death of Dick Steele, who is killed in an airplane crash.

As in other works of the period, "Marcia of the Doorstep" reveals Burroughs' political and social conditioning and his acceptance of the prejudices of the day. There is a repetition of his views in three familiar areas. Radicals and communists are derided. When Dick Steele refers to the "burden" workers are carrying because of "parasites" like the playboy van Spiddle, Della remarks, "Getting to be a regular little Bolshevik, eh?" She points out that van Spiddle's spending creates work for others, and scoffs at the concept of financial equality—a world of this type "would be about as dull and impossible as the orthodox Christian conception of Heaven."

Ashton, in commenting upon the angry complaints of certain crew members, notes that "they've been inoculated with IWW virus" and speaks with scorn of their labor leaders who "live off the fat of the land" and "do it without labor at the expense of the damn fools upon whose ignorance and credulity they play. . . ."

Burroughs demonstrates some prudish morality in Jack Chase's disapproval of women who usurp "the prerogative vulgarities and vices of men," these being smoking, drinking, and swearing. Chase remarks to Patsy that "We all approve of it . . . for the other fellow's women." Yet, "Marcia of the Doorstep" contains an odd, sexually-tinged scene of a type never used by Burroughs. Marcus first hooks his wife's garters and then is summoned by Marcia to come to her room and pull down her brassiere "so it won't show." The un-Burroughesque nature of the brief scene makes it seem that he was doing this in an attempt to emulate the newer style of frank realism in literary stories. He may have hoped that it would make the story more salable, but the scene appears inappropriate and awkward.

In the lifeboat episode the horrifying prospect of cannibalism appears; Burroughs had last resorted to this in *The Return of Tarzan* where a party including Jane and Clayton, adrift in a lifeboat, take part in a gruesome "Lottery of Death." In "Marcia of the Doorstep" Pilkins, one of the sailors, discusses the past of Bledgo, the most dangerous of the mutineers, who had been shipwrecked before; rescued after being adrift for three weeks, Bledgo looked "as fat and chipper as he is today, but they say the boat smelt awful." The bestial, half-crazed Bledgo now runs amuck, attempts to kill one of the men and bites a piece out of his shoulder.

Aware of the excessive length of "Marcia of the Doorstep," Burroughs went through the manuscript making numerous deletions. Long passages, many of them redundant, and even whole pages are scratched out in pencil. A middle section and the long closing scene are reduced through the use of insert pages. On October 30, 1924, in rejecting the story, Davis commented that it would make a first-class book and then added his criticisms:

. . . there is so much diversity, so many characters and scenes, so many threads, the coming together of which is so far apart, that it would be fatal to publish it in a monthly magazine in serial form. No reader could remember the complications in this novel for a period of five, six or possibly seven months; the time required in view of its length to complete it in serial segments.

Later submissions produced no results. To Horace Liveright (Boni & Liveright) on June 3, 1925, in sending the manuscript Ed noted he had made "some slight changes" and added dolefully, "I am afraid you will not like the story." Liveright's rejection—"It is not our sort of book. . . ."—confirmed Ed's fears. He was frank in his reply that "people much more experienced than I have told me I had no business trying to write anything other than highly imaginative fiction" and also admitted that he had not sent the story to Bray at McClurg because he *knew* the editor would not like it. Other rejections came from *Redbook,* the *Saturday Evening Post,* and *Love Story Magazine.* Clearly, "Marcia of the Doorstep" was not fated to appear in print.

With the purchase by Davis for $2,150 of "The Moon Men," a revision of the unsalable "Under the Red Flag," came some bantering remarks about Ed's obvious plan for a sequel, made evident in the concluding page of the story. On October 20, 1924, Davis wrote, "The Jews may be 'God's Chosen People,' but you are His chosen author. You could take any one of the psalms, make it 100,000 words in length, and then leave a string

ARGOSY
ALL-STORY
WEEKLY

A sequel to
"The Moon
Maid"

Edgar Rice Burroughs
Creator of TARZAN *writes*
The Moon Men

10¢ PER COPY   FEBRUARY 21   BY THE YEAR $4.00

"The Moon Men" cover of Argosy All-Story Weekly, *February 21, 1925.*

dragging for a second verse." About the sequel, its theme being a "feudal state" existing in California of the future, Davis was encouraging, but suggested that Ed use actual locations of the contemporary "Golden West" in developing this story of a region lapsing into decadence. Ed adopted this idea, and on May 14, 1925, sent "The Red Hawk" to the editor.

The summer brought a return to Mars, with the sixth of the series in progress. The story, at first titled "A Weird Adventure on Mars," was finished on November 16. With the invention of a new hero, Ulysses Paxton, an infantry captain in the United States Army, Burroughs makes him the second earthman to be transported to Mars. From Paxton, as the story opens, comes a letter describing his serious injuries in battle, and how, as he lay on the verge of death, he followed the example of his idol, John Carter, stretched out his arms imploringly toward Mars, and then found himself drawn "through the trackless wastes of interplanetary space."

Paxton at once becomes an associate of the brilliant surgeon Ras Thavas of Barsoom. A very old man, Thavas, in his "House of the Dead," stores the bodies of young men and women, preserving both the living and the dead for use in transplants. The living include the beautiful Valla Dia, purchased as a slave and kept in a state of suspended animation for ten years, at which time her youthful body is exchanged for that of the aged Xaxa the Jeddara (Queen) of Phundahl. In the operation, witnessed by Paxton, the surgeon Thavas demonstrates an astonishing skill: ". . . at the end of four hours he had transferred the brain of each woman to the brain pan of the other, deftly connected the severed nerves and ganglia, replaced the skulls and scalps and bound both heads securely with his peculiar adhesive tape, which was not only antiseptic and healing but anaesthetic, locally, as well." The blood of Valla, reheated, and with a chemical solution added, is then exchanged for the blood of the older woman Xaxa, who is now the possessor of youth and beauty. Thavas, devoid of all sentiment, performs with the detached and objective attitude of the scientist.

Because he believed that the Earthman Paxton, a stranger on Mars, could be trusted, Thavas had chosen him as his assistant. The aged scientist, above all, needed someone who could learn his surgical techniques, and when the necessity arose, exchange his worn-out body for that of a younger man. Paxton, now thoroughly skilled, agrees to perform the operation, but imposes a condition. He had fallen in love with the exquisite Valla Dia at sight and is determined that her body shall be returned to her. Thavas, having no choice, promises to make the transference if Xaxa is brought to his laboratory. The remainder of the story develops from this incredible task Paxton has set for himself. He must journey to the distant Phundahl, somehow kidnap the most powerful woman in the kingdom, Xaxa, and carry her back to the laboratory where the surgery can take place.

In this 1925 story, Burroughs' plot, which may have appeared bizarre, contained the substance of "things to come" in modern transplants. The storage of bodies and vital organs is a present-day medical practice. A description of the transplants could well apply to standard procedures of today or the next decade:

I removed the kidneys from a rich old man, replacing them with healthy ones from a young subject. The following day I gave a stunted child new thyroid glands. A week later I transferred two hearts and then, at last, came the great day for me—unassisted, with Ras Thavas standing silently beside me, I took the brain of an old man and transplanted it within the cranium of a youth.

A further projection of the future is evident in a device called the "equilibrimotor," designed for individual flying. It is described as a "broad belt" which is filled with a Barsoomian ray of propulsion that, by exerting a counterforce against the pull of gravity, helps to maintain a person's equilibrium. The remainder of the apparatus consists of a small radium motor and a sturdy, light wing that can be manipulated with hand levers.

As in *The Gods of Mars,* Burroughs cannot resist ridiculing a blind, superstitious belief in religion. The people of Phundahl worshipped the god Tur, and at the temple followed a ritual which they never presumed to question. Before various idols they might lie prone or bump their heads on the floor, or, on occasion, crawl madly in a circle. In all cases money was dropped in a receptacle.

Burroughs presents a significant aspect of his philosophy in the scene that follows. Paxton, upon hearing the worshippers recite "Tur is Tur, Tur is Tur" before two different idols, remarks that in both cases the sounds are identical. Dar Tarus corrects him, insisting that at first they said, "Tur is Tur," while at the second idol they reversed it. Dar Tarus asks, "Do you not see? They turned it right around backwards, which makes a very great difference." Paxton could not detect the "difference," and because of this, was again accused of a lack of faith.

Of course Burroughs' invention of the word "Tur" for the

Phundahlian God is deliberate. The worshippers are really saying, "Rut is Rut." In this scene Burroughs is commenting upon the follies of all blind religious custom, whether on earth or on Mars. But in addition, he is emphasizing a danger. Through years of ritualistic behavior and unquestioning conformity, one may lose the power of seeing things rationally. Paxton, a stranger, not confined in the Phundahlians' particular rut, could apply simple reasoning. About religion as mere jargon chanted automatically, Burroughs is saying that whether one mumbles it backward or forward, it remains meaningless.

With the completion of "A Weird Adventure on Mars," Ed's procedure, as usual, was to submit the manuscript to Munsey. In August 1925 Bob Davis had departed for six months of vacation and travel; his visit to Los Angeles, where he noted his intention to see a "million relatives," included a stopover with the Burroughs family. Replacing Davis was Matthew White, Jr., and his reaction to the Martian manuscript was both unexpected and disturbing to Ed. On November 27, in rejecting the story, White noted, ". . . the present vein you are writing in does not suit the *Argosy* as did your Tarzan stories. We do not find them tense enough in action, rapid enough in action, gripping enough in situations." White indicated that if the choice were his, he would not have accepted "The Red Hawk." Icily formal, in contrast to Davis' bantering remarks, White closed with a statement about writing something "strictly in line with the kind of story the *Argosy* requires. . . ."

Irked and bewildered, Ed put the story aside, uncertain whether to submit it elsewhere. On March 10, 1926, he expressed his feelings to Joseph Bray, explaining that he was a "little sore" about the rejection, "possibly more by the tone of the man's letter . . . than anything else." Because of the extended relationship with Munsey, Ed felt he was entitled to better treatment. He could not restrain his anger: "Therefore, they can go to hell as far as I am concerned until they ask me for another story." He added, "I know it was not Bob's fault, but after all it is the Frank A. Munsey Company that I am dealing with and the letter I received from them was official."

In April, Davis, who had been traveling around the world, returned to his desk; Frank A. Munsey had died. To Ed, Davis remarked that one of the happiest experiences of his trip was "meeting the Burroughs family at their own table." He also advised that two of his books were being published that year, one titled *Over My Left Shoulder,* containing an editor's reminiscences about events and personalities, and the other, *Ruby Robert, Alias Bob Fitzsimmons,* an account based upon Davis' personal association with the prizefighter. In 1897, on assignment from C. M. Palmer, business manager of the *New York Journal,* and with specific instructions from William Randolph Hearst, Davis set out to contact Fitzsimmons before his scheduled fight with Corbett. Hearst, whose plan was to sign Fitzsimmons to an agreement for thirty days prior to the fight and twenty-four hours after, explained the conditions to Davis: "We are paying Fitzsimmons for his silence. He cannot speak to anyone, write to anyone, pose for photographs, or carry on any intercourse whatsoever except through you or in your presence. . . ." For this agreement Fitzsimmons was offered ten thousand dollars, half upon signing and the remainder following the fight. Martin Julian, the fighter's manager, after some persuasion signed the agreement, and Davis at once joined the training group, accompanying them to Carson City, Nevada. He described himself humorously as Fitzsimmons' private secretary. In his book, besides reporting the fight, in which Corbett was knocked out, Davis added colorful anecdotes about Fitzsimmons.[32]

oncerning "A Weird Adventure on Mars," Ed, on April 20, notified Davis that the story had been "packed away" in the vault "with an accompaniment of a few briny tears." Despite his joking, it was evident that he was losing patience with the Munsey Company. He had hoped they would sign an agreement to take his entire output; their refusal to do this and their rejections of "Marcia of the Doorstep" and his latest Mars story put a severe strain upon the relationship. Street & Smith had also returned "Marcia of the Doorstep," and when editor Charles Agnew MacLean, in September 1926, wrote to request Burroughs' submissions for *Popular Magazine,* Ed in annoyance reminded him of this recent rejection. The material MacLean sought was painfully obvious to Ed. MacLean spoke of "a wild hope" that Ed might be interested in doing another *Tarzan* story. Ed forwarded "A Weird Adventure on Mars" to him, and the ensuing correspondence, a contest of price proposals and counter-proposals for a *Tarzan* story, lasted for two years and achieved a new record for futility.

On October 30 MacLean had returned the Mars story, commenting that the theme was "too bizarre and shocking." He followed oddly with an admission that it was "extremely easy to read" and confessed, ". . . I kept reading it long after I knew that it would not be advisable for us to publish it." As negotiations continued, Ed determined that if MacLean wanted only a *Tarzan* story, he must pay high for it, and quoted a price of ten cents a word. With the contest moving into 1927, Ed became more irritable: "We seem to be working at cross-purposes. You want to buy a Tarzan story and I want to sell a Martian story. I think you are very foolish not to buy it. . . ." On March 2 MacLean explained that he could not accept the "rather repellent features" of this particular Martian story.[33] During the course of this bickering, Ed had submitted the story to the *Elks Magazine,* where it was rejected. The title change to "Vad Varo of Barsoom" could not make the story more palatable.[34]

The Burroughs response to MacLean's use of "repellent" offered logic and example that were grimly humorous. A story far more repellent, *The Chessmen of Mars,* had been successful in both magazine and book form. In mentioning the kaldanes who were all brain, and "bred" human bodies to carry them about, Ed noted they also devoured these bodies. "They were utterly horrid. There was also another race of delightful people who stuffed their dead and posed them on balconies outside their homes as well as in the corridors of their palaces." The transplanting of brains from one head to another, as described in "Vad Varo of Barsoom," in Ed's opinion was hardly as "gruesome" as the breeding and eating of human bodies. Ed submitted a gambling proposition to MacLean: if the new Mars story did not increase *Popular Magazine's* circulation, the editor would not have to pay anything for it. Despite this free-trial concession, MacLean could not be persuaded to accept the story.[35]

On April 19, 1927, replying to a query by Hugo Gernsback, editor of *Amazing Stories,* about available material, Burroughs offered "Vad Varo of Barsoom" for $1,250. To the struggling Experimenter Publishing Company this was a stiff price. Gernsback, noting that "at the present stage of *Amazing Stories'* development, we would not be justified in paying the amount you ask, . . ." made a counter-proposal. "Vad Varo of Barsoom" would be published in a yearbook of best stories, issued by *Amazing Stories* in July, and selling for fifty cents, double the price of the magazine. If this were satisfactory, Gernsback would pay the amount demanded. Burroughs quickly agreed, but in the months that followed, a delay in payment brought some heated correspondence.[36] The selection of a title for the story became an immediate problem. On May 9 Gernsback wired for permission to rename it "Xaxa of Mars," stating, "The long name will interfere with sale. . . . Word Mars should be in

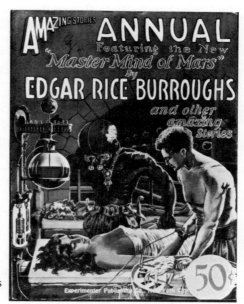

"Master Mind of Mars"
cover of Amazing Stories
Annual, *July 1927.*

Cover of Tarzan, Lord of
the Jungle, *1928; J. Allen*
St. John, illustrator.

title in our opinion." Burroughs granted Gernsback a free hand, but when the annual appeared, the story assumed a new and final title—"The Master Mind of Mars."

While the MacLean dealings remained at an impasse, Ed, from summer 1926-27, completed and sold two *Tarzan* stories elsewhere. These were "The Tarzan Twins," a juvenile, and "Tarzan, Lord of the Jungle." Through his hesitation MacLean had lost his chance to acquire the latter story, but on October 17 the editor quoted the remarkable rate of ten cents a word for a *Tarzan* story, the highest price he had "ever paid anyone," and stipulated that it must be "really good." That nothing but a Tarzan story would interest him was made evident by his rejection on December 20 of the second of Burroughs' ventures into Indian-white-man conflict, "Apache Devil."

It was not until June 1928 that Ed finished the story, "Tarzan and the Lost Tribe," and sent it to *Popular Magazine*. Based upon the past difficulties, the reaction might have been anticipated. MacLean, seriously ill, was not scheduled to return to work for several months, but the magazine editors, highly disappointed, rejected the story, commenting, ". . . it is not a real Tarzan story, which we had hoped to get from you, and for which our offer was made." Ed had conceived a story of a lost Roman civilization, later to be retitled "Tarzan and the Lost Empire." The editors complained that "almost none of the action takes place in the jungle. . . ." They conceded that the story was "quite fascinating indeed," but claimed, "the balance of appeal is on the side of readers who are interested in archaeology and history (imaginative)."[37] Ed's disgust with the entire matter, the culmination of two years of correspondence, was indicated in his "No Ans." scrawled across the top of the editors' letter.

The cross-exchanges with various editors had often involved wrangling over prices or revisions and had at times produced impatience or exasperation on Burroughs' part; however, this correspondence could produce an unmatched brand of sarcasm and humor, as evidenced by letters between newspaper editors and Burroughs. In December 1926 the *Kansas City Star* rejected "The Mad King" for serialization and added a comment that it was a motion picture scenario. Burroughs, on the seventeenth, wrote to Louis Mecker, serial editor, to express surprise at the statement and to point out that "The Mad King" was a novel, had appeared as a serial in a magazine and had been published by McClurg. He remarked "The motion picture rights to this story have not been sold, nor was it written for motion picture purposes. In fact, none of my stories have been written for the screen, nor am I sufficiently conversant with motion picture production to write a scenario. I am sorry that you were misinformed. . . ."

Mecker, in his answer of the twenty-second, noted the assurance that "The Mad King" *was* a novel and agreed that other newspapers had purchased it with this belief: "All of this only goes to show how preconceived ideas may affect one's convictions. I examined 'The Mad King' myself and came to the conclusion that it was a motion picture scenario, although, like you, I have no technical knowledge of the construction of these scenarios."

Continuing, Mecker turned to Shakespeare for an example:

When Hamlet and Polonius stood gazing at the sky, it was Polonius's opinion that a certain cloud form resembled a whale (if I remember correctly), but Hamlet remarked "Methinks it is a camel," Polonius at once conceded, " 'Tis backed like a camel." You and the Boston Post and the New York World all feel that "The Mad King" is a novel. And sure enough, now that you suggest it, methinks 'tis backed like a novel, but for the rest of it me still thinks 'tis very like a motion picture scenario.

Burroughs, hardly to be outdone in this type of sarcasm, and never one to concede the last word to anybody, proceeded on the twenty-eighth to demolish Mecker: "Many thanks for your delightful letter of December 22nd. The Kansas City Star is to be congratulated on having discovered Shakespeare, and I am encouraged to believe that three hundred years hence it will discover the Burroughs classics and commence to increase its circulation accordingly."

An exchange of a lighter nature, involving the *Daily World* of Tulsa, Oklahoma, was initiated on November 18, 1927, when Burroughs inquired why the newspaper had never used his stories serially; he wondered if there were any "condition" that he could correct. From A. X. Hallinan, Sunday editor, came a terse response scrawled on Burroughs' letter: "Not enough sex appeal!"

In the summer of 1926 Burroughs finally began to write a story based upon an idea that had appealed to him seven years earlier. The procedure of making mental notes about story material, filing them away in a corner of his mind, and then reviving the idea at the appropriate time, had been adopted by him on various occasions in the past. An inquiry to *The American Boy* in September 1919 about the market for a story featuring an Apache Indian boy had been followed by a request to the Chicago Field Museum for information about Apache life. In October of that year he expressed his admiration of the Apaches to

Davis, referred to "the atrocities committed on them by whites," and sought approval of his idea to create a young Apache warrior "similar to Tarzan." He could turn the Apache into a "regular Tarzan," he explained, through the use of a plot involving a kidnapped white child raised by the Indians.

On October 8, 1925, Burroughs contacted H. C. Paxton, editor of *The Country Gentleman,* and commented about "tying up" his next Western story with the Geronimo campaign. He also spoke of the crossing of the Mormons from Illinois to Utah as another idea. Later he complained about the difficulty of finding information about Geronimo. His hopes for years had been to be accepted by a prestige market of this type, and he made it plain he was writing the story to specifically meet the requirements of the Curtis publication. On June 8, 1926, he was careful to explain a new direction in his story idea: "I find records of innumerable instances in which white children were captured by Apaches and reared by them as members of their own tribes, and in this fact I saw the possibility of a romantic character that might be likened to an Apache Tarzan." Ed noted that with this theme the story "would be written from the viewpoint of the Apache." The plot would center about a white boy who "would be unaware that he was not an Indian"; Ed referred to a true-life situation concerning a white girl abducted by the Indians who afterward married a chief, and who, many years later, upon being captured by the white men, so resembled the other Indian squaws that it was difficult to identify her as a white woman. Ed stressed that he would not start the story until this approach was approved by Paxton, and until the rate of payment was established.

In correspondence with Ed, Paxton, speaking for "The Oldest Agricultural Journal in the World," had indicated that his magazine was not interested in the standard Burroughs fare of *Tarzan* or other-planet works. It was only Ed's shift to the Western, "The Bandit of Hell's Bend," that changed Paxton's attitude. Now, in approving the Apache plot, Paxton and editor Loring A. Schuler commented that there was "abundant foundation for a Tarzan of the Apaches kind of book," but cautioned Ed to limit the flights of his imagination—he would have "to hold far closer to the probabilities" than he had in *Tarzan*. The price was generous, "not less than $5,000—more if the quality of the tale warranted a better price."[38]

An immediate obstacle to an agreement arose before the story was begun. The Curtis policy required that all rights be sold and that second serial publication in newspapers not be permitted. Book, dramatic, and motion picture rights would be reassigned to the author after the story appeared in the magazine. Ed had stubbornly adhered to his practice of selling only the first serial rights ever since he had unknowingly lost the rights to several of his earliest works. But he was so anxious to break into a media of this type whose reputation was above the *Argosy-All Story,* that he abandoned the rule he had maintained since 1912 and agreed to Paxton's conditions.[39]

In noting the "paucity of authentic information relative to Apaches," especially their "pre-reservation life," Ed claimed he had bought every book on the subject, and after reading and rereading ten volumes had found so many contradictions that he was compelled "to take considerable license" in his writing. He stressed that he was not utilizing his personal knowledge of the Apaches to any great extent, because his experiences had given him "an extremely biased and one-sided impression:" "I knew them then from the soldier's and white man's point of view and even in that day they were still hated and hunted like coyotes or mountain lion, our Apache scouts never travelling across country alone without being in actual danger of being fired upon by the first cowboy or prospector who saw them, and everyone that I talked with being absolutely convinced that there was no good in them."[40]

The precautions Ed had taken to work closely with Paxton and accede to his wishes did not bring the desired result. On December 3, 1926, in a letter distinguished by its vagueness, Paxton and Schuler rejected "The War Chief of the Apaches," describing it as "not quite the serial we should offer our readers." Other phrases were equally meaningless. Without question the story would have "a distinct appeal for many readers"; the choice of a serial "is a matter that calls for prayerful thought." Baffled, Ed sought specific reasons, speculating in confusion about the possible weaknesses in the story. He wondered if his detailed account of the Apache Shoz-Dijiji, in his early years, had been the cause: ". . . I was anxious, probably over-anxious, to develop the reader's understanding of the training and environment of Apaches from childhood to the end that some of their cruel and inhuman practices might not make them wholly abhorrent in his eyes."[41]

He wanted to know if the story was "too horrible" or if the white characters were "too crude," confessing that he thought this might be the problem, and "as a sop," of which he was really ashamed, had arranged for the girl, Wichita Billings, to be taken into the home of an army officer to make her "a little more presentable in the eyes of polite society." He explained he had known many whites of this type years before in Arizona, Idaho, and Utah, and found these pioneers of the '70s and '80s to be "almost universally ignorant, illiterate, uncouth, and unclean," although they often possessed "sterling characteristics" that more than balanced their defects. He added, "Knowing them as I did, I could not honestly place a sweet, marcelled, grammatical heroine in this environment and claim that she was part of it."[42]

On December 28 Paxton explained the reasons for the rejection. Surprisingly, they had little relationship to those Ed had conjectured. Paxton conceded that the white man's dealings with the Indians became "one of the most shameful chapters in American history." But in his opinion the average American still did not understand this and clung to the old view of the redskin as "a savage and heartless marauder." Paxton's remaining comments provided a depressing revelation as to the type of material *The Country Gentleman* fed to its readers. He noted that "Pocahontas and, to a lesser degree, Squanto are romantic figures; Cooper won sympathy for his redskin characters; but the average reader has no such feeling towards any of the Plains Indians. . . ." Thus, Paxton insisted, a serial written from the Indian's side would have only a limited appeal. Yet, Ed had explained his intention to write the story from the Apache's viewpoint, and Paxton had not objected at that time.

Paxton's main objection, however, was still to come. While admitting that Ed's story could have "genuine literary and historic value," he finally let the cat out of the bag: ". . . the most effective use of savage peoples in fiction is where the red or brown or black man is shown as the staunchly loyal follower of the white leader, and where there is the opportunity for the striking contrast between characters of different races." Plainly, *The Country Gentleman* wanted nothing to do with realism; the reference to Cooper's sentimental romances about the noble savage made that clear; the desired Indian was a well-tamed, well-behaved "white" Indian. And equally clear was the fact that the magazine would not print a story containing the truth (which Paxton had already conceded) that the Apache was a victim of white aggression, cruelty, and greed.

In his many hours of research, and in the great care he had taken to develop an authentic Apache background, which of course, when combined with Shoz-Dijiji's own viewpoint was bound to create a sympathetic picture of the Apaches, Ed, for

Paxton's purposes, had wasted his time. He might just as well have devised a flimsy, trite romance about the Indians, with no concern for realism or for an actual depiction of their customs and habits.

It is true that to a certain extent Ed was writing as a reformer; his indignation about the white man's behavior is forcefully presented. "The War Chief of the Apaches" contains numerous examples of antiwhite propaganda and typical Burroughs comments about the destructive effects of our supposed "civilization":

> . . . fewer men died at the hands of the six tribes of the Apaches than fell in a single day of many an offensive movement during a recent war between cultured nations.
>
> Had he (Shoz-Dijiji) had the cultural advantages of the gorgeous generals of civilization he might have found the means to unloose a poison gas that would have destroyed half the population of Sonora.

Certainly, this condemnation of the white man, and Ed's attempt to interpret the Apache's bloodthirsty deeds as a justifiable retaliation for worse acts committed by the whites, would hardly be viewed by Paxton as acceptable material for his readers.

"The War Chief of the Apaches" is especially remarkable for its details of tribal customs, of religious rites, and of Indian costumes and equipment. All of these become the background to the raising of the white infant, Andy MacDuff, whose father, a Scotch pioneer, and mother, the granddaughter of a Cherokee Indian, had been murdered by the Apaches. The infant, renamed Shoz-Dijiji, grows to manhood unaware of his white blood, and lives under the protection of such great Apache chiefs as Cochise and Geronimo. Burroughs' determination to develop the Apache life faithfully and accurately caused him to copy the most reliable versions of Indian terms he could find. These, undoubtedly formidable for the reader, included such terms as *pindah-lickoyee,* white-eyes; *izze-kloth,* sacred medicine cord; *chidin-bikungua,* house of spirits (heaven); and *hodden-tin,* a sacred powder. The story is also complicated by the use of such Apache tribal names as the *Be-don-ko-he,* the *Cho-ko-ken,* the *Chi-hen-ne,* and the *Chi-e-a-hen,* and by a large number of individual names and special words: the hero, *Shoz-Dijiji,* (meaning "black bear"); *Go-yat-thay,* the Indian name for Geronimo; *Nakay-do-klunni,* the medicine man; *Ish-kay-nay,* the Indian girl; *tzi-daltai,* an amulet; *es-a-da-ded,* a primitive drum. In his adoption of these numerous Indian words and a great many others, taken from

ARGOSY

ALL-STORY WEEKLY

APRIL 16

PRICE 10¢

The War Chief

by Edgar Rice Burroughs

"The War Chief" cover of Argosy All-Story Weekly, *April 16, 1927.*

supposedly authentic sources, Burroughs has far exceeded the number of words he invented for his Mars and *Tarzan* languages.

Burroughs' understanding of the type of story he did not want, one repeating the cliché of the romanticized and tamed "noble savage," and his extreme care in developing a realistic picture of Apache life, make "The War Chief of the Apaches" an outstanding novel. Unfortunately, in the later sections as he departs from realism and contrives incidents to round out his plot, the story is not as strong. The introduction of a white heroine, Wichita Billings, with whom Shoz-Dijiji falls in love; the convenient death of his Indian sweetheart; the inconsistency Shoz-Dijiji displays in his bloodthirsty mission of revenge against the whites, while at the same time killing members of his own tribe in order to rescue Wichita and her friends; and the unfinished ending with the sequel to come—all of these contribute to weakening the powerful effect achieved in the first half of the novel.

Its title shortened to "The War Chief," the novel appeared in *Argosy-All Story* in 1927 and was published by McClurg in the same year. For the book Burroughs compiled a brief glossary. His main research sources, noted on his worksheet, consisted of ten books.[43] In his use of one of the sources, *Trailing Geronimo,* Burroughs corresponded with the author, Anton Mazzanovich, and sent him a copy of *The War Chief.* On November 7, 1927, Ed explained that he had not received *Trailing Geronimo* until *The War Chief* was almost completed, and remarked, ". . . as soon as I did get it I took advantage of the historical information and the local color which it contained." Ed spoke of his days with the Seventh Cavalry at Fort Grant, the Apache scouts he had known there, and the futile efforts of the troops to capture the Apache Kid. He was frank in admitting that the publications about Apache life were often contradictory, and that an informed reader might readily dispute certain points presented in *The War Chief.*

A year later, after he had completed the sequel, *Apache Devil,* Ed somewhat apologetically commented to Mazzanovich, "As a writer . . . you will appreciate the fact that the hero must have redeeming qualities in order to win the sympathy of the reader, and so you can forgive the improbable character as long as I did not make him a full blood Apache, which would have made him impossible."[44]

Hugh Thomason, a former Michigan Military Academy schoolmate, wrote to thank Ed for the copy of *The War Chief.* Explaining that he had known Geronimo well, Thomason described him as "a devil incarnate," and recalled, "One day he sharpened a little pine stick; opened up a small vein in his forearm, and printed his name on his photograph for me."[45] Thomason, himself an author, sent Ed a magazine with one of his stories, published under the pen name "Jack MacLeod." In his reply Ed listed all his sources and also referred to a book, *Lives of Famous Indian Chiefs,* by Norman B. Wood which stated that Geronimo had blue eyes.[46]

Once *The War Chief* had been completed, the customary dealings with the Munsey Company and McClurg began. Matthew White, the new *Argosy All-Story* editor, had suggested a shortened title, and Ed, on January 11, 1927, noted that the single word "Apache" might create an impression of a Parisian Apache. Ed confessed he was "not keen" about the titles "The Big Chief" or "A Good Indian." On May 23, with only the first novel finished, Ed revealed that his plans included a series of three. He wrote jokingly, "Shoz-Dijiji will not marry the white girl until the third story of the series. I have found that it pays to prolong the agony." He also explained this to Bray: "In the third and concluding volume of the series he [Shoz-Dijiji] will be a cowpuncher or ranch foreman and everything will end happily by his getting the girl. New and original stuff!"[47] After *Apache Devil* had been written, Ed, his plans apparently changed, made no attempts to produce a third story.

While praising *The War Chief,* Bray commented "there is a little too much history in it." He thought the opening was too slow and appeared dubious about the "unpleasant" incidents, such as the scalping of the three prospectors which "creates in one a feeling of disgust." He conceded, however, that the current trend was toward realism and that the War Chief would have committed these bloodthirsty acts. With both White and Bray, Ed became severe about errors or changes in the proofs. Because of the intensive research he had devoted to his Indian stories, he was especially determined that the original manuscript should be followed.

On July 1, 1927, in returning the manuscript and galley proofs of *The War Chief* to Bray, he expressed a blunt disapproval of unauthorized changes in the story. His hesitancies of the early writing period were largely overcome. Having attained success through his own imagination and driving effort, he now could afford to be independent, to be stern with his editors. His letter to Bray, frosty and firm, was a series of instructions that he expected the editor to follow:

The manuscript should be read carefully for grammatical errors, many of which your readers missed.

They should not attempt to alter my copy or change my style. I spent half a day putting back into the galley proof that which had been deleted from the manuscript.

I write into my stories the things that I wish there. If they happen to offend the sensibilities of a proofreader or an editor, I am sorry, but no one has the right to do more than suggest changes—not make them.

In noting that many changes had been made in his books in the past, he accepted the blame, conceding that he had been "too busy or too lazy" to check the proofs carefully. He intended to do so in the future. Concerning items removed from *The War Chief* and then returned by him, he admitted there was one that might bring up a question, a paragraph ending, "Holy Mary sat on the sidelines and rooted for the Mexicans." Ed assumed that the editor had considered this sacrilegious. "It is, however, neither sacrilegious nor disrespectful," he commented. "It is only familiar."

He had often spoken of his deficiency in grammar, and it seemed to him in the matter of corrections, *this* was the proper and necessary province of the editors, but one that they usually overlooked. "I am both faulty and careless in my English and I am very anxious to have my mistakes corrected. . . . but I most emphatically object to having my stuff cut to pieces and whole paragraphs deleted without being consulted in the matter." Interestingly, he expounded his philosophy about the Indians: he had taken great care to treat the Indians fairly in the story, to tell the truth and yet try to win the reader's sympathy. In doing this, he explained, he was compelled to make comparisons between the Indians and the "civilized" whites, these often proving unfavorable to the white man. Above all, he hoped the reader would understand about the Indians, "that everything connected with their life and activity on the war trail was in the nature of religious rites, which puts a very different aspect upon their characters than if it were assumed that they were merely black hearted murderers." He noted that these paragraphs, supporting the Indians' side, were the ones largely deleted. About the glossary of Apache words that he enclosed, he spoke of the various sources from which they had been drawn; none of these could be considered authoritative. ". . . I think there is no authority on the Apache language."[48]

Ed's struggle with McClurg to maintain the realistic aspects of *The War Chief* were far from over. Upon viewing the sample jacket of the forthcoming book, he irately wired his disappointment to Bray. On July 5, 1927, he wrote in disgust:

The figure of the Indian is not of an Apache, it does not look like an Indian and is homely as Hell. I did not mind so much when I saw it on the magazine cover, but I was nearly sick when I saw that you had adopted it for the book, as I was sure St. John would do something really worth while for it.

There is nothing of the atmosphere or coloring of Arizona in the foliage or background; in fact, the whole thing is atrocious and if the picture can kill sales, I am confident that this one will.[49]

Bray's contention that Ed was expecting "an Adonis" on the cover brought an angry reply. Ed referred to his many months of research and to the one hundred dollars he had spent for books. He described the jacket in strong terms: its effect would be to put the story "in the yellow covered, dime novel category at the first glance. It is cheap and tawdry and untrue." Those who see it will feel "that the text is as worthless and as full of errors as the jacket." He was insultingly frank: "You do not have to tell me why this jacket was selected. It was solely because it was bought cheap from Munsey and a couple of hundred dollars saved. If I wrote my stories for you in that spirit, you would not buy them."[50] He admitted that the decision lay with McClurg—he had no voice in the matter. *The War Chief,* published on September 15, 1927, contained the objectionable jacket.

That month an old friend, General Charles King, wrote to praise the book, and in his letter of October 4 Ed noted, "I endeavored to write the story from the viewpoint of an Apache; in fact, as though I were an Apache, and without permitting racial prejudices to influence me." This same attempt to present an objective appraisal of the Apaches was illustrated also in correspondence with John W. LaRue, Literary Editor of *The Cincinnati Enquirer.* After thanking LaRue for a "very kind review" of *The War Chief,* Ed brought up a question suggested by this review: "Are Indians really as dirty as we are accustomed to think them?"

Ed, on September 29, offered a detailed defense of the Indians:

Unquestionably some tribes are less fastidious than others and it is true that they have not the facilities for cleanliness that modern engineering and plumbing have given us, but my experi-

ence has been that, with equal facilities, the Indian is as cleanly as the white man.

To support his views, he returned to incidents of the past, recalling the period when he owned a stationery store in Pocatello, Idaho; the store was located inside an Indian reservation. ". . . many Indians came into my place and, of course, I came in contact with them to some extent. If these people had been infested with vermin, it seems to me I should have acquired a few myself, but I never did." He also remembered how in New Mexico he had purchased a blanket "off the back of a buck," and although he wore it for a week without having it cleaned, he found no evidence of vermin.

His most interesting recollection was about the Apache scouts who accompanied the troops of the Seventh Cavalry in Arizona. Ed insisted they were much cleaner than the soldiers; he spoke of the "considerable time and labor" they would spend in constructing one of their primitive Turkish baths. They prepared a circular excavation and lined it with boulders, upon which they built a fire.

When the boulders became superheated, the embers were removed and a light wickiup constructed around the pit. They then went in with pails of water which they threw on the stones. After this steam bath they took a plunge in the river.

Concerning the ordinary enlisted man of that period, Ed recalled that a soldier in the field for as long as two months might not take a bath at all: ". . . from personal experience of the pioneer stock that won the West from the Indians, I think I may state, without fear of refutation, that they were about the dirtiest people in the world." Aware of the accusation that the older Indian women were quite fat, Ed responded, "pound for pound, they have not, I think you will admit, much avoirdupois advantage over the fat dowagers hiding behind their diamonds at the opening of a grand opera season."

The last of the 1926 stories, "The Tarzan Twins," Burroughs' first juvenile, was begun on November 16 but not finished until January 15, 1927. A request for a book designed for boys eight to twelve had come from Dr. J. C. Flowers of the Gerlach-Barklow Company, a firm that had acquired the P. F. Volland Company. On receiving Flowers' inquiry, Ed revealed that he had been planning to come to Chicago and would discuss the matter there. The two men met on June 7, 1926, but in the months that followed, Ed was reluctant to commit himself, mainly because of his health (he had been recovering from the flu), and also because of his strenuous writing schedule. In letters to Theodore R. Gerlach, the Volland president, Ed made clear his interest in writing a juvenile, which, he noted, "would be in the nature of an experiment. . .", and surprisingly, after saying he could not guarantee completion by March 1927, indicated he might deliver it by the first of the year.[51]

On November 23 Ed submitted an outline of "The Tarzan Twins" to Gerlach and explained that he was writing the story for children about fourteen years old and that he did not intend to change either his style or his subject matter. "I am simply omitting the love interest and using two boys about fourteen years of age as the principal characters," he wrote. "Otherwise, it will be very much like my Tarzan stories." With the story half finished, a suggestion came from Gerlach's office: could one of the twins be a girl? This idea, Ed replied, had occurred to him but he had abandoned it for several reasons. During the Twins' adventures in the jungle, they revert to primitive living and are "practically stripped of clothing." Illustrations of the boys in their scanty, savage costumes would appeal to the young readers, but, obviously, a juvenile book could not feature drawings of a half-clothed girl. Ed also believed that a girl would slow down the action.

Gerlach's displeasure upon hearing that the "Twins" would actually be cousins, brought a reassurance from Ed: this relationship would not detract in any way from the story. Ed then revealed an inspiration that was hardly unexpected. He would devise a sequel with a girl in it, if Gerlach desired one.[52] After the completion of the 21,000-word "Tarzan Twins" and the receipt of a $500 advance royalty, problems at once arose. Volland, in February 1927, complained that the story was too short and requested that from three to seven thousand words be added. Ed replied irritably, stating that an addition of this length would require as much work as he had devoted to the entire story. Experience had also taught him that changes often weakened the original work.[53]

More important reasons for lengthening "The Tarzan Twins" soon emerged. Both Flowers and Margherita Osborne, the editor, agreed that the characters of the two boys had not been adequately developed, and that contrary to the usual Burroughs stories, "The Tarzan Twins" contained little of the vital, colorful African background. Miss Osborne suggested, ". . . you could show some of the wonder and beauty of the native tribes, as well as their outlandishness. . . ." Flowers wanted "the development of manhood in which physical and mental courage were combined." Unfortunately, since the Volland staff had accurately pinpointed the weakness of the story, Ed brusquely rejected the suggestions, making it plain that the payment was the main factor: "I contracted to write a story of a given length for a stated royalty which starts at 5c a copy and increases to 7½c a copy, dependent upon sales. . . . If I had been told that a longer manuscript was desired, the royalties that I should have asked would have been greater. . . ." It would have been far easier, he stressed, to revise the story at the time he was writing it, than to attempt the changes now.[54]

Undoubtedly overawed by Ed's curt rejection, his positive attitude and the prestige of the Burroughs name, Flowers acceded, apologizing for the requested changes. He wrote, ". . . your opinion in this matter should be better than ours. . . . I do not want to take the position of being an able critic in any sense. . . an author like yourself, who has had long years of experience, should be in a much better position to judge. . . ." He agreed to publish the story in its original form.

Volland's unenthusiastic view of "The Tarzan Twins" was duplicated by *Youth's Companion* early in 1927, with a prompt rejection. In proceeding with plans for publication, Volland chose Douglas Grant as illustrator; he prepared the full pages by painting them first in oil on canvas. On August 8 Ed forwarded the dedication for the book: "To Joan, Hulbert and Jack, who were brought up on Tarzan stories, this volume is affectionately dedicated by their father." A month later Ed expressed his approval of Grant's illustrations, and on October 10, *The Tarzan Twins* was published. The book at once won an award from the American Society of Graphic Arts as an example of fine bookmaking, but Ed, while noting his pleasure over this recognition, commented irritably about a different matter: *"The Tarzan Twins* is too fine a piece of bookmaking to be marred by errors which might easily have been obviated by another careful proof reading."[55]

The early sales of the book were encouragingly high; on February 29, 1928, Margherita Osborne, the editor, reported that in the preceding four months 6,715 copies had been sold and that the total would have been greater if *The Tarzan Twins* had been issued with a jacket rather than a box. The dealers claimed that the boxed books were necessarily placed on counters with the juveniles for younger children. By the fall it became evident that the sales were poor; the change from a box to an attractive jacket brought little improvement.

Ed had his own theories as to the failure. These, for the first time, included an admission of the weaknesses in his writing: he believed that he had "unconsciously" been guilty of "writing down" for the juvenile market. He was convinced that children of about fifteen years preferred adult literature. He offered a list of other causes:

. . . the cover illustration was a handicap. . . it showed the boys so very small in comparison to Tarzan, suggesting that it was a book about very young children. . . . Another handicap may have been the title, which I believe now should have been "Tarzan and the Twins" . . .[56]

At the same time he attempted a comparison between his book and the children's stories written by Kipling:

I recall the effect of Kipling's "Just So" stories. I do not know that they flopped, although they did as far as I was concerned, notwithstanding the fact that I was an ardent Kipling admirer, and in view of my own experience and what I have learned from it, I think that Kipling made the mistake of writing down to a juvenile audience.

To Volland on April 1, 1929, he mentioned the "unquestioned flop" of *The Tarzan Twins,* and suggested the measures that might be taken to rescue the book. These included enlarging the size of the volume to remove it from the juvenile class and giving it a new jacket with the Twins made larger alongside of Tarzan. ". . . Everything about the character of Tarzan should carry the suggestion of the grim and mysterious dangers of the jungle; neither he nor the boys should be shown smiling." These measures were not carried out, and in the passing years the sales of *The Tarzan Twins* practically vanished. On July 20, 1932, Francis H. Evans, Volland vice-president, noted that the accrued sales since 1927 had totaled only $449, not even equalling the $500 advance Ed had received.

The Tarzan Twins features the escapades of the fourteen-year-old boys Dick and Doc, really cousins, who look alike and are distantly related to Lord Greystoke. The boys, one British and one American, while attending school in England are invited to spend two months on Tarzan's African estate. In the adventures that follow they leave the train to investigate the jungle, become lost, and are captured by cannibals. They make friends of two native prisoners, Bulala, a Negro, and Ukundo, a pygmy. Doc's skill in sleight-of-hand impresses the cannibals and causes them to believe he has magical powers; as a result, the boys' lives are spared. With Ukundo's aid they escape and are later rescued in the jungle by Tarzan and his group of Waziri.

The flimsy story is almost plotless, and as Volland correctly maintained, Burroughs, possibly in his effort to "write down," omitted all of his customary rich detail of the jungle and the animals. Burroughs had commented that boys of about fifteen were reading his adult novels, and he must have been aware that the jungle setting and the personified animals, such as Numa and Tantor, were providing part of the fascination. Yet he devoted no space to this. An even more serious shortcoming occurs because of the light, joking tone of the story. This is produced mainly through the dialogue of Dick and Doc which remains bantering even as they encounter fearful dangers. Because of this, the "perils" create neither interest nor excitement for the reader. *The Tarzan Twins* fails to develop the tension and conflict vital to an adventure story.